Handbook of Gender and Women's Studies

Handbook of
Gender and Women's Studies

Edited by Kathy Davis,
Mary Evans and Judith Lorber

London • Thousand Oaks • New Delhi

© SAGE Publications Ltd 2006

First published 2006

Apart from any fair dealing for the purposes of research or private study, or criticism or review, as permitted under the Copyright, Designs and Patents Act, 1988, this publication may be reproduced, stored or transmitted in any form, or by any means, only with the prior permission in writing of the publishers, or in the case of reprographic reproduction, in accordance with the terms of licences issued by the Copyright Licensing Agency. Enquiries concerning reproduction outside those terms should be sent to the publishers.

SAGE Publications Ltd
1 Oliver's Yard
55 City Road
London EC1Y 1SP

SAGE Publications Inc.
2455 Teller Road
Thousand Oaks, California 91320

SAGE Publications India Pvt Ltd
B-42, Panchsheel Enclave
Post Box 4109
New Delhi 110 017

British Library Cataloguing in Publication data

A catalogue record for this book is available from the British Library

ISBN-13 978-0-7619-4390-7
ISBN-10 0-7619-4390-0

Library of Congress Control Number: 2005927695

Typeset by C&M Digitals (P) Ltd., Chennai, India
Printed in Great Britain by The Cromwell Press Ltd, Trowbridge, Wiltshire
Printed on paper from sustainable resources

Contents

Contributors		viii
Acknowledgements		xvii
Introduction *Kathy Davis, Mary Evans, and Judith Lorber*		1

I CURRENT STATE OF WOMEN'S STUDIES, GENDER STUDIES, AND STUDIES OF MEN — 11

1. The Life and Times of Academic Feminism — 13
   Clare Hemmings

2. The Shadow and the Substance: The Sex/Gender Debate — 35
   Wendy Cealey Harrison

3. Changing Studies on Men and Masculinities — 53
   Jeff Hearn and Michael S. Kimmel

II CULTURAL REPRESENTATIONS AND CRITIQUES — 71

4. Gendered Cultures — 73
   Gabriele Griffin

5. The Social Foundations of the Sacred: Feminists and the Politics of Religion — 92
   Bronwyn Winter

6. The Crisis in Masculinity — 109
   David Morgan

III KNOWLEDGE — 125

7. Clearing Ground and Making Connections: Modernism, Postmodernism, Feminism — 127
   Carolyn DiPalma and Kathy E. Ferguson

8 Women Knowing/Knowing Women: Critical–Creative
Interventions in the Politics of Knowledge 146
Lorraine Code

9 Gender, Change, and Education 167
Diana Leonard

IV GLOBALIZATION AND THE STATE 183

10 Gender in a Global World 185
Miri Song

11 Insiders and Outsiders: Within and Beyond
the Gendered Nation 196
Barbara Einhorn

12 Towards a New Theorizing of Women, Gender, and War 214
Dubravka Zarkov

13 Mothers and Muslims, Sisters and Sojourners:
The Contested Boundaries of Feminist Citizenship 234
Baukje Prins

V WORK AND FAMILY 251

14 Gender and Work 253
Rosemary Crompton

15 Gender, Care, and the Welfare State 272
Clare Ungerson

16 Blending into Equality: Family Diversity and
Gender Convergence 287
Molly Monahan Lang and Barbara J. Risman

VI INTIMATE RELATIONSHIPS AND SEXUALITIES 305

17 Thinking Straight, Acting Bent:
Heteronormativity and Homosexuality 307
Chrys Ingraham

18 Foregrounding Friendship: Feminist Pasts,
Feminist Futures 322
Sasha Roseneil

19 Transgendering: Blurring the Boundaries of Gender 342
Wendy McKenna and Suzanne Kessler

| VII | **EMBODIMENT IN A TECHNOLOGICAL WORLD** | **355** |

20	Gendered Bodies: Between Conformity and Autonomy *Sharyn Roach Anleu*	357
21	The Natural World and the Nature of Gender *Irmgard Schultz*	376
22	From Science and Technology to Feminist Technoscience *Jutta Weber*	397

| VIII | **MAKING CHANGE** | **415** |

23	Moral Perspectives: Gender, Ethics, and Political Theory *Joan C. Tronto*	417
24	Having It All: Feminist Fractured Foundationalism *Sue Wise and Liz Stanley*	435
25	From Autonomy to Solidarities: Transnational Feminist Political Strategies *Manisha Desai*	457
26	Utopian Visions	469
	A World Without Gender? *Judith Lorber*	469
	Getting Real: Contextualizing Gender *Mary Evans*	474
	Feminist Politics of Location *Kathy Davis*	476

| Index | 481 |

Contributors

Sharyn Roach Anleu is Professor of Sociology at Flinders University, Adelaide, and a past president of the Australian Sociological Association. She was one of three editors of the *Journal of Sociology* and is the author of *Law and Social Change* (Sage, 2000). She has just completed a fourth edition of *Deviance, Conformity and Control* (Pearson Education, Sydney, 2005). Her areas of research include legal regulation of reproduction, women and the legal profession, and criminal justice processes. She is currently undertaking research with Kathy Mack on magistrates and their courts in Australia.

Lorraine Code is Distinguished Research Professor of Philosophy at York University in Toronto, and a Fellow of the Royal Society of Canada. In addition to numerous articles and chapters in books, and four co-edited books, she has published *Epistemic Responsibility* (University Press of New England, 1987), *What Can She Know? Feminist Theory and the Construction of Knowledge* (Cornell University Press, 1991), and *Rhetorical Spaces: Essays on (Gendered) Locations* (Routledge, 1995). She is General Editor of the Routledge *Encyclopedia of Feminist Theories* (2000), editor of *Feminist Interpretations of Hans-Georg Gadamer* (Pennsylvania State University Press, 2003), and with Kathryn Hamer has translated Michèle Le Doeuff's *Le Sexe du savoir* as *The Sex of Knowing* (Routledge, 2003). Her latest book is *Ecological Thinking: The Politics of Epistemic Location* (Oxford University Press, 2006). She is currently working on questions generated by the new epistemologies of ignorance, on knowing across differences, and on developing a moral epistemology sensitive to vulnerability.

Rosemary Crompton is Professor of Sociology at City University, London. She has researched and published widely in the areas of stratification and employment, particularly women's employment. Her books include *Class and Stratification* (Polity, 1998) and *Restructuring Gender Relations and Employment* (Oxford University Press, 2000). She is currently working on a book entitled *Employment and the Family*, to be published by Cambridge University Press, and beginning a new project linked to the Economic and Social Research Council Gender Equality Network (GeNet). She is a past editor of *Work, Employment and Society*.

Kathy Davis is Senior Researcher at the Research Institute of History and Culture (OGC) at Utrecht University, the Netherlands. Born in the United States, she has taught psychology and women's studies at various universities in the Netherlands. She is the author of *Dubious Equalities and Embodied Differences* (Rowman & Littlefield, 2003), *Reshaping the Female Body* (Routledge, 1995), *Power Under the Microscope* (Foris, 1988), and the editor of *Embodied Practices: Feminist Perspectives on the Body* (Sage, 1997) as well as several books on gender, power, and discourse. She is currently finishing a book on feminist knowledge and how it travels, based on the feminist classic on women's health, *Our Bodies, Ourselves*. Together with Mary Evans, she is editor of the *European Journal of Women's Studies*.

Manisha Desai is Acting Director, Women and Gender in Global Perspectives, Associate Professor of Sociology, and Associate Director of the Program in South Asia and Middle Eastern Perspectives at the University of Illinois, Urbana–Champaign. Her areas of interest are social movements, gender, globalization and human rights. She is currently finishing a book, *Rethinking Globalization* (Rowman & Littlefield). She has published two edited books, *Women's Issues in Asia and Oceania* (Greenwood, 2003) and *Women's Activism and Globalization: Linking Local Struggles with Transnational Politics* (Routledge, 2002, with Nancy Naples). She has also published numerous articles and book chapters; the latest one is 'Transnational Feminist Politics: The Face of Women's Movements Post-Beijing' for a special issue of the *International Social Science Journal* on Beijing Plus Ten. She has also worked as a Senior Programme Officer with UNESCO in its Gender, Equality and Development Section.

Carolyn DiPalma is Associate Professor Emerita of Women's Studies at the University of South Florida. Her research interests include epistemology and method, feminist theory, body politics, feminist pedagogy, and women's health. Her publications include essays in the *Journal of Medical Humanities, Theory & Event, Configurations: A Journal of Literature, Science and Technology, Asian Journal of Women's Studies, Intertexts, Women's Studies Quarterly*, and in *The Teacher's Body: Embodiment, Authority, and Identity in the Academy* and *Reader's Guide to Women's Studies*. She is co-editor of *Teaching Introduction to Women's Studies: Expectations and Strategies* (Bergin & Garvey, 1999).

Barbara Einhorn is Reader in Gender Studies and Director of Graduate Studies in the School of Social Sciences and Cultural Studies at the University of Sussex. She has published on issues of gender, citizenship, civil society, nation, and women's movements, especially in the context of transformation in Central and Eastern Europe. Her publications include *Cinderella Goes to Market: Citizenship, Gender and Women's Movements in East Central Europe* (Verso, 1993) and *Citizenship in a Uniting Europe: From Dream to Awakening*

(Palgrave Macmillan, 2006). She is currently working on a book project provisionally entitled *No Homecoming: Narratives of 'Home' and Belonging, Exile and Return*, which is concerned with questions of nation and identity, 'home', and belonging in German–Jewish multiple migrants.

Mary Evans is Professor of Women's Studies at the University of Kent, Canterbury, where she has taught Women's Studies and Sociology for over thirty years. With Kathy Davis, she is the editor of the *European Journal of Women's Studies*. Her main research interests have been in feminist theory and literature. Recent publications include *Missing Persons: The Impossibility of Auto/Biography* (Routledge, 1999), *Love: An Unromantic Discussion* (Polity, 2003), *Gender and Social Theory* (Open University Press, 2003), and *Killing Thinking* (Compendium Books, 2004). The last publication reflects her most recent interest in modernity as bureaucracy and its impact on intellectual life.

Kathy E. Ferguson is Professor of Women's Studies and Political Science at the University of Hawai'i. She teaches and writes about feminist theories and research methods, contemporary critical theory, and global/national/local militarisms. She is currently writing a book on Emma Goldman's political thinking and co-editing a volume on gender and globalization in Asia and the Pacific. Her books include *Oh, Say, Can You See? The Semiotics of the Military in Hawai'i*, with Phyllis Turnbull (University of Minnesota Press, 1999) and *The Man Question: Visions of Subjectivity in Feminist Theory* (University of California Press, 1993).

Gabriele Griffin is Professor of Gender Studies at the University of Hull. Her research centers on Women's Studies as a discipline and on women's contemporary cultural production. Among her recent publications are *Contemporary Black and Asian Women Playwrights in Britain* (Cambridge University Press, 2003) and *Thinking Differently: A Reader in European Women's Studies* (Zed Books, 2002; co-edited with Rosi Braidotti). She is co-founding editor of the journal *Feminist Theory*. In recent years she has worked extensively on EU-funded projects; in October 2003 she completed 'Women's Employment, Equal Opportunities and Women's Studies' (www.hull.ac.uk/ewsi), and between 2004 and 2007 she is co-ordinating a project on integrated research methods for the humanities and social sciences.

Wendy Cealey Harrison was, until recently, Senior Lecturer in Sociology at the University of Greenwich, London, and is now is Head of its Learning and Quality Unit. She is the author, with John Hood-Williams, of *Beyond Sex and Gender* (Sage, 2002) and of a number of articles on the work of Judith Butler and on the reconceptualization of gender and sexual difference. Her research interests lie predominantly in the field of post-structuralist theory and psychoanalysis and, in particular, in the ways in which their insights can be reconciled with more conventional forms of natural-scientific enquiry. She is a member of the International Neuro-Psychoanalysis Society.

Jeff Hearn is Professor, Swedish School of Economics, Helsinki; Linköping University; and University of Huddersfield. He was previously Research Professor, University of Manchester, and has worked at the Universities of Bradford, Oslo, Tampere and Åbo Akademi. His books include: *'Sex' at 'Work'* (Palgrave Macmillan, 1987/1995), *The Sexuality of Organization* (Sage, 1989), *Men in the Public Eye* (Routledge, 1992), *Men as Managers, Managers as Men* (Sage, 1996), *Hard Work in the Academy* (Helsinki University Press, 1999), *Gender, Sexuality and Violence in Organizations* (Sage, 2001), *Information Society and the Workplace* (Routledge, 2004), and *Handbook of Studies on Men and Masculinities* (Sage, 2005), and *European Perspectives on Men and Masculinities* (Palgrave Macmillan, 2006). He is co-editor of the journal *Men and Masculinities*. He was Principal Contractor of the EU Research Network 'The Social Problem of Men' and is currently researching 'Men, Gender Relations and Transnational Organising, Organisations and Management'.

Clare Hemmings is Senior Lecturer in Gender Studies at the Gender Institute, London School of Economics and Political Science. Her current research and teaching are divided into three overlapping areas of enquiry in gender and sexuality studies: critical practices and histories, patterns of institutionalization, and cultural translation. Her first book *Bisexual Spaces* was published by Routledge in 2002, and she is currently completing a second book, *Telling Feminist Stories*.

Chrys Ingraham is Professor of Sociology, Director of the Helen M. Upton Center for Women's Studies at Russell Sage College, Troy, NY. A specialist in feminist theory, gender studies, social inequality, popular culture, and social theory, Ingraham is a leading international contributor to the field of critical heterosexual studies. She is author of 'The Heterosexual Imaginary: Feminist Sociology and Theories of Gender', in the journal *Sociological Theory* (1994), co-editor of *Materialist Feminism: A Reader in Class, Difference, and Women's Lives* (Routledge, 1997), author of *White Weddings: Romancing Heterosexuality in Popular Culture* (Routledge, 1999), and editor of *Thinking Straight: The Power, the Promise, and the Paradox of Heterosexuality* (Routledge, 2005).

Suzanne Kessler is Kempner Distinguished Professor of Psychology and Dean of the School of Natural and Social Sciences at Purchase College, State University of New York. She is the author of *Lessons From the Intersexed* (Rutgers University Press, 1998) and co-author of *Gender: An Ethnomethodological Approach* (University of Chicago Press, 1978) as well as author of many articles on the social construction of gender.

Michael S. Kimmel is Professor of Sociology at State University of New York at Stony Brook. His books include *Changing Men* (Sage, 1987), *Men Confront Pornography* (Meridian Books, 1990), *Men's Lives* (6th edition, Allyn and Bacon, 2003), *Against the Tide: Profeminist Men in the United States, 1776–1990* (Diane Publishing Company, 1992), *The Politics of Manhood* (Temple University Press, 1996), *Manhood: A Cultural History* (Oxford University Press, 1996), *The Gendered Society* (2nd edition, Oxford University Press, 2003), *Handbook of Studies on Men and Masculinities* (Sage, 2005), *The Gender of Desire* (SUNY Press, 2005), and *The History of Men* (SUNY Press, 2005). He is editor of *Men and Masculinities*, an interdisciplinary scholarly journal, a book series on Men and Masculinity at the University of California Press, and the Sage Series on Men and Masculinities. He is the spokesperson for the National Organization for Men Against Sexism (NOMAS) and lectures extensively on campuses in the United States and abroad.

Molly Monahan Lang is Assistant Professor of sociology at Baldwin–Wallace College, Berea, OH, where she teaches a variety of courses including Family, Social Inequalities, SPSS: Data Analysis, and Caregiving in Society. Her previous research on violence against women in families can be seen in *Journal of Marriage and Family*. She has also researched the challenges and inequalities faced in a particular kind of caregiving work (hospice), as it undergoes the process of rationalization.

Diana Leonard is Professor of Sociology of Education and Gender at the Institute of Education, University of London and Honorary Professor at Deakin Universtiy, Melbourne. She has published extensively on the sociology of gender and the family, including *Familiar Exploitation: A New Analysis of Marriage in Contemporary Western Societies* (with Christine Delphy, Polity, 1992, reprinted 1996) and conducted research on gender and learning among 10-year-olds, violence resilient (secondary) schools, and, currently, the long-term consequences of single- and mixed-sex schooling. Her other interests include diversity in the experiences of doctoral students, as published in *A Woman's Guide to Doctoral Studies* (Open University Press, 2001) and a report on the *Experiences of International Students in UK Higher Education* for UKCOSA: The Council for International Education, 2003.

Judith Lorber is Professor Emerita of Sociology and Women's Studies at Brooklyn College and the Graduate School, City University of New York. She is the author of *Breaking the Bowls: Degendering and Feminist Change* (W.W. Norton, 2005), *Gender Inequality: Feminist Theories and Politics* (Roxbury, 3rd edition, 2005), *Gender and the Social Construction of Illness* (Altamira, 2nd edition, 2002, with Lisa Jean Moore), *Paradoxes of Gender* (Yale University Press, 1994; Italian translation, *L'Inventione dei sessi*; German translation, *Gender-Paradoxien*), and *Women Physicians: Careers, Status and Power* (Tavistock, 1984). She is co-editor of *Revisioning Gender* (Sage, 1999, with Myra Marx Ferree and Beth B. Hess) and *The Social Construction of Gender* (Sage, 1991, with Susan A. Farrell). She is the Founding Editor of *Gender & Society*, official publication of Sociologists for Women in Society.

Wendy McKenna is Associate Professor of Psychology at Barnard College and Professor of Sociology at Purchase College, State University of New York. She is a certified sex educator and a licensed psychologist. She is co-author of *Gender: An Ethnomethodological Approach* (University of Chicago Press, 1978). Her most recent writing is on the topic of transgender.

David Morgan has recently retired from the Sociology Department at the University of Manchester. He holds a part-time appointment at Norwegian University of Science and Technology, Trondheim. He is the author of several books and articles on masculinities and family studies, including *Discovering Men* (Routledge, 1992) and *Family Connections* (Polity, 1996). He is a former President of the British Sociological Association.

Baukje Prins is Assistant Professor of Philosophy at the University of Groningen, the Netherlands. She is the author of *Voorbij de onschuld* (Beyond Innocence, 2nd revised edition, 2004), on the Dutch discourse on ethnic minorities and multiculturalism. Currently she is working on a book with the provisional title *Een (on)gewone klas* (Accidental Classmates), on the history and dynamics of everyday inter-ethnic relationships in the Netherlands since the early 1960s. She has been an editor of the (Dutch) journal of philosophy *Krisis*, and is currently editor of *Migrantenstudies*. She has been a visiting researcher at the History of Consciousness Program at the University of California, Santa Cruz, and at the Institute for Women's Studies, University of Lancaster.

Barbara J. Risman is Alumni Distinguished Research Professor at North Carolina State University in Raleigh. She is the author of *Gender Vertigo: American Families in Transition* (Yale University Press, 1998) and nearly two-dozen articles, including 'Gender as Structure: Theory Wrestling with Activism' in *Gender & Society*. She is the co-chair of the Council on Contemporary Families, a national organization of experts dedicated to providing information to the public and the media about the changes currently taking place in families.

Sasha Roseneil is Professor of Sociology and Gender Studies at the University of Leeds, and Professor II in the Centre for Women's Studies and Gender Research at the University of Oslo. She is the author of *Disarming Patriarchy* (Open University Press,1995) and *Common Women, Uncommon Practices: The Queer Feminisms of Greenham* (Cassell, 2000). She is one of the founding editors of the journal *Feminist Theory*. She is also editor or co-editor of *Stirring It: Challenges for Feminism* (Taylor & Francis, 1994), *Practising*

Identities (Macmillan, 1999), *Consuming Cultures* (Macmillan, 1999), *Globalization and Social Movements* (Palgrave, 2000), and special issues of *Citizenship Studies* (2000), *Feminist Theory* (2001, 2003), *Current Sociology* (2004), and *Social Politics* (2004). Her latest book is *Sociability, Sexuality, Self* (Routledge, 2007).

Irmgard Schultz is one of the founders of the Institut für sozial-ökologische Forschung (ISOE, Institute for Social-ecological Research) in Frankfurt am Main, Germany. She is currently the head of ISOE's research department on 'Everyday Ecology and Consumption'. Her main fields of research are concepts of transdisciplinary and gender-integrated environmental studies. Since the 1980s, she has published many feminist essays and books on gender and the environment. Together with Ines Weller she co-edited *Gender and Environment* (IKO-Verlag, 1995); and with Andreas Nebelung and Angelika Poferl she co-edited *Geschlechterverhältnisse, Naturverhältnisse* (Leske and Budrich, 2001).

Miri Song is Senior Lecturer in Sociology at the University of Kent, Canterbury. She is a Korean–American who has lived in the UK since 1991. Her books include *Choosing Ethnic Identity* (Polity, 2003) and *Helping Out: Children's Labor in Ethnic Businesses* (Temple University Press, 1999). Her research interests include 'race' and ethnic identity, immigrant adaptation, the second generation, and Internet use by minority groups.

Liz Stanley is Professor of Sociology at the University of Edinburgh. Formerly editor of *Sociology* and of *Women's Studies International Forum*, she is also founding editor of *Sociological Research Online* and *Auto/Biography*. Her recent books include *Imperialism, Labour and the New Woman: Olive Schreiner's Social Theory* (Sociology Press, 2002) and *Mourning Becomes… Post/Memory, Commemoration and the Concentration Camps of the South African War* (Manchester University Press and Rutgers University Press, 2006).

Joan C. Tronto is Professor of Political Science at Hunter College, City University of New York. Her scholarly writings are in feminist ethics, political theory, and women in politics in the United States. Her essays have appeared in *Signs, Hypatia, Feminist Studies, Feminist Theory*, and in numerous anthologies. She is a proponent for using care ethics as a basis for political theory and public policy, an argument expounded in her book *Moral Boundaries: A Political Argument for an Ethic of Care* (Routledge, 1993), currently being translated into French and Italian. She also co-edited a volume with Cathy Cohen and Kathy Jones, *Women Transforming Politics* (New York University Press, 1997), and is currently completing a book, *Democratic Caring*, forthcoming from New York University Press.

Clare Ungerson is Emeritus Professor of Social Policy at the University of Southampton, and currently Honorary Professor of Social Policy at the University of Kent, Canterbury. She has published widely on urban policy and race relations and on gender and social policy, often using a cross-national perspective. Her books include *Policy is Personal: Sex, Gender and Informal Care* (Tavistock, 1987), *Women and Social Policy – A Reader* (Palgrave Macmillan, 1996), *Gender and Caring – Women, Work and Welfare in Britain and Scandinavia* (Harvester Wheatsheaf, 1990). Most recently, she has directed a research project funded as part of the British Economic and Social Research Council 'Future of Work Programme', which looked at the way informal unpaid care carried out by kin is being 'commodified' and paid within many modern welfare states.

Jutta Weber is Guest Professor at the Centre for Interdisciplinary Studies at the University of Duisburg-Essen. She also works at the Department for Philosophy of Science, University of Vienna, on a project, 'Sociality with Machines' in the field of 'social robots' and software agents (http://www.univie.ac.at/soziale_maschinen/). Her main interests are science and technology studies, epistemology, philosophy of science, social and feminist theory. Recent publications include: 'Helpless machines and true loving caregivers: a feminist critique of recent trends in human– robot interaction', *Journal of Information Communication and Ethics in Society* (2005), *Umkämpfte Bedeutungen: Naturkonzepte im Zeitalter der Technoscience* (Contested Meanings: Concepts of Nature in the Age of Technoscience) (Campus, 2003). She is currently working on a book on robotics, gender and techoscience studies.

Bronwyn Winter is a Senior Lecturer in the Department of French Studies at the University of Sydney. Her research areas include: women, culture, ethnicity and religion, human rights, militarism and globalization, feminist theory, and lesbian politics. Recent publications include: *September 11, 2001: Feminist Perspectives* (contributing co-editor with Susan Hawthorne, Spinifex Press, 2002), republished in 2003 by Raincoast Books as *After Shock*; 'Fundamental Misunderstandings: Issues in Feminist Approaches to Islamism', in the *Journal of Women's History* (2001); 'Pauline and Other Perils: Women in Australian Right-Wing Politics', in *Right-Wing Women* (2002). Forthcoming work includes: 'Religion, culture and women's human rights', *Women's Studies International Forum*; 'Secularism aboard the Titanic: feminists and the debate over the hijab in France', *Feminist Studies*. Work in progress: books on the French hijab debate and on women, culture, and domination.

Sue Wise is Professor of Social Justice and Social Work at Lancaster University. Her main research interests are concerned with the exploitation and oppression of children. Among her books are *Breaking Out: Feminist Research and Feminist Consciousness* (Routledge, 1983) and *Breaking Out*

Again: Feminist Ontology and Epistemology (Routledge, 1993), both written with Liz Stanley.

Dubravka Zarkov is Senior Lecturer in Gender, Conflict and Development Studies at the Institute of Social Studies, The Hague. Her research and teaching are on gender and violent conflict, with a focus on intersectionality of gender and on media representations of war and violence. Her regional interest is in former Yugoslavia and South Asia. She co-edited *The Postwar Moment: Militaries, Masculinities and International Peacekeeping* (Lawrence and Wishart, 2002, with Cynthia Cockburn). Her forthcoming books are *The Fe/Male Body and the Productive Power of Violence: On 'Media War' and 'Ethnic War' in Former Yugoslavia* (Duke University Press, 2006) and *Gender, Violent Conflict, Development: Challenges of Practice* (Zubaan/Kali for Women, 2006). She is a member of the Advisory Council of Women's Initiative for Gender Justice.

Acknowledgements

The editors would like to take this opportunity to thank first and foremost the many contributors to this collection, who have written papers which so much enhance women's and gender studies. Our thanks to all our authors for their chapters and for their help in making the various additions and changes so swiftly and surely. We owe an equal debt to Karen Phillips of Sage for first suggesting that this handbook should be compiled and for her grace and assistance (and that of her colleagues) in the many months of preparation.

Finally, Mary Evans would like to thank her co-editors for their endless support and sisterly concern at a difficult time. In large part, the handbook has emerged out of the collective enterprise that is feminism, and we hope that it will make a contribution to its ongoing dialogues.

Kathy Davis
Mary Evans
Judith Lorber

Introduction

Kathy Davis, Mary Evans, and Judith Lorber

The *Handbook of Gender and Women's Studies* is first and foremost an indication of the coming of age of academic work on women and the meaning of gender in the twenty-first century. This area of study, born out of second-wave feminism, has initiated and enabled the rethinking and the rewriting of previously taken-for-granted understandings of gender and its place in the social and the symbolic world. As this handbook demonstrates, no discipline in the university curriculum remains untouched by the intervention of thinking about gender.

This process, accomplished in the past forty years, has overturned previous certainties about the fixed order and meaning of gender. As the chapters in this collection demonstrate, there is no subject or context which cannot be seen differently when examined through the lens of 'gender thinking.' Although no author in this handbook would claim to represent the consensus of this new understanding of the world, all would agree on the centrality of gender to any coherent understanding of the world.

The handbook shows the theoretical plurality and diversity of gender and women's studies, and also demonstrates the political and national range of gendered thinking. Even if the historical roots of feminism lie in the European Enlightenment, the growth of the subject has not been subject to the same geographical limits. The handbook is, in the same way as feminism itself, literally international. Both the editors and the authors are drawn from different countries and different academic interests, but what is shared is greater than what is distinct: namely, a commitment to extending our understanding of arguably the greatest human division, that between female and male. In these pages, readers can find comprehensive reviews of the literature on gender in particular contexts. Just as significantly, the authors also suggest ways in which the existing richness and excitement of work on gender can be further extended. All in all, this handbook attests to the dynamic global work-in-progress on gender.

CONCEPTUAL ISSUES

The concept of women's studies, thirty-five years ago a radically new idea in an academic world where White Western men were considered the generalized 'human,' is now well enough established to have been complemented by gender studies and studies of men and masculinities. Each of these areas includes elements of the other areas, but in examining the current state and future potential of gender and women's studies, we take as our focus the research and theories that have developed around women, and, more recently, around gender as encompassing women and men in relation to each other. In addition to analyzing women's and men's interactions and the processes of domination and oppression of women by men, gender studies, more so than women's studies, has focused on the way the organization and structure of society itself and its cultural and knowledge productions are gendered.

By gendered, we mean the division of people into two differentiated groups, 'men' and 'women,' and the organization of the major aspects of society along those binaries. The binary divisions override individual differences and intertwine with other major socially constructed differences – racial categorization, ethnic grouping, economic class, age, religion, and sexual orientation – which interact to produce a complex hierarchical system of dominance and subordination. Gender divisions not only permeate the individual's sense of self, families, and intimate relationships, but also structure work, politics, law, education, medicine, the military, religions, and culture. Gender is a system of power in that it privileges some men and disadvantages most women. Gender is constructed and maintained by both the dominants and the oppressed because both ascribe to its values in personality and identity formation and in appropriate masculine and feminine behavior. Gender is hegemonic in that many of its foundational assumptions and ubiquitous processes are invisible, unquestioned, and unexamined.

There is still debate over whether a focus on *gender* rather than on *women* undoes the accomplishments of the past thirty-five years in bringing women and women's standpoints to the forefront in research, knowledge, and cultural production. Some scholars of women's studies are concerned that the concept of gender neglects sexual and emotional differences between women and men. For the more psychoanalytically minded, the concept of gender is too sociological and may obscure the centrality of the sexed body for understanding our culture. Others have worried that gender may water down the powerful concept of *patriarchy* as the source of women's oppression. Patriarchy, to some scholars of women's studies is much more encompassing than gender, in that it reflects the violence and misogyny that imbues many of the social and emotional encounters of women and men. More recently, the concept of gender has been criticized for not doing justice to the intersectionality of women's (and men's) multiple identities and the ways they are shaped by other socially constructed categories of difference.

A central concern of many of the authors is with the way in which the 'masculine' (whether as behavior or as a conceptual system) is both rewarded and hegemonic because it is taken for granted as the dominant perspective. Challenging the hegemony of the masculine in its many shapes and forms has been the prime endeavor of second-wave feminism, but as numerous feminists have pointed out, that hegemony is institutionalized in complex and subtle ways. Social prohibitions clearly excluding or discriminating against women are easy to challenge and dispute (always assuming a form of civic society which allows such challenges), but more difficult to confront are those patterns of discrimination that have the appearance of either universality or the authority of the 'natural.'

One of the more famous binary oppositions posed in the history of second-wave feminism was outlined by Sherry Ortner in 'Is Female to Male as Nature is to Culture?' In that paper (first published in 1972), Ortner proposed that Western thinking in the years since the Enlightenment had been founded on the assumption that men inhabited the domain of understanding and rational thought, while women's 'natural' habitat was that of reproduction and the care of others, those 'naturally' vulnerable and unable to care for themselves. Despite Mary Wollstonecraft's best efforts (in 1792), it has taken over 200 years to challenge effectively those traditions and ideologies which locate women 'outside' knowledge, and hence outside the realms of power. We can recognize – as authors in this collection collectively do – the evolving global paradigms that impinge on the autonomy and well-being of women. It is another question of how those paradigms might be resisted or countered. Two strands are possible in considering this issue: one is to revisit those apparent certainties about the normative order of the world in order to define an agenda which is more assuredly both feminist and gendered. The other is to consider the transformation of the realm of the personal and public which has taken place in the West since the 1960s and ask if these 'new' people (or certainly people acting within new normative boundaries) will, through the politics of the personal, transform public politics.

These arguments and debates in the theory and scholarship of women's and gender studies draw on Western second-wave feminism, that explosion of creative and critical energy that played a large part in the recent transformation of Western civil society and its pedagogy. As the slogan of the 1960s states, 'the personal is political,' and that concept, in challenging the division of public and private which had been part of Western assumptions since the nineteenth century, came to overturn many previously held divisions and distinctions between the world of men and the world of women. That distinction was, of course, always more ideal than real, but the repudiation of different spheres was one that second-wave feminism claimed as a platform from which to demand the reordering of the social and intellectual world.

Women's studies was thus first the claim by women for the study of women, a paradigm shift in focus which would (and did) demonstrate the biases of the academy's male-centered viewpoint. Gender studies was made possible through this process of the recovery of women: once the human subject had been gendered, there arose the possibility of extending the knowledge of the complexity of human gender to the study of both women and men and their interactions in the personal, in civil society, and in public and political life.

CURRENT STATE OF WOMEN'S STUDIES, GENDER STUDIES, AND STUDIES OF MEN

In this context, it is entirely appropriate that the chapter that opens this collection, 'The Life and Times of Academic Feminism' by Clare Hemmings, raises those issues which have always been of concern to scholars working in women's/gender studies, namely, the question of the disciplinary status of women's/gender studies and the relationship of the area (or discipline, depending on how the debate is resolved) to the institutional context of the academy. Far from being a matter of intellectual history, women's/gender studies is very much a matter of the present and future, as Hemmings argues: 'I remain in thrall to a thirty-year endeavor that has developed an institutional life that intersects with, but cannot be reduced to, feminist political movements, and that has been brave enough to take its own history and presumptions as critical objects of inquiry' (p. 14). To be critical of others is never problematic, to be critical of one's own positions is something unknown in the academy, and it extends that project of 'humanization' where second-wave academic feminism began.

In the second chapter, 'The Shadow and the Substance: The Sex/Gender Debate,' Wendy Cealey Harrison lays out the complexities of the intersection of sex and gender, taking the debate beyond the foundational assumption of the distinction between them that second-wave feminists originally promulgated. She asserts that the exciting and challenging work that remains to be undertaken in feminism is research that recognizes and understands the biological yet 'takes full account of the fact that human beings are pre-eminently social and cultural creatures who, in shaping the world around them, also shape themselves' (p. 35).

The growing acceptance of gender studies saw the parallel burgeoning of studies of men and masculinities. Jeff Hearn and Michael Kimmel, in 'Changing Studies on Men and Masculinities,' review the material which has made explicit the dynamics of gender as applied to men as well as women, and has problematized the meaning of 'masculinity.' As they comment, 'Men's outlooks and culturally defined characteristics were formally generally the unexamined norm for religion, science, citizenship, law and authority' (p. 53), but gender studies has shifted that assumption towards the now general analysis that masculinity, quite as much as femininity, is socially constructed. Yet in their concluding remarks, Hearn and Kimmel point out that research on the social construction of gender remains a 'First World' concern and that theories about gender which 'de-construct' biological gender have so far largely made an impact mostly in those rich societies where biology, in all senses of human identity and human need, is more likely to be negotiable.

CULTURAL REPRESENTATIONS AND CRITIQUES

It is the changing meaning of gender in modernity that is the focus of the chapters by Gabriele Griffin and David Morgan in the part on cultural representations and critiques. Addressing this key question, Griffin in 'Gendered Cultures' and Morgan in 'The Crisis in Masculinity' pursue ideas, first voiced at the beginning of the twentieth century, about the ways in which ideological change has made previously traditional expectations about gender redundant. Griffin highlights how shifts in discourse from 'women' to 'gender' have impacted on cultural practices, generating popular interest in women's performance, film, and popular cultural work. She documents how the 'cultural turn' has changed the content of women's and gender studies courses around the world.

In the second chapter in this part, Bronwyn Winter points out in 'The Social Foundations of the Sacred: Feminists and the Politics of Religion' that religion is constitutive of social organization and power relations and central to the collective and individual internalization of cultural identity. To the extent that feminists have challenged long-standing taboos in religious belief and practice, they have created major changes in traditional religions, yet they have not been able to resolve the question of whether symbols of religious identity that mark women, such as Islamic veiling, are demeaning or distinctive.

The 'crisis' in masculinity to which Morgan refers is the moral panic about what seems to be – to some men – the claiming of public and institutional space by women. As he points out, this 'crisis' tells us as much about the fragility of masculinity as about the strength of the feminine; nevertheless, he cites evidence which suggests that 'structures of male power are remarkably resilient' (p. 116). To many feminists, that remark would be judged as one of the great understatements of the twentieth and twenty-first centuries. Yet, as Morgan goes on to point out, while gender identities and differences are remarkably resistant to social change, they are always complicated by differences of class and ethnicity. Those whose social status is not dominant, which includes women, have challenged the traditional and conventional with their 'outside' perspectives and views 'from below.'

KNOWLEDGE

An important contention of second-wave feminism is that the shaping of the world takes place through the production of knowledge. Thus, those who control and influence that production create the intellectual world we live in. The chapters in this part are particularly concerned with the ways that women's and gender studies have problematized the taken-for-granted meaning of gender. All three chapters argue that feminist standpoints have forced rethinking and reframing of research and scholarship, and have left deep marks in what and how we think and know.

Carolyn DiPalma and Kathy Ferguson in 'Clearing Ground and Making Connections: Modernism, Postmodernism, Feminism,' tackle one of the most important debates within academic feminism, namely, between modernism and postmodernism, showing how this debate has left a lasting imprint on feminist scholarship. Rather than resolving the debate, they argue that feminist thinking is best served by productively engaging with tensions between modern and postmodern thinking. Lorraine Code, in 'Women Knowing/Knowing Women: Critical–Creative Interventions in the Politics of Knowledge,' shows how feminist critical, gender-sensitive, and political inquiries have produced not only better but different knowledge by creating epistemic standards 'stringent enough to enable knowers to participate intelligently in the world, both physical and human' (p. 148).

In 'Gender, Change, and Education,' Diana Leonard reviews the many changes that have taken place in educational practice and notes the assimilation of women into both the institutions and values of schools and universities. At the same time, she observes the shift towards 'gender-blind' educational policies, a shift which, she notes, can frequently obliterate the interests of women. The drift towards the 'masculine' remains very powerful, entrenched as the masculine has been within the discourses of both Western religion and philosophy.

GLOBALIZATION AND THE STATE

Gender politics with the goal of more structural change are played out in national and international arenas. In the four chapters on globalization and the state, the authors confront state-sanctioned differences between women and men as citizens and members of particular nations with particular national identities and ideologies. If gender politics are complex within societies, they reach the heights of Byzantine complication between societies. Western assumptions about gender in the twenty-first century generally take for granted a formal equality of citizenship; outside the West, this equality cannot be taken for granted. Global agendas and rhetoric about 'democracy' and 'freedom' are sometimes deeply flawed by their limited appreciation of gender difference.

Miri Song points out in 'Gender in a Global World,' the very important role for feminist interventions that do not ignore local differences and diverse cultures. Song makes evident the erasure of gender in most mainstream writings about globalization, and the relationship between the global and the local; that is 'glocal'.

In 'Insiders and Outsiders: Within and Beyond the Gendered Nation,' Barbara Einhorn presents vivid evidence about the difference political change can make to women and gender politics: the dismantling of state socialism in Eastern Europe and the coming of what is described as the 'free' market radically altered women's ability to participate in civil society.

The erasure of gender provides an important context for Dubravka Zarkov's chapter, 'Towards a New Theorizing of Women, Gender, and War.' Women over the centuries, but most notably in the twentieth century, as in *Three Guineas* by Virginia Woolf, have observed that war and organized violence are the province of men. The responsibilities of citizenship involve understanding the motivations for war and military action, yet while Western nations assume that this responsibility will be shared by women and men, none of them fully integrates women into the military. Some definitions of the 'feminine' remain resistant to transformation; yet just as certainly, women are as likely as men to be the civilian victims of violence and aggression. In 'Mothers and Muslims, Sisters and Sojourners: The Contested Boundaries of Feminist Citizenship,' Baukje Prins takes this discussion to the heart of our individual dilemmas as citizens and feminists, asking who we should include as our 'co-citizens' in a world which is increasingly global. The conclusions drawn by the authors are pessimistic about the possibilities of a specifically feminist resistance to the globalization of evermore brutal neo-liberal economies and unprecedented global militarization.

WORK AND FAMILY

One of the major challenges to traditional thinking has been the feminist confrontation of the intersection of the public and the personal in work organizations, families, caregiving, and the welfare state. The transforming impact of second-wave feminism on state policies about social care and welfare provision is founded on distinctions between women and men which largely assume stable gendered behavior. We know, for example, that the majority (although not all) of family carers are women, but in saying this we also have to recognize the cultural baggage implicit in that recognition. The precise nature of that cultural baggage and how it is changing under the impact of new thinking about men and women workers, family members, and caretakers is the subject of the chapters in the part on work and family.

The conventional understanding of gender, as Rosemary Crompton in 'Working with Gender' and Clare Ungerson in 'Gender, Care, and the Welfare State' point out, underpins much of the structure of the labor market, paid and unpaid caregiving, and the welfare state. Ungerson and Crompton draw on the particular case of the British welfare/labor structure, but their essays make the more general point that while gender is paramount in defining the organization of paid work and patterns of unpaid work, these aspects of society are also complicated by factors of racial and ethnic discrimination. Europe in general has far more extensive welfare provisions (notably in health services) than the United States, but other global divisions exist which demand further attention to the different extent of the impact of gender on the individual lives of women and men.

Molly Monahan Lang and Barbara Risman, in 'Blending into Equality: Family Diversity and Gender Convergence,' argue that recent changes in families are increasingly minimizing the differences in women's and men's roles. If that convergence continues and becomes normalized (which is, of course, a matter of conjecture), it may arguably be the case that divisions of gendered behavior and ideologies about them will be overtaken by radical social changes and realignments.

INTIMATE RELATIONSHIPS AND SEXUALITIES

Even more drastic changes in gender and sexuality are outlined by Chrys Ingraham, Sasha Roseneil, and Wendy McKenna and Suzanne Kessler. These authors take as their subject matter the question of gender, sexuality, and intimate relationships; their shared argument is the social construction, and indeed the possible deconstruction, of gender and sexual identities. Although second-wave feminism drew on the rhetorical possibilities of the binary distinction between female and male, women and men, and homosexuals and heterosexuals, feminists at the beginning of the twenty-first century increasingly look beyond those binaries to the theoretical and social possibilities of what Ingraham, in 'Thinking Straight, Acting Bent: Heteronormativity and Homosexuality,' describes as 'thinking (and acting) bent.'

Ingraham proposes a major challenge to feminists and others who want to change the sex/gender system: to recognize the power of 'thinking straight'; that is, thinking in terms of heterosexuality (not gender) as the dominant social paradigm. Change, she argues, must take place by undermining the hegemony of heterosexuality. Roseneil, in 'Foregrounding Friendship: Feminist Pasts, Feminist Futures,' suggests that focusing on friendship enables a challenge to the heteronormativity of the social sciences, and makes visible 'some of the radical transformations in the organization of intimate life which characterize the early twenty-first century' (p. 324). Taking the transformations even further, McKenna and Kessler in 'Transgendering: Blurring the Boundaries of Gender' lay out the ways that this phenomenon 'radically deconstructs the meaning of gender categories and presents feminist scholars with possibilities for linking theory and practice' in producing social change (p. 344).

EMBODIMENT IN A TECHNOLOGICAL WORLD

The body, the environment, and science and technology are the focus of three chapters that explore the intersection and interaction of gender, bodies, and technology. The authors point out the various tensions that exist between the individual choices which women make (or wish to make) and the social norms defining women's social position. In 'Gendered Bodies: Between Conformity and Autonomy,' Sharyn Roach Anleu argues that conformity to gender norms, while more restrictive for women than for men, does not always compromise or reduce women's autonomy and power.

Indeed, as Irmgard Schultz suggests in 'The Natural World and the Nature of Gender,' the concept of the feminine can play a key part in rethinking social organization. For example, the ideas of 'provident economy' and 'everyday life ecology,' ideas drawn from gendered perspectives about the conduct of daily life, take women's experience as the conceptual basis for the renegotiation of social relationships, in this case the particularly sensitive relationship of women and men to nature. In 'From Science and Technology to Feminist Technoscience,' Jutta Weber interprets recent cultural studies of science and technology as reactions to the feminist reorganization of knowledge.

MAKING CHANGE

The final part explores the possibilities for creating social change. The contributions in this handbook do not share the same political aims or strategies or, for that matter, moral views. In 'Moral Perspectives: Gender, Ethics, and Political Theory,' Joan Tronto explores the way people develop their moral views, and how those moral views are so deeply structured by context. Nevertheless, Tronto points out that the ethic of care is now an undisputed part of feminist challenges to the conventional post-Enlightenment assumption that individual citizens must be free to act in their own interests. For feminists, an ethic of care means responsibility for others as well. The concept of autonomy and agency, therefore, must encompass the recognition of that responsibility.

The goal of knowledge that accurately reflects our gendered lives is widely accepted by feminists, but there are major disagreements about how to do the research that will produce that knowledge. In 'Having It All: Feminist Fractured Foundationalism,' Sue Wise and Liz Stanley offer a 'toolkit' for practical use that they suggest will produce 'unalienated feminist knowledge.' In political activism, as Manisha Desai points out in 'From Autonomy to Solidarities: Transnational Feminist Political Strategies,' the aims of feminists vary considerably if one takes a transnational perspective.

In the final chapter, we offer our own utopian views on what social changes we would most like to see, and how these can be accomplished. At this point in the twenty-first century, the study of gender, in all its many forms, offers an endlessly challenging way of thinking through, and past, the banal rhetoric of public politics. One of the paradoxes of the twenty-first century is that as intellectual life allows increasing doubt and speculation about the clarity of previously entrenched 'natural' categories, including male and female, it brings, as Judith Lorber argues in 'A World Without Gender?', the possibility of 'degendering' to the fore as a viable form of resistance to existing gendered social orders. Against the backdrop of global inequalities of power and a growing tendency towards fundamentalist politics, Mary Evans in 'Getting Real: Contextualizing Gender' reminds us that the task for feminism is to be critical of its liberal underpinnings, even as it remains committed to preserving its longing for a more egalitarian and democratic future for women and men. Taking a transnational perspective, Kathy Davis, in 'Feminist Politics of Location,' concludes on a hopeful note. With a little 'geographical imagination,' a feminism of the future may become the site for dialogues across cultural, regional, and national borders. Taken together, we provide a vision of how women's and gender studies can become a richly subversive challenge to the authoritarian construction of knowledge and an opportunity for a radical politics of social justice and transformation.

REFERENCES

Ortner, Sherry (1972) 'Is Female to Male as Nature is to Culture?' *Feminist Studies*, 1: 5–31.
Wollstonecraft, Mary (1988) *A Vindication of the Rights of Woman*. New York: W. W. Norton.
Woolf, Virginia (1992) *Three Guineas*. Oxford, Oxford University Press.

Part I
CURRENT STATE OF WOMEN'S STUDIES, GENDER STUDIES, AND STUDIES OF MEN

1

The Life and Times of Academic Feminism

Clare Hemmings

This chapter re-examines two debates central to the current state of Gender and Women's Studies. The first is known as the autonomy/integration debate, which asks whether feminist enquiry should seek to influence the academy from within particular disciplines, or establish itself as a separate 'discipline' drawing on interdisciplinary theories and methods. In critiquing dominant modes of evaluating institutional success in this context, I provide an overview of the current state of academic feminism from a range of intellectual and geographical positions. The second debate concerns the 'proper name' of academic feminism. Here I focus on the proliferation of writing which condemns or endorses an institutional move from Women's Studies to Gender Studies, suggesting that we need to situate such claims in the geographical and as well as theoretical contexts from which they arise. Throughout this chapter, I stress the importance of thinking through academic feminist institutionalization as having a 'life of its own', one that is negotiated and renewed on a daily basis, rather than one whose meaning is predominantly referential.

INTRODUCTION

Joan Wallach Scott suggestively describes Women's Studies as 'a place of anxiety and irritability…but also one of great energy and vitality' (1997: iv). Marilyn Jacoby Boxer echoes Scott's ambivalence, insisting that 'to partake of Women's Studies is to dwell in an incubator of optimism – despite the field's obduracies, penuries, blindnesses, fallacies and disputes' (2003: xiii). And Beverley Skeggs bemoans the fact that 'the vibrantly energetic Women's Studies lovingly described by Ailbhe Smyth (1992) is taking a kicking and we are the body bags' (1995: 483), ending her otherwise crushing indictment of consumer culture's impact on Women's Studies in the UK with the rousing reminder that it 'is in these conditions that we will continue to fight'

(p. 483).[1] While invested commentary on the academic institutionalization of feminism is enormously diverse in many respects, it tends to share this strong affective tone, frequently weighing its difficulties against its pleasures and responding to both with equal fervour.

As an academic in Gender Studies, I also reside in those anxieties and vitalities. Deeply committed to feminist higher education though I am, some days I can't shift my feelings of gloom. In the UK, each year brings news of more closures of undergraduate Women's and Gender Studies departments, despite continued and diverse interest in feminist research and pedagogy and growth in some specific areas at the graduate level (such as gender and development). While academics are consistently encouraged to apply for external funding to give them much needed leave in departments starved of resources, feminist research remains unrecognized as distinct by the primary funding bodies, and thus interdisciplinary feminist applications are at a considerable disadvantage. In addition, the increasing bureaucratization of academic life in general means that curriculum development, pastoral care of students, and research are frequently squeezed out by audits, meetings, and the struggle for basic resources (Deem and Johnson, 2003; Gray, 2003; Knights and Richards, 2003).[2] My heart sinks when I see my in-tray, the list of meetings with students and colleagues, the cursed email in my inbox, and the possibility of research today trickles away – again. But such crowding at least delays the more persistent anxieties that have a different temporality and that can ruin the summer I thought I was looking forward to. Is feminist academic work valuable? If it used to be, is it still? Is mine? What do feminist academics think we are doing?

And then again, some days I fairly float to work. I teach feminist thought! I write about the social world from a feminist perspective! This is partly individual – it is a good life. I teach graduate Gender Studies at a well-funded UK institution, we have good student numbers, we are not facing imminent closure (for now). These days also serve to reframe those anxieties. Those demanding students are the same ones who thirst for feminist knowledge, push it to its limits, and make the connections that allow feminist thought to expand beyond itself and thus remain, or become, useful and relevant. They are motivated and ruthless in their critical judgements. On such days, it should be noted, so that you do not go away with the impression that students always carry the burden of my own sense of usefulness (a quite dreadful academic feminist habit), I am reminded why *I* am committed to an academic feminist project.

I remain in thrall to a thirty-year endeavour that has developed an institutional life that intersects with, but cannot be reduced to, feminist political movements, and that has been brave enough to take its own history and presumptions as critical objects of enquiry. In the process, academic feminism has developed a dizzying interdisciplinary array of epistemological and methodological tools that allow us to understand and challenge social and political realities globally. It has not done so on its own, but it most certainly has done so. And there is plenty of life in the young (you name it) yet.[3]

You may see your own perspective represented in some parts of my opening account, but the affective tensions I have described are more fundamental to academic feminism than straightforward identification or dis-identification might suggest. The histories of the last three decades of academic feminist institutionalization are structured by these prevalent themes of loss or progress. Commentators tend to privilege one over the other, such that the institutionalization of feminism emerges either as a relentless march away from real feminist politics and towards professionalization and bureaucratization (Griffin and Hanmer, 2001; Messer-Davidow, 2002; Stanley and Wise, 2000; Stromquist, 2001), or as a welcome increase in the variety of tools in the feminist store cupboard, with a particular emphasis on the political importance of challenging the fantasy of lost feminist unity that grounds the previous narrative (Adkins, 2004; Huffer 1998; Roof, 1997; Stacey, 1993; Wiegman, 2000). My own introduction emphasizes both bureaucratization and transformation, and I began this chapter by locating myself as a way of flagging from the outset the central role of biography in determining whether anxiety or vitality dominates a particular account of academic feminist institutionalization. My story would be very different if I worked in an under-resourced institution, if my post were temporary or part-time, as so many Women's and Gender Studies jobs are, if I were a research professor with dedicated research assistance, or if I were the lone feminist researcher teaching in a disciplinary context.

In the rest of this chapter, I take forward the question of location to re-examine two abiding debates within academic feminism. The first is known as the autonomy/integration debate, which asks whether feminist enquiry should seek to influence the academy from within particular disciplines, or establish itself as a separate discipline drawing on interdisciplinary theories and methods. It is in this context that I aim to provide a partial account of the current state of play of feminist work within the academy,[4] highlighting the material contexts of institutionalization of feminist work over the commonly abstract debates that circulate on this issue. The second debate concerns the 'proper name' of academic feminism. Here I focus on the proliferation of writing which condemns or endorses an institutional move from Women's Studies to Gender Studies, suggesting that we need to situate such claims in the geographical as well as theoretical contexts from which they arise.

Throughout this chapter, I stress the importance of thinking through academic feminist institutionalization as having a 'life of its own', one that is negotiated and renewed on a daily basis, rather than one whose meaning is predominantly referential. I see this project as a direct challenge to a feminist imagination dominated by the counterproductive myth of 'the selfish feminist academic'– the one who has abandoned her sisters to 'serve only

[her] professional interests and those of patriarchy and the male ruling class' (Evans, 1982: 61). The myth of the selfish feminist academic only works if we retain the image of her opposite of course: the political doer Mary Evans ironically dubs 'the true believer' (1982: 70). Such a perverse pairing means that academic feminist production can only be understood as lacking, as subject to an imagined feminist golden age before institutionalization, or a future full of political (which is to say non-institutional) redemption. This myth thus prioritizes easy scapegoating over the painstaking task of teasing out the specific contributions and challenges of thirty years of academic institutionalization of feminism.

INSTITUTIONAL ROUTES

In large part, debates about autonomy versus integration of feminist research and teaching within the academy are questions of strategy. Some feminists have argued that integration into existing disciplines is essential if change within the academy as a whole is to occur and be sustained, and further that ghettoization of feminist work will not advance its efforts for transformation of social or academic worlds (SIGMA report, 1995; Smyth, 1992; Stanley, 1991).[5] Alternatively, feminists favouring autonomy stress the importance of providing a space for feminist dialogue across disciplinary interests and investments (Bowles and Klein, 1983: 13), and the importance of ensuring the development of intellectual as well as institutional autonomy (Braidotti, 2002: 288; Griffin and Hanmer, 2001). For these authors, autonomy is also more likely to generate a dynamic environment for student–staff interaction, including the development of innovative pedagogies and assessment methods (Deats and Lenker, 1994; Jackson, 2004). Both perspectives have been rigorously critiqued. Integration as a strategy is likely to put enormous pressure on individuals or small groups of feminist academics both to 'write to the [disciplinary] audience' concerned (Bowles and Klein, 1983: 7), and to fill the feminist gaps in the existing disciplinary curriculum and supervision arrangements. In addition, the replacement of feminist staff is harder to guarantee, being more subject to the intellectual and political investments of those with power in the department or discipline concerned. Yet autonomy can also isolate feminist departments, centres, or institutes, making them vulnerable to marginalization or closure. And if disciplinary integration has been abandoned, closure of an autonomous unit can effectively wipe out feminist research and teaching at a given institution.

There are two main responses to the opposition of autonomy and integration as described above. Most commentators now take the view that a combination approach is the most desirable and sustainable one (Bergman, 2000: 52; SIGMA report, 1995). Jackie Stacey, Ann Phoenix, and Hilary Hinds thus argued in the early 1990s that Women's Studies needs to work 'within disciplines to challenge and transform them, and [seek] some autonomy through which to develop new models and understandings' (1992: 5). This sentiment was reinforced a decade later by Rosi Braidotti, who stressed the importance of understanding Women's Studies as both 'a critical project in so far as it examines how science perpetuates forms of discrimination and…exclusion' and 'a creative field that opens up alternative spaces' for feminists to take stock of our own critical history and imagine our future differently (Braidotti, 2002: 288).

A second approach tends to see autonomy as evidence of the *fullest* institutional achievement, through which the various other levels of institutionalization of feminist research and pedagogy can be measured (Barazzetti and Leone, 2003: 5–7; Silius, 2002).[6] The latter may be useful as a temporary methodological necessity, perhaps, but such a developmental history privileges the experiences in countries where autonomy has already been (albeit partially) achieved – the UK, the Netherlands, and Australia, for example – or where autonomy is suited to the particular system of higher education, but hotly contested – most notably the United States. But a straightforward 'combination' approach is rather dissatisfying too, since it specifies an ideal rather than speaking directly to specific institutional strategies for sustainability of feminist work. I believe it is more useful to focus on the tensions that attend both the autonomy and integration approaches and on the material conditions in which the differences are negotiated than it is to seek to resolve the issue abstractly in a straightforward 'additive' mode.

In the majority of national contexts, the institutionalization of feminist knowledge within the academy is intimately linked to broader feminist social movements. Frequently known as the 'academic arm' of the women's movement, a strong presence of such a movement seems to have been a precondition for feminist academic institutionalization in the United Kingdom, the United States, and Germany, for example (Silius, 2002). The lack of such movements is frequently cited as a central reason for delayed academic institutionalization in Central and Eastern Europe (Corrin, 1992; Papic, 2002). Yet this trajectory is not singular, or developmental, in any simple way – indeed the two are frequently in tension. In her discussion of women's groups in Serbia and Montenegro, for example, Andjelka Milić indicates that women's organizing was present in urban centres in the former Yugoslavia throughout the 1970s (2004), indicating that there must have been a different reason for the lack of academic feminist institutionalization in that context. In Italy, which had a strong feminist movement in the 1970s, grassroots opposition to feminist intervention (autonomy or integration as strategies aside) in the academy was so fierce that Women's Studies only existed as a separate intellectual endeavour outside the academy until very recently (Barazzetti, 2000; Silius, 2002: 23). Similarly, in France, post-May 1968 feminist intellectual production was stronger in non-institutionalized contexts, such as the Cahiers du Grif collective, than in universities (Braidotti, Vonk, and van Wichelen, 2000: 167; Silius, 2002: 17).

In sites where feminist research and teaching were institutionalized early, debates about the dangers of depoliticization of feminist knowledge have been ongoing. Some discussants have insisted that university-level Women's and Gender Studies should be considered as one of several sites of struggle over knowledge production and not be privileged as primary (Barazzetti and Leone, 2003: 20; Lees, 1991: 90–91). The history of feminist knowledge production across Europe includes adult education (Kelly and Pearson, 1983), the establishment of independent publishers and academic journals, feminist libraries and documentation centres, and the use of interdisciplinary media, including art and film.

Within the academy, the struggle to resist institutional depoliticization has combined an ongoing emphasis on collaborative work and transformative pedagogy with an insistence on maintaining activist, community, and policy links.[7] The extent to which these principles have been instigated and maintained in contemporary academic contexts varies enormously, as one might expect. Across Europe, the link between degree-level courses in Women's and Gender Studies and non-governmental policy development is well established, with students frequently using their degrees as stepping stones to careers in the NGO sector (Griffin and Hanmer, 2001; Silius, 2002).[8]

Yet it would be rather hasty to reify this 'academia into policy' route as straightforwardly preserving the integrity of feminist knowledge production. In the UK, the reduction in public spending on education has been accompanied by an increasing bureaucratization of the NGO sector to carry the burden of public sector service delivery (Griffin and Hanmer, 2001), hardly a self-evidently progressive arena. And I would also argue that policy intervention is not self-evidently transformative of gender relations in the long term. Writing from the perspective of the former Yugoslavia, Zarana Papic cautions that unless policy intervention is matched by concomitant cultural shifts in gender perceptions and expectations, policy advances are easily lost in the event of a regime change (2002).

While the relationship between intellectual and activist struggles has a clear effect on whether academic institutionalization of feminist research and pedagogy has occurred, the factor most directly influencing longevity of feminist courses or centres is the nature of local, national, or international institutional support. In national contexts where higher education is modular, expansionist, and employment directed, Women's or Gender Studies saw a boom in the 1980s and 1990s. A combination of demand from the new influx of women into higher education and staff vision to promote and meet that demand meant that a large number of Women's or Gender Studies courses at undergraduate and graduate levels were established in the United States, the UK, the Netherlands, and some Scandinavian countries during that time (Skeggs, 1995: 479; Stacey, Phoenix, and Hinds, 1992: 4; Threadgold, 2000: 44). Autonomy could thus be argued for and sometimes granted, if grudgingly, on the basis of parity rather than special treatment.

In most of these contexts, autonomy has been easier to achieve and sustain at the graduate level rather than undergraduate level because of the perceived need for a disciplinary undergraduate background in the first instance. Strangely, here, Women's or Gender Studies is imagined both as too narrow (biased) and too broad (interdisciplinary) to constitute a discipline in its own right. In the United States, where entry into graduate school is understood to mark the beginning of disciplinarity proper, after a broad-based undergraduate education, Women's and Gender Studies have taken a much greater hold at the undergraduate level, but for similar reasons.[9]

In contexts where higher education remains formally disciplinary and resolutely hierarchical, such as France and Italy, Women's or Gender Studies has not been able to generate the same level of internal institutional support and has thus either not expanded beyond individual course provision or has relied on the international reputation of individual feminists to force institutional approval.[10] As a result, integration rather than autonomy is usually the only viable option within the institutions concerned, and lecturers frequently introduce feminist history, concepts, and contexts via courses with more neutral disciplinary names.

There is another increasingly significant route enabling the academic institutionalization of feminist research and teaching: external funding from government or equal opportunities agencies or funding from international agencies such as the World Bank, for whom 'gender' might be said to be the new agenda. In both Spain and Finland, for example, Women's Studies is predominantly funded by equal opportunities agencies (Silius, 2002: 29, 31), and in India, the thirty-two independent women's studies centres have arisen as a direct result of international and government agency support (Jain and Rajput, 2003: 19).

In a very real sense, then, one could argue that the success or otherwise of feminist academic institutionalization in different national contexts is predominantly a question of markets. And importantly, academic markets, like all markets, are subject to change. British feminist academics writing in the early to mid 1990s were aware that student demand and a 'market-led economy for higher education' (Skeggs, 1995: 497) were the core reasons for the blossoming of undergraduate Women's Studies at that time, and indeed we have subsequently been hit by an equally rapid decline in those student numbers, which has lead to cutbacks and closures as many departments and institutions struggle to survive.

While the field continues to attract large numbers of graduate students (mostly overseas students), particularly in the context of joint degrees with development, social policy, or media, and an interested student can take pathways or individual courses in women's or gender issues in almost any university in the country, undergraduate programmes have been decimated. At this point, all UK single honours programmes have closed, and increasing numbers of autonomous centres, departments, or institutes have had to move into larger departments to survive in any form.

Commentators see two main reasons for this decline in the UK. First, the abolition of grants and introduction of fees for undergraduate degrees has reduced the number of mature students returning to education and created a dominant student culture of utilitarianism over idealism (Griffin and Braidotti, 2002: 4; Silius and Tuori, 2003: 17; Stromquist, 2001: 382). In this fee-paying context, given that most students are unlikely ever to have encountered Women's or Gender Studies as an area of academic enquiry before attending university, let alone appreciate the high level of employability of its graduates, it is unsurprising that the appeal of a single honours degree in Women's or Gender Studies has dwindled.

Second, pervasive cultural understandings of feminism as anachronistic mean that students steer clear of feminist programmes, particularly in light of the need to make their degree 'count' on the open market (Griffin and Hanmer, 2001: 43).[11] While the changing fortunes of UK higher education clearly play an important part in explaining this particular decline, it is critical to stress that not all academic areas of enquiry are positioned equally in relation to its logic. In a recent survey conducted by the Feminist and Women's Studies Association (UK and Ireland), feminist academics remarked on the inconsistent application of 'the numbers game' across their particular institutions. Other departments with low recruitment were frequently protected rather than dissolved, and the calculation of the numbers themselves varied according to the needs of the institution.

The feelings of isolation experienced by many UK feminist academics in this climate are compounded by broader institutional attacks on the life of Women's and Gender Studies. National funding bodies continue to refuse to recognize Women's and Gender Studies as fields of enquiry in their own right, meaning that, as suggested above, feminist grant applications are less likely to be evaluated by experts in the field and financial support for emerging feminist scholars is increasingly difficult to obtain. The Research Assessment Exercise (RAE)[12] that dominates contemporary UK academic life has axed the Women's Studies sub-panel for the 2008 round subsuming it with the Sociology sub-panel.[13]

The precipitous closure of undergraduate programmes in Women's and Gender Studies in the UK must be placed within this broader ideological context of devaluation of feminist research and training. It is difficult to be a feminist academic in the UK currently and not feel alternately angry and helpless in the face of these institutional blows. For this reason alone, perhaps, a less nationally delimited analysis can be helpful.

As suggested, Women's Studies in the UK was one of the countries swift to take up the market opportunities presented in the 1980s and early 1990s, and as one might expect, the same is true now in other national contexts. Women's or Gender Studies is currently growing in Germany, Spain, Portugal, and New Zealand, where higher education is in a period of reorganization. In contexts where there is ongoing support from equal opportunities or international agencies, the situation is currently stable (Griffin and Braidotti, 2002: 4). There is also hope that the reframing of higher education in line with the Bologna Declaration (1999) will provide a new context of student demand and institutional support for Women's and Gender Studies across Europe.[14] While not underestimating the competition-led nature of the Bologna Declaration, the European Women's Studies Thematic Network (Athena) has been actively exploring positive applications of this change (Silius, 2002: 19, 22), with particular emphasis on its potential value in consolidating a European Women's Studies curriculum and institutionalized exchange networks for staff and students.

A challenging development in the UK has been the increase of international students pursuing Women's and Gender Studies Masters and PhD programmes. In departments or programmes where growth in student numbers has been sustained, this can be largely attributed to the global demand for interdisciplinary, autonomous degree programmes in Women's and Gender Studies that the UK is well placed to meet. In market terms, the UK can currently provide interdisciplinary academic feminist training in a range of arenas and with an increasing number of specialties, which other national contexts cannot.[15] At the graduate Gender Institute at the London School of Economics, where I teach, student numbers are high and growing, but they are predominantly international students, many from the United States, while numbers of UK students are in decline (for the reasons suggested above).

Within this context, students are particularly keen to take graduate courses that have an international, development, or globalization focus, since these both reflect their located interests and arguably offer the greatest employment prospects for Women's and Gender Studies graduates. As gender, and with it Gender Studies, can no longer (if they ever could) be thought of in national terms, the teachers of Women's and Gender Studies in the UK need to find a way to respond creatively to the current market without simply echoing its demands.

Academic feminists have no alternative but to seize the moments when institutional and/or international changes move in our favour, but opportunism must be met with plans for sustainability if we are not to keep on watching the contexts built up over years disappear when national and international circumstances alter. I have been suggesting that debates about autonomy and integration need to be situated within particular institutional, national, and international frames if the arguments are not to remain abstract. The institutionalization of feminist work in higher education is too uneven and precarious a process to have a single developmental ideal imposed upon it. Nor can we propose a dual, combined approach in anything other than the abstract. Instead, academic feminist debate needs to stress located, translatable sustainability to identify the best ways to enable feminist work to flourish.

WHAT'S IN A NAME?

In the uneven thirty-year process of academic institutionalization of feminist knowledge, a dispute has occurred over the proper name of this project. While some sites retain the title Women's Studies, others have shifted to, or named new programmes, Gender Studies, Women's and Gender Studies, or the more descriptive 'Gender and...'[16] These questions of naming are anything but neutral, and one's theoretical position on the issue tends to be directly linked to intellectual biography and to national or international location. I have privileged the naming question over many others in this chapter because a given author's response to the issue is frequently a platform for engagement with concerns about the institutionalization of feminist work more generally.

Those who resist naming academic feminist work anything other than Women's Studies do so for compelling reasons. Most broadly, Gender Studies is perceived as representative of a desire for academic neutrality in the hope of accessing institutional rewards (Stromquist, 2001: 374–375). It is thus commonly seen as a deliberate depoliticization of an academic feminist project, all the more regrettable where the change is internally decided, and not externally forced. Commentators have been concerned that a primary effect of this renaming will be to open up what historically has been a vibrant, safe, women-only environment to include men (Evans, 1991; Richardson and Robinson, 1994). This potential invasion is theorized in several ways: as related to literal bodies (men will feel more comfortable in something called Gender Studies); as facilitated by the alliance between feminism and queer theory, which may privilege gay male experience; and as a shift to studying 'gender relations' over the experience and construction of womanhood, with its risk of an attendant consolidation of the heteronormative framing of gender as 'complementarity'. Renate Klein takes the strongest position on this last issue, rephrasing Gender Studies 'hetero-relations studies' (1991: 81). As Stacy Gillis and Rebecca Munford point out, these objections to Gender Studies are typically situated within a more general anger at the academic attacks on the 'very category of "woman"' (2003: 6), precipitated by the very worst invasion of all, that of poststructuralism into the academy.

Poststructuralism is credited with authoring 'a shift of attention from the basic issue of women's subordination' (Aaron and Walby, 1991: 5) towards a concern with language over material reality (Segal, 2000: 26; Stromquist, 2001: 373). Without 'woman' as the subject and object of feminism, what we are left with are 'fragmented bits and pieces, vagueness and uncertainty' (Klein, 1991: 83). To abandon Women's Studies in favour of Gender Studies is thus to have been 'lured' (Evans, 1991: 73) away not only from the 'proper object' (Butler, 1994) of enquiry, women, but from feminism itself. Wendy Brown's insistence that the final deconstruction of the 'woman' of 'Women's Studies' propels us towards an inevitable, and not to be lamented, return to disciplinarity would seem to prove the point (1997).

As anyone familiar with contemporary feminist theory might anticipate, the counter-arguments concerning the 'proper name' of feminism within the academy foreground the same issues but value them differently. Thus, the alliances between 'Gender Studies, queer, transgender and postcolonial theories' (Gillis and Munford, 2003: 6) are seen as essential to the survival of feminism in the academy, and as cause for celebration not retrenchment. Contests over the 'proper object' of feminism are seen as arising out of a positive political desire to recognize both 'other' marginal subjects and other marginalized fields within the academy (Braidotti and Butler, 1994; Zalewski, 2003). The argument is that in order for the desire for connections with Lesbian and Gay or Queer Studies, Transgender Studies, and Ethnic Studies to be understood as genuine, it will not always be appropriate (or ethical) to privilege a female body in terms of gendered meaning. Thus, in relation to Transgender Studies, for example, the mobilization of a female body as foundational has been theorized as part of an invalidation of transgender experiences (Wilton, 2000). Challenges to the grounding of Women's Studies in the category 'woman' usually supplement these with the delineation of gender as a theoretically and politically useful category of analysis that need not (though it may) take woman as its object (Martin, 2001; Scott, 1988; Spivak, 1981). Gender Studies is in this way thought through as part of a theoretical and political shift towards coalition within the specific context of the academic institutionalization of feminist work.

The debates I have outlined above are underpinned by maintaining a clear opposition between Women's Studies and Gender Studies in the first place. The two are consistently articulated as entirely separate projects with distinct objects and distinct subjects, and, importantly, as *chronologically* distinct. It is this rhetorical separation that allows Diane Richardson and Victoria Robinson to imagine a feminist choice about which one we want – 'should we welcome [Gender Studies]…or should we be critical?' (1994: 11) – as if feminist commentators were not already staked within the debates and located in areas other than Women's Studies. Richardson and Robinson's question only makes sense if we assume that those making such a choice are *first of all* located in Women's Studies. In fact, both 'sides' bolster their claims by situating the debates chronologically. Advocates of Women's Studies tend to frame Gender Studies simply as a rejection of the former, while advocates of Gender Studies repeatedly position Women's Studies as irredeemably essentialist and anachronistic, as *over* if one is at all theoretically sophisticated.[17] In fixing the meaning of these designations as predominantly relational, both 'camps' ignore the myriad institutional and national or international contexts in which Women's Studies and Gender Studies have developed either independently or in mutually exclusive ways.

The assumption that advocating Gender Studies over Women's Studies or vice versa is an endorsement of either poststructuralism or material accounts of womanhood is simultaneously to assume that these designations mean the same thing everywhere. In this respect, the Women's Studies/Gender Studies debates are remarkably Anglo-American in their frames of reference, while rarely being located in them as such. Thus Brown's (1997) advocacy of a return to disciplinarity for feminist scholars reflects her location in the US academy, where Women's Studies has made relatively little impression at the graduate level, and most feminist scholars have graduate, which is to say disciplinary, expertise to facilitate such a return. That the US situation is anomalous and thus in need of careful rather than abstract translation (Spivak, 1993) is ignored both in Brown's own recommendations for the international field of Women's and Gender Studies and in the transnational adoption of her arguments (Zalewski, 2003).

In contrast, my first critique of a fixed, chronological opposition between Women's and Gender Studies concerns the varied institutional contexts of their emergence, and is thus partly a way of tracing an institutional history of academic feminism. In most Scandinavian countries, for example, the translation of 'gender' into 'genus' in NGO and governmental sites has facilitated the dominance of 'genus studies' in the academy (Braidotti, 2002: 294). Kari Jegerstedt argues that the widespread use of 'genus studies' (with the exception of Finland) appropriately reflects and consolidates the prioritization of equal opportunities in academic feminist environments (2000). There is no history of displacement of Women's Studies in this context, and no sense of 'genus' as a neutral term. Additionally, in the 2000s, the global currency of 'gender' has increased to such an extent that it seems folly indeed to continue to think through the meaning of Gender Studies only in terms of an abandonment of an interest in women's subordination. The shift from 'women in development' to 'gender and development' in this particular interdisciplinary arena means that 'Gender Studies' as a designation is more likely to attract funding and students, and to facilitate interdisciplinary and international alliances in ways that cannot previously have been anticipated.

Let me be clear: I am not arguing for a celebration of plurality of meaning for its own sake. Located meanings of Gender Studies or its translations need to be examined in their own right precisely because they present new opportunities for assimilation and co-optation of feminist values, not because they are immune from these. While Gabriele Griffin and Rosi Braidotti are optimistic about the ways in which academic feminism can offer a potent challenge to nationalism within Europe by challenging the normative use of gender as the basis of national identifications (2002: 12), the linguistic and cultural foundation of 'gender' in 'genre' and thus 'species' in many countries makes guarding against its interpretation as part of a nationalist strategy focusing on 'gender purity' particularly important.[18] And while governmental or NGO support of Gender Studies may provide opportunities for feminist research not otherwise available, there are both practical and theoretical problems with an unqualified endorsement of this direction. Such support can signal a potential loss of intellectual self-determination or the watering down of academic feminists' transformative agenda. Bearing in mind the trenchant critiques of a gender and development agenda by transnational feminist theorists, we cannot afford to celebrate the international context of Gender Studies in narrow Anglo-American institutional terms either.[19]

'Women's Studies' as an institutional designation also has a varied history that cannot be reduced to its imagined past reliance on an inert conception of womanhood, from the perspective of Gender Studies as an imagined cutting edge. Again an international approach is instructive. As a term, 'Women's Studies' is a US import, but its translation into multiple contexts where English is not the native tongue has also transformed its meaning, linguistically and theoretically (Braidotti, 2002: 285). In Finland, for example, 'woman' already has multiple meanings – both biological and cultural – and Women's Studies is thus preferred over Gender Studies, which does not translate in the same way (Braidotti, 2002: 293). Theoretically, Griffin and Braidotti celebrate the ways in which, in European feminist sites that are grounded in continental philosophical traditions, the 'Woman' of 'Women's Studies' does not refer to the complement of Man, but to 'a multilayered and complex subject that has taken her distance from femininity'. In their European framing, the subject of Women's Studies becomes 'the subject of quite another story, a subject-in-process, who can figure as an example of the kind of transformation Europe…[needs] to undergo' (2002: 12). Here it is a European incarnation of Women's Studies more than Gender Studies that is most closely aligned with the mission of problematizing 'woman' in dominant discourse.

At its most radical, this project disarticulates 'the feminine' from the female body, challenging the necessary correlation between the two, as suggested by the mission statement of Les Etudes Féminines at the University of Paris VIII, which insists that 'le féminine d'Etudes Féminines ne revoie pas nécessairement à des sujets de sexe féminin' (Berger, 2004).[20] While in the United States a thorough deconstruction of 'woman' has suggested the death of Women's Studies as a discipline, then, in France, the Netherlands, and Finland, the deconstruction of 'woman' might be said to constitute the ground of that discipline.

Women's and Gender Studies spaces are resonant with these different histories and contexts. As indicated above, academic feminism in many Western contexts is increasingly international in terms of its student body, staff mobility, and syllabus content. The hierarchical valuation of academic institutions globally means that more people come to study in the UK from India, say, than vice versa. But this hierarchization is further complicated for students wanting feminist education because of the uneven nature of institutionalization of feminist work in different countries, as discussed above. Students who want to work on feminist issues will frequently have to travel to obtain specialist training or to have feminist teaching of any kind.[21] There is a flow from North America to the UK for students wanting specialist training in gender and development or gender and social policy at the Masters level, for example, because of the particular pattern of institutionalization in the United States. Students from Italy are likely to take up places in the Netherlands, Germany, France, or the UK because of the difficulty in obtaining recognition for interdisciplinary feminist work in the strictly disciplinary Italian system. Australian Women's and Gender Studies courses draw significantly on nearby South East Asian contexts (Magarey and Sheriden, 2002). Feminist academics, as well as students, are often forced (and sometimes choose) to relocate to follow jobs, as feminist institutes, departments, and courses open and close, or to follow their hearts or the prospect of promotion. Writing about Australian Women's Studies, indeed, Susan Magarey and Susan Sheriden note that most of the 'home-grown' feminist academics in Australia come from, or have moved, elsewhere (2002: 139–140).

Academic feminism thus truly does produce nomadic professional subjects (Braidotti, 1994). The flow of staff and students between and among these sites makes academic feminism an interesting place to be, albeit one dense with contradictions. While an international staff and student body is cause for celebration in many ways, it needs to be situated in the context of forced migration, the financial privilege of elites, and the cornering of the global student market by a few leading universities (Rizvi and Walsh, 1998). Recent wars in former Yugoslavia, for example, have forced many feminist academics to disperse to other countries, notably France and Italy. And of course it is usually only the richest students who can afford to chase qualifications across continents.[22]

The increasingly international background of staff and students occupying academic feminism means that we cannot afford to reproduce Anglo-American universalization for pedagogical reasons, too. In an extremely international space like the LSE Gender Institute, meanings are negotiated *in situ* as staff and students recognize and misrecognize each other's histories and locations through the terms they use. If particular students and staff reject Women's Studies and claim Gender Studies to describe their curriculum and environment, this can only be the beginning of further investigation. A US student may claim Gender Studies in order to mark her or his interest in Queer Studies, for example, while a seemingly similar claim from an Indian student is at least as likely to mark an interest in questions of economic redistribution over cultural and political identity. When UK, Italian, and French students insist that Women's Studies be considered the proper name of their academic endeavours, they may well be marking out intellectual, disciplinary, and political locations more different than they are similar. It is these tensions and unexpected alliances that I believe need to form the fertile ground for debates about Women's and Gender Studies in order to ensure that we are not working with outdated or provincial models of academic feminist institutionalization.

AGAINST FEMINIST NOSTALGIA

Given the range of theoretical, historical, and political ways of assessing the relationship between Women's Studies and Gender Studies, the domination of the debate by clear-cut positions for or against seems difficult to account for. My suspicion is that Women's and Gender Studies are kept chronologically and politically distinct in part because of feminist intellectual biography. As I suggested at the outset of this chapter, the chronologization of these debates intersects with and relies on broader positions on the decline or regeneration of (academic) feminism. Thus, the lament at the naming of academic feminism anything other than Women's Studies frequently chimes with the conviction that this was always bound to happen. Poststructuralism, with its UK and US impetus towards Gender Studies, provides retrospective evidence in support of the suspicion that the project of academic institutionalization of feminism was apolitical all along (Ehrenreich, 1990: 176). Recent millennium special issues of interdisciplinary academic feminist journals reflecting on the past, present, and future of academic feminist endeavour are peppered with articles bemoaning the loss of feminist unity in the face of intellectual and cultural fragmentation.[23] In such a narrative, lost feminist politics is always nostalgically invoked through reference to its contemporary absence, and personal experiences of 'the declining passion for politics evident in many veteran feminists' (Segal, 2000: 19) or 'the end of the exciting feminist intellectual milieu I once moved in' (Ehrenreich, 1990: 176) are generalized as representative of feminist experience in general. The alternative position relishes poststructuralist challenges to Women's Studies, producing a rather different narrative of a move away from false unity and towards a valuation of difference (Adkins, 2004; Wiegman, 2000).

My resistance to the first narrative is that it seems unable to concede that many feminists experienced the coincidence of poststructuralism and feminism precisely as political. I was one of those feminists, coming to left-wing politics in my early twenties, reading Black and postcolonial feminist theory in the late 1980s and early 1990s, finding it shed enormous light on the problems I was experiencing making sense of Black feminist resistance to 'reclaim the night' marches. On coaches on the way to marches against violence against women, my poststructuralist comrades and I debated whether 'woman' was still a useful category of analysis in the political present. Those of us who thought it was preferred an Irigarayan perspective of 'woman' as in excess of the hom(m)osexuality we were resisting (Irigaray, 1985), while those of us who had recently been reading *Gender Trouble* argued passionately in favour of the political importance of the parodic inside (Butler, 1990). Poring over my dog-eared copy of *The Epistemology of the Closet*, I was able to make connections between previous marches against Clause 28, the Alton Bill, and the Poll Tax through Eve Kosofsky Sedgwick's analysis of the heteronormativity of the public/private divide (Sedgwick, 1991). (And here I burst into song)

'Those were the days, my friends…' and lately I have been wondering in turn, following Ehrenreich, where that 'exciting poststructuralist feminist intellectual milieu *I* once moved in' has gone.

Historiographic critique of my own narrative is harder, of course, because it requires my accepting that my own feminist intellectual biography may not provide a satisfactory narration of what Klein termed 'the passion and the politics' (1991: 75) of academic feminism for all partaking of it, or for all time. To begin to think through my own narrative myopia here, it makes sense to start from the knowledge that my own nostalgia, and therefore conservatism, makes me passionately resistant to contemporary claims that poststructuralism failed to take account of 'the material', 'the body', 'the psyche', and so on. I bristle in the face of a current intellectual certainty that the 'linguistic turn' was or is an evacuation rather than a re-evaluation of 'the political', witnessing, it seems, my formative political experiences, friendships, passions rendered useless, immaterial, redundant. My saving grace is that this, at least, is a lesser charge than that of essentialism.

As I differentiate myself from those I claim are more doggedly attached to myths than I am (lost unity? Oh come on!), I fatally lock myself into a reductively generational chain of feminist meaning, imperative to my continued occupation of the political and intellectual high ground. Perhaps you can guess what is coming next. As Segal and Ehrenreich are in relation to me, so I, too, am over-invested in insisting that those who come 'after' me are unquestionably less political, less interested in transformation, more concerned with their own career advancement than the project of transforming gender relations. From the duped before me to the duplicitous after me, the properly deconstructive subject saves the day again. That was close; I was in danger of having to challenge my own nostalgia for a moment there.

I am struggling here to show how important it is that I *do* challenge my own nostalgia, so that histories of feminist meaning and academic feminist change do not become embarrassing reflections of individual, generational, or geographical location, with their attendant sleights of hand and moral certitude. Such histories cannot be other than linear, since they seek to position a particular subject, and not others, as the heroine of feminist theory, and they are thus resistant to a thorough examination of difference within both the past and present.

We need to start our histories of academic feminism from an assumption of difference and contest, an attention to subordinate as well as dominant knowledges in the present, to open up a range of possible futures rather than predictable outcomes. In the process, we have to accept that we do not know in advance who the authors of these futures will be, and really to believe this, rather than merely to write this here, is very hard indeed. For academic feminism, whatever its designation, to remain as current, inspiring, and useful as it has been for the last thirty years, I feel that those of us working within it need to be prepared to do at least three things. First, we must adopt a reflexive approach that openly interrogates the relationship between the histories of feminist theory that we tell and our own intellectual biographies. Nostalgia cannot be the ground of any meaningful life, still less one committed to political and collective transformation. Second, following Braidotti, we need to become skilled in the science of 'cultural translation' (2002: 302) in order to negotiate with precision and familiarity the linguistic, geographical, and cultural contexts that make up a contemporary academic feminist terrain. I see this method as a workable challenge to the spatially and temporally locked perspectives I have been addressing throughout this chapter. Third, and as I hope I have begun to do here, we should foreground the painstaking work of mapping and evaluating the specific conflicts and insights produced by many years of academic institutionalization of feminist research and pedagogy. Only then can academic feminist strategies for change, not only answerable to an imagined political outside but internally viable, be sustained.

NOTES

1 The aspect of consumer culture Skeggs is referring to here is the student demand to be taught from a perspective reflecting their existing convictions. Skeggs identifies the ways in which this 'demand' can lead to tensions between feminist staff and postfeminist students, and indeed this tension has scarcely been eased by the introduction of fees for UK higher education.

2 Joanna de Groot terms this familiar situation the alienated labour of academic feminists (1997).

3 Different people might want to anthropomorphize academic feminism in different ways – woman, queer, androgyne, man, exile? – or indeed not anthropomorphize it at all – cyborg, monster?

4 This partiality reflects the proliferation of work on the development of the interdisciplinary arena of Women's and Gender Studies. As Marilyn Boxer notes, in her account of that development in a US context, it is no longer possible to read everything that has been published on the subject (2003: xvii). It also reflects my knowledge about predominantly Western feminist contexts of institutionalization.

5 The SIGMA report on Women's Studies provided detailed information on Women's Studies teaching and research in universities and colleges across Europe. It made recommendations for a combined European strategy for improving Women's Studies educational provision. See http://women-www.uia.ac.be/women/sigma/index.html.

6 A clear exception to either position is Wendy Brown's call for feminist academics to 'return' to disciplinary engagement (1997). Her argument is that Women's Studies itself is not viable in an era of deconstruction of identity categories, however, rather than an endorsement of one or other side of an autonomy versus integration debate.

7 To give just a few examples, the Women's Education, Research and Resource Centre (WERRC) at University College, Dublin (est. 1983), and the Belgrade Women's Studies Center in Serbia and Montenegro (est. 1992) provide a range of open-access courses and maintain strong community links. See http://www.ucd.ie/werrc/ and http://www.zenskestudie.edu.yu/ respectively. The Anveshi Research Centre for Women's Studies in India (Jain and Rajput, 2003) and the Institute for Women's and Gender Studies at the American University in Cairo (Altorki, 2000) both prioritize activist, community, and voluntary sector links in their educational provision.

8 The context for this route is now increasingly international, as suggested by the popularity of courses and degrees in gender and development, a shift in emphasis that underscores the importance of and demand for global perspectives in feminist pedagogy more broadly.

9 In 2003 there were only ten graduate degree-awarding Women's or Gender Studies departments or centres in the United States, as compared to hundreds of undergraduate major and minor concentrations in Women's or Gender Studies (Boxer, 2003).

10 This is a particular problem in contexts where supervision of doctoral students is dependent upon a supervisor having the appropriate certification that only comes with very high levels of seniority (Barazzetti and Leone, 2003), producing a self-perpetuating cycle of exclusion and marginalization.

11 Susan Faludi most famously identified this cultural trend as a 'backlash' (1992). The success of the 'backlash' is the widespread belief that men and women now have equality, despite overwhelming evidence to the contrary (Whelehan, 2000).

12 The RAE is the national evaluation of academic research output that determines the research money allocated to each department. It takes place every six to seven years, when four pieces of published research per individual are graded and an overall departmental grade established. The exercise is enormously divisive in that it mitigates against projects that take considerable time to set up (Lewis, 2000), creates a counter-productive culture of competition (Knights and Richards, 2003), results in conservative, mainstream work over innovation (Lee and Harley, 1998), and subjects interdisciplinary work to disciplinary evaluation. While 'allowance' is made for maternity or other forms of necessary leave within the exercise, anyone on the job market without the requisite four in the lead-up to the exercise is at a considerable disadvantage.

13 While the sociology draft guidelines assure concerned researchers that interdisciplinary gender research will be evaluated by a sub-panel of experts, Women's and Gender Studies as an independent field of inquiry has been effectively undermined in this assessment process.

14 The Bologna Declaration aims to harmonize divergent EU higher education systems, creating Europe-wide co-operation and competition. It heralds the introduction of a 3 + 1/2 system – three-year BA courses followed by one- or two-year Masters programmes (Barazzetti and Leone, 2003: 17–18).

15 An integration approach at this point in time and space would thus be disastrous for many European Gender and Women's Studies contexts, since it is precisely the most developed independent programmes that are attracting this international student body, filling the niche not offered elsewhere.

16 Individual courses and the very occasional institute might use the term 'feminist'.

17 Both claims rather dangerously reinforce the broader cultural and institutional conviction that feminism has had its day.

18 Anastasia Posadskaya makes this argument in relation to Russia (1994), Theodossia-Soula Pavlidou in relation to Greece (2000), and Eva Bahovec in relation to Slovenia (2000).

19 The critiques of gender and development are many and varied, but as someone outside the field of Development Studies, I have found the collections by the following authors very helpful: Kum-Kum Bhavnani, John Foran, and Priya Kurian (2003); Rosi Braidotti, Ewa Charkiewicz, Sabine Hausler, and Saskia Wieringa (1994); Inderpal Grewal and Caren Kaplan (1994); and Marianne Marchand and Jane Parpart (1995).

20 Translation: 'the feminine of Feminine Studies does not necessarily refer back to those subjects sexed female'.

21 From its inception, the Athena network of European Women's Studies has focused on the facilitation of student movement within Europe. This focus recognizes the uneven development of opportunities for feminist research and pedagogy across European sites, and represents the desire to make feminist research and pedagogy more accountable to the specificities of a broad range of contexts (Griffin and Braidotti, 2002).

22 It is important to note that this situation similarly advantages academics and students without dependants or caring responsibilities.

23 These special editions include the following: (1999) 'Snakes and Ladders: Reviewing Feminisms at Century's End', *Feminist Review*, 61; (2000) 'Feminisms at a Millennium', *Signs*, 25(4); and (2000) 'At the Millenium: Interrogating Gender', *Women: a Cultural*

Review, 11(1–2). For a discussion of the specific techniques used to create and sustain these narratives see Clare Hemmings (2005). More examples are integrated into my discussion as a whole, but see also Susan Gubar (1998; 1999), Martha Nussbaum (1999), and Sylvia Walby (2000).

REFERENCES

Aaron, Jane and Walby, Sylvia (1991) 'Introduction: Towards a Feminist Intellectual Space', in J. Aaron and S. Walby (eds), *Out of the Margins: Women's Studies in the Nineties*. London: Falmer Press. pp. 1–6.

Adkins, Lisa (2004) 'Passing on Feminism: from Consciousness to Reflexivity?', *European Journal of Women's Studies*, 11: 427–444.

Altorki, Soraya (2000) 'The Institute for Gender and Women's Studies – The American University in Cairo', *The Making of European Women's Studies, Volume III*, Athena/Universiteit Utrecht: 46–50.

Bahovec, Eva (2000) 'A Short Note on the Use of "Sex" and "Gender" in Slavic Languages', *The Making of European Women's Studies, Volume I*, Athena/Universiteit Utrecht: 44–45.

Barazzetti, Donatella (2000) 'Women's Studies and the Feminist Movement in Italy', *The Making of European Women's Studies, Volume I*, Athena/Universiteit Utrecht: 87–91.

Barazzetti, Donatella and Leone, Mariagrazia (2003) 'The Institutionalisation of Women's Studies Training in Europe', 'Comparative Data Report 2', *Employment and Women's Studies: The Impact of Women's Studies Training of Women's Employment in Europe*, The University of Hull.

Berger, Anne Emmanuelle (2004) 'Historiques des Etudes Féminines', 'Horizons de Recherches', website for Etudes Féminines a Paris VIII, http://julienas.ipt.univ-paris8.fr/~etudfem/position.html

Bergman, Solveig (2000) 'Women's Studies in the Nordic Countries: Organisation, Strategies and Resources', *The Making of European Women's Studies, Volume II*, Athena/Universiteit Utrecht: 51–66.

Bhavnani, Kum-Kum, Foran, John, and Kurian, Priya (eds) (2003) *Feminist Futures: Re-imagining Women, Culture and Development*. London: Zed Books.

Bowles, Gloria and Klein, Renate Duelli (1983) 'Introduction: Theories of Women's Studies and the Autonomy/Integration Debate', in G. Bowles and R. D. Klein (eds), *Theories of Women's Studies*. London: Routledge. pp. 1–26.

Boxer, Marilyn Jacoby (2003) *When Women Ask the Questions: Creating Women's Studies in America*. Baltimore, MD: The Johns Hopkins University Press.

Braidotti, Rosi (1994) *Nomadic Subjects: Embodiment and Sexual Difference in Contemporary Feminist Theory*. New York: Columbia University Press.

Braidotti, Rosi (2002) 'The Uses and Abuses of the Sex/Gender Distinction in European Feminist Practices', in G. Griffin and R. Braidotti (eds), *Thinking Differently: A Reader in European Women's Studies*. London: Zed Books. pp. 285–307.

Braidotti, Rosi and Butler, Judith (1994) 'Feminism By Any Other Name', *Differences: a Journal of Feminist Cultural Studies*, 6(2–3): 27–61.

Braidotti, Rosi, Charkiewicz, Ewa, Hausler, Sabine, and Wieringa, Saskia (1994) *Women, the Environment and Sustainable Development: Towards a Theoretical Synthesis*. London: Zed Books.

Braidotti, Rosi, Vonk, Esther, and van Wichelen, Sonja (2000) 'Historical Dossier on the Making of European Women's Studies: France – Introduction', *The Making of European Women's Studies, Volume II*, Athena/Universiteit Utrecht: 167–169.

Brown, Wendy (1997) 'The Impossibility of Women's Studies', *Differences: a Journal of Feminist Cultural Studies*, 9(3): 79–101.

Butler, Judith (1990) *Gender Trouble: Feminism and the Subversion of Identity*. New York: Routledge.

Butler, Judith (1994) 'Against Proper Objects', *Differences: a Journal of Feminist Cultural Studies*, 6(2–3): 1–27.

Corrin, Chris (1992) 'Women's Studies in Central and Eastern Europe', in H. Hinds, A. Phoenix and J. Stacey (eds), *Working Out: New Directions for Women's Studies*. London: Falmer Press. pp. 124–133.

Deats, Sara and Lenker, Lagretta (1994) *Gender and Academe: Feminist Pedagogy and Politics*. Lanham, MD: Rowman and Littlefield.

Deem, Rosemary and Johnson, Rachel (2003) 'Risking the University? Learning to be a Manager-Academic in UK Universities', *Sociological Research Online*, 8(3), http://www.socresonline.org.uk/8/3/deem.html

De Groot, Joanna (1997) 'After the Ivory Tower: Gender, Commodification and the "Academic"', *Feminist Review*, 55: 130–142.

Ehrenreich, Barbara (1990) 'The Professional-Managerial Class Revisited', in B. Robbins (ed.), *Intellectuals: Aesthetics, Politics, Academics*. Minneapolis: University of Minnesota Press.

Evans, Mary (1982) 'In Praise of Theory: the Case for Women's Studies', *Feminist Review*, 10: 61–74.

Evans, Mary (1991) 'The Problem of Gender for Women's Studies', in J. Aaron and S. Walby (eds), *Out of the Margins: Women's Studies in the Nineties*. London: Falmer Press. pp. 67–74.

Faludi, Susan (1992) *Backlash: The Undeclared War Against Women*. London: Chatto and Windus.

Gillis, Stacy and Munford, Rebecca (2003) 'Introduction', 'Special Issue: Harvesting Our Strengths: Third Wave Feminism and Women's Studies', *Journal of International Women's Studies*, 4(2): 1–11.

Gray, A (2003) 'Cultural Studies at Birmingham: The Impossibility of Critical Pedagogy', *Cultural Studies*, 17(6): 767–782.

Grewal, Inderpal and Kaplan, Caren (eds) (1994) *Scattered Hegemonies: Postmodernity and Transnational Feminist Practices*. Minneapolis: University of Minnesota Press.

Griffin, Gabriele and Braidotti, Rosi (2002) 'Introduction: Configuring European Women's Studies', in G. Griffin and R. Braidotti (eds), *Thinking Differently: A Reader in European Women's Studies*. London: Zed Books. pp. 1–28.

Griffin, Gabriele and Hanmer, Jalna (2001) 'Background Data Report: UK', *Employment and Women's Studies: The Impact of Women's Studies Training of Women's Employment in Europe*, The University of Hull.

Gubar, Susan (1998) 'What Ails Feminist Criticism?', *Critical Inquiry*, 24: 878–902.

Gubar, Susan (1999) 'Critical Response II: Notations in Media Res', *Critical Inquiry*, 25: 380–396.

Hemmings, Clare (2005) 'Telling Feminist Stories', *Feminist Theory*, 6(2): 115–139.

Huffer, Lynne (1998) *Maternal Pasts, Feminist Futures: Nostalgia, Ethics, and the Question of Difference*. Palo Alto, CA: Stanford University Press.

Irigaray, Luce (1985) *Speculum of the Other Woman*. Cornell, NY: Cornell University Press.

Jackson, Sue (2004) *Differently Academic? Developing Lifelong Learning for Women in Higher Education*. Dordrecht Kluwer Academic.

Jain, Devaki and Rajput, Pan (eds) (2003) *Narratives from the Women's Studies Family: Recreating Knowledge*. New Delhi: Sage.

Jegerstedt, Kari (2000) 'A Short Introduction to the Use of "Sex" and "Gender" in the Scandinavian Languages', *The Making of European Women's Studies, Volume I*, Athena/Universiteit Utrecht: 39–41.

Kelly, Liz and Pearson, Ruth (1983) 'Women's Studies: Women Studying or Studying Women', *Feminist Review*, 15: 76–80.

Kitch, Sally L. (1998) 'Ph.D. Programs and the Research Mission of Women's Studies: the Case for Interdisciplinarity', 'Forum – Graduate Education in Women's Studies: Paradoxes and Challenges', *Feminist Studies*, 29(2): 435–447.

Klein, Renate D. (1991) 'Passion and Politics in Women's Studies in the 1990s', in J. Aaron and S. Walby (eds), *Out of the Margins: Women's Studies in the Nineties*. London: Falmer Press. pp. 75–89.

Knights, D. and Richards, W. (2003) 'Sex Discrimination in UK Academia', *Gender, Work and Organization*, 10(2): 213–238.

Lee, Frederick S. and Harley, Sandra (1998) 'Peer Review, the R. A. E. and the Demise of Non-Mainstream Economics', *Capital and Class*, 66: 23–51.

Lees, Sue (1991) 'Feminist Politics and Women's Studies: Struggle, Not Incorporation', in J. Aaron and S. Walby (eds), *Out of the Margins: Women's Studies in the Nineties*. London: Falmer Press. pp. 90–104.

Lewis, J. (2000) 'Funding Social Science Research in Academia', *Social Policy and Administration*, 34(4): 365–376.

Magarey, Susan and Sheridan, Susan (2002) 'Local, Global, Regional: Women's Studies in Australia', *Feminist Studies*, 28(1): 129–152.

Marchand, Marianne and Parpart, Jane (eds) (1995) *Feminism/Postmodernism/Development*. London: Routledge.

Martin, Biddy (2001) 'Success and Failures', in E. Bronden and M. Kavka (eds), *Feminist Consequences: Theory for the New Century*. New York: Columbia University Press. pp. 353–380.

Messer-Davidow, Ellen (2002) *Disciplining Women: From Social Activism to Academic Discourse*. Durham, NC: Duke University Press.

Milić, Andjelka (2004) 'The Women's Movement in Serbia and Montenegro at the Turn of the Millennium: a Sociological Study of Women's Groups', *Feminist Review*, 76: 65–82.

Nussbaum, Martha (1999) 'The Professor of Parody', *The New Republic*, 22 February: 37–45.

Papic, Zarana (2002) 'Europe after 1989: Ethnic Wars, the Fascistization of Civil Society and Body Politics in Serbia', in G. Griffin and R. Braidotti (eds), *Thinking Differently: A Reader in European Women's Studies*. London: Zed Books. pp. 127–144.

Pavlidou, Theodossia-Soula (2000) 'Modern Greek "Gender"', *The Making of European Women's Studies, Volume I*, Athena/Universiteit Utrecht: 42–43.

Posadskaya, Anastasia (1994) *Women in Russia: a New Era in Russian Feminism*. London: Verso.

Richardson, Diane and Robinson, Victoria (1994) 'Theorizing Women's Studies, Gender Studies and Masculinity: The Politics of Naming', *The European Journal of Women's Studies*, 1: 11–27.

Rizvi, Fazal and Walsh, Lucas (1998) 'Difference, Globalisation, and the Internationalisation of Curriculum', *Australian Universities' Review*, 41(2): 7.

Roof, Judith (1997) 'Generational Difference; or, the Fear of a Barren History', in D. Looser and E. A. Kaplan (eds), *Generations: Academic Women in Dialogue*. Minneapolis: Minnesota Press. pp. 69–87.

Scott, Joan (1988) *Gender and the Politics of History*. New York: Columbia University Press.

Scott, Joan (1997) 'Women's Studies on the Edge: Introduction', *Differences: a Journal of Feminist Cultural Studies*, 9(3): i–v.

Sedgwick, Eve Kosofsky (1991) *Epistemology of the Closet*. London: Harvester Wheatsheaf.

Segal, Lynne (2000) 'Only Contradictions on Offer', *Women: a Cultural Review*, 11(1–2): 19–36.

Silius, Harriet (2002) 'Women's Employment, Equal Opportunities and Women's Studies in Nine European Countries – a Summary', *Employment and Women's Studies: The Impact of Women's Studies Training on Women's Employment in Europe*, The University of Hull.

Silius, Harriet and Tuori, Salla (2003) 'Professionalisation of Women's Studies Graduates (Including Academic Profession) in Europe', 'Comparative Data Report 6', *Employment and Women's Studies: The Impact of Women's Studies Training of Women's Employment in Europe*, The University of Hull.

Skeggs, Beverley (1995) 'Women's Studies in Britain: Entitlement Cultures and Institutional Constraints', *Women's Studies International Forum*, 18(4): 475–485.

Smyth, Ailbhe (1992) 'Women's Studies and "The Disciplines"', *Women's Studies International Forum*, 15(5–6): 615–617.

Spivak, Gayatri Chakravorty (1981) 'French Feminism in an International Frame', *Yale French Studies*, 62: 154–184.

Spivak, Gayatri Chakravorty (1993) 'The Politics of Translation', *Outside in the Teaching Machine*. New York: Routledge. pp. 179–200.

Stacey, Jackie (1993) 'Feminist Theory: Capital F, Capital T', in V. Robinson and D. Richardson (eds) (1997) *Introducing Women's Studies: Feminist Theory and Practice*. New York: New York University Press. pp. 54–76.

Stacey, Jackie, Phoenix, Ann, and Hinds, Hilary (1992) 'Working Out: New Directions for Women's Studies', in H. Hinds, A. Phoenix and J. Stacey (eds), *Working Out: New Directions for Women's Studies*. London: Falmer Press. pp. 1–10.

Stanley, Liz (1991) 'Feminist Auto/Biography and Feminist Epistemology', in J. Aaron and S. Walby (eds), *Out of the Margins: Women's Studies in the Nineties*. London: Falmer Press. pp. 204–219.

Stanley, Liz and Wise, Sue (2000) 'But the Empress has No Clothes! Some Awkward Questions about "the Missing Revolution" in Feminist Theory', *Feminist Theory*, 1(3): 261–288.

Stromquist, Nelly (2001) 'Gender Studies: A Global Perspective of their Evolution, Contribution, and Challenges to Comparative Higher Education', *Higher Education*, 41: 373–387.

Threadgold, Terry (2000) 'Gender Studies and Women's Studies', *Australian Feminist Studies*, 15(31): 39–48.

Walby, Sylvia (2000) 'Beyond the Politics of Location: The Power of Argument in a Global Era', *Feminist Theory*, 1(2): 189–206.

Whelehan, Imelda (2000) *Overloaded: Popular Culture and the Future of Feminism*. London: Women's Press.

Wiegman, Robyn (2000) 'Feminism's Apocalyptic Futures', *New Literary History: a Journal of Theory and Interpretation*, 31(4): 805–825.

Wilton, Tamsin (2000) 'Out/Performing Our Selves: Sex, Gender and Cartesian Dualism', *Sexualities*, 3(2): 237–254.

Zalewski, Marysia (2003) 'Is Women's Studies Dead?', *Journal of International Women's Studies*, 5(2): 1–35.

2

The Shadow and the Substance
The Sex/Gender Debate

Wendy Cealey Harrison

In spite of the foundational implications of the distinction between 'sex' and 'gender' for feminism, this chapter seeks to explore ways of reconciling the two concepts, so that a unified field of feminist research could be developed, one that encompasses consideration of bodies in the analysis of the social and cultural and that identifies in those bodies, and the interpretation of those bodies, the unmistakable impact of the social and cultural environments within which they exist. This requires recognizing that the mind that creates these environments is both brain and social and cultural product.

The challenge for feminism is to produce a social science that recognizes and understands the biological, without taking biological characteristics as a given, and a biology that takes full account of the fact that human beings are pre-eminently social and cultural creatures who, in shaping the world around them, also shape themselves. It is in this latter area that some of the most exciting developments could lie for a feminist biology.

INTRODUCTION

The sex/gender distinction has been essential to the full flowering of second-wave feminism. The point of making that initial distinction, however, was not to create two concepts, but to allow the concept of gender to take off. And take off it did. There followed over thirty years of enormously productive feminist scholarship, which made evident that what the term 'gender' uncovered was a vast and intellectually fertile domain. This handbook is itself testament to the complexity and richness of this new terrain. But accepting the straightforward existence of something called 'sex', which was not – at least initially – to be an area of investigation for feminism, meant that there was something obdurate embedded at the edges of feminist scholarship that never quite went away.

Quite early in its history, Christine Delphy declared herself disappointed by the concept of 'gender', which had failed, she said, to live up to the promise it carried in embryo: in remaining tied to the concept of 'sex', it had not 'taken wing' but had 'on the contrary seemed to cling onto its daddy' (1984: 24–5). She was dismayed to find that the term 'gender' was so often to be found in composites such as 'sex/gender' or 'sex and gender', in which the forward slash or the 'and' denoted the fact that 'gender' had not separated itself from, but always resided with, 'sex'.

In a sense, the adoption by feminists of the distinction between 'sex' and 'gender' originally proposed by John Money (1965) and theorized by Robert Stoller (1968), however radical its impetus and consequences, embodied a concession. This concession is evident in Ann Oakley's first formulation of the feminist concept of gender, and that is that there were 'natural' differences between the sexes which were self-evident and undeniable: 'The constancy of sex must be admitted,' she said, 'but so also must the variability of gender' (1972: 16). Yet Oakley's own work indicated quite clearly that variability was not the sole prerogative of gender. In *Subject Women* (1981: 54–5), she pointed out, for example, the impact of social situations on testosterone levels in animals, research that has since been confirmed by human studies (Bernhardt et al., 1998). Nevertheless, although the very notion of 'sex' has lately come to seem far more problematical than it used to, and there have now been a number of forays by feminist scholars into the realm of the biological, 'sex' continues to act as something of a lodestone in the study of gender, a taken-for-granted binary divide in the population which unambiguously classifies all human beings, alive or dead.

The concession that was tacitly embodied in Oakley's formulation has returned to haunt feminism. Casual internet searches reveal a wealth of ruminations on the reinvigorated topic of 'nature' versus 'nurture', with a return to the claim – believed successfully dispelled and dismissed by feminism in the 1970s – that there are ineradicable behavioural and psychological characteristics peculiar to women (or in a more 'progressive' vein, peculiar to women and to men) which cannot be wished away by feminist social scientists as the products of social and cultural construction. 'Gender', in other words, is under threat as a concept. Even Delphy herself talks of the 'social *aspect* of the sexual dichotomy' (1984: 24), as if there were something basic and irrefutable about the dichotomy between the sexes as a biological reality.

But before we simply fall into line and concede what looks like the inescapable biological case, it is worth opening up the whole issue of biology for scrutiny. What R. W. Connell described as the 'doctrine of natural difference', the conviction of the foundational character of biological difference for gender, forms for many people, he says, 'a limit *beyond which thought cannot go*' (1987: 66, emphasis added). Indeed, acceptance of the idea that there are fundamental and foundational differences between the sexes is sometimes actively embraced by feminists as an acknowledgement of the specificity of women's experience in the flesh. Not only does the doctrine of natural difference imply that sex forms the bedrock, the foundation for gender, but the assumption is, as Oakley's statement indicates, that sex has constancy: it is a 'matter of fact', based in a stable biological reality, which by definition does not alter.

One problem, then, lies in what precisely it would mean for the concept of 'gender' to take wing, as Delphy had hoped it would do. For there appears to be an unavoidable sense in which gender is 'about' sex, which makes it difficult to see how gender could cease to be, as Delphy puts it, set on 'anatomical sex like the beret on the head of the legendary Frenchman' (1984: 25). Although the concept of 'gender' first came into being in order to address the potential discrepancy between an individual's anatomy and their attribution of identity to themselves (so that, for example, someone could be anatomically male but see themselves as female), the notion that gender in some sense elaborates on, or builds on, sex, and that sex is a given, seems to obey a compelling logic.

Both of those ideas, the notion that sex is a given and that it is somehow foundational and more 'real' and solid than gender, however, are open to question – on different kinds of grounds admittedly, as we shall see in what follows, but neither should be taken for granted. The apparent solidity and reality of sex is strongly associated with the idea that it is bodies ('sex') that have substance, where minds and relationships ('gender') do not. The idea of what she called the 'materiality' of sex was investigated by Judith Butler in her 1993 book *Bodies That Matter*. In a complex philosophical discussion, she unpicks the contradictions involved in endorsing the claim that the body is somehow outside and beyond minds, relationships, and language (1993: 1–32). How did it come to be the case, she asks, that sex is seen as something irreducible, in other words as something which is essentially outside and beyond human thought?

It is this apparent integrity and solidity to 'sex' that provides the basis for Delphy's disappointment. Particularly problematical for the fate of the concept of 'gender', she says, is the fact that, although 'sex' can be spoken of without 'gender', the same is not true the other way around. In remaining tied to 'sex', Delphy argued, 'gender' becomes no more than a gesture, a way of paying lip-service to the social aspects. As the dependent term in the pair, 'gender' has a tendency to collapse back onto what is regarded as primary: 'sex'. The powerful way in which this collapse operates in all our lives is perfectly encapsulated by a transsexual quoted in Suzanne Kessler and Wendy McKenna's pioneering book, *Gender: An Ethnomethodological Approach*, who said: 'Gender is an anchor, and once people decide what you are they interpret everything you do in the light of that' (1978: 6). The weight in that anchor is 'sex', or to be more precise, genitalia, which, as Kessler and McKenna point out, represent the biological insignia which are seen to indicate, indeed determine whether someone is male or female, and are therefore attributed to them as of right. These 'cultural genitals' are those that it is believed people possess under their clothing, or if not, *ought* to possess, as a legitimate member of their gender category. Gender attribution is therefore in a sense always genital attribution: 'The cultural genitals (not some configuration of biological material) are the foundation for any gender attribution made'[1] (Kessler, 1998: 86). This means that the collapse of 'gender' onto 'sex' goes even further than Delphy suspects, since 'sex' to all intents and purposes amounts to 'genitals'.

In keeping with this insight, Delphy's attempt to retrieve the concept of 'gender' from this collapse lies in exposing what is for her the fact that 'sex' is not a fundamental and incontrovertible reality but a marker, the marker used by a discriminatory and oppressive social system to differentiate between superordinate and subordinate groups of people. 'Sex' marks out the exploited group, women. For Delphy, then, 'sex' is not a matter of fact; rather, sexual differentiation serves a social purpose in patriarchal exploitation. 'Women' and 'men' are social, not biological categories, and the very clarity of the distinction between them, both in practical terms and in terms of discourses, is about the maintenance of what Delphy sometimes describes as two castes within the population. The alleged differences between the sexes are identified, and indeed 'found' to exist, in order to construct the hierarchy between the two. The traits identified, where indeed they exist, would otherwise be no more important than the difference between having blue eyes and having green eyes. One could summarize this by saying that 'sex' is to sexism as 'race' is to racism.

Although persuasive, this point of view seems to go against the grain of common sense, as if it were essentially counter-intuitive. Both Delphy's notion of 'sex' as a marker and Kessler and McKenna's use of the notion of 'cultural genitals' seem to call forth the rejoinder that there really is such an entity as sex and there really are such things as genitalia: their *uses* may be social, but their reality is incontrovertible. Against such views, there will also always be those who, as Simone de Beauvoir pointed out over half a century ago (1972 [1949]: 14), will rush to make the claim that women simply *are not* men and to insist that the difference between the sexes is the most fundamental of human differences, which it is at best foolish and at worst detrimental to ignore. Indeed, with the recent ascendancy of biologistic explanations in general, and the increasing prestige of genetics in particular, feminism is now faced with something like the return of the repressed, the idea that maybe there really are differences between the sexes, differences which might have implications for the ways in which women and men should be treated.

WOMEN ARE BUT MEN TURNED OUTSIDE IN

One of the most revolutionary and compelling pieces of research of the 1990s, however, is to be found in Thomas Laqueur's luminous book, *Making Sex: Body and Gender from the Greeks to Freud*. It dislocates our commonsense understanding of what 'sex' and 'gender' are and how they might be related to one another. Put briefly, what Laqueur argues is that 'sex' is a concept which was invented at a particular point in time in our culture. 'Sex' as a biological entity was 'made' rather than simply discovered, and brought into being for reasons other than the scientific.

Not only did the idea of 'sex' not always exist, but in the past – before about 1800 in Europe – bodies were seen in radically different ways from those we take for granted. Far from our ancestors living in a world in which sex was a fundamental reality given by biology, the primary reality for them was a divine order, an order in which bodies were oddly insubstantial things. Women's and men's bodies in pre-Enlightenment accounts are indices of a metaphysical reality – literally a reality beyond the physical – a reality more profound and more fundamental than the presence and disposition of organs, like penis or uterus. Indeed the disposition of organs shows a mutability which would simply provoke incredulity in us: a girl chasing her swine suddenly springs an external penis and scrotum (for vaginas were assumed to be internal ones – penises turned outside in); men associating too much with women lose the more perfect hardness of their bodies and regress towards effeminacy (Laqueur, 1990: 7). As Caroline Walker Bynum (1989) has pointed out in another context, bodies do strange and remarkable things – male bodies lactate; the bodies of female saints are miraculously preserved after death – but these phenomena are related to a completely different understanding of what bodies *are*. As Laqueur puts it, rather than bodily morphology providing evidence of an underlying biological reality, instead it merely 'makes vivid and more palpable a hierarchy of heat and perfection that is in itself not available to the senses' (1990: 27).

Prior to the Enlightenment, what Laqueur calls the 'one-sex model' described woman as a lesser version of man, in whom a lack of 'vital heat' caused her to retain inside her body structures that in men would have been on the outside: 'women are but men turned outside in', as early nineteenth-century doggerel would have it (1990: 4). Men themselves would, in Christian theology, have been placed below the diverse orders of the angels, but above the whole of the animal kingdom. What emerges after the Enlightenment to replace this view is the notion, familiar to us, of a fundamental polarity between the sexes based upon discoverable biological differences: 'No longer would those who think about such matters regard woman as a lesser version of man along a vertical axis of infinite gradations but rather as an altogether different creature along a horizontal axis whose middle ground was largely empty' (1990: 148).

So important is this sense of an empty middle ground between the sexes, of a no-(wo)man's land that separates them and that no human being should occupy, that surgery carried out on the genitalia of intersexed infants effectively sets out to create it. Suzanne Kessler (1998: 43) points out that there are published guidelines for clitoral and penile size, which are devised so as to leave a clear 1.5 cm gap between the two sets of measurements. The result is that clitoral lengths above the stipulated maximum will tend to be surgically reduced, while penises below the required dimensions could even lead to the reassignment of the child to a gender deemed more appropriate to the size of his genital.

The temptation, of course, would be simply to say that our ancestors got it wrong, that scientific advances have revealed the ideas behind the 'one-sex model' to be a myth. But Laqueur does not allow us such comforting rationalizations. The historical evidence reveals that the reconsideration of the nature of women and men which is the basis of our understanding occurs roughly 100 years before the scientific discoveries that are brought to bear to support it: 'In place of what, in certain situations, strikes the modern imagination as an almost perverse insistence on understanding sexual difference as a matter of degree, gradations of one basic male type, there arose a shrill call to articulate sharp corporeal distinctions' (Laqueur, 1990: 5). What is also marked after 1800 is that bodies are being thought of in a different way, as the foundation and guarantor of particular sorts of social arrangements (1990: 29). As Laqueur puts it, 'no one was much interested in looking for evidence of two distinct sexes until such differences became politically important' (1990: 10).

SEX AS A MOTIVATED INVENTION?

What Laqueur's book suggests, then, is that 'sex' is a motivated invention, born, if you like, of gender. In that sense, he might seem to agree with Delphy. He demonstrates very clearly the inextricable link between the ways in which bodies are imagined and what we would now recognize as the political and cultural imperatives of gender. More importantly, what he suggests is that the body does not automatically give itself to be interpreted in this or that particular way: 'Two sexes are not the necessary, natural consequence of corporeal difference. Nor, for that matter, is one sex' (1990: 243). This contention is in part an issue about the body itself, as something which is not as unambiguous as it first appears, and in part a point about human knowledge. Talking of the anthropological literature, he has a wonderful description of the way in which human purposes, symbolism, frameworks of interpretation, and even fantasy can act to transform things that appear to have an unassailable reality into something rich and strange:

> The cassowary, a large, flightless, ostrich-like, and, to the anthropologist, epicene bird, becomes to the male Sambian tribesman a temperamental, wild, masculinized female who gives birth through the anus and whose feces have procreative powers; the bird becomes powerfully bisexual. Why, asks the ethnographer Gilbert Herdt, do people as astute as the Sambia 'believe' in anal birth? Because anything one says, outside of very specific contexts, about the biology of sex, even among the brute beasts, is already informed by a theory of sameness and difference. (1990: 19)

Laqueur's point is that human beings impose their own symbolic order onto what he calls a world of continuous shades of difference and similarity. Particular symbolic configurations make little sense to an outsider, and the same object may well appear in widely differing ways within different systems of meaning. Quoting Claude Lévi-Strauss's example about the sagebrush, *Artemisia*, and the variable parts it plays in association with other plants in a Native American ritual, Laqueur says: 'No principle of opposition could be subtler than the tiny differences in leaf serrations that come to carry such enormous symbolic weight' (1990: 19).

In short, carving out what is empirical reality from human purpose is no straightforward matter. Our obvious rejoinder might be to reach for the scientific method as the guarantor that what *we* are dealing with when *we* look at cassowaries, sagebrush, or indeed male and female bodies in their infinite variety is what is *really* there. Unfortunately, as in every other area of scientific work, a set of methodological protocols certainly provides some assistance, but it does not supply any guarantees.

Some of the most interesting recent work, such as that of feminist biologists like Anne Fausto-Sterling (1989; 1992; 2000), has been invaluable in uncovering the gendered assumptions embedded in the supposedly cool neutrality of biological research on 'sex'. The places in which such gendered assumptions are to be found can be quite subtle and surprising. In an article written as early as 1989, entitled 'Life in the XY Corral', Fausto-Sterling identified the complex ways in which gendered assumptions entered into such obscurely technical issues as the role of the cell nucleus and gene activity in embryological development. She makes the case that these assumptions downplay other vital contributory factors, not least of which is the part played by the cytoplasm of the egg cell. Her more general point is 'not that political philosophies cause bad theory choice, but that there are often several fairly good accounts of existing data available. Which theory predominates depends on much more than just how well the data and the facts fit together' (1989: 324).

Does that mean, though, that our whole idea of 'sex' is, as Delphy suggests, a politically constructed fiction? Well, not necessarily. But we do now have to think very hard about how we should henceforth regard the scientific discoveries associated with the idea of 'sex' that to us seem so unimpeachable precisely because they are scientific. We might all be familiar with the idea that the science of sexuality can be host to some dubious gendered assumptions, as Emily Martin (1991) pointed out in her article on the romance of the egg and the sperm. But none of us doubts the existence of egg and sperm. Indeed, Laqueur finds himself in some difficulty here because, on the one hand, he quite clearly believes that scientific advances *have* taken place, talking of certain beliefs about sex as 'patently absurd', while on the other, he argues that the whole science of difference is misconceived (1990: 21–2). There is simply no discussion of biological realities that does not have its admixture of value, desire, and social and political exigency:

> Sex, like being human, is contextual. Attempts to isolate it from its discursive, socially determined milieu are as doomed to failure as the *philosophe's* search for a truly wild child or the modern anthropologist's efforts to filter out the cultural so as to leave a residue of essential humanity. And I would go further and add that the private enclosed stable body that seems to lie at the basis of modern notions of sexual difference is also the product of particular, historical, cultural moments. It too, like opposite sexes, comes into and out of focus. (Laqueur, 1990: 16)

We might then logically suppose that even eggs and sperm themselves – regardless of any romance they may be engaged in – are to be cast into doubt. Laqueur clearly wants to resist any such notion, and what he describes as the erosion of the 'body's priority over language'. He identifies what he calls a powerful tendency among feminists to empty sex of its content by arguing that natural differences are really cultural. He also says, however, quoting Maurice Godelier, that 'society haunts the body's sexuality'. He describes his own work and much feminist scholarship in general as caught in the tensions of this contradictory formulation, 'between nature and culture; between "biological sex" and the endless social and political markers of difference'. The analytical distinction between sex and gender, he suggests, 'gives voice to these alternatives and has always been precarious'. 'We remain poised,' he goes on, 'between the body as that extraordinary fragile, feeling and transient mass of flesh with which we are all familiar – too familiar – and the body that is so hopelessly bound to its cultural meanings as to elude unmediated access' (1990: 11–12).

Judith Butler suggests that talking about the social construction of the natural appears to produce 'the cancellation of the natural by the social':

> Insofar as it relies on this construal, the sex/gender distinction founders…if gender is the social significance that sex assumes within a given culture…then what, if anything, is left of 'sex' once it has assumed its social character as gender?…If gender consists of the social meanings that sex assumes, then sex does not *accrue* social meanings as additive properties, but rather *is replaced by* the social meanings it takes on; sex is relinquished in the course of that assumption, and gender emerges, not as a term in a continued relationship of opposition to sex, but as the term which absorbs and displaces 'sex'. (1993: 5, original emphasis)

We cannot, however, remain poised over a precarious analytical distinction between 'sex' and 'gender', in which the former at least comes into and out of focus, nor can we simply obliterate what is designated by the term 'sex' by bringing it under the heading of 'gender' as that is commonly understood.

THE HAUNTING OF THE BODY'S SEX

An abiding theme of the last decade has been the feminist dilemma of how we should think about the body and 'sex' in a context in which we are aware that what we have now come to think of as 'gender' plays a major role. Attempts have been made both to recoup and recognize what are deemed to be the biological realities of women's lives (often indistinguishable from those things with which opponents of feminism had weighed women down in the past) and, by contrast, virtually to dissolve what Laqueur calls that 'transient mass of flesh' into something which appears at first sight to be nothing but social meanings. Since neither provides a satisfactory alternative, we have to find a way not so much of maintaining what Butler describes as 'a continued relationship of opposition' between 'gender' and 'sex', as of bringing them together and reconciling them.

One way of doing so is to begin to see the relationship between 'sex' and 'gender' less like a relationship between chalk and cheese, and rather more in terms of what Laqueur points out is the impossibility of ever entirely separating the body and our understanding of it from its socially determined milieu. Part of this reconceptualization involves dismantling the taken-for-grantedness of 'sex' as a form of categorization for human beings and examining the ways in which such a categorization is built. As early as 1932, a biologist called John Lillie pointed out that 'sex', rather than being an entity, was just a label which covered our total impression of the differences between women and men. This view is confirmed by contemporary biological research, which is increasingly breaking down what we label 'sex' into its component parts, so that we would now say that it takes a number of quite complex processes to come together and cohere in order to produce what we would spontaneously identify as a male or female human being.

One of the sharpest and fastest ways to arrive at an understanding of the complexity of what lies under the heading of 'sex' is to look at those who disturb our conventional sexual categories, for example transsexuals, but more especially, the intersexed. In this context, undoubtedly one of the most significant pieces of work of the last twenty-five years has been Michel Foucault's (1980) case history of *Herculine Barbin*, the hermaphrodite who was brought up as a girl but was subsequently reassigned to the male sex, a reassignment that resulted in her suicide. It is with Herculine that we first see doctors assuming that underneath her indeterminate anatomy was hidden what she *really* was and striving to decipher 'the true sex that was hidden beneath ambiguous appearances' (1980: viii). As Foucault points out, it is the moment in history when hermaphrodites stop being people in whom a combination of sexual characteristics can be found (and who might therefore be allowed to choose what they wished to be) and become those whose bodies deceptively hide their real identities, their *true* sex, which the expertise of the doctors can detect. At that point in time, our world becomes one in which, Foucault says, sexual irregularities are henceforth to be seen to belong to the realm of chimeras, those fictions which represent errors in the most classically philosophical sense; in other words, 'a manner of acting which is not *adequate to reality*' (1980: x, emphasis added).

Hermaphrodites, or what we would now call the intersexed, become – in a notion which is entirely familiar to us – 'errors' of nature, a way in which reality is not adequate to itself. This is the point at which we could say that 'sex' as an ontological category, as something that defines us in the depths of our being, is born. Herculine had the misfortune to live on the cusp of this new world, in which the intersexed are no longer able to be themselves (providing they did not behave in a licentious manner and take advantage of their ambiguity by having sex with both women and men alike), but had to be redefined as 'really' something else, a man or a woman. With Herculine's case history, we can also watch the doctors strive to identify what might be the *real* markers of sex. Despite concluding that Herculine had both vagina and clitoris, the clinching element for them is the presence of testes and spermatic cords (even though there are no sperm), which leads them to conclude that, upbringing notwithstanding, Herculine is really a man. There is, in other words, an alignment of the components of sex in such a way as to tidy up the picture, to produce a clear binary divide when the empirical evidence provided by Herculine's body defied all attempts to place it categorically on one side or the other of that sexual divide. It marks the moment when a conviction is born that even if the elements that make up a sexed creature do not line up, they *ought to*.

Fausto-Sterling's research indicates just how persistent the notion is that all of the processes necessary to the creation of a sexed being automatically fall into place to produce a clear binary divide in the population, and that there is, furthermore, a single 'key' that locks the whole thing into place. Criticizing the work of David Page et al. (1987) who set out to look for a master 'sex-determining locus' in the Y chromosome of male mammals, she points out just how many different items we might regard as key to identifying sex:

> In both XX males and XY females, then, what does the notion of a sex-determining gene mean? Is maleness decided on the basis of external genital structure? Often not, since sometimes physicians decide that an individual with female genitalia is really a male and surgically correct the external structures so that they match the chromosomal and hormonal sex. Is it the presence of an ovary or testis that decides the matter? If so, oughtn't the gonad to have germs cells in it to 'count'? Or is it enough to be in the right place and to have the right superficial histological structure? There are no good answers to these questions because EVEN biologically speaking sex is not such an either/or construct. Page and co-workers chose to leave some of the messy facts out of their account, which makes the story look much cleaner than it actually is. (1989: 328–9)

Maybe, then, egg and sperm are not as obvious as they might at first appear to be? If Fausto-Sterling is right, can we any longer be sure that, even if we can see them under the microscope, our interpretations of egg and sperm are really correct? What mechanism can we use to separate them clearly from the admixture of social and cultural concerns with which we imbue them?

Even if we are led to doubt the correctness of our interpretations, however, awareness of this kind does not lead us to obliterate their existence merely because our understanding of them is bound up with the imperatives of the world in which we live. The key lies in recognizing that entities like egg and sperm, even if they seem pristinely biological, do not come into being in that pristine a way for us: we only come to know them in what are very precisely definable social contexts. The strength of their capacity to exist independently, and therefore in some sense their scientific longevity, is marked by the extent to which they can continue to exist and their existence be confirmed in other, quite different contexts. Put very simply, if recognition of egg and sperm allow *in vitro* fertilization to take place successfully, we can be fairly sure that they are what we assume them to be.

Take the notion of sex hormones, which are not only a consistent feature of our world, but, as pharmaceutical preparations, some of the most widely consumed of all drugs (not least in the form of the contraceptive pill). Should the idea that they are social constructs necessarily imply that this is all that they are, or that their social meaning in some sense cancels their biological reality? Nelly Oudshoorn's 1994 book *Beyond the Natural Body: An Archaeology of Sex Hormones* would suggest not. The hormones do, nevertheless, emerge from their history as constructs, quite literally things that were built. But they are built of a combination of things, both 'natural' and 'social': the concepts that inform their discovery, the investigative context in which that discovery takes place, the professional rivalries and relationships that shape how they come to be described, the manner in which the substances are isolated chemically, the uses to which they are put, the clinical settings in which they are deployed. The sense that emerges from Oudshoorn's book is that hormones can be both socially constructed and historically specific and yet also what we would recognize conventionally as 'material objects' that have a defined effect on the world around them, in this case on the bodies of those that ingest them.

One obvious way in which they can be regarded as socially constructed is to be found in the very name given to them as 'sex' hormones. As Oudshoorn points out, part of the ideas that surrounded their discovery was that, like the portion of the Y chromosome researched by Page et al. (0.2 per cent of it!), they might just provide the key to what made women women and men men, something which is reflected in their subsequent extensive clinical uses in the restoration of 'femininity' to post-menopausal women. The expectation that they might provide the key to sex was, however, belied by the discovery not only that women, for example, secrete testosterone (the allegedly 'male' hormone) but also by the fact that oestrogen was first isolated in the urine of, not mares, but stallions.

The social construction of the 'sex hormones', then, is about much more than words and social meanings – although it is about those, too. In a more profound sense, they are socially constructed through the wide range of elements that contributed to their birth and maintain and sustain their existence thereafter. Oudshoorn makes the point that science encompasses much more than theories and facts: it involves laboratories, investigative techniques, relationships between scientists, commercial settings, complex instrumentation, a whole social reality that also entails a range of what she calls 'material conditions' and 'material effects' (1994: 13). Therefore, when we look at such seemingly simple ideas as that of 'egg' and 'sperm', we need to be alive not only to the ways in which the facts and the theories have been put together but to the whole context in which the objects they identify exist, a complex combination of 'social' and 'natural' elements. And when we focus in on the concepts of 'egg' and 'sperm' themselves, we have to remember the differences that are wrought in those concepts by the assumptions with which we imbue them. Thinking of the egg as a large mass that simply waits passively for the arrival of an aggressive little sperm provides for a very different picture from the idea of an egg cell whose outer membrane draws the sperm in or whose cytoplasm plays a key role in embryological cell differentiation (Fausto-Sterling, 1989: 322).

BODY AND SOUL

There is, nevertheless, another way that we can think about the complexity of the processes that need to combine in order to produce what we spontaneously recognize as male or female human beings. One of the major insights of Kessler and McKenna's early work (1978) was that when we make a judgement that someone is male or female, what we use in doing so is all of a piece. For that reason and because that process obeys some key social rules, they describe it not as the attribution of 'sex' but as 'gender attribution'.[2] In that sense, they also refuse to differentiate between the processes employed by biologists in categorizing people into one sex or another and the processes used by the rest of us. And there is a kind of wisdom in this.

What we are seeing when we make the instantaneous gesture of classifying someone as female or male is a seamless combination of the biology of the body and the social and cultural context in which that body exists. In spite of the early tussles between feminists and anti-feminists over whether or not a particular feature belonged more properly to 'gender' or to 'sex', in practice the two are indistinguishable from one another. There will never be any natural experiment in which we might find out what the sexed body entails entirely outside the ways in which it, and the person whose body it is, has been gendered. Seeing 'sex' and the body as socially constructed, therefore, could also mean looking at the ways in which the body might itself be shaped by a social and cultural context. Connell, in keeping with Marx's notion that human beings transform the material world they encounter, including themselves and their own lives, talks of the practical transformation of the human body in its encounter with culture. 'In the reality of practice,' he says, 'the body is never outside history and history is never free of bodily presence and effects on the body' (1987: 87). As an example, he describes the way in which particular combinations of force and skill become strongly cathected (in other words, emotionally charged) aspects of an adolescent boy's life. These owe as much to fantasy as they do to activity, and together they produce a model of bodily action and bodily conformation whose result is, as Connell puts it, 'a statement embedded in the body':

> The social definition of men as holders of power is translated not only into mental body-images and fantasies, but into muscle tensions, posture, the feel and texture of the body. This is one of the main ways in which the power of men becomes 'naturalized,' i.e. seen as part of the order of nature. (1987: 85)

In fact, of course, one needs to go beyond the generality of men as a social grouping, not merely in terms of the inflections produced by class or culture, but towards the kind of cultural detail provided by, say, Loïc Wacquant in *Body and Soul: Notebooks of an Apprentice Boxer* (2003). Wacquant – who, incidentally, proposes the idea of a somatic sociology – charts his own training as, and transformation into, a boxer, describing the notion of the pugilist's honour, which requires that the boxer develop the mental resolve to fight on, regardless of pain or discomfort and possible or even actual injury. In other words, the process of becoming a boxer involves not only the creation of a particular kind of body but also the shaping of a whole moral and psychological universe inhabited by the boxer.

An analogous point can be made about developing the body of a classical ballet dancer, who, in a much more systematic way than the general incorporation of masculinity into the body of the adolescent boy, learns quite precisely what the body of a dancer should *feel* like and the appropriate mental attitudes to accompany and foster success as a dancer. In that process, the body itself is literally reshaped – it becomes a particular kind of object, with distinctive musculature and capabilities – but so too, as the title of Wacquant's book indicates, does the soul. Body and mind – musculature and skill, fantasy and conceptualization – are indivisible here. Furthermore, this melding has to be understood to go much further than mere morphology; it has to be taken right through to the biochemistry of body and brain. What is happening here is quite literally an incorporation, the creation of a particular way of incarnating masculinity, femininity, or even a transgendered status, in the body. We shape ourselves at the very moment in which we are shaped.

Although these forms of incorporation describe very well the way in which gender goes considerably beyond the apparently insubstantial questions of minds and relationships, understanding of these processes tends to be limited to the sociology of the body. What is lacking here is much recognition or investigation into the potential for transformation of the human body from within biology. There is ample attention paid within the pages of the journal *Body & Society*, for example, to both the symbolic aspects and the lived experience of such forms of incorporation as those of, say, women body builders, but a relative lack of engagement within the biological sciences with the ways in which social, psychological, and cultural elements interface with the physiology of the body. The general way in which transformation of the body is conceptualized is limited by an assumption, familiar to us from athletic competition and the controversy over the use of banned substances (now not even describable as drugs), that the body sets limitations to this process. There is, apparently, only so much transformation any body can take. If anything, this assumption is strengthened where sexual difference is concerned, as if it were there to form a counterweight to disturbance caused by the contemporary blurring of gender boundaries and the fact that we are routinely witness to transsexual reassignments that are so effective they would be undetectable without prior knowledge.

FISHES LIVE IN THE SEA

There is some evidence that we have barely begun to understand the potential malleability of the body, malleability of the kind that was so graphically illustrated over half a century ago by W. B. Cannon's investigation into what he called 'voodoo death', the situation in which someone with no apparent physiological abnormalities dies following a curse by a witch doctor (Cannon, 1942; Sternberg, 2002).[3] Biological research and the prevalence and popularity of genetic explanations are largely driving in the opposite direction.

Part of the revived rhetoric of sexual difference currently in circulation is the injunction to accept that there might be fundamental genetic, hormonal, physiological, and psychological differences between the sexes with which we must all come to terms, and we seem to be particularly enjoined to deny any malleability in the distinction between women and men. In that context, our current behaviours and ways of being are believed to reveal our natural boundaries.

Erving Goffman describes this rather complacent approach to human behaviour in *Gender Advertisements* (1979) when he identifies the little bit of folk wisdom that underpins the ways in which we consider ourselves and naturalize our own behaviours:

> There is a wide agreement that fishes live in the sea because they cannot breathe on land, and that we live on land because we cannot breathe in the sea. This proximate, everyday account can be spelled out in ever increasing physiological detail, and exceptional cases and circumstances uncovered, but the general answer will ordinarily suffice, namely an appeal to the nature of the beast, to the givens and conditions of his existence, and a guileless use of the term 'because.' Note, in this happy bit of folk wisdom – as sound and scientific surely as it needs to be – the land and the sea can be taken as there prior to fishes and men, and not, contrary to genesis – put there so that fishes and men, when they arrived, would find a suitable place awaiting them. (1979: 6)

This little parable about the fishes draws attention to the fact that we tend to explain what happens and how we behave by dint of an appeal to 'the very conditions of our being'. There is a deeply held belief in our culture, which we apply to ourselves in relation to what Goffman calls 'gender displays', that objects are passively informing about themselves through the imprints they leave on the surrounding environment, that they give off unintended signs of what it is that they are: 'they cast a shadow, heat up the surround, strew indications, leave an imprint; they impress a part picture of themselves' (1979: 6). As human beings, says Goffman, we learn not only how to convey and express who we are to others, but also to abide by our own conceptions of expressivity, to convey that characterological expression as if it were natural and unavoidable. In terms of gender, we not only learn to be a particular kind of object, but to be 'the kind of object to which the doctrine of natural expression applies…We are socialized to confirm our own hypotheses about our natures' (1979: 7). We learn how to behave and then, like learning to ride a bicycle, we forget that we once wobbled and found the whole thing improbable and impossible, and it all comes naturally. The lack of conscious intentionality in a large part of our performance then supplies its 'naturalness'.

Not to take account of this latent reflexive capacity in human behaviour is crucially to miss a trick. It is not merely that we can be self-conscious about particular encounters and our behaviours within them, or indeed about the whole repertoire we have at our disposal, it is that we need to have an understanding that behaviours are the behaviours of whole bodies in social settings, and it is for this reason that Goffman begins by considering gender displays under the heading of ethology. The application of ethology to human beings, however, is often interpreted to mean a reduction and simplification of human behaviours to some allegedly more primitive state of affairs (take Desmond Morris's *The Naked Ape* as a caricatural example), which belies and bypasses the sophistication of the cultures within which human beings operate and negotiate their being.

Thus, the gender displays we supply to others to provide background information about our sex and our selves are no different in kind from the 'background information' that an eighteenth-century slave owner might employ in addressing his slaves, or a twenty-first-century motorist in responding to a police officer. They represent our own staging of something which quite literally *embodies* discourse and conceptualization, fantasy, social and psychological knowledge, and so on, and it is there to set the terms of the engagement. Anyone who has ever watched a parent dealing with a child in a way which is markedly different from the way one would deal with one's own child is testament to these processes: the tone of voice that is rather too loud for someone standing a mere two feet away, the slowed-down speech patterns that imply some notion of the essential idiocy of children – all of these attest to a common way of conceptualizing the status and capabilities of the child, some of which they share with those defined as 'elderly' and with foreigners who, perversely, refuse to speak English. In a more complex vein, in *Counting Girls Out*, Valerie Walkerdine and her co-authors give some enlightening descriptions of the ways in which the respective behaviours of middle-class and working-class mothers towards their children reveal assumptions about what a 'good mother' is and how she should conduct herself in relation to her child – the middle-class-mother-as-educator, for example, for whom 'every possible permutation of events, actions and conversations becomes a "not-to-be-missed" opportunity for a valuable lesson' (Walkerdine et al., 1989: 46).

The fact of such a staging also being a 'statement in the body' naturalizes the performance, for what could be more 'natural' than the body? The overloud tone of voice used with children, the elderly, or foreigners is clearly simply that which is deemed necessary. From the point of view of either the actor or the recipient of any such performance, it is all a matter of knowing who one is dealing with. The marked particularity of persons, or for that matter the specification of objects in the natural world (dangerous or benign snakes, for example), is there merely to allow one to know how to respond appropriately, safely, and in a way that allows for some prediction of the outcome.

It would certainly be naïve therefore to downplay the way in which human beings actively negotiate and shape such processes, including the representation of their sex. The biological underpinnings are not the impoverished *reductio ad absurdum* given to us by much contemporary evolutionary psychology, but the potential province of a new and dynamic feminist biology – a socio-biology in the true sense. Until and unless we recognize the unity of these processes, of the complex human biological apparatus and the sophisticated psychological and social engagements created by that apparatus, which in its turn shape its creator, we shall be condemned to miss the point in terms of 'sex' and 'gender' and the relationship between them.

NOTES

1 In fact, when Kessler and McKenna's book was first published, there was arguably only a single genital being attributed, the penis, with men being defined as possessing a penis and women as lacking one, just as any good Freudian might have expected. More recently, in *Lessons from the Intersexed*, Kessler suggests that there is some evidence that vaginas may now be emerging as cultural genitals, although 'there are no cultural clitorises' (1998: 157, n.15). This is in keeping with the dominance of a reproductive imperative in the way in which women's bodies are read. So it is not only that gender attribution and genital attribution can be considered synonymous, it is that the only legitimate cultural genitals for women are arguably those which are tied to, the potential at least, of reproduction.

2 Kessler and McKenna face a similar problem to that confronted by Laqueur insofar as they have difficulty accommodating the biological itself in their argument about the primacy of gender attribution. Speculating as to whether or not infants have an inherent capacity to detect the difference between the sexes prior to their learning the rules for gender attribution and about the fact that small children are better at 'seeing through' the attempts by transsexuals to 'pass' in their chosen gender, Kessler and McKenna find themselves

resorting to a concept of 'gender' differentiation, which they endeavour to explain, not entirely successfully, as the identification of whether someone is 'the same' as oneself or not, 'perhaps in terms of some basic reproductive criteria' (1978: 166–67). The quotation marks around the term 'gender' in that formulation reveal the tension within it.

3 Claude Lévi-Strauss (1977) explains 'voodoo death' as being produced by the shock of the withdrawal of all social anchorage points from the person being cursed, who is effectively declared dead. This is, to all intents and purposes, the dissolution of their social personality. The result is that their physical integrity thereby collapses with, amongst other things, a catastrophic and ultimately lethal drop in blood pressure.

REFERENCES

Bernhardt, Paul C. et al. (1998), 'Testosterone Changes during Vicarious Experiences of Winning and Losing among Fans at Sporting Events', *Physiology and Behavior*, August 65(1): 59–62.

Butler, Judith (1993), *Bodies That Matter: On the Discursive Limits of 'Sex'*, New York, Routledge.

Bynum, Caroline Walker (1989), 'The Female Body and Religious Practice in the Later Middle Ages', in Michael Feher et al. (eds), *Fragments for a History of the Human Body*, New York, Zone, pp. 161–219.

Cannon, Walter B. (1942), '"Voodoo" Death', *American Anthropologist*, 44: 169–81.

Connell, R.W. (1987), *Gender and Power: Society, the Person and Sexual Politics*, Cambridge, Polity Press.

de Beauvoir, Simone (1972 [1949]), *The Second Sex*, Harmondsworth, Penguin.

Delphy, Christine (1984), *Close to Home: A Materialist Analysis of Women's Oppression*, Diana Leonard (trans.), London, Hutchinson.

Fausto-Sterling, Anne (1989), 'Life in the XY Corral', *Women's Studies International Forum*, 12(3): 319–31.

Fausto-Sterling, Anne (1992), *Myths of Gender: Biological Theories about Women and Men*, New York, Basic Books.

Fausto-Sterling, Anne (2000), *Sexing the Body: Gender Politics and the Construction of Sexuality*, New York, Basic Books.

Foucault, Michel (1980), *Herculine Barbin, Being the Recently Discovered Memoirs of a Nineteenth-Century Hermaphrodite*, Richard McDougall (trans.), Brighton, Harvester Press.

Goffman, Erving (1979), *Gender Advertisements*, London, Macmillan.

Kessler, Suzanne (1998), *Lessons from the Intersexed*, New Brunswick: NJ, Rutgers University Press.

Kessler, Suzanne and McKenna, Wendy (1978), *Gender: An Ethnomethodological Approach*, Chicago: University of Chicago Press.

Laqueur, Thomas (1990), *Making Sex: Body and Gender from the Greeks to Freud*, Cambridge: MA, Harvard University Press.

Lévi-Strauss, Claude (1977), 'The Sorcerer and his Magic', *Structural Anthropology*, Claire Jacobson and Brooke Grundfest Schoepf (trans.), Harmondsworth, Penguin.

Martin, Emily (1991), 'The Egg and the Sperm: How Science Has Constructed a Romance Based on Stereotypical Male–Female Roles', *Signs*, 16(3): 485–501.

Money, John (1965), 'Psychosexual Differentiation', in John Money (ed.), *Sex Research: New Developments*, New York, Holt, Rhinehart and Winston.

Oakley, Ann (1972), *Sex, Gender and Society*, London, Temple Smith.

Oakley, Ann (1981), *Subject Women*, Oxford, Martin Robertson.

Oudshoorn, Nelly (1994), *Beyond the Natural Body: An Archaeology of Sex Hormones*, New York, Routledge.

Page, David; Mosher, Rebecca; Simpson, Elizabeth M. C.; Mardon, Graeme; Pollack, Jonathan; McGillivray, Barbara; de la Chapelle, Albert and Brown, Laura G. (1987) 'The Sex-determining Region of the Human Y Chromosome Encodes a Finger Protein', *Cell*, 24(December): 1091–1104.

Sternberg, Esther M. (2002), 'Walter B. Cannon and "'Voodoo' Death": A Perspective from 60 Years on', *American Journal of Public Health,* 92: 1564–6.

Stoller, Robert (1968), *Sex and Gender: On the Development of Masculinity and Femininity*, London, Hogarth Press.

Wacquant, Loïc (2003), *Body and Soul: Notebooks of an Apprentice Boxer*, New York, Oxford University Press.

Walkerdine, Valerie and the Girls and Mathematics Unit (1989), *Counting Girls Out*, London, Virago Press.

3

Changing Studies on Men and Masculinities

Jeff Hearn and Michael S. Kimmel

Gender research and women's studies has made the dynamics of gender explicit and has also made masculinity visible as gendered ideology, named men as gendered, and problematized the position of men. Recent years have seen a considerable expansion of explicitly gendered research and scholarship on men and masculinities. Where men's outlooks and culturally defined characteristics were formerly the unexamined norm for religion, science, citizenship, law, and authority, the new scholarship recognizes the specificity of different masculinities and increasingly investigates their genealogies, structures, and dynamics. The chapter begins by discussing the framing and naming of studies on men and masculinities in relation to feminism and critical gender scholarship. Thereafter, men and masculinities are analysed as socially constructed, with the interweaving of men's gender status and other social statuses. Epistemological and methodological issues are explored, along with implications of studies for political and policy issues. The chapter concludes with a commentary on the future of the field.

INTRODUCTION: FRAMING STUDIES ON MEN AND MASCULINITIES

The impulse to develop the field of gender research and women's studies has come primarily from feminists. Those making gender visible in contemporary scholarship and in public forums have mainly been women, and the field has been very much inspired by addressing research questions about women and gender relations. At the same time, revealing the dynamics of gender also makes masculinity visible as a central concept of gendered ideology, names men as gendered, and problematizes the position of men.

Studies of men and masculinities stand in a complex relation to women's studies and feminism. The question of 'men' has long been on feminist agendas and part of women's studies and gender research in the United States. Jalna

Hanmer (1990) lists fifty-six feminist publications 'providing the ideas, the changed consciousness of women's lives and their relationship to men – all available by 1975' (pp. 39–41). In the 1980s there were a number of feminist theoretical consolidations regarding men (hooks, 1984; O'Brien, 1981), and feminist and mixed-gender conference debates on men (Friedman and Sarah, 1982; Hearn and Morgan, 1990; Jardine and Smith, 1987). More recent feminist initiatives have suggested a wide variety of analyses of men and ways forward for men (Adams and Savran, 2002; Gardiner, 2002; Schacht and Ewing, 1998).

Feminism has demonstrated many theoretical and practical lessons for men, though men seem to keep ignoring or forgetting most of them. One is that the understanding of gender relations has to involve attention to questions of power. Another is that to transform gender relations, and specifically men's continued dominance of much of social life, means changes not only in what women do and are but also in what men do and are.

Thus, where men's outlooks and culturally defined characteristics were formerly the unexamined norm for religion, science, citizenship, law, and authority, the new scholarship recognizes the specificity of different masculinities and, increasingly, investigates their genealogies, structures, and dynamics. This process has now been active for more than twenty-five years in the United States and has produced a large and interesting body of research that focuses on men and masculinities.

This research interest has been developed by feminist scholars and a relatively small number of men scholars and from a variety of perspectives and relations to feminism – from anti-feminist to ambiguous and ambivalent to pro-feminist.[1] However, the object of study – men and masculinities – needs to be distinguished from the producers of studies on men and masculinities – women, men, or women and men together. This distinction sometimes appears to be an area of confusion, especially for non-pro-feminist men, who may assume, erroneously, that they have or should have privileged status over women when it comes to studying men.

NAMING STUDIES ON MEN AND MASCULINITIES

It is perhaps not so surprising with the relative flurry of activity on men and masculinities that there might be disputes over the framing and naming of the subject area. There is some debate about what to call this field of knowledge. Some scholars have used the terms *masculinity studies* or *male dominance studies* or *critical studies on men* to describe the field. Others have called this area of enquiry *men's studies*.

However, men's studies is not an accurate corollary to women's studies, since women's studies made both women *and* gender visible. Nor is it a corrective to the perceived defects of women's studies made by anti-feminist scholars, who seem to say, 'Well, you have *your* women's studies, but what about us men?' In short, the phrase men's studies often suggests a defensive reaction to women's studies rather than a building on its original insights about gender.

Women's studies offered a corrective to the androcentric bases and biases of the traditional scholarly canon, and its signal success has been to create a new discipline, along with libraries and book series devoted to women's lives. Today, in fact, any book that does not have the word 'women' in it is a book in 'men's studies' – but we call it 'literature', 'history', or 'political science'.

We have named this chapter Changing Studies on Men and Masculinities to distinguish between studies of men as corporeal beings and masculinities – the ideologies and attitudes that are associated with those corporeal beings. We use the term *masculinities* to make it clear that there is no one singular masculinity, but that masculinity is elaborated and experienced by different groups of men in different ways. Such a framing more accurately reflects the nature of contemporary work, which is inspired by, but not simply parallel to, feminist research on women.

MEN AND MASCULINITIES AS SOCIALLY CONSTRUCTED

All human cultures have ways of accounting for the positions of women and men and different ways of picturing the patterns of practice we call masculinities. The combination of empirical description and secular explanation that constitute social science took shape during the later nineteenth century, at the high tide of European imperialism. The colonial frontier was a major source of data for European and North American social scientists writing on sexuality, the family, and women and men. There was, thus, a situational, socially constructed, and global dimension of gender in Western social science from its earliest stage (Connell, 2002).

However, an evolutionary framework of progress (with Western White men as the apex) was largely discarded in the early twentieth century. The first steps towards the modern analysis of masculinity are found in the psychologies pioneered by Freud and Adler. Psychoanalysis demonstrated that adult character was not predetermined by the body but was constructed through emotional attachments to others in a turbulent process of growth (Connell, 1994). In the next generation, anthropologists such as Malinowski and Mead emphasized cultural differences in these processes and the importance of social structures and norms. By the mid-twentieth century, these ideas had crystallized into the concept of sex roles.

Masculinity was then understood in psychology, social psychology, sociology, and anthropology as an internalized role or identity, reflecting a particular (in practice often meaning US or Western) culture's norms or values, acquired by social learning from agents of socialization such as family, school, and the mass media. Under the influence of women's liberation, gay liberation, and even men's liberation, the male role was subject to sharp criticism (Pleck and Sawyer, 1974). In the United States, the idea of men's studies as an academic field emerged out of debates sparked by this critique (Massachusetts Institute of Technology, 1979).

In the social sciences, the concept of a male sex role has been critiqued as ethnocentric, lacking in a power perspective, and positivistic (Brittan, 1989; Eichler, 1980; Kimmel, 1987). In its place, broader social construction perspectives highlighting issues of social power have emerged (Carrigan, Connell, and Lee, 1985; Kaufman, 1987), along with critiques of the dominance of heterosexuality, heterosexism, and homophobia (Frank, 1987; Herek, 1986). Two major sets of power relations have thus been addressed: the power of men over women (heterosocial power relations), and the power of some men over other men (homosocial power relations). These twin themes inform contemporary enquiries into the construction of masculinities.

The concept of masculinities in the plural has been extremely important over the last twenty years in widening the analysis of men and masculinities within the gender order (Brod, 1987; Brod and Kaufman, 1994; Carrigan et al., 1985; Connell, 1995). It has supplanted the concept of the male sex role and is generally preferred to other terms, for example manhood or manliness. Conceptual work emphasized social structure as the context for the formation of particular masculinities (Connell, 1987; Hearn, 1987; Holter, 1997), with some recent authors emphasizing that masculinities are constructed within specific discourses (Petersen, 1998). Detailed life-history and ethnographic research provide close descriptions of multiple and internally complex masculinities (Mac an Ghaill, 1994; Messner, 1992; Segal, 1997; Wetherell and Edley, 1999). There is also a growing debate and critique around the concepts of masculinities and hegemonic masculinity from a variety of methodological positions, including the historical (MacInnes, 1998), materialist (Donaldson, 1993; Hearn, 1996; 2004; McMahon, 1993), and poststructuralist (Whitehead, 2002).

The construction of men and masculinities can be explored with many different scopes of analysis and sets of interrelations, including the social organization of masculinities in their global and regional iterations; institutional reproduction and articulation of masculinities; the organization and practices of masculinities within a context of gender relations, that is how interactions with women, children, and other men express, challenge, and reproduce gender inequalities; and individual men's performance, understanding, and expression of their gendered identities.

Many scholars have explored the institutional contexts in which such masculinities are articulated and constructed. Masculinities do not exist in social and cultural vacuums but rather are constructed within specific institutional settings. Gender, in this sense, is as much a structure of relationships within institutions as it is a property of individual identity. For example, locating the construction of masculinities within families, workplaces, schools, factories, and the media are promising areas for research.[2]

METHODOLOGIES FOR STUDYING MEN AND MASCULINITIES

A wide range of research methods have been used to study men and masculinities, including social surveys; statistical analyses; ethnographies; interviews; and qualitative, discursive, and deconstructive approaches, as well as various mixed methods. An explicitly gendered focus on men and masculinities can lead to the rethinking of particular research methods. Michael Schwalbe and Michelle Wolkomir (2002) have set out some key issues to be borne in mind when interviewing men; Bob Pease (2000) has applied memory work in researching men; and David Jackson (1990) has developed men's critical life-history work.

Historical research has also traced the emergence of new and situational masculinities and the institutions in which they arise. These have included both dominant (Davidoff and Hall, 1990; Hall, 1992; Hearn, 1992; Kimmel, 1997; Tosh, 1999; Tosh and Roper, 1991) and resistant (Kimmel and Mosmiller, 1992; Strauss, 1982) forms of masculinities at home, in work, and in political and cultural activities. Important historical work has been done from gay history (Mort, 2000; Weeks, 1990) and from colonies of settlement such as New Zealand and Natal on schools and military forces (Morrell, 2001b; Phillips, 1987).

Social scientific perspectives in studies on men and masculinities necessarily draw on a number of traditions. While not wishing to play down debates and differences between traditions, the broad, critical approach to men and masculinities that has developed in recent years can be characterized in a number of ways, by:

- a *specific*, rather than an implicit or incidental, *focus* on the topic of men and masculinities;
- taking account of *feminist, gay, and other critical gender scholarship*;
- recognizing men and masculinities as *explicitly gendered* rather than non-gendered;
- understanding men and masculinities as *socially constructed, produced, and reproduced* rather than as somehow just 'naturally' one way or another;
- seeing men and masculinities as *variable and changing* across time (history) and space (culture), within societies, and through life courses and biographies;
- emphasizing men's relations, albeit differentially, to *gendered power*;
- spanning both *the material and the discursive* in analysis;
- interrogating the *intersecting of gender with other social divisions* in the construction of men and masculinities. It is to this last point that we now turn.

INTERWEAVING MEN'S GENDER STATUS WITH OTHER SOCIAL STATUSES

Men are not simply or only men. Although men and masculinities are our explicit focus and are understood as explicitly gendered, men and masculinities are not formed by gender alone. Men and masculinities are shaped by differences of, for example, age, class, disability, ethnicity, racialization. Men's gender status intersects with racial, ethnic, class, occupational, national, global, and other socially constructed and defined statuses. The gendering of men exists in the intersections with these other social divisions and social differences.

The intersection of social divisions has been a very important area of theorizing in critical race studies, Black studies, postcolonial studies, and kindred fields (Awkward, 2002; hooks, 1984; Morrell and Swart, 2005; Ouzgane and Coleman, 1998). Paradoxically, it might be argued that as studies of men and masculinities deconstruct the gendering of men and masculinities, other social divisions come to the fore and are seen as more important. Part of the long-term trajectory of gendered studies of men could thus be the deconstruction of gender (Lorber, 1994; 2000).

Very promising research is being carried out on differences and intersectionalities among men by racial group, class, sexuality, age, and the like, and the intersections of these axes of identity and social organization. For example, discussion of the relations of gender and class can demonstrate the ways in which different classes exhibit different forms of masculinities and the ways in which these both challenge and reproduce gender relations among men and between women and men. A key issue here is how men relate to other men, and how some men dominate other men. Men and masculinities are placed in both cooperative and conflictual relations with each other – in organizational, occupational, and class relations – and also in terms defined more explicitly in relation to gender, such as family, kinship, sexuality, and gender politics.

Some intersectional research on masculinities has used ethnographic methods to explore the constructions of masculinities. For example, Matt Gutmann (1996) has investigated the construction of masculinity among poor men in Mexico City, and Loïc Wacquant (2004) has conducted participant observation among poor Black young men training to become Golden Gloves boxers in Chicago. Such ethnographic works take the analysis inside gender construction and examine how meanings are made and articulated among men themselves.

The intersectional perspective links with research on the impacts of globalization or glocalization on local gender patterns: men's employment, definitions of masculinity, and men's sexuality (Altman, 2001). Analysis of masculinities and men's place in the gender order has become a worldwide undertaking, with emphasis on local differences. Although most empirical research is still produced within the developed countries, global perspectives are increasingly significant (Cleaver, 2002; Pease and Pringle, 2002). In his recent work, R. W. Connell (1998; 2005) has explored the ways in which certain dominant versions of masculinities are rearticulated in the global arena as part of the economic and cultural globalization project by which dominant states engulf weaker states.

EPISTEMOLOGICAL ISSUES

In studying men, certain epistemological considerations recur. We may ask:

- what form of and assumptions about epistemology are used, more or less consciously?
- who is doing the studying, with what prior knowledge, and with what positionality?
- what is being studied – in this case, what is counted as 'men' or to do with 'men'?
- what is the relation between those studying men and the men studied?
- in what specific social contexts, especially academic, do the above activities take place? (Hearn, 2003)

This last point is especially important. The gendering of epistemology, along with the gendered analysis of academic organizations, has tremendous implications for rethinking the position and historical dominance of men in academia and how their dominance structures what counts as knowledge (Connell, 1997; Hearn, 2001). A gendered focus on men can be applied to academia, suggesting rereadings of non-gendered traditions and 'classics' within mainstream social science, in terms of their implicit and explicit conceptualizations of gender, women, and men (Morgan, 1992).

There are various approaches to epistemology, both generally and in studying men. According to rationalist epistemology, ideas exist independently of experience, in some way derived from the structure of the human mind or existing independently of the mind. We might 'know', for example, the 'essence' of 'deep masculinity', as in the work of Robert Bly and the mythopoetics. It is very difficult to prove or disprove such knowledge: *we know* what men are like, even if evidence appears otherwise.

In contrast, empiricists deny that concepts exist prior to experience. For them, knowledge is a product of human learning, based on human perception. Thus, men are studied by sense perceptions, whether through one's own or more systematically, through the perceptions of others, as indicative of how men are. This epistemology remains at the base of much mainstream social science on men. Focusing on perception, however, brings its own complications – misunderstandings and illusions – that show that perception does not always reveal the world as it 'really is'.

There are problems with both the rationalist and the empiricist epistemologies, and certainly so in their extreme forms. Kant, and subsequently many other critical thinkers, sought to develop some form of synthesis between them: people certainly do have knowledge that is prior to experience, for example the principle of causality. Kant held that there are a priori synthetic concepts, but empirical knowledge is also important. Many others have expanded this critical insight and developed forms of knowledge that mix elements of rationalism, empiricism, and critical reflection, whether through an emphasis on meaning and interpretation, as in hermeneutics, or through a more societally or socially grounded analysis of knowledge, as in the Hegelian–Marxist tradition and feminist and various other, indeed multiple, standpoint theories (Harding, 1991).

Standpoint traditions – the view that knowledge is shaped by social position – inform much of the development of feminist and pro-feminist critical studies on men. In this view, the positioning of the author in relation to the topic of men, as a personal, epistemological, and indeed geopolitical relation, shapes the object of research and the topic of men and masculinities in a variety of ways. Such positionings include, for example, treating the topic non-problematically (through taking for granted its absence or presence), through sympathetic alliance with those men studied or the contrary subversion of men, or with ambivalence, in terms of alterity (i.e. the recognition of various forms of otherness between and among men), or through a critical relation to men (Hearn, 1998). These differentiations are partly a matter of individual political choices and decisions in positioning, but increasingly the importance of the more structural, geopolitical positioning is being recognized. Postcolonial theory has shown that it matters whether analysis is being conducted from within the West, the global South, the former Soviet territories, the Middle East, or elsewhere. Thus, history, geography, and global politics matter in epistemologies and ontologies in studying men.

What may appear obvious and open to straightforward empirical data gathering is not so simple. One might argue that different knowledge is available to men than women, or to feminists, pro-feminists, or anti-feminists. Such differences arise from socially defined experiences and standpoints. A useful contrast can be drawn between more individually defined standpoint theory, which prioritizes knowledge from the individual's identity politics, and more socially contextualized standpoint theory, which sees knowledge as a collective production linked to historical political positions and circumstances that are not necessarily rooted in individual identity politics.

We find the collective variant of standpoint theory more compelling than the individual viewpoint. A collective understanding of standpoint theory can usefully inform research designs in highlighting gendered power relations in the subjects and objects of research and in the research process itself. It can also assist the production of more explicitly gendered and grounded knowledge about men, masculinities, and gender relations. Emphasizing the researcher's social position is not to suggest a deterministic account of the impact of the researcher on the research process; rather, the social position of the researcher is *relevant* but not all-encompassing. Positionality is especially important in researching certain topics and sites, but the relevance and impact of the social position of the knower is likely to vary considerably with different kinds of research situations, sites, materials, and questions. The topic of men is not unified, ranging from broad theoretical analyses to specific social situations, which might be individual or men-only or mixed-gender.

Studying men cannot be left only to men. Men's knowledge of themselves is at best limited and partial, at worst violently patriarchal. The idea that only men can study men (or that only women can study women) links social position to bodies. This idea can be seen as essentialist biologism, but it also recognizes the importance of bodies (and, for that matter, emotions) to the production of knowledge. Exploration of the embodied nature of knowledge, in relation to both researcher and researched, is an important epistemological concern that is often an unexamined subtext in the research process.

POLITICAL AND POLICY ISSUES

The growth of research on men and masculinities reflects a diverse public and policy interest, ranging from boys' difficulties in school to men's violence.[3] Research is paralleled by the development of admittedly extremely uneven policy debates at local, national, regional, and global levels. The motivations for such policy initiatives can also come from varied political positions, ranging from men's rights to pro-feminism to the emphasis on differences between men, whether by social class, age, sexuality, ethnicity, and racialization (Messner, 1997).

In the rich countries, including Japan, Germany, and the United States, and in some less wealthy countries, including Mexico and Brazil, the late 1980s and 1990s saw rising media interest and public debate about boys and men. Mainly focused on social problems such as unemployment, educational failure, and domestic violence, but also discussing men's changing identities, these debates have different local emphases. In Australia, the strongest focus has been on problems of boys' education (Lingard and Douglas, 1999). In the United States, more attention has been given to interpersonal relationships and ethnic differences (Kimmel and Messner, 2003). In Japan, there has been a challenge to the 'salaryman' model of middle-class masculinity (Taga, 2005). In the Nordic region, there has been more focus on gender equity policies and men's responses to women's changing position (Lundberg, 2001). In Latin America, especially Mexico, debates have addressed the broad cultural definition of masculinity in a long-standing discussion of 'machismo', its roots in colonialism, and effects on economic development (Adolph, 1971; Gutmann and Viveros Vigoya, 2005).

In most of the developing world, these debates have not emerged, or have emerged only intermittently. In the context of mass poverty, the problems of economic and social development have had priority. However, questions about men and masculinities emerged in development studies in the 1990s, as feminist concerns about women in development led to discussions of gender and development and the specific economic and political interests of men (White, 2000).

Such debates also have different emphases in different regions. In Latin America, particular concerns arose about the effects of economic restructuring. Men's sexual behaviour and role in reproduction are addressed in the context of population control policies and sexual health issues, including HIV/AIDS prevention (Valdés and Olavarría, 1998; Viveros Vigoya, 1997). In Southern Africa, regional history has given debates on men and masculinities a distinctive focus on race relations and on violence, both domestic and communal (Morrell, 2001a). In the Eastern Mediterranean and Southwest Asia, cultural analysis of masculinity has particularly concerned modernization and Islam, the legacy of colonialism, and the region's relationship with contemporary Western economic and military power (Ghoussoub and Sinclair-Webb, 2000).

Locally and regionally, there are various attempts to highlight problems both created by and experienced by men and boys and to initiate interventions, such as boys' work, youth work, anti-violence programmes, men's health programmes. There is growing interest in the interventions against men's violence at both global (Ferguson et al., 2004) and local (Edwards and Hearn, 2005) levels. Stratification issues, both of gender and other divisions, are clearly relevant at both national and global levels.

Several national governments, most prominently in the Nordic region but also elsewhere, have promoted men's and boys' greater involvement in gender equality agendas. Regional initiatives include those in the European Union and the Council of Europe. The multinational study by the collaborative European Union's 'The Social Problem of Men' research project (Critical Research on Men in Europe, CROME) is an attempt to generate a comparative framework for understanding masculinities in the new Europe. The goal is to remain sensitive to cultural differences among the many countries of that continent and to the ways in which nations of the EU are, to some extent, developing convergent definitions of gender. Here we see both the similarities across different nations and variations among them as well, as different countries articulate different masculinities (Hearn et al., 2004; Hearn and Pringle, 2006; Pringle et al., 2005).

By the late 1990s, the question of men and masculinity was also emerging in international forums, such as diplomacy and international relations (Zalewski and Parpart, 1998), the peacekeeping operations of the United Nations (Breines, Connell, and Eide, 2000), and international business (Hooper, 2000). The UN and its agencies have also been at the forefront in the field of men's health and HIV/AIDS prevention and intervention.

An interesting convergence of women's and men's issues has taken place at the UN. Following the world conferences on women that began in 1975, there has been an increasing global debate on the implications of gender issues for men. The Platform for Action adopted at the 1995 Fourth World Conference on Women said:

> The advancement of women and the achievement of equality between women and men are a matter of human rights and a condition for social justice and should not be seen in isolation as a women's issue...The Platform for Action emphasises that women share common concerns that can be addressed only by working together and in partnership with men towards the common goal of gender equality around the world.[4]

Since 1995, these issues are increasingly being taken up in the UN and its various agencies and in other transgovernmental organizations' policy discussions. For example, the UN's Division for the Advancement of Women in 2003 organized a worldwide online discussion forum and expert group meeting in Brasilia on the role of men and boys in achieving gender equality as part of its preparation for the 48th session of the Commission on the Status of Women, with the following comment:

> Over the last decade, there has been a growing interest in the role of men in promoting gender equality, in particular as the achievement of gender equality is now clearly seen as a societal responsibility that concerns and should fully engage men as well as women. (Division for the Advancement of Women, United Nations (2003a: 1)[5]

THE FUTURE OF THE FIELD

While it is not possible to predict the future of a field of research with any precision, it may be possible to identify emerging problems and approaches that are likely to be fruitful. There is, first, the task of developing the picture on a world scale. The social scientific record is very uneven; research on men and masculinities is still mainly a First World enterprise. There is far more research in the United States than in any other country. There are major regions of the world where research even partly relevant to these questions is scarce – including China, the Indian subcontinent, and Central and West Africa. To respond to this lack is not a matter of sending out First World researchers with existing paradigms. That has happened all too often in the past, reproducing, in the realm of knowledge, the very relations of dominance and subordination that are part of the problem. Forms of cooperative research that use international resources to generate new knowledge of local relevance need to be developed.

Next, there are several issues that seem to be growing in significance. The most obviously important is the relation of masculinities to those emerging dominant powers in the global political economy. Organization research has already developed methods for studying men and masculinities in corporations and other organizations (Cockburn, 1983; 1991; Collinson and Hearn, 1996; 2005; Kanter, 1977; Ogasawara, 1998). It is not difficult to see how this approach could be applied to transnational operations, including international capitalist corporations and military organizations, although it will call for creative cooperation.

There are also new or relatively underdeveloped perspectives that may give greater insight even into well-researched issues. The possibilities of poststructuralist theory are now well discussed, although there are doubtless new applications to be found. These could include combining the insights of poststructuralism with more materially grounded analyses of men and masculinities, whether as controllers of power and resources, or as excluded and marginalized. More broadly, there is still much to be done in developing interdisciplinary scholarship; for example, bringing together research on men from the social sciences and the humanities.

At the same time, the possibilities in postcolonial theory are still little explored (Morrell and Swart, 2005; Ouzgane and Coleman, 1998), and they are very relevant to the transformation of a research field historically centred in the First World. Analysis of both political and economic transformations, militarism, and neo-imperialism are seriously underdeveloped (Higate, 2003; Novikova and Kambourov, 2003), as is political and economic analysis more generally. Most discussions of men and gender acknowledge the importance of power and the world of work but do not carry them forward into analyses of a gendered economy. Economic inequality is crucial to understanding the link between masculinity and violence, and the same may be argued for other masculinity issues (Godenzi, 2000).

There are other long-standing significant problems that have remained under-researched. A notable example is the personal development of masculinities in the course of growing up. How children are socialized into gender was a major theme of sex role discussions, and when the male role literature went into a decline, this problem seems to have stagnated. All the debate about boys' education has produced little new developmental theorizing. However, a variety of approaches to development and social learning exist (ethnographic, psychoanalytic, cognitive) along with excellent models of fieldwork (Thorne, 1993).

An interdisciplinary research agenda on these issues would certainly move our understanding of men and masculinities a long way forward. Nevertheless, understanding is mainly worth having if we can do something with it to create a more gender-just world. Therefore, the uses of knowledge and the relationship between research and practice must be key issues for the development of this field.

ACKNOWLEDGEMENTS

We are very grateful to R. W. Connell for his cooperation in developing some of these ideas (see Connell, Hearn, and Kimmel, 2005), and to Judith Lorber for editorial comments.

NOTES

1 There are Web-based and other bibliographic resources available, including *The Men's Bibliography*, constructed by Michael Flood (2004), now in its 13th edition.

2 Research collections and reviews are available on a wide variety of social institutions, including crime (Messerschmidt, 2005), violence (DeKeseredy and Schwartz, 2005), the military (Higate, 2003; Higate and Hopton, 2005), family (Adams and Coltrane, 2005), fatherhood (Marsiglio and Pleck, 2005), health (Sabo, 2005), sport (Messner, 2005), welfare (Pringle, 1995; Popay, Hearn, and Edwards, 1998), transgender (Ekins and King, 2005), and nation (Nagel, 2005).

3 In this volume, see Morgan, Leonard.

4 The Platform for Action adopted by the Fourth World Conference on Women, 15 September 1995, paragraph 3 (United Nations, 2001: 17).

5 A number of very informative documents on the challenges facing men in different parts of the world that were part of this preparation are available online (Division for the Advancement of Women, 2003b). These should be read along with the subsequent Report to the Secretary-General on 'The role of men and boys in achieving gender equality' (Division for the Advancement of Women, 2003c).

REFERENCES

Adams, M., and Coltrane, S. (2005). Boys and men in families: The domestic production of gender, power and privilege. In M. Kimmel, J. Hearn, and R. W. Connell (eds), *Handbook of studies on men and masculinities* (pp. 230–248). Thousand Oaks, CA: Sage.

Adams, R., and Savran, D. (eds) (2002). *The masculinity studies reader*. Malden, MA: Blackwell.

Adolph, J. B. (1971). The South American macho: Mythos and mystique. *Impact of Science on Society*, 21(1): 83–92.

Altman, D. (2001). *Global sex*. Chicago: University of Chicago Press.

Awkward, M. (2002). Black male trouble: The challenges of rethinking masculine difference. In J. K. Gardiner (ed.), *Masculinity studies and feminist theory* (pp. 290–304). New York: Columbia University Press.

Breines, I., Connell, R. W., and Eide, I. (eds) (2000). *Male roles, masculinities and violence: A culture of peace perspective*. Paris: UNESCO.

Brittan, A. (1989). *Masculinity and power*. Oxford: Blackwell.

Brod, H. (ed.) (1987). *The making of masculinities*. London: Unwin Hyman.

Brod, H., and Kaufman, M. (eds) (1994). *Theorizing masculinities*. Thousand Oaks, CA: Sage.

Carrigan, T., Connell, R. W., and Lee, J. (1985). Toward a new sociology of masculinity. *Theory and Society*, 14: 551–604.

Cleaver, F. (ed.) (2002). *Masculinities matter! Men, gender and development*. London: Zed.

Cockburn, C. K. (1983). *Brothers*. London: Pluto.

Cockburn, C. K. (1991). *In the way of women*. London: Macmillan.

Collinson, D. L., and Hearn, J. (eds) (1996). *Men as managers, managers as men: Critical perspectives on men, masculinities and managements*. London: Sage.

Collinson, D. L., and Hearn, J. (2005). Men and masculinities in work, organizations and management. In M. Kimmel, J. Hearn, and R. W. Connell (eds), *Handbook of studies on men and masculinities* (pp. 289–310). Thousand Oaks, CA: Sage.

Connell, R. W. (1987). *Gender and power: Society, the person and sexual politics*. Cambridge: Polity Press.

Connell, R. W. (1994). Psychoanalysis on masculinity. In H. Brod and M. Kaufman (eds), *Theorizing masculinities* (pp. 11–38). Thousand Oaks, CA: Sage.

Connell, R. W. (1995). *Masculinities*. Cambridge: Polity Press.

Connell, R. W. (1997). Long and winding road: An outsider's view of U.S. masculinity and feminism. In B. Laslett and B. Thorne (eds), *Feminist sociology: Histories of a movement* (pp. 151–164). New Brunswick, NJ: Rutgers University Press.

Connell, R. W. (1998). Men in the world: Masculinities and globalization. *Men and Masculinities*, 1(1): 3–23.

Connell, R. W. (2002). *Gender*. Cambridge: Polity Press.

Connell, R. W. (2005) Globalization, imperialism, and masculinities. In M. Kimmel, J. Hearn, and R. W. Connel (eds), *Handbook of studies of men and masculinities* (pp. 71–89). Thousand Oaks, CA: Sage.

Connell, R. W., Hearn, J., and Kimmel, M. (2005). Introduction. In M. Kimmel, J. Hearn, and R. W. Connell (eds), *Handbook of studies on men and masculinities* (pp. 1–12). Thousand Oaks, CA: Sage.

Davidoff, L., and Hall, C. (1990). *Family fortunes: Men and women of the English middle class 1780–1850*. Chicago: University of Chicago Press.

DeKeseredy, W. S., and Schwartz, M. D. (2005). Masculinities and interpersonal violence. In M. Kimmel, J. Hearn, and R. W. Connell (eds), *Handbook of studies on men and masculinities* (pp. 353–366). Thousand Oaks, CA: Sage.

Division for the Advancement of Women, United Nations. (2003a, September 24). *Aide-memoire for the expert group meeting on the role of men and boys in achieving gender equality*. Retrieved 20 September 2004, from http://www.un.org/womenwatch/daw/egm/men-boys2003/aide-memoire.html

Division for the Advancement of Women, United Nations. (2003b, September 24). 'The role of men and boys in achieving gender equality'. Expert Group Meeting, organized by DAW, in collaboration with UNDP, ILO, and UNAIDS, 21–24 October 2003, Brasilia, Brazil. Retrieved 20 May 2004, from http://www.un.org/womenwatch/daw/egm/men-boys2003/documents.html

Division for the Advancement of Women, United Nations. (2003c, December 22). 'The role of men and boys in achieving gender equality'. Thematic issue before the Commission: The role of men and boys in achieving gender equality. Report to the Secretary-General. Retrieved 20 May 2004, from http://www.un.org/womenwatch/daw/csw/csw48/Thematic1.html

Donaldson, M. (1993). What is hegemonic masculinity? *Theory and Society*, 22: 643–657.

Edwards, S. S. M., and Hearn, J. (2005). *Working against men's 'domestic violence': Priority policies and practices for men in intervention, prevention and societal change*. Strasburg: Council of Europe.

Eichler, M. (1980). *The double standard: A feminist critique of feminist social science*. London: Croom Helm.

Ekins, R., and King, D. (2005). Transgendering, men, and masculinities. In M. Kimmel, J. Hearn, and R. W. Connell (eds), *Handbook of studies on men and masculinities* (pp. 379–394). Thousand Oaks, CA: Sage.

Ferguson, H., Hearn, J., Holter, Ø. G., Jalmert, L., Kimmel, M., Lang, J., Morrell R., and de Vylders, S. (2004). *Ending gender-based violence: A call for global action to involve men*, Stockholm: SIDA. Available at: http://www.sida.se/content/1/c6/02/47/27/SVI34602.pdf

Flood, M. (2004). *The men's bibliography: A comprehensive bibliography of writing on men, masculinities, gender, and sexualities*. Retrieved 21 September 2004, from http://www.xyonline.net/mensbiblio/

Frank, B. (1987). Hegemonic heterosexual masculinity. *Studies in Political Economy*, 24: 159–170.
Friedman, S., and Sarah, E. (eds) (1982). *On the problem of men*. London: Women's Press.
Gardiner, J. K. (ed.) (2002). *Masculinity studies and feminist theory*. New York: Columbia University Press.
Ghoussoub, M., and Sinclair-Webb, E. (2000). *Imagined masculinities: Male identity and culture in the modern Middle East*. London: Saqi Books.
Godenzi, A. (2000). Determinants of culture: Men and economic power. In I. Breines, R. Connell, and I. Eide (eds), *Male roles, masculinities and violence: A culture of peace perspective* (pp. 35–51). Paris: UNESCO.
Gutmann, M. C. (1996). *The meanings of macho: Being a man in Mexico City*. Berkeley, CA: University of California Press.
Gutmann, M. C., and Viveros Vigoya, M. (2005). Masculinities in Latin America. In M. Kimmel, J. Hearn, and R. W. Connell (eds), *Handbook of studies on men and masculinities* (pp. 114–128). Thousand Oaks, CA: Sage.
Hall, C. (1992). *White, male and middle-class: Explorations in feminism and history*. New York: Routledge.
Hanmer, J. (1990). Men, power and the exploitation of women. In J. Hearn and D. Morgan (eds), *Men, masculinities and social theory* (pp. 21–42). London/New York: Unwin Hyman/Routledge.
Harding, S. (1991). *Whose science? Whose knowledge? Thinking from women's lives*. Milton Keynes: Open University Press.
Hearn, J. (1987). *The gender of oppression: Men, masculinity and the critique of Marxism*. Brighton: Wheatsheaf.
Hearn, J. (1992). *Men in the public eye: The construction and deconstruction of public men and public patriarchies*. London: Routledge.
Hearn, J. (1996). 'Is masculinity dead?' A critical account of the concepts of masculinity and masculinities. In M. Mac an Ghaill (ed.), *Understanding masculinities: Social relations and cultural arenas* (pp. 202–217). Milton Keynes: Open University Press.
Hearn, J. (1998). Theorizing men and men's theorizing: Men's discursive practices in theorizing men. *Theory and Society*, 27: 781–816.
Hearn, J. (2001). Academia, management and men: Their connections and implications. In A. Brooks and A. MacKinnon (eds), *Gender and the restructured university* (pp. 69–89). Buckingham: Open University Press.
Hearn, J. (2003). Epistemologies for studying men. In *Developing studies on men in the Nordic context. A report on men's cultures and networks conference, 4 October 2002* (pp. 53–65). Helsinki: Finnish Council for Equality between Women and Men/Oslo: Nordic Institute for Women's Studies and Gender Research. Available at: http://www.tasa-arvo.fi/ta-neuv/julkaisut.php3
Hearn, J. (2004). From hegemonic masculinity to the hegemony of men. *Feminist Theory*, 5: 97–120.
Hearn, J., and Morgan, D. (eds) (1990). *Men, masculinities and social theory*. London: Unwin Hyman/Routledge.
Hearn, J., and Pringle, K., with members of Critical Studies on Men in Europe (2006). *European perspectives on men and masculinities*. Houndsmill: Palgrave Macmillan.
Hearn, J., Müller, U., Oleksy, E., Pringle, K., Chernova, J., Ferguson, H., Holter, Ø. G., Kolga, V., Novikova, I., Ventimiglia, C., Lattu, E., Tallberg, T., and Olsvik, E. (2004). *The European Research Network on Men in Europe: The Social Problem and Societal Problematisation of Men and Masculinities. Volumes 1 and 2*. Brussels: European Commission. http://improving-ser.jrc.it/default/show.gx?Object.object_id=TSER----000000000000121D&_app.page=show-TSR.html
Hearn, J., Pringle, K., Kolga, V., Müller, U., Novikova, I., and Oleksy, E. (2005). *European perspectives on men and masculinities*. Houndmills: Palgrave.
Herek, G. M. (1986). On heterosexual masculinity: Some consequences of the social construction of gender and sexuality. *American Behavioral Scientist*, 29: 563–577.
Higate, P. (ed.) (2003). *Military masculinities: Identity and the state*. Westport, CT: Praeger.

Higate, P., and Hopton, J. (2005). War, militarism and masculinities. In M. Kimmel, J. Hearn, and R. W. Connell (eds), *Handbook of studies on men and masculinities* (pp. 432–447). Thousand Oaks, CA: Sage.

Holter, Ø. G. (1997). *Gender, patriarchy and capitalism: A social forms analysis.* Oslo: University of Oslo.

hooks, b. (1984). *Feminist theory: From margin to center.* Boston: South End Press.

Hooper, C. (2000). Masculinities in transition: The case of globalization. In M. H. Marchand and A. S. Runyan (eds), *Gender and global restructuring: Sightings, sites and resistances* (pp. 59–73). London: Routledge.

Jackson, D. (1990). *Unmasking masculinity: A critical autobiography.* London: Unwin Hyman/Routledge.

Jardine, A., and Smith, P. (eds) (1987). *Men in feminism.* London: Methuen.

Kanter, R. M. (1977). *Men and women of the corporation.* Boston: Basic Books.

Kaufman, M. (1987). *Beyond patriarchy: Essays by men on pleasure, power and patriarchy.* Toronto: Oxford University Press.

Kimmel, M. (ed.) (1987). *Changing men: New directions in research on men and masculinity.* Newbury Park, CA: Sage.

Kimmel, M. (1997). *Manhood in America: A cultural history.* New York: Free Press.

Kimmel, M., and Messner, M. A. (eds) (1988). *Men's lives* (1st edition). New York: Macmillan.

Kimmel, M., and Messner, M. A. (eds) (2003). *Men's lives* (6th edition). Boston, MA: Allyn and Bacon.

Kimmel, M., and Mosmiller, T. (eds) (1992). *Against the tide: Pro-feminist men in the United States, 1779–1990. A documentary history.* Boston, MA: Beacon.

Lingard, B., and Douglas, P. (1999). *Men engaging feminisms: Pro-feminism, backlashes and schooling.* Buckingham: Open University Press.

Lorber, J. (1994). *Paradoxes of gender.* New Haven, CT: Yale University Press.

Lorber, J. (2000). Using gender to undo gender. *Feminist Theory*, 1: 79–95.

Lundberg, C. (ed.) (2001). Mannen. *Fronesis*, 8 (special issue).

Mac an Ghaill, M. (1994). *The making of men: Masculinities, sexualities and schooling.* Buckingham: Open University Press.

MacInnes, J. (1998). *The end of masculinity: The confusion of sexual genesis and sexual difference in modern society.* Buckingham: Open University Press.

Marsiglio, W., and Pleck, J. H. (2005). Fatherhood and masculinities. In M. Kimmel, J. Hearn, and R. W. Connell (eds), *Handbook of studies on men and masculinities* (pp. 249–270). Thousand Oaks, CA: Sage.

Massachusetts Institute of Technology. (1979). *Men's studies bibliography* (4th edition). Cambridge, MA: Human Studies Collection, Humanities Library, MIT.

McMahon, A. (1993). Male readings of feminist theory: The psychologization of sexual politics in the masculinity literature. *Theory and Society*, 22(5): 675–696.

Messerschmidt, J. W. (2005). Men, masculinities, and crime. In M. Kimmel, J. Hearn, and R. W. Connell (eds), *Handbook of studies on men and masculinities* (pp. 196–212). Thousand Oaks, CA: Sage.

Messner, M. A. (1992). *Power at play: Sports and the problem of masculinity.* Boston, MA: Beacon.

Messner, M. A. (1997). *Politics of masculinities: Men in movements.* Thousand Oaks, CA: Sage.

Messner, M. A. (2005). Still a man's world? Studying masculinities and sport. In M. Kimmel, J. Hearn, and R. W. Connell (eds), *Handbook of studies on men and masculinities* (pp. 313–325). Thousand Oaks, CA: Sage.

Morgan, D. H. J. (1992). *Discovering men.* London: Routledge.

Morrell, R. (ed.) (2001a). *Changing men in southern Africa.* London: Zed.

Morrell, R. (2001b). *From boys to gentlemen: Settler masculinity in colonial Natal, 1880–1920.* Pretoria: UNISA Press.

Morrell, R., and Swart, S. (2005). Men in the Third World: Postcolonial perspectives on masculinity. In M. Kimmel, J. Hearn, and R. W. Connell (eds), *Handbook of studies on men and masculinities* (pp. 90–113). Thousand Oaks, CA: Sage.

Mort, F. (2000). *Dangerous sexualities: Medico-moral politics in England since 1830* (2nd edition). London: Routledge.
Nagel, J. (2005). Nation. In M. Kimmel, J. Hearn, and R. W. Connell (eds), *Handbook of studies on men and masculinities* (pp. 397–413). Thousand Oaks, CA: Sage.
Novikova, I., and Kambourov, D. (eds) (2003). *Men and masculinities in the former Soviet countries*. Helsinki: Kikimora, Aleksantteri Institute, University of Helsinki.
O'Brien, M. (1981). *The politics of reproduction*. London: Routledge & Kegan Paul.
Ogasawara, Y. (1998). *Office ladies and salaried men: Power, gender, and work in Japanese companies*. Berkeley, CA: University of California Press.
Ouzgane, L., and Coleman, D. (1998). Postcolonial masculinities: Introduction. *Jouvert: A Journal of Postcolonial Studies*, 2(1). Retrieved 10 December 2003, from http://social.chass.ncsu.edu/jouvert/v2i1/con21.htm
Pease, B. (2000). *Recreating men: Postmodern masculinity politics*. London: Sage.
Pease, B. and Pringle, K. (eds) (2002). *A man's world: Changing men's practices in a globalized world*. London: Zed.
Petersen, A. (1998). *Unmasking the masculine: 'Men' and 'identity' in a sceptical age*. London: Sage.
Phillips, J. (1987). *A man's country? The image of the Pakeha male: A history*. Auckland: Penguin.
Pleck, J. H., and Sawyer, J. (eds) (1974). *Men and masculinity*. Englewood Cliffs, NJ: Prentice Hall.
Popay, J., Hearn, J., and Edwards, J. (eds) (1998). *Men, gender divisions and welfare*. London: Routledge.
Pringle, K. (1995). *Men, masculinities and social welfare*. London: UCL Press.
Pringle, K., Hearn, J., Ferguson, H., Kambourov, D., Kolga, V., Lattu, E., Müller, U., Nordberg, M., Novikova, I., Oleksy, E., Rydzewska, J., Šmídová, I., Tallberg, T., and Niemi, H. (2005). *Men and masculinities in Europe*. London: Whiting and Birch.
Sabo, D. (2005). Men's health studies: An overview. In M. Kimmel, J. Hearn, and R. W. Connell (eds), *Handbook of studies on men and masculinities* (pp. 326–352). Thousand Oaks, CA: Sage.
Schacht, S. P., and Ewing, D. (eds) (1998). *Feminism and men: Reconstructing gender relations*. New York: New York University Press.
Schwalbe, M. L. and Wolkomir, M. (2002). Interviewing men. In J. F. Gubrium and J. A. Holstein (eds), *Handbook of interview research* (pp. 203–219). Thousand Oaks, CA: Sage.
Segal, L. (1997). *Slow motion: Changing masculinities, changing men* (2nd edition). London: Virago.
Strauss, S. (1982). *Traitors to the masculine cause*. Westport, CT: Greenwood Press.
Taga, F. (2005). East Asian masculinities. In M. Kimmel, J. Hearn, and R. W. Connell (eds), *Handbook of studies on men and masculinities* (pp. 129–140). Thousand Oaks, CA: Sage.
Thorne, B. (1993). *Gender play: Girls and boys in school*. New Brunswick, NJ: Rutgers University Press.
Tosh, J. (1999). *A man's place: Masculinity and the middle-class home in Victorian England*. New Haven, CT: Yale University Press.
Tosh, J., and Roper, M. (eds) (1991). *Manful assertions: Masculinities in Britain since 1800*. London: Routledge.
United Nations. (2001). *Beijing declaration and platform for action*. New York: United Nations Department of Public Information.
Valdés, T., and Olavarría, J. (eds) (1998). *Masculinidades y equidad de género en América Latina* (Masculinities and equity of gender in Latin America). Santiago: FLACSO/UNFPA.
Viveros Vigoya, M. (1997). Los estudios sobre lo masculino en América Latina: Una producción teórica emergente (Studies on the masculine in Latin America: An emerging conceptual development). *Nómadas*, 6: 55–65.
Wacquant, L. (2004). *Body and soul*. New York: Oxford University Press.
Weeks, J. (1990). *Coming out: Homosexual politics in Britain, from the nineteenth century to the present* (rev. edition). London: Quartet.

Wetherell, M., and Edley, N. (1999). Negotiating hegemonic masculinity: Imaginary positions and psycho-discursive practices. *Feminism and Psychology,* 9(3): 335–356.

White, S. C. (2000). 'Did the earth move?' The hazards of bringing men and masculinities into gender and development. *IDS Bulletin,* 31(2): 33–41.

Whitehead, S. M. (2002). *Men and masculinities: Key themes and new directions.* Cambridge: Polity Press.

Zalewski, M., and Parpart, J. (eds) (1998). *The 'man' question in international relations.* Boulder, CO: Westview Press.

Part II

CULTURAL REPRESENTATIONS AND CRITIQUES

4

Gendered Cultures

Gabriele Griffin

This chapter charts the changing ways in which gender has figured in cultural production by feminist women since the 1970s, highlighting how shifts in discourse from 'women' to 'gender' have impacted on cultural practices and analyses. It suggests that the feminist archaeological/genealogical project of the 1970s and 1980s which served to change cultural canons by inserting women's work into them was predicated upon an unproblematized notion of women as socio-cultural entities whose identity as women was not in question. Debates about differences among women, rather than only between women and men, resulted in shifts in cultural preoccupations that increasingly led to the notion of femininity as constructed and gender as performance. This shift also marked a rise in interest in women's performance, film, and popular cultural work during the 1980s and 1990s, fuelled not least by advances in biotechnology. The 'cultural turn' in the social sciences of the 1990s created significant feminist work on the inter-relationship between the body, technology, and science which highlighted the increasing differences in content of women's/gender studies courses around the world. Technology and women's cultural positioning in the collapsing public and private spheres of globalized cultures are likely to dominate feminist agendas in the twenty-first century.

INTRODUCTION

The recognition that cultures are gendered has permeated women's intellectual work throughout the twentieth century. The anthropological writings of Margaret Mead, the literary criticism of Virginia Woolf, the writings of Gertrude Stein, the collages of Hannah Höch, for instance, all reveal a preoccupation with the gendered nature of culture that has antecedents in previous centuries but which began to be historicized predominantly during the last century. For the purposes of this chapter, I shall concentrate on the period from the late 1970s onwards to indicate how gender has manifested itself in the Northwestern cultures of Europe and the United States, and how those manifestations have been analysed. As part of that process, I shall discuss the ways in which the language we use to speak about gender has changed during that period and the implications of those changes.

In writing about 'culture', I shall focus on 'concrete sets of *signifying practices* – modes of generating meaning – that create *communication orders* of one kind or another' (Polity Press, 1994: 2), and discuss 'high' cultural forms such as literature, performance, and art, as well as 'popular' cultural forms, such as cinema and television. My concern is to show how certain ways of manifesting and thinking about gender were expressed through particular signifying practices and modes of communication.

THE POWER OF BINARIES

One of the most powerful drivers of the women's liberation movement of the 1970s was the notion that women as a category of human beings universally shared a culturally completely entrenched experience of oppression by men. This experience was considered to be the foundation on which women should bond to make political and economic claims for equality with men. On its basis, two propositions were articulated. One was the binary divide between men and women, a divide that itself had a long cultural history in Western thinking and had been the basis on which women's oppression by men was justified (Grimshaw, 1986; Lloyd, 1984) the other, that 'sisterhood [was] global' (Morgan, 1984). The latter led to generalizations on behalf of women – in hindsight perhaps unjustified – such as Radicalesbians' wonderful assertion: 'What is a lesbian? A lesbian is the rage of all women condensed to the point of explosion' (Radicalesbians, 1970: 17). But under the impact of these propositions, women began to demand spaces of their own, their place in the public sphere, the reform of the private sphere, and proper recognition of their contributions to society. The talk was of 'women' and of 'sex', not of 'gender', and, as the Convention for the Elimination of All Discrimination Against *Women* (CEDAW) (1975; my emphasis) indicates, the focus of the 1970s and early 1980s was on women as biocultural entities whose identity as *women* was not in question. Correspondingly, the first women's studies courses to emerge in the United States and other Anglophone countries during the 1970s and early 1980s had women as an unproblematized category at their centre.

The claims of the women's liberation movement on behalf of women were fuelled by two perceptions: the need to assert presence – that of women – and the need to explain absence or silence – also that of women. Rozsika Parker and Griselda Pollock, for instance, wrote of the 1970s that 'a dominant concern of women artists both inside and outside the Artists' Union was the male monopoly on exhibition space, not only within the establishment but in the new alternative galleries then opening in London' (1987: 13). Similarly, Tillie Olsen's *Silences* (1980) was intended as 'a powerful witness to great cultural loss' to account for an absence, already noted by Virginia Woolf in *A Room of One's Own* (1929), of women from literature. Women, viewed as objects and consumers of culture,[1] began to assert their presence as subjects and producers of culture, not only within their immediate generation but also in relation to those preceding. This stance generated one of the major feminist cultural projects of the 1980s, the archaeological–genealogical 'thinking back through [our] mothers' (Woolf, 1929: 93). Across a vast range of signifying practices, women began to account for the absence of women from cultural production, to create genealogies, histories, and maps of women whose work had been suppressed in cultural histories, and to analyse this work.

This feminist project changed the cultural landscape of Northwestern countries significantly and within a very short period of time. The work of many 'forgotten' women writers, artists, musicians, travellers, dressmakers, filmmakers, designers, photographers, playwrights, poets, and other cultural producers was rediscovered or uncovered, documented, reproduced, and analysed. In women-dominated academic disciplines such as literature and sociology, but also in history, art history, philosophy, archaeology, and other such subjects, feminist academics began 'the long march through the institutions' to integrate their newly recovered cultural foremothers' work into the canons of their academic field. Thus, where women educated in the period until the mid-1970s in literature, for example, were unlikely to encounter women writers other than Jane Austen and George Eliot, by the mid-1980s, virtually all English courses in the UK included 'women's writing' as one of their key and most popular modules in undergraduate courses, and writers such as Alice Walker and Virginia Woolf were routinely taught. These courses became one of the axes on which women's and gender studies degrees were built during the 1980s.

The reproduction of 'forgotten' cultural works by women was accompanied by a new scholarly–critical apparatus that underpinned the notion of a history of women's cultural work shaped by their sex-specific position in society. It resulted in classics such as Kate Millet's *Sexual Politics* (1969), Elaine Showalter's *A Literature of Their Own* (1977), Sandra M. Gilbert and Susan Gubar's *The Madwoman in the Attic* (1979), Ann Oakley's *Subject Women* (1981), and Rozsika Parker's and Griselda Pollock's *Old Mistresses: Women, Art and Ideology* (1981). These texts produced powerful analyses of the cultural and economic oppression of women within and through patriarchy,[2] and served as key texts on 'women's writing' and 'women and representation' courses within women's and gender studies.

This revolution in educational content was in part made possible by the numerous feminist cultural production sites for women's work that, staffed by women, sprang up in the Northwestern countries. (Many of these sites disappeared by 2004.) Publishing houses such as Virago, the Women's Press, Daughters Inc., Naiad Press, and Onlywomen Press were established by women with feminist ideological agendas, intent on transforming women's cultural, social, political, and economic lives by empowering them through reflecting back to women and articulating *their* experiences and views. The mid-1970s to the mid-1980s thus proved an enormously productive era for women whose cultural work began to find voice, support, and recognition. Feminist newspapers and journals such as *Spare Rib* and *Emma* appeared; publishers produced series such as 'Mothers of the Novel' by Pandora, 'Plays by Women' by Methuen, and the 'Feminist Sci-fi' series that the Women's Press inaugurated. Even staid presses such as Oxford University Press understood that there was now a market for 'forgotten' works by women and produced Charlotte Lennox's *The Female Quixote* in its 'World Classics' series in 1989. These texts enabled women academics to intervene in the canons of their subjects and to present their students with female role models of cultural creativity, thus suggesting the possibility of female subjecthood and agency in culture.

Feminist sci-fi created worlds separate from men and ruled by women promulgating conventionally womanly qualities, such as communalism, nurturance, and non-violence (Elgin, 1984; Gearhart, 1980; Russ, 1975; Wittig, 1969). Some of these texts came complete with inventions of new languages to articulate women's experiences. Suzette Haden Elgin (1984: Appendix n.p.), for instance, invented Láadan, which contained words such as *óothanúthul* to mean 'spiritual orphanhood; being utterly without a spiritual community or family', or *radama*, which meant 'to non-touch, to actively refrain from touching'. These utopias had their origins partly in the anti-war movements of the 1960s and 1970s, and partly in the feminist perception, articulated in Adrienne Rich's *Diving into the Wreck* (1973), for instance, that men – through war, pollution, violence, and exploitation – are responsible for the gradual destruction of the world, and that 'The Will to Change' (Rich, 1971) required a separation of women from men.

Feminist sci-fi was only one of the means by which women began to 'appropriate' cultural forms that had been dominated by men. 'Gender and genre' began increasingly to be featured in courses on 'women's writing' as women began to appropriate and investigate popular genres, such as the detective novel, pulp fiction, and romance. Indeed, it was largely through this engagement with popular genres that popular culture began to take hold in women's studies courses in the mid-1980s, since these popular genres tended to be produced in textual as well as in televisual and filmic forms. The TV series *Cagney and Lacey*, featuring two women detectives, became as popular as the detective novels of Val McDermid, Claire McNab, and Sarah Dreher were to a lesbian readership. Popular culture – as became particularly evident in the interrogation of Harlequin romances, of Mills and Boon pulp fiction, and of the novels of Ann Bannon, for example – far from being analysed as a way of duping the unsuspecting masses, was reclaimed as a form that afforded its women consumers the satisfactions they lacked in their real-life encounters with their men partners. Understanding female pleasure in consumption became an important feature of these recuperations.

FEMALE/FEMININE SPECIFICITIES

The archaeological/genealogical project and women's new cultural assertiveness went hand in hand with the search for female specificity, the notion that women's cultural production had traits and properties particular to women and derived from the specificity of their experience as distinct from that of men. Virginia Woolf had already articulated such potential difference in *A Room of One's Own* when she wrote:

> I will only pause here one moment to draw your attention to the great part which must be played in [the future of fiction] so far as women are concerned by physical conditions. The book has somehow to be adapted to the body, and at a venture one would say that women's books should be shorter, more concentrated, than those of men, and so framed that they do not need long hours of steady and uninterrupted work…[T]he nerves that feed the brain would seem to differ in men and women, and if you are going to make them work their best and hardest, you must find out what treatment suits them. (Woolf, 1929: 74)

Woolf's notion that 'the book must somehow be adapted to the body' sprang from her complex and contradictory views of the importance of biology for cultural destiny – in the section quoted above, she proposes a necessary correlation between physiology and cultural production, grounded in her understanding of the biological differences between women and men.

Those differences were seized upon in the 1970s and early 1980s as part of the attempt to uncover and map women's specificity and to account for the differences – assumed, ascribed, and real – in women's and men's cultural productions and productivity. The case for the promotion of women's cultural production per se was partly made on the basis of its specificity and difference from that of men. Feminist linguists, for instance, attempted to show that women use language differently from men, revealing through their usage the internalization of the state of inferiority, dependency, and inarticulateness to which women have been reduced in patriarchy, as well as their assumed 'natural' tendency to be more supportive, cooperative, communicative, and nurturant than men (Spender, 1980). There was a connected and highly visible movement to reduce sexism in language through the invention of terms such as 'Ms' instead of 'Mrs' or 'Miss' to move beyond the pressure on women to identify their marital status (Miller and Swift, 1980). There were also attempts to create dictionaries sensitive to and expressive of women's language, women's use of language, and women's relation to language (Daly, 1978; Daly with Caputi, 1987; Mills, 1989; Wittig and Zeig, 1976).

Women's new cultural assertiveness, indexed by the attempt to create languages for/by women, was part of an attempt to celebrate women and women's specificity by focusing on revaluing aspects of their selves that were abjected within patriarchal culture (Kristeva, 1980). The celebration included, importantly, women's bodies, specifically their vaginas and their menstrual cycle, regarded as quintessential aspects of women's particularity. Famously, US artist Judy Chicago created 'The Dinner Party' in the 1970s. It was a triangular multimedia installation of a table with thirty-nine china plates decorated with symbolic vaginas, all depicting women's achievements, and designed to re-vision 'the Last Supper from the point of view of those who'd done the cooking throughout history' (Chicago, 1975: 210). The same idea was later used in British playwright Caryl Churchill's *Top Girls* (1984), whose opening scene featured a reimagining of the Last Supper. Feminists (re)claimed the artist Georgia O'Keeffe, whose flower paintings were adored for vulval connotations that seemed to be a celebration of the vagina, vaginal lips, and the clitoris. They also (re)claimed Frieda Kahlo's paintings, which, *inter alia*, feature the abject female body.

The portrayal of women's bodies in art aroused strong reactions. Rozsika Parker's piece on British artist Judy Clark's 'Body Works' exhibition, for example, was introduced with the following paragraph:

> Judy Clark's recent exhibition aroused extreme reactions. While several women critics were swept into pseud's corner by their enthusiasm for the exhibition and the Tate was buying one of her works, many others were appalled. Judy makes works of art out of matter that is usually hidden or thrown away. She takes dust, urine, nail parings, menstrual blood etc., and mounts them with clinical care, creating an effect not unlike a museum cabinet. Her self-portrait consisting of hairs from all parts of her body and fluids from her nine orifices could hardly be further from the sweet plastic image of women celebrated in pop art. (1974: 37)

This introduction illustrates the over-investment within dominant culture in certain forms of femininity and feminine bodies (hairless, non-leaking, without menstruation, un-bodied indeed except in the plastic guise of the Barbie Doll), which prompted feminists to create new images of women and to expose their status as cultural constructs. This double exposure–celebration was evident as much in the installations of Mary Kelly as it was in the collages of Barbara Kruger or the photographs of Cindy Sherman.

The reclamation of women's bodies by women went hand in hand with the reclamation of women's minds, partly derived from the anti-psychiatry movement of the 1960s and early 1970s. States and conditions, until then viewed within patriarchal culture as denoting women's mental incapacity and inferiority, were re-figured as strategies of female survival in a hostile, male-centred environment. Thus, 'hysteria' and post-natal depression in particular were reinterpreted by both feminist artists and feminist critics as women's ways of coping with worlds unsuited to their emotional needs. The poetry of Emily Dickinson, the diary of Alice James, Charlotte Perkins Gilman's novella *The Yellow Wallpaper* (1892), and H D's *Her* (1927) were all rediscovered and reread as part of that phenomenon. Novels such as Sylvia Plath's *The Bell Jar* (1963), Eva Figes' *Days* (1974), Marie Cardinal's *The Words to Say It* (1975), and Janice Galloway's *The Trick is to Keep Breathing* (1989) offered similar contemporary commentaries. The lives of writers such as Virginia Woolf, Anne Sexton, and Sylvia Plath were re-examined from this same perspective. Sigmund Freud's case histories of hysterics were reread and reinterpreted by feminist artists working in a variety of media to reveal the inadequacy of psychoanalysis in enabling women to deal with their lives and suggesting, perhaps over-optimistically, that women's psychosomatic responses to their experiences of oppression had liberatory potential. 'Women and Madness' became one of the topics – part of the 'Women and…' tradition – which were commonplace in many women's studies courses.

Questions of women's relation to their body and the cultural manifestation of that relation were central to the work of certain feminist theorists living in France, in particular Luce Irigaray (1974; 1977), Julia Kristeva (1974; 1977) and Hélène Cixous (1981a; 1981b). Responding to a biographically based sense of displacement regarding their country of birth in the case of Kristeva and Cixous and within patriarchy, the influence of psychoanalytic thinking, and the interrogation of language as 'man-made', these feminists began a celebratory re-visioning of the relation of the maternal to language. They juxtaposed the semiotic (understood as utterances based on instinctual and bodily drives, the pre-linguistic state of the infant who still experiences unison with the mother, *jouissance*, the cyclical, the repetitive, the polysemic – that is, utterances with indeterminate or multiple meanings) with the symbolic (utterances governed by the entry into language, the law of the father, repression of instinctual and bodily drives, linearity, prohibition, closure through singularity of meaning). Kristeva and Cixous (together with Clément, 1975) suggested that the semiotic, as manifested in certain cultural forms, particularly but not only in poetic writing and in performance, had the potential to disrupt the symbolic order.

Neither Kristeva nor Cixous attributed the capacity for producing *écriture féminine* (translated into English as 'writing the body') – as cultural work that manifested the traits of the semiotic came to be known – exclusively to women; indeed, Kristeva's work was critiqued for its failure to engage with women's cultural work in preference to explorations of writings by men. However, both viewed the relation of the semiotic to the maternal as a key disruptive force against the dominance of the masculine order in culture and associated the production of *écriture feminine* significantly with women and also with gay men.

Although the notion of an *écriture feminine* was severely critiqued by materialist feminists and by feminist critics who thought that the process of the translation of bodily drives into signifying practices remained unexplained by Kristeva's and Cixous' work (for example, Jones, 1985), it nonetheless proved highly suggestive as an explanatory model for experimental, avant-garde, postmodern cultural work, such as the writings of Clarice Lispector and Christine Brooke-Rose, and the performance work of Mnouchkine and Pina Bausch. The concept of *écriture feminine* thus became very influential during the 1980s in disciplines such as English, theatre, and performance studies. Increasingly, performance, the female body as spectacle in a diversity of settings, came under interrogation.

In contrast to Kristeva and Cixous, Irigaray centred her theoretical work much more on female morphology. Juxtaposing the unitary penis (or the phallus as its symbolic expression) with the two labia of the vagina and the clitoris, Irigaray posited a decentred female sexuality whose diffusion disrupts the phallic order, the symbolic as expressive of a male cultural economy. She argued that women are both literally and metaphorically *The Sex Which Is Not One* (1977). As such, women operate outside the male-centred or phallogocentric culture, requiring its revaluation based on women supporting each other rather than seeking support from men. It was this latter idea, based on the notion of an absolute difference between women and men, which made Irigaray's work particularly popular among Italian feminists.

DIFFERENCES

In Italy, the sense of women's difference from men resulted in a movement outside of academic institutions and inspired by reading the work of cultural foremothers, such as Virginia Woolf, to promote a new socio-symbolic contract between women, necessitated by the view that women were outside of men's economy in every sphere. The Milan Women's Bookstore Collective (1990) suggested that women's empowerment and participation in culture and in the public sphere more generally could only come about through women empowering each other, achieved via an explicit contract, based on trust, between 'the woman who wants to know' (that is, a woman with less knowledge and fewer resources) and 'the woman who knows' (a more powerful woman). Italian feminism was one of the few feminist contexts that focused significantly on theorizing the unequal relations among women as opposed to the unequal relations between men and women.

Italian feminism never gained the same popularity as French feminism in the Anglophone world. The work of one of French feminism's key theorists, Luce Irigaray, did not generate anything like the reception afforded to Kristeva and Cixous. The popularity of the different feminist theorists in part depended on the very different receptions of psychoanalytic theory in France, Italy, and Germany, where psychoanalysis was integrated into feminist political practice (see Sapegno, 2002) and the Anglophone countries, where feminism was more strongly invested in materialist and empirical traditions. In those countries, socialist feminism played a greater role than it did in continental Europe.

What feminisms in all Western countries during the 1970s and until the mid-1980s shared was a sense that women were constructed as the new redeemers, capable of promoting change through activating their specificities in the service of that change. This included the re-figuring of the meaning of 'woman' and 'womanhood', since 'woman' stood – within patriarchal culture – for all that was secondary, and more radically, since the notion of 'woman' was, as some argued, itself invested with patriarchal values. Simone de Beauvoir's (1949) dictum that 'One is not born, one becomes a woman' was picked up in particular by lesbian writers such as Monique Wittig (1981) and Marilyn Frye (1990) to argue that 'woman' as a category was not natural but socio-cultural, and therefore inscribed with patriarchal values. The latter made 'woman' a construct of the male imaginary, utterly separate from what actual women were really like, and thus rendered the term 'woman' to describe those usually subsumed under that heading useless for the purposes of connoting these same people.

This prising apart of the connotations of 'woman' from the denoted women had its antecedents in a process that had already set in during the late 1970s, namely, the debates among women about their differences from each other. Lesbians and Black women, women from working-class backgrounds, women with disabilities, and women from Third World countries had all begun to question the notion that women constitute a unitary category subsumable under the assumption that 'sisterhood is global'. Betty Friedan's *The Feminine Mystique* (1963) in particular came in for severe criticism for failing to recognize that 'the problem that has no name' as she called it, which besets the young suburban wife who wants more than husband, home, and children, was hardly shared by all women (hooks, 1984). A shift occurred in feminist rhetoric, away from the focus on differences between women and men, and towards an exploration of differences among women. The 1980s saw a huge rise in cultural producion from women who are Black, lesbian, working class, and diversely able, fuelled by a newly legitimated assertiveness of women from different backgrounds and with diverse agendas and needs.

One of the most powerful developments was the emergence of literature by Black American feminist women such as Alice Walker, Toni Morrison, Paule Marshall, Ntozake Shange, Audre Lorde, and Maya Angelou, whose work was widely represented in curricula throughout the Northwestern world. Their writing reworked histories of slavery and racial oppression to foreground the narratives of women's experiences of those histories, and did so in high-cultural forms (Walker's *The Color Purple* (1982), for instance, was an epistolary novel). Their work indicted not only White people but also Black men for failing Black women through incest, domestic violence, abuse, abandonment, and neglect. Their indictments of Black men caused major debates within Black communities in which Black women insisted on their right to speak out against oppressive practices within their own communities, while Black men argued that it was a betrayal of the Black race in the face of oppression from Whites (Wallace, 1990). The focus within Europe on Black American feminist writing during the 1980s conveniently and regrettably drew attention away from the cultural work by women from diverse ethnic backgrounds creating that work within Europe. Black and Asian women in the UK, Algerian women in France, Turkish women in Germany, and Arab women in Sweden continued to have great difficulties to achieve cultural visibility.

One reaction to African American feminist writing was the emergence of so-called Third World voices. Promoted through the advocacy of the need for subaltern studies, it enabled the voices of women from the poorest countries in the world, such as India and Latin America, to be heard. Its best-known proponent is Gayatri Chakravorty Spivak, whose *In Other Worlds: Essays in Cultural Politics* (1988) inaugurated feminist engagement with the concept of subaltern studies and with the question of 'Third World' women's cultural production. This work shifted the focus away from fiction, which was predominant in Black American feminist work, to autobiography, a form that became extensively theorized by feminists during the 1980s and 1990s (for example, Evans, 1999; Smith, 1987; Stanley, 1992). Autobiographies, in particular of women engaged in revolutionary and resistance movements, became the dominant Third World cultural expression read in Northwestern countries. Chief among these was perhaps *I, Rigoberta Menchú; An Indian Woman in Guatemala* (1984), for which the eponymous heroine won the Nobel Peace Prize in 1992. Mahasweta Devi's (1988) story 'Draupadi', championed by Gayatri Chakravorty Spivak, was made into a successful film, 'The Bandit Queen'. These texts reinforced the importance of the recognition of differences among women.

Another source of the recognition of differences among women were the so-called sex wars among lesbians: in the 1980s, 'vanilla sex' was juxtaposed with more aggressive forms of sexual behaviour, such as sado-masochism. Just as 'women of colour' differentiated themselves from White women and from each other and exploded the notion of a 'universal' Black woman, so lesbians began to lay claim to a diversity of identities. The lesbian feminism of the 1970s was repudiated in favour of a revival of the butch/femme dynamic associated with 1950s' bar culture (Nestle, 1992) and the use of strap-on dildos and sado-masochistic sex (Califia, 1988). This aggressive lesbian sexuality was condemned by some lesbian feminists as an expression of penis envy (Jeffreys, 1994). Nevertheless, this 'lesbian sexual revolution' spawned a wide range of performance work and literature, including lesbian erotica, fiction, plays, poetry, and research into lesbian sexual history. This work re-engaged with issues of role-playing in lesbian culture and became a key contributor to the shift from 'women' to 'gender' in culture during the 1990s, a shift that was spearheaded by Judith Butler's *Gender Trouble* (1990).

GENDER-BENDING

Role-playing within lesbian culture, in particular the adoption of accoutrements associated with certain kinds of masculinity or femininity such as moustaches and lipsticks, helped to generate the concept of 'gender-bending', of playing with gender while refusing to be identified with either the masculine or the feminine sex. Out of it arose a new debate about sexual and cultural identities, in part subsumed within 'queer theory', which challenged conventional thinking about sex, sexuality, and gender identity (Smyth, 1992).

The distinction between sex as a biological given and gender as a form of acculturation, widely taken for granted during the 1970s and early 1980s, unravelled with developments in biotechnology. Cultural theory began to question the objectivity of science, the fixity of biology, and the teleology of sexo-cultural destinies in favour of an understanding, underpinned by the work of postmodern theorists such as Michel Foucault and Jacques Derrida, that all material manifestations are culturally mediated and therefore malleable. In this view, biology and the body as conventionally conceived are portrayed as themselves the products of certain forms of acculturation and as such are not 'given' but 'made'.

Queer theory, gender-bending, and challenges to biological givens undid many of the binaries on which, at the very least, much feminist thinking had been based. The classic distinction between female and male, on which the feminist politics of the 1970s had been founded, began to dissolve. In popular culture, that dissolution was played out through figures like the singers David Bowie, Madonna, and k.d. lang. Lesbian culture saw the emergence of a debate about sexo-cultural identity through the rise of voices from within the transsexual and, increasingly, the more diverse transgender communities, which had been excluded from the women-only venues of lesbian culture (Bornstein, 1994). It also saw the emergence of the drag king (Volcano and Halberstam, 1999), a gender-bending figure outside the binary gender regime.

POPULAR CULTURES

Many of these changes in women's cultures during the 1990s were accompanied by debates about power and identity that shifted attention away from the feminist preoccupations of the 1970s and early 1980s,[3] and onto issues of sexual identity and power structures. The 1990s thus saw a focus on the re-sexualization (Grosz and Probyn, 1995) and the empowerment of women (Wolf, 1994), encapsulated in popular cultural figures such as Lara Croft and Buffy the Vampire Slayer or, within mainstream culture, the ladette, the pretty woman who can hold her own among the lads in terms of drinking, sexual assertiveness, and the pursuit of money, fame, and career. The American TV series *Sex and the City* became emblematic of this figure.

Some viewed cultural phenomena such as Madonna or *Sex and the City* as liberatory for women, part of the g-r-r-r-l culture that emerged during the 1990s. That culture was embodied, *inter alia*, in the zap actions of the Guerrilla Girls who sought to assert women's place in culture through witty and provocative interventions designed to expose cultural gender bias. Indeed, being witty, provocative, assertive, in-your-face, publicly visible, and politically concerned were the hallmarks of g-r-r-r-l culture. Its growling (hence 'g-r-r-r-l') refusal to be conventionally 'girly', while claiming a heterosexually assertive femininity, became one of the trademarks of 1990s' feminism.

Others were more sceptical of the emancipatory potential of ladette culture. Indeed, one might argue that the gun-toting Lara Croft, the aggressive sexuality of certain contemporary singers, the promotion of sado-masochism among women, and other similar phenomena have resulted in a masculinization of female culture, not matched, significantly, by a feminization of masculine cultures. Despite repeated pronouncements of masculinity in crisis, especially since the decline of certain major male-dominated industries such as steel, coal, and shipbuilding since the early 1980s, there has not been a significant cultural swing in male mainstream cultures towards traits conventionally associated with the feminine.[4] Instead, it has resulted in a sense of vacuum regarding male role models, increasingly filled by a perception of young men's rising lawlessness on the one hand, and their preoccupation with a new consumerism on the other (Campbell, 1993).

The masculinization of women's cultural production is one way to think about the plays of Sarah Kane (2001), for instance, the British playwright whose suicide in 1999 articulated a violence against self that had already made her plays infamous. Her work marks the collapse of gender distinctions in culture in favour of a rise in violence, aggression, breakdown of family, community, and relation through action-packed narratives that centre principally on the violent expression of power structures between people whose only way of relating to each other is through domination, humiliation, and degradation – by men of women, by women of men, by men of men, and women of women. A very recent version of this phenomenon were the by-now notorious images of the American woman, Pfc. Lynndie England, degrading and sexually humiliating male Iraqi prisoners of war in the infamous Abu Ghraib Prison in Bhagdad. The sense of outrage was doubly unsettling to feminists (Ehrenreich, 2004; Enda, 2004.)

Kane's plays produce, in condensed and shocking form, a tabloid view of the world dominated by incest, rape in many different forms, war, murder, abuse, domestic violence, sadistic brutalization, the collapse of the very fabric of environments. These events exist outside a moral order, uncontained by value systems that transform, transcend, or redeem them. They speak to both a radical enfranchisement and a radical disenfranchisement effect of worlds without moral orders. It is worth noting that this kind of work, described by some as 'post-feminist', has been difficult to integrate into feminist cultural preoccupations other than through the, in a sense quite dated, notion that the writer is a woman.

The backlash against feminism, that is 1970s' feminism, which was documented by Susan Faludi (1992) and Marilyn French (1992), led to debates, already hinted at in the preceding paragraph, about the possibilities of 'post-feminism' (Coppock, Haydon, and Richter, 1995; Modleski, 1991) and ushered in a new kind of heterosexually invested feminism as articulated by Naomi Wolf (1991), for example. This trend was accompanied by the rise of consumerism and the commodification of identities:

> When, in my travels, I asked women who hated the word 'feminism' to describe to me a version of feminism that could capture their aspirations, they replied with striking unanimity, 'That Nike ad. You know – "Just do it."' (The phrase that was most often quoted by 'insider' feminists, in contrast, was Audre Lorde's quote about the master's tools never dismantling the master's house.) (Wolf, 1994: 49)

The changes in women's position in Northwestern countries since the 1970s, including women's greater participation in education and in the labour market, opportunities for control over one's reproductivity through contraception and abortion, changes in the possibilities for and attitudes towards divorce and cohabitation, mean that women, especially younger women who had grown up in the 1980s, increasingly think of equality between women and men as something that has been achieved. The dead hand of conservatism has further depoliticized them so that the issue of consumption became a key concern in the feminisms of the 1990s, stimulated by the conservatively inspired propagation of 'choice' as the fuel firing consumerist, individualist, and anti-communitarian attitudes.

GENDER/S, BODIES, AND TECHNOLOGY

That notion of 'choice' has also been consistently replayed in the debates around gender/s, bodies, and technologies that have been a mainstay of 1990s' culture. 'Gender' replaced 'women' as the term of reference within many feminist debates, for both good and ill. Those roots of this change, which connected to the refusal of the term 'woman' as invested with male-centred values and to an anti-essentialist attitude towards the meaning of 'woman', helped women to engage with diversity among themselves and revealed the extent to which men were also not a unitary category. Especially in film, these roots led to an explosion of the production of gender-bending movies, such as those by the Spanish film maker Pedro Almodovar, and films such as *Torchsong Trilogy, Priscilla, Queen of the Desert, She Must be Seeing Things, Paris is Burning, Boys Don't Cry*, and performance pieces such as Claire Dowie's monologues (1996), which were widely used in women's/gender studies courses, and afforded women the opportunity to consider gender outside of conventional norms.

The roots of the replacement of 'women' with 'gender', however, that connected to the equal opportunities policies which had led to equality discourses proclaiming the end of the need for feminism were much more problematic. It was through those routes that popular cultural forms showing women as on a particular kind of par with men (equally violent, equally sexually voracious, equally ruthless), as epitomized by the female stalker movie *Fatal Attraction*, or indeed by *Sex and the City*, became popularized. In fact, they showed how unliberated women still were from the heterosexist norms that measured women's worth – properly and not least internalized by many women themselves – in terms of their affiliation with a man, and repositioned women as ultimately at the behest of their instincts and emotions, unredeemed by reason of any kind.

A different set of developments of the 1990s came from the so-called 'cultural turn' in the social sciences, advanced by one phenomenon particularly important for the 1990s and the arena in which the most important feminist interventions of that decade were made: the culturalization of the 'hard' sciences. Advances in biotechnology and in gene modification technology in particular, impacting directly on people's daily lives through crises in food production and changing possibilities of medical intervention in reproduction, for instance, led to major political campaigns to enhance 'the public understanding of science', not least because governments were not prepared to bear the costs of errors of judgement.

Within feminism, that culturalization of the sciences went hand in hand with an explosion of writing on the body, and, indeed, within feminist cultural production one might describe the 1990s as the decade of the body. Its antecedents were the debates about test-tube babies and *in vitro* fertilization which had come to a specifically gendered head when a team of male doctors facilitated the birth, in 1978, of Louise Brown, the first so-called test-tube baby. The proliferation of medically assisted reproductive technologies led to a flurry of scientific, medical, legal, and cultural activity in which women's 'ownership' of reproduction was increasingly called into question, culturally underpinned by films such as the *Aliens* series, for instance, and the powerful and sustained revival of Mary Shelley's novel *Frankenstein* (1818). Body preoccupations also led to feminist interrogations of the cultural manufacture of the female body (Bordo, 1993; Gatens, 1996; Grosz, 1994) and to a new destabilization of the body as a given biological entity.

One effect of this sense of the body as 'made' or 'achieved' rather than given was an extensive feminist engagement with body modification, in particular through plastic surgery, but also through sport, as detailed in the film *Pumping Iron II*, for instance. The malleability and cultural manufacture of gender, replayed as the malleability and cultural manufacture of the body, created fierce debates about such interventions (Davis, 1995; 2003). The debates about cosmetic surgery and other body modifications were imbricated in the feminist discourse about female genital mutilation, race oppression through the privileging of the White body as the beauty norm, women's 'right to choose', and the ethics of bodily intervention in general.

Symptomatic of those debates about the body was the work of French artist Orlan (1993) who infamously staged a series of body modification operations during the 1990s that were simultaneously transmitted into galleries around the world in which she tellingly declared '*ceci est mon corps…ceci est mon logiciel…*' (this my body…this is my software…) and sought to explore the use of plastic surgery for the purposes of self-transformation. Some feminists interpreted such transformations as reflections of the repressive nature of heterosexist body regimes that encourage women to work towards 'unnatural' body shapes through diet, fitness, and intervention regimes that are ideologically problematic and questionable health risks, while others interpreted them as enabling women to take control of their bodies and be the shape they choose.[5]

The association of body with software made in Orlan's work is telling because of the pervading sense in the 1990s and into the twenty-first century of the imbrication of technology in body manufacture. The meaning of changes in technology for women and in culture has become one of the most important preoccupations of women's and gender studies in recent years. Within this context, feminists have been particularly concerned to analyse the culturally specific and gendered nature of both science and technology, thus becoming mediators in the struggle for the public's understanding of science through the medium of culture.[6] One of the most abiding images for that struggle is the figure of the 'cyborg', manufactured by Donna Haraway to account for the imbrication of technology in the body and the dissolution between the boundaries of 'natural' and 'un- or non-natural' body/body parts: 'A cyborg is a cybernetic organism, a hybrid of machine and organism, a creature of social reality as well as a creature of fiction' (1991: 149). Feminists' reading of technology has centred extensively on the impact of virtual technologies and environments such as cyberspace on our understanding of gender (Stone, 1996; Wolmark, 1999) and on questions of the post-human body. As such it has served not only to insist on the body as manufactured but also on the potential for change that such understanding entails.

MATERIAL REALITIES: OTHER HORIZONS

The cultural turn in the social sciences which has led, *inter alia*, to a cultural turn in the syllabi of women's and gender studies courses in Northwestern countries and in the Anglophone countries around the world is radically different from the kinds of agendas which dominate women's and gender studies courses in other regions of the world. The Asian Institute of Technology, for instance, has as two of its objectives 'to facilitate increased participation of Asian women in professions in science, technology, environment, and resource management' and 'to gain for women access to the status and authority in the larger society that participation in technological planning and decision-making bring' (Griffin, 2002: 23). Here, a different kind of instrumentality prevails, concerned with the education of a new ruling elite of professionals and a preoccupation with the material conditions of women's lives that has become an increasingly smaller part of the agenda of women's studies in Northwestern countries.

Such instrumentality is frequently born out of a continuing or indeed only awakening recognition that women's material conditions remain atrocious in many parts of the world, with little access to resources and self-determination of any kind. As an effect of globalization, such instrumentality is additionally and equally importantly born out of the demands of supranational organizations such as the World Bank and the International Monetary Fund that women *as a resource* be utilized more effectively in the development of Third World economies. The resourcing of women – giving them resources and using them as resources – thus becomes a key issue for feminism, requiring critical engagement in a context where the seduction of resources (being given grants, investments, etc.) may lower resistance to the interrogation of the meanings of that resourcing.

As the twenty-first century progresses, technological developments in relation to the material conditions under which they occur will probably remain a key area of debate among feminists. 'Gender' has replaced 'women' as the term of reference in many feminist discourses, even though the meaning of 'gender' in the context of supranational and development agendas, for example, remains 'women'. As culturally conservative and culturally progressive environments achieve greater proximity in Northwestern Europe and beyond, and as certain cultural and economic contexts are becoming 'feminized', it becomes possible to envisage renewed battles over the cultural positioning of women and 'woman' in the collapsing public and private spheres that characterize the early twenty-first century.

NOTES

1 It is worth noting that women in the shape of the muse (as servants to men's cultural production) and as bearers of culture (in the context of nationalism and war) had occupied service functions in relation to both men and culture.

2 The term 'patriarchy' has become both deeply unfashionable since the 1980s and highly contested since it is thought that the 'rule of the father' has been superceded by the 'rule of the brothers', that is by cohorts of younger males rather than by a single all-powerful father figure.

3 It is, perhaps, worth remembering here that the seven demands of the women's liberation movement were: (1) equal pay; (2) equal education and job opportunities; (3) free contraception and abortion on demand; (4) free twenty-four hour nurseries, under community control; (5) legal and financial independence; (6) an end to discrimination against lesbians; (7) freedom from intimidation by the threat or use of violence or sexual coercion, regardless of marital status. An end to the laws, assumptions, and institutions that perpetuate male dominance and men's aggression towards women. (Feminist Anthology Collective, 1981).

4 One cultural phenomenon, however, that has arisen in this context, is the production of films from the Northern industrial UK about men's needs to become spectacular bodies and insert themselves in cultural forms associated with women as an antidote to the end of the industries that occupied them (for example, *The Full Monty*; *Billy Elliott*; *Brassed Off*).

5 See Roach Anleu, in this volume.

6 See Weber, in this volume.

REFERENCES

Bordo, Susan (1993) *Unbearable Weight*. Berkeley, CA: University of California Press.
Bornstein, Kate (1994) *Gender Outlaw*. London: Routledge.
Butler, Judith (1990) *Gender Trouble*. London: Routledge.
Califia, Pat (1988) *Macho Sluts*. Boston, MA: Alyson Publications.
Campbell, Beatrix (1993) *Goliath: Britain's Dangerous Places*. London: Methuen.
Cardinal, Marie (1975; repr. 1983) *The Words to Say It*. London: Picador.
Chicago, Judy (1975; repr. 1982) *Through the Flower: My Struggle as a Woman Artist*. London: Women's Press.
Cixous, Hélène (1981a) 'Sorties', in Elaine Marks and Isabelle de Courtivron (eds), *New French Feminisms*. Brighton: Harvester Press. pp. 90–8.
Cixous, Hélène (1981b) 'The Laugh of the Medusa', in Elaine Marks and Isabelle de Courtivron, (eds), *New French Feminisms*. Brighton: Harvester Press. pp. 245–64.
Cixous, Hélène and Catherine Clément (1975; trans. 1986) *The Newly Born Woman*. Manchester: Manchester University Press.
Coppock, Vicki, Deena Haydon, and Ingrid Richter (1995) *The Illusions of Post-Feminism*. London: Taylor & Francis.
Daly, Mary (1978) *Gyn/ecology*. Boston, MA: Beacon Press.
Daly, Mary, with Jane Caputi (1987) *Webster's First Intergalactic Wickedary of the English Language*. Boston, MA: Beacon Press.
Davis, Kathy (1995) *Reshaping the Female Body*. New York: Routledge.
Davis, Kathy (2003) 'Surgical Passing', *Feminist Theory* 4: 73–92.
de Beauvoir, Simone (1949; repr. 1953) *The Second Sex*. Harmondsworth: Penguin.
Devi, Mahasweta (1988) 'Draupadi', in Gayatri Chakravorty Spivak, *In Other Worlds*. London: Routledge. pp. 179–96.
Dowie, Claire (1996) *Why is John Lennon Wearing a Skirt? And Other Stand-up Theatre Plays*. London: Methuen.
Ehrenreich, Barbara (2004) 'Feminism's Assumptions Upended.' *Los Angeles Times*, 16 May: http://www.latimes.com
Elgin, Suzette Haden (1984) *Native Tongue*. New York: Daw Books.
Enda, Jodi (2004) 'Female Face of Abuse Provokes Shock', Women's Enews, 10 May: http://www.womensenews.org/article.cfm?aid=1828
Evans, Mary (1999) *Missing Persons: The Impossibility of Auto/biography*. London: Routledge.
Faludi, Susan (1992) *Backlash: The Undeclared War Against Women*. London: Chatto and Windus.
Feminist Anthology Collective (1981) *No Turning Back: Writings from the Women's Liberation Movement 1975–1980*. London: Women's Press.
Figes, Eva (1974) *Days*. London: Faber and Faber.
French, Marilyn (1992) *The War Against Women*. London: Hamish Hamilton.
Friedan, Betty (1963) *The Feminine Mystique*. Hasmondsworth: Penguin.
Frye, Marilyn (1990; repr. 1992) 'Willful Virgin or Do You Have to Be a Lesbian to Be a Feminist?', in M. Frye, *Willful Virgin*. Freedom, CA: The Crossing Press.
Galloway, Janice (1989) *The Trick is to Keep Breathing*. London: Minerva.
Gatens, Moira (1996) *Imaginary Bodies*. London: Routledge.
Gearhart, Sally Miller (1980) *The Wanderground*. Watertown, MA: Persephone Press.
Gilbert, Sandra M. and Susan Gubar (1979) *The Madwoman in the Attic*. New Haven, CT: Yale University Press.
Gilman, Charlotte Perkins (1892; repr. 1981) 'The Yellow Wallpaper', in A. J. Lane, (ed.), *The Charlotte Perkins Gilman Reader*. London: Women's Press.
Griffin, Gabriele (2002) 'Co-option or Transformation? Women's and Gender Studies Worldwide', in Heike Flessner and Lydia Potts (eds), *Societies in Transition – Challenges to Women's and Gender Studies*. Opladen: Leske and Budrich. pp. 13–32.
Grimshaw, Jean (1986) *Feminist Philosophers: Women's Perspectives on Philosophical Traditions*. Brighton: Wheatsheaf Books.

Grosz, Elizabeth (1994) *Volatile Bodies*. Bloomington: Indiana University Press.
Grosz, Elizabeth and Elspeth Probyn (eds) (1995) *Sexy Bodies: The Strange Carnalities of Feminism*. London: Routledge.
H[ilda] D[oolittle] (1927; pub. 1981) *Her*. New York: New Direction Books.
Haraway, Donna J. (1991) *Simians, Cyborgs, and Women*. London: Free Association Press.
hooks, bell (1984) *Feminist Theory: From Margin to Center*. Boston, MA: South End Press.
Irigaray, Luce (1974, trans. 1985) *Speculum of the Other Woman*. Trans. Gillian C. Gill. Ithaca, NY: Cornell University Press.
Irigaray, Luce (1977, trans. 1985) *This Sex Which Is Not One*. Trans. Catherine Porter. Ithaca, NY: Cornell University Press.
Jeffreys, Sheila (1994) *The Lesbian Heresy*. London: Women's Press.
Jones, Ann Rosalind (1985) 'Writing the Body: Toward an Understanding of *l'écriture féminine*', in Judith Newton and Deborah Rosenfelt (eds), *Feminist Criticism and Social Change*. London: Methuen. pp. 86–104.
Kane, Sarah (2001) *Complete Plays*. London: Methuen.
Kristeva, Julia (1974; trans. 1984) *Revolution in Poetic Language*. New York: Columbia University Press.
Kristeva, Julia (1977; trans. 1980) *Desire in Language*. Oxford: Basil Blackwell.
Kristeva, Julia (1980; trans. 1982) *Powers of Horror: An Essay on Abjection*. New York: Columbia University Press.
Lloyd, Genevieve (1984) *The Man of Reason: 'Male' and 'Female' in Western Philosophy*. London: Methuen.
Menchú, Rigoberta (1984; repr. 1992) *I, Rigoberta Menchú: An Indian Woman in Guatemala*. London: Verso.
Milan Women's Bookstore Collective (1990) *Sexual Difference: A Theory of Social-Symbolic Practice*. Bloomington: Indiana University Press.
Miller, Casey and Kate Swift (1980) *The Handbook of Non-sexist Writing for Writers, Editors and Speakers*. London: Women's Press.
Millett, Kate (1969; repr. 1977) *Sexual Politics*. London: Virago.
Mills, Jane (1989) *Womanwords*. London: Longman.
Modleski, Tanja (1991) *Feminism without Women*. London: Routledge.
Morgan, Robin (1984) *Sisterhood is Global*. Harmondsworth: Penguin.
Nestle, Joan, (ed.) (1992) *The Persistent Desire: A Butch-Femme Reader*. Boston, MA: Alyson Publications.
Oakley, Ann (1981) *Subject Women*. London: Martin Robinson.
Olsen, Tillie (1980) *Silences*. London: Virago.
Orlan (1993) *Ceci est mon corps...ceci est mon logiciel....* London: Black Dog.
Parker, Rozsika (1974) 'Body Works', *Spare Rib* 23: 37–8.
Parker, Rozsika and Griselda Pollock (1981) *Old Mistresses: Women, Art and Ideology*. London: Routledge & Kegan Paul.
Parker, Rozsika and Griselda Pollock (eds) (1987) *Framing Feminism: Art and the Women's Movement 1970–1985*. London: Pandora.
Plath, Sylvia (1963) *The Bell Jar*. London: William Heinemann.
Polity Press (1994) *The Polity Reader in Cultural Theory*. Cambridge: Polity Press.
Radicalesbians (1970; repr. 1988) 'The Women Identified Woman', in Sarah Lucia Hoagland and Julia Penelope, (eds), *For Lesbians Only: A Separatist Anthology*. London: Onlywomen Press, 1988. pp. 17–21.
Rich, Adrienne (1971; repr. 1984) 'The Will to Change', in A. Rich, *The Fact of the Doorframe*. New York: W.W. Norton. pp. 111–46.
Rich, Adrienne (1973; repr. 1984) 'Diving into the Wreck', in A. Rich, *The Fact of the Doorframe*. New York: W.W. Norton. pp. 147–84.
Russ, Joanna (1975) *The Female Man*. New York: Bantam Books.
Sapegno, Serena (2002) 'Psychoanalysis and Feminism: A European Phenomenon and its Specificities', in G. Griffin and R. Braidotti (eds), *Thinking Differently*. London: Zed Books. pp. 110–26.

Showalter, Elaine (1977; repr.1978) *A Literature of Their Own*. London: Virago.
Smith, Sidonie (1987) *A Poetics of Women's Autobiography: Marginality and the Fictions of Self-Representation*. Bloomington: Indiana University Press.
Smyth, Cheryl (1992) *Lesbians Talk Queer Notions*. London: Scarlet Press.
Spender, Dale (1980) *Man Made Language*. London: Routledge & Kegan Paul.
Spivak, Gayatri Chakravorty (1988) *In Other Worlds: Essays in Cultural Politics*. London: Routledge.
Stanley, Liz (1992) *The Auto/biographical I*. Manchester: Manchester University Press.
Stone, Allucquère Rosanne (1996) *The War of Desire and Technology at the Close of the Mechanical Age*. Cambridge, MA: MIT Press.
Volcano, Del LaGrace and Judith Halberstam (1999) *The Drag King Book*. London: Serpent's Tail.
Walker, Alice (1982) *The Color Purple*. New York: Harcourt Brace Jovanovich.
Wallace, Michele (1990) *Black Macho and the Myth of Superwoman*. New York: Dial Press.
Wittig, Monique (1969; repr. 1972) *Les Guérillères*. London: Picador.
Wittig, Monique (1981; repr. 1992) 'One is Not Born a Woman', in M. Wittig, *The Straight Mind and Other Essays*. London: Harvester Wheatsheaf. pp. 9–20.
Wittig, Monique and Sande Zeig (1976; repr. 1980) *Lesbian Peoples: Materials for a Dictionary*. London: Virago.
Wolf, Naomi (1991) *The Beauty Myth*. New York: William Morrow.
Wolf, Naomi (1994) *Fire with Fire: The New Female Power and How It Will Change the 21st Century*. London: Vintage.
Wolmark, Jenny (ed.) (1999) *Cybersexualities*. Edinburgh: Edinburgh University Press.
Woolf, Virginia (1929; repr. 1983) *A Room of One's Own*. London: Granada.

5

The Social Foundations of the Sacred

Feminists and the Politics of Religion

Bronwyn Winter

This chapter looks at religion as a sociocultural, political, economic, and historical phenomenon, rather than as a personal question of faith or notions of transcendence, the sacred, the taboo, or the divine. In other words, it looks at religion as constitutive of social organization and power relations and the codification thereof, and as such, as central to the collective and individual internalization of cultural identity. It gives a broad overview of the late twentieth-century development of Western and non-Western feminist study and critiques of religion, then looks at some contemporary debates that cut across different religions – the question of interpretation and authenticity, secularism and atheism, the search for spirituality, and lesbians and religion – as well as at the particular case of the Islamic headscarf as a marker of gender, ethnic, and religious identity in a post-9/11 context.

INTRODUCTION

While I do not take it as a given that a need for spirituality or a concept of the divine are a *necessary* part of the human condition, it is apparent that at this point in time and to the best of my knowledge, there exists no society – and thus no culture – without some form of religious belief that underpins its dominant value system. These religious beliefs can be examined from the perspective of their sacred components or the personal faith of their adherents. This chapter, in contrast, looks at religion as a sociocultural, political, economic, and historical phenomenon and examines the ways that religions reflect the codification of social organization and power relations. From this sociocultural perspective, religion can be seen as often central to collective and individual internalization of cultural identity.

Following an initial development of this analytical framework, I will give a broad overview of the late twentieth-century development of Western and non-Western feminist study and critiques of religion. Next, I will look at the particular case of the Islamic headscarf as a marker of gender, ethnic, and religious identity in a post-9/11 context, as it exemplifies the polarization and heatedness of debates in which religion becomes imbricated with questions of racism and political hegemony and resistance, and in which women become the emblems of 'cultural identity'. Finally, I will discuss some of the contemporary feminist debates that cut across Western and non-Western religions: interpretation and 'authenticity', secularism and atheism, the search for spirituality, and lesbians and religion.[1]

RELIGION AS CONSTITUTIVE OF CULTURE AND POLITICAL POWER

The postulate that religion has to do with power and hierarchy incorporates two apparently contradictory, but, in fact, complementary ideas: religion is part of the masculinist power structure within which social relations become gendered (and class-stratified, racialized, and so on), and religion is a vehicle through which power and hierarchy can be challenged, subverted, overthrown, or modified. The co-existence of these two functions of religion has formed a central premise of a number of feminist writings on the subject.[2] This body of work argues that religions are not fixed entities existing in some eternally abstract space untouched by humans but are dynamic, adapting to socio-historical and geo-political contexts and, indeed, play a decisive role in shaping them. Feminists look at the development of different schools of thought within religions to bolster their claim that religion, whatever its uses for individuals, has evolved through processes of struggles for political power, whether the religion is the agent of assertion of power, direct resistance to it, or a means of finding a transformative space for disempowered groups during a period of socioeconomic upheaval. Unsurprisingly, periods of upheaval or resistance have tended to favour women's manœuvring within religions, as within other social institutions, although this is not universally the case. At the same time, even those religions that may have started as a form of dissent against a dominant order or questioning its values (Christianity and Buddhism come immediately to mind) have over time become part of the dominant social, political, and economic order through their clergy's association with societies' elites.

Religions, however strongly proselytizing they may be, have adapted to local cultural, political, and economic contexts to produce different variants and hybridities. In many parts of West Africa, for example, Islamic leaders are also tribal spiritual elders. In the French Caribbean, Louisiana, and Brazil, elements of Christianity were incorporated by slaves into African religions to produce the new religion of voudou, which has been historically, and continues to be, symbolic of popular culture and resistance to oppression both from White colonizers and the so-called *mulâtres*, the minority of 'mixed race' who benefited from greater privileges under colonial rule.

A final important point to make with regard to religion and power is that prior to the rise of the modern nation-state, religious institutions had control over education (and still do to a great extent). As a consequence, religious values have informed the type of education that people receive, and religious institutions have provided the primary means of access to education, which in many parts of the world and for many centuries was largely denied to girls outside religious orders.[3] Three comments need to be made here. First, the role of religions in education not only had class and gender dimensions but also colonial dimensions through the missionary movement, for example (Donaldson and Kwok, 2002). Second, religious institutions have not always been instruments of exclusion; they have sometimes been the means of access to literacy for the poor. Third, the education of girls within religion-based states is unlikely to be ultimately liberating for women. Women in Khomeinist Iran, for example, were among the most highly educated in the Muslim world at the time, but they were not more liberated than their sisters in many other Muslim countries (Chafiq, 1991).

FEMINIST CRITIQUES OF RELIGION

Like feminist questionings of other institutions and values within and outside the academy, feminist studies in religion began by seeking to render visible the invisible: (a) women, and (b) androcentric or masculinist methodologies and values.[4] Just as feminists questioned other areas considered off-limits for political debate, such as marriage, housewifery, childrearing, and compulsory heterosexuality, feminists interrogating religion and studies of religion asked: 'Why this taboo? What is its social context? Who benefits from it? Why is venturing into this discursive terrain made so difficult for us? What might we discover/uncover that may be of use to women if we do venture there?'

Western feminist critiques

The field of feminist studies of and in religion developed within the West, and like other areas of women's studies, found and continues to find its major impetus in the United States, as might be expected, given the preponderant role of the United States in the development of women's studies for reasons of political, economic, and cultural power. Notwithstanding important developments elsewhere (for example, writings published by Kali for

Women in India or ASR in Pakistan), feminist studies on and in religion continue to be driven, to a large extent, by US preoccupations, even when the critiques are 'non-Western'.

This observation, however, warrants some commentary. First, as concerns the development of the area of women's critique, historical study, and exegesis within studies of religion, or the very possibility for women of undertaking study in religion, there is some evidence of later development in the United States. A famous case in point is that of Mary Daly, who, unable to enrol in a PhD programme in theology in the United States, went to Switzerland to do it instead; her book *The Church and the Second Sex* was a result (Daly, 1965). Rita Gross has also written of the difficulties she encountered at the University of Chicago when she first undertook a feminist critique of conventional (masculinist) methodology in the study of religion (Gross, 1994a). Second, the fact that feminist studies in religion may have initially developed as a modern university discipline within the West does not mean that there was no presence of women engaging critically with religious traditions prior to this, within or outside the West.[5]

Feminist study of and in religion as it developed from the late 1960s/early 1970s in the United States focused initially on women in relation to Christianity. Another area that developed fairly early was work on women and Judaism. The 1982 anthology *Nice Jewish Girls* (Beck, 1982) was among the first, and rare, works to deal explicitly with lesbians within 'malestream' religious/cultural traditions. Feminist studies of and in religion also very quickly picked up on the feminist spirituality movement and rediscoverings and revalidations of historically marginalized or vilified religious traditions (Christ and Plaskow, 1979; Spretnak, 1982).

Like other feminist scholars at that time, however, early feminist theologians were lonely pioneers in their field, particularly in the comparative study of religion. A turning point in putting feminist theology and intercultural study of religion on the map was the founding in 1985 of the US journal *Feminist Studies in Religion* (the founding editors were Judith Plaskow and Elisabeth Schüssler Fiorenza).

Non-Western critiques

More recently, an increasing volume of work on non-Western religions by feminists of non-Western backgrounds has been made available to an international readership through the interest in the West for 'postcolonial' studies. This work has centred on four main areas. First, it has involved a re-evaluation of women's personal and political engagement with religion, even in its more conservative expressions, as a vehicle for popular expression of resistance against an oppressive state or against an imperial power (Donaldson and Kwok, 2002; Eck and Jain, 1986; Haddad and Findly, 1985). Second, it has provided a space for feminist exegesis within non-Western religious traditions, as well as comparative/intercultural theological study (Becher, 1990; Parsons, 2002; Women Living Under Muslim Laws, 1997). Third, it has questioned what has been seen as a hegemonic Western feminist standpoint, according to which all religion is patriarchal and necessarily disempowering for women (Afshar, 1998; Donaldson and Kwok, 2002; Jeffery and Basu, 1998). Fourth, as with other areas of postcolonial studies, it has challenged the 'ways that the study of religion has participated in and contributed to the epistemic violence maintained by western studies and narrations of the Other' (Donaldson and Kwok, 2002: 15).

As early as the mid-1970s, non-Western feminist critical writing on non-Western religions was being published in the West (for example, Mernissi, 1975). More recently, a considerable body of feminist scholarship has explored the relationship between women, religious conservatism, and the state, both within and outside the West (Bacchetta and Power, 2002; Sarkar and Butalia, 1995). That relationship is generally seen as detrimental to women, although not universally so (Brink and Mencher, 1997). Much of that writing has also examined ways in which women have been complicit with religious conservatism, for reasons that range from the need for unity in anticolonial liberation struggles or identification with an ethnic minority, to the right-wing/antifeminist politics of the women in question (Jeffery and Basu, 1998; Moghadam, 1994; Bacchetta and Power, 2002). Over a similar period, scholarship on women's human rights and feminist critiques of cultural relativism have increasingly brought religion and religious identity under scrutiny in investigations of whether and in what ways women's human rights and religion and/or cultural particularism may be 'competing claims' (Cohen, Howard, and Nussbaum, 1999; Gustafson and Juviler, 1999; Mayer, 1995; Rao, 1995).

The case of the *hijab*

The points I wish to raise here may not be limited to discussions of Islam, but in a so-called post-9/11 global context, it is Islam that has become the focus of much highly charged debate around religion, politics, cultural 'difference', and women.

Feminist scholars have long observed that women's bodies, appearance, and behaviour are one of the major contested sites in debates over nation, culture, ethnicity, and religion (Enloe, [1989] 1990). In debates over the *hijab* (Islamic headscarf), or 'veiling', what are at issue are sexualizing 'orientalist' overtones, twentieth-century histories of colonization and ensuing Muslim anticolonial nationalism and identity politics, and the rise of twentieth-century Muslim fundamentalist movements (Lazreg, 1994; Shirazi, 2001; Winter, 2001; Yegenoglu, 1998). Debates over the *hijab* have perhaps been waged most exhaustively and emotively in France, where the so-called 'headscarves affair' of 1989 triggered what has been called a 'national psychodrama' and was much spoken of internationally (Bloul, 1994; Winter, 1996), although, at that time, feminists were largely marginalized from the public debate. More recently, the French law on banning religious dress or adornment in public schools[6] has been widely criticized, although significant numbers of French citizens of Muslim background have come out strongly in support of France's so-called 'intransigent' secularism.[7] The debate has spawned a plethora of articles and books, including, this time, many that are explicitly feminist (for instance, Djavann, 2003; *Prochoix* 25, 2003).[8] The 'headscarf debate' is also being waged in a number of other countries, such as the UK, where Shabina Begum, a 15-year-old secondary school student, was expelled in 2002 for wearing the *jilbab* (a form of Islamic dress that covers all but the face and hands) and lost her appeal to the British High Court in 2004.[9] In Turkey, there was a furore in October 2003 during the celebration of the eightieth anniversary of the Turkish Republic over the outlawing of the *hijab* at official functions. In Singapore, an appeal against the secular dress code in schools (which outlaws the *hijab*) was lodged in 2002 with the High Court.

In a post-9/11 context, the *hijab* has increasingly become the symbol of a demonized Islam and of the victims (both material and symbolic) of that demonization. A polarization has occurred between right-wing and/or neo-colonial and neo-orientalist Western views of all Islam as fundamentalist and/or terrorist and an identity politics (defended by the Western left wing) that sweeps under the carpet the very real existence of fundamentalism (including fundamentalist lobbies behind defences of the *hijab* in the name of multiculturalism and antiracism). More importantly for feminist debate, the deployment of the *hijab* as a marker of cultural or religious identity has tended to make it difficult to find a discursive space in which to speak critically, from a feminist perspective, of the *hijab* as – first and foremost – a gender marker. This is not to say that one should not be cognisant of the choices made by young women to don the *hijab* as a marker of identity or protest, or as part of a quest for cultural roots from which they feel their parents may have become disconnected (Gaspard and Khosrokhavar, 1995). There is also, as in any so-called postcolonial context, the problem of appropriation and the search for authenticity: Whose identity is authentic? Can a Western woman criticize fundamentalist manipulation of the *hijab* in the same way that a woman of Muslim background might be able to? But then, is the latter really able to? How much space is given to secular voices among Muslim-background women?

At this point, it appears easier for Western women who have converted to Islam and donned the *hijab* to have a voice in certain academic and political circles than it is for women of Muslim backgrounds who argue against the *hijab*.[10] This may be related to the difficulty more generally of arguing for secularism or atheism in relation to some non-Western religions or cultural traditions, as such arguments are criticized as Western and even imperialist. Such arguments against Westernness, however, do not appear to be put as vehemently in relation to other Western practices as they are in relation to women's rights (Chanda, 2003).

FEMINIST RELIGIOUS DEBATES

In addition to critiques of particular religions and religious practices, feminists have engaged in debates that cut across different religions – the question of interpretation and authenticity of religious texts, the challenge of secularism and atheism, the search for a spirituality meaningful to women, and the place of lesbians in religious traditions that condemn homosexuality.

The question of interpretation and the search for authenticity

Foundational religious texts can be polyvocal, ambiguous, or fragmentary, with ensuing difficulties for interpretation, which will thus tend to depend on what other values one associates with the exercise of one's religion. As concerns religions without written traditions, 'foundational texts' are transmitted through oral traditions, which can be even more open to dispute, as there is no recorded source to refer to.

For example, a *cause célèbre* in Australia in the 1990s involved opposition by Indigenous women in South Australia to the construction of a bridge to connect the mainland to Hindmarsh Island. A group of women elders maintained that the island was a sacred site for secret women's business. Construction was therefore stalled. Subsequently, men – and some other women – from the same tribe claimed that the first group of women had been lying for the purposes of saving the island from increased tourism. A Royal Commission was formed in 1996, and the transcript of its findings fills 6,670 pages. The final result was that the proposed bridge and marina ended up being built. In this case, authenticity was disputed, and it is indicative of the scant weight given within Australia to women's voices in general and Indigenous women's voices in particular that the women protesting were discredited as liars (Bell, 1999; Hindmarsh Island Bridge Royal Commission, 1996).

Others have argued that texts referring to roles of women within religions cannot be properly understood without understanding the contexts in which they were produced. In relation to ancient Rome, for example, vestal virgins were for a long time considered to have a role comparable to that of nuns in Catholicism, but more recent scholarship, including a retraction by one of the main scholars who argued for the comparison with nuns, has indicated that vestal virgins had considerably more power and were indeed priests in their own right (Beard, 1995). In other words, attempts to apply modern understandings and modern experiences of discrimination against women to totally different historical, geographical, or cultural frameworks can easily lead to gross misinterpretations.[11] Even attempts at historical contextualization are tricky, for the versions of history that filter through to us are not only those that have been preserved but also those that we are explicitly seeking. For example, many Muslim women have sought to demonstrate the positive values of Islam in relation to advances in women's rights. Others, however, have argued that Mohammed's first wife, Khadidja, an independent businesswoman who was fifteen years older than he was, was very much a product of Jahilia (pre-Islamic) society. Mohammed remained monogamously married to her until her death, after which he took a child-wife, 'Aïsha, and became polygamous. What had changed in the interim? He had written the bulk of the Koran and institutionalized polygyny and men's control of women (Ahmed, 1992: 42–43).

Historical contextualization has also been used to 'let men off the hook'. Rita Gross, for example, has written of the Buddha's sexism that:

> though enlightened regarding certain deep spiritual truths, [he] was not entirely free of the social conditioning of his times. I do not believe that enlightenment entails a timelessly perfect social conscience or universal scientific and historical knowledge. Therefore, it did not occur to the Buddha to encourage women to be equal to men in their unconventionality and counter-cultural activities. (Gross, 1994b: 5–6)

Although the way Gross frames the concept of enlightenment may be internally coherent (that is, plausible or valid within the context of the Buddhist belief system), one could plausibly ask why the Buddha's enlightenment was so limited with regard to women. Why should we accord a leniency to the Buddha or Mohammed that we do not grant, for example, to Marx, Rousseau, and other thinkers whose limited social vision has been criticized by feminists? Moreover, 'authenticity' and 'tradition' can be invented (Hobsbawm and Ranger, 1983). For example, in the debates over the *hijab* discussed above, it is often overlooked that in many places where wearing it is claimed in the name of 'cultural identity', the *hijab* is not, in fact, a garment indigenous to the country or ethnic group in question.

It is ironic that those seeking authenticity and original meanings often appear to be doing one of two somewhat contradictory things. Either they are using a recontextualization in a past time and, often, different place, to argue for interpretations that may somehow transcend time and place, or they are seeking to purify the text of any temporal or spatial contextualization in order to interpret it appropriately for a very specifically located audience. Religions, however, are not simply accretions of foundational texts or images of the (largely mythified) history or collective memory of the origins of that religion's conception of the divine, but institutions and practices that are necessarily imbricated with social relations, and which evolve through time and place (Winter, 2001). The quest for authenticity is not necessarily useless, but claims of authenticity must take into account the context in which those making the claim are situated, including the very here-and-now politics of searches for original meanings.

Secularism and atheism

In the 1970s and early 1980s, the feminist debate on religion seemed to centre on two questions: Why bother? And if we do bother, how might we bother? In more recent times, the debate, at least as it is constituted within the Western English-speaking world and in particular the United States, appears to centre more on finding demarcation lines between expressions of religion that are demonstrably 'bad' for women and those that are 'good'. The underlying assumption in this debate is that there is something inherently and indisputably positive about religion which feminists can, should, and will uncover. This shift is arguably due to increased volume and sophistication of feminist debate on religion, including discussions concerning both the polyvocality of religious traditions and the contexts within which women operate. In some of these contexts, as I noted earlier, engaging with religion as an emancipatory oppositional force can carry demonstrable benefits for women. It may also be due to the assumption of secularization and the separation of church and state in the West as a given, although such separation is clearly tenuous.[12] Religion exercises a far greater influence in the West than is often assumed, from the organization of public holidays and mass cultural celebrations around Christian festivals to continued government funding of private Christian schools and Christian underpinnings of legislation, in particular that governing family relations and financial arrangements. Nationally and internationally established religions and politically influential religious lobbies also oppose the exercise of women's reproductive rights and lesbian and gay rights.[13]

Outside the West, or even within ethnic minorities within the West, the question 'Why bother?' is usually not even on the agenda, as secularism is simply not perceived as an option. Much focus has consequently been given to the question of how women might best engage positively with religion and use its more progressive elements strategically – notably, although not exclusively, with relation to Islam. Since secularism is not a given in these contexts, it is perhaps all the more important to argue for it, as it has been, for example, by Muslim-background feminists in France who support the outlawing of religious insignia in schools (for example, Djavann, 2003). Indeed, even though women engage with religious traditions for varied reasons, working solely within religion and particularly within a religion-based state will ultimately limit the outcomes that feminists will be able to achieve (Moghadam, 2001: 44–45).

The search for spirituality

Given the close imbrication of religion and culture, it is perhaps understandable that after quite strident feminist critiques of religion and lack of intercultural awareness by Western feminists, there should be a wave of literature that revalidates religion and the cultural traditions of which religions are part. Feminists do work in many ways and in many areas, and that great diversity and polyvocality are also among feminism's great strengths, for they enable us to deal with a complex and changing world while still finding some sort of common language, however imperfect, through which we can communicate with each other across the globe and recognize each other's values and struggles as feminist. Another of feminism's great strengths is that everything is open to question – nothing is taboo, including women's engagement with religion and claims for positive spiritual outcomes. It is only by continuing to open up debate that feminism's great transformative potential can be realized.

The women's spirituality movement in the United States has been important in opening up avenues for greater gender equality and feminist and lesbian voices within more mainstream religions. Feminists have variously defined spirituality as a form of transcendence or striving for perfection or peace at an individual level, and for connection with other living beings, with the earth and/or with the various elements that make up our cosmos. Spirituality may involve deity figures, but most often, in feminist terms, corresponds to a search for the spiritual power within. Carol Christ explained the need for the feminist spirituality movement in the following terms: 'because religion has such a compelling hold on the deep psyches of so many people, feminists cannot afford to leave it in the hands of the fathers... Symbol systems cannot simply be rejected, they must be replaced' (Christ, 1979: 274–275). Christ further wrote that 'the strength and independence of female power can be intuited by contemplating ancient and modern images of the Goddess' (p. 277). Revalorizing female figures that have been demonized within masculinist ideology is a feminist strategy that has been used in many areas (for example, lesbian revalorizing of the butch dyke), and it is thus unsurprising that such strategies have also been used within religions – Kali and Lilith are oft-cited examples (King, 1989).

The search for a feminist spirituality has questioned Western monotheism and its misogyny and sparked a notable interest by Western feminists in what are seen as more positive values of non-Western religions (Buddhism in particular, but also mysticism within other traditions, such as Sufi Islam; North American, Australasian, and Pacific Indigenous spirituality; and Jewish kabbalah). This interest was in part a product of a more general late 1960s/early 1970s Western protest-movement fascination with 'Eastern' spirituality, and has produced writings by Western feminist converts to those religions (for example, as concerns Buddhism, Farrer-Halls, 2002; Klein, 1995).

Such interest by Western feminists in non-Western religions and spirituality may address some concerns about the ethnocentrism of Western feminist work on religion.[14] Others, however, have cautioned against superficial Western cultural appropriation of non-Western cultures and traditions, and in particular against the Western assumption that somehow non-Western religions are less misogynist or more positive for women. For example, the worship of the feminine and of goddesses within Hinduism has been critiqued as being inscribed within masculinist logic and serving male-supremacist power structures (Hiltebeitel and Erndl, 2000).

Lesbians and religion

A growing body of work that sits as much within the field of lesbian and gay or queer studies as it does within feminist, women's, or gender studies has looked at religion and homosexuality. This work has accompanied developments and areas of activism within the wider lesbian and gay community, such as the formation of houses of worship for gay and lesbian congregations, the Rainbow Sash movement within the Catholic Church, the increasingly high profile given to the ordination of lesbian and gay pastors and rabbis, and more generally, lesbian and gay activism against religious conservatism, notably in the West. These activities have been accompanied by studies developed quite early in relation to Christianity and, to a lesser extent, Judaism; the majority of work done continues to concern those traditions.[15]

One of the major gaps in feminist scholarship on religion concerns critical engagement by lesbians with religious traditions outside Judaism, Christianity, or women's spirituality. It is perhaps less the case concerning those religions' attitudes to lesbianism and lesbians, including literary representations (see, for example, Machacek and Wilcox, 2003; Vanita and Kidwai, 2000), although even here, most of the work on lesbians is subsumed under studies of homosexuality and religion, which mainly discuss male homosexuality with often only scant or no references to lesbians (for example, Leyland, 1998; 2000; Swidler, 1993). Concerning the history of lesbianism and religion and critical engagement of lesbians with non-Western religion in modern times, the corpus of scholarship is much smaller, for several reasons (see, for example, on India, Bacchetta, 2002; Thadani, 1996; Vanita, 2001).

First, there is generally less scholarship widely available about women and religion outside Christianity and Judaism – although there is much on women and Islam from a postcolonial perspective or within a context of writings on women, religion, and the state or women and fundamentalism, some of which has been referred to here. Second, it is more difficult for lesbians to be 'out' in countries outside the Western world, and there is therefore less writing on lesbians and anything at all, let alone lesbians and religion.[16] Third, many cultural and religious traditions either do not conceive of homosexuality in the same terms as in the West (Vanita, 2001), or have ignored homosexuality or obliterated written documentation of it. Finally, within some traditions that may at this point be less accommodating of lesbianism than some areas of modern Christianity and Judaism, lesbians may be less likely to engage with those traditions than to reject them outright. Until there is more lesbian writing from some of the countries in question, however, this last hypothesis remains to be proven. The feminist world perhaps needs a second, lesbian-focused version of a groundbreaking US feminist anthology on feminism and racism (Hull, Scott, and Smith, 1982): 'All the lesbians are white, all the Muslim/Hindu/Zoroastran/Voudou/etc women are straight: but some of us are brave.'

CONCLUSION: WHITHER FEMINIST STUDY OF RELIGION?

Critiques of religion as bound up with power and hierarchy, and even as a patriarchal institution, certainly did not start with the contemporary feminist movement, but feminist study of and in religion has, like feminist involvement in other areas of society and intellectual endeavour, uncovered women's presence in the history of religions, both as actors within religion and as rebels against it. It also has provided new critique of the relationship between religious institutions and masculinism, and reinterpreted religions from a feminist perspective. In doing so, feminists have deepened understandings of the relationships between religion, culture, and politics, opened up new debates in theology and exegesis, and created spaces for women not only to articulate their refusal of religion and have some measure of safety and support in doing so, but also to move to positions of influence within religions and, hopefully, change the institutions from within. Postcolonial feminist readings of racialized women's identification or strategic alliances with religion have brought us more sophisticated understandings of the plurivocality of the world's religions and the ways in which they are mobilized as vehicles not only of women's oppression but also of women's resistance and empowerment.

Some notes of caution must, however, be sounded, especially within the global context in which we find ourselves in the early years of the third millennium, where fundamentalisms of all creeds and colours are on the rise, and the slender and fragile gains that women have made are seriously threatened the world over. It is true that in moving into prominent roles in religions or cultural traditions, women gain a social status and personal empowerment that they might not otherwise have had. It is also true, however, that access to high status within a masculinist framework is not in itself feminist. Moreover, women who move to prominence within religions may *already* have socioeconomic advantages that assist their progress. For example, women who are prominent within the main Algerian fundamentalist movement and political party, the Islamic Salvation Front (FIS), have testified to their feelings of empowerment as women through their activism (Taarji, 1991), but that does not render the politics of the FIS somehow acceptable in feminist terms. The women who take leadership roles within the FIS are for the most part young university students or graduates. In a country with a significant rural population where illiteracy, particularly for women, remains a problem, these women are hardly grappling with social disadvantage to start with.

As concerns feminist campaigns for accession of women to positions of leadership within religions (through ordination or otherwise) and the growing visible presence of lesbians among the ranks of women who are ordained, the jury probably remains out on whether the religions in question are fundamentally changed, just as it does on the question of, for example, the changes brought to political parties, parliaments, the police force, corporations, trade unions, and the military by the increased presence of women in their senior ranks. If one is to agree with Carol Christ that religions, as such pervasive and deeply internalized sociocultural phenomena, should not be left solely in the hands of the men, then theoretical and practical strategies for the ordination and advancement of women religious leaders can be seen as a good thing. But it does not necessarily mean that their religious institutions will be feminist in promoting gender equality, women's perspectives, and so on, especially if the deities and liturgies remain male-dominated.

It is difficult to make forecasts on where feminist studies of religion may go next, but it would seem that there is a need for further research into the areas of masculinity and religion, lesbianism and religion, the history of women and what may be called feminist activity in today's world religions (especially outside Christianity) as well as in religions of the ancient world, and the interaction of religion and culture. I would also like to see comparative feminist studies of religion as a polyvocal sociopolitical force both within and between different religions and critical studies of both the history and contemporary politics of secularism, atheism, and the resurgence of religious fundamentalist political movements in new or reinvented guises. I thus look forward to continued and lively debate on feminism and religion: whether we should bother, and if so, why we should, how we might, and what we may stand to gain or lose from doing so.

ACKNOWLEDGEMENTS

Many thanks to Iris Wielders for her invaluable assistance with editing the first draft of this chapter.

NOTES

1 It is not my concern here to discuss theological debates over faith and interpretation. Nor is it my intent to provide an overview of 'women in world religions'. I have neither the space nor the expertise to fulfil either of these briefs. I thus refer readers to a number of well-regarded reference works available on the subject (for example, Holm, 1994; King, 1995; Larrington, 1992; Machacek and Wilcox, 2003; Christ and Plaskow, 1989; Sharma, 1994a, 1994b; Sharma and Young, 1999).

2 As covered in various works (see, for example, Berktay, 1998; Christ and Plaskow, 1979; Douglas, 1999; Eck and Jain, 1986; Haddad and Findly, 1985; Spretnak, 1982).

3 Contemporary examples include the denial of schooling to all Afghan girls by the Taliban and now to married women by the Karzai government (Winter, 2002: 451–452).

4 By 'androcentric' I mean 'centred on men' (to the exclusion of women, or the subsuming of women's experience within men's), whereas by 'masculinist' I mean 'ideologically and practically designed to consolidate male domination' (so that even where there are representations of women/focus on women, these may serve the interests of male supremacy and not feminism).

5 As can be found in various works (see, for example, Badran and Cooke, 1990; Cahill, 1996; Haddad and Findly, 1985; Keller and Ruether, 1995).

6 *Journal officiel* N°65, 17 March 2004, p. 5190: www.legifrance.gouv.fr

7 For example, the Movement for Secular Muslims (www.wluml.org) and Manifeste des Libertés (www.manifeste.org), both launched petitions defending progressive values and the rights of women and opposing religious obscurantism. Muslim religious leaders were among the signatories of the first petition, and the second, which was signed by Muslim intellectuals, also denounced antisemitism and defended homosexual rights.

8 A number of feminist articles are accessible through the feminist website sisyphe.org.

9 The judge ruled that her human rights had not been infringed and that the Luton secondary school's uniform policy 'was aimed at the proper running of a multi-cultural, multi-faith secular school' (news.bbc.co.uk/2/hi/uk_news/education/3808073.stm).

10 One widely recognized 'expert' on Islam and on Muslim women in Australia is an Anglo-Celtic convert to Islam whose name is now Jamila Hussain, who studied at an Islamic university in Malaysia and has written a well-known and well-regarded textbook on Islam (2003).

11 My thanks to Kathryn Welch for bringing this to my attention.

12 The separation of church and state is questionable in the United States, given both the country's national motto and the significant political influence of the Christian right in the aftermath of George W. Bush's 2004 re-election.

13 The international influence is evidenced both by the fact that the Holy See has the status of a 'member country' of the UN, and by the influence (often through intimidation) of Christian fundamentalist groups in both governmental and non-governmental delegations to UN conferences on women, population, and human rights.

14 See Audré Lorde's critique of Daly's *Gyn/ecology* (Daly, 1979; Lorde, 1984). Kwok Pui-Lan (2002) has examined such critiques and suggested a 'postcolonial' reading of Daly.

15 Found in various works (Beck, 1982; Gearhart and Johnson, 1974; Jakobsen and Pellegrini, 2003; Macourt, 1977; Stuart, 2002; Sweasey, 1997).

16 It is significant that I have found only one book by an out Muslim lesbian who engages critically with and *within* Islam – and she lives in Canada (Manji, 2003). Another recent publication of note is the first anthology published in English by and about Israeli lesbians, which includes a chapter by an orthodox lesbian (Frankfort-Nachmias and Shadmi, 2005).

REFERENCES

Afshar, Haleh (1998) *Islam and Feminisms: An Iranian Case-Study*. Basingstoke/New York: Macmillan/St. Martin's Press.

Ahmed, Leila (1992) *Women and Gender in Islam: Historical Roots of a Modern Debate*. New Haven, CT: Yale University Press.

Bacchetta, Paola (2002) 'Re-Scaling Trans/national "Queerdom": 1980s Lesbian and "Lesbian" Identitary Positionalities in Delhi'. *Antipode*, special issue 'Queer Patriarchies, Queer Racisms, International', 34: 947–973.

Bacchetta, Paola and Power, Margaret (eds) (2002) *Right-Wing Women: From Conservatives to Extremists Around the World*. New York: Routledge.

Badran, Margot and Cooke, Miriam (eds) (1990) *Opening the Gates: A Century of Arab Feminist Writing*. London: Virago.

Beard, Mary (1995) 'Re-reading (Vestal) Virginity', in Richard Hawley and Barbara Levick (eds), *Women in Antiquity: New Assessments*. London/New York: Routledge.

Becher, Jeanne (ed.) (1990) *Women, Religion and Sexuality: Studies on the Impact of Religious Teachings on Women*. Geneva: World Council of Churches Publications.

Beck, Evelyn Thornton (ed.) (1982) *Nice Jewish Girls: A Lesbian Anthology*. Watertown, MA: Persephone Press.

Bell, Diane (1999) *Ngarrindjeri Wurruwarrin: A World That Is, Was, and Will Be*. Melbourne: Spinifex.

Berktay, Fatmagül (1998) *Women and Religion*, trans. Belma Ötüs-Baskett. Montreal, New York and London: Black Rose Books.

Bloul, Rachel A. D. (1994) 'Veiled Objects of (Post)-Colonial Desire: Forbidden Women Disrupt the Republican Fraternal Space', *Australian Journal of Anthropology* 5(1–2): 113–123.

Brink, Judy and Mencher, Joan (eds) (1997) *Mixed Blessings: Gender and Religious Fundamentalism Cross Culturally*. New York and London: Routledge.

Cahill, Susan (ed.) (1996) *Wise Women: Over Two Thousand Years of Spiritual Writing by Women*. New York and London: W.W. Norton.

Chafiq, Chahla (1991) *La Femme et le Retour de l'Islam. L'expérience Iranienne*. Paris: Le Félin.

Chanda, Geetanjali Singh (2003) '(Other) Feminisms – (Other) Values', *Hecate* 29(2): 62–71.

Christ, Carol P. (1979) 'Why Women Need the Goddess: Phenomenological, Psychological, and Political Reflections', in Carol P. Christ and Judith Plaskow (eds), *Womanspirit rising: A Feminist Reader in Religion*. San Francisco: Harper and Row, pp. 273–287.

Christ, Carol P. and Plaskow, Judith (eds) (1979) *Womanspirit rising: A Feminist Reader in Religion*. San Francisco: Harper and Row.

_____ (eds) (1989) *Weaving the Visions: New Patterns in Feminist Spirituality*. San Francisco: Harper Collins.

Cohen, Joshua, Howard, Matthew, and Nussbaum, Martha C. (1999) *Is Multiculturalism Bad for Women? Susan Moller Okin with Respondents*. Princeton, NJ: Princeton University Press.

Daly, Mary ([1965] 1975) *The Church and the Second Sex*. New York: Harper and Row.

_____ ([1978] 1979) *Gyn/Ecology: the Metaethics of Radical Feminism*. London: Women's Press.

Djavann, Chahdortt (2003) *Bas les Voiles!* Paris: Gallimard.

Donaldson, Laura E. and Kwok, Pui-Lan (eds) (2002) *Postcolonialism, Feminism and Religious Discourse*. New York and London: Routledge.

Douglas, Kelly Brown (1999) *Sexuality and the Black Church: A Womanist Perspective*. Marynoll, NY: Orbis Books.

Eck, Diana L. and Jain, Devaki (eds) (1986) *Speaking of Faith: Cross-Cultural Perspectives on Women, Religion and Social Change*. New Delhi: Kali for Women.

Enloe, Cynthia ([1989] 1990) *Bananas, Beaches and Bases*. Berkeley, CA: University of California Press.

Farrer-Halls, Gill (2002) *The Feminine Face of Buddhism*. Alresford: Godsfield Press.

Frankfort-Nachmias, Chava and Shadmi, Erella (eds) (2005) *Sapho in the Holy Land: Lesbian Existence and Dilemmas in Contemporary Israel*. New York: State University of New York Press.

Gaspard, Françoise and Khosrokhavar, Farhad (1995) *Le Foulard et la République*. Paris: La Découverte.

Gearhart, Sally and Johnson, William R. (eds) (1974) *Loving Women/Loving Men: Gay Liberation and the Church*. San Francisco: Glide Publications.

Gross, Rita (1994a) 'Studying Women and Religion: Conclusions Twenty-Five Years Later', in Arvind Sharma (ed.), *Today's Woman in World Religions*. New York: State University of New York Press, pp. 327–361.

_____ (1994b) 'Buddhism', in Jean Holm (ed.), with John Bowker, *Women in Religion*. London: Pinter, pp. 1–29.

Gustafson, Carrie and Juviler, Peter (eds) (1999) *Religion and Human Rights: Competing Claims?* Armonk, NY and London: M.E. Sharpe.

Haddad, Yvonne Yazbeck and Findly, Ellison Banks (eds) (1985) *Women, Religion and Social Change*. New York: State University of New York Press.

Hiltebeitel, Alf and Erndl, Kathleen M. (eds) (2000) *Is the Goddess a Feminist? The Politics of South Asian Goddesses*. New York: New York University Press.

Hindmarsh Island Bridge Royal Commission (1996) Transcript of Proceedings: www.library.adelaide.edu.au/gen/H_Islnd/

Hobsbawm, Eric and Ranger, Terence (1983) *The Invention of Tradition*. Cambridge: Cambridge University Press.

Holm, Jean (ed.), with John Bowker (1994) *Women in Religion*. London: Pinter.

Hull, Gloria T., Scott, Patricia Bell, and Smith, Barbara (eds) (1982) *All the Women Are White, All the Blacks Are Men, But Some of Us Are Brave: Black Women's Studies*. New York: Feminist Press.

Hussain, Jamila (2003) *Islam: Its Law and Society* (2nd edition). Leichhardt, NSW: Federation Press.

Jakobsen, Janet R. and Pellegrini, Ann (2003) *Love the Sin: Sexual Regulation and the Limits of Religious Tolerance*. New York/London: New York University Press.

Jeffery, Patricia and Basu, Amrita (eds) (1998) *Appropriating Gender: Women's Activism and Politicized Religion in South Asia*. New York/London: Routledge.

Keller, Rosemary Skinner and Ruether, Rosemary Radford (eds) (1995) *In Our Own Voices: Four Centuries of American Women's Religious Writing*. San Francisco: Harper Collins.

King, Ursula (1989) *Women and Spirituality: Voices of Protest and Promise*. Basingstoke: Macmillan.

_____ (ed.) (1995) *Religion and Gender*. Oxford: Basil Blackwell.

Klein, Anne Carolyn (1995) *Meeting the Great Bliss Queen: Buddhists, Feminists and the Arts of the Self*. Boston, MA: Beacon Press.

Kwok, Pui-Lan (2002) 'Unbinding Our Feet: Saving Brown Women and Feminist Religious Discourse', in Laura E. Donaldson and Kwok Pui-Lan (eds), *Postcolonialism, Feminism and Religious Discourse*. New York/London: Routledge, pp. 62–81.

Larrington, Carolyne (ed.) (1992) *The Feminist Companion to Mythology*. London: Pandora.

Lazreg, Marnia (1994) *The Eloquence of Silence. Algerian Women in Question*. New York/London: Routledge.

Leyland, Winston (ed.) (1998) *Queer Dharma: Voices of Gay Buddhists*. San Francisco: Gay Sunshine Press.

_____ (2000) *Queer Dharma, Vol. 2: Voices of Gay Buddhists*. San Francisco: Gay Sunshine Press.

Lorde, Audré (1984) 'An Open Letter to Mary Daly', in Audré Lorde, *Sister Outsider: Essays and Speeches*. Freedom, CA: Crossing Press, pp. 66–71.

Machacek, David W. and Wilcox, Melissa M. (eds) (2003) *Sexuality and the World's Religions*. Santa Barbara, CA: ABC-CLIO.

Macourt, Malcolm (ed.) (1977) *Towards a Theology of Gay Liberation*. London: SCM Press.

Manji, Irshad (2003) *The Trouble with Islam: A Muslim's Call for Reform in Her Faith*. Toronto: Random House.

Mayer, Ann Elizabeth (1995) 'Cultural Particularism as a Bar to Women's Rights: Reflections on the Middle Eastern Experience', in Julia Peters and Andrea Wolper (eds), *Women's Rights, Human Rights: International Feminist Perspectives*. New York and London: Routledge, pp. 176–188.

Mernissi, Fatima (1975) *Beyond the Veil: Male-female Dynamics in a Modern Muslim Society*. Cambridge, MA: Schenkman.

Moghadam, Valentine M. (ed.) (1994) *Identity Politics and Women: Cultural Reassertions and Feminisms in International Perspective*. Boulder, CO: Westview Press.

_____ (2001) 'Feminism and Islamic Fundamentalism: A Secularist Interpretation', *Journal of Women's History* 13(1): 42–45.

Parsons, Susan Frank (ed.) (2002) *The Cambridge Companion to Feminist Theology*. Cambridge: Cambridge University Press.

Prochoix 25, Special issue *Voile*, Summer 2003.

Rao, Arati (1995) 'The Politics of Gender and Culture in International Human Rights Discourse', in Julia Peters and Andrea Wolper (eds), *Women's Rights, Human Rights; International Feminist Perspectives*. New York and London: Routledge, pp. 167–175.

Sarkar, Tanika and Butalia, Urvashi (eds) (1995) *Women and Right-Wing Movements: Indian Experiences*. London and New Jersey: Zed Books.

Sharma, Arvind (ed.) (1994a) *Today's Woman in World Religions*. Albany, NY: State University of New York Press.

—— (ed.) (1994b) *Religion and Women*. Albany, NY: State University of New York Press.

Sharma, Arvind and Young, Katherine K. (eds) (1999) *Feminism and World Religions*. Albany, NY: State University of New York Press.

Shirazi, Faegheh (2001) *The Veil Unveiled: The Hijab in Modern Culture*. Gainesville: University Press of Florida.

Spretnak, Charlene (ed.) (1982) *The Politics of Women's Spirituality: Essays on the Rise of Spiritual Power within the Feminist Movement*. New York: Anchor Books.

Stuart, Elizabeth (2002) *Gay and Lesbian Theologies: Repetitions with Critical Difference*. Aldershot: Ashgate.

Sweasey, Peter (1997) *From Queer to Eternity: Spirituality in the Lives of Lesbian, Gay and Bisexual People*. London/Washington, DC: Cassell.

Swidler, Arlene (1993) *Homosexuality and World Religions*. Valley Forge, PA: Trinity Press International.

Taarji, Hinde (1991) *Les Voilées de l'Islam*. Paris: Balland.

Thadani, Giti (1996) *Sakhiyani: Lesbian Desire in Ancient and Modern India*. London: Cassell.

Vanita, Ruth (2001) *Queering India: Same-Sex Love and Eroticism in Indian Culture and Society*. New York and London: Routledge.

Vanita, Ruth and Kidwai, Saleem (eds) (2000) *Same-Sex Love in India: Readings from Literature*. New York: St. Martin's Press.

Winter, Bronwyn (1996) 'Learning the Hard Way: The Debate on Women, Cultural Difference and Secular Schooling in France', in John Perkins and Jürgen Tampke (eds), *Europe: Retrospects and Prospects*. Manly, NSW: Southern Highlands Publishers, pp. 203–213.

—— (2001) 'Fundamental Misunderstandings: Issues in Feminist Approaches to Islamism' and 'Naming the Oppressor, Not Punishing the Oppressed: Atheism and Feminist Legitimacy', *Journal of Women's History* 13(1): 9–41 and 53–57 respectively.

—— (2002) 'If Women Really Mattered', in Susan Hawthorne and Bronwyn Winter (eds), *September 11, 2001: Feminist Perspectives*. Melbourne: Spinifex, pp. 450–480.

Women Living Under Muslim Laws (1997) *For Ourselves: Women Reading the Qur'an*. Lahore: Women Living Under Muslim Laws.

Yegenoglu, Meyda (1998) *Colonial Fantasies: Towards a Feminist Reading of Orientalism*. Cambridge: Cambridge University Press.

6

The Crisis in Masculinity

David Morgan

Discussions about a 'crisis in masculinity' are widespread. This idea of a crisis can be formulated as a relationship between some immediate experiences and responses on the part of men (young men in particular) which are linked to changes in employment, the family, and the gender order and which together are constituted as a more general crisis. Focusing mainly on issues of health and education, this chapter argues that it is possible to talk about a crisis in relation to specific groups of men. Whether these specific issues can be taken as a sign of a more generalized crisis is less clear.

INTRODUCTION

It is likely that the word 'crisis' is one of the most frequently used words in contemporary discourse, with an increasingly wide range of application. We may talk of personal crises, or crises in particular institutions such as those to do with education or health care, or at a more global level. Thus, we may talk of a 'crisis in Western civilization' or a widespread 'legitimation crisis' (Habermas, 1976). Notions of a crisis in masculinity clearly belong at this more global level, although it might also be expected to have repercussions at an individual or an institutional level.

Dictionary definitions of crisis tend to distinguish between two distinct but overlapping sets of meanings. The more specific meanings refer to vitally important or decisive turning points which could result in recovery (as in the case of a serious illness) or rapid decline and collapse. Logically, whether a crisis is of this kind can only be determined at some time after the event, when the collapse or recovery has taken place. The other set of meanings refers, more generally, to 'times of difficulty, insecurity and suspense in politics or commerce' (*Oxford English Dictionary*, 1989), although this meaning could undoubtedly be extended to other areas of social life. Most discussions of 'the crisis in masculinity' tend to be of this kind of generality, although not without suggestions of the former meanings of some kind of turning point, a sense that things cannot continue as they are for much longer. It is possible, therefore, to distinguish between a crisis *in* masculinity (something more specific and focused and presumably capable of resolution) and a crisis *of* masculinity, where the whole sets of practices and discourses implied by this term are in question. Perhaps another way of expressing these differences is in terms of a contrast between a crisis and a contradiction, where the latter cannot be changed without some fundamental alteration in the wider system as a whole.

More generally, the notion of crisis conveys a sense of widespread serious concern, located within an identifiable time period and representing some kind of convergence of different forces, events, changes, and anxieties. In this chapter, I intend to provide a critical interrogation of the idea of a 'crisis in masculinity'. I begin with an outline of some provisional models of this crisis as a way of exploring the supposed links between sets of indicators of a crisis, changes in particular social institutions together with wider societal changes, including changes in the idea of masculinity and of what it means to be a man. I then go on to explore some of the hypothesized symptoms of the crisis in more detail, focusing on issues to do with education, health (including suicide), and anti-social behaviour. I then outline some critical issues associated with this crisis model. Here I look at some overlaps in the experiences of young men and women, consider questions of 'whose crisis?', explore some issues of timing and historical change and general questions to do with the interpretation of the evidence of crisis.

THE CRISIS IN MASCULINITY: SOME PROVISIONAL MODELS

The idea of a crisis in masculinity usually consists of three causally related elements. At the more immediate or individual level there is a set of symptoms or indicators. These might include health-related indicators, including suicide rates, educational under-performance, and criminal or anti-social behaviour. I shall consider these in more detail in the next section. At the most general, societal, level there are a range of changes which are seen as having far-reaching implications. These are chiefly changes in the economy and the gender order but may also include changes in the family and patterns of intimate living. The notion of a crisis in masculinity provides a link between these wider structural changes and the more individualized effects. One of many examples of this kind of model is provided by Stephen Frosh, Ann Phoenix, and Rob Pattman when they write of:

> an apparent 'crisis' in contemporary forms of masculinity, marked by uncertainties over social roles and identity, sexuality, work and personal relationships – and often manifested in violent or abusive behaviours towards self and others. (2002: 1)

Possible roots of this crisis are to be seen in the collapse of 'traditional' men's work, the growth of a technological culture that cannot be passed on from generation to generation, the rise of feminism, and challenges to dominant forms of rationality.

It is important to remember the difference between the idea of a 'crisis in masculinity' and a 'crisis in patriarchy', although very often the structure of the argument is quite similar. Thus, Manuel Castells writes about the erosion of patriarchalism citing 'the inseparably related processes of the transformations of women's work and the transformation of women's consciousness' as key elements which themselves arise out of the growth of the informational global economy, technological changes in reproduction, and the struggles of women themselves (1997: 135). Within this process, Castells lays considerable stress on the 'undoing of the patriarchal family' (p. 136). He notes male anger (including violence and abuse) as one set of responses to these transformations. R. W. Connell (1995) writes of a crisis within the gender order as a whole, one aspect of which might be seen as an erosion of what he calls the patriarchal dividend. This is a dividend from being a man in a patriarchal society 'in terms of honour, prestige and the right to command' together with a more material set of benefits. The patriarchal dividend has not, by any means, been eroded completely, but it has been adversely affected by wider shifts in the labour market and the division of labour and the impact of feminism.

Hence, it is argued that the 'crisis' of masculinity is something to do with wider social and economic changes. While there are some variations in the changes noted as being of significance and the relative weighting to be accorded to these factors, there would seem to be a broad agreement that the following are of significance:

(a) Changes in the labour market and the patterns of work, which would include the decline of heavy industries and, hence, strong physical labour and the development of the service economy. Linda McDowell, for example, notes that two-thirds of British workers are now employed in the service sector, a sector which itself embraces a variety of different working conditions (2003: 27). We may also include here the growth of flexible working practices and the erosion, at least in some areas, of the idea of a working career or a job for life, both of which having been associated with masculine identities. Other writers might add globalization as a factor underlining many of these economic changes or as an influence in its own right.

(b) Changes in the family and in patterns of intimate life, which would include the rise in divorce rates (more frequently initiated by women), challenges to a dominant heterosexual model, and the rise of single-parent households, again more often than not headed by women. All these changes, as Castells (1997) argues, represent a challenge to the patriarchal family. One particular aspect of this challenge, partially associated to these changes in family and household and partially to the economic changes indicated above, is the loss or a weakening of links to fathers (Frosh, Phoenix, and Pattman, 2002: 225).

(c) Changes in the positions of women in the labour market, politics, education, and all other spheres of social and economic life. These changes, in part the result of struggles by women themselves, are clearly linked, in a variety of ways, to the other changes listed above.

As has already been indicated, there is a time dimension to this model. In a simple causal model, of course, the structural changes take place prior to the individual responses. One variation is some kind of generational model. Perhaps the most influential version of this model is Susan Faludi's *Stiffed*, which is subtitled *The Betrayal of the Modern Man* (1999). Faludi notes many of the factors cited by other writers: the collapse of relatively secure employment in work that had strong identifications with notions of masculinity and the erosion of the heroic models of masculinity that might have been present during the Second World War and the immediate post-war years. For new generations of men, the kinds of promise held out to their fathers and grandfathers of a relatively straightforward confirmation of a masculine identity no longer obtained. Faludi's account goes beyond most of the other arguments, including the commercialization of sport, which undermines the intimate and gendered relationship between a man and the team he supports, and the development of an 'ornamental culture', which pervades work as well as leisure. The generational model, therefore, is roughly one of a cohort of men socialized within one framework of assumptions but encountering social situations based on quite different assumptions in later life. Faludi, noting the painful accounts which many men give of their relationships to their fathers, sees links between the public betrayals and the more individualized 'paternal betrayals'. While it is possible to argue against many of Faludi's specific arguments, the idea of a generational effect is quite persuasive and seems to be an integral part of the overall model, whether it is made explicit or not.

The argument, therefore, would be that these changes (some of which have taken place over a long period of time) have had an impact on the lives, experiences, and responses of individual men. Mediating between the changes and the experiences are notions of masculinity and of what it means to be a man. In short, it is argued, these constructions are becoming less clear, less positively valued, and less dominant.

SOME KEY 'SYMPTOMS' OF THE CRISIS

Discussions of the crisis in masculinity frequently begin with a range of 'symptoms' or indicators which are read as signs of a deeper, gendered crisis. Frequently the focus is on the lives and experiences of young men and boys:

On the face of it there certainly seems to be a 'boys problem'. Boys are now under-performing compared to girls in nearly all subjects at GCSE; the less well qualified can be difficult to employ and as a result often struggle to construct stable and fulfilling lives; boys commit about three times as much crime as girls; and they are generally perceived as far more anti-social in their general conduct than girls. Much of the damage they do is to themselves. Boys are far more likely to attack each other than to attack girls, and the suicide rate for young men between the ages of 15 and 24 has almost doubled since 1976 and is far higher than the corresponding figure for young women. The image of young men is now so poor that they are often presented in the popular media as a dubious risk as partners for young women. (O'Donnell and Sharpe, 2000: 1)

Similar lists may be found in other studies. The implication is that these apparently different indicators are signs of an underlying crisis. The fact that the focus is on young men suggests that we are dealing with a cohort or a generational issue and that, without some outside interventions, these effects are likely to reproduce themselves through subsequent generations.

The key points of concern are issues of health and education. There has been a growing set of issues about men's health focusing not simply on specifically male conditions such as prostate cancer but, rather, on a wider range of concerns which are said to reflect both men's life styles and the overall relationships between men, health, and their bodies (Sabo and Gordon, 1995). Life style issues include questions of risk-taking (accidents, sexually transmitted diseases, alcohol and drug abuse) while the more general issues concern men's apparent unwillingness to seek medical advice. Much of this concern might be said to reflect long-standing practices of men which have only come to the fore as a consequence of this recent focus on men's health. If these 'symptoms' represent a crisis, it is a crisis of long duration.

However, there are more specific health issues which might be more directly related to a sense of crisis. One example might be a recorded fivefold increase in liver failure among men in the last thirty years (Laurance, 2003), an increase that can be associated with heavy drinking. Concerns about 'binge drinking' among the young have grown in recent years, although the extent to which it can be attributed to a crisis in masculinity rather than a continuation of masculine practices in times of relative affluence is still an open question.

A more serious area of concern is rising suicide rates among young men. One recent article states: 'Suicide is one of the principal causes of premature mortality in young adults in industrialised countries' (Gunnell, Middleton, Whitley, Dorling, and Frankel, 2003). It notes a doubling in the rates for males aged 45 or under over the last fifty years, compared with declines recorded for women and older men. The concern is particularly with men in the younger age groups, especially those between 25 and 34. The authors note that these increases parallel increases in other well-documented risk factors, such as 'unemployment, divorce, alcohol and drug abuse, and declines in marriage' (p. 606). Several of these adverse trends are also highly correlated with each other. Concerns with suicide rates are not confined to

Britain but may also be found in other parts of Europe and the United States (McDowell, 2003: 60).

The other main area of concern is education, more specifically the relative under-performance of boys at school as compared with girls. As with suicide and other health issues, these concerns are not confined to Britain but are manifested in many parts of Europe, Australia, and North America (Arnot, David, and Weiner, 1999; Connell, 2000; Epstein, Ellwood, Hey, and Maw, 1998; McDowell, 2003; Yates, 1997). In relation to the debate in Britain, the *Guardian* of 14 August, 2003 had the headline 'Girls continue to outstrip boys in exams – and the gap is widening'. Variations on this story (associated with the publication of 'A' level results, the examinations which determine university entry to a large extent) have appeared regularly over the past few years (Arnot et al., 1999). Lower down the school years, we find boys continuing to under-perform in English, although the differences are less marked in maths and science. Looking at behaviour, boys are almost five times more likely than girls to be permanently excluded from school (Office for National Statistics, 2003: 58 and 59).

The apparent failure of boys, in relation to girls, at all levels of schooling is usually attributed to a rejection of academic or school-based values and a greater tendency to play around, have a laugh, or engage in various forms of anti-social behaviour with other boys. In terms of the overall model, the ultimate causes might be seen in terms of changes in the labour market, especially as they affect young working-class men. Reduced opportunities here contribute to an increasing sense of alienation from school, seen as having little relevance to life beyond school. Intervening between the wider economic structural changes and the individual responses on the part of boys are peer group pressures which stress that there is something uncool, unmasculine, or possibly homosexual about showing an interest in schoolwork. Some recent British research suggests that these attitudes and trends are now beginning to carry over into universities (*Times Higher Education Supplement*, 2003: 8).

In Britain, the popular term for the factors leading to educational failure and other symptoms has been 'the new laddism'. The phenomenon has been presented in magazines and television programmes as a positive endorsement of some of the practices of young men, including alcohol consumption, rejections of school or work-based values, sexism, and general 'loutish' behaviour. To some, this 'new laddism' is part of an overall male backlash against the rising presence of women in many areas of social life and against feminism in particular.

In general, therefore, an exploration of these particular 'symptoms' (and of the various explanations given for them) fleshes out the tentative model presented in the previous section. We have some widespread and far-reaching structural changes in the areas of work and the family leading to a perceived, and possibly actual, loss of male power, especially for young men, who experience a loss of continuity over the generations. Alternatively, as some have suggested, the 'male breadwinner' ideology persists in times where it is of little relevance (Arnot et al., 1999: 125). The opportunities apparently open to previous generations in terms of steady employment and family building seem to be much more in question. A smooth transition to adulthood is no longer guaranteed. This loss of power, position, and identity leads to various forms of retreatism or aggression. Actual manifestations are underperformance at school, engagement in life-threatening activities, and, in some cases, suicide.

SOME CRITICAL ISSUES

There is a certain plausibility about the idea of a 'crisis in masculinity'. The focus on young men rather than men in general suggests that there is something about this specific point in time which brings about a particular dislocation between expectations and reality. What we appear to be witnessing is an over-determined phenomenon whereby a variety of trends and processes converge to produce a crisis or, at the very least, a sense of crisis. To slightly reformulate the argument, these points of convergence include:

(a) Structural changes in work and employment which bear especially upon young men and their expectations. We may also point to changes in the family which equally appear to undermine previous expectations to do with fatherhood and the idea of the provider.
(b) A series of responses and practices on the part of men, especially young men, which, while they have been part of men's culture for some generations, seem less and less in tune with modern times. These would include peer groups and group solidarities most obviously manifested in the cultures of 'the lads'.
(c) Features associated with men and masculinity for some generations which seem to inhibit more positive responses on the part of men to the difficulties of late modernity. These would include an unwillingness to share or to articulate personal or emotional problems.

However, while the outline of the argument for the crisis of masculinity has a degree of plausibility there are also some reasons for scepticism. Without detracting from the seriousness of some of the elements in the argument, youthful suicides for example, the overall framework of understanding and interpretation can be questioned. The most obvious point of question is the one raised at the beginning of the chapter, namely, that despite all the public talk about such a crisis, men still maintain a dominant position in key political, military, economic, and religious institutions as well as in many areas of sport, media, and entertainment. Moreover, whatever questions might be made about the particular performances of such men, they are rarely assessed in terms of problems to do with their gendered identities.

Some of the limitations of the simple crisis model are instructive and require treatment in some more detail. The first is that the evidence is not always as straightforward or clear cut as it might seem. In the case of studies of young men, the individuals who might be supposed to be most 'at risk' are not necessarily so. For example, data from the British Household Panel Study of over 1,000 young people found lower levels of self-esteem and higher levels of 'negative self-efficacy' for girls as compared with boys (ESRC, 2002). Girls tended to report greater unhappiness and were more likely to get into 'negative spirals' in their adolescent years. Furthermore, there were no gender differences discovered for truancy and drinking, although boys were more likely to be involved in risky behaviour. A more qualitative study of boys in two different 'deprived areas' (where one might expect the 'crisis' thesis to be especially relevant) certainly found signs of opposition to school and uncertainties about the world of work, but also found a sense of masculinity combined with aspirations for domestic security (McDowell, 2003). Put another way, whatever problems these boys and young men encountered in the move from school to work (and these were often real and immediate), they could not be directly attributed to something called 'the crisis of masculinity'.

In any event, there were often considerable overlaps between the experiences of young men and young women, the differences representing tendencies rather than clear-cut oppositions. For example, while attention has been focused on the suicide rates of young men, some countries, other than England and Wales, have also experienced rising rates for young women (Gunnell et al., 2003: 595). Within England and Wales, young women aged 15–24 years old have not experienced the overall decline in female suicide rates. At the very least, such counterindicators should advise a measure of caution in moving from suicide rates to some relatively global crisis of masculinity. Another area of overlap between boys and girls is in the area of 'binge drinking'; indeed, the concern has recently been focused on the practices of young women, which may reflect the persistence of some more 'traditional' ideas about gender and alcohol.

There is also reason to have some reservations about some of the key points in the model to do with changes in work and working practices. One study called into question some of the more sweeping assumptions about the feminization of work (Bradley, Erickson, Stephenson, and Williams, 2000). The authors argue that it is possible to talk of feminization of the labour market (in that there are more women taking up jobs and more jobs open to women) but that occupations are becoming feminized only to a limited degree and work itself not at all. In other words, the labour market is still highly gendered and unequal, and there is still a close, if weakening, association between work and masculine identity. They conclude: 'Structures of male power are remarkably resilient and the feminisation of the labour market does not amount to a female takeover' (p. 91) For the school-leavers in McDowell's study, the experience of work in itself (rather than the gendered character of any particular job) and the structure that it gave to the week often provided a basis for the construction of a sense of identity. Further, these young men still found themselves working with other men and to have male friends; few, if any, expressed any anxiety about their masculinity (McDowell, 2003).

I have argued that the idea of 'crisis' conveys, in part at least, a 'sense of widespread social concern'. However, we need to ask 'whose concern?' It cannot be automatically assumed that this sense of concern about the current state of masculinity is widely or evenly distributed throughout Western society. A glance at the newspapers or television news broadcasts would seem to suggest that many men, as they go about their daily business at international conferences, in corporate meetings, or on the sports field, are relatively secure in their position, as men, in the world. What we are talking about is a set of claims about a current crisis, claims which may or may not be justifiable but which do not necessarily reflect obvious and widespread concerns on a more day-to-day basis. To some extent, sociological analysis of 'moral panics' (Thompson, 1998), a social construction of areas of moral or political concern made by definable groups or individuals, may be more relevant here.

Turning away from more generalized notions of crisis to the crisis in or of masculinity, we need to ask to whom or to what does the word 'crisis' apply? In the first place, it could refer to individual men. Individual men may feel some sense of unease or uncertainty which is in some ways bound up with their sense of themselves as men. There may be increasing doubts as to what it means to be a man, how to behave as a man in particular situations, or whether particular gendered identities (such as being a father or a breadwinner) continue to have any significance or value. The idea of a crisis would seem to suggest that this sense of unease applies to individual men in sufficient numbers to justify the use of such a strong descriptive term. We have seen that there are some signs of individual unhappiness, although there is less evidence to suggest that the sum total of these individual experiences and practices constitutes a crisis, or that there is a more general, diffuse sense of gender panic on the part of men.

Second, the sense of crisis may be said to apply to 'masculinity'. This is itself a troublesome term and these troubles are only partially resolved by using the term in its plural form. We still need to ask whether this crisis applies to all the masculinities that are on offer or whether it is particularly associated with what Connell and others have identified as 'hegemonic masculinities' (Connell, 1987; 1995). Further, are we simply dealing with discourses about or representations of masculinity or, as McDowell suggests, 'collective social practices' (2003: 12)? While it can be argued that there is an increasing area of debate and contestation about the public representations of masculinities, there would seem to be less evidence of a crisis in terms of 'collective social practices'.

Finally, we may be referring to a crisis of (or in) 'patriarchy'. Again, this is a problematic and much debated term but refers to what Bethan Benwell calls 'masculinity as a power project', as distinct from masculinity as an 'identity project' (2003a). We are referring to sexual politics and gendered practices on the part of men (see Walby, 1990). Patriarchy is linked to masculinity, but there is also some degree of individual variation:

> If there is a crisis or crises in masculinities, then patriarchy too must be under stress, and very likely severe stress…Once men begin to lose belief in their masculinity, then it is a sure sign that patriarchy itself is losing credibility. (O'Donnell and Sharpe, 2000: 89)

A crisis in patriarchy is something at a more institutional, possibly global, level and refers to the supposed erosion of the power of men across a wide range of institutions (Castells, 1997). In somewhat similar terms, Connell rejects the terminology of a 'crisis of masculinity' and refers to a crisis of the gender order as a whole (1995). Patriarchy is certainly under challenge; simply to use the word is to indicate that the sets of practices denoted by the term are no longer taken for granted. But it is by no means certain that this sense of debate and challenge has yet been transformed into a global crisis. Further, what evidence we have of a 'crisis of masculinity' does not necessarily signify a crisis in patriarchy; at least, not yet.

A further set of problems arises when the more complex relationships among gender, class, ethnicity, and nationality are considered. David Jackson writes of 'gender absolutism', by which he means that gender is seen as a single or overwhelming influence on behaviour and attitudes (1998: 82). All the discussions of educational under-performance on the part of boys also emphasize that the issues are confounded by class and ethnicity, and these qualifications also apply when health issues are considered. Thus, the problem is rarely simply one of boys or young men; the focus is increasingly on young working-class men and, within this category in Britain, men from an Afro-Caribbean background. There is less evidence of a crisis among middle-class White boys who do not usually have to confront racism on a daily basis and who frequently have enough social and cultural capital to cope with changes in work and economic life. Similarly, there are national variations. Despite the concerns about British men and their health, they, in common with Swedish men, have experienced a rise in life expectancy which puts them near the top in terms of this index for most of Europe. However, these advantages seem to be concentrated amongst men in the higher socio-economic groups (Laurance, 2003).

There are two conclusions that emerge from these particular findings. One is that if we are to continue to talk of a crisis of masculinity, we must recognize that the effects of this crisis are mediated by other social divisions, underlining the importance of talking about 'masculinities' rather than 'masculinity'. Men in different classes and racial ethnic groups may have quite different sets of life experiences and life chances, and so the crisis might be less evident among hegemonic men than among men who are more marginalized or subordinated. The other conclusion is that while there are some similarities in experiences across different countries, it would be difficult to talk about a 'global' crisis of masculinity. For perhaps the majority of men globally, issues of masculinity are probably even less likely to be seen as problematic than they are in parts of the more developed world. Put simply, they have more urgent matters to worry about than their masculine identity. There may be localized crises in other countries, about particular codes of honour or patterns of machismo in Latin American or Mediterranean cultures, for example. Constructions of masculinity do vary in different cultures, and while there is an increasing range of forces and pressures that have a global impact, the ways in which these interact with masculinities is likely to be very complex. Some of the simpler claims of a 'crisis of masculinity' might be guilty of adopting a somewhat over-gendered and probably ethnocentric view of the world.

A farther critical issue is the supposed novelty of the current 'crisis'. Michael Kimmel, in an influential article (1987), argued that masculinity has been constructed as being in crisis on at least two previous occasions, in Restoration England (1688–1714) and in the United States just prior to the First World War (1880–1914). In both historical contexts, there were concerns expressed about the attempts on the part of women to renegotiate their positions within marriage and within the wider society. In both periods, there were concerns about the alleged effeminacy of the nation's manhood, and both were times of considerable economic and political upheaval. Prior to the First World War, Kimmel argues, there were three responses on the part of men to this sense of crisis: an anti-feminist backlash, an assertion of masculinity, and the development of a pro-feminist movement on the part of men.

Perhaps this argument cannot be taken too far. For one thing, these earlier concerns are about the supposed decline of masculinity and manliness and the need for the development of more moral fibre. More recent concerns, on the other hand, are in part about the dysfunctions inherent in the idea of masculinity itself or, at least, in more exaggerated versions of hyper-masculinity which emerge in response to social and economic changes. Further, these earlier 'moral panics' (if that is what they were) were even more confined to a limited section of society than the men who arouse the more recent anxieties. However, Kimmel's argument serves as a reminder to question the claimed novelty of the crisis in masculinity.

Linked to this question about the supposed novelty of the crisis of masculinity is a wider one about the uses of history in social analysis. In talking about a crisis, some kind of comparison with the past is being implied. To talk of a crisis now or impending implies some relatively stable or steady state in the past. In much of the literature some distinction is usually made between 'now' and something called 'traditional' masculinity. For example, McDowell writes:

> For young men in particular it is a difficult time to negotiate the transitions to adulthood and pathways to employment when traditional ways of becoming a man are increasingly less available. (2003: 4)

Similarly, Jonathan Rutherford writes:

> In the age of the informational and service economy, certain traditional ways of being male, rooted in the industrial revolution, and its domestic division of labour, are becoming obsolete. (2003: 1)

The word 'obsolete', frequently used in discussions of this kind, is significant, implying as it does some previous functional linkage between modes of masculinity and the wider economic, political, and social order. But there is also, frequently, a moral dimension as well. Stephen Whitehead and Frank Barrett, for example, refer to the 'social and cultural disapproval of traditional masculinity' (2001: 6).

Temporally, the comparison of the present with the past may refer to a long drawn-out crisis, usually beginning with the Industrial Revolution and continuing up to the present day. Confusingly, here, the word 'traditional' is used to refer to what others might call 'modern'. Alternatively, the crisis may refer to a somewhat shorter period, one usually associated with late modernity and beginning roughly somewhere in the period following the Second World War. At a more individual level, men may be making some kind of contrast with their parents' or grandparents' generations. Whatever the contrast, the notion of crisis clearly implies that 'traditional' or 'conventional' masculinity is increasingly coming into conflict with other changes in society, especially within the gender order. Such assumptions and usages of history are not necessarily wrong, but they are frequently, from a historical perspective, unexamined.

A final problem with the talk of the crisis of masculinity is that it is a construction from the outside, from an external observer or analyst. This problem has two aspects. First, it tends to present men as simply reacting to certain external stimuli, changes in the economy or in the family or in the gender order as a whole. Thus, while suicide may be one possible response to a set of interlinked changes in employment and family relationships, it is clear that it is only one response among several. There was one suicide in McDowell's small sample of twenty-four boys, which means that the other twenty-three, with varying degrees of success, attempted to do the best with the limited resources available to them. In terms of gender politics, the development of hyper-masculinity or the expression of an anti-feminist backlash are only two of a range of possible responses, as Kimmel suggests in relation to his historical evidence.

Second, a model is drawn up as, among other things, an interpretative framework for certain trends in education and health, which takes little account of the actual perceptions or understandings of men or boys themselves. There is little evidence of men themselves talking about a crisis in terms of their identities as men. Expressed anxieties are to be found in terms of work and employment or possibly in men's relationships with women or their futures as family men. There are expressions (say comparing present generations with earlier generations) which recognize that things are changing, but it is difficult to find any clear articulations of a sense of crisis on the part of men themselves. This might not conclusively discredit the whole idea. Part of the crisis, it may be argued, is that men often find it difficult to give expression to their deepest feelings, and these inabilities are themselves part of the crisis. Or, again, some understandings of masculinity inhibiting shared emotions may militate against any expression of apparent weakness. However, any deep exploration of the crisis of masculinity (rather than the difficulties faced by particular sets of individual men) must at some stage come to grips with men's own understandings and constructions of the problem.

CONCLUSION

So, is there a crisis of masculinity? It might be useful to turn to some of the suggested distinctions at the beginning of this chapter that suggest ways of breaking down this question. In the first place, therefore, we are asking whether there is a crisis in masculinity, that is within particular groups of men or individual men. The evidence suggests that it is possible to talk about some sense of crisis here, one largely generated by changes within work and employment and, possibly, within the wider gender order, but one which is always mediated by class and ethnicity. The extent to which these problems reflect a wider crisis is open to question, however.

If we are talking about a crisis of masculinity, that is a crisis in the representations of and discourses around dominant or hegemonic masculinity, then the matter is less clear cut. Certain understandings of masculinity seem to have a long history and do not show clear signs of erosion; the idea of the man as 'provider', for example. However, these continuities are less apparent in some countries (Norway, for example) and it would appear that certain constructions of masculinity to do with violence and aggression are increasingly under challenge. There would seem some sense that these manifestations are less acceptable and possibly even represent dysfunctional or obsolete forms of masculinity. Elsewhere, it is possible to see some beginnings of a critique of rationality and its association with a masculine construction of the world. At the very least, it could be argued that issues of masculinity are increasingly open to critical scrutiny. Further, it can be argued that there is an increasing sense of uncertainty about what it means to be a man. Older, more hegemonic constructions (of manliness, for example) no longer have the apparent certainty that they once did.

Whether all this amounts to a crisis in patriarchy is even more complex. Castells was probably correct in identifying certain more or less global changes that are having or will have an effect on the apparent solidity of patriarchal institutions, especially the family. More generally, a sense of crisis in and of masculinity must have some kind of effect on patriarchal structures themselves. However, it might also be argued that patriarchy is showing considerable resilience in responding to these trends and that new constructions of masculinity (global male elites, for example) might be taking place to redefine and rework patriarchal power. The patriarchal dividend may be smaller, less secure, and less widely available, but there is little doubt that it still exists. Indeed, it is possible that focus on some aspects of the crisis in masculinity may reinforce patriarchal institutions through an over-emphasis on the theme of 'men as victims'.

There is little doubt that there is considerable talk about a crisis for men, at least some men, and within some versions of masculinity. But there is also a need to be much more precise and definite about the nature and character of the crisis and the links between its various manifestations. There is also a need to look beyond the concerns of North America or Europe and develop a more complex comparative analysis, sensitive to local meanings and experiences. Further, there is a continuing need to focus on the actions and perceptions of men and women themselves and the ways in which they seek to respond to and change the conditions of their own lives.

REFERENCES

Arnot, M., David, M., and Weiner, G. (1999) *Closing the Gender Gap: Post-war Education and Social Change* Cambridge: Polity.
Benwell, Bethan (2003a) 'Introduction: Masculinity and men's lifestyle magazines' in Benwell, Bethan (ed.), *Masculinity and Men's Lifestyle Magazines* Oxford: Blackwell/Sociological Review pp. 6–30.
Benwell, Bethan (ed.) (2003b) *Masculinity and Men's Lifestyle Magazines* Oxford: Blackwell/Sociological Review.
Bradley, H., Erickson, M., Stephenson, C., and Williams, S. (2000) *Myths at Work* Cambridge: Polity.
Castells, Manuel (1997) *The Power of Identity* (Vol. 2 of 'The Information Age') Oxford: Blackwell.
Connell, R. W. (1987) *Gender and Power* Cambridge: Polity.
Connell, R. W. (1995) *Masculinities* Cambridge: Polity.
Connell, R. W. (2000) *The Men and The Boys* Cambridge: Polity.
Epstein, D., Ellwood, D., Hey, V., and Maw, J. (eds) (1998) *Failing Boys? Issues in Gender and Achievement* Buckingham: Open University Press.
ESRC (2002) *Youth, Citizenship and Social Change: Research Briefing No. 15* Brighton.
Faludi, Susan (1999) *Stiffed: The Betrayal of the Modern Man* London: Chatto and Windus.
Frosh, S., Phoenix, A., and Pattman, R. (2002) *Young Masculinities: Understanding Boys in Contemporary Society* Basingstoke: Palgrave.
Guardian (2003) 'Girls Continue to Outstrip Boys in Exams – And the Gap is Widening' 14 August, p. 12.
Gunnell, D., Middleton, N., Whitley, E., Dorling, D., and Frankel, S. (2003) 'Why are suicide rates rising in young men but falling in the elderly? A time-series analysis of trends in England and Wales 1950–1998' *Social Science and Medicine* 57: 595–611.
Habermas, J. (1976) *Legitimation Crisis* London: Heinemann.
Jackson, David (1998) 'Breaking out of the binary trap: boys' under-achievement, schooling and gender relations' in Epstein, D., Ellwood, D., Hey, V., and Maw, J. (eds), *Failing Boys? Issues in Gender and Achievement* Buckingham: Open University Press pp. 77–95.
Kimmel, Michael S. (1987) 'The contemporary "crisis" of masculinity in historical perspective' in Brod, H. (ed.), *The Making of Masculinities* London: Allen and Unwin pp. 121–154.

Laurance, Jeremy (2003) 'Good news: UK men live longer. Bad news: only if they are rich' *Independent* 9 July, p. 3.

McDowell, Linda (2003) *Redundant Masculinities? Employment Change and White Working Class Youth* Oxford: Blackwell.

O'Donnell, Mike and Sharpe, Sue (2000) *Uncertain Masculinities: Youth, Ethnicity and Class in Contemporary Britain* London: Routledge.

Office for National Statistics (2003) *Social Trends* No. 33 London: The Stationery Office.

Rutherford, Jonathan (2003) 'Preface' in Benwell, Bethan (ed.), *Masculinity and Men's Lifestyle Magazines* Oxford: Blackwell/Sociological Review pp. 1–5.

Sabo, Donald and Gordon, David Frederick (eds) (1995) *Men's Health and Illness: Gender, Power and The Body* Thousand Oaks, CA: Sage.

Thompson, Kenneth (1998) *Moral Panics* London: Routledge.

Times Higher Education Supplement (2003) 31 October, p. 8.

Walby, Sylvia (1990) *Theorizing Patriarchy* Oxford: Blackwell.

Whitehead, Stephen M. and Barrett, Frank S. (eds) (2001) *The Masculinity Reader* Cambridge: Polity.

Yates, L. (1997) 'Gender equity and the boys' debate: what sort of challenge is it?' *British Journal of Sociology of Education* 18: 337–347.

Part III

KNOWLEDGE

7

Clearing Ground and Making Connections
Modernism, Postmodernism, Feminism

Carolyn DiPalma and
Kathy E. Ferguson

This chapter provides a brief introduction to some of the most interesting debates in modernism and postmodernism, describes how those debates find expression in feminist inquiries, and offers a brief vision of feminist pursuits informed by those debates. Key points of contestation are shaped by four overall convictions: (1) the terms modernism and postmodernism are fundamentally relational, and strategically illuminating these shifting relations can be productive; (2) gender is brought to visibility as an analytical category somewhat differently in modern and postmodern thinking; (3) feminist energies produce a particular stance toward method, a set of expectations toward various practices of inquiry; and (4) feminist thinking is best served by productively engaging tensions between modern and postmodern thinking.

INTRODUCTION

Numerous debates within feminism move among issues and opinions associated with modernism/modernity and those associated with postmodernism/postmodernity. However, these terms shift and slide around one another with tricky agility; it is difficult to pin them down for examination or judgment. Lawrence Cahoone suggests that the term 'modernism' has been used in a 'famously ambiguous way' (1996: 13), while the authors of a feminist glossary flag modernism as 'a contested category which has dominated the writing of twentieth-century literary history' (Andermahr, Lovell, and Wolkowitz, 2000: 169). Michel Foucault remarked in his 1976 lectures at the Collège de France that we are stuck with the term 'modern' because there is no other word we can use, and that the term has become completely devoid of meaning (2003: 80).

The term 'postmodernism' fares little better; the same feminist glossary finds 'an almost infinite variety of pathways and combinations' within this term, throwing so broad a net as to catch 'most of the major social theorists of the second half of the twentieth century' (Andermahr et al., 2000: 209). Linda Nicholson describes the postmodern critique of modernity as 'wide ranging,' explaining that it 'focuses on such diverse elements as the modern sense of the self and subjectivity, the idea of history as linear and evolutionary, and the modernist separation of art and mass culture' as well as 'the idea of transcendent reason' (1990a: 3). Kwame Appiah goes farther, fearing to enter 'the shark-infested waters around the semantic island of the postmodern' (1997: 423).

Each of these authors sketches a struggle between the need for these concepts and the impossibility of figuring out what they mean. If these terms are so difficult to apprehend, how is it that we continue to try to do so? And what feminist goals does this continued struggle serve? Following the advice of those who preceded us, we do not offer precise definitions of 'modernism' and 'postmodernism.' Instead, we sketch a map of some key points of contestation between the vague territories implied by their usage. Our incursions into this turbulent political and intellectual space are shaped by four overall convictions.

First, the terms are fundamentally relational; they take their meaning and do their work within the implied or explicit relations they sustain to one another. As we frame our inquiry around the key terms *modern* and *postmodern*, we implicitly constitute these categories as at least somewhat unified and oppositional; this move is useful in ways we sketch below, but is unhelpful in unpacking the diverse kinds of arguments that reside within each category. In other words, in order to compare postmodern and modern thinking we have to push the differences *within* the categories to the background so that the differences *between* them can emerge. This analytic move could itself be thought of as modern in that it depends on solidly bounded categories conceived as mutually incompatible; our challenge is to make this oversimplification worthwhile both by using it to illuminate key debates and by calling it into question through strategies that continually bring the two kinds of thinking into relation with one another.

Second, gender is brought to visibility as an analytic category in both modern and postmodern thinking, but in somewhat different ways. The modern vector has enabled feminists to recognize and name the inconsistent expectations of gender as a problem requiring redress, and to seek greater gender equality or revolutionary transformations in gender order. The postmodern vector has nudged feminists toward taking gender as a verb: 'to gender' is something one does, something that is done in discourses and material structures. While the more modern feminist thinkers generally take gender as an aspect of life that we have found and then look for ways to make it work differently, the primarily postmodernist thinkers tend to take gender as a category we have produced and then look for strategies for inventing it otherwise.

Third, feminism's encounter with the world of method is both uncertain and robust. There is a relationship between feminist analyses of the world and the methods used to produce/express those analyses. Engaging with the questions raised by the vectors of modernism and postmodernism while staying open to the concerns of those seeking a particular method that earns the descriptor 'feminist,' our inquiry takes feminist energies to produce, not a particular method, but *a stance toward method*, a set of expectations that we bring to a variety of practices of inquiry.

Fourth, feminist thinking and acting is best served by seeking engaging ways to connect modern and postmodern thinking, to work within the problematic relations, and to find the tensions productive rather than crippling.

MODERN AND POSTMODERN: SHIFTING MEANINGS AND PRODUCTIVE RELATIONS

Modern

While we eschew the search for precise meanings, we nonetheless find the dictionary (*Oxford English Dictionary On-line*; *Webster's New Twentieth Century Dictionary*) a useful place to start: not because it pins down definitions, but because it flags multiple possible meanings that might be pursued. The English word 'modern' comes from the Latin term *modernus*, meaning 'of the present time,' and the Latin word *modus*, or measure. While some literary theorists entertain a tradition that confines 'modernism' largely to the twentieth century (Groden and Kreiswirth, 1994: 512), broader conversations among critical theorists, which we are using in this chapter, sketch the modern as that which interrupted and transformed European feudalism. Some combination of capitalism, secularism, individualism, rationalism, humanism, and liberal democracy became hegemonic, while class and race warfare, gender disturbances, anti-colonial frictions, and feudal remnants interrupted and complicated the dominant vectors of power. Modern thinking, anchored in and indebted to the Enlightenment, typically 'lays claim to a certain exclusivity of insight' (Appiah, 1997: 425) in various domains – one best route to knowledge, one superior truth, one ultimate ground of politics, one best narrative of history.

Feminist scholars have both claimed a place for women within the modern, as do historians Natalie Davis and Arlette Farge (1993), and noted women's forced exclusion from it, as in Joan Kelly-Gadol's (1977) famous essay 'Did Women Have a Renaissance?' and David Noble's (1993) history of women's exclusion from European scientific and religious traditions. The logic of these inquiries pursues the question consistently posed by Cynthia Enloe (2001) – where are the women? – in order to understand and demonstrate 'the reality of women's lives' (Davis and Farge, 1993: 2). These inquiries require feminists to have some idea, no matter how qualified, of who counts as women and what counts as real.

The kind of thinking associated with the modern has been crucial to feminist arguments for women's emancipation. Foucault goes so far as to see in modernity 'a society whose historical consciousness centers not on sovereignty and the problem of its foundation, but on revolution, its promises, and its prophecies of future emancipation' (2003: 80). Foucault's lectures track the transfigurations of modern scientific, economic, and political revolutions, their mutations through racial, national, and class struggles, and the reassertions of sovereignty in pursuit of state-centered reformulations of revolutionary promises; however, he sees little gender turbulence in these otherwise dynamic relations. Yet the measure of the modern for feminism can be taken in large part from the resources modern thinking provides to name gender as a category of analysis rather than an unremarkable fact of life, to critique male dominance as oppression rather than nature or divine order, and to seek women's rights and liberation through political reforms or revolutionary transformation.

Postmodern

Perhaps the most obvious meaning of postmodern takes *post* to be a prefix meaning after, behind, later, suggesting a linear sequence – modern is followed by postmodern, just as feudalism was followed by modernity. Here *postmodern* is grammatically like *postwar* – simply the period after the modern. Jean-François Lyotard (1979), for example, names the postmodern as the successor to the modern, and *The Glossary of Feminist Theory* refers to postmodernism as 'a new condition of society' (Andermahr et al., 2000: 207). David Harvey (1990) theorizes postmodernism as a distinctive historical condition emerging in the late twentieth century out of successive waves of space/time compression and the accompanying pressures of capital accumulation. Cahoone refers to this view as 'historical postmodernism' because it takes the political, economic, and cultural organization of modernity to have changed sufficiently to count as a 'novel world' (1996: 17).

Yet the term postmodern could summon a different grammar – rather than relegating *post* to the subordinate position of prefix, with *modern* as the anchoring root term, *postmodernism* might be a compound word, a coming together of two equal meanings. The noun *post* comes from the Latin *ponere*, to place. In noun form, post can mean a place, notably a place where troops are garrisoned, aid is offered, or trading occurs. *Post modern*, here, would be grammatically more like *post office* or *post exchange*. Postmodernism as a noun + noun combination could be the place from which to take the measure of the modern. Taking the measure of the modern might best be done from the perspective of the postmodern, since modernity does not come clearly into focus until one can be, at least to some degree, outside of it. The postmodern could be a site from which one can get a fuller view of the modern, an outpost or incursion into the modern, a place where one can get one's bearings, gather some resources, pause before reentering.

Continuing our dictionary explorations, in verb form *post* can mean 'to put up on a wall…or other conspicuous place'; 'to announce, publicize, or advertise by posting notices'; 'to hasten, to travel with speed…to inform, as of events.' To get at this potential meaning, *post* needs to become an infinitive: *[to] post modern* could be, grammatically, like *to post a message* or, going back to the original meaning of *modus*, *to post the measure*. Postmodernism as a verb + noun combination could be that which announces the modern. Instead of warning people against trespassing by posting notices, postmodernism invites people to trespass on the modern. A post can 'denounce by a public notice' and can 'publish a name…as lost or missing.' [To] postmodern is to denounce some aspects of the modern and to point out that other parts are lost or missing. Postmodernism could be that which keeps us well posted on the working of the modern.

In any of these grammatical formulations, postmodernism is clearly a way of thinking indebted to the modern. The exclusivities that various modernist philosophies and institutions have claimed – science's claim to be the best route to knowledge; rationalist or realist thinkers' assumptions of an unchanging foundation for understanding; Marxist narratives of the transcendent grounds of history; liberals' assertions about a primary origin of psychology or politics – are disrupted by postmodern responses. The loose family of ideas gathering under the term *postmodernism* brings a dispersing, pluralizing energy to the unities of the modern; it is a 'space-clearing gesture' (Appiah, 1997: 432) pushing against various realisms and challenging their legitimating narratives. Yet these multiplying strategies can be pursued in a variety of ways. Because modernism tends to narrate history as a process of evolution or a sequence of stages, the first grammar of postmodern, in which *post* is a prefix, is actually the modernist understanding of the term. The alternative grammars, in which *post* becomes a noun (a place) or a verb (an act), recruit postmodern energies to define themselves. While this sort of word play is itself evocative of postmodernism, it also fits us out with two additional points of entry into the modern–postmodern relation: as a site from which to investigate the modern, and as a way of announcing/informing/transgressing it. These playful invitations to think the relation differently do not replace the more common reference to historical sequence, but they provide useful feminist supplements to it.

Postmodern thinking has been vital to feminist attempts to trouble the limits of gender as a category of analysis and to make feminist expectations of gender into uncomfortable nodes for internal questioning. The alternative grammar of feminist postmodernism permits and encourages active exploration and transgression of gender prospects, power, and performance from multiple strategic points. In short, postmodern feminism examines the liberatory costs and benefits of thinking gender differently.

MODERN AND POSTMODERN INTERPRETATIONS OF GENDER

Gender can be understood as both the social or cultural organization of sexual difference and as a system of power relations privileging men and masculinity as prior to and more worthy than women and femininity. Contemporary gender thinking often sways between two arguments: one for gender's relentless persistence, as seen, for example, in women's lower wages, greater vulnerability to violence, exclusion from power, or devastation by globalization; a second for gender's dislocation – as shown in practices of performativity that queer and amplify gender categories, as well as through discourses and technologies of production, representation, and abjection. Gender analysis, framed in modern terms, becomes a way of empowering women to struggle against male dominance and to imagine their own liberation. In modern feminist conversations, the concept of gender shifted from a property of grammar and developed to move away from biological foundations grounded in the concept of sex (male and female) and toward more abstract cultural underpinnings (masculine and feminine). Gayle Rubin's term 'sex/gender system,' meaning a 'set of arrangements by which a society transforms biological sexuality into products of human activity,' was very influential on this point in the mid-1970s (1997: 28).

Yet, many also questioned this separation as overly sterile and as refusing to recognize overlapping links in diverse constraints and pressures informing both biology *and* culture. Gender, framed in postmodern terms, offers a site from which to problematize the gender categories that modernism produces and requires and to muster resources for trespassing against those categories. By conferring gender in increasingly explicit terms, modernism declares the presence of gender. However, the demands of maintaining order, delineating meaning, and avoiding the possibility of questions for any category are persistent. Modernism's desire for clarity produces an abstract yet constant need for category fortification against absent but anticipated difficulties. Postmodern gender thinking requires the presence and certainty of modern gender thinking in order to have a site of confidence on which to wield troubling questions about category assumptions, differences, excesses, and limitations. In this sense, postmodern gender thinking does not simply come after modern, but helps to produce it by serving as the implicit (needed) absence through which a (definitive) presence can be figured. Judith Lorber (1993) provides an example of this dynamic in her examination of biological foundations as ideological productions that have worked to reinforce the assumptions of sex and gender as dichotomous variables. Other examples of this enterprise include Thomas Laqueur's (1990) investigation into historical changes from a one-sex model of natural law (with male as telos) to a two-sex model, based on an increasing faith in science which, by the eighteenth century, claimed empirically provable different male and female bodies; Suzanne Kessler's (2000) analysis of the key role of penis size in the 'dilemma' of ambiguous genitalia; and Anne Fausto-Sterling's (2000) inquiry into the culturally informed scientific practices of gender politics and the construction of sexuality.

By looking briefly at feminist engagements around questions of subjectivity, intersectionality, power and politics, and knowledge and representation, we can illuminate some of the shared conversations and abiding tensions inhabiting modern/postmodern struggles within feminist thinking about gender.

Subjectivity

Modern energies have largely directed feminists toward claiming subjectivity for women to gain entry into the domains of rights-bearing or revolution-making subjects. Feminist developmental psychologists, most famously Carol Gilligan (1982), have named and investigated ways of thinking and judging in women's voice; feminist standpoint theorists such as Nancy Hartsock (1983) have looked to women's productive and reproductive labor as the potential grounds upon which a feminist viewpoint can be achieved. These approaches offer a subject-centered hermeneutic in which a self, understood relationally, is a source of knowledge and action in the world; these approaches also predictably raise fears, such as those expressed by Denise Riley (1988) and Diana Fuss (1990), that claiming a particular subjectivity for women will lead to essentialism (attributing a timeless essence to all women, as patriarchal theorists frequently do).[1] In turn, others, including Hartsock (1990) and Jane Flax (1987), express counter-fears that subjectivity as a stable ground for knowledge is being questioned by postmodernism just when women are in a position to claim a coherent subject position for themselves.

Postmodern approaches to subjectivity typically focus on subjects as the outcome rather than the source of historical processes and power relations. For example, Judith Butler's (1990) arguments for performativity, approaching gender as something one *does* rather than something one is, problematize expectations of regulative modernist gender categories. Focusing on the doing of gender rather than on the identity of a subject prior to the doing, Butler (1990) invites postmodern energies to deconstruct the presumed foundations of all subject positions and at the same time alarms some, including Seyla Benhabib (1992), who fear that this sort of feminism will lead to a 'theory without addresses, that is, without real women or men' to rally and recruit (Humm, 1995: 217).

Intersectionality

Another aspect of the discussion of gender as framed in contrasting modern and postmodern terms stresses the need to connect gender to race, class, age, sexuality, disability, and other vectors of power. Both modern and postmodern feminist thinkers would likely agree that gender always operates in relation to such other vectors. The differences are in the ways these thinkers name and govern such relations of meaning and power. The modern move incorporates the intersections of gender, race, class, etc., by multiplying the available subject positions that women might occupy, proliferating the categories with which gender is required to work: 'white working class lesbians,' for example, or 'disabled women of color.'[2] While to multiply gender is in some ways to destabilize it, the mandate to name a coherent subject position from which various subalterns can speak tends to restabilize the (multiplied) categories around the intersection of terms most needed to protest subordination.

Postmodern feminists generally agree that gender does not stand alone as an analytic category and must be considered in relation to other salient practices of power, but postmodern thinking multiplies gender practices with the goal of disrupting them altogether rather than reconsolidating a better set. The impossibility of ever completing the list that usually starts with 'gender, race, class...' accounts for what Butler (1990) calls 'the embarrassed etc.' at the end of such sets; rather than expecting closure, the postmodern move sees feminist inquiry as best served by understanding gender as always already intertwined with other analytic and political energies.[3]

The postmodern move is not exhausted through resisting and trespassing modern concerns; rather, the move proceeds toward an internal critique of postmodernism's own reliance on presence and absence, focusing on and questioning the tugs and pulls within webs of relations that work together to momentarily (if at all) produce a glimpse of something that might be (always already mistakenly) taken to be gender. Elsa Barkley Brown points to this aspect when she states 'all women do not have the same gender,' arguing that although Black women may be recognized as both raced and gendered, 'one cannot write adequately about the lives of white women in the United States *in any context* without acknowledging the way in which race shaped their lives' (1997: 276, emphasis in original).[4] Going beyond the insistence that gender is something we *do*, these thinkers multiply and mobilize genders to the point that gender becomes impossible in the sense that no useful generalizations about it can be made, and thus the term becomes difficult to use at all.[5]

Power and politics

Feminism's liberal and radical struggles for political change have generally tried to unify women and their allies to win changes in the laws, policies, or practices of states, organizations, or social movements. Such political activities generally reflect a modern understanding of power as force and politics as struggle, although feminists may at the same time strive among themselves to enact power as empowerment and politics as cooperation.[6] These two contrary pulls generally go together because no matter how ecumenically feminists define 'our side' and how inclusively we act toward each other, there is still 'the other side' whose advocates have to be confronted and persuaded or defeated.

Feminisms operating under postmodern declensions do not so much dispute as dislocate the parameters of politics of struggle. Postmodern feminism works on two political levels: to insist that we acknowledge and respond to difference or otherness, to 'let difference be' by lightening the hand of order and diminishing demands for conceptual or historical mastery; and to locate the workings of power prior to and productive of the subjects said to wield it.[7] The 'space-clearing operations' (Appiah, 1997) of postmodern politics playfully or ruthlessly track down the remnants of modern faith in a unified subject or singular trajectory of change; while the modernistically inclined may or may not appreciate the political energy involved in clearing a space, they are apt to answer, 'fine, but what, exactly, are we supposed to *do* in this space once it has been opened?'

Knowledge and representation

Feminism with a modern face generally operates with a considerable debt to a stable distinction between appearance and reality. While some feminists talk about explaining the world by seeking valid and reliable knowledge to represent reality, and others talk more about understanding the world by uncovering the hidden or distorted meaning standing behind surface accounts, both approaches are dependent on a stable relation between language and the world that language apprehends.[8] Postmodern feminists, in contrast, problematize representation by seeing it as productive of reality claims rather than reflective of a prior grounds or foundation.[9]

Like most speakers for oppressed groups, feminists speaking with a modern inflection see a resource embedded in their subordination: being on the margins of the social order gives us a fuller and more complete view of the world, puts us 'in a better position to speak the truth' (Foucault, 2003: 53). The postmodern face of feminism problematizes claims to truth because knowledge, in this view, is the outcome of and has its very conditions of possibility in power relations. Knowledge here appears not so much as a truth but as a 'truth-weapon' (Foucault, 2003: 54) or a truth-effect. Practices of representation then become not transparent vehicles or even dense narratives but mobile fields of power within which meaning is constructed and clarity achieved through insistence.[10]

FEMINIST STANCES TOWARD METHODS OF INQUIRY

Feminist intellectual work ranges across modern and postmodern methods, methodologies, and epistemologies. This range of inquiry is not well captured by conventional distinctions between empirical and normative or quantitative and qualitative, since feminist inquiry is generally informed by political commitments exceeding these distinctions. Recognizing the difficulty of discussing feminist method, Sandra Harding (1987a; 1987b) teases out questions of method, methodology, and epistemology intertwined in both feminist and traditional research discourses. Working primarily within a modern frame of inquiry, Harding describes research methods as 'techniques for gathering evidence,' methodology as 'a theory and analysis of how research should proceed,' and epistemology as 'issues about an adequate theory of knowledge or justificatory strategy' (1987a: 2).

However, approaching research and methods from a postmodern position confounds the still-useful categories of method, methodology, and epistemology, and articulates available stances along another axis of differentiation. Recalling that *postmodern* can allude to the site from which to take the measure of the modern, a postmodern take on feminist research methods suggests a different set of distinctions among research practices, one based on what each is able to accomplish. We suggest three groupings of feminist research activities – explanation, understanding, and disruption – organized within categories that reflect the self-understanding of the participants as well as the achievements and limitations of each from the point of view of the others. These categories capture moments of method/methodology/epistemology clusters, rather than fully characterizing people or studies or arguments. Each category reflects a different expectation about the work that scholarship is intended to perform; each, when pursued exclusively, has built-in limitations; each puts useful pressure on the others. They are all 'empirical' in that they all identify data to be recorded, reported, and analyzed; the difference is in (a) what counts as data and (b) what one does with the data.

Approaches and expectations

The first category, 'explanation,' is familiar within conventional social scientific practices; it asks: 'how are X and Y related?' or 'what causes X?' This approach seeks to explain something, to identify patterns, to establish cause and effect relations, perhaps to predict future occurrences. Compelling explanations allow one to build models, to identify trends or patterns, and to claim clarity and/or objectivity for one's accounts. 'Explanation' is primarily rooted in a modern conception of scientific inquiry and knowledge production; it assumes a stable connection between words and things and then strives for the most accurate (or least inaccurate) available account.

The second category, 'understanding,' is an interpretive approach that also usually relies upon a stable relation between language and the world it conceives. 'Understanding' is a narrative inquiry; it asks, 'what does X mean?' This approach analyzes available interpretive possibilities, articulates contesting cultural contexts, and contrasts one interpretation with another. It does its work by pushing its categories (for example, class analysis, gender analysis, etc.) farther and farther into the world; it often takes an historical approach, looking at the production of contrasting understandings over time. This approach is good at contesting the prevailing stories with counter-stories, with creating alternative accounts of things. 'Understanding' is obliged to modernism in its attempt both to properly interpret appearances and to search for distortions of reality by those in power.

The third approach, 'disruption,' is a genealogical or postmodern approach; disruptive research approaches ask, 'why are we asking this question?' It is historical, working to denaturalize categories and question claims to knowledge by asking 'how does it come to be?' It tends to destabilize all meaning claims and is good at calling attention to the will to truth that inhabits inquiry. Disruptive strategies find, behind every set of appearances, another set of appearances; unlike modernism, there is no stable 'there,' it is appearances all the way down.

Limitations and strengths

Feminist inquiry benefits when the strengths of each approach are brought into a contentious and productive conversation with one another. Yet each is susceptible to reductionism, to being overly simplified.

Ruthlessly pursued, 'explanation' tends to be ahistorical, to avoid the more postmodern move of looking at the process of coming to meaning. It is good at highlighting important relationships between factors (often called 'variables'), and good at giving us useful stories about the material world, but its unexamined roots in modernism make it generally unaware of itself as a story. Yet the explanatory approach is not reducible to positivism, in that it can be employed with greater awareness of its own self-constitution.

Ruthlessly pursued, 'understanding' tends to assume, with modernism, that there is an order waiting to be found behind the misleading appearances that veil reality. The 'there' that is out there is complex, and requires careful interpretation, but it can be grasped through the proper stance of attunement, or unambiguous use of language, or a full historical accounting. However, it tends to neglect its own role in putting this order in place by the act of reaching for it. The reductionist version immunizes itself against surprises by framing its inquiries in ways that eliminate ideas or events that do not fit the dominant narrative. Yet 'understanding' is not reducible to the clearly modernist practices of universalizing or essentializing grand theory; it can provide an analytic frame while still making the more postmodern move of calling attention to the limits of that frame.

Ruthlessly pursued, 'disruption' makes it difficult to articulate political commitments because its debt to a postmodern stance means every value is subject to further deconstruction, every story to further unraveling. Any truth claim becomes problematic, so it is hard to distinguish between those one can embrace and those one rejects. The reductionist version of genealogy is frequently decried as relativism because it does not provide stable, more modernist grounds for choice. Yet by insisting on the limits and costs of even the most compelling stories, it resists its own will to power by offering a more chastened vision of alternatives.

Examples and epistemology

Feminist explanatory inquiry is exemplified in much work on political economy, women and politics, women and development, and other areas in which the end result requires the clarity necessary for generating a solution, resolution, or policy recommendation. Work by, for example, Roberta Spalter-Roth and Heidi Hartmann (1999), Ruth Dixon-Mueller (1991), and Christine Bose (1991) marshal facts as data from which to advance hypotheses, build models, and offer findings. Their techniques for gathering evidence (method) require identifying and collecting facts to serve as data upon which they employ a gender-driven analysis. The results of this analysis (methodology) will reveal the ways in which examining women as a group, or gender as a category, provides information that would otherwise escape notice. Their focus on explanation tends to foreground observation and reason while backgrounding epistemology. Implicitly, the theory of knowledge that impels this work is some version of the familiar correspondence theory of truth, in which accuracy of fit between words and things can be achieved by choosing words with care and cautiously defining terms.

For feminist interpretation (also sometimes referred to as hermeneutics), understandings are produced by engaging stories for the purposes of finding richer and fuller accounts of meaning. The techniques for gathering evidence (method) identify relevant sites of representation, including narratives, documents, or other texts, as data to be analyzed. The methodology entails reading those stories with meticulous attention to submerged details, exposing the arrangements of power that hide parts of the story, and uncovering more complete connotations. Such unveiling opens the possibility of different stories, new meanings, and altered arrangements of power. Much work in feminist ethnography, object relations theory, and standpoint theory, including that done by Nancy Hartsock (1983; 1990), Patricia Hill Collins (1991), Nancy Chodorow (1978), and Beth Roy (1998), operates largely within an interpretive frame. Epistemologically, interpretive work relies on exposing the ordered reality that stands behind misleading appearances, holding responsible the powerful interests that created those appearances, and advocating a different and better order.

Feminist disruptions are explicitly postmodern; they purposefully take their data from conflicting locations, recognize multiple meanings actively in play, and trace their consequences. Like interpretive understandings, genealogical disruptions look for data in practices of representation, including narratives, documents, and other symbolic sites; disruptive inquiries ask how we come to have these stories, what the limits are of intelligibility within stories, and what the effects are of their circulation. Disruptive approaches read against the grain to expose unarticulated dependencies and complicities among claims to meaning and to mark the limits and exclusions entailed in realms of intelligibility. Much writing by Joan Wallach Scott (1988; 1992), Judith Butler (1990; 1999; Butler and Scott, 1992), Donna Haraway (1985; 1988; Haraway and Goodeve, 2000), Wendy Brown (1995; 2003), Toni Morrison (1990), and Laura Hyun Yi Kang (2002) employs multifaceted deconstructive energies in making the familiar strange. Epistemologically, this approach elicits the capriciousness within any appearance of order, flagging the costs of grand narratives, the seduction of origin stories, and dangers in the will to power over truth.

CULTIVATING FEMINIST RELATIONS

While some feminist discussions continue to assert the priority of either modern or postmodern perspectives, more commonly, the value of each is acknowledged and some constructive, or at least livable, relation is sought between them. For example, Kathi Weeks urges feminists to get beyond 'the stagnation of our thinking' that accompanies a sterile paradigm debate between mutually incompatible positions (1998: 155). Gayatri Chakravorty Spivak calls for these contrasting energies to 'become persistent interruptions of each other' (1987: 249). Simply picking a 'winner' becomes untenable once the contributions of each are recognized as needed for feminist intellectual and political projects. Similarly, after sketching the ways in which modern and postmodern energies tug in opposing directions, any straightforward synthesis of the ideas has been rendered unworkable; further, the idea of a synthesis of competing views into a larger and coherent whole is itself deeply implicated in modern perspectives and quite inhospitable to the deliberate unfinishedness of postmodern thinking.

There is both a theoretical richness and a pragmatic usefulness in approaching these debates not for the purpose of declaring one side true or virtuous while the other is false or vicious, but rather to ask what sorts of questions each approach most adequately explores and what kinds of politics each one can help us to accomplish.[11] Given that feminists need both kinds of thinking to energize our work, and that inevitable frictions are produced by their conversations, what is a feminist to do? Several responses to this dilemma have been offered.

Strategic essentialism

One of the first feminist thinkers to usefully tackle the tension between the cherished incompatibilities of postmodern and modern (in her case, Marxist) thinking is Gayatri Chakravorty Spivak (with Ellen Rooney, 1997). Luce Irigaray's earlier poetic feminist explorations of mimesis, while sometimes read as naturalizing women, anticipate strategic essentialism by using the tool of unfaithful replication to combat fixed ideas. Spivak's term 'strategic essentialism' proposes a way into, rather than a way out of, these feminist dilemmas. To use essential understandings strategically, Spivak argues, is to employ an 'embattled concept-metaphor' needed in feminist struggles despite the dangers it poses (1997: 358). 'The strategic use of an essence as a mobilizing slogan or master word like *woman* or *worker* or the name of a nation is, ideally, self-conscious for all mobilized. This is the impossible risk of a lasting strategy' (1997: 358). Noting that 'a strategy is not a theory,' Spivak encourages us to hold onto the deconstructive energies made available by our theories to problematize the stabilizing moves that strategy requires. Strategic essentialism is a tension-filled space flagging 'the dangerousness of something one cannot not use' (1997: 359).

Rooney, in her conversation with Spivak, notes that 'it remains difficult to engage in feminist analysis and politics if not "as a woman"'(1997: 357). The 'essentialism' in the concept allows us 'to speak not simply as feminists but as women, not least against women whose political work is elsewhere' (1997: 357). The 'strategy' preceding and guiding the essentialism locates its political heart, its dream, not in a 'formal resolution of the discontinuity between women and feminisms' (1997: 357) but in needed political energy to keep struggles, including struggles among women, animated and engaged.

In her 1999 Preface to *Gender Trouble*, Butler similarly explores 'the important strategic use' of claims to universality; such claims 'can be proleptic and performative, conjuring a reality that does not yet exist, and holding out the possibility for a convergence of cultural horizons that have not yet met' (pp. xvii–xviii). Both Spivak (with Rooney, 1997) and Butler (1999) cherish the utopian hopes sketched by 'a future-oriented labor of cultural translation' (p. xviii) in which possibilities are kept alive because we need them.

Irony and counterpoint

Haraway (1985; Haraway and Goodeve, 2000) and others have brought irony to the table as an art and technique for holding together ideas that are both necessary and incompatible. 'Irony,' Haraway argues, 'is about contradictions that do not resolve into larger wholes, even dialectically, about the tension of holding incompatible things together because both or all are necessary and true. Irony is about humor and serious play' (1985: 65). The arts of irony enable feminism's justice projects by allowing us to act politically without ignoring the complexity of competing ideas or pretending that contradictions have been resolved into a consistent program.[12] Irony facilitates the juggling acts needed for coalition politics, in which partial convergences of agendas replace stable fusions of identity or permanent political homes.[13]

Brown's argument for counterpoint, 'a deliberate practice of multiplicity that exceeds simple opposition and does not carry the mythological or methodological valence of dialectics or contradiction' (2003: 367), is, despite her disclaimer, similar to irony as sketched above.[14] The musical juxtaposition of contrasting elements can 'bring out the complexity that cannot emerge through a monolithic or single melody' (2003: 367). Counterpoint, like irony, recruits modern and postmodern energies to put pressure on one another, 'holding together the inherent slide of gender on the one hand and the powers comprising regimes of male dominance on the other' (2003: 367). Counterpoint and irony become tactics to multiply fields of meaning and to keep contrary impulses in play so they can enrich and contest one another.

Local use of global theory

Another approach to these tensions calls on the theoretical purchase offered by universalist or global understandings married to the situated complexities of local applications and investments. Haraway 'insists on situatedness, where location is itself a complex construction as well as inheritance' (2000: 160). Both politics and knowledge are implicated in this move toward the local: 'objectivity,' Haraway argues, 'is always a local achievement' (2000: 161). Foucault argued that postmodern thinkers can still call on the modern: while he objected to the 'inhibiting effect specific to totalitarian theories, or at least – what I mean is – all-encompassing and global theories' he nonetheless found in them 'tools that can be used at the local level' (2003: 6). The use of such tools locally has meant we have 'cut up, rip[ped] up, torn to shreds, turned inside out, displaced, caricatured, dramatized, theatricalized' the 'theoretical unity of their discourse' (2003: 6). Such appreciative assaults on the coherence of the modern in the service of local critique suggest 'a sort of autonomous and noncentralized theoretical production, or in other words a theoretical production that does not need a visa from some common regime to establish its validity' (2003: 6).

In her work on transnational women's movements, Amrita Basu (2003) seems to take Foucault's advice. Basu suggests it may be time to rethink the bumper sticker 'Think Globally, Act Locally,' and replace it with 'Think Locally, Act Globally' (2003: 68). Basu's concerns are generated by local receptions of transnational feminist campaigns:

> Women's groups most enthusiastically have supported transnational campaigns against sexual violence in countries where the state is repressive or indifferent and

women's movements are weak. Conversely, transnationalism has provoked more distrust in places where women's movements have emerged, grown, and defined themselves independently of Western feminism. (2003: 74)

Grappling with the 'tearing up' and 'turning inside out' of local women's movements in relation to transnational feminist networks, she calls for continued conversations: 'global visions need to be further infused with local realities, while appreciating that the local is not merely local, but infused with global influences' (2003: 76).

Each of these engagements with the intersections of modern and postmodern feminist thinking offers resources for continuing to think/act the disruptions of the postmodern in connection with the unities of the modern. Future directions for feminist thinking are likely to build upon these efforts to stay open to contradictory meanings, to remain honest about enduring frictions, and to keep moving toward feminist political goals.

NOTES

1 For a discussion that grapples with this tension in the feminist context of 'standpoint theory' and 'situated knowledges' see Ingrid Bartsch, Carolyn DiPalma, and Laura Sells (2001: 129–139).

2 See, for example, Audre Lorde (1984).

3 See, for example, Norma Alarcon (1997), Kang (2002), and Trinh Minh-ha (1989).

4 Another example: David Eng (2001).

5 Our thanks to Kathleen Earle for her help in thinking through this literature.

6 For further elaboration of differences between power and empowerment, see Kathy Ferguson (1996); and, for another perspective, Peggy Chinn (2001).

7 For exploration of the ontological backdrop and political fall-out of the demand for mastery, see William Connolly (1988).

8 See, for example, Catharine MacKinnon's (1987) analysis of the solid gender grounding of the state and Brown's critique (1995).

9 See Scott's (1992) essay, 'Experience,' for a key example; Scott articulates the concept of 'women's experience,' which is a starting point for much modern feminist thinking, as itself an outcome of prior discursive practices. See also Luce Irigaray's (1985a; 1985b) inquiry into the underrepresented forms of the feminine as a critique of the structures of representation.

10 Scott's (1988) presentation of the testimony in the Sears case demonstrates some of the difficulties/impossibilities of communication between these positions. See also: Geoffrey Bowker and Susan Leigh Star's (1999) discussion of communities of practice and boundary infrastructures.

11 Our invitation could itself be called a postmodern approach to the modern/postmodern relation in that it shifts attention away from 'is it true?' and toward 'what can it do?' However, this move, while attractive, invites us into an infinite regress that we decline for political reasons.

12 For further discussion see Kathy Ferguson (1993: 27–35, 178–183).

13 See Bernice Johnson Reagon (1983).

14 Brown (1997) contrasts the simultaneity of many voices in gumbo ya ya and jazz with the singularity of classical music, arguing for recognizing the creative productivity active in non-linear relationships.

REFERENCES

Alarcon, Norma (1997). 'The Theoretical Subject(s) of *This Bridge Called My Back* and Anglo-American Feminism,' in Linda Nicholson (ed.), *The Second Wave: A Reader in Feminist Theory*. New York: Routledge. pp. 288–99.

Andermahr, Sonya, Terry Lovell, and Carol Wolkowitz (eds) (2000). *A Glossary of Feminist Theory*. New York: Oxford.

Appiah, Kwame Anthony (1997). 'Is the "Post" in "Postcolonial" the "Post" in "Postmodern"?', in Anne McClintock, Aamir Mufti, and Ella Shohat (eds), *Dangerous Liaisons: Gender, Nation and Postcolonial Perspectives*. Minneapolis: University of Minnesota Press. pp. 420–444.

Bartsch, Ingrid, Carolyn DiPalma, and Laura Sells (2001). 'Witnessing the Postmodern Jeremiad: (Mis)Understanding Donna Haraway's Method of Inquiry,' *Configurations: A Journal of Literature, Science, and Technology* 9(1): 127–64.

Basu, Amrita (2003). 'Globalization of the Local/Localization of the Global: Mapping Transnational Women's Movements,' in Carole R. McCann and Seung-Kyung Kim (eds), *Feminist Theory Reader: Local and Global Perspectives*. New York: Routledge. pp. 68–77.

Benhabib, Seyla (1992). *Situating the Self: Gender, Community and Postmodernism in Contemporary Ethics*. Cambridge: Polity.

Bose, Christine (1991). 'Household Resources and Women's Work: Factors Affecting Gainful Employment at the Turn of the Century,' in Mary Margaret Fonow and Judith A. Cook (eds), *Beyond Methodology: Feminist Scholarship as Lived Research*. Bloomington: Indiana University Press. pp. 197–225.

Bowker, Geoffrey C. and Susan Leigh Star (1999). *Sorting Things Out: Classification and Its Consequences*. Cambridge, MA: MIT Press.

Brown, Elsa Barkley (1997). '"What Has Happened Here?" The Politics of Difference in Women's History and Feminist Politics,' in Linda Nicholson (ed.), *The Second Wave: A Reader in Feminist Theory*. New York: Routledge. pp. 272–287.

Brown, Wendy (1995). *States of Injury: Power and Freedom in Late Modernity*. Princeton, NJ: Princeton University Press.

Brown, Wendy (2003). 'Gender in Counterpoint,' *Feminist Theory*, 4(3): 365–368.

Butler, Judith (1990). *Gender Trouble: Feminism and the Subversion of Identity* (10th anniversary edition, 1999). New York: Routledge.

Butler, Judith and Joan Wallach Scott (eds) (1992). *Feminists Theorize the Political*. New York: Routledge.

Cahoone, Lawrence (ed.) (1996). 'Introduction,' in *From Modernism to Postmodernism: An Anthology*. Cambridge, MA: Blackwell.

Chinn, Peggy L (2001). *Peace and Power: Building Communities for the Future*. (5th edition). Boston, MA: Jones and Bartlett.

Chodorow, Nancy (1978). *The Reproduction of Mothering*. Berkeley: University of California Press.

Collins, Patricia Hill (1991). 'Learning from the Outsider Within: The Sociological Significance of Black Feminist Thought,' in Mary M. Fonow and Judith A. Cook (eds), *Beyond Methodology: Feminist Scholarship as Lived Research*. Bloomington: Indiana University Press. pp. 35–59.

Connolly, William (1988). *Political Theory and Modernity*. New York: Basil Blackwell.

Davis, Natalie Zemon and Arlette Farge (eds) (1993). *A History of Women: Renaissance and Enlightenment Paradoxes*. Cambridge, MA: Harvard University Press.

Dixon-Mueller, Ruth (1991). 'Women in Agriculture: Counting the Labor Force in Developing Countries,' in Mary M. Fonow and Judith A. Cook (eds), *Beyond Methodology: Feminist Scholarship as Lived Research*. Bloomington: Indiana University Press. pp. 226–247.

Eng, David (2001). *Racial Castration: Managing Masculinity in Asian America*. Raleigh, NC: Duke University Press.

Enloe, Cynthia (2000). *Maneuvers: The International Politics of Militarizing Women's Lives*. Berkeley: University of California Press.

Enloe, Cynthia (2001). *Bananas, Beaches and Bases* (updated edition). Berkeley: University of California Press.

Fausto-Sterling, Ann (2000). *Sexing the Body: Gender Politics and the Construction of Sexuality*. New York: Basic Books.

Ferguson, Kathy E. (1993). *The Man Question: Visions of Subjectivity in Feminist Theory*. Berkeley: University of California Press.

Ferguson, Kathy E. (1996). 'Feminist Thinking on Women and Power,' *Asian Women* 2(Spring): 1–16.

Flax, Jane (1987). 'Re-membering the Selves: Is the Repressed Gendered?', *Michigan Quarterly Review* 26(1): 92–110.

Fonow, Mary M. and Judith A. Cook (eds) (1991). *Beyond Methodology: Feminist Scholarship as Lived Research*. Bloomington: Indiana University Press.

Foucault, Michel (1980). *An Introduction,* Vol. 1 of *The History of Sexuality* (trans. Robert Herley). New York: Random House.

Foucault, Michel (2003). *Society Must Be Defended* (trans David Macey, (ed.), Mauro Bertani and Allessandro Fontana). New York: Picador.

Fuss, Diana (1990). *Essentially Speaking: Feminism, Nature and Difference*. New York: Routledge.

Gilligan, Carol (1982). *In A Different Voice*. Cambridge, MA: Harvard University Press.

Groden, Michael, and Martin Kreiswirth (eds) (1994). *The Johns Hopkins Guide to Literary Theory and Criticism*. Baltimore, MD: Johns Hopkins University Press.

Haraway, Donna (1985). 'A Manifesto for Cyborgs: Science, Technology, and Socialist Feminism in the 1980s,' *Socialist Review* 15(March–April): 65–107.

Haraway, Donna (1988). 'Situated Knowledges: The Science Question in Feminism and the Privilege of Partial Perspectives,' *Feminist Studies* 14(Fall): 575–599.

Haraway, Donna and Thyrza Nichols Goodeve (2000). *How Like a Leaf (an interview with Thyrza Nichols Goodeve)*. New York: Routledge, 2000.

Harding, Sandra (1987a). 'Is There a Feminist Method,' in Sandra Harding (ed.), *Feminism and Methodology*. Bloomington: Indiana University Press. pp. 1–15.

Harding, Sandra (ed.) (1987b). *Feminism and Methodology*. Bloomington: Indiana University Press.

Hartsock, Nancy C. M. (1983). *Money, Sex, and Power: Toward a Feminist Historical Materialism*. New York: Longman.

Hartsock, Nancy C. M. (1990). 'Foucault on Power: A Theory for Women?', in Linda Nicholson (ed.), *Feminism/Postmodernism*. New York: Routledge. pp. 157–175.

Harvey, David (1990). *The Condition of Postmodernity: An Enquiry into the Origins of Cultural Change*. Cambridge, MA: Blackwell.

Humm, Maggie (1995). *The Dictionary of Feminist Theory* (2nd edition). Columbus, OH: Ohio State University.

Irigaray, Luce (1985a). *Speculum of the Other Woman* (trans. Gillian C. Gill). Ithaca, NY: Cornell University Press.

Irigaray, Luce (1985b). *This Sex Which Is Not One* (trans. Catherine Porter and Carolyn Burke). Ithaca, NY: Cornell University Press.

Kang, Laura Hyun Yi (2002). *Compositional Subjects: Enfiguring Asian-American Women*. Durham, NC: Duke University Press.

Kelly-Gadol, Joan (1977). 'Did Women Have a Renaissance?', in Renate Bridenthal and Claudia Koonz (eds), *Becoming Visible: Women in European History*. Boston, MA: Houghton Mifflin. pp. 137–164.

Kessler, Suzanne J. (2000). *Lessons from the Intersexed*. New Brunswick, NJ: Rutgers University Press.

Laqueur, Thomas (1990). *Making Sex: Body and Gender from the Greeks to Freud*. Cambridge, MA: Harvard University Press.

Lorber, Judith (1993). 'Believing is Seeing: Biology as Ideology,' *Gender & Society* 7: 568–581.

Lorde, Audre (1984). 'Age, Race, Class, and Sex: Women Redefining Difference,' in *Sister Outsider: Essays and Speeches*. Trumansburg, NY: Crossing Press. pp. 114–123.

Lyotard, Jean-François (1979). *The Postmodern Condition*. Minneapolis: University of Minnesota Press.

MacKinnon, Catharine A. (1987). *Feminism Unmodified: Discourses of Life and Law*. Cambridge, MA: Harvard University Press.

McCann, Carole R. and Seung-Kyung Kim (eds) (2003). *Feminist Theory Reader: Local and Global Perspectives*. New York: Routledge.

Morrison, Toni (1990). *Playing in the Dark: Whiteness and the Literary Imagination*. New York: Vintage Books.

Nicholson, Linda (1990a). 'Introduction,' in Linda Nicholson (ed.), *Feminism/Postmodernism*. New York: Routledge. pp. 1–16.

Nicholson, Linda (ed.) (1990b). *Feminism/Postmodernism*. New York: Routledge.

Nicholson, Linda (ed.) (1997). *The Second Wave: A Reader in Feminist Theory*. New York: Routledge.

Noble, David (1993). *A World Without Women: The Christian Clerical Culture of Western Science*. New York: Alfred A. Knopf.

Reagon, Bernice Johnson (1983). 'Coalition Politics: Turning the Century,' in Barbara Smith (ed.), *Home Girls: A Black Feminist Anthology*. New York: Kitchen Table: Women of Color Press. pp. 356–368.

Riley, Denise (1988). *Am I that Name? Feminism and the Category of 'Women' in History*. Minneapolis: University of Minnesota Press.

Roy, Beth (1998). 'Goody Two-Shoes and the Hell-Raisers: Women's Activism, Women's Reputations in Little Rock,' in Kathleen M. Blee (ed.), *No Middle Ground: Women and Radical Protest*. New York: New York University Press. pp. 96–131.

Rubin, Gayle (1997). 'Traffic in Women: Notes on the "Political Economy" of Sex,' in Linda Nicholson (ed.), *The Second Wave: A Reader in Feminist Theory*. New York: Routledge. pp. 27–62.

Scott, Joan Wallach (1988). 'Deconstructing Equality-Versus-Difference: Or, The Uses of Poststructuralist Theory for Feminism,' *Feminist Studies* 14(1): 33–50.

Scott, Joan Wallach (1992). 'Experience,' in Judith Butler and Joan Wallach Scott (eds), *Feminists Theorize the Political*. New York: Routledge. pp. 22–40.

Spalter-Roth, Roberta and Heidi Hartmann (1999). 'Small Happiness: The Feminist Struggle to Integrate Social Research with Social Activism,' in Sharlene Hesse-Biber, Christina Gilmartin, and Robin Lydenberg (eds), *Feminist Approaches to Theory and Methodology: An Interdisciplinary Reader*. New York: Oxford University Press. pp. 333–347.

Spivak, Gayatri Chakravorty (1987). *In Other Worlds: Essays in Cultural Politics*. New York: Methuen.

Spivak, Gayatri Chakravorty, with Ellen Rooney (1997). '"In a Word": Interview,' in Linda Nicholson (ed.), *The Second Wave: A Reader in Feminist Theory*. New York: Routledge. pp. 356–378.

Trinh, T. Minh-ha (1989). *Woman, Native, Other*. Bloomington: Indiana University Press.

Weeks, Kathi (1998). *Constituting Feminist Subjects*. Ithaca, NY: Cornell University Press.

8

Women Knowing/Knowing Women
Critical–Creative Interventions in the Politics of Knowledge

Lorraine Code

Concentrating on interconnections between gender and epistemology, particularly in the Anglo-American world since the beginning of second-wave feminism, this chapter traces a history of departures from a view of epistemology as an a priori normative inquiry which could fulfill its mandate only by producing apolitical, impersonal, experience-remote analyses of necessary and sufficient conditions for knowledge 'in general.' Feminist epistemologists have demonstrated how a gender-sensitive, avowedly political inquiry can produce knowledge good of its kind and epistemic standards stringent enough to enable knowers to participate intelligently in the world, both physical and human. Moving through the early taxonomy of feminist empiricism, standpoint theory, and postmodernism to the multiple directions feminist epistemology has subsequently taken, the chapter concludes by outlining the promise of new conceptual frameworks generated out of such modes of inquiry as agential realism, situated knowledges, naturalized epistemology, ecological thinking, and the complex questions posed by epistemologies of ignorance.

INTRODUCTION

The gender question in epistemology arises urgently, if often tacitly, with respect to how women know and are known, who claims to know them and why, what conception of 'the knowing subject' informs and inflects the operative conception of knowledge through which claims by and about women are adjudicated, and how knowledge is situated, formally and morally–politically. Although in mainstream Anglo-American philosophy the sex/gender of the knower is accorded no epistemological significance, feminists have shown how the gender question is always implicated, even if not explicitly, with hierarchies of power and privilege that structure social orders according to asymmetrical attributions of credibility, cognitive authority, and expertise; hierarchies whose effects in patriarchal societies are to consign women (and other Others) to positions of the unknown, unknowing, and unknowable.

Analyzing the state of play in epistemology in the early twenty-first century, Rae Langton (2000) shows how feminist inquiry has revealed that in matters of knowledge, women get left out, or get hurt. Normative, regulative conceptions of what counts as knowledge and who is a legitimate knower generate a social imaginary where there is no legitimate space for women to claim cognitive authority, credibility, or acknowledgement. The universal pretensions of the story of knowledge told by and about men mask its partiality in both senses of the word, thus rendering women's lives invisible. Nor is this erasure merely a sin of omission to be expiated by 'letting women in': received conceptions of knowledge hurt women, for the ideal objectivity at their center also objectifies women. Langton writes, 'Objectification is a process of projection supplemented by force, whose result is that women are made subordinate…women really come to have at least some of the qualities that are projected onto them' (2000: 140). Her conclusion that ignorance masquerading as knowledge of women's lives, experiences, and situations harms women amounts, emblematically, to a diagnosis of the effects of the *androcentricity* feminists have exposed at the core of mainstream epistemology ever since they began deconstructing its gender-neutral posture.

Epistemology's professed gender-neutrality is continuous with its commitment to determining a priori, necessary, and sufficient conditions for 'knowledge in general' and refuting skepticism, thus sustaining claims to apolitical universality. Knowledge worthy of the name is conceived as a rational, intellectual product whose validity holds across 'contingent' details of gender, racial and ethnic identity, class, age, sexual orientation, and the particularities of affect, situation, and materiality. Hence the very idea of a *feminist* epistemology was long dismissed as oxymoronic and outrageous. In contrast to explicitly gender-focused feminist inquiry in moral and political philosophy which developed into an impressive body of critical–constructive inquiry in the 1960s and 1970s, gender issues in epistemology were late additions to the feminist agenda. Suggestions that gendered interventions could be required in epistemology, philosophy of science, and even logic were dismissed as preposterous manifestations of ideological excess. Knowledge, science, and logic, by definition, stood secure as guardians of objectivity and truth, protected from the vagaries of gender politics. To preserve its objective, impartial detachment, orthodox epistemology eschewed any idea of taking subjectivity into account.[1]

UNSETTLING THE ASSUMPTIONS

In the early 1980s, Lorraine Code's article 'Is the Sex of the Knower Epistemologically Significant?' (1981), Sandra Harding and Merrill Hintikka's landmark text *Discovering Reality: Feminist Perspectives on Epistemology, Metaphysics, Methodology, and Philosophy of Science* (1983), and Alison Jaggar's *Feminist Politics and Human Nature* with its chapter on epistemology (1983) began to unsettle these sedimented assumptions. Feminists moved the question 'whose knowledge are we talking about?' to a central place in epistemology, where it interrogated the patterns of authority and expertise, incredulity, acknowledgement, and advocacy that enable or constrain epistemic agency in Western societies. Feminist epistemologists have analyzed women's circumscribed access to cognitive authority, shown how the credibility accorded to testimony varies with the gender of the testifier and the social standing of those prepared to confer or withhold acknowledgement, and demonstrated how experiential evidence is devalued, in contrast to scientifically credentialed, putatively objective knowledge, abstracted from people's desires, circumstances, and social–political positioning.

Since the early 1980s, feminist epistemologists have produced work so meticulous, sophisticated, and varied as to disrupt most of the fundamental presuppositions of traditional theories of knowledge, expanding the scope of critical investigation well beyond their formal constraints. Having established the epistemological significance of the sex of the knower, they have moved to expose the androcentricity of the epistemological project in its received forms. Androcentricity – the principal, overarching charge – implies deriving from and being relevant principally to men's experiences. Without, implausibly, charging men 'in general' with conspiring to ensure the hegemony of 'their' knowledge while suppressing 'women's ways of knowing', feminists have exposed a remarkable congruence between evolving ideals and values of ideal (i.e., White, educated, propertied, heterosexual) masculinity throughout Western cultural, philosophical, and social history since pre-Socratic times, and values constitutive of the highest forms of rationality and most authoritative forms of knowledge (Bordo, 1987; Keller, 1985; Lloyd, 1984).[2] The psychosocial norms affluent White male children are nurtured to embody are the very ones to equip them for a life of detached, objective, putatively knowledgeable control in a public world of work and deliberation. Regulative epistemological ideals – even such apparently incontestable ideals as objectivity, autonomy, and impartiality – affirm the value of these traits. The androcentricity of orthodox theories of knowledge derives from these ideals, distilled from abstract conceptions of the experiences of this group of privileged men. But orthodox epistemologies are not generically man-made, nor have all men participated equally in their making. Thus, androcentricity alone is too crude a charge, for theories of knowledge perpetuate power–privilege asymmetries as much according to interconnected racial, class, religious, ethnic, age, physical ability, and other differentials as to any univocal sex/gender system. Hence, a viable successor epistemology must simultaneously address diverse subjectivities and embodied positionings, and pose critical questions about knowledge 'in general'. Indeed, in feminist and other post-colonial critiques, the very idea of 'knowledge in general' is drained of content.

Post-positivist theories of knowledge have, nonetheless, represented themselves as apolitical on principle. Working with formal conceptions of knowledge, remote from the experiences, practices, and situations of 'real knowers' (the phrase is Alcoff's, 1996) of any gender, they have maintained a dispassionate distance from the knowledge-producing activities they purport to explain and adjudicate. This disinterested stance promises a maximally objective approach, protected from vested interest, subjective idiosyncrasy, and specificities of ideology, circumstance, and place. Unsurprisingly, such a stance offers real, embodied, situated knowers minimal guidance for understanding, evaluating, negotiating, and interpreting how the diverse, quotidian effects of established knowledge or the complexities of ordinary, or specialized, epistemic negotiations and quandaries shape their everyday lives. Orthodox epistemology presupposes a standardized knower who is everyone and no one (yet whose experiences and assumptions are strikingly congruent with those of privileged White men), and abstract, formal models of knowledge that do not travel well into the situations and problems where real people need to know. Yet while claiming to transcend the everyday, epistemology is neither self-contained within philosophy nor isolated from people's lives. In their trickle-down effects in institutions of knowledge production and secular settings, theories of knowledge – and the knowledge they legitimate, the knowers to whom they accord epistemic authority, and the exclusions they enact – are shaped by and shape a dominant social–political imaginary of mastery and control. Thus, they participate in the structural ordering of societies and communities according to uneven distributions of authority and expertise, power and privilege.

The epistemologies of modernity, which evolved from the intellectual achievements of the Enlightenment with a later infusion of positivist–empiricist principles, coalesce around ideals of objectivity and value-neutrality, where objectivity requires a detached, neutral approach to subject matters existing in publicly observable spaces, separated from knowers/observers and making no claims on them. Value-neutrality elaborates this detachment: bona fide knowers have no vested interest in the objects of knowledge; no reason to seek knowledge other than the pursuit of 'pure' inquiry. These ideals are best suited to regulate the knowledge-making of people so well situated, materially and otherwise, as to believe in the possibility of a 'view from nowhere' (Nagel, 1986) – of performing what Donna Haraway (1991: 189) calls 'the god-trick' – thereby escaping the constraints of location within specific bodies, the messiness of material circumstances, the vagaries of affect, and the responsibilities of sociality. In affluent societies, such beliefs are possible mainly for White, able-bodied, educated, men who are neither too young nor too old, and whose wives take charge of everyday encumbrances: hence the androcentricity and the racial, cultural, historical, class, and other 'centricities' of Anglo-American epistemology.

Ideal knowers are neutral spectators, and objects of knowledge are separate from them, inert items which yield observationally verifiable knowledge. Each knower is separately accountable to the evidence, while the assumption is that *his* knowledge is replicable by anyone in identical circumstances. Knowers are substitutable for one another: each can act as a 'surrogate knower,' can put himself in anyone else's place and know just what he would know (La Caze, 2002; Scheman, 1991: 181). Objectivity and value-neutrality presuppose a homogeneous 'human nature,' separately realized in each self-sufficient knower. In the name of autonomy, they discredit communal deliberations in which knowledge is negotiated and established, and erase connections between knowledge and power. The implication is that if knowers cannot see 'from nowhere,' from an observation position that could be anywhere and everywhere, they cannot produce reliable knowledge. Resistance to deviating from a 'normal' (meaning male-derived) medical model in studying women's symptoms as they experience and report them is but one pertinent example. It exposes a conviction that 'special interest groups' cannot be objective; their experiences and circumstances cannot yield knowledge. So long as women – or Blacks, gays, indigenous people, the working classes, the disabled, the elderly – are thus designated, their concerns will not figure on epistemological or political agendas with those of the dominant. Their lives will not count as worth knowing nor the injustices in their situations worth addressing.

For these epistemologies, knowledge enables its possessors to predict, manipulate, and control their situations, both animate and inanimate, both human and more-than-human. Where the fact/value distinction regulates inquiry, the belief prevails that because value judgments (e.g., 'sexual harassment is humiliating,' 'abortion is wrong') cannot be verified empirically; they reduce to expressions of *feeling*, which must be prevented from distorting 'the facts.' Research cannot legitimately be inspired, governed, or justified by such values as feminist, anti-racist, or gay and lesbian advocacy commitments. These prohibitions sustain the 'myth of the neutral man,' presumed capable of representing everyone's interests objectively, and of knowing women and other Others better than they know themselves. By contrast, women and other Others produce only partial, subjectively interested knowledge. Within this conceptual frame, epistemological projects perpetuate assumptions about what counts as knowledge and whose knowledge merits acknowledgement, thereby confirming the very presuppositions around which their theories of knowledge are constructed.

In what follows I show, first in some readings of the history of philosophy and then of the gender-saturated character of scientific ideals, methods, and practice, how deconstructing the conceptual underpinnings of the ideals of reason, knowledge, and objectivity exposes their androcentricity. From the historical discussion, I proceed to delineate the contours of an early philosophy-of-science-derived taxonomy for feminist epistemologies, before explaining how feminists have ceased to work strictly within its categories.

FEMINIST INTERVENTIONS

With reference to the regulative concepts and character ideals that have shaped the dominant epistemic imaginary, feminist analyses of epistemological androcentricity owe a significant debt to three theorists who, in the 1980s, exposed the historical and cultural specificity of such putatively perennial ideals as reason and rationality, objectivity, and knowledge itself. Genevieve Lloyd's *The Man of Reason* (1984), Evelyn Fox Keller's *Reflections on Gender and Science* (1985), and Susan Bordo's *The Flight to Objectivity* (1987) created conceptual possibilities literally unimaginable in Anglo-American philosophy before these analyses appeared in print.

In a meticulous rereading of canonical texts of Western philosophy from the pre-Socratics to Simone de Beauvoir, Lloyd discerns a striking coincidence, through historical variations, between definitions, symbolisms, and ideals of masculinity and of Reason. Reason is not something people simply come across in the world. It is symbolically, metaphorically constituted all the way down: its constitution in association with ideal masculinity demarcates a rational domain inaccessible, or accessible only with difficulty, to people whose traits, possibilities, and attributes do not coincide with those of ideal White masculinity. The conceptual–symbolic dichotomies such alignments generate – mind/body, reason/emotion, objective/subjective, abstract/concrete are typical samples – align descriptively and evaluatively with a male/female dichotomy to underwrite the symbolism that represents masculinity as a regulative character ideal, defined in stark contrast to and repudiation of 'the feminine.' Universally valid knowledge is claimed as a product of rational endeavor, uncontaminated by opinion, emotion, or particularity, which are associated with (stereotypical) femininity. Rational knowledge, as Langton (2000) suggests, excludes women and thereby hurts them.

Keller's and Bordo's 1980s analyses are more psycho-social than symbolic, yet their engagement with the gendered conceptual apparatus of Western philosophy is continuous with Lloyd's. For Bordo, Cartesian objectivism derives from a seventeenth-century 'flight from the feminine,' testifying to a conviction that *the* epistemological task, both practical and theoretical, was to tame the chaos of 'the female universe' (see also Bordo, 1999). Only from a stance of self-controlled objectivity conceptualized as *masculine*, and removed from the particularities of time, place, idiosyncrasy, embodiment, and a fortiori from the object itself, could a knower achieve this project. Indebted to object-relations theory, Bordo reads the requirements of objectivism as strategies to dispel a pervasive (masculine) anxiety produced by separation from the mother and, derivatively, from 'reality.'

For Keller, too, conceptions of rationality, objectivity, and a will to dominate nature inform an ideal of masculinity and contribute to institutionalizing a 'normal science' adapted to the traits of (male) practitioners. Her respect for scientific achievements and methods is palpable; yet she too discerns alignments between dominant conceptions of reason, masculinity, knowledge, and scientific practice, as clearly in the philosophy of Plato and Bacon as in the exclusions effected by twentieth-century science. In an equivalently path-breaking text for feminist inquiry, Keller reads the scientific establishment's failure to accord timely recognition to geneticist Barbara McClintock (who ultimately was awarded a Nobel Prize) as occasioned by McClintock's divergent (from the masculine norm) scientific style (Keller, 1983). These works count among the texts – and producers of the contexts – which, at a conceptual level, explicitly or implicitly made feminist epistemology possible.

Cognizant of a range of conceptual possibilities generated out of these analyses, feminists have worked within and against received epistemologies, drawing on those of their resources that withstand critical scrutiny while contesting their exclusionary, oppressive, and harmful effects. Feminist epistemology requires more radical transformations than the old 'add women and stir' adage can offer. Few epistemologists seek to achieve feminist ends simply by introducing women into the population of accredited knowers and adding 'women's issues' to the subject matter of epistemology, leaving sedimented conceptions of reason and knowledge unchallenged. Yet most resist positing essentialized 'women's ways of knowing' which run parallel to, but do not disturb, the entrenched epistemic imaginary.[3] No longer constructing idealized accounts of what abstract knowers should do, feminists ground normative conclusions in the demands faced by real, embodied, specifically located knowers endeavoring to construct knowledge that can serve people well in real-world (and/or real scientific/social scientific) circumstances.

Because of physical science's eminence in the Western world as the declared site of the best, most sophisticated knowledge humankind has achieved, with methods more reliable than any hitherto known, it is no surprise that the formative analyses of gender and epistemology came from philosophy of science. Yet the scope of feminist epistemology is broader than and different from that of feminist philosophy of science, although commitments to common causes allow for innovative cross-fertilizations.

Among the most influential works of the 1980s was Sandra Harding's *The Science Question in Feminism*. Starting from philosophy of science, Harding (1986; 1993) proposed a taxonomy for differentiating among feminist approaches to questions of knowledge and science. She discerned three strands of inquiry, labeling them feminist empiricism, feminist standpoint theory, and feminist postmodernism. The ordering marked degrees of radicality, with empiricism remaining closest to traditional theories of scientific knowledge and postmodernism departing most sharply from them, challenging them at their roots. This taxonomy has been superseded as feminists have realized that neither science projects nor epistemologies of everyday life can be summed up so neatly and as the postmodern import of the entire project has been variously conceived. Yet because these categories characterized so much critical debate in the late 1980s and the 1990s, I begin with a sketch of empiricism and standpoint theory, separately and in their overlapping commitments, and continue by showing how postmodernism in its multiple modalities both differs from and concurs with them. The point to remember, however, is that many feminist and post-colonial knowledge projects do not fit neatly into these categories, separately or combined.

Despite differences in their political stances and points of origin, standpoint and empiricist feminism do not diverge from one another as sharply as their distinct titles suggest. Empiricists for whom strong objectivity is a regulative ideal are closer to standpoint theorists than the seemingly stark divisions between the categories suggest, and standpoint theorists are often realists in ways close to those that mark empiricist projects. Moreover, all three feminist epistemologies are postmodern to varying degrees in rejecting such fundamental tenets of the Enlightenment project as belief in a universal, homogeneous human nature, in universal conceptions of knowledge, reason, and morality, and in the need to transcend the specificities of lives and situations.

FEMINIST EMPIRICISM

Consistently with traditional empiricist principles, feminist empiricists such as Helen Longino (1990; 2002) and Lynn Hankinson Nelson (1990; Nelson and Nelson, 2003) hold that knowledge requires a basis in empirical evidence. Otherwise, it cannot enable people to move capably about the physical world and engage effectively with diverse social, political, and 'natural' situations. Such claims pertain to everyday knowledge and to scientific and other academic knowledge across the disciplines. Feminists part company, however, with classical empiricists' requirement that evidence must come from ideal observation conditions where knowers figure as self-reliant, neutral information-processors whose access to 'the evidence' is assured by their simply encountering it. Such knowers are separate and interchangeable, since specificities of their bodily and subjective locations are erased for analytic purposes. A model of evidence as self-announcing, and knowers as individually, uniformly ready to receive it (knowledge as found, not made), which feminist empiricists contest, dominates classical empiricist claims about everyday knowledge, and natural and social scientific knowledge.

Although, *ex hypothesi*, post-positivist empiricism discounts historical, gendered, locational cognitive differences as biases or aberrations – individual errors to be eradicated and thence disregarded in formal justification – feminist empiricists argue that knowledge is indelibly shaped by its creators: it bears the marks of their gendered and other epistemic locations. Despite its alleged empirical–experiential grounding, traditional empiricism presupposes an abstract conception of experience, where differences are homogenized under one dominant conception of knowledge and knowers. In practice, this conception again mirrors and replicates the lives and experiences its (usually White, prosperous, educated male) creators are positioned to consider exemplary.

Producing secular *and* scientific knowledge that is neither androcentered nor tainted by racism, classism, sexism, or other oppressive–exclusionary biases is the goal of feminist empiricists. They reaffirm science's impressive achievements in the laboratory and in everyday lives, enabling many human beings to live knowledgeably and well. But their guiding claim is that a rigorous yet unabashedly value-laden empiricism (i.e., informed by feminist values) can produce more adequate knowledge than one whose practitioners are ignorant of the epistemic effects of their specificity, especially of their complicity in sustaining a hierarchical sex/gender system. It can enable inquirers to see, and work to explicate, evidence that slips through the conceptual grids non-feminists rely on. Investigators thus become as accountable to epistemic communities as to the evidence, and details of subjectivity, epistemic location, and interests are likewise opened to empirical scrutiny and count among conditions for the possibility of knowledge. The idea is that politically informed inquiry generates 'strong objectivity,' more objective than an objectivity whose self-definition bypasses the circumstances of its own possibility (Harding, 1991; 1993). Objectivity is enhanced by feminist-informed cognizance (and racial, class, and other 'difference'-sensitive awareness) of the effects of subjective positioning for achieving good observations and deriving sound conclusions. Components of knowers' epistemic locations thus require analyses as rigorous as the evaluations of the knowledge claims he/she/they advance(s).

The leading neo-empiricist feminist epistemologies of the 1990s eschew enclosed, uni-linear conceptions of accountability (from observer to evidence), to move toward socially located theories of knowledge, frequently derived from philosophy of science. Longino's contextual empiricism advances a view of science as social knowledge, examining background assumptions for their constitutive part in knowledge production and evaluation (1990; 2002). She emphasizes the contribution of critical social reception in making knowledge possible, declaring people's relation to a cognitive community as significant as their relation to the objects and content of knowledge (2002: 122–123). Neither scientific nor secular inquiry, then, is presumed value-free, as classical empiricists insist: cultural and social values form the background assumptions, embedded in communal wisdom, from which inquiry is generated. These assumptions require critical scrutiny at the level where they shape conceptualizations of research projects, hypotheses that guide and regulate inquiry, and taken-for-granted beliefs about what counts as evidence and what merely as irrelevant aberration. Diverse background assumptions, Longino shows, can produce radically different readings of 'the same' natural phenomena. Yet paradoxically, background assumptions are often invisible to those whose thinking they shape, so that internal investigations may fail to expose them. Hence the need for critical 'outsider' voices to sustain community standards of respect for evidence, accountable cognitive agency, and reliably collaborative knowledge-seeking. Objectivity becomes an explicitly social achievement.

Nelson, whose *naturalized* empiricism elaborates W. V. O. Quine's conception of knowledge as consisting of webs of belief, eschews classical empiricism's concentration on evaluating monologic knowledge claims formally structured as 'S knows that *p*' or multiples thereof, to propose a conception of beliefs embedded in theories, evolving holistically as the theories are tested against new evidence, and introduced into diverse contexts (Nelson, 1990; Nelson and Nelson, 2003). She commends Quine's 'naturalistic epistemology' for its turn toward studying real human knowledge-making as contrasted with idealized, stylized knowledge claims, while moving beyond Quine to expose gender, race, and class-insensitivities embedded in received theories of social science, including the scientific psychology which, for Quine, is where human cognitive activity should be studied. Longino and Nelson engage in critical social–cultural rereadings of background assumptions or webs of belief that perpetuate the androcentricity both of scientific ideology and of more secular epistemologies of everyday life.

Feminist empiricists of the 1990s thus shifted attention from exclusive concentration on knowledge itself to questions about who knows, and how. Yet empiricists pose these questions at a different level from theorists who avow a Marxist and/or postmodern influence. Even for feminist empiricists who reject abstract individualism, the new knowing subject often emerges as separate and relatively self-contained, capable of formulating knowledge claims monologically and independently, even while presenting them for communal critique. The community emphasis redistributes burdens of evidence-gathering and proof, and reconfigures patterns of accountability to transform epistemic practice. But even feminist empiricists like Nelson, for whom agents of knowledge are not individuals but communities, pay scant attention to how knowing subjects and communities are themselves socially/communally produced within power-saturated structures of domination and subordination.

STANDPOINT THEORISTS

Standpoint theorists part company with feminist empiricists in their refusal of individualism and their focus on power as it infuses knowledge production throughout the social–material world. Not even a rigorously feminist empiricism, they argue, offers sufficiently radical analyses of the historical–material circumstances that produce experience, knowledge, and subjectivity. Constructing an analogy between women's epistemic position under patriarchy and the proletarian economic position under capitalism, they argue that just as capitalist ideology represents proletarian subordination to the bourgeoisie as natural, so patriarchal ideology represents women's subordination to men as natural. Just as Marxists take material–historical experiences of proletarian lives as their starting point, so feminist standpoint theorists start from women's experiences in material–historical circumstances where power is distributed according to a hierarchical sex/gender system, with men occupying the positions of epistemic, and other, privilege. Nancy Hartsock (1983), Dorothy Smith (1987; 1990), Hilary Rose (1983; 1994), Patricia Hill Collins (1990), and Sandra Harding (1991) were the principal articulators of feminist standpoint epistemology in the 1980s and 1990s.

A feminist standpoint must not be confused with a 'women's standpoint,' theirs simply by virtue of their femaleness, nor is it an interchangeable perspective which any woman (or feminist man) could occupy by deciding to do so. It is a hard-won product of consciousness-raising and social–political engagement that exposes the false presuppositions of the 'myth of the neutral man' on which domination and subordination rely. Just as the purpose of Marxist consciousness-raising was to enable the proletariat to understand that their subordination was not caused by defects in their 'nature' and to demonstrate the contingency of the social order represented as natural, so the purpose of feminist consciousness-raising is to enable women to recognize their experiences of oppression *as* oppressive, not natural, to understand them as artifacts of a social order designed to ensure masculine supremacy. The goal is to empower women to recognize the validity of their experiences, in defiance of a long history of men speaking for and about women and claiming to know them better than women could know themselves. Yet the aim is not to substitute a new tyranny of experientialism, where experiential reports are inviolable and closed to critical analysis, but to create space where experiences can be interpreted and debated in open, democratic processes of feminist-informed collectivity and solidarity.

Standpoint theorists contend that the detailed, strategic knowledge the oppressed acquire of the workings of the social order just to function within it can become a resource for undermining that order. Their project is not to aggregate women around a unified or representative standpoint, but to acknowledge women's diverse material, domestic, intellectual, and professional labor as knowledgeable practices, and their marginalized experiences as affording an epistemic privilege unavailable to those whose lives are so replete with material goods and social–political authority that they need not understand the structures that make them possible: they can remain ignorant. Haraway puts it well: 'There is no single feminist standpoint because our maps require too many dimensions for that metaphor to ground our visions. But the feminist standpoint theorists' goal of an epistemology and politics of engaged, accountable positioning remains eminently potent' (1991: 196).

Standpoint theorists eschew goals of determining necessary and sufficient conditions for knowledge in order to establish its starting points and testing grounds in women's experiences. Empiricism – feminist or otherwise – cannot offer sufficiently radical analyses of the structural factors shaping women's practices and consciousness in the everyday world, where authoritative knowledge derives from the experiences of the dominant. Locating investigators on the same plane as the investigated, bringing their social, material, political, racial, economic, and sexual situations – the power and privilege that naturalize hierarchical arrangements – as sharply into focus as traditional 'objects of knowledge,' standpoint theorists contest epistemic neutrality. They expose patterns of dominance and subordination in which knowledge is produced and legitimated, showing that even allegedly disinterested empirical science demands scrutiny for the forces that produce both its successes and its failures. Thus, they aim to achieve transformative understandings of social structures that devalue women's labor and accord its practitioners minimal social–political authority, especially within the privileged structures of such professions as law, medicine, academia, and the corporate world.[4]

FEMINIST POSTMODERNIST EPISTEMOLOGIES

Most feminist epistemologies could be labeled postmodern if only because of the critical distance they variously take from the regulative conceptions of knowledge and subjectivity constitutive of the epistemologies of modernity. Postmodern feminists who explicitly own the label tend to take a more radical stance vis-à-vis knowledge and subjectivity than feminist empiricists or standpoint theorists, but separating them should not blur the connections among them. Indebted to psychoanalytic and literary theory and 'continental' philosophy in its various modalities, feminist postmodernists highlight the opaque, often contradictory aspects of subjectivity, while concentrating on the effects of embodiment – of bodily specificity – and on differences, especially corporeal, as they inflect and are inflected by material, racial, class, sexual, and other politics of difference.

Their flavor is apparent in Kathleen Lennon and Margaret Whitford's *Knowing the Difference* (1994): the editors characterize the postmodernism of the essays in the volume as entailing a 'recognition that all of our interactions with reality are mediated by conceptual frameworks or discourses… themselves…historically and socially situated…[and that] fragmentation and contradictions are inevitable and we will not necessarily be able to overcome them' (1994: 5; see also Hekman, 1990). Yet the tensions these contradictions enact generate the very energies feminist epistemologists need to negotiate the complexities of situations where objective, well-established facts are required to contest oppression, together with a measure of strategic skepticism to guard against a too-easy closure that could block attention to differences. Such projects often require both affirming politically informed identities and allegiances and remaining wary of the tendencies of identity politics and political categories to impose hard-edged structures when events and circumstances require openness to critical–transformative intervention. Many postmodern feminists work from a conviction that knowledge and power interpenetrate, so knowledge can only ever be partial, again in two senses of the word: it is always incomplete, and it comes from and speaks to particular interests and social groups.

With respect to power, feminists have engaged, ambivalently, with Michel Foucault, and especially his view of the 'micro-physics' of power permeating the social order as capillaries run imperceptibly through human bodies (Barrett, 1991; Foucault, 1980). Power, thus, is not owned by individual agents: it is exercised in social practices and legitimated within disciplinary mechanisms of surveillance, regulation, and classification. It is as productive as it is negative or repressive: it produces discourses, pleasures, meanings, subversive resistance. Such analyses make room for explaining how the sexual control of women's bodies is ubiquitously experienced and enacted, even when it comes from nowhere in particular. They show how 'subjugated knowledges' such as women have to acquire can infiltrate the gaps and interstices of allegedly seamless epistemic positions. Yet some feminists charge Foucault with ignoring macro-structures of power whose effects for women are palpable in global labor practices; others for advancing no viable conception of agency, just when women and other Others are claiming an agency from which they have long been excluded (Hartsock, 1990).

Women's experiences – their erasure, integrity, veracity – figure centrally in standpoint and postmodern projects: feminist research and activism recognize how women's experiences are consigned to invisibility throughout Western history in malestream thought and action. But feminists also insist that experience rarely 'speaks for itself,' and experiences are rarely unmediated, as classical empiricist rhetoric implies: hence, standpoint theorists' emphasis on consciousness-raising. Even the most vivid private experience often requires interpretive negotiation to expose its patterns of embeddedness in larger social structures and to enable experiencers and interpreters to understand how it is mediated by biographical and social–cultural location (Scott, 1992). Postmodern emphasis on subjectivity's instability and opacity moves these issues to a level where the contestability of experience and of identity claims invoked to ground it has to be balanced against feminist commitments to take women's experiences seriously. Feminists thus tread a perilous path between a tyranny of authoritarian expertise that discounts the veracity of women's experiences and those of other marginalized, oppressed people and a tyranny of 'experientialism' that shields first-person experiential claims from critical–interpretive challenge or can yield only what Sonia Kruks calls 'an epistemology of provenance' where 'knowledge arises from an experiential basis…so fundamentally group-specific that others, who are outside the group and who lack its immediate experiences, cannot share that knowledge' (2001: 109). Feminist social scientists are particularly aware of these issues (see, for example, di Leonardo, 1991); feminist biographers and biologists have to develop an interpretive sensitivity to discern and contest the effects of mechanisms of power even in seemingly straightforward observations and experiential reports.

SITUATED KNOWLEDGES

Since the mid-1990s, in philosophy of science and elsewhere, feminist epistemology has resisted containment in the categories set out in Harding's 1986 taxonomy, although many researchers continue to draw on the theoretical resources and research practices empiricist, standpoint, and postmodern feminists make available, while rarely claiming exclusive allegiance to one position. Often in reciprocally instructive dialogue with philosophers of science, feminist epistemologists who do not concentrate on gender in the natural sciences are engaged in interdisciplinary, cross-disciplinary projects where epistemological assumptions are unearthed and analyzed locally within such specific domains and practices as social science, law, medicine, moral deliberation, and policy-making.

Moving away from philosophy of science does not amount to rejecting scientific findings. Many domains I have mentioned – notably law and medicine – are crucially reliant on state-of-the-art science, and feminists in these areas may be as conversant with feminist philosophy of science as with the epistemology specifically pertinent to their own research and practice. Others turn to literature and cultural production as sites of knowledge-making that interrogate the complacency of mainstream assumptions about knowledge, power and privilege, sexuality and gender, racial and ethnic categories, and social class, age and disability. Their findings often illuminate issues in quite different feminist domains. To cite one extra-scientific example, Patricia Williams's mappings of the lived effects of systemic racism produce knowledge specific to a professional Black woman's (local) experiences in the urban, northern United States, which is translatable by analogy to racism and issues of epistemic accountability in other situations (1991; 1997). Producing natural histories of human beings in their myriad everyday epistemic activities, both professional and private, and in institutions of knowledge production, these multi-layered, multi-directional projects also *naturalize* epistemology. They challenge the boundaries traditionally delineated with reference to physical science and modeled on scientific method to show that knowledge issues run through and shape human lives in ways no monologic, disinterested theory could address (Hubbard, 1990; Stanley, 1992).

Haraway's 'Situated Knowledges' (1991), whose influence cannot be overestimated, is a centerpiece of these inquiries. It offers feminist successor epistemologies a particularly effective interpretive tool. Haraway argues for the political necessity of maintaining a commitment to objectivity – to learning to see well – while recognizing the implausibility of assuming everyone could see in the very same way. That, she says, is 'the god-trick of seeing everything from nowhere' or the imaginary of neutral, replicable knowers facing infinitely replicable objects of knowledge. 'Seeing well,' she contends, does not just happen: it is cognizant of its particularity and the accountability requirements specific to its location, and aware of 'the critical and interpretive core of all knowledge.' Embodied knowers engage with objects in the world, whose agency and unpredictability unsettle any hope of perfect knowledge and control, nor do these embodied knowers comprise a homogeneous group. In ecofeminist philosophy, Haraway finds one place where feminists recognize that 'we are not in charge of the world' (1991: 191, 199), a thought she pursues with increased sophistication and subtlety in *Modest_Witness* (1997). Haraway's 'seeing well' preserves an empiricist–realist belief in a world independent of knowers, about which they can be right or wrong. Her emphasis on situatedness and materiality accords with standpoint theorists' and postmodern critiques of the unified, perfectly knowable subject and object of the Enlightenment legacy, even as her work exceeds the confines of those categories.

An equally powerful recognition that 'we are not in charge of the world' comes from Karen Barad's 'agential realism' (1996; 2002) which, like Haraway's work but starting from physics, moves beyond realism-versus-constructivism to develop an account of *intra-actions* from which subjects and objects are constituted. Agential realism claims recognition for the agency of material entities and of human discursive practices: the *phenomena* it knows are not mere representations of a passive nature awaiting a disinterested knower, but specific *intra-actions* of the human and non-human, material and discursive, natural and cultural. It incorporates a call for accountability, provides a viable alternative to essentialism, and offers enlarged conceptions of human and material agency.

Although it is not grounded in physical science, Lorraine Code's position is residually empiricist in acknowledging the physical, material, and social world's resistance to casual restructuring or intervention. Emphasizing the specificity of epistemic agents and cognitive circumstances, the position claims affinities, also, with standpoint theory and postmodernism. Arguing that persons are 'second persons' whose achieved subjectivity is interactive, dialogic, deliberative, it accords knowing other people exemplary status, analogous to the status traditionally accorded knowing middle-sized material objects. Responsive knowledge of/about people is less reductive, more adequate to the heterogeneous constructive–negotiative–interpretive features of everyday evidence-gathering than standard empiricism. Endorsing a methodological pluralism indebted to Foucault's work on 'local knowledges,' and wary of homogenizing people, artifacts, material objects, and events as 'objects' of knowledge, under a unified model; it resists assuming that 'one size fits all' to work by analogy and dis-analogy, from situation to situation. Hence its pluralism. Contesting a too-exclusive (traditional) focus on perception and memory as sources of knowledge, this approach redirects attention to testimony and the multiple patterns of incredulity that acknowledge or dismiss it according to whose it is, who is speaking, within power-infused structures of authority and expertise (Code, 1987; 1991; 1995; 2006).

In her most recent work, Code locates these patterns in an ecological model of knowledge and subjectivity, in a (naturalized) understanding of cognitive interdependence and the radical interdependence of human lives and the natural–social world (Code, 2006). Both commendatory and critical of Quinean 'naturalized epistemology,' she applauds its shift from idealized abstraction and a priori analysis toward studying real epistemic practices, while contesting the idea that natural science alone produces knowledge worthy of the name, thus allowing scientists to evade questions about how they select 'the natural,' how laboratory specimens, behaviors, and findings translate into more ordinary epistemic moments, how items are isolated for controlled study or results achieved, analyzed, and circulated. Although 'ecological naturalism' locates this project within a naturalistic frame, it moves outside the laboratory to diverse knowers, circumstances, institutions, and places where knowledge is constructed and evaluated. Ecology talk functions metaphorically and literally in this project, signaling engagement in naturalist–materialist analyses of practices specific to institutions of knowledge-production and everyday lives, exposing inequalities implicated in standards of judgment, authority, and expertise, thereby working toward democratic, responsible epistemic communities. 'Situation' and place are constitutive, if not determinative, of how problems are defined, evidence recognized, read, and interpreted, and epistemic agency exercised: thus, situation and place are not merely context or backdrop. Their constraining and enabling factors need to be charted in concert with investigations of the knowledge produced there.

Moving to a different interaction with twentieth-century epistemology, Linda Alcoff's *Real Knowing* investigates the promise of *coherentist* epistemology for feminist projects (1996; 2003). Juxtaposing such central mainstream analytic figures as Hilary Putnam, Richard Rorty, and Donald Davidson with the 'continental' philosophy of Hans-Georg Gadamer and Michel Foucault, Alcoff turns to historical conceptions of truth, arguing that 'historicizing' truth neither renders it irrational nor prompts a descent into unreason. In Gadamerian hermeneutic interpretation and his conception of experience as meaningful, and thus open to interpretation at its most basic level, Alcoff finds an *immanent* metaphysics or ontology of truth which 'poses an interaction between knower and known out of which truth is produced…immanent to the domain of lived reality rather than completely transcendental to any human practice or context.' Situating Gadamer's engagement with questions of knowledge, Alcoff argues that he offers a way of conceptualizing the locatedness of knowers 'not as a detriment but as a necessary condition for knowledge' (1996: 66, 79). Her reading of Foucault goes beyond relationships between power and knowledge to address his archaeological and genealogical methods as exposing the limits and constitutive forces shaping human knowledge. The positions she analyzes contribute to a larger project of immanent critique and to standards of evaluation based in demonstrable coherence. Working within texts and practices, she contends that epistemologists must always, self-reflexively, question the legitimacy of their claims to know or to speak for others, or about real-world events.

NEW DIRECTIONS: A SAMPLING

In the new millennium, some feminist epistemologists have turned away from standpoint and/or postmodern theory toward pragmatism, realism, pluralism: positions as critical of the (imagined) excesses of postmodernism and the limitations of standpoint theory as indebted to them, and creative in proposing new directions. Three examples will convey a sense of how these lines of thought are developing. Some US feminists find in John Dewey's pragmatism a valuable resource, particularly because he accords centrality to practices and practical activities in his philosophy of experience, represents theory and practice as intertwined in science and in everyday knowledge, and sees in common sense a way of overcoming dualisms that plague philosophy. Feminists are drawn to this focus on practices and on the differences they make in the real world, as well as to pragmatist claims for the social nature of knowledge and justification. Yet, in Lisa Heldke's words, they are mindful of Dewey's failure to see 'the everyday activities of women's work' as practices worthy of analysis (2002: 255).

Starting from Dewey's theory of inquiry, yet moving creatively beyond it, Shannon Sullivan develops a conception of 'transactional knowing,' where bodies are in ongoing transactions with one another and with the physical and social world; experience is neither incontestably given nor foundational but open to reflective interpretation in which no one position or perspective claims privilege (2001: esp. ch. 6). She names her position a pragmatist–feminist standpoint theory for which knowing is a mode of *experimental* investigation. Knowers investigate problematic situations with the goal of developing solutions capable of effecting changes in their lives and the world, both human and more than human.

Critical of postmodernism's excessive distrust of identity politics, Paula Moya develops 'a postpositivist realist position': a theoretical 'pragmatism' for which objectivity is 'a theory-dependent, socially realizable goal' (2001: 444). She charges postmodern contestations of identity politics and objectivity with failing to empower Chicana and other 'difference' feminists to name and claim the oppressions they experience, consequent upon their marginalized identities, and to address the factuality of physical–material objects and events that sustain their specific forms of oppression. Cognizant of needing to avoid a dogmatism that solidifies and essentializes identities and conceptions of reality, she argues for the political cogency of a position capable of grounding 'the complex and variable experiences of the women who take on the identity *Chicana* within the concrete historical and material conditions they inhabit' (p. 479). It is rooted in specificities of US Chicana lives, yet translatable by analogy and dis-analogy across diverse circumstances where social identities are causally linked to, yet not determinative of the experiences, and thus the knowledge, of any knower(s).

Feminists drawn to pragmatism as it informs and underpins ethical–political situations have enlisted its resources to show that realism in feminist epistemology need not escalate into dogmatism, nor identity claims into essentialism. Their views are partially compatible with Miranda Fricker's claims for a pluralism 'capable of honouring the everyday insight (whose feminist theoretical expression originates in standpoint theory) that social differences give rise to differences in the perspectives in which the world is viewed, and that power can be an influence in whose perspectives seem rational' (2000: 160). These are some of the creative, innovative ways feminist epistemologists address the gender question in the early twenty-first century.

A different inspiration for twenty-first century feminist inquiry comes from projects that show how a 'politics of unknowing' fosters and condones ignorance, thereby preserving the temptations and illusions a god's-eye view still offers. According to Charles Mills, White Western society is founded on a *Racial Contract* which 'prescribes…an inverted epistemology, an epistemology of ignorance…[which produces] the ironic outcome that whites will be unable to understand the world they themselves have made' (1997: 18). This idea has opened the way for exploring the implications of an epistemology of ignorance, capable of exposing the exclusions and silencings effected by the pretensions and presuppositions of hegemonic epistemologies.[5]

Comparable unknowings characterize 'the epistemology of the closet' which, for Eve Kosofsky Sedgwick, simultaneously gives 'an overarching consistency to gay culture and identity' throughout the twentieth century, and is 'the defining structure for gay oppression' (1990: 68, 71). Kosofsky Sedgwick analyzes the liberatory promise and the dangers of coming out, where oppositions between gay and straight as different, clearly defined, and readily knowable 'natural kinds' are assumed, while the conceptual apparatus for thinking about homo/heterosexual definitions is markedly impoverished. In consequence, an impasse paralyzes debates between 'minoritizing and universalizing views of homosexual definition.' It attests to stark asymmetries of gender and to heterosexist oppression. Kosofsky Sedgwick warns against the damage a too-swift move toward an artificially achieved congruity would enact in a still-fragile, incoherent political and private situation.

These changes make space for analyses of ignorance, willed or inadvertent, as productive of the exclusions and harms Langton (2000) names: ignorance that allows, condones, and legitimates the perceptions of the 'arrogant eye,' characterized by Marilyn Frye as that of the arrogant perceiver who 'coerces the objects of his perception into satisfying the conditions his perception imposes' (1983: 67). Contesting the power of that eye, with the innumerable 'unseeings,' harms and misconceptions its deliverances have generated in Western societies, is a guiding motivation of feminist inquiry into the gendering of epistemology and the knowledge it has to interrogate.

NOTES

1 I address this issue in Code (1995).
2 The *locus classicus* is Lloyd (1984).
3 An exception is Mary Field Belenky, Blythe McVicker Clinchy, Nancy Rule Goldberger, and Jill Mattuck Tarule (1986). For a critical discussion of their position, see Code (1991: 251–262).
4 For a comprehensive, critical evaluation of standpoint debates, see Alison Wylie (2003).
5 Much of this new work was presented at the conference 'Epistemologies of Ignorance,' Pennsylvania State University, March 2004.

REFERENCES

Alcoff, Linda (1996). *Real Knowing: New Versions of the Coherence Theory* (Ithaca, NY: Cornell University Press).
_____ (2003). 'Gadamer's Feminist Epistemology.' In Lorraine Code (ed.), *Feminist Interpretations of Hans-Georg Gadamer* (University Park: Pennsylvania State University Press).
Barad, Karen (1996). 'Meeting the Universe Halfway.' In Lynn Hankinson Nelson and Jack Nelson, (eds), *Feminism, Science, and the Philosophy of Science* (Dordrecht: Kluwer).
_____ (2002). 'Posthumanist Performativity: Toward an Understanding of How Matter Comes to Matter.' *Signs: Journal of Women in Culture and Society* (28:3, 801–831).
Barrett, Michèle (1991). *The Politics of Truth* (Stanford, CA: Stanford University Press).
Belenky, Mary Field, Blythe McVicker Clinchy, Nancy Rule Goldberger, and Jill Mattuck Tarule (1986). *Women's Ways of Knowing* (New York: Basic Books).
Bordo, Susan (1987). *The Flight to Objectivity* (Albany: State University of New York Press).
_____ (1999). *Feminist Interpretations of René Descartes* (University Park: Pennsylvania State University Press).
Code, Lorraine (1981). 'Is the Sex of the Knower Epistemologically Significant?' *Metaphilosophy* (12:3 and 4). Reprinted with 1986 Postscript in Terence Bynum and William Vitek (eds) (1988) *Applying Philosophy* (New York: Metaphilosophy Foundation).
_____ (1987). *Epistemic Responsibility* (Hanover, NH: University Press of New England).
_____ (1991). *What Can She Know? Feminist Theory and the Construction of Knowledge* (Ithaca, NY: Cornell University Press).
_____ (1995). 'Taking Subjectivity Into Account.' In *Rhetorical Spaces: Essays on (Gendered) Locations* (New York: Routledge). Revised from Linda Alcoff and Elizabeth Potter (eds) (1993). *Feminist Epistemologies* (New York: Routledge).
_____ (2006). *Ecological Thinking: The Politics of Epistemic Location* (New York: Oxford University Press).
Collins, Patricia Hill (1990). *Black Feminist Thought* (New York: Harper Collins; 2nd edition, New York: Routledge, 2000).
di Leonardo, Michaela (1991). 'Contingencies of Value in Feminist Anthropology.' In Joan E. Hartman and Ellen Messer-Davidow (eds), *(En)Gendering Knowledge* (Knoxville: University of Tennessee Press).
Foucault, Michel (1980). *Power/Knowledge: Selected Interviews and Other Writings 1972–77*. Ed. Colin Gordon; trans. Colin Gordon, Leo Marshall, John Mepham, and Kate Soper (New York: Pantheon).

Fricker, Miranda (2000). 'Feminism in Epistemology: Pluralism without Postmodernism.' In Miranda Fricker and Jennifer Hornsby (eds), *The Cambridge Companion to Feminism in Philosophy* (Cambridge: Cambridge University Press).
Frye, Marilyn (1983). 'In and Out of Harm's Way.' In *The Politics of Reality* (Freedom, CA: Crossing Press).
Haraway, Donna (1991). '"Situated Knowledges": The Science Question in Feminism and the Privilege of Partial Perspective.' In *Simians, Cyborgs, and Woman* (New York: Routledge).
_____ (1997). *Modest_Witness@Second_Millenium. FemaleMan_Meets_OncoMouse*^{TM} (New York: Routledge).
Harding, Sandra (1986). *The Science Question in Feminism* (Ithaca, NY: Cornell University Press).
_____ (1991). *Whose Science? Whose Knowledge? Thinking From Women's Lives* (Ithaca, NY: Cornell University Press).
_____ (1993). 'Rethinking Standpoint Epistemology: What Is "Strong Objectivity"?' In Linda Alcoff and Elizabeth Potter (eds), *Feminist Epistemologies* (New York: Routledge).
Harding, Sandra and Merrill Hintikka (eds) (1983). *Discovering Reality: Feminist Perspectives on Epistemology, Metaphysics, Methodology, and Philosophy of Science* (Dordrecht: Reidel).
Hartsock, Nancy C. M. (1983). *Money, Sex, and Power* (Boston: Northeastern University Press).
_____ (1990). 'Foucault on Power: A Theory for Women?' In Linda Nicholson (ed.), *Feminism/Postmodernism* (New York: Routledge).
Hekman, Susan (1990). *Gender and Knowledge* (Boston: Northeastern University Press).
Heldke, Lisa (2002). 'How Practical is John Dewey?' In Charlene Haddock Siegfried (ed.), *Feminist Interpretations of John Dewey* (University Park: Pennsylvania State University Press).
Hubbard, Ruth (1990). *The Politics of Women's Biology* (New Brunswick, NJ: Rutgers University Press).
Jaggar, Alison (1983). *Feminist Politics and Human Nature* (Totowa, NJ: Rowman and Littlefield).
Keller, Evelyn Fox (1983). *A Feeling for the Organism: The Life and Work of Barbara McClintock* (New York: W. H. Freeman).
_____ (1985). *Reflections on Gender and Science* (New Haven, CT: Yale University Press).
Kruks, Sonia (2001). *Retrieving Experience* (Ithaca, NY: Cornell University Press).
La Caze, Marguerite (2002). *The Analytic Imaginary* (Ithaca, NY: Cornell University Press).
Langton, Rae (2000). 'Feminism in Epistemology: Exclusion and Objectification.' In Miranda Fricker and Jennifer Hornsby (eds), *The Cambridge Companion to Feminism in Philosophy* (Cambridge: Cambridge University Press).
Lennon, Kathleen and Margaret Whitford (eds) (1994). *Knowing the Difference: Feminist Perspectives in Epistemology* (London: Routledge).
Lloyd, Genevieve (1984). *The Man of Reason* (Minneapolis: University of Minnesota Press, 2nd edition, 1993).
Longino, Helen (1990). *Science as Social Knowledge* (Princeton, NJ: Princeton University Press).
_____ (2002). *The Fate of Knowledge* (Princeton, NJ: Princeton University Press).
Mills, Charles (1997). *The Racial Contract* (Ithaca, NY: Cornell University Press).
Moya, Paula (2001). 'Chicana Feminism and Postmodern Theory.' *Signs: Journal of Women in Culture and Society* (26:2, 441–483).
Nagel, Thomas (1986). *A View From Nowhere* (Oxford: Oxford University Press).
Nelson, Lynn Hankinson (1990). *Who Knows. From Quine to a Feminist Empiricism* (Philadelphia: Temple University Press).
Nelson, Lynn Hankinson and Jack Nelson (eds) (2003). *Feminist Interpretations of W. V. O. Quine* (University Park: Pennsylvania State University Press).
Rose, Hilary (1983). 'Hand, Brain and Heart: Towards a Feminist Epistemology for the Sciences'. *Signs: Journal of Women in Culture and Society* (9:3, 93–96).

_____ (1994). *Love, Power, and Knowledge* (Cambridge: Polity Press).

Scheman, Naomi (1991). 'Who Wants to Know? The Epistemological Value of Values.' In Hartman, Joan E. and Ellen Messer-Davidow (eds), *(En)Gendering Knowledge* (Knoxville: The University of Tennessee Press). Reprinted in Naomi Scheman (1993). *Engenderings* (New York: Routledge).

Scott, Joan Wallach (1992). '"Experience".' In Judith Butler and Joan W. Scott (eds), *Feminists Theorize the Political* (New York: Routledge).

Sedgwick, Eve Kosofsky (1990). *The Epistemology of the Closet* (Berkeley, CA: University of California Press).

Smith, Dorothy (1987). *The Everyday World as Problematic* (Toronto: University of Toronto Press).

_____ (1990). *The Conceptual Practices of Power* (Toronto: University of Toronto Press).

Stanley, Liz (1992). *The Auto/Biographical I* (Manchester: Manchester University Press).

Sullivan, Shannon (2001). *Living Across and Through Skins* (Bloomington: Indiana University Press).

Williams, Patricia J. (1991). *The Alchemy of Race and Rights* (Cambridge, MA: Harvard University Press).

_____ (1997). *Seeing a Color-Blind Future* (New York: Farrar, Straus and Giroux).

Wylie, Alison (2003). 'Why Standpoint Matters.' In Robert Figueroa and Sandra Harding (eds), *Science and Other Cultures* (New York: Routledge).

9

Gender, Change, and Education

Diana Leonard

This chapter reviews the many changes that have taken place in educational theory and practice over the last forty years and discusses the causes and effects of the assimilation of women into both the institutions and values of schools and universities. It notes a recent shift back towards supposedly 'gender-neutral' educational policies in richer nations, which frequently overlook the specific interests of girls and women. It argues for resisting this through knowledge of our own educational history and more exchange of ideas between countries of the North and South.

INTRODUCTION

One of the main concerns of feminists in many countries in the late nineteenth and early twentieth centuries was the opening up of education to girls and women – both for personal development, including the reading of sacred texts, and as a means of access to paid employment. Since the education provided for the sons of the upper, middle and poor classes was itself then sharply differentiated, so too was the first education provided for girls. It was also unevenly provided between rural and urban settings. Schools were often single gender, or else boys and girls entered and worked within them separately. But across the board, such education as there was for girls directed them primarily towards a domestic future rather than employment or other forms of public life. The curriculum for girls was more limited and inferior to that provided for boys.

In England in the 1870s, for instance, girls from impoverished families were less likely than their brothers to get any schooling at all, especially if they were needed at home to help domestically or to earn a wage, or if money was not available to pay the costs of education for more than one or two of the siblings in a large family. Girls from 'respectable' working-class backgrounds were educated to be, first, servants in the houses of the upper and middle classes and then, later, the non-employed wives and mothers of working-class men and boys. So they learned traditional womanly skills such as sewing and laundry rather than arithmetic, which was seen as an unnecessary skill. Girls from wealthier backgrounds were often educated at home by governesses, with a focus on French, music, and other 'accomplishments'.

The leaders of the first wave of feminism had to struggle hard to provide academic secondary and boarding schools for girls to match those long available for their brothers. They faced arguments that education might upset not only women's deferential demeanour but also their reproductive physiology. Lagging behind the United States and parts of the Commonwealth, some UK universities admitted small numbers of women from the late nineteenth century and early twentieth centuries (for example, London in 1878), though others held out much longer – women were only awarded full degrees at the University of Cambridge in 1948 – and there were attempts to offer women a different curriculum. They were not allowed to study medicine but offered domestic science.

Feminist history has been important in tracing and rewriting the history of education, including not only girls' and women's education generally and the history of particular institutions and the teaching profession, but also the lives, aims and achievements of feminist educational activists and reformers. However, research on educational establishments (whether schools or higher education) and on the teaching profession is not a high-status area within either the academy or feminism (Stone,1994). Education is also a difficult area to cover in a general and brief way because there are several different major systems even within the West, each with national and regional and neo-colonial variants. It is also an arena with frequently changing policies as politicians try to use schools and universities to develop or spread national cultures, and, lately, to improve national economic competitiveness. This chapter will therefore be based primarily on discussion of the UK and the United States over the past forty years, with some information on others for contrast, ending with a brief reference to low- to medium-income countries.

RECENT HISTORY

In all Western countries, universal basic (primary/elementary) education was established by the time of the First World War, and there were also secondary and boarding schools and colleges available for middle- and upper-rank girls to parallel those for boys. Most children therefore attended school for at least six years, and literacy and numeracy were seen as important skills. Mixed-gender schooling was introduced into many elementary schools at times and places when there would otherwise have been no provision for girls, and it also became seen as 'progressive'; so new coeducational secondary schools were established in the private sector from the turn of the twentieth century. Coeducation was partly a response to fears of homosexuality in single-gender schools and partly a concern to support and stabilize future roles in the ideal family. However, some private and religious schools and colleges in the United States, UK and Australia continue to be single-gender and this remains a mark of 'elite' secondary schooling.

After the Second World War, in democratic Western countries, the focus was on socio-economic differences in education – how schools reproduced social class inequalities by streaming by 'ability' and through having differences in the types (academic and vocational) and quality of schools. (In countries such as Spain and Greece, which were dictatorships in the 1950s and 1960s, attention to socio-economic issues occurred only later.) Education reformers also wanted to change the continuing elitist nature of higher education so as to 'tap the pool of ability' in the population as a whole. The concerns of politicians and the focus of research therefore became the widening of what had previously been a 'ladder' for able working-class children into a wide 'staircase' of progress into secondary schooling, through the raising of the school-leaving age from 12 years to 14 and then 16 and the provision of both more vocational colleges and more free or affordable university places.

When all state-provided elementary/primary schools and most state/public secondary schools were coeducational, any issues of girls' continuing disadvantage were thought to have been resolved. Girls and young women were seen as having access to substantially the same educational institutions and the same curricula as boys and men. Any differences which remained, for instance in subject choice or the very gender-segregated nature of vocational training, were seen as due to 'natural' interests and abilities and to be generally appropriate for the different future lives of men and women.

TEACHING AS A GENDERED OCCUPATION

School teaching itself is an interesting occupation from a gender perspective. The teaching labour force in primary/elementary schools in most countries consists mainly of women and that of higher education predominantly of men, but there are national differences in whether secondary school teaching is largely a woman's occupation (as in the United States and Israel) or one which also attracts a sizeable proportion of men (as in Germany and Greece). However, both men and women teachers have been seen as needed in mixed primary/elementary schools, to meet the specific needs of both boy and girl pupils. Consequently, so-called 'sex antagonisms' dominated teaching in the first half of the twentieth century. They split the occupation and its trade unions and prevented it from attaining full professional status. Many agreed that school principals/heads, like heads of families, should generally be men and that 'a man teacher should not have to serve under a woman'. But there were also single-gender unions in several countries (for example, Canada and the UK). The men's unions argued that men should get more money than women because it was harder to attract men into teaching. Those men already in the job were known to be less well qualified than women teachers, but it was felt that the situation would get worse if women were given equal pay. There have also been marriage bars on women in teaching and amazing arguments as to the sorts of women who were appropriate for the job – young, attractive women, who would in due course get married and stop teaching to raise a family – and worries about the warping effects of spinster teachers on boys.

Over time, however, women acquired formally equal access to school teaching and headship/administration, and by the 1960s had formally equal pay and opportunities for promotion, though in practice men still enjoyed more senior positions with higher incomes. Colleges and universities were especially slow to allow women to teach, and certain subjects were deemed 'not proper for women to know about' until the 1930s and 1940s. There were also far fewer women students in universities in many countries until the 1970s – and many who might have gone to university went instead to colleges for teacher or nurse training.

THE RE-EMERGENCE OF CONCERN WITH FEMINISM AND EDUCATION

Into the consensus that gender equality had been achieved in schools in the West, even if boys and girls still had different interests and chose different subjects and careers, there erupted the new social movements of the late 1960s and 1970s. These were notably concerned with racism (in countries where there was a heterogeneous population) and sexism. Many European countries were considerably influenced by writings from the United States, where the women's liberation movement drew on ideas and organizing strategies from the civil rights and Black Power movements, though there was also a long tradition of Scandinavian work on equal opportunities in education. In some countries, the women's movement was never very strong, and many relied on translations of English or French work, which were slow in coming. But in all cases, activism on schooling, and even for greater access to higher education, lagged somewhat behind demands for equal rights in employment and for more equitable family division of labour, contraception and abortion, and efforts to get women's issues taken seriously by political parties. However, by the mid 1970s, second-wave feminist work on education was well underway, stressing continuing inequalities and that so-called 'natural' interests were socially constructed and constrained.

For English-speakers concerned with early childhood and schooling, the new concept of gender was key. But wherever one deems the balance lies (whether it is mainly a question of nature or, as most feminists claimed, 99 per cent nurture), education involves a political choice socially either to encourage or to minimize 'natural' potentials. That is to say, it can seek either to stress and encourage differences and divisions between boys and girls or to minimize them, and early second-wave feminists sought to minimize gender differences, arguing that men and women have equal intellectual capacities and rights to education. Teachers should provide the same knowledge, skills and experience to girls and boys and have the same expectations of them. However, because of historical inequalities, it was argued that there was a need to increase the importance of currently devalued 'feminine' subject areas and attributes (which include valuing teaching itself and childcare generally) and to direct more teacher time and attention to girls to even out the balance. Binary division of skills inhibits everyone, and it is as bad for boys not to engage in art, languages and dance in school as it is for girls to be kept out of (or to develop a dislike for) technical subjects and science. But in a gender-divided society, where masculine attributes are more rewarded, the employment and social costs for girls are greater.

The mid 1970s to the mid 1980s were exciting times in schools, colleges, and universities in the United States and the UK. Feminist activists formed women's groups for support and consciousness-raising and to discover and explore new issues. Their concerns were, first, to put gender (back) onto the educational map, and then to explore its parameters, stressing ideology and the power of ideas: how schools and universities reproduce not only the economic, social and cultural capital of class relations but also those of gender, race and ethnicity.

Feminists questioned the content of what was taught and learned formally and informally in schools and investigated educational progression and occupational outcomes, producing very creative work in curriculum development, classroom management, and school policies. New empirical, ethnographic or action research was undertaken involving teacher–researchers and school inspectors as well as academics. The problems investigated included how much more teacher attention was given to boys, the continuing differences in the curriculum offered to boys and girls, and career consequences. Feminists noted that even when girls had access to the same curriculum as boys, the content was weighted towards boys' interests, including what books were read. In examinations, having a female (or a foreign) name at the top of an exam paper affected judgements of its worth. Such studies were often quite basic and positivistic, and 'race' and gender issues were initially often considered separately, and also separately from social class. But the work did serve to map the field and had 'street credibility'.

This grassroots activity was assisted by the enactment of new racial and gender anti-discrimination legislation which covered educational institutions, and new equal opportunities commissions with responsibilities for enforcing the law. In addition, the US and UK governments were particularly concerned with attracting more women into science and engineering, and so they cooperated with feminists in pioneering a number of research projects and action initiatives. Some sought to change the focus of school science in order to interest girls, and there were also efforts to ensure girls got access to resources in schools and to encourage them to continue with science at university.

COEDUCATION DEBATES REVISITED

The question of girls' disadvantages in science courses reopened the issue of the merits of coeducation in the UK. A report from the school inspectorate in 1975 had pointed out that girls were less likely to take physics in coeducational than in single-gender schools and boys were less likely to take history and languages. This came as a surprise. Many girls-only schools in the 1950s had not had appropriate laboratories and it was thought that it was this that held girls back. But even when there were facilities available to girls, as when a boys and a girls school amalgamated, girls were still under-represented in science. Since feminists themselves seemed to have disproportionately attended single-gender schools, there was a resurgence of the belief that girls did better in single-gender schools (Spender, 1982; Spender et al., 1980), even if boys did better in mixed schools. Some subsequent research has suggested that it is more a matter of the type of school – most selective schools were single-gender – but the issue remains open.

At the same time, adult education classes also began to provide women-only women's studies courses in response to staff and students' interests, and higher education saw the start of courses, again attended almost exclusively by women students, which not only added women to course material but also focused centrally on them and/or drew on feminist theory. These courses often encountered considerable opposition. The history of the establishment of full degrees in women's studies of necessity differed by country, given the variety of educational systems. They were established at undergraduate level in the United States earlier than in Europe, but options within mainstream degrees were common by 1980 in, for instance, Denmark, France, Germany, and the UK.

At this point, 'woman-friendly' pedagogy and women-oriented curricula began to be explored. The move into higher education, and the entry of women into knowledge-producing posts in universities ('the storming of the ivory tower'), were important because the women's movement as a whole required the production of new knowledge from a radical, feminist perspective. Women were entering the universities as undergraduates in greater numbers, but only a low proportion, around 15–17 per cent, of those doing PhDs were women in the early 1970s (Leonard, 1997). This meant not only poor career prospects for women as faculty in colleges and universities, but also that women made relatively little contribution to creating valued and legitimized knowledge.

THE 1980s: DIVERSITIES AND COMPLEXITIES

By the mid 1980s, feminism had achieved great success in raising awareness of girls' situations in schools in the United States and the UK (though less so in France, Japan, or Israel) and in persuading teachers, principals, local state/government employees, and some politicians of the need to appoint specialists to give advice on whole-school policies to tackle discrimination. The Australians coined the word 'femocrat' for the increasing number of women who worked in bureaucracies but were appointed because of their feminist knowledge and practical experience. Staff in schools, and more rarely in colleges and universities, were given time out to attend meetings to discuss the issue of girls' education, and one or more teachers per school or college were given responsibility for coordinating work and to plan and evaluate their own small-scale projects. Women's studies was fully established as a separate, though under-funded, field of study at postgraduate and undergraduate level in universities, and women's centres were established in colleges, especially in the United States, giving advice and campaigning for safety on campus, childcare provision, and women's sports.

As in the women's movement as a whole, there were sometimes heated debates as to the causes of women's subordination/oppression and what was primarily in need of change in education. Some teachers, advisers and researchers involved in gender work in schools, the equal opportunities commissions, and various established women's organizations argued a liberal, individualized account. They saw the issue as one of adjusting a (physically based) binary relationship which was socially out of balance and inequitable. They spoke of sex-role stereotyping and role models, and stressed trying to change attitudes, in particular the attitudes of senior people such as headteachers and principals. For them, education was a privileged site for instigating social change. Gender discrimination was declared inefficient, and examples were given of better, more effective practice. If that did not work, they would use the law to require equal treatment.

Others, mostly grassroots feminist organizations and social researchers, took a more structural and conflictual approach, claiming that education contributed to the social reproduction of an exploitative patriarchal system. Education was a difficult tool to use for change since it had been established for the opposite purpose – maintaining social continuity and dominant class structures. But for those who worked within schools and colleges, it was certainly a site where men's power had to be contested.

This latter group was, however, itself divided between those who stressed the advantages of gender (and racial) divisions to capitalism and those who saw primarily men as being advantaged by a patriarchal system which existed alongside capitalism. The former critiqued 'classic' Marxist and neo-Marxist sociologists of education, showing that schools reproduced not only gender but also class (and other) inequalities; while the latter stressed the ways in which boys physically dominated classrooms and playgrounds and harassed girls and certain other boys and women teachers, both verbally and physically. Both critiqued the bias towards boys' and men's interests in education, including which knowledge and skills were valued and which areas (including sports) were seen as the source of schools' and colleges' prestige.

The middle-class and White focus of earlier work on education was contested from the start by Black feminists, but by the 1980s, more accounts of the educational experiences of working-class and disadvantaged ethnic women existed and there was more recognition of student differences. Similarly, from the mid 1980s, there was pressure to recognize the experiences of gay and lesbian young people growing up and 'coming out' in schools and their difficult experiences as adolescents: one in five had seriously considered or attempted suicide. There was increased awareness that many children were not raised by heterosexual couples, but by single and lesbian or gay parents. Various groups started to produce resources to give more diverse and 'positive images' of minority ethnic households and homosexual lifestyles. This included stocking and indexing books showing diverse lives in school libraries and discussing homosexual cultures in history and English literature classes as well as in strictly defined 'sex education' lessons. There were also efforts to recruit more Black staff, particularly in nursery schools, and to prevent openly homosexual staff from being dismissed from teaching jobs in schools, though this was the least acceptable face of feminism and suffered substantial backlash.

With increasing numbers of higher education faculty interested in feminist research, postgraduate work in women's studies expanded rapidly and associated research challenged the very nature of the disciplines – in many cases, such as sociology, political studies, and geography, revitalizing them. Similarly challenging work also emerged in the field of education – for instance, Jane Rowland Martin's critique of the classic philosophers of education (1985), and the problematizing of the 'boy as norm' standards of developmental psychology (Chodorow, 1978; Gilligan, 1977; Walkerdine, 1984). There was also a particular focus, including from pro-feminist men, on gender and teaching as a gender-segregated labour market (Apple, 1986), and how this affected the nature of teachers' work and its maternal subtext (Grumet, 1988) and men's and women's moral orientation to caring and institutional practices (Noddings, 1984; 1992). Feminist educational theory also developed a particular focus on diversity and identity, including Queer and postcolonial arguments.

THE 1990s: DECONSTRUCTION AND SOME RECONSTRUCTION

Feminist (and other) attempts at critical educational reform have subsequently been overtaken and undermined by political conservatism. Major changes were swiftly put in place across many educational systems from the late 1980s and, despite a rhetoric of enhanced teacher power and professionalism, in the United States and the UK, teachers' daily lives in school and college classrooms have became more controlled. Centralized direction and standardization of the curriculum and pedagogy have been instigated where not already present, with reductive accountability through various evaluation or 'quality assurance' schemes. The central purpose of education has become to improve the levels of student achievement and students' future employability, so as to ensure national development and competitiveness, rather than for broader personal development or as a means of social engineering – to redistribute resources towards disadvantaged groups. Education is certainly not currently encouraged to be a source of social critique, much less of resistance to the powerful.

Adapting to rapid change has occupied much of teachers' and lecturers' time and attention and greatly increased their work load. Combined with job insecurity for many, it has left little time for activism or even reflection. Instead, there has arisen a trust in managed change – in school improvement and 'evidence-based practice' – and a stress on the potential of management and leadership. Both have received a mixed response from feminists. It has been noted that the overall concern with improved standards and effectiveness and efficiency in education tends to homogenize students and to be antipathetic to work on equity. A commitment to evidence-based practice sits ill with the general lack of monitoring of the effects of recent changes and often includes a dismissal of qualitative feminist research data. But feminists do mostly remain committed to getting more women into school and university administration, and they are hopeful that their values and styles will improve education (Blackmore, 1999). Relative success has been claimed by a number of women who have attained senior positions and then reflected on their careers, looking at how they position themselves and are positioned in their efforts to make a difference (David and Woodward, 1998; Kolodny, 1998).

Whether due to the general decline in the women's movement and an associated decline of most grassroots feminist activism in schools and colleges, or the dwindling of government support for equal opportunities work, the 1990s have seen a return to the view that the problem of girls' education has been solved, and a resurgence of focus on boys. However, this is no longer based simply on an assumption of boys' greater importance, or rationalized as their mattering more because they will be the mainstay of the labour market and the breadwinners for households, as in the 1950s. Instead, it is based principally on concern for boys' 'underachievement' in tests and examinations: that is to say, on their not doing at least as well as girls. Academic results are improving across the board in many industrialized countries, but girls are improving their test results faster and are seen to be now substantially outperforming boys. Moreover, women now comprise a majority of the undergraduates – and in the United States this is described as a 'feminization' of the universities. It is therefore being argued that there is a need to put in place some sort of special provision for boys, such as special reading support. It is even being argued that girls have been unfairly advantaged by one or other recent changes – feminist initiatives to make the curriculum or pedagogy more girl-friendly, evaluation of students on their coursework rather than exams – and that these changes should be reversed.

Countering such knee-jerk reactions is complex. We can question the quality of the tests themselves and point out that some statistically significant gender differences may not be socially significant. We can also point out that the visibility of differences between girls' and boys' performance today is partly due to the greater stress on schools' results, and that such differences have existed for some time. We can also point to the longevity of explanations which see boys as having potential and girls as only doing well because of luck or the way they are taught. We can also stress that, while gender differences are discussed in terms of (all) boys and (all) girls, in fact the patterns vary by racial and ethnic group, and socio-economic background remains a more critical differentiator of school performance than gender. But this does not make the perception that boys are losing out disappear. It is not surprising that there has been considerable writing in this field that stresses the interplay of multiple factors and the difficulty of disentangling causes (Arnot, David and Weiner, 1999; Salisbury and Riddell, 2000).

To the extent that girls in many industrial countries are now getting better exam results than boys at 16 and 18, after being behind in previous decades (and this is the case only in certain subjects), the difference is certainly partly due to most girls now foreseeing a very different future from their grandmothers, and so looking to obtain different things from their education. From the 1970s to 1990s there were radical changes in women's participation in Western labour markets (although of course there had long been differences between, say, Finland and the Netherlands, between different regions within one country, between ethnic groups, and migrants and indigenous populations). Women have also wanted to reduce their economic dependency when given the opportunity, and, with a reduced stability of marriage, have seen it as likely that they might need to be self-supporting for some if not all of their lives. Even if women do marry, all households now need two incomes, and middle-class men breadwinners (where present) can experience periods of unemployment, as working-class and Black men have for many years. Employment opportunities are also now greater for women due to the decline in the birth rate. Finally, some of the changes in educational performance may be due to feminist and government interventions to prevent pupils making early gender-stereotyped subject choices, and to it having become more socially acceptable for girls to be competitive.

However, it is the simple statement that 'girls are doing better', or that their school behaviour is more appropriate than boys' anti-school 'laddishness', which provides headlines; and the public stress on gender differences is having consequences for how young people see themselves. Pupils, too, read newspapers and make identifications based on the accounts of gender proclaimed within them. Meanwhile, some teachers and parents continue to discipline (have resumed disciplining?) boys with threats about how it is shameful not to do as well as girls and exposing boys' poorer reading performance. The result is a resurrection of 'gender antagonisms' in education, including the aforementioned concern to shift resources to boys, combined with calls to repeal equity legislation in the United States and the re-emergence of biologistic explanations for differences between (all) boys and (all) girls.

While some of the concern with boys' performance is perhaps misplaced and certainly over-simplified, there is, however, legitimate cause for concern with some of the educational problems of certain groups of boys in Western societies, as well as their contribution to, and their being the main victims of, violence and crime in and out of schools. There are worryingly high rates of male adolescent suicide – though girls also self-harm, often through eating disorders, while not directly killing themselves. These issues for boys and young men led to a surge of research on masculinity/ies, including work on masculinity and education, in the 1990s. Some took a 'pity the poor boys' line and reasserted men's rights, but a larger and more significant group of feminists and pro-feminist men pioneered a raft of work stressing how hegemonic forms of masculinity in every setting involve assertions of heterosexuality and the sexual harassment of women and non-hegemonic men. These performances, based on popularity, physicality, toughness, skill, speed, and interest in sports and sexual prowess, express and reconfirm hierarchical power relations within groups of men and boys, inside and outside educational institutions.

Much of this work, along with parallel work on femininities since the early 1990s, has drawn on post-structuralist and sometimes psychoanalytic theory. These perspectives stress the fluidity and constant reconstruction of gender: how social differences and inequalities are constantly reconstructed and performed in micro interactions in schools. That is to say, authors argue that educational systems do not simply act upon pre-existing social differences which are brought into schools, colleges, and universities, but rather that teachers, pupils, and others in educational institutions actively *re*-construct and constantly modify gender and their own identities. They also insist that while there are always gender dimensions to any educational social interaction, it is never just a question of gender, but of other social differences too (including class, racial and ethnic hierarchies, sexuality, ability, and physical size), all interacting in constant flux. Unlike the first work on gender in children's books in the 1970s, which used content analysis and influenced authors to produce non-sexist alternative books, recent work stresses that texts have no stable meanings and can be read in a variety of ways, though too great a departure from expectations will provoke resistance. Thus, authority has been shifted from the text to the interpretation of the text and to analysis in terms of discourses and relativized 'regimes of truth'. There are undoubted strengths to such modes of analysis, but there are also drawbacks in terms of political mobilization and as guides to future practice because accounts are being based on very specific local events.

CURRENT TRENDS

Because gender is now firmly tied to boys' academic performance, it has been possible to get funding to do research on gender in the English-speaking West, and such projects, together with doctoral theses and the wide-ranging interests of individual academics, have provided increasingly sophisticated (often ethnographic) research on girls and boys and young men and women's identities, and the interconnections of gender, racial ethnicity, class, and education. The academic field is therefore flourishing, though there is a tightening government grip on what counts as 'good' research to guide policy. 'Systematic reviews', overviews of 'what works' (see Archer, 2003), and a preference for 'scientific', randomized control testing are being promoted. Meanwhile the academic field of gender and education is separated from grassroots feminist activism. Hence there is currently little *practical* concern with improving girls' and women's school and college experience, at least in the UK.

But if we look only at gender in educational *studies*, the future looks exciting, as we can see new avenues being opened up. To take just a few examples: with increased education taking place outside of schools, there is important work being done on the effects of media and marketing on gender (and age) segmentation in children's and youth culture (Kenway and Bullen, 2001). With globalization, there are renewed cross-national studies of the role of education in nation-building and citizenship (Arnot and Dillabough, 2000); and there is, finally, the beginnings of a dialogue between debates on gender and education in the West and those on gender and development in low- to medium-income countries (Unterhalter, 2003).

Feminists have sought to stress the importance of including women in development planning since the 1970s. They first stressed the importance of investing in women's education because it would help lower fertility rates, reduce infant morality, increase efficiency, and improve per capita GDP, but this 'women and development' (WID) concern progressed into a more politically oppositional 'gender and development' (GAD) argument in the 1980s. The latter stresses the effects of structured gender inequalities on women and the need for both immediate and practical effects and improvements and longer-term, strategic changes. The longer-term aims include challenges to discrimination entrenched in law and around sexuality, the consequences of lack of political representation, and discrimination in the workplace. But GAD demands have seldom included reference to formal education – according to Nelly Stromquist (1995), because the state was seen as such an ambiguous partner when seeking to transform gendered social relations.

However, GAD-influenced projects did often include efforts to improve women's literacy because NGOs and new social movements usually included adult basic literacy as part of their mobilization strategies. This was especially the case in Latin America, where they were influenced by Paulo Freire's radical pedagogy (2000).

By the 1990s, the concept of 'empowerment' was widely used in critiques of the WID/human capital/World Bank approach; and even though the term was loosely formulated, Naila Kabeer (1999) did manage to develop proposals for ways in which the various elements of 'empowerment' might be measured. She included consideration of the effects of education on women and the consequences of not taking inequalities in the state distribution of education seriously. So, by the time of the key UNESCO conference in Jomtien in 1990, which proposed the Millennium Development Goal of Education for All by 2005, girls' education had become a key concern, and the proportion of girls who have access to at least primary education became a key performance indicator.

As a consequence, the large numbers of children and especially girls who are not in school, and of women who are illiterate, continue to be an important object of research for many ministries of education and for large development agencies and their consultants and associated academics, working in (generally Western) universities. The official approach remains statistical and focused on problems of access and retention, but there is now some focus on what goes on inside poor schools and on the lives and values of teachers and of what is transmitted by teacher–educators. That is to say, there are now the beginnings of qualitative research and some ethnography of gender in small NGOs and individual schools and districts in low- to medium-income countries. There are also accounts of gender and learning and of gender and educational management and administration, so we have a better idea of what happens once girls and women do have 'access' to education.

However, such qualitative research in Southern countries is still only tenuously tied into theoretical debates in Western sociology, cultural studies, and women's studies, and it is barely influenced by Western feminist methodological discussions. Conversely, the concept of 'empowerment' has had little influence on Western feminist educational thinking. It has anyway now been somewhat superseded in development circles by Amartya Sen's capability approach, developed in relation to education by Martha Nussbaum (2000) and practically by UNICEF in its rights-based programming. But this approach is also little used in the West (Sen, 1999).

Most low- to medium-income countries lack the large base of educated women who have been so important to Western feminism and women's studies, so they have little research based on reflection by teachers (or by former teachers who are now educators in universities and colleges). They are also as yet little influenced by postmodern thinking on development (i.e. by postcolonial or post-development theory and its critiques of development practice and methodologies for thinking about the 'Third World') or by this approach to research on schooling. In return, the North could learn a lot from the literature in the South on the importance of not restricting one's view of education to a single country (or district or a few schools) and the educational implications of wider political, economic, and social changes, including the role of major inter-governmental organizations, and especially of global dialogues and international connections.

CONCLUSION

Women's movements have always recognized the importance of writing women's history, and not only to record events and give credit to past activists, but, more importantly, to try to analyse recent events and evaluate causal interconnections. We need currently to know much more about the relationship between education and the labour market, family relationships, changing social policies, and social movements. While there have been some moves in this direction, including autobiographies (e.g. David, 2003; Weiner, 1994), there remain many gaps and a general lack of a comparative perspective which would note differences and similarities between countries and regions.

We still need to evaluate fully how the women's liberation movement came to develop in Western countries, especially given the conservative cultural practices and stated policy aims of the curriculum and pedagogy of their schools in the 1950s and 1960s (Middleton, 1988). We need to look at what was achieved in the 1980s and to determine how much was due to changes in central government policy and how much to now-disparaged social movements and local institutions. In the UK, the 1980s' initiatives were ended abruptly, and so few evaluations were made of such equity projects (see Leonard, 2000), but feminists world-wide can learn from the work conducted in Australia (Kenway, Willis, Blackmore, and Rennie, 1997).

For policy-makers, contemporary history has several drawbacks. It is retrospective when they want information on what to change for the future. It shows the complexity of social structures and processes and how policies directed at one area can have unintended consequences elsewhere, rather than providing simple answers. It also clarifies how the implementation of educational policy is diverted by the imperatives of politicians who make short-term decisions to get themselves re-elected, the media seeking sensational stories, and individual litigation by parents and students, especially in the United States in regard to sexual harassment (Stein, 1999).

Writing our own history is, however, important to feminists in education because we need to let newcomers to the field, including new recruits to teaching, know about past gender politics. Most do not know what has been tried in the past and the reason why some initiatives succeeded and others failed. Changes in women's position in society, and especially in education, are often presented as having 'just happened' as society 'moves forward', rather than being the fruit of struggles. Moreover, girls still feel alienated from traditionally male subjects and have gendered career expectations, while a minority of boys still dominate the classroom environment and may impede girls' learning. Teachers still have lower expectations of girls than boys, and find boys more stimulating to teach. Equity issues may have been largely buried by the recent focus on the importance of education to national competitiveness, the stress on supposedly gender-neutral efficiency and effectiveness, and the potential of new management systems to spearhead change. New rigid curricula may have undermined the spaces boys and girls used to have to discuss and explore issues of gender and sexuality, and the teacher-training courses today may not deal with gender (either not at all or not in any detail) or be taught by people who have no specialist knowledge in this field. But writing our own history can renew our reflexivity about our changing conditions, our possibilities as researchers, and how political concerns and theory and research interact, and so encourage us to keep putting gender and girls' issues back onto the table.

REFERENCES

Apple, M. (1986) *Teachers and Texts: a political economy of class and gender relations in education*. New York: Routledge.

Archer, L. (2003) 'Evidence-based practice and educational research: When "what works" doesn't work…', in C. Skelton and B. Francis (eds), *Boys and Girls in the Primary Classroom*, Buckingham: Open University Press.

Arnot, M. and Dillabough, J.-A. (2000) *Challenging Democracy: international perspectives on gender, education and citizenship*. London: RoutledgeFalmer.

Arnot, M., David, M., and Weiner, G. (1999) *Closing the Gender Gap: postwar education and social change*. Cambridge: Polity Press.

Blackmore, J. (1999) *Troubling Women: feminism, leadership and educational change*. Buckingham: Open University Press.

Chodorow, N. (1978) *The Reproduction of Mothering: psychoanalysis and the sociology of gender*. Berkeley and Los Angeles: University of California Press.

David, M. (2003) *Personal and Political: feminisms, sociology and family lives*. Stoke-on-Trent: Trentham.

David, M. and Woodward, D. (eds) (1998) *Negotiating the Glass Ceiling: careers of senior women in the academic world*. London: Falmer Press.

Freire, P. (2000) *Pedagogy of the Oppressed* (30th anniversary edition), trans. Myra Bergman Ramos. London: Continuum International.

Gilligan, C. (1977) 'In a different voice: women's conceptions of the self and morality', *Harvard Educational Review* 47: 481–517.

Grumet, M. (1988) *Bitter Milk*. Amherst: University of Massachusetts Press.

Kabeer, N. (1999) *The Conditions and Consequences of Choice: reflections on the measurement of women's empowerment*. New York: United Nations Research Institute for Social Development (UNRISD).

Kenway, J. and Bullen, E. (2001) *Consuming Children: education-entertainment-advertising*. Buckingham: Open University Press.

Kenway, J., Willis, S., Blackmore, J., and Rennie, L. (1997) *Answering Back: girls, boys and feminism in schools*. St Leonards, NSW: Allen and Unwin.

Kolodny, A. (1998) *Failing the Future: a dean looks at higher education in the twenty-first century*. Durham, NC: Duke University Press.

Leonard, D. (1997) 'Gender issues in doctoral studies', in N. Graves and V. Varma (eds), *Working for a Doctorate: a guide for humanities and social sciences*. London: Routledge.

Leonard, D. (2000) 'Teachers, femocrats and academics: activism in London in the 1980s', in K. Myers (ed.), *Whatever Happened to Equal Opportunities in Schools? Gender equality initiatives in education*. Buckingham: Open University Press.

Middleton, S. (1988) 'Researching feminist educational life histories', in S. Middleton (ed.), *Women and Education in Aotearoa*. Sydney: Allen and Unwin.

Noddings, N. (1984) *Caring: a feminine approach to ethics and moral education*. Berkeley, CA: University of California Press.

Noddings, N. (1992) *The Challenge to Care in Schools*. New York: Teachers College Press.

Nussbaum, M. (2000) *Women and Human Development*. Cambridge: Cambridge University Press.

Rowland Martin, J. (1985) *Reclaiming a Conversation*. New Haven, CT: Yale University Press.

Salisbury, J. and Riddell, S. (eds) (2000) *Gender, Policy and Educational Change: shifting agendas in the UK and Europe*. London: Routledge.

Sen, A. (1999) *Development as Freedom*. Oxford: Oxford University Press.

Spender, D. (1982) *Invisible Women: the schooling scandal*. London: Writers and Readers Publishing Cooperative.

Spender, D. et al. (eds) (1980, revised edition 1988) *Learning to Lose: sexism and education*. London, Women's Press.

Stein, N. (1999) *Classrooms and Courtrooms: Facing Sexual Harassment in K-12 Schools*. New York: Teachers College Press.

Stone, L. (ed.) (1994) *The Education Feminism Reader*. New York, Routledge.

Stromquist, N. (1995) 'Romancing the state: gender and power in education', *Comparative Education Review*. 39(4): 423–454.

Unterhalter, E. (2003) 'Gender, basic education and development: a review of literature'. Background paper for the opening session of the DfID, Institute of Education/Oxfam project 'Beyond Access: gender, education and development'. London: Institute of Education.

Walkerdine, V. (1984) 'Developmental psychology and the child-centred pedagogy: the insertion of Piaget into early education', in J. Henriques et al. *Changing the Subject: psychology, social regulation and subjectivity*. London: Methuen.

Weiner, G. (1994) *Feminisms in Education: an introduction*. Buckingham: Open University Press.

Part IV
GLOBALIZATION AND THE STATE

10

Gender in a Global World

Miri Song

Work about globalization has been very wide-ranging and comes to quite different conclusions about the implications of globalization for different societies and groups. The focus of this chapter will be a critical discussion of the grand pronouncements which are often made about globalization, whether they be in relation to the economic, cultural, or political realms. Work on globalization, I argue, needs to be tempered by more empirically based investigations into the highly variable effects of this phenomenon. First, I examine the overly celebratory and breezy claims made about diasporic minority identities within the context of globalization. Second, I discuss the erasure of gender in most mainstream writings about globalization. In doing so, I explore some of the difficulties which arise when we think within a 'global' framework.

WHAT IS GLOBALIZATION?

It is now heard everywhere: we live in an increasingly global world, or 'global village' (McLuhan, 1964). Generally speaking, globalization entails the increased interconnections of social, economic, cultural, and political life, and has resulted in the spread of capitalist market relations and a truly interconnected global economy.[1] Another key aspect of globalization is the way in which information and communications technology has resulted in 'time–space compression' which links distant lands and lives together (Harvey, 1989).

There are various arguments made about the effects of globalization in virtually every sphere of life. For instance, there is an ongoing debate about whether there is such a thing as a global economy, or whether it is even a recent development. For the hyperglobalists, such as Kenichi Ohmae (1996), contemporary globalization defines a new era in which people everywhere are increasingly subject to the disciplines of the global marketplace. Such a view of globalization generally privileges an economic logic, and some proponents of this view celebrate the emergence of a single global market and the principle of global competition as the harbingers of human progress. In response to such claims, analysts such as Paul Hirst and Graham Thompson (1996) argue that while globalization has become a fashionable concept in the social sciences, it is essentially a myth which conceals the reality of an internationalized economy which is neither new nor unprecedented. They would also deny that nation-states have lost control over key aspects of their economies, especially in relation to various domestic social policies.

Related to this debate, some analysts (the 'declinists') argue that the nation-state's autonomy and legitimacy, more generally, is very much in decline (Featherstone and Lash, 1995; Giddens, 1999; Held, McGrew, Goldblatt, and Perraton 1999; Ohmae, 1996). Yet others (the 'sceptics') argue, for a variety of reasons, that nation-states still play an absolutely vital part in the contemporary global context, in terms of both their international roles and their ability to determine domestic social policies (Hirst and Thompson, 1996). Furthermore, nation-states are said to be bolstered by nationalist sentiments and feelings which are of continuing importance for people all around the world (Smith, 1990).

Another widely debated topic is the hegemonic influence of Western culture and ideology and its effects on the rest of the world. Francis Fukuyama (1992) famously declared 'the end of history' and the triumph of liberal capitalism, thus heralding a global unity which was previously unthinkable. He claimed, in the aftermath of the fall of the Berlin Wall and the then incipient dismantling of the Soviet Union, that the war of ideas and ideologies was at an end, and that the future would be devoted to the resolution of rather mundane economic problems. This line of thinking was rebutted by the controversial claim that, contrary to a kind of global harmony emerging, we are headed for a major 'clash of civilizations,' in which the great divisions among humankind and the dominating source of conflict will be cultural (Huntington, 1993).

Many writers now observe that globalization is a dialectical process, meaning that rather than producing a uniform set of changes, globalization consists of mutually opposed tendencies (Featherstone, 1990; Giddens, 1990). For example, this dialectical process can be illustrated by the tendencies toward cultural homogenization *and* cultural differentiation (Hall, Held, and McGrew, 1992). Globalization is sometimes interpreted as a process of gradual homogenization dictated by the West, whether it be in the clothes we wear or the food we eat (Latouche, 1996; Ritzer, 1996). At the same time, globalization can engender emotionally laden forms of nationalisms (Smith, 1990) and a return to the mythic certainties of the 'old traditions' (Morley and Robins, 1995), which refute any conception of a genuinely representative and collective identity and experience.

Yet others have argued that while national identities are declining, new hybridized identities are emerging (Appadurai, 1990; Pieterse, 1994):

> By compressing time and space, globalization forces the juxtaposition of different civilizations, ways of life, and social practices. This both reinforces social and cultural prejudices and boundaries whilst simultaneously creating 'shared' cultural and social spaces in which there is an evolving 'hybridisation' of ideas, values, knowledge and institutions. (Hall et al., 1992: 75).

As a result of these processes, more and more people are said to be involved with more than one culture (Hannerz, 1990).

The dynamics associated with globalization, and modernity more generally, are said to destabilize established identities (Calhoun, 1994; Giddens 1990). Increasingly, peoples' sense of their ethnic identities and affiliations are said to be relativized and shaped by our greater consciousness of the interconnections of people and societies around the world (Featherstone, 1990; Robertson, 1992). Globalization and the shifting and multifaceted nature of ethnic identification in many Western societies are especially relevant in relation to second-, third-, and fourth-generation 'diasporic' minority people, who are negotiating their senses of home and belonging within multiethnic societies, such as the United States and Britain.

While most analysts are centrally concerned with the effects of globalization and the processes underlying it, still others are interested in globalization, 'not simply [as] an empirical force that has changed the everyday realities of people's lives, but [as] *a discursive condition*, currently being reproduced within academia and outside it' (Franklin, Lury, and Stacey, 2000: 4). For them, globalization is an open-ended process without known outcomes.

This brief overview should impart a sense of the wide-ranging discussions and debates concerning globalization. Given the massive number of publications on globalization to date, and the very diverse perspectives and disciplines of scholars in the field, I cannot provide an exhaustive account of how globalization is theorized or documented. The focus of this chapter will be a critical discussion of the grand pronouncements which are often made about globalization, especially in the economic, cultural, and political realms. I argue that work on globalization needs tempering by empirically based investigations into its effects. I will first examine the overly celebratory claims made about diasporic minority identities, and then I will discuss the erasure of gender in most mainstream writings about globalization. In doing so, I will explore some of the difficulties inherent in thinking 'globally.'

GLOBALIZATION: AN OVERLY CELEBRATORY DISCOURSE

In some of the literature on globalization and diaspora (though these terms encompass an admittedly diverse array of work), the postmodern emphasis on fluid identities and positionings is far too celebratory. It emphasizes the freedom with which diasporic minorities – the 'subject' or 'subaltern' – are able to mine connections and identities in relation to their real or imagined 'homeland' and their country of residence (Bhabha, 1994; Featherstone, 1996; Pieterse, 1994). For example, Mike Featherstone points to the 'extension of cultural repertoires and an enhancement of the resourcefulness of groups to create new symbolic modes of affiliation and belonging' (1996: 74). For Homi Bhabha (1994), marginal, betwixt, and between postcolonial migrants are a real force to be reckoned with, and diasporas are liberating forces against oppressive state structures and exclusionary nationalisms. Some also argue that new, more contingent forms of allegiance and identity are making the nation-state largely obsolete (Glick-Schiller, 1999).

There is no question that contemporary understandings of cultural and ethnic identity must be anti-essentialist and capable of conceptualizing change and multiple forms of affiliations which can transcend national borders. While I would agree that agency and the choices made about ethnic identity are extremely relevant for ethnic minority peoples (Song, 2003), the politics and dynamics of diasporic peoples' ethnic affiliations and identifications are far more constrained and subject to negotiation than suggested by the rather breezy celebrations of diaspora and hybridity. Not all diasporic people may be equally successful in their efforts to assert hybridized identities or to occupy and enunciate a 'third space.'

Some of the theoretical work on globalization and diaspora lacks concrete articulations of the specific local and national structures which shape and constrain diasporic groups and individuals around the world. In addition, much of this work obscures the differential ability of postcolonial peoples to realize their desired positionings and identifications. The 'subject' is rarely discussed in sufficiently concrete context, and often seems to be floating around in an ether of endless possibilities. It is important to weave together a framework which takes into account both the analysis of cultural politics and the political economy of specific histories and geopolitical situations (Ong, 1999).

The celebration of these interstitial spaces between cultures, which are inhabited by diasporas, migrants, refugees, and exiles, is problematic because it tends to obscure the ways in which the material specificities of both geographical location and the racialized body mediate one's ability to negotiate one's belonging and status in a given society. Place, class, gender, 'race,' and nationality all intertwine in complex ways in constraining the opportunities available to diasporic individuals. True, globalization has enabled the emergence of culturally hybrid identities, but not all hybridized subjects occupy the same social and political space. The key idea – that with globalization comes the relativization of identities – is overstated, in that it tends to overlook the very real consequences of the differential embodiment and status associated with different kinds of 'races,' gender, and class. Not only is some global discourse too abstract and celebratory, it also tends to treat globalization as a gender-neutral process.

GENDER IN GLOBALIZATION

Most mainstream work on globalization has had very little to say about gender inequalities and the experiences of women in different regions of the world. Given the widespread acknowledgement that globalization can divide as well as unite (Bauman, 1998; Robertson, 1992), analysts readily point to the unequal outcomes of globalization, especially in relation to different parts of the world, such as the 'North' and the 'South' (though these terms themselves are being contested). Yet relatively few writers on globalization make more than a passing reference to how the processes and effects of globalization may be gendered.

While many women scholars, such as Saskia Sassen (1998) and Doreen Massey (1994), address the dynamics and processes associated with globalization in their work, writing on the subject of globalization (and the discourse of globalization) has been dominated thus far by men. In fact, a very diverse array of feminist scholars, such as Cynthia Enloe (1990) and Elspeth Probyn (1996), talk about issues which are clearly related to globalization – such as inequalities, belonging, and place – without recourse to the language of globalization.

Most theorizing on globalization has been macro-level and has implied a gender-neutral thrust to the ongoing processes associated with it. For instance, in *Runaway World* (1999), Giddens talks persuasively about how globalization is reshaping our lives. Giddens is sensitive to the fact that much of the scholarship on globalization is highly abstract: 'Globalization isn't only about what is "out there", remote and far away from the individual. It is an "in here" phenomenon too, influencing intimate and personal aspects of our lives' (p. 12). While he makes the *de rigueur* references to women and family life, he says very little of substance on this topic. According to Giddens: 'Traditional family systems are becoming transformed, or are under strain, in many parts of the world, particularly as women stake claim to greater equality' (p. 12). While this pronouncement is not in any obvious way wrong, it is so general as to be virtually meaningless.

There is a great deal of scholarship which seems adept at documenting, in detail, the complex workings of global trade and finance or the remit of contemporary nation-states without a consideration of how these complex processes may be gendered. As a result, mainstream scholarship on globalization, dominated by men, is devoid of analyses of how gendered processes are generated, maintained, and changed by the complexity of globalization. In recent years, some feminist scholars have begun to challenge the highly abstract, gender-neutral discussion of globalization. In a recent special issue of *International Sociology*, 'Gender matters: studying globalization and social change in the 21st century,' Esther Ngan-ling Chow (2003) argues that mainstream theorizing about globalization '[ignores] how globalization shapes gender relationships and people's lives materially, politically, socially and culturally at all levels…In particular, women's voices and lives are virtually absent from much theoretical discussion on globalization.' Chow goes on to point out that 'when the gender issue is discussed, the focus tends to be on the effects of globalization on women rather than on the effects of gender on globalization' (p. 444).

Gender clearly matters for understanding what globalization is and how it is shaped by gendered hierarchies and ideologies, which in turn shape gendered institutions, relationships, and the experiences and identities of women and men (Chow, 2003). The underlying logics of globalization in capitalist production, market rationality, transnational corporations, and trade liberalization are themselves gendered processes based upon institutional arrangements which perpetuate unequal power relationships between women and men (Kimmel, 2003). Global production networks which have experienced significant growth, such as export production, sex work, and domestic service, are gendered, and there are systematic linkages between the global expansion of production, trade, and finance and the increase of women in these networks (Pyle and Ward, 2003).

Diverse forms of transnational migration arise in the context of globalization, including the dense network of economic and social relationships which are illustrative of the growing interconnectedness of societies around the world. Transnational migration can also involve family survival strategies, which are gendered. When Filipina women migrate to Rome to work in domestic service, they are acting as key breadwinners for their families in the Philippines. As a consequence of globalization and debt crisis, the Philippines is now the largest labor-exporting Asian country, and has approximately 5–7 million overseas Filipino workers in more than 160 countries, including Italy (Lindio-McGovern, 2003: 514). Ligaya Lindio-McGovern sees Filipina migrant women's work as domestic servants in Italy as an example of the changing transnational division of labor in which the intersection of gender, class, racial ethnicity, and nationality ends up reinforcing global inequalities.

Thus, the feminization of export labor offers insights into how globalization can result in the widening gap between the richer and poorer countries, as well as the close intersection of gender/race/ethnicity/nationality/ 'North–South' in the processes and practices of what we call 'globalization' in its many forms. Other feminist analyses of women's migrant labor in the past have argued that some women can benefit from particular forms of transnational migration. For instance, women's contributions to family survival strategies via the formation of transnational households can empower women (Boyd, 1989; Morokvasic, 1984).

The operation of global, transnational corporations cannot be understood properly without a consideration of the gender norms, though largely unspoken, underlying employment practices in such firms. In her study of Korean transnational companies based in New York City, Jo Kim (2004) found that one's ethnic identity (or the attributions of such an identity by the management in these firms), as either predominantly Korean or predominantly American (in the case of Korean Americans who were raised in the United States), was used to impose and justify biased organizational work practices. Kim observed that for feminized tasks, such as typing, serving coffee, and drafting documents, the Korean managers tended to ask the 'Korean' Korean American women staff, assuming a 'common cultural understanding' with them, which they assumed they would not have with 'Americanized' Korean American women subordinates. In such settings, gendered hierarchies and practices are interwoven with ethnic hierarchies and practices.

What more and more studies of globalization reveal is that analyses of gender cannot be extricated from its combination with national, racial, ethnic, and class contexts. For instance, the experiences of domestic service workers who migrate abroad underscore how simplistic the notion of the First/Third World split is, and how inadequate it is to make sense of today's international politics (Enloe, 1990: 193). Not only do affluent White women hire Mexican women in the United States, but wealthy women in other developing countries hire poor women from the 'Third' World – for instance, Filipina maids are employed in affluent Middle Eastern households, such as in Jordan and Saudi Arabia, where they are often sexually abused and beaten.

GLOBALIZATION AND TRANSNATIONAL FEMINIST MOVEMENTS

Feminist scholarship about globalization is now growing, and feminists are asking a wide array of questions which have not been sufficiently addressed thus far. In theorizing the constitutive effects of the global in making worlds, bodies, selves, and futures, Franklin et al. (2000) say that they are increasingly interested in not what gender is, but what it does, as an open-ended and contested process. As mentioned earlier, Chow argues that rather than confining our inquiries to how globalization impacts on gender, we need to ask how the enactment and embodiment of gender impacts upon the many processes which make up globalization.

In recognizing the gendered dynamics and processes of globalization, we must avoid making unfounded generalizations. It is now axiomatic in feminist theory and practice that 'woman' is not a unitary homogeneous category, especially in the context of globalization. In fact, feminist ways of knowing are inherently perspectival and culture-bound. As Chandra Mohanty has noted: 'The assumption of women as an already constituted and coherent group with identical interests and desires, regardless of class, ethnic or racial location, implies a notion of gender or sexual difference or even patriarchy which can be applied universally and cross-culturally' (1988: 242). A universalizing gender analysis is no more legitimate within the context of globalization than it was before globalization became a household term in the early 1990s. While a sweeping analysis of the gendered dimensions of globalization may be tempting, given the near invisibility of gender in most mainstream writings about globalization, gender is a master status which makes such a task not only difficult, but rather dangerous. This is the case whether we are talking about gendered divisions of labor or the kinds of childcare which are available to working mothers – across various societies.

Is there any reason to think that the effects of globalization are resulting in greater interconnections or shared experiences and interests of women worldwide? In 1985, Avtar Brah (1996) attended the International Women's Conference in Nairobi. Over 10,000 women from more than 150 countries gathered to address questions of women's 'universal' subordination as a 'second sex.' According to Brah, the most striking aspect of this conference was the heterogeneity of women's social conditions. Brah's observations dating back to 1985 are probably no less resonant now – when our awareness of being in the throes of globalization is high: 'The issues raised by the different groups of women present at the conference, especially those from the Third World, served to underline the fact that issues affecting women cannot be analysed in isolation from the national and international context of inequality' (Brah, 1996: 102; see also Mohanty, 1988).

However, there is some evidence of feminist dialogue and movements which transcend societal borders and raise questions about what constitutes women's rights, who is to define such rights, and the politics of cultural relativism. Violence against women is an issue that arrived relatively late in the international women's movement, differing from the classic issues of suffrage, equality, and discrimination, around which women have long mobilized. Violence was one of the four issues given special prominence at the UN Conference on Women in Beijing in 1995 (Keck and Sikkink, 1998). The focus on violence included not just sexual violence such as rape, but also female infanticide (in China, for example), differential access to food and medical care for girls, and forms of genital mutilation of girls.

In the early 1990s, the issue of violence against women coalesced around the Global Campaign for Women's Human Rights. Coordinated at Rutgers University in the United States, it was based on the groundwork of international networks and local groups in many countries. This campaign 'offers an unusually clear example of global moral entrepreneurs consciously strategizing on how to frame issues in a way likely to attract the broadest possible global coalition' (Keck and Sikkink, 1998: 185).

The emergence of the issue of violence against women as an international issue shows how two previously separate transnational networks – around human rights and women's rights – began to converge and mutually transform each other. What was previously seen as a 'women's issue' became related to 'human rights' issues and global discourses. Recent scholarship about how women's rights may be interpreted and employed in Muslim societies, such as Pakistan, illustrates the intellectual and political challenge of implementing what some non-Western people may regard as a questionable Western import. Anita Weiss (2003) investigates Pakistan's response to becoming a state party to the United Nations' Convention on the Elimination of All Forms of Discrimination Against Women (CEDAW). She argues that what actually does (and does not) constitute discrimination against women, and how the state might act to eliminate such discrimination against women, both legally and socially, is, to say the least, a tricky business, if the implementation of CEDAW is to be acceptable to local mores and values in Pakistan. Such case studies are crucial for future feminist analyses of globalization, in order to avoid the highly abstract, vague social theory which permeates much of the existing mainstream scholarship on globalization.

CONCLUSION

It is imperative that globalization is not regarded as a set of anonymous, gender-neutral forces, but rather as processes shaped (and contested) by specific groups, nations, alliances, and movements. We must remember that globalization is quite uneven in its effects – in its 'power geometry' (Massey, 1994).

Sassen is hopeful that the ascendance of an international human rights regime and the participation of a large variety of non-state actors in the global arena will provide 'a space where women can gain visibility as individuals and as collective actors, and come out of the invisibility of aggregate membership in a nation-state exclusively represented by the sovereign' (1998: 99). Here, Sassen points to the need for women to work at least partly outside of the state, through non-state groups and networks. Gendered analyses of globalization are needed to reveal the specificity of global–local linkages mediated by nation-states, international organizations, and regional networks (Chow, 2003).

But in bringing gender into our understandings of globalization, we should avoid generalizations about gender and globalization. In particular, we need to move away from overly broad debates about whether globalization is 'good' or 'bad' in terms of its effects on women. Such a question can only make sense in a much more qualified form: For whom and in what place is this particular aspect of globalization good or bad? To what extent do women in specific societies support or contest certain aspects of globalization? On the one hand, globalization can create new employment opportunities for some women and hence foster economic independence and greater life choices, albeit limited. For example, when Nike opens a factory in Vietnam, many young women hope to obtain jobs at this factory. At the same time, such jobs, made possible by the dominance of global transnational companies, can be regarded negatively, in terms of the feminization of labor in segregated and low-paying sectors, whether it is the 'nimble fingers' needed in electronic assembly and textile work, or the making of Nike trainers. Women (both within and across societies) are bound to disagree about whether certain aspects of globalization are predominantly positive or negative.

In conclusion, the growing number of studies on globalization demonstrates that analyses of gender cannot be extricated from its relationship with national, ethnic, and class contexts. In recognizing the gendered dynamics of globalization, we must not make the mistake of making generalized claims about the effects of globalization on 'women' as a unitary group.

NOTE

1 As discussed in many references (see Boli and Thomas, 1999; Giddens, 1990; Hoogvelt, 1997; Massey, 1994; Reich, 1991; Robertson, 1992; Waters, 1995).

REFERENCES

Appadurai, Arjun (1990) 'Disjuncture and difference in the global cultural economy,' in M. Featherstone (ed.), *Global Culture*, London: Sage, 295–310.
Bauman, Zygmunt (1998) *Globalization: The Human Consequences*, Cambridge: Polity Press.
Bhabha, Homi (1994) *The Location of Culture*, New York: Routledge.
Boli, John and Thomas, George (1999) *Constructing World Culture*, Stanford, CA: Stanford University Press.
Boyd, M. (1989) 'Family and personal networks in international migration', *International Migration Review*, vol. 23, no. 3, 638–70.
Brah, Avtar (1996) *Cartographies of Diaspora*, London: Routledge.
Calhoun, Craig (1994) 'Social theory and the politics of identity,' in C. Calhoun (ed.), *Social Theory and the Politics of Identity*, Oxford: Blackwell, 9–36.
Chow, Esther Ngan-ling (2003) 'Gender matters: studying globalization and social change in the 21st century,' *International Sociology*, vol. 18, no. 3, 443–60.
Enloe, Cynthia (1990) *Bananas, Beaches, and Bases*, Berkeley, CA: University of California Press.
Featherstone, M. (1990) 'Global culture: an introduction,' in M. Featherston (ed.), *Global Culture* London: Sage, 1–14.
Featherstone, M. (1996) 'Localism, globalism, and cultural identity,' in Rob Wilson and Wilmal Dissanayake (eds), *Global/Local*, Durham, NC: Duke University Press.
Featherstone, M. and Lash, S. (1995) 'Globalization, modernity and the spatialization of social theory: an introduction,' in M. Featherstone, S. Lash, and R. Robertson (eds), *Global Modernities*, London: Sage, 1–24.
Franklin, S., Lury, C., and Stacey, J. (2000) *Global Nature, Global Culture*, London: Sage.
Fukuyama, Francis (1992) *The End of History and the Last Man*, London: Hamish Hamilton.
Giddens, Anthony (1990) *The Consequences of Modernity*, Cambridge: Polity Press.
_____ (1999) *Runaway World*, London: Profile Books.
Glick-Schiller, Nina (1999) 'Transmigrants and nation-states,' in Charles Hirschman, Phil Kasinitz, and Josh DeWind (eds), *Handbook of International Migration*, New York: Russell Sage.
Hall, Stuart, Held, David, and McGrew, Anthony (eds) (1992) *Modernity and its Futures*, Milton Keynes: Open University Press.
Hannerz, Ulf (1990) 'Cosmopolitans and locals in world culture,' in M. Featherstone (ed.), *Global Culture*, London: Sage, 237–52.

Harvey, David (1989) *The Condition of Postmodernity*, Oxford: Blackwell.
Held, David, McGrew, A., Goldblatt, D. Perraton, J. (1999) *Global Transformations*, Stanford, CA: Stanford University Press.
Hirst, Paul and Thompson, Grahame (1996) *Globalization in Question*, Cambridge: Polity Press.
Hoogvelt, Anke (1997) *Globalisation and the Postcolonial World*, Basingstoke: Macmillan.
Huntington, Samuel (1993) 'The clash of civilizations,' *Foreign Affairs*, vol. 72, no. 3, 22–49.
Keck, Margaret and Sikkink, Kathryn (1998) *Activists Beyond Borders*, Ithaca, NY: Cornell University Press.
Kim, Jo (2004) '"They are more like us": the salience of ethnicity in the global workplace of Korean transnational corporations,' *Ethnic and Racial Studies*, vol. 27, no. 1, 69–94.
Kimmel, M. (2003) 'Globalization and its mal(e)contents,' *International Sociology*, vol. 18, no. 3, 603–20.
Latouche, Serge (1996) *Westernization of the World*, Cambridge: Polity Press.
Lindio-McGovern, Ligaya (2003) 'Labor export in the context of globalization,' *International Sociology*, vol. 18, no. 3, 513–34.
Massey, Doreen (1994) *Space, Place and Gender*, Cambridge: Polity Press.
McLuhan, Marshall (1964) *Understanding Media*, London: Routledge.
Mohanty, Chandra (1988) 'Under Western Eyes,' *Feminist Review*, no. 30, 238–51.
Morley, David and Robins, Kevin (1995) 'Reimagined communities? New media, new possibilities,' in David Morley and Kevin Robins, *Spaces of Identity: Global Media, Electronic Landscapes and Cultural Boundaries*, New York: Routledge.
Morokvasic, M. (1984) 'Birds of passage are also women,' *International Migration Review*, Special issue on women immigrants, vol. 18, no. 4, 886–907.
Ohmae, Kenichi (1996) *The End of the Nation State*, London: Harper Collins.
Ong, Aihwa (1999) *Flexible Citizenship*, Durham, NC: Duke University Press.
Pieterse, Jan N. (1994) 'Globalization as hybridisation,' *International Sociology*, vol. 9, no. 2, 11–34.
Probyn, Elspeth (1996) *Outside Belongings*, London: Routledge.
Pyle, J. and Ward, K. (2003) 'Recasting our understanding of gender and work during global restructuring,' *International Sociology*, vol. 18, no. 3, 461–89.
Reich, Robert (1991) *The Work of Nations*, New York: Knopf.
Ritzer, George (1996) *The McDonaldization of Society*, Thousand Oaks, CA: Pine Forge Press.
Robertson, R. (1992) *Globalization*, London: Sage.
Sassen, Saskia (1998) *Globalization and its Discontents*, New York: New Press.
Smith, Anthony (1990) 'Towards a global culture?', in M. Featherstone (ed.), *Global Culture*, London: Sage, 171–92.
Song, Miri (2003) *Choosing Ethnic Identity*, Cambridge: Polity Press.
Waters, Malcom (1995) *Globalization*, London: Sage.
Weiss, A. (2003) 'Interpreting Islam and women's rights,' *International Sociology*, vol. 18, no. 3, 581–601.

11

Insiders and Outsiders
Within and Beyond the Gendered Nation

Barbara Einhorn

This chapter examines the intimate relationship of gender, nation, and nationalism, both in scholarship and in the lives of real people. It begins by showing how scholarly attempts to define the nation have, historically, omitted gender, both as a key social variable and as a tool of analysis. Feminist interventions since the late 1980s have breathed new life into considerations of the ways in which not only gender, but sexuality, 'race', class, and religion play into, and are in turn affected by, nationalist projects. Underlying both notions of nation and the politics of nation-building is a gendered power politics. The deployment of gender and sexuality in the politics of national reproduction helps to forge close links between nationalism and militarism. The chapter considers how the language of citizenship and the practices of transnational feminism might serve to contest and transcend the political limitations and the exclusionary tendencies of nationalism.

INTRODUCTION

This chapter considers how processes of nation-building rely on gendered discourses and symbolic representations. These discourses have material, embodied consequences for both insiders and outsiders, especially when the nation feels itself to be under threat or during periods of actual inter- or intra-national conflict. Nationalist discourses interact with political institutions and manipulate social and cultural practices to imprint gendered identities on embodied subjects, attempting to make them malleable within the power struggles of the nation-building (or nation-defending) process. I demonstrate the interplay of gendered discourses with normative notions of sexuality, class, 'race', and religion in the service and reproduction of the national idea. In discussing how the language of citizenship might facilitate contestation of the gendered hierarchies naturalized by nationalist discourses, I pay tribute to the transformative potential of feminist initiatives enacting a 'transversal politics' across the boundaries of nationalist conflicts (Cockburn, 1998; 2004; Yuval-Davis, 1997).

THE NATION AS A CONCEPT

The nation is an elusive entity. Despite frequent conflation of the two concepts, it is not synonymous with the nation state. The nation is an amorphous 'idea', an 'imagined community' (Anderson, 1983). Yet nationalists usually intend it to map onto a particular geographical territory or ethnic community in their intention to create a political state. The idea that nationalist strategies aim to translate ideologies of belonging into political statehood is contested by theorists who hold that the nation brings together those with allegiance to a shared cultural heritage (Smith, 1991: 74). Such theorists see the nation as timeless and immutable, hence fundamentally ahistorical and 'natural'. For Eric Hobsbawm, this 'naturalization' forms part of a process of 'inventing traditions' (1983: 1).

The need for norms of behaviour and traditional practices to be continually reinvented through ritual hints both at the precariousness of imputed homogeneity within the national community and at the centrality of gender in articulating and perpetuating the sense of national belonging. Somebody has to invoke and perform the rituals that reinforce these norms and to inculcate them into the next generation in order to ensure historical continuity. This 'somebody' is woman-as-mother-of-the-nation (Peterson, 1994), with the nation construed as 'metaphoric kinship' (Eriksen, 1993: 108; Smith, 1991: 79), or as 'family-writ-large' (Golden, 2003: 85).

The nation is in fact both political – in striving to create a state or to defend national boundaries – *and* cultural, representing a set of values and meanings inscribed in 'a system of cultural representation' (Hall, 1992: 292). Yet nationalism as an ideology can be enlisted either in the support of political modernization or in support of a backward-looking traditionalism, and has therefore often been referred to as 'Janus-faced'.[1] Nations can emphasize their 'shared socio-cultural attitudes and historical memories'; they can also manifest 'disrespect for and animosity towards other peoples (racism, xenophobia, anti-Semitism)' (Alter, 1994: 3). Most nations define themselves negatively, *against* (imputed) Others. As communities, they tend to be *ex*clusive, not *in*clusive.

While nations claim a unity of *insiders* against *outside* groups, they are in fact neither homogeneous nor united. The issue of power emerges here, not only as an issue of power *over* Others, but as a hierarchy of power *among* 'insider' groups in the struggle for 'authentic' national identity.[2] It is here that gendered – and sexualized – discourses creep in, defining who belongs to the national body and disciplining those who do not, setting dominant 'insiders' against 'enemies within' (Kofman, Phizacklea, Raghuram, and Sales, 2000: 37). Tamar

Mayer argues that the nation was 'produced as a heterosexual male construct, whose "ego" is intimately connected to patriarchal hierarchies and norms' (2000a: 6). Sheila Allen reminds us that 'both in social science and in practice, women have been defined as the "Other"' within (1998: 55). Men take on the duty of policing shared norms, ensuring that women enact their allotted roles in the national drama and causing tension between women who conform and any who resist. Nationalist discourses also discipline men who fail to perform normative masculinity. Leslie Dwyer confirms that 'the repression and policing of sexualities labelled as aberrant' have made them the scapegoats of nationalist narratives (2000: 27–8).

EARLY FEMINIST STUDIES OF NATIONALISM

According to Cynthia Enloe, 'as insightful and helpful' as Benedict Anderson and other theorists were 'in charting new ways to think about the creation of nationalist ideas, they left nationalists…ungendered' (1993: 231). Much academic scholarship on the nation still remains both gender-blind and disembodied.[3] Yet 'international politics and global political economy impact directly and often violently upon the bodies of actual people' (Pettman, 2000: 52).

Enloe pioneered the feminist challenge to theories of nationalism, showing that international affairs, the realms of diplomacy, inter-state relations, and (inter)national conflicts were not exclusively the preserve of men. She uncovered apparently obvious truths, namely that diplomacy depended on the charms of diplomatic wives, that international affairs and trade would founder without the input of (largely) women secretaries,[4] and that militaries depend not only on women support staff, but also on the sexual services of women. From this insight, she concluded that 'making women invisible hides the workings of both femininity and masculinity in international politics' (1989: 11).

Most early feminist contributions to scholarship on the nation focused on the ways in which nationalist discourses manipulated and instrumentalized otherwise invisible women. They primarily highlighted how nationalism depicted women-as-objects, exploited women-as-symbols, and affected women-as-victims. In their path-breaking text *Woman-Nation-State*, Floya Anthias and Nira Yuval-Davis elaborated five ways in which women figured in the national project, as: biological reproducers of the ethnic collectivity; reproducers of the boundaries between ethnic/national groups; agents in the ideological reproduction of the group's ethical and cultural identity; symbolic signifiers of group differences; and active participants in national identity struggles (1989: 7). Kumari Jayawardena (1986) was the first to argue that struggles for national liberation in former colonial countries in Asia initially empowered their female participants.

The involvement of women activists in nation-building projects and the successes of nationalist movements in introducing emancipatory measures have also been documented for Poland, Korea, Finland, Israel, and Palestine. Yet most accounts agree that while these activists subordinated gender-based demands to the goal of national independence, their mobilization resulted in neither the establishment of women's organizations nor the adoption of feminist agendas after the achievement of national independence. Rather, 'normalization' processes tended to return women to 'their "accustomed place"' (Jayawardena, 1986: 259; see also Fidelis, 2001; Juntti, 1998; Kim, 1996; Marakowitz, 1996; Sharoni, 1998: 1070).

It is understandable that many early feminist theorists of nationalism concentrated exclusively on women. In doing so, they 'for the most part, neglected to analyze *men* as an equally constructed category' (Mayer, 2000a: 5; emphasis in original). Four years after her ground-breaking *Bananas, Beaches and Bases* (1989), Enloe noted that 'because we still know too little about women's experiences of nationalism, we have left ourselves ignorant of men – as men – in the histories of nationalism [and] the uses of masculinity in the mobilization of national consciousness' (1993: 236).

RECENT FEMINIST SCHOLARSHIP ON NATIONALISM

Recent feminist scholarship has therefore stressed the decisive impact of notions of *masculinity* on definitions of national identity, power, and hegemony. This work enhances earlier discussions about how nationalisms construct and functionalize women through discourses of appropriate *femininity*. Increasing emphasis has been placed on gender relations as relations of (unequal) power in nationalist projects, for 'masculinity and femininity are not "independent" categories…but are defined in *oppositional* relation to each other' (Peterson and Runyan, 1999: 8).

Establishing the pertinence of gender to nation requires us to understand that 'the notion of nation always suggests a project of power' (Cockburn, 1998: 37). Since this project has always been dominated by men, 'nationalist ideologies, strategies, and structures have served to update and so perpetuate the privileging of masculinity' (Enloe, 1993: 229, 323; 2004: 102–4). Nationalist ideologies rely on constructions of masculinity and femininity to 'naturalize' power struggles over who gets to define what the nation stands for. Nations are thus not just 'systems of cultural representation', but also 'constitutive of people's identities through social contests that are frequently violent and always gendered' (McClintock, 1997: 89).

NATION, GENDER, AND SEXUALITY

Notions of nation are intimately intertwined with, indeed depend upon, the manipulation of rigid gender norms, such that 'despite many nationalists' ideological investment in the idea of popular *unity*, nations have historically amounted to the sanctioned institutionalisation of gender *difference*' (McClintock, 1995: 353). Gender difference as mythic stereotype gets translated into political dicta and behavioural norms for present-day women and men.

'Woman' is depicted in the iconography of the nation as the *Motherland*, the title of the massive statue by Evgenii Vuchetich that dominates Volgograd (Warner, 1985: plate 1). Eric Hobsbawm identifies such 'personification of "the nation" in symbol or image…as with Marianne or Germania' as part of the process of 'inventing traditions…[which] we should expect…to occur more frequently when a rapid transformation of society weakens or destroys the social patterns for which "old" traditions had been designed' (Hobsbawm, 1983: 4,7). Hobsbawm explains here why nationalist fervour is highest in times of social upheaval or perceived external threat. Despite stereotypes of a weak femininity in need of defence by masculinized militarism, the personification of the nation as Mother Russia, Marianne, or Britannia reveals gender ambivalence and sexual ambiguity. All three appear as part mother, part warrior maiden. Vuchetich's super-sized Motherland may have breasts and child-bearing hips, but her muscular physique and warlike posture, brandishing a sword, emulate the stance of male warriors. Eugene Delacroix's famous painting of *Liberty Leading the People* renders her gown as having slipped, revealing breasts either erotic or motherly, depending on the viewer. Yet she wields a flag in one hand and a bayonet in the other as she stands dominant on a mound, surrounded by the bodies of dead patriotic warriors.[5] Britannia is always depicted as a warrior, with helmet and shield over-riding the soft folds of her gown.[6]

Symbolic constructions of woman as the embodiment of nation decisively affect the behaviour and room for movement afforded actual women. Yet these 'tropes of femininity' are double-edged in more ways than one. First, they reveal 'the disparity between the symbolic power of feminine images and women's material conditions of inferior social, economic, and political status in a range of locations' (Chan, 2003: 581–2). Second, they stress that national identity is not fixed, but always under construction.

'Man' is depicted as the 'warrior-hero' or the 'citizen-warrior', entrusted with the almost sacred duty to defend the homeland (Mayer, 2000a: 11; Peterson, 1994). This mythological role necessitates (in real time and real terms) men protecting – and policing – the sexuality and reproductive function of the ethnic/national group's women. In this way, 'the metaphors of nation-as-woman and woman-as-nation suggest how women, as bodies and cultural repositories, become the battleground of group struggles' (Peterson, 1994: 79; see also Peterson, 1996: 7). Thus, the gendered divisions of *symbolic* national identity signal *material* relationships of unequal power in which 'through control over reproduction, sexuality, and the means of representation, the authority to define the nation lies mainly with men' (Mayer, 2000a: 2). In George Mosse's early formulation, women provide 'the backdrop against which men determine[d] the fate of the nation' (1985: 23).

It may seem obvious from this exposition that sexuality is inextricably entwined with gender in nationalist ideology, but with few exceptions (Mosse, 1985; Parker, Russo, Sommer, and Yaeger, 1992), this connection was missed in scholarship on the nation until very recently.[7] Now it has been recognized that nationalist discourses use 'images and practices of sexuality [as] the malleable means of reproducing homogeneous and bounded communities' (Dwyer, 2000: 27). Women's sexuality is seen as threatening the idealized vision of woman-as-nation. It is therefore sanctified and robbed of its unruly potential in images of powerful and protective – but definitely asexual – national motherhood (Einhorn, 1993: 223).

Historically, the threat of unrestrained sexuality was evident in the British imperial project that sought both to domesticate the exotic Other and – through images of the unbridled sexuality of 'the natives' – to discipline both the British working classes and Jews, constructed as ethnic Others, in the 'Mother country' (Gilman, 1985; McClintock, 1995). For British colonists, 'the imperial conquest of the globe found both its shaping figure and its political sanction in the prior subordination of women as a category of nature'. In nineteenth-century Britain, empire and nationhood rested on a metaphor of family arranged as a gendered hierarchy. Paradoxically, the taming of femininity this implied 'took different forms in different parts of the world'. Middle-class British women were constrained within a regime requiring their sexual – and racial – purity. Meanwhile, 'Arab women were to be "civilized" by being undressed (unveiled), while sub-Saharan women were to be civilized by being dressed [in clean, white, British cotton]' (McClintock, 1995: 24, 31, 47, 61, 357–8). Inderpal Grewal sees 'home' and 'harem' as 'useful spatial tropes by which female subjects were constructed in both England and India within a colonial context that linked patriarchal practices' (1996: 56; also 5–6, 38–9).

Nationalist ideologies deploy 'us' versus 'them' narratives in which 'our women are always "pure" and "moral" while their women are "deviant" and "immoral"' (Mayer, 2000a: 10). Such mythologized models of national virtue personified are one side of a duality that offers women only two possible roles, 'the infantilized angel of the house and the victimized whore' (Grewal, 1996: 41). Both these roles deny women subjectivity and agency.

As if to illustrate this binary, Russian immigrant women in Israel are cast as prostitutes (disruptive of the national community) whom Israeli women – as 'mothers-of-the-nation' (custodians of the nation's moral values) – seek to educate (Golden, 2003: 86).[8] 'Othering' via stereotypes also applies to Russian men who are depicted as 'mafia'. In Israel, where, as Deborah Golden argues, notions of ethnicity figure larger than those of citizenship as tags of belonging, these gender stereotypes have acted as 'national cautionary tales' (2003: 96–7).

Normative notions of appropriate (heterosexual) sexuality in narratives of the nation leave many women and men within the nation in a precarious situation (Allen, 2000; Peterson, 1999). Such norms place compliant women on a pedestal through a symbolic equation of femininity with maternity, but simultaneously proscribe non-procreative and/or non-heterosexual sexuality. Dangerous sexuality is seen as emanating from either 'enemies' within, or the 'Other' nation's men. As potentially either rape victims, or, worse still, the enemy's whores, women in nationalist conflicts are ascribed only two roles: passive victimhood or active treason.

Both Women in Black in Israel, whose weekly silent vigils protest the occupation of Palestine, and Women in Black in Belgrade, protesting the conflicts in former Yugoslavia in the 1990s, drew (and draw) insults from passers-by couched in terms of disloyal sexuality. In Jerusalem, the women are seen as metaphorically 'sleeping with the enemy', and cursed as 'Arab fuckers' and 'Arafat's whores' (Helman and Rapoport, 1997: 690–1; Women in Black, 2001). In remarkably similar terms, Belgrade Women in Black were called 'motherfuckers', 'Shiptar bitches', or 'bloody Turks' (Bozinovic, Zajovic, and Zarkovic, 1998: 8–9).[9] An essentially *political* opposition to state strategies becomes reinterpreted as *national* and *sexual* betrayal, treason against an ethnically conceived national community (Golden, 2003: 93–4).

For men, too, the presumption that masculinity means heterosexual virility expressed through aggression against Others constrains and stigmatizes not only homosexuals, but also objectors to militaristic national projects. An example is 'the US military…[which] fosters a model of transcendent national citizenship that is closely aligned with heterosexual masculinity' (Allen, 2000: 310). Both gays and opponents of militarism are labelled pejoratively as effeminate, not 'real' men, thus as being of the *wrong* gender. Such negative typecasting is especially prevalent when the nation perceives itself as under threat in terms of either demographic decline, which requires heteronormative 'performance' of masculinity as procreative sex, or outside attack, which requires men to act as warriors. In former Yugoslavia, men who dared to oppose militarist conflict in the early 1990s were labelled not 'real' Serbs or Croats and/or denigrated as homosexuals (Zarkov, 1995: 112). Similarly, men of the 'enemy' ethnicity were derided as 'fairies' (Ugresic, 1998: 118). These discourses constructed 'violence-oriented masculinity' as the only way for patriotic men to demonstrate their claim to ethnic–national belonging and 'real' manhood (Korac, 1996: 137).

THE POLITICS OF NATIONAL REPRODUCTION

Nationalist narratives slide easily from the iconography of nation-as-woman to the construction of woman-as-nation, figuring women as 'Mother Earth', the fecund body of the nation. This narrative is translated into a moral imperative requiring women both to 'represent' the nation through moral virtue and social norms, and to reproduce the national/ethnic group in biological as well as cultural terms. While the politics of national reproduction require policing the sexual activity of both men and women, women balance on a particularly narrow tightrope. They may be adulated as 'mothers-of-the-nation', but are 'always suspect (potentially disloyal)' (Mostov, 2000: 98), because they may choose to express their sexuality – or worse still, to procreate – with the 'wrong' men (Nagel, 1998: 259; Yuval-Davis, 1996; 1997).

Injunctions to 'bear babies for the nation' generally have a racist and/or classist subtext. US population policies differentiate women according to both racial or ethnic group and class in a nation state 'conceptualized as a racialized national family' (Hill Collins, 1999: 126–7). In Singapore, 'a dangerous agenda of racial and class manipulation' was evident in an extraordinary 1983 attack on 'the nation's mothers' by Prime Minister Lee Kuan Yew. He lambasted highly educated Chinese women for failing to reproduce. The none-too-subtle subtext pitched their presumed ethnic and class superiority against the 'inordinate reproductive urges' of under-educated, working-class women of Malay and Indian ethnic origin (Heng and Devan, 1992: 344–5).

Israeli women are given positive incentives to have more children in the 'demographic race' to avoid ethnic dominance by the Palestinians (Yuval-Davis, 1997: 30). The 'white plague' rhetorically cited by Serb politicians to chastise Serbian women as delinquent (i.e. reluctant) mothers, conjured images of Serbs swamped by ethnic Albanians whose women were no more than 'baby factories' or 'demographic reactors' (Bracewell, 1996: 26–7; Mostov, 2000: 98–9). Yet such appeals rarely succeed, encountering active or passive resistance by the 'insider' women to whom they are addressed. Ironically, a Serb politician's call in the early 1990s to 'all Serbian women to give birth to one more son in order to carry out their national debt' was not even designed to promote demographic growth (Zajovic, 1993: 26). Rather, it signalled women's patriotic duty to bear sons who could be sacrificed for an abstract idea of the motherland (Bracewell, 1996; Kesic, 2002/2004: 65).

The instrumental use of gendered stereotypes in the name of national reproduction becomes most evident in the intimate inter-relationship of nationalism and militarism. It is epitomized in constructions of women as the 'Motherland' whom masculinized and militarized citizen–soldiers are enjoined to defend by killing 'enemy' men and defiling their women.[10] Dubravka Ugresic describes the nationalist struggle in former Yugoslavia as 'a masculine war. In the war, women are post-boxes used to send messages to those other men, *the enemy*.' She cites a 1991 TV programme in which the President of Croatia handed out medals to the widows and mothers of '*brave Croatian knights* who had *laid down their lives on the altar of the homeland*' (1998: 119, 121–2; emphasis in original).[11]

Rape in war is the ultimate expression of the link between nationalism and militarized masculinity, since its deliberate purpose is to destroy the culture and the very identity of the 'enemy' by polluting 'his' seed and thus disrupting the ethnic purity and continuity of the Other community (Hansen, 2001: 60; Salecl, 1994: 16–17; Seifert, 1996). Rape in war thus operates both as military strategy and as personal violation. The 'enemy's' women are attacked simultaneously as 'female Other' and 'ethnic Other' (Morokvasic, 1998: 81;

Zarkov, 1995: 115; 2001). The 2003 Iraq War demonstrated how national military might provides the rationale for male as well as female 'enemies' to be denigrated via their sexuality. While the involvement of American women soldiers in sexually humiliating Iraqi men prisoners apparently countered simplistic views of women as always and only the victims of masculinized militarism, the routine rape and sexual abuse of Iraqi women prisoners in the very same Abu Ghraib Prison received a much more muted media reception (Harding, 2004; Paul, 2003; Wilkinson, 2004).

INTERSECTIONS OF NATION WITH GENDER, RELIGION, ETHNICITY, AND CLASS

Constructions of national identity depend on fixed notions of gender difference. The combination with other markers of difference, such as religion, ethnicity, and class, creates powerfully marked discourses that promote exclusionary practices both *within* and *between* national communities. Cockburn argues that exclusionary nationalisms can only be overcome by changes in the gender order, for just 'as patriarchy and ethno-nationalism are partners in theory, sexism and racism are partners in practice'. She feels that 'women stepping out of line in terms of gender can be specially effective activists for change in the ethnic order' (2004: 198).

Religion is a vital ingredient in the potent mix constituting national narratives. In many Catholic countries, the Virgin Mary is seen as symbolizing the nation. In Poland, the Black Madonna of Czestechowa is faceless. She wears a crown, denoting her as Polonia, Queen of Poland. Her unattainable 'holy' purity is transmuted for mere mortal women into the heroic image of *Matka Polka*, the 'Polish Mother'. This image honours the Polish women who defended hearth and home, keeping Polish national culture alive while their men were resisting foreign invasion during the 150-year period up to the First World War when Poland had virtually ceased to exist as a nation (Einhorn, 1993; Kramer, 2005; Ostrowska, 1998). Images of the nation as Madonna equate femininity with chastity and asexual maternity. This kind of iconography depicts the spectre of female sexuality as a portent of danger and destruction, unless domesticated and subjugated to the national project.

In Ireland too, the Virgin Mary is cast as Queen of Ireland. Not only has Mary 'been used as a symbol of the Irish nation's moral purity', but in her image, contemporary 'Irish women and the female body are particularly targeted as strategic to the conservative battle to preserve the Irish nation and its moral alterity with respect to Europe' (Martin, 2000: 71, 78). National identity is linked with maintaining Irish bans on abortion and divorce. A religious pamphlet published in 1994 'explicitly states that the separation of sexual intercourse from reproduction in Ireland represents *the death of the nation*' (Martin, 2000: 76–7; emphasis in the original).

The current rise of fundamentalist discourses in all monotheistic religions synthesizes with nationalist narratives in which religious dogma unites with racist myths and strategies. Many extreme right-wing groups in the United States, for example, subscribe to religious fundamentalism while espousing 'an American sense of nationhood [that] depends greatly on creating myths about white male supremacy' (Mayer, 2000a: 11).

In India, contemporary ideologues of Hindutva (Hindu nationalism) draw on a combination of gender and religious differences. In an attempt to counter the negative feminization of Indian men propagated by the British, they at once appropriate British colonial precepts of 'Christian manliness' and paradoxically 'reinvent tradition' by masculinizing Hindu deities: 'The disengaged, androgynous, divine Ram has become a masculine Hindu warrior' (Banerjee, 2003: 173). This imagery is manipulated in the name of political goals, such as those of the Bharatiya Janata Party (BJP) based on the idea of 'one nation, one people, and one culture'. Sikata Banerjee fears that while 'more moderate proponents of Hindutva will perhaps emphasize ideas of Hindu pride and cultural dominance…radical followers will agitate for acts of war against the "other" or "enemy" of the Hindu nation, be it Islam or Christianity' (2003: 172).

Class difference is also implicated with gender in discourses of nationalism, albeit often more covertly than religion or ethnicity. In Belarus, 'national issues…are mostly manifestations of…class formation', which Elena Gapova sees as 'the major social process in the post-Soviet world'. In this process, 'class necessarily includes the emergence, or rather the reconfiguration, of masculine privilege'. Both nationalism and class formation can be seen to 'demand specific gender arrangements and invoke particular symbolic representations of men and women…in which men are subjects and agents, and women are redefined as sexualized or private objects' (2002: 641, 654).

Ethnicity was cast as the basis for national belonging in the 'ethno-nationalisms' that emerged in the 1990s' conflicts in Bosnia and Kosovo.[12] Another perceived foundation of national identity is shared language. Yet the case of former Yugoslavia demonstrates clearly that strongly exclusionary nationalisms do not necessarily emerge from neatly separate ethnic, linguistic, or religious communities. Nor do the discourses of nationalism necessarily reflect people's lived realities. Both Bosnian Muslims and Orthodox Serbs are ethnically Slavic peoples (Allen, 1998: 50). Inter-marriage over many generations among Croats, Serbs, and Bosniaks further blurred ethnically conceived lines of demarcation (Meznaric, 1994: 82). Serbo-Croat was, until the hostilities, the language spoken by all warring parties. The desire on all sides to distinguish themselves as fundamentally different from '*enemies* who were their *brothers* until a short time before' prompted the invented claim that no such language existed (Ugresic, 1998: 122; emphasis in original).

Racism is endemic in nationalist claims of internal cultural or social cohesion, especially at times of instability or crisis (Kofman et al., 2000: 38). Discriminatory racism has been seen as the dominant characteristic – and hence also the legacy – of British imperialism (Allen, 1998: 59). More recently, there are perceptions that 'the British nation is a myth', a racist construct with which not many of the country's citizens identify, especially not young Black and Asian people in London who see 'Englishness' as synonymous with being 'White' (Phoenix, 1995: 29). Contemporary English nationalism operates 'as an exclusionary force to deny racialized minorities a British/English identity with full rights of citizenship' (Allen, 1998: 59).

NATIONALISM, CITIZENSHIP, TRANSNATIONALISM

The most fundamental problem with nationalist discourse is that it casts women as symbolic markers and policy objects, not as active political subjects. Women feature as vessels of national reproduction or as rationale for national contests, but rarely as national actors (McClintock, 1995: 354). Deniz Kandiyoti encapsulates this:

> Wherever women continue to serve as boundary markers between different national, ethnic and religious collectivities, their emergence as full-fledged citizens will be jeopardized, and whatever rights they may have achieved during one stage of nation-building may be sacrificed on the altar of identity politics during another. (1991: 435)

Spike Peterson has argued that as long as 'the motherland is female, but the state and its citizens-warriors are male', effective political and state power will remain defined in terms of masculine norms (1994: 80). The essentialist difference-based discourses and exclusionary practices of nationalism label women both within and outside the nation as Other, setting women against men but also compliant women against dissenting women. In this process, they also limit women's ability to attain political subject status, to access citizenship rights, and to engage in collective struggles for gender equality.[13]

It is possible to counter the difference-based language of nationalism with the language of universalism. However, this must be done in a contextualized way that acknowledges and does not attempt to erase the real differences in power between women and men, and between women and women, both within and across national communities. Chandra Talpade Mohanty argues that 'in knowing differences and particularities, we can better see the connections and commonalities because no border or boundary is ever complete or rigidly determining'. There is a double need: both 'for women of different communities and identities to build coalitions and solidarities across borders', and for political campaigns *within* borders, using the universalist language of citizenship to counter the essentialist and exclusionary language of nationalism (2003: 226).

From a gender perspective, the main reason to rehabilitate the language of citizenship is that the national state retains the power to confer citizenship rights. Reports of the death of the nation state in the context of processes of economic and political globalization are premature (Einhorn, 2006; Jacques, 2004;

Rai, 2003). While supranational political entities (such as the EU or the UN) can in some instances override national states in forcing compliance with equality legislation, their power to do so depends on grassroots pressure within nation states (Hoskyns, 1996; Rai, 2003: 19; True and Mintrom, 2001). In most cases, it is still the national state upon which individuals can make claims for social entitlements; and which has the power to include or exclude from citizenship.

I would argue that the language of citizenship is more effective in contesting discursive nationalist and neo-conservative exclusions than the discourse of human rights. For while there has been some success in translating feminist claims that women's rights are human rights into international legislation, notably in the case of rape in war, it remains true that ultimately policies formulated at an international level (UN, EU) require the nation state as the locus of enforcement (Werbner and Yuval-Davis, 1999: 2–1). It is also at the level of the national state rather than in the international arena that feminist political struggles can achieve a loosening of nationalist strictures on women and men.

In Croatia, during the transition 'from a multiethnic federation to an ethnically founded sovereign nation state...women's bodies [became] symbolic, then real battlefields on which all kinds of wounds, discrimination and violence [were] inflicted', Vesna Kesic asserts. While men could be attacked on the basis of their ethnicity, 'the focus of the attack was still their political or ideological standpoint'. By contrast, 'women's sexuality was always targeted, even when the real stake of the campaign was their ethnic belonging or political standpoint'. During this period, women 'almost disappeared from public life', comprising only 5.4 per cent of Croatia's first independent parliament. In the 1999 elections following the end of rule by the ultra-nationalist Hrvatska Demokratska Zajednica (HDZ, Croatian Democratic Union) women won 21 per cent of parliamentary seats (Kesic, 2002/2004: 79–80).[14]

Just as there is a need for feminist organizing to overcome gender-based and intra-women inequalities within nation states, so there is an increasing demand for transnational feminist networking to overcome both the exclusionary practices of closed nationalist entities and the structures of gender inequality inherent in them (Mackie, 2001).[15] Cynthia Cockburn documents inspiring examples of women working across ethnic, religious, and nationalist divides. Working with women in Bosnia, Israel, Northern Ireland, and Cyprus, she shows how women acknowledge and respect their differences while maintaining a willingness to work through the pain suffered as a result of their respective positionings within nationalist conflicts. Without attempting to subsume, eliminate, or resolve those differences, women in these projects have engaged in difficult dialogue in order to create strategic political alliances (1998; 2004). In doing so, they apply – or enact – what Nira Yuval-Davis has called 'transversal politics', aiming not for homogeneity or unity, but for an inclusive approach to the common problems inherent in gendered nationalisms (1997).[16]

'Transversal politics' involves a search for commonalities while not denying, nor yet being derailed by, differences. It requires the acknowledgement of differences in power as well as in political, ethnic, or religious identities. Most of all, 'it demands a shared vision of the nature and goal of the dialogue, including a sense of a shared future' (Cockburn, 2004: 38–40). Transversal politics can thus be seen as both successful contestation of nationalism and a form of coalition politics across the divides of national and other differences; in other words, a form of transnational citizenship practice. It offers some hope of transcending the narrow confines of gendered and exclusive nationalisms en route to the achievement of mutual respect and understanding between peoples, across the divides of gender, class, ethnic, national, and religious differences.

ACKNOWLEDGEMENTS

I would like to thank Cynthia Cockburn, Diane Neumaier, Paul Oestreicher, Charlie Sever, Eileen Yeo, Nira Yuval-Davis, and the editors for their helpful and supportive feedback.

NOTES

1 For the Janus-faced nature of nationalism see Gapova (1998), Kandiyoti (1991: 432), Werbner and Yuval-Davis (1999: 14). The Janus image is itself gendered, with women depicted as 'the atavistic and authentic body of national tradition', 'embodying the nation's conservative principle', thereby implicitly contrasted with modernizing men (McClintock, 1995: 358–9). For the relationship between gender-differentiated bodies and the historical birth of the nation-state see Sluga (1998: 101–3).

2 Cynthia Cockburn shows how the Partition Line between Greek and Turkish Cyprus both defines national entities and creates divisions within them, 'not least between those who adopt the new separate identities and those who refuse them' (2004: 38).

3 Theorists of nation who elide gender include Anderson (1983), Gellner (1997), Hobsbawm (1983), Hosking and Schöpflin (1997), Ignatieff (1993), and Smith (1991). *Nationalism – The Reader* (Hutchinson and Smith, 1994) includes just two chapters by women (and a co-authored one) out of forty-nine. Only one of these two focuses on women and nationalism (taken from Anthias and Yuval-Davis, 1989). None focus on the impact of gender. For a critique, cf. Racioppi and O'Sullivan See (2000: 21).

4 Enloe puts it succinctly: 'If secretaries went out on strike, foreign affairs might grind to a standstill' (1989: 9).

5 Marina Warner discusses how 'oscillation between these two different meanings of the breast is constant after the first Revolution in France, and it reflects swings between accepting woman as an active agent of change or desiring her to remain a passive source of strength' (1985: 282).

6 The image of Britannia as victorious warrior was lampooned by Raymond Briggs in his anti-war book depicting Margaret Thatcher as the 'Old Iron Woman' (1984).

7 See Dwyer (2000), Golden (2003), Mayer (2000a: 3), Julie Mostov (2000), Peterson (1999).

8 See Einhorn (1993: 221–4), Kandiyoti (1991: 441–2), Nagel (1998: 256).

9 On Women in Black in Israel see Jacoby (1999). On Women in Black in Serbia, see Korac (1996: 139), Jasmina Lukic (2000: 410), Women in Black (2001).

10 On the intimate, gendered links between nationalism and militarism, see Enloe (1993: 229, 245; 2000), Mayer (2000a: 11), Mosse (1995: 171). Gendered paradigms are deployed selectively in nationalist discourse. In Nazi Germany, it was the Fatherland, not the Motherland, in whose name women were to breed 'pure' Aryan stock and men were to kill stigmatized Jews and 'lesser' peoples. In Israel, the seemingly inevitable association of masculinity with militarism is paradoxical (Mayer, 2000b: 284, 297). On the one hand, it rests on twin poles: 'the casting of Woman as Other' and the simultaneous feminization of both Holocaust survivors and Diaspora Jews (Lentin, 1996: 89ff.). On the other hand, women too have the patriotic duty to serve in the armed forces, fulfilling a triple role as 'citizen warriors, workers and mothers' (Bryson, 1998; Levy, 2000).

11 On media representations of the war in former Yugoslavia see Lukic (2000) and Zarkov (1997).

12 On ethno-nationalism in former Yugoslavia see Bracewell (1996), Korac (1996), Morokvasic (1998), Mostov (2000), and Zarkov (1995).

13 For nationalism's limitations on women's rights as active political subjects see Kesic (2002/2004: 80), Mayer (2000a: 19), McClintock (1997: 89–90), and Werbner and Yuval-Davis (1999: 1, 28).

14 'The HDZ ruled Croatia from 1990–1999 under their president Franjo Tudjman. In November 2003, the HDZ returned to power under their president and prime minister Ivo Sanader, who has pledged a new image as a moderate conservative party committed to Croatia's reintegration into Europe' (www.babe.hr, accessed 19 May 2005, translated by Jelena Djordjevic; cf. also Geshakova, 2003).

15 On transnational feminisms, see Kaplan and Grewal (1999), Mackie (2001), and Moallem (1999).

16 As Yuval-Davis acknowledges, the concept of 'transversal politics' was first developed by Italian feminist anti-war activists. However, she has elaborated it in relation to the discourses of both nationalism and citizenship, while Cockburn has illustrated its applicability in projects designed to overcome national conflicts (Yuval-Davis, 1997: 125–32; Cockburn, 1998; 2004).

REFERENCES

Allen, Holly (2000) 'Gender, Sexuality and the Military Model of US National Community', in: Mayer, T. (ed.) *Gender Ironies of Nationalism: Sexing the Nation*, London and New York: Routledge, pp. 309–28.

Allen, Sheila (1998) 'Identity: Feminist Perspectives on "Race", Ethnicity and Nationality', in: Charles, N. and Hintjens, H. (eds), *Gender, Ethnicity and Political Ideologies*, London and New York: Routledge, pp. 46–64.

Alter, Peter (1989; 2nd edition. 1994) *Nationalism*, London: Edward Arnold.

Anderson, Benedict (1983, revised edition 1991) *Imagined Communities: Reflections on the Origins and Spread of Nationalism*, London and New York: Verso.

Anthias, Floya and Yuval-Davis, Nira (1989) *Woman-Nation-State*, London: Macmillan.

Banerjee, Sikata (2003) 'Gender and Nationalism: The Masculinization of Hinduism and Female Political Participation in India', *Women's Studies International Forum*, 26(2): 167–79.

Bozinovic, Neda, Zajovic, Stasa, and Zarkovic, Rada (eds) (1998) *Women for Peace*, Belgrade: Women for Peace.

Bracewell, Wendy (1996) 'Women, Motherhood and Contemporary Serbian Nationalism', *Women's Studies International Forum*, Special Issue on *Links across Differences: Gender, Ethnicity, and Nationalism*, 19(1–2): 25–33.

Briggs, Raymond (1984) *The Tin-Pot Foreign General and the Old Iron Woman*, London: Hamish Hamilton.

Bryson, Valerie (1998) 'Citizen Warriors, Workers and Mothers: Women and Democracy in Israel', in: Charles, N. and Hintjens, H. (eds), *Gender, Ethnicity and Political Ideologies*, London and New York: Routledge, pp. 127–45.

Chan, Suzanna (2003) Review of *Art, Nation and Gender: Ethnic Landscapes, Myths and Mother Figures by*, Cusack, T and Breathnach-Lynch, S. (eds), *Women's Studies International Forum*, 26(6): 581–2.

Cockburn, Cynthia (2004) *The Line: Women, Partition and the Gender Order in Cyprus*, London and New York: Zed Books.

Cockburn, Cynthia (1998) *The Space between Us: Negotiating Gender and National Identities in Conflict*, London and New York: Zed Books.

Collins, Patricia Hill (1999) 'Producing the Mothers of the Nation: Race, Class and Contemporary US Population Policies', in: Yuval-Davis, N. and Werbner, P. (eds), *Women, Citizenship and Difference*, London and New York: Zed Books, pp. 118–29.

Dwyer, Leslie K. (2000) 'Spectacular Sexuality: Nationalism, Development and the Politics of Family Planning in Indonesia', in: Mayer, T. (ed.), *Gender Ironies of Nationalism: Sexing the Nation*, London and New York: Routledge, pp. 25–64.

Einhorn, Barbara (2006) *Citizenship in a Uniting Europe: From Dream to Awakening*, Basingstoke: Palgrave Macmillan.

Einhorn, Barbara (1993) *Cinderella goes to Market: Citizenship, Gender and Women's Movements in East Central Europe*, London and New York: Verso.

Enloe, Cynthia (2004) *The Curious Feminist: Searching for Women in a New Age of Empire*, LA: University of California Press.

Enloe, Cynthia (2000) *Maneuvers: The International Politics of Militarizing Women's Lives*, Berkeley, Los Angeles, London: University of California Press.

Enloe, Cynthia (1993) *The Morning After: Sexual Politics at the End of the Cold War*, Berkeley, Los Angeles, London: University of California Press.

Enloe, Cynthia (1989) *Bananas, Beaches and Bases: Making Feminist Sense of International Politics*, Berkeley, CA: University of California Press and London: Pandora Press.

Eriksen, Thomas Hylland (1993) *Ethnicity and Nationalism: Anthropological Perspectives*, London: Pluto Press.

Fidelis, Malgorzata (2001) '"Participation in the Creative Work of the Nation": Polish Women Intellectuals in the Cultural Construction of Female Gender Roles, 1864–1890', *Journal of Women's History*, 13(1): 108–25.

Gapova, Elena (2002) 'On Nation, Gender, and Class Formation in Belarus…And Elsewhere in the Post-Soviet World', *Nationalities Papers*, 30(4): 639–62.

Gapova, Elena (1998) 'Women in the National Discourse in Belarus', *European Journal of Women's Studies*, 5(3–4): 477–88.

Gellner, Ernest (1997) *Nationalism*, London: Weidenfeld and Nicolson.

Gellner, Ernest (1983) *Nations and Nationalism*, Oxford: Basil Blackwell.

Geshakova, Julia (2003) '2003 and Beyond: Are the Balkans Swinging Back Toward Nationalism?', Radio Free Europe/Radio Liberty: www.rferl.org/features/2003/12/101 22003162621.asp, accessed 19 May 2005.

Gilman, Sander (1985) *Difference and Pathology: Stereotypes of Sexuality, Race, and Madness*, Ithaca, NY and London: Cornell University Press.

Golden, Deborah (2003) 'A National Cautionary Tale: Russian Women Newcomers to Israel Portrayed', *Nations and Nationalism*, 9(1): 83–104.

Grewal, Inderpal (1996) *Home and Harem: Nation, Gender, Empire and the Cultures of Travel*, Leicester: Leicester University Press and Durham, NC: Duke University Press.

Hall, Stuart (1992) 'The Question of Cultural Identity', in: Hall, S. et al. (eds), *Modernity and Its Futures*, Milton Keynes: Open University Press, pp. 273–326.

Hansen, Lene (2001) 'Gender, Nation, Rape: Bosnia and the Construction of Security', *International Feminist Journal of Politics*, 3(1): 55–75.

Harding, Luke (2004) 'The Other Prisoners', *Guardian*, 20 May, G2: 10–11.

Helman, Sara and Rapoport, Tamar (1997) 'Women in Black: Challenging Israel's Gender and Socio-Political Orders', *British Journal of Sociology*, 48(4): 681–700.

Heng, Geraldine and Devan, Janadas (1992) 'State Fatherhood: The Politics of Nationalism, Sexuality and Race in Singapore', in: Parker, A., Russo, M., Sommer, D., and Yaeger, P. (eds), *Nationalisms and Sexualities*, New York and London: Routledge, pp. 343–64.

Hobsbawm, Eric (1983) 'Inventing Traditions', in: Hobsbawm, E. and Ranger, T. (eds), *The Invention of Tradition*, Cambridge: Cambridge University Press, pp. 1–14.

Hosking, Geoffrey and Schöpflin, George (eds) (1997) *Myths and Nationhood*, London: Hurst.

Hoskyns, Catherine (1996) *Integrating Gender: Women, Law and Politics in the European Union*, London and New York: Verso.

Hutchinson, John and Smith, Anthony D. (eds) (1994) *Nationalism – The Reader*, Oxford: Oxford University Press.

Ignatieff, Michael (1993) *Blood and Belonging: Journeys into the New Nationalism*, London: Macmillan.

Jacoby, Tami Amanda (1999) 'Gendered Nation: A History of the Interface of Women's Protest and Jewish Nationalism in Israel', *International Feminist Journal of Politics*, 1(3): 382–402.

Jacques, Martin (2004) 'Strength in Numbers', *Guardian*, 23 October.

Jayawardena, Kumari (1986) *Feminism and Nationalism in the Third World*, London: Zed Books and New Delhi: Kali for Women.

Juntti, Eira (1998) 'On Our Way to Europe: Finnish Women's Magazines and Discourse on Women, Nation and Power', *European Journal of Women's Studies*, 5(3–4): 399–419.

Kandiyoti, Deniz (1991) 'Identity and Its Discontents: Women and the Nation', *Millennium: Journal of International Studies*, 20(3): 429–43.

Kaplan, Caren and Grewal, Inderpal (1999) 'Transnational Feminist Cultural Studies: Beyond the Marxism/Poststructuralism/Feminism Divides', in: Kaplan, C., Alarcon, N., and Moallem, M. (eds), *Between Woman and Nation: Nationalisms, Transnational Feminisms, and the State*, Durham, NC and London: Duke University Press, pp. 349–64.

Kesic, Vesna (2002/2004) 'Gender and Ethnic Identities in Transition', in: Ivekovic, R. and Mostov, J. (eds), *From Gender to Nation*, Ravanna: A Longo Editore, reprinted New Delhi: Zubaan, an associate of Kali for Women, pp. 63–80.

Kim, Kyung-Ai (1996) 'Nationalism: An Advocate of, or a Barrier to, Feminism in South Korea', *Women's Studies International Forum*, Special Issue on *Links across Differences: Gender, Ethnicity, and Nationalism*, 19(1–2): 65–74.

Kofman, Eleonore, Phizacklea, Annie, Raghuram, Parvati, and Sales, Rosemary (2000) *Gender and International Migration in Europe*, London and New York: Routledge.

Korac, Maja (1996) 'Understanding Ethnic-National Identity and Its Meaning: Questions from a Woman's Experience', *Women's Studies International Forum*, Special Issue on *Links across Differences: Gender, Ethnicity, and Nationalism*, 19(1–2): 133–44.

Kramer, Anne-Marie (2005) 'Gender, Nation and the Abortion Debate in the Polish Media', in Tolz, Vera and Booth, Stephenie (eds), *Nation and Gender in Contemporary Europe*, Manchester: Manchester University Press, pp. 130–48.

Lentin, Ronit (1996) 'A *Yiddishe Mame* Desperately Seeking a *Mame Loshn*: Toward a Theory of the Feminization of Stigma in Relations Between Israelis and Holocaust Survivors', *Women's Studies International Forum*, Special Issue on *Links across Differences: Gender, Ethnicity, and Nationalism*, 19(1–2): 87–98.

Levy, Edna (2000) 'Women Warriors: The Paradox and Politics of Israeli Women in Uniform', in: Ranchod-Nilsson, S. and Tetreault, M. A. (eds), *Women, States and Nationalism*, London and New York: Routledge, pp. 196–214.

Lukic, Jasmina (2000) 'Media Representations of Men and Women in Times of War and Crisis: The Case of Serbia', in: Gal, S. and Kligman, G. (eds), *Reproducing Gender: Politics, Publics, and Everyday Life after Socialism*, Princeton, NJ: Princeton University Press, pp. 393–423.

Mackie, Vera (2001) 'The Language of Globalization, Transnationality and Feminism', *International Feminist Journal of Politics*, 3(3): 180–206.

Marakowitz, Ellen (1996) 'Gender and National Identity in Finland. An Exploration into Women's Political Agency', *Women's Studies International Forum*, Special Issue on *Links across Differences: Gender, Ethnicity, and Nationalism*, 19(1–2): 55–63.

Martin, Angela K. (2000) 'Death of a Nation: Transnationalism, Bodies and Abortion in Late Twentieth Century Ireland', in: Mayer, T. (ed.), *Gender Ironies of Nationalism: Sexing the Nation*, London and New York: Routledge, pp. 65–88.

Mayer, Tamar (2000a) 'Gender Ironies of Nationalism: Setting the Stage', in: Mayer, T. (ed.), *Gender Ironies of Nationalism: Sexing the Nation*, London and New York: Routledge, pp. 1–25.

Mayer, Tamar (2000b) 'From Zero to Hero: Masculinity in Jewish Nationalism', in: Mayer, T. (ed.), *Gender Ironies of Nationalism: Sexing the Nation*, London and New York: Routledge, pp. 283–308.

McClintock, Anne (1997) '"No Longer in a Future Heaven": Gender, Race and Nationalism', in: McClintock, A., Mufti, A., and Shohat, E. (eds), *Dangerous Liaisons: Gender, Nation, and Postcolonial Perspectives*, Minneapolis and London: University of Minnesota Press, pp. 89–112.

McClintock, Anne (1995) *Imperial Leather: Race, Gender and Sexuality in the Colonial Contest*, New York and London: Routledge.

Meznaric, Silva (1994) 'Gender as an Ethno-Marker: Rape, War, and Identity Politics in the Former Yugoslavia', in: Moghadam, Valentine M. (ed.), *Identity Politics and Women: Cultural Reassertions and Feminism in International Perspective*, Oxford: Westview Press, pp. 76–97.

Moallem, Minoo (1999) 'Transnationalism, Feminism, and Fundamentalism', in: Kaplan, C., Alarcon, N., and Moallem, M. (eds), *Between Woman and Nation: Nationalisms, Transnational Feminisms, and the State*, Durham, NC and London: Duke University Press, pp. 320–48.

Mohanty, Chandra Talpade (2003) '"Under Western Eyes" Revisited: Feminist Solidarity through Anticapitalist Struggles', in: Mohanty, C. T., *Feminism without Borders: Decolonizing Theory, Practicing Solidarity*, Durham, NC and London: Duke University Press, pp. 221–52.

Morokvasic, Mirjana (1998) 'The Logics of Exclusion: Nationalism, Sexism and the Yugoslav War', in: Charles, N. and Hintjens, H. (eds), *Gender, Ethnicity and Political Ideologies*, London and New York: Routledge, pp. 65–90.

Mosse, George L. (1995) 'Racism and Nationalism', *Nations and Nationalism*, 1(2): 163–73.

Mosse, George L. (1985) *Nationalism and Sexuality: Middle Class Morality and Sexual Norms in Modern Europe*, Madison, WI: University of Wisconsin Press.

Mostov, Julie (2000) 'Sexing the Nation/Desexing the Body: Politics of National Identity in the Former Yugoslavia', in: Mayer, T. (ed.), *Gender Ironies of Nationalism: Sexing the Nation*, London and New York: Routledge, pp. 89–112.

Nagel, Joanne (1998) 'Masculinity and Nationalism: Gender and Sexuality in the Making of Nations', *Ethnic and Racial Studies*, 21(2): 242–69.

Ostrowska, Elzbieta (1998) 'Filmic Representations of the "Polish Mother" in Post-Second World War Polish Cinema', *European Journal of Women's Studies*, 5(3–4): 419–36.

Parker, Andrew, Russo, Mary, Sommer, Doris, and Yaeger, Patricia (eds), (1992) *Nationalisms and Sexualities*, New York and London: Routledge.

Paul, Ari (2003) 'Human Rights Watch Report Critical of Coalition's Ability to Protect Women', *Baghdad Bulletin*, 20 July: http://www.baghdadbulletin.com/pageArticle.php?article_id=63

Peterson, V. Spike (1999) 'Sexing Political Identities/Nationalism as Heterosexism', *International Feminist Journal of Politics*, 1(1): 34–65; reprinted in: Ranchod-Nilsson, S. and Tetreault, M.A. (eds), (2000) *Women, States, and Nationalism*, London and New York: Routledge, pp. 54–80.

Peterson, V. Spike (1996) 'The Politics of Identification in the Context of Globalization', *Women's Studies International Forum*, Special Issue on *Links across Differences: Gender, Ethnicity, and Nationalism*, 19(1–2): 5–15.

Peterson, V. Spike (1994) 'Gendered Nationalism', *Peace Review*, Special Issue on *Nationalism and Ethnic Conflict*, 6(1): 77–84.

Peterson, V. Spike and Runyan, Ann Sisson (1999, 2nd edition) *Global Gender Issues*, Boulder, CO: Westview Press.

Pettman, Jan Jindy (2000), 'Writing the Body: Transnational Sex', in: Youngs, G. (ed.), *Political Economy, Power and the Body: Global Perspectives*, Basingstoke and London: Macmillan; New York: St. Martin's Press, pp. 52–71.

Phoenix, Ann (1995) 'Young People: Nationalism, Racism and Gender', in: Lutz, H., Phoenix, A., and Yuval-Davis, N. (eds), *Crossfires: Nationalism, Racism and Gender in Europe*, London and East Haven, CT: Pluto Press, pp. 26–47.

Racioppi, Linda and O'Sullivan See, Katherine (2000) 'Engendering Nation and National Identity', in: Ranchod-Nilsson, S. and Tetreault, M. A. (eds), *Women, States and Nationalism*, London and New York: Routledge, pp. 18–35.

Rai, Shirin M. (2003) 'Institutional Mechanisms for the Advancement of Women: Mainstreaming Gender, Democratizing the State', in: Rai, S.M. (ed.) *Mainstreaming Gender, Democratizing the State: Institutional Mechanisms for the Advancement of Women*, Manchester and New York: Manchester University Press, pp. 15–39.

Salecl, Renata (1994) 'The Fantasy Structure of War: The Case of Bosnia', in: Salecl, R. *The Spoils of Freedom: Psychoanalysis and Feminism after the Fall of Socialism*, London and New York: Routledge, pp. 11–20.

Seifert, Ruth (1996) 'The Second Front: The Logic of Sexual Violence in Wars', *Women's Studies International Forum*, Special Issue on *Links across Differences: Gender, Ethnicity, and Nationalism*, 19 (1–2): 35–44.

Sharoni, Simona (1998) 'Gendering Conflict and Peace in Israel/Palestine and the North of Ireland', *Millennium: Journal of International Studies*, 27(4): 1061–89.

Sluga, Glenda (1998) 'Identity, Gender, and the History of European Nations and Nationalism', *Nations and Nationalism*, 4(1): 87–111.

Smith, Anthony D. (1991) *National Identity*, Harmondsworth: Penguin.

True, Jacqui and Mintrom, Michael (2001) 'Transnational Networks and Policy Diffusion: The Case of Gender Mainstreaming', *International Studies Quarterly*, 45: 27–57.

Ugresic, Dubravka (1998) 'Because We're Just Boys', in: Ugresic, D. *The Culture of Lies: Antipolitical Essays*, translated by Celia Hawkesworth, London: Phoenix House, pp. 113–27.

Warner, Marina (1985) *Monuments and Maidens: The Allegory of the Female Form*, London: Weidenfeld and Nicolson.

Werbner, Pnina and Yuval-Davis, Nira (1999) 'Introduction: Women and the New Discourse of Citizenship', in: Werbner, P. and Yuval-Davis, N. (eds), *Women, Citizenship and Difference*, London and New York: Zed Books, pp.1–38.

Wilkinson, Tracy (2004) 'A Double Ordeal for Female Prisoners', *Los Angeles Times*, 11 May.

Women in Black (2001) 'Women in Black', *Peace News*, no. 2443: 22–5.

Yuval-Davis, Nira (1997) *Gender and Nation*, London, Thousand Oaks, CA, New Delhi: Sage.

Yuval-Davis, Nira (1996) 'Women and the Biological Reproduction of "The Nation"', *Women's Studies International Forum*, Special Issue on *Links across Differences: Gender, Ethnicity, and Nationalism*, 19(1–2): 17–24.

Zarkov, Dubravka (2001) 'The Body of the Other Man: Sexual Violence and the Construction of Masculinity, Sexuality and Ethnicity in the Croatian Media', in: Moser, C. O. N and Clark, F. C. (eds), *Victims, Perpetrators or Actors? Gender, Armed Conflict and Political Violence*, London and New York: Zed Books, pp. 69–82.

Zarkov, Dubravka (1997) 'Pictures of the Wall of Love: Motherhood, Womanhood and Nationhood in Croatian Media', *European Journal of Women's Studies*, 4(3): 305–40.

Zarkov, Dubravka (1995) 'Gender, Orientalism and the History of Ethnic Hatred in the Former Yugoslavia', in: Lutz, H., Phoenix, A., and Yuval-Davis, N. (eds), *Crossfires: Nationalism, Racism and Gender in Europe*, London and East Haven, CT: Pluto Press, pp. 105–20.

Zajovic, Stasa (ed.) (1993) *Women for Peace*, Belgrade: Women in Black.

12

Towards a New Theorizing of Women, Gender, and War

Dubravka Zarkov

This chapter presents a search for new theoretical and analytical approaches to gender and violent conflict by investigating feminist analyses of two specific issues: sexual violence against women as a gender-specific war strategy and women's participation in war and violence. These two issues most aptly reflect recent debates about the limits and biases of classical feminist approaches to violent conflict and militarism and offer possibilities for innovative thinking. This chapter is not written as a review of feminist studies of war and violent conflict. One could even question the existence of *a* field, as war and different types of violent conflict are studied by feminists in many different disciplines.

The chapter will first reflect on some of the main theoretical premises of the classical feminist studies of war and challenges they faced in the 1990s. Then studies of sexual violence against women and women's participation in violent conflicts will be discussed by juxtaposing different perspectives and bringing in debates that challenge classical approaches and engage in alternative theorizing.

CLASSICAL FEMINIST STUDIES REVISITED

Feminists in any academic discipline have always had to counter hegemonies present within their discipline's theoretical and geo-political traditions, not just hegemonies along the line of gender. The hegemonic position of Western academia, for example, has offered an advantage to Western feminists and feminists living in the West, prioritizing their theorizing against the knowledge produced in other parts of the world. Thus, not surprisingly, much of now classical feminist scholarship on war and militarism produced in the 1980s has often foregrounded the experiences of Western women and

Western perspectives on women's engagements in and against wars and militant movements in other parts of the world.

The equality-versus-difference debate underpins this Western bias.[1] It is a product of two fundamentally different feminist projects – liberal feminists' struggle to counter discrimination and secure women's equal access to all social spheres, especially those perceived as exclusively men's, and radical feminists' struggle to preserve the presumed (essential) difference between nurturing femininity and violent masculinity and to build a society based upon the qualities of the former. This debate produced a rich, complex, and diverse body of feminist knowledge about war. Studies focused on the relationships between women and war (especially the two world wars) rallied around the idea that dramatic social transformations caused by wars and women's engagements in different 'war efforts' (be it in war industries or in the fighting) offer a chance for lasting change in gender relations and a long-term effect on women's emancipation and empowerment. Other studies addressed the same relationship using essentialized notions of feminine-cum-maternal care and peace-loving as their stating points.[2] Yet others analysed women's participation in national militaries (both in the West and in the Third World) or in militant, separatist, and guerrilla movements, arguing that women's presence could and would eventually bring about transformation of masculinist institutions, such as the military.[3]

These studies have, on the one hand, made immensely valuable contributions to our understanding of the relationships between women, gender, and war, and of the construction of militarism through notions of femininity and masculinity and their impact on women's lives. On the other hand, they have also produced the key analytical frameworks and tools through which women's experiences and the relevance of gender have been approached, often assuming a direct conceptual link between women's agency and women's participation in armies, militaries, and wars as potentially empowering and emancipatory, especially when linked to anti-colonial or anti-fascist movements.

However, there is a huge 'but' in these conceptualizations. It concerns the nature of the army, military, or violent conflict in which women took part. That is, when these were seen as oppressive, hegemonic, or unjust, feminists seldom analysed the lives of women who joined them, and women's agency disappeared from view. Such an attitude seems to have to do with the general feminist uneasiness of the time with women's participation in politics that can be characterized as right wing: nationalist, racist, or religious fundamentalist movements, communal violence, or terrorist actions. It seems that feminist discourse of men's oppression of women has been for long ill-equipped for perceiving women active in right-wing political groups and militant movements.

Nevertheless, there have been studies that analysed the lives of women belonging to, or associated with, movements, armies, and militaries whose definition could hardly be accurate without words such as oppressive or hegemonic. The study of German women in the Nazi movement by Claudia Koontz (1986) has been one of these exceptions, inspiring other studies, such as Jacklyn Cock's (1992; 1994) analysis of the lives of women in the White South African Defence Force (SADF), against the backdrop of apartheid.[4] Cock compared the role of women in the SADF in maintaining the racist and sexist social order of South Africa with that of Nazi women in Germany, who (like Nazi women in Koontz's analysis) contributed to the power of an oppressive state 'by preserving the illusion of love in an environment of hatred' (1994: 154). She also compared the position of women in the SADF with the position of women in the MK, an armed wing of the African National Congress. She concluded that women's roles in the SADF were extended into the men's sphere, but not fundamentally changed. Women in the MK, on the other hand, were incorporated into rather new roles. While the SADF 'cultivated subordinate and decorative notion of femininity', the ideology of MK 'sometimes involved a denial of femininity' (p. 161). Whatever the differences between the two, Cock asserts that in both the SADF and the MK, combat played a fundamental role for defining women's position within the military. Those women who participated in combat were – sometimes, and very selectively – allowed to participate in the heroic myths and historic narratives of their communities; others were relegated to insignificance (p. 159).

Classical feminist studies of militarism have defined combat as one of the most important factors that defined the position of women within Western militaries, marking an ultimate difference between men and women.[5] As an exclusive preserve of men, combat was analysed as the core axis around which femininities and masculinities in most of the militaries and wars have been constructed. However, during the Second World War, Russian and Yugoslav partisan women were fighting on the front lines, as is true for women in many liberation movements in the Third World. Therefore, the neat political, ideological, and theoretical constructions of combat as exclusively masculine crumble when perspectives and experiences are not Western European or North American. Reviewing feminist literature on women militants in Eritrea, Vietnam, Namibia, South Africa, Nicaragua, and South Asia, and comparing it with literature on the United States, Sarala Emmanuel (2004) points out that the sexual division of labour in many militant movements in the Third World did not exclude women from combat. Second, some of the support services provided by women – usually associated with the domestication of femininity within militaries – have actually been highly politicized. Thus, even when women were excluded from combat, they were not necessarily excluded from the spheres of political relevance. Consequently, Emmanuel concludes, these distinctions reflect Eurocentrism in feminist theoretical frameworks that still assume the split between the public and private and continue to link masculinity with the public, and femininity with the private, even when realities of women defy such neat divisions.

These realities became evermore complex in the late 1980s and the early 1990s, both theoretically and geo-politically. Theoretically, many of the basic feminist premises produced in the West have been questioned by the rising power of marginalized feminist groups within the West (Black, lesbian, migrant) and from the Third World. The post-modern turn in feminism, often coming from totally different perspectives and with totally different premises, further destabilized classical feminist theoretical assumptions. Sometimes the two met in highly prominent and visible feminists from the Third World working in Western academia, bringing in not only different theories but, ultimately, different strategies for political action. New theorizing has resulted in undermining some of the classical feminist concepts conceived within modernist feminist discourses, such as agency, emancipation, and empowerment, and their relationship. New strategizing has made feminist knowledge produced by Third World feminists both more prominent in the West and more relevant to feminist analysis of Western as well as global realities, not just Third World realities.

These theoretical and strategic trajectories go hand in hand, indicating the unsettling of Western feminist hegemony in the production of feminist knowledge by the growing presence of Third World feminists. There is also a growing demand within global feminist movements that new theoretical reflections and political solidarities be developed to suit the changing geo-political situation of the late 1980s and early 1990s.[6] Simply put, new wars opened new questions for feminism. Women soldiers participated in the Falklands and the Gulf War, stirring up old debates and posing new challenges to classical feminist studies of war and militarism developed in the early 1980s.

One of these challenges was how to analyse links between gender and other social relations of power, and especially other social identities that seem to have gained in visibility and relevance in these wars. It was obvious, for example, that the British and American women soldiers fighting in the Falklands and the Gulf War became multiple symbols – of nation, racial identity, ideology, emancipation, and modernity – and as such, served the purpose of defining the Self and the Other.[7]

Wars in Rwanda and the former Yugoslavia in the early 1990s made the links between gender and communal identities even more painfully clear. They brought about yet another challenge to feminist theorizing: intersections of these identities with gender-based sexual violence against women as a war strategy. As I will argue, they also mark a shift from classical feminist focus on women's agency to women's victimization in war. In the 1990s, the increasing participation of women in communal violence and nationalist-cum-religious movements in India and South Asia has posed very different questions about the intersectionality of gender, collective identities, and violence, and stirred up some of the old debates about the concept of agency and its link to empowerment and emancipation.

STUDYING SEXUAL VIOLENCE IN WAR

In her analysis of war rapes in Bosnia and Croatia, Rhonda Copelon pointed out that war rape 'takes many forms, occurs in many contexts, and has different repercussions for different victims' (1993: 213). She asserted that each instance of rape has its own dimension that must not be taken for granted, but that specificity does not mean uniqueness or exclusivity:

> The rape of women in the former Yugoslavia challenges the world to refuse impunity to atrocity as well as to resist the powerful forces that would make the mass rape of Muslim women in Bosnia exceptional and thereby restrict its meaning for women raped in different contexts. It thus demands recognition of situational differences without losing sight of the commonalities. To fail to make distinctions flattens reality; and to rank the egregious demeans it. (p. 214)

Although she never states it explicitly, Copelon's warnings come as a reaction to the fact that the rapes in Bosnia and Croatia were ranked by many feminists, in the region and in the West, as the worse in human history, as unique and exceptional.[8] This assumption of exceptionality can be challenged by more recent studies of the prevalence of sexual violence in African wars[9] and earlier studies of rapes in South Asian violent conflicts, and can be attributed to the ambiguous positioning of Bosnia both within and outside of the 'symbolic continent of Europe' (Bakic-Hayden and Hayden, 1992). Its symbolic inclusion into Europe made rapes there more visible and more relevant for Western feminist theorizing on war rapes, compared with, for example, rapes during the Rwandan Civil War. The violence in Rwanda remained for a long-time quite invisible theoretically in Western feminism, although it mobilized women's organizations and feminist NGOs across the globe.[10] The wars in Yugoslavia, in contrast, caused an enormous academic production in a wide range of disciplines.[11]

The symbolic exclusion of Bosnia and Yugoslavia from Europe affected the way relationships between women, gender, and war in the region were theorized and ultimately created a shift in Western feminist theorizing on war. While studies on sexual violence against women in wars contributed hugely to our understanding of the intersections between gender, sexuality, collective identities, and violence, feminist studies of Yugoslav and, later, the Rwandan war in the late 1990s largely focused on studies of war rapes. Consequently, the concept of gender-based violence was reduced to sexual violence. More importantly, classical feminist studies of women and war shifted from a conceptualization of agency and empowerment to theoretically and politically much more problematic conceptualization of sexual victimization.

This new prominence, centrality, even, of the raped female victim in feminist studies of war could be traced to specific theoretical and political perspectives within feminism. On the one hand, in classical feminist theorizing on war, it is a direct, albeit paradoxical consequence of the centrality of the concept of agency and its relation to empowerment and emancipation. Informed by modernist discourses that split the social realities of women into private passivity and public activity, women's engagement in militaries and wars with arms in their hands was easy to conceptualize as emancipatory and empowering within a feminist framework of public agency. The victimhood of civilian women was thus a mirror image of such an understanding of agency. As already indicated, geo-politics has a role to play, too. Eurocentrism, racism, and Orientalism made sure that there have always been women and regions that have been seen as more empowered and emancipated than others. Thus, it was also very easy to perceive some of them entirely through the prism of victimization. Not surprisingly, women in the Balkan and African wars have been among the latter.

On the other hand, the centrality of the rape victim for feminist studies of war in the 1990s can be linked to the classical Western feminist conceptualization of peacetime rapes. Probably the most significant feminist work for understanding peacetime sexual violence was Susan Brownmiller's book *Against Our Will: Men, Women and Rape*, first published in 1975. Brownmiller analysed rape as the most powerful means of men's control over women. In her words, through rape '*all men* keep *all women* in a state of fear' (Brownmiller, 1986: 5; emphasis in the original). Susan Griffin (1971) contributed to the same perspective by asserting the reality of women's constant fear of rape and the defining social condition of that fear as 'rape culture'.

For many feminists, these analyses have remained unshaken truth twenty years after Brownmiller published her book, although she herself has criticized the 'rape victim identity' in 1993, while writing about rapes in Bosnia (Brownmiller, 1993). Catherine Niarchos, however, referring to Bosnia, states: 'All women know a great deal about rape, whether or not we have been its direct victims. Rape haunts the lives of women on daily basis' (1995: 650). The inevitability of female rapability inscribed in this paradigm has consequences: if women are already defined as rapable, then rape defines femininity as violability and becomes a female mode of being, and simultaneously ascribes propensity to rape as an essential prerogative of maleness. These definitions, paradoxically, reinforce the greatest of all gender distinctions, assuming, once again, the omnipotence of men and the absolute powerlessness of women. The context of war – when a man is invariably defined as a soldier and a woman as an innocent civilian – further underscores the inevitability of female violability and powerlessness and allows for the erasure of women's agency.

The fatal linkage between femininity, sexual violence, and victimization has repercussions for legal remedies of war-time rapes. Julie Mertus (2004) shows how victimization was at play at the International Criminal Tribunal for former Yugoslavia, where testimonies of raped women were turned into legal narratives that benefited either the prosecution or the defence, but hardly the women themselves. As both the defence and the prosecution focused on the acts of violence, within which description of the victim's and perpetrator's body parts and the actions of the perpetrator figured prominently, the victim's testimony was broken into a staccato of questions and answers, and the testifying woman was reduced to a dismembered and passive victim. Thus the very act of agency – the public testifying at the court – is turned into an act that reproduces the woman's victimization, if not into an act of victimization in itself. Showing instances of women's defiance to such victimizing legal practice, Mertus (2004: 112) is weary of the enthusiasm of 'the (mainly western) champions of "universal justice"' who have not yet learned the lesson of the limits of legal response to rape.[12] She concludes that legal processes like the Tribunal hardly bring a possibility for closure for the witness, and that the visibility of the victim is not necessarily followed by recognition and respect. Thus, she argues for alternative legal and non-legal modes of justice – truth commissions, memory projects, and 'people's tribunals' – wherein the narrative of violence would be controlled by the witness.

However, Antjie Krog (2001) and Chiseche Mibenge (forthcoming) show that there is no easy access to justice for women who experienced sexual violence in conflicts in South Africa and Rwanda. In both places, public witnessing of sexual violence had to be replaced by special closed hearings in order to protect women from contempt, intimidation, violence, and even death that testifying in public could expose them to. The point to consider here is that the struggle between feminist exposure and social erasure of rape against women in wars belongs to complex dynamics of different relations of power within which the rapes and the victims are given meaning. In other words, visibility of the raped women, be it in feminist texts, in legal practice, or in local communities, will depend on the differential place their bodies have within the given feminist, legal, or local community. And this is certainly not a fixed place.

Urvashi Butalia's (1993) work on the partition of India, for example, very clearly shows that the visibility and recognizability of a victim depends on the very specific political context. She notes that within Hindu and Sikh communities, those remembered in ritual commemorations of partition today are not the raped women, but rather the so-called 'martyred' women – those killed by members of their own families and communities *in order not to be raped* by the 'enemy'. They are remembered by their communities, often by individual name and place of residence, precisely because they were *not raped*. The lives of those who were actually raped, or those who would have rather risked being raped than killed by their own relatives, were not written about in the popular booklets celebrating 'martyrdom', which are currently sold to schoolchildren on street corners (p. 24).[13]

Selective and differential visibility of the rape victim has relevance in the Sri Lankan conflict, too. The Tamil Tiger militant women raped by government forces are awarded a public space – and with it all the glory of the martyr – within the Tamil community only if and when they are already dead or killed. Raped women were systematically silenced when trying to talk about their experience of sexual violence while they were still alive (de Mel, 2001). Or, as Emmanuel (2004) shows, their sexual violation – while they are still 'innocent civilians' – is turned by researchers and propaganda makers alike into a story of motivation for joining the Tigers. At the same time, the symbol of the raped woman is regularly used for propaganda and other purposes by both the Sri Lankan government and the Tamil separatist movement, and so is the practice of sexual violence itself.[14]

Thus, social and cultural norms and specific political contexts affect the visibility of the victim of sexual violence by providing or withdrawing the discursive space within which the victim can speak or be spoken about. Diana Taylor (1993) and Biljana Kašić (2000), for example, both point to the links between violated female bodies and the voicelessness in the representation of women victims in Argentina and Bosnia, asserting that the muteness of the female victim went hand in hand with the appropriation of her pain and her voice for political purposes (dictatorship, nationalism).

So how are we then to study sexual violence in wars in a way that neither jeopardizes the plight of women who have been raped, nor takes sexual victimization as the ultimate destiny of women in war? Following Copelon's suggestion of recognizing differences 'without losing sight of the commonalities', one could argue for comparative studies of sexual violence against women in different violent conflicts and other political and violent contexts, such as, for example, colonial violence, as well as for more critical exchange between studies of peace rapes and war rapes.

An interesting comparative study of rapes in the former Yugoslavia and South Asia is that of Hayden (1998), who examined not only the meanings and functions of rape but also strategies of rape avoidance in different communal conflicts and mass violence in India. Further comparisons of rapes in the two regions come from feminists writing on sexual violence during the partition of India in 1947; they cite the female body as one of the primary sites of communal violence.[15] The accounts of 'rapes, of women being stripped naked and paraded down streets, of their breasts being cut off, of their bodies being carved with religious symbols of the other community' (Butalia, 1993: 14) indicate that the violence functioned in the production of collective identities. Ritu Menon and Kamla Bhasin (1998: 43) assert that the divisions between India and Pakistan were 'engraved ... on the women ... in a way that they *became* the respective countries, indelibly imprinted by the Other' (emphasis in the original). According to Menon and Bhasin (1998) this symbolic geography of the sexually violated female body and its role in the construction of collective identities was a significant similarity between the violence against women during partition and during the wars in Bosnia and Croatia. According to Mibenge (forthcoming), similar acts of violence against women, or their dead bodies, were also seen in Rwanda, indicating further possibilities for comparative analysis of the symbolic value of the violated female body in the production of collective identities.

In addition to comparative studies of rapes of women in wars in different regions, cross-disciplinary scholarship may also bring new insights. Black studies, post-colonial studies, and masculinity studies seem to be especially relevant here. On the one hand, they too are concerned with the specific socio-political context within which sexual violence is perpetrated. On the other hand, they bring in the subject of male victims of sexual violence. However controversial this subject may be for feminism, it actually offers new theoretical perspectives and insights.

Post-colonial and Black studies have asserted that rape functions within time-and-space-specific political contexts. In her analysis of rape in colonial India, Jenny Sharpe (1991: 36–37) pointed out that colonialism was a 'signifying system' within which the meanings of rape were produced. Susan Pedersen (1991: 662) asserted the same when describing the concerns of colonial administrators in Kenya that their interfering with 'native issues' regarding Kenyan women could endanger the sexual safety of White women. Analysing the history of slavery and racism, Valerie Smith (1998) argued that slavery, lynching of Black men, and rape of Black women informed the construction of racial and gender identities in America.[16] James Messerschmidt (1998), for example, explicitly analyses lynching and castrating of Black men in relation to White masculinity and femininity. He asserts that the construction of Black masculinity through sexual violence against White women plays an essential role in obscuring racist violence against Black men.

The latter research, and many other studies of masculinity, show that male bodies also carry attributes of specific collective identities and functions as symbols of ethnically, racially, or religiously defined communities. It is this symbolic value of the male body for the community that exposes men to violence, including sexual violence, during a conflict. Not surprisingly, however, men as victims of gender-specific violence in armed conflicts and war have only recently received attention from feminists. War in Bosnia has again been the one that alerted some researchers to the fact that men have also been assaulted sexually, and that this assault appears to be as systematic as that against women, although the number of assaulted men was never indicated in the UN reports.[17]

The research on sexual victimization of men in violent conflict, while still in its inception, is important for feminist studies of war precisely because it cautions us to avoid fatal linkages between femininity and victimization. While the female rape victim is often publicly visible in the West, the male victim is still mostly invisible. This public invisibility of the male victim of sexual violence is not only due to the prevalence of the dominant associations of masculinity with power and heterosexuality, but also due to the position of the violated male body within specific social contexts. Sexual violence and torture of Iraqi prisoners in the Abu Ghraib Prison in Baghdad is an apt example. The unprecedented exposure and high visibility of the naked bodies of Iraqi prisoners in the Western media (from press to TV to Internet) is a result of their social status in the West – their 'Otherness'. Violated and humiliated naked bodies of soldiers of Western militaries serving in Iraq have not been, and will probably never be, exposed that way.

The study of sexual violence against women and men and a comparison of the meanings of the rape of women and the rape of men during violent conflict carry potential far beyond the present conceptualization. What has already been done quite extensively is an investigation of the intersections of femininity and other social identities and power relations, such as those of race, class, ethnicity, and religion, and the role of sexual violence therein. But what needs further exploration is what sexual violence tells us about the intersections of masculinity, race, ethnicity, and religion. In short, research into sexual violence defines both differences between femininities and masculinities and differences within them.

Finally, researching sexual violence against both women and men brings a focus on female and male sexuality and homo/heterosexuality. As already discussed, the selective and differential concern with women's sexual vulnerability, or female sexuality as violability, is part and parcel of war strategies of violence against women. This violable sexuality of women has almost become a dominant framework of feminist analysis of sexual violence against women in war, but, as Anita Roy (1997) pointed out, not everywhere around the globe is female sexuality constructed as timid, passive, and violable. Focusing on gendered sexualities is not enough. One also has to ask how norms of (hetero)sexuality intersect with notions of femininity and masculinity and definitions of collective identity within a particular violent conflict, and how this impacts upon war realities, including, but not limited to, sexual violence against women and men alike.

STUDYING WOMEN'S PARTICIPATION IN VIOLENT CONFLICT

Wars in the former Yugoslavia and Rwanda were not the only ones relevant for change in classical feminist theorizing on women and war. Other wars have also challenged established feminist thinking. The NATO war against Serbia over Kosovo in 1999 and the wars in Afghanistan in 2001 and in Iraq in 2003, justified by the doctrine of 'humanitarian wars' and 'pre-emptive strikes' and the discourse of the 'war on terror', have further exposed, each in a different way, some of the limitations in classical feminist theorizing on violent conflict and a need for new approaches.[18]

Throughout the 1990s, feminist conceptualizations of wars, violent conflicts, and militarization have been changing. After the study of *women* in violent conflict and its aftermath, *femininity and masculinity* became much more prominent tools of analysis. Then studies of women's and girls' *experiences* of war were joined by studies focused on *representations* of femininities and masculinities in various war narratives, on the genderdness of narratives and practices, on links between gendered identities, violence, and the military, and (much less so) on the changing nature of warfare.[19]

The concepts of *women's agency* and *empowerment through war* became ever more important for the global feminist movement. Thanks to feminist efforts in 2000, the United Nations adopted Resolution 1325, which demanded inclusion of women's anti-war efforts in every step of the official political and social processes that transforms a society from war to peace. Resolution 1325 also asked for due attention to women's informal ways of doing peace-politics and for preserving gains that women acquired during times of conflict.

Theoretically, the analyses of women's agency in and against war continued through studies of women's anti-war activism, individual and collective resilience and survival strategies, and community work and leadership.[20] However, the old optimism about the long-term impact of changes in gender roles during war has been losing strength. Judy El-Bushra's recent work is probably the most significant in this respect. She sends two grim warnings. First, while gender roles do change in violent conflicts (sometimes dramatically), and women do take greater responsibilities within the household and community, institutional supports that 'would provide women with decision-making power consistent with these new and more responsible roles have been slow in coming' (2004: 169). In other words, *gender relations* may stay intact, even when *gender roles* change. El-Bushra asserts that 'the ideological underpinnings of gender relations have barely been touched at all and may even have become further reinforced through conflict' (p. 169). Second, she notes that analysing how gender becomes utilized in preserving different political and economic orders is only one side of a coin. The other is that violent conflict and war are used to preserve gender orders. Theoretically, this point has been made earlier,[21] but there were no empirical studies to prove it. El-Bushra's work on several states in Africa shows how violent conflict becomes a means of preserving, achieving, and reclaiming the lost prerogatives of dominant masculinity (such as property, control, and social status) as well as dominant gender hierarchies.

Much feminist work on militarization of women's lives – be it through direct participation in the military or through professional and family associations – also continues to rely on the concept of women's agency and empowerment. But here too, the straightforward link of militant agency to emancipation and empowerment was undermined to quite an extent. First, women's presence in the military does not seem to change the masculinist nature of these institutions, nor does it contribute to the general advancement of women's social position – quite the contrary. Cynthia Enloe (2000), for example, shows that defending the rights of women soldiers in the US military may impact negatively on the rights of civilian women affected by the US militarism. For example, US feminists fighting for women soldier's rights against harassment, sexual violence, and gender discrimination did ally with the lesbian and gay movement fighting homophobia in the military, but *not* with feminists working with prostitutes around military bases or military wives. Still, Enloe insists that women's soldiering may, 'under certain conditions', advance the cause for all women (p. 287). As a case in point she gives an example of exposing the cover-up of the rape of a woman soldier by a male soldier in the US press. Such an exposure of a cover-up, Enloe argues:

> can tear away the legitimizing camouflage that has sustained that military as a symbol of national pride and security…[c]an make that military appear to many citizens for the first time to be little more than a men's club…[A] state official … may become confused. Although state confusion is not as invigorating to witness as state transformation, it can be revealing. And revelation can alter consciousness. (p. 287)

This perspective is extremely optimistic, but also utterly unrealistic, and it further exposes the limits of some of the dominant feminist theoretical approaches to wars and militaries, women's participation in them, and their gendered implications.

Second, the wars of the 1980s and 1990s and those of the twenty-first century confirmed the fact that women soldiers and militants are here to stay, not only as enlightened freedom fighters in liberation movements of the Third World, nor in presumed democratic Western militaries fighting fascism and totalitarianism, but in wars both gruesome and horrid, not only among the oppressed, but also among the aggressors. These women and their actions may well be contributing to the maintenance of national or international social orders based on oppression and exclusion. Their actions may well be part and parcel of male-defined ideologies and projects. But they are neither blind, manipulated victims of patriarchal social orders, nor are they empowered or emancipated in the way feminists usually define emancipation and empowerment.

As some of the old political and theoretical certainties of feminism crumbled, at least two things seem to have become evident: first, women's agency, emancipation, and empowerment are not necessarily linked only to liberating and progressive movements. Second, agency, emancipation, and empowerment may not be the best framework at all for studying women's diverse positioning within violent conflict, including women's participation in violence.

The region in which both of these points have been taken most seriously in feminist theorizing on violent conflict is South Asia. There, a body of knowledge has been steadily growing on women's diverse positioning within a range of very different violent conflicts. In India, women have participated in militant formations of the RSS,[22] in riots in 1984, in the destruction of the Ayodhya Mosque in 1992, in communal violence in Bombay in 1992 and 1993, and in separatist movements in Kashmir, Assam, and Punjab. Women also took part in the communal violence in Gujarat, and in Maoist insurgency in Nepal, and separatist militant movements in Sri Lanka. These are all very different violent conflicts, with different histories and trajectories. Their effects on women and women's engagements in them are also very diverse. But it seems that this diversity as well as the overwhelming presence of women on the side of those who inflict violence has forced feminists in the region to re-examine the old theoretical tools and search for the new ones.

Anita Roy once remarked that, for India, '1947 was a moment of triumph not only for anti-colonial nationalism but also for communalism' (1997: 261). Today, one could add, communalism marks the triumph of women's will to violence. It is not surprising then that many feminists writing on women and violence in South Asia and especially in India criticize '"traditional" feminist concerns with violence, in which women are cast as victims', for their failure 'to account for instances in which violence is perpetrated *by* women', and for their continuous gendering of violence as 'male' (Roy, 1997: 260; emphasis in original).[23] The old feminist assumption that women cannot be active in right-wing political movements in any other way but as 'manipulated and separated from each other in the service of a male-defined project' (Seidel, 1988: 6) is increasingly seen as outdated among South Asian feminists. Roy even suggests that this assumption tells more about feminism of the North – 'willfully and perversely blind to the specificities of different women's experiences' – than about the women on the right (1997: 261). Darini Rajasingham-Senanayake (2001: 111) further criticizes secular feminists in South Asia who see women's political violence as a 'black hole' and part of 'a male patriarchal project', and militant women as 'pawns and victims in the discourse of nationalist patriarchy', while Tanika Sarkar and Urvashi Butalia (1995: 4) argue that women on the right 'bring with them an informed consent and agency, a militant activism' of their own.

In their work, Rajasingham-Senanayake (2001), Patricia Jeffery (1999), and Butalia (2001) suggest that feminist analysis of gender and violent conflict needs rethinking, as concepts such as agency and empowerment no longer offer satisfactory frameworks. First, radical right-wing politics are both appropriating feminist language and offering emancipation and empowerment. This practice seems to be especially true for the Hindutva nationalist movement in India. Figuring prominently as followers as well as leaders of the movement, Hindutva women have defied feminist imagery of victimized or manipulated women who simply catch the crumbs of privilege falling from patriarchal tables around which men leaders make all the difference. As Paola Bacchetta and Margaret Power point out, 'women in the right are neither dupes of right-wing men nor less powerful replicas of them', they 'consciously choose to support and help build the projects of which they are part. In so doing, right-wing women carve out a space and identity for themselves and enhance the ability of their right wings to implement their agenda' (2002: 3). The consequence of such engagements of women in the Hindutva movement is empowerment. However limited, conditional, and controversial this empowerment might be,[24] women's activism in Hindutva has a 'palpable impact on women in the public sphere' (Deshpande, 1997: 197); it politicized femininity and expanded the 'horizons of domesticity'. By becoming a 'communal subject' within the Hindutva movement, 'woman has stepped out of a purely iconic status to take up an active position as a militant' (Sarkar, 1995: 188).

Second, some South Asian feminists argue that the modernist concept of agency is too reductive, as it recognizes only political and public activism, thus missing a much broader social and cultural context of women's engagement in violence outside of clearly defined political movements and public spheres.[25] Far from being either the starting points or the central concepts of feminist theorizing of women's soldiering or sexual victimization in war, agency and victimization should be, as South Asian feminists suggest, only two among many other narratives of women's positioning within a violent conflict. Instead of assuming the presence of either agency or victimization, a feminist studying a violent conflict should rather ask when and how agency and victimization are prioritized in the experiences and representations of war, what other narratives of women's and men's positioning within the war there are, and how they are obscured or denied.

CONCLUSION

Two regional conflicts during the 1990s have inspired many feminists to study sexual violence against women – former Yugoslavia/Bosnia and Rwanda/Africa. One region seems so far to inspire many studies of women's participation in violent conflict – South Asia. In all of these regions women – and men – have been sexually violated, and have taken part, directly and indirectly, in violence. In the wars through which the former Yugoslavia disintegrated, men have been exposed to systematic sexual violence, and women fought as volunteers and within regular armies. Women have been tried at the International Criminal Tribunal for Rwanda for participating in genocide. In some of the African wars, girls and young women, as abducted or co-opted soldiers, commit gruesome crimes. But in the case of the Balkans and Africa, feminist studies have focused almost exclusively on raped women, while in the case of South Asia, sexual violence against women and their participation in communal violence have both attracted feminist attention.

Still, it is clear that these violent conflicts, with sexual violence against women and women's participation in violence, have challenged classical feminist thinking about women, war, and militancy, and have raised questions with significant theoretical and strategic consequences. New feminist studies contributed hugely to intersectional analyses of gender and collective social identities, although, to a large extent, with assumptions about female sexual violability as the starting point. Thus studies of war were sometimes reduced to studies of war rape. New studies have also challenged the conceptualization of agency, empowerment, and emancipation, leading feminists to abandon the assumption that these make their presence felt only within progressive, liberating movements. Many have already noted that geo-politics and feminist theorizing about war seem to be related. If this is so, then the unsettling of the hegemony of Western feminism offers an enormous opportunity for rethinking some basic theoretical and strategic principles, for the benefit of a better understanding of present-day global realities.

NOTES

1 Among classical works on war, militarism, and masculinity (see e.g. Elshtain, 1987; Enloe, 1983; 1989; Huston, 1982; Lloyd, 1986; Segal, 1987), there are collections as well (e.g. Macdonald, 1987).

2 For essentialized differences between feminine–maternal–peace-loving–feminist politics and masculine–war-waging politics see especially Sara Ruddick (1989; 1993) and Klaus Theweleit (1993). See also Tarja Cronberg (1997) on Russian women working in military industry.

3 Jean Bethke Elshtain (1987) suggests that women's participation in armed struggles could subvert essentialist representations of women as peace-loving. Nira Yuval-Davis (1997) argues that demand for equality also demands participation in the military. Dyan Mazurana (2002) and Jolanda Bosch and Desiree Verweijn (2002) argue that an influx of women in the peace-keeping militaries could have a transforming effect.

4 See also Elaine Unterhalter (1987).

5 See also examples by Yuval-Davis (1985) for women in the Israeli Army and Lydia Sklevicky (1989) for partisan women in the Yugoslav army during the Second World War. According to Gilda Zwerman (1994) the same applies to women in clandestine armed organizations in the United States.

6 I especially refer here to works of Chandra Talpade Mohanty (2003) and Inderpal Grewal and Caren Kaplan (1994).

7 See Gill Seidel and Rennte Gunther (1988) for the Falklands and Abouali Farmanfarmaian (1992) and Christine Forde (1995) for the Gulf War.

8 For a thorough overview of theoretical approaches to rapes in Bosnia see Elissa Helms (1998) and Dubravka Zarkov (forthcoming).

9 For the prevalence and forms of sexual violence during violent conflicts in Africa and elsewhere and for responses by NGOs and human rights groups see especially Indai Lourdes Sajor (1998), Clotilde Twagiramariya and Meredeth Turshen (1998). For the post-war sexual violence and its consequences see Sheila Meintjes, Anu Pillay, and Meredeth Turshen (2001).

10 Lately, more studies of the Rwandan war are available in the West, although these are often from Western authors. See, for example, Enloe (2000) on rapes and Myriam Gervais (2004) on Rwanda's women personal, economic, and socio-political security after the conflict, respectively. See also Twagiramariya and Turshen (1998) on sexual politics and Mibenge (forthcoming) on Rwandan tribunals.

11 For a review see Zarkov (forthcoming).

12 This lesson was learned by both the witnesses and the women's NGOs in Rwanda, where, after being unhappy with the Court proceedings, witnesses and their associations refused cooperation with the International Criminal Tribunal for Rwanda and stalled the process for more than a year. Similar events may be happening to the International Criminal Court (ICC) in The Hague, according to stories coming from women's NGOs from Uganda and the Democratic Republic of Congo, with regard to the cases to be

taken up by the ICC, as women's NGOs there are unhappy with the ICC's handling of the cases (information from personal contact with members of Women's Initiative for Gender Justice, The Hague).

13 The communalization of women's bodies during and after partition did not end in rapes, abductions, and forced conversion and marriages. As the states of India and Pakistan were established, the project of 'recovery' started, with the objective of bringing the abducted women back to their 'rightful' religious communities. The women who, after abduction, conversion, and marriage gathered their lives in their new communities were uprooted and displaced once again. This time, however, the children that were born as a result of the new marriages were not allowed to go back with the mothers. Thus, for example, Hindu women from India who were abducted and married to Muslim men in Pakistan had to leave their children in Pakistan. Clearly, India, which praised itself as a secular state, defined the children through the religion of their fathers (Butalia, 1993).

14 See also Rajasingham-Senanayke (2001) and Peries (1998).

15 As discussed in various references (see Butalia, 1993; 1997; 2001; Menon and Bhasin, 1993; 1996; 1998). The estimates range from 25,000 to 29,000 Hindu and Sikh women and 12,000 to 15,000 Muslim women who were abducted and raped, forced into conversion and marriage (Butalia, 1993; 1997).

16 Within the racist discourses, the rape of White women has been made most visible precisely in cases when the rapist is not White. See, for instance, research by Chris Grover and Keith Soothill (1996), who point out that the press in Britain still most often reports – in most gruesome detail – the rape of White women by Black and Asian men.

17 For details and analysis of UN reports about sexual violence against men in the Bosnian War, see Augusta DelZotto and Adam Jones (2002), Jones (2001), and Zarkov (2001). For sexual torture against male prisoners in the context of political violence see Sahika Yuksel (1991). For invisibility and unrecognizability of sexual violence against men see Harry Van Tienhoven (1993).

18 One could even say that these wars exposed the lack of feminist theorizing on war, as some of the most important debates on war and violent conflict, such as those on 'greed vs. grievance' or on 'new wars,' have been actually proceeding without much feminist input.

19 For literary and cultural representations of gender and war see especially collections by Helen Cooper et al. (1989), Miriam Cooke and Angela Woollacott (1993), and the study of the First World War by Billi Melman (1998), who redefines both the war (including the decades that led to it, and the decades after it, that were an introduction to the Second World War) and Europe (including its colonial and imperial domains of power). For the changing nature of war, see, for example, Schott (1996).

20 As presented in various references (see, for example, Afshar and Eade, 2004; Meintjes et al., 2001; Turshen and Twagiramariya, 1998).

21 See especially Robert Connell (2002).

22 RSS (Rashtriya Swayam Sevak Sangh) is a militant, radical, nationalist Hindu organization established in 1924 by an activist in the Indian Independence movement. Its contemporary recruitment policies still target pre-adolescent boys, who are trained in semi-military camps in an authoritarian fashion, with a strong emphasis on physique, moral character, and national/religious purity. The organization also has a women's wing. RSS members have been implicated in much of the communal violence in India.

23 For early critical work on women's violent and right-wing agency see Bacchetta (1996) and Sarkar and Butalia (1995). For recent studies, see Bacchetta (2002), Amrita Basu (1999), Butalia (2001), de Mel (2001), Jeffery (1999), and Rajasingham-Senanayake (2001).

24 See the debate in Paula Banerjee (2001), Basu (1999), Butalia (2001), and Jeffery (1999).

25 See Jeffery (1999) on political agency and Ritu Manchanda (2001) on women's violent agency within the domestic sphere – through support of the militancy and violence of their family members, especially sons.

REFERENCES

Afshar, H. and Eade, D. (eds) (2004) *Development, Women and War: Feminist Perspectives*, Oxford: Oxfam.

Bacchetta, P. (1996) 'Hindu Nationalist Women as Ideologues: The Sangh, the Samiti and Differential Concepts of the Hindu Nation', in Jayawardena, K. and de Alwis, M. (eds), *Embodied Violence: Communalizing Women's Sexuality in South Asia*, New Delhi: Kali for Women, pp. 126–167.

Bacchetta, P. (2002) *The Nation and the RSS: Gendered Discourse, Gendered Action*, New Delhi: Kali for Women.

Bacchetta, P. and Power, M. (eds) (2002) *Right Wing Women: From Conservatives to Extremists Around the World*, New York: Routledge, pp. 1–15.

Bakic-Hayden, M. and Hayden, R. (1992) 'Orientalist Variations on the Theme "Balkans": Symbolic Geography in Recent Yugoslav Cultural Politics', *Slavic Review* 52(1): 1–16.

Banerjee, P. (2001) 'Between Two Armed Patriarchies: Women in Assam and Nagaland', in Manchanda, R. (ed.), *Women, War and Peace in South Asia: Beyond Victimhood to Agency*, Thousand Oaks, CA: Sage.

Basu, A. (1999) 'Hindu Women's Activism in India and the Questions it Raises', in Jeffery, P. and Basu, A. (eds), *Resisting the Sacred and the Secular: Women's Activism and Politized Religion in South Asia*, New Delhi: Kali for Women, pp. 167–184.

Bosch, J. and Verweijn, D. (2002) 'Enduring Ambivalence: the Dutch Armed Forces and their women recruits', in Cockburn, C. and Zarkov, D. (eds), *The Postwar Moment: Militaries, Masculinities and International Peacekeeping*, London: Lawrence and Wishart, pp. 122–145.

Brownmiller, S. (1986) *Against Our Will – Men, Women and Rape*, New York: Bantam Books.

Brownmiller, S. (1993) 'Making Women's Bodies Battlefields', in Stiglmayer, A. (ed.), *Mass Rape – The War against Women in Bosnia-Hercegovina*, Lincoln and London: University of Nebraska Press, pp. 180–183.

Butalia, U. (1993) 'Community, State and Gender: On Women's Agency during Partition', *Economic and Political Weekly* 24 April, New Delhi, India, pp. 12–24.

Butalia, U. (1997) 'A Question of Silence: Partition, Women and the State', in Lentin, Ronit (ed.), *Gender and Catastrophe*, London and New York: Zed Books, pp. 92–110.

Butalia, U. (2001) 'Women and Communal Conflict: New Challenges for the Women's Movement in India', in Moser, C. O. N. and Clark, F. C. (eds), *Victims, Perpetrators of Actors? Gender, Armed Conflict and Political Violence*, London and New York: Zed Books, pp. 99–113.

Cock, J. (1992) *Women and War in South Africa*, London: Open Letters.

Cock, J. (1994) 'Women and the Military: Implications for Demilitarization in the 1990s in South Africa', *Gender and Society* 8(2): 152–169.

Connell, R. W. (2002) 'Masculinities, the reduction of violence and the pursuit of peace', in Cockburn, C. and Zarkov, D. (eds), *The Postwar Moment: Militaries, Masculinities and International Peacekeeping*, London: Lawrence and Wishart, pp. 33–40.

Cooke, M. and Woollacott, A. (eds) (1993) *Gendering War Talk*, Princeton, NJ: Princeton University Press.

Cooper, H. et al. (eds) (1989) *Arms and the Woman: War, Gender and Literary Representation*, Chapel Hill: University of North Carolina Press.

Copelon, R. (1993) 'Surfacing Gender: Reconceptualizing crimes against women in time of war', in Siglmayer (ed.), *Mass Rape – The war against Women in Bosnia-Hercegovina*, Lincoln: University of Nebraska Press, pp. 197–218.

Cronberg, T. (1997) 'The Feeling of Home: Russian Women in the Defense Industry and the Transformation of their Identities', *European Journal of Women's Studies* 4(3): 263–282.

de Mel, N. (2001) 'Agent or Victim? The Sri Lankan Woman Militant in the Interregnum', in *Women and the Nation's Narrative. Gender and Nationalism in Twentieth Century Sri Lanka*, New Delhi: SSA, pp. 203–232.

DelZotto, A. and Jones, A. (2002) 'Male-on-male Sexual Violence in Wartime: Human Rights' Last Taboo?', paper presented to the Annual Convention of the International Studies Association (ISA), New Orleans, LA, 23–27 March 2002.

Deshpande, S. (1997) 'Book Review', *Thamyris*, 4(1): 195–199.
El-Bushra, J. (2004) 'Fused in combat: gender relations and armed conflict', in Afshar, H. and Eade, D. (eds), *Development, Women, and War. Feminist Perspectives*, Oxford: A Development in Practice Reader, pp. 152–171.
Elshtain, J. B. (1987) *Women and War*, New York: Basic Books.
Emmanuel, S. (2004) *Re-Examining Feminist Discourses on Female Militancy: a Critical Analysis of Writings on the Women of the Liberation Tigers of Tamil Eelam*, MA Thesis Institute of Social Studies, The Hague.
Enloe, C. (1983) *Does Khaki Become You? The Militarization of Women's Lives*, London: South End Press.
Enloe, C. (1989) *Bananas, Beaches, Bases: Making Feminist Sense of International Politics*, London: Pandora.
Enloe, C. (2000) *Maneuvers: The International Politics of Militarizing Women's Lives*, Berkeley, Los Angeles, London: University of California Press.
Farmanfarmaian, A. (1992) 'Sexuality in the Gulf War: Did you measure up?' in *Genders* 13(Spring): 1–29.
Forde, C. (1995) '"Women warriors": Representation of Women Soldiers in British Daily Newspaper Photographs of the Gulf War (January to March 1991)', in Maynard, M. and Purvis, J. (eds), *(Hetero)sexual Politics*, London: Taylor & Francis, pp. 108–123.
Gervais, M. (2004) 'Human security and reconstruction efforts in Rwanda: impact on the lives of women', in Afshar, H. and Eade, D. (eds), *Development, Women and War. Feminist Perspectives*, Oxford: Oxfam, pp. 301–314.
Grewal, I. and Kaplan, C. (eds) (1994) *Scattered Hegemonies: Postmodernity and Transnational Feminist Practices*, Minneapolis: University of Minnesota Press.
Griffin, S. (1971) 'Rape: The All-American Crime', *Ramparts*, September: 2635.
Grover, C. and Soothill, K. (1996) 'Ethnicity: The search for rapist and the press', *Ethnic and Racial Studies* 19(3): 567–584.
Hayden, R. (1998) 'Rape and Rape Avoidance in Ethno-National Conflicts: Sexual Violence in Liminalized States', *American Anthropologist* 102(1): 27–41.
Helms, E. (1998) *Representation of wartime rape in Bosnia-Herzegovina: Nationalism, Feminism, and International Law*, MA Thesis University of Pittsburgh.
Huston, N. (1982) 'Tales of War and Tears of Women', *Women's Studies International Forum* 5(3/4): 271–282.
Jeffery, P. (1999) 'Agency, Activism and Agendas', in Jeffery, P. and Basu, A. (eds), *Resisting the Sacred and the Secular: Women's Activism and Politized Religion in South Asia*, New Delhi: Kali for Women, pp. 221–243.
Jones, A. (2001) 'Genocide and Humanitarian Intervention: Incorporating the Gender Variable', *Journal of Humanitarian Assistance*. Retrieved 9 February 2006, from www.jha.ac/articles/1080.htm.
Kašić, B. (2000) 'The Aesthetic of the Victim Within the Discourse of War', in Slapsak, S. (ed.), *War discourse/women's discourse. Essays and case studies from Yugoslavia and Russia*, Ljubljana: Topos, pp. 271–283.
Koontz, C. (1986) *Mothers of the Fatherland: Women, the Family and Nazi Politics*, London: Cape.
Krog, A. (2001) 'Locked into Loss and Silence: Testimonies of Gender and Violence at South Africa Truth Commission', in Moser, C. O. and Clark, F. (eds), *Victims, Perpetrators or Actors? Gender, Armed Conflict and Political Violence*, London: Zed Books, pp. 203–216.
Lloyd, G. (1986) 'Selfhood, war and masculinity', in Pateman, C. and Gross, E. (eds), *Feminist Challenges: Social and Political Theory*, Boston, MA: Allen and Unwin.
Macdonald, S. (1987) 'Drawing the Lines: Gender, Peace and War. An Introduction', in S. Macdonald, P. Holden, and S. Ardener (eds), *Images of Women in Peace and War*, London: Macmillan and Oxford University Women's Studies Committee, pp. 1–26.
Manchanda, R (2001) 'Where Are the Women in South Asian Conflicts?', in Manchanda, R. (ed.), *Women, War and Peace in South Asia: Beyond Victimhood to Agency*, New Delhi, Thousand Oaks, CA, London: Sage.

Mazurana, D. (2002) 'International peacekeeping operations: to neglect gender is to risk peacekeeping failure', in Cockburn, C. and Zarkov, D. (eds), *The Postwar Moment. Militaries, Masculinities and International Peacekeeping*, London: Lawrence and Wishart, pp. 41–50.

Meintjes, S., Pillay, A., and Turshen, M. (eds) (2001) *The Aftermath. Women in post-conflict transformation*, London: Zed Books.

Melman, B. (1998) *Borderlines: Genders and Identities in War and Peace (1870–1930)*, London: Routledge.

Menon, R. and Bhasin, K. (1993) 'Recovery, Rupture, Resistance: Indian State and Abduction of Women during Partition', *Economic and Political Weekly* 24 April, New Delhi, India, pp. 2–11.

Menon, R. and Bhasin, K. (1996) 'Abducted Women, the State and Questions of Honour: Three Perspectives on the Recovery Operation in Post-Partition India', in Jayawardena, K. and de Alwis, M. (eds), *Embodies Violence: Communalizing Women's Sexuality in South Asia*, New Delhi: Kali for Women, pp. 1–32.

Menon, R. and Bhasin, K. (1998) *Borders and Boundaries: Women in India's Partition*, New Delhi: Kali for Women.

Mertus, J. (2004) 'Shouting from the Bottom of the Well. The Impact of International Trails for wartime Rape on Women's Agency', *International Feminist Journal of Politics* 6(1): 110–128.

Messerschmidt, J. (1998) 'Men Victimizing Men: The Case of Lynching, 1865–1900', in Bowker, J. (ed.), *Masculinities and Violence*, London: Sage, pp. 125–151.

Mibenge, C. (forthcoming) 'The right to access to a remedy for victims of wartime sexual violence: A case study of Rwanda (1994–2004)', in Zarkov, D. (ed.), *Gender, Violent Conflict, Development: Challenges of Practice*, New Delhi: Zubaan.

Mohanty, C. Talpede (2003) '"Under Western Eyes" Revisited: Feminist Solidarity Through Anticapitalist Struggle', *Signs*, 28(2): 499–535.

Niarchos, C. (1995) 'Women, War and Rape: Challenges Facing the International Tribunal for the Former Yugoslavia', *Human Rights Quarterly* 17(4): 649–690.

Pedersen, S. (1991) 'National Bodies, Unspeakable Acts: The Sexual Politics of Colonial Policy-making', *Journal of Modern History*, 63: 647–680.

Peries, S. (1998) 'Metamorphosis of the Tamil Woman in the Nationalist War for Elam', Paper presented at the Women in Conflict Zone Network Conference, York University, Toronto, Canada.

Rajasingham-Senanayake, D. (2001) 'Ambivalent Empowerment: The Tragedy of Tamil Women in Conflict', in Manchanda, R. (ed.), *Women, war and peace in South Asia: Beyond victimhood to agency*, London, New Delhi, Thousand Oaks, CA: Sage, pp. 102–130.

Roy, A. (1997) 'Introduction: Cultural Studies, Violence and Femininity', *Women, a cultural review* 8(3): 259–263.

Ruddick, S. (1989) *Maternal Thinking*, Boston, MA: Beacon Press.

Ruddick, S. (1993) 'Notes Toward a Feminist Peace Politics', in Cooke, M. and Woollacott, A. (eds), *Gendering War Talk*, Princeton, NJ: Princeton University Press, pp. 109–127.

Sajor, I. L. (ed.) (1998) *Common Grounds. Violence against Women in War and Armed Conflict Situations*, Philippines: ASCENT.

Sarkar, T. (1995) 'Heroic Women, Mother Goddesses: Family Organization of Hindutva Politics', in Sarkar, T. and Butalia, U. (eds), *Women and Right-Wing Movements: Indian Experiences*, London and New York: Zed Books, pp. 181–215.

Sarkar, T. and Butalia, U. (1995) *Women and Right-Wing Movements. Indian Experiences*, London and New York: Zed Books.

Schott, R. M. (1996) 'Gender and "Postmodern War"', *Hypatia* 11(4): 19–29.

Segal, L. (1987) *Slow Motion: Changing Masculinities, Changing Men*, London: Virago.

Seidel, G. (ed.) (1988) *The Nature of the Right: A Feminist Analysis of Order Patterns*, Amsterdam/ Philadelphia: John Benjamin Publishing Company.

Seidel, G. and Gunther, R. (1988) '"Nation" and "family" in the British media reporting on the "Falklands conflict"', in Seidel, G. (ed.), *The Nature of the Right: A Feminist Analysis of Order Patterns*, Amsterdam/Philadelphia, John Benjamin Publishing Company, pp. 115–128.

Sharpe, J. (1991) 'The Unspeakable Limits of Rape: Colonial Violence and Counter-insurgency', *Genders* 10: 25–47.

Sklevicky, L. (1989) 'Emancipated Integration or Integrated Emancipation: The Case of Post-Revolutionary Yugoslavia', in Angerman, A. et al. *Current Issues in Women's History*, London: Routledge, pp. 93–108.

Smith, V. (1998) *Not Just Race, Not Just Gender. Black feminist readings*. New York: Routledge.

Taylor, D. (1993) 'Spectacular Bodies: Gender, Terror and Argentina's "Dirty War"', in Cooke, M. and Woollacott, A. (eds), *Gendering War Talk*, Princeton, NJ: Princeton University Press, pp. 20–40.

Theweleit, K. (1993) 'The Bomb's Womb and the Genders of War (War Goes on Preventing Women from Becoming the Mothers of Invention)', in Cooke, M. and Woollacott, A. (eds), *Gendering War Talk*, Princeton, NJ: Princeton University Press, pp. 283–317.

Twagiramariya, C. and Turshen, M. (1998) '"Favours" to give and "Consenting" Victims. The Sexual Politics of Survival in Rwanda', in Twagiramariya, C. and Turshen, M. (eds), *What Women Do In Wartime. Gender and Conflict in Africa*, London: Zed Books, pp. 101–117.

Unterhalter, E. (1987) 'Women Soldiers and the Unity in Apartheid South Africa', in S. Macdonald, P. Holden, and S. Ardener (eds), *Images of Women in Peace and War*, London: Macmillan and Oxford University Women's Studies Committee, pp. 100–121.

Van Tienhoven, H. (1993) 'Sexual torture of male victims', *Torture* 3(4): 133–135.

Yuksel, S. (1991) 'Therapy of sexual torture', Paper presented at the XI World Sexology Congress, 18–22 June, Amsterdam, the Netherlands.

Yuval-Davis, N. (1985) 'Front and Rear: The sexual division of labor in the Israeli army', *Feminist Studies* 11(3): 649–676.

Yuval-Davis, N. (1997) *Gender and Nation*, London: Sage.

Zarkov, D. (2001) 'The Body of the Other Man: Sexual Violence and the Construction of Masculinity, Sexuality and Ethnicity in Croatian Media', in Moser, O. and Clark, F. (eds), *Victims, Perpetrators or Actors? Gender, Armed Conflict and Political Violence*, London: Zed Books, pp. 69–82.

Zarkov, D. (forthcoming) *The Fe/Male Body and the Productive Power of Violence: On 'Media War' and 'Ethnic War' in former Yugoslavia*, Durham, NC: Duke University Press.

Zwerman, G. (1994) 'Mothering on the Lam: Politics, Gender Fantasies and Maternal Thinking in Women Associated with Armed Clandestine Organizations in the United States', *Feminist Review* 47: 33–56.

13

Mothers and Muslims, Sisters and Sojourners
The Contested Boundaries of Feminist Citizenship

Baukje Prins

Three tendencies can be discerned in feminist theories of citizenship: the first aims at the inclusion of women as full-fledged citizens, the second opts for a reversal of the dominant conceptions of citizenship, and the third deconstructs existing dichotomous frameworks of citizenship in order to develop feminist reconceptualizations of liberal democracy. Each of these outlooks generates a different perspective on one of the most nagging questions in contemporary feminist theory: how do the political aims of feminism and multiculturalism relate to one another? Each of these perspectives is confronted with the tacit assumption that citizenship involves the position of members of a nation-state. Current processes of globalization appear to undermine this conception of citizenship. For feminists, a conception of citizenship beyond the nation-state brings up urgent questions, such as: should we aim at global justice for all women world-wide, or does our civic responsibility require us to primarily care for our co-citizens? As feminist citizens, who do we count as part of our community?

INTRODUCTION

In the early 1990s, many feminist philosophers found that the practice of the women's movement as well as those of other new social movements could be articulated most adequately in terms of citizenship. The classical political vocabulary of citizenship seemed to offer a viable alternative to the vocabularies that until then had been dominant in feminist political theory: the individualistic, rights-oriented discourse of liberalism, and the structuralist, interest-oriented perspectives of socialism and Marxism. Citizenship-talk made room for the political role of social groups and communities, and it emphasized the value of the attachment to and active participation in those communities. The focus on citizenship, moreover, enabled feminist theorists to rethink the political struggles and achievements of the women's movement as part of a much larger process of democratization which had evolved in the modern Western world since the American and French Revolutions.

Recent feminist reflections on citizenship are confronted by two nagging questions. The first concerns the relation between the political projects of multiculturalism and feminism: how can we reconcile the justified demand of minority groups for recognition of their religious, ethnic, or cultural identity with the feminist goal of the individual autonomy of women? Some feminists argue that multiculturalism is 'bad for women' because it tends to lock them up within the confines of their traditional, often patriarchal communities and actually hands them over to the power of the men in those communities. Others perceive multiculturalism not as opposed to, but rather as allied to the feminist project: just as women have fought for the equal valuation of differences among women, so are ethnic or cultural groups asking for recognition of their differences. To reformulate this controversy in terms of citizenship: whereas some are deeply concerned that the granting of specific cultural rights to members of ethnic and cultural groups will privilege the men of these groups and violate the civil, political, and social rights of the women, according to others the recognition of religious and cultural identity is nothing less than an example of the further democratization of Western societies and of the inclusion of previous outsiders as legitimate members of civil society.

The second issue concerns the relationship between feminist struggles aimed at equality and justice for women and struggles for more global justice between developed and developing countries. The nagging question here is: who, as feminist citizens, do we reckon to be part of our community? Should we aim at global justice for all women world-wide, or does our civic responsibility require us to primarily care for our co-citizens? This nagging question, as will become clear, is due to a tacit assumption at the heart of contemporary political theories, namely, that the territorial domain of the nation-state is the only political community that can endow individuals with the status, rights, and privileges of citizenship.

In this chapter, I will distinguish three different feminist strategies regarding feminist citizenship: the strategy of inclusion, the strategy of reversal, and the strategy of displacement. The meaning, usefulness, and limitations of each will be assessed by exploring how it handles the much disputed issue of multiculturalism versus feminism. I will argue that the strategy of displacement seems to offer the best conceptual tools to steer a middle way between the radical affirmation and a wholesale rejection of multiculturalism. I will conclude with some reflections on how the current process of globalization not only affects the position of women world-wide in different and often contradictory ways, but also fundamentally challenges each of the three kinds of feminist citizen-talk discussed in this chapter. However, before diving into these specific debates, it seems wise to retreat for one moment and first get an idea of the relationship between feminism and political theory in general.

FEMINISM AND POLITICAL THEORY

Feminist practice and theory can be named *political* projects, in so far as they initiate processes of public negotiation and struggle over the right to equal participation in the exercise of government – over oneself as well as over one's community. Feminist interventions are aimed at the equality of opportunities for each woman to develop her talents, to realize her ambitions, and to attain the same socio-economic status as men. Political activities which seek to establish more equality belong to the 'official-political sphere' (Fraser, 1997). They focus on problems that can be handled by existing governmental and social institutions. Demands put forward here focus on the acquisition of rights, backed by official legislation. If successful, these interventions result in the inclusion of women in the existing social and political order. However, for the transformation of such a *de jure* equality into *de facto* equality, a different kind of political activity is needed. These are activities which aim to describe matters previously defined as apolitical, for instance the economy, culture, or family life, into political problems of exploitation, injustice, or exclusion. Such practices of *politicization* involve the public contestation of dominant interpretations of codes of conduct, needs, interests, and identities. They make public what was formerly considered private. By exposing what is usually perceived of as necessary and natural as in fact contingent and socially constructed, transformative political practices redefine what looked like inevitable fate into changeable circumstances. Such activities belong to the sphere of the 'discursive-political' (Fraser, 1997).

In the 1970s feminists confronted modern liberal thought with the slogan 'the personal is the political'. Until then, it was taken for granted that the spheres of social relationships and personal life should be regarded as 'private' domains, as spheres of freedom with which the state ought not interfere. On the one hand, government should interfere as little as possible with citizens' activities in the public sphere. On the other hand, individuals' most personal thoughts and projects should not be curbed either, not by state regulations, nor by civil conventions and social expectations. Hence, civil society counts as 'private' when opposed to the state, but as 'public' when opposed to the personal.

'The personal is the political' also takes issue with this tripartite liberal–romantic framework for neglecting yet another public–private divide, between the public and domestic or family life. Many feminist critics have pointed out how liberal thought failed to theorize the very domain which serves to constitute and legitimize the framework of liberal political philosophy (Squires, 1999: 27). On the one hand, the family is the realm of intimate relationships, based on values of love and care rather than economic gain, political power, or social status. On the other hand, the family is a public institution: marriage is a contract which regulates the rights and responsibilities of spouses, and parents have legal custody over their children. Hence, the family emerges as a 'private' realm when opposed to civil society, but as a 'public' institution when contrasted to the personal life of an individual.

A final deconstructive move implied in 'the personal is political' involves the politicization of our intimate 'inner' life. Feminists put much effort into exposing the variegated ways in which our most personal needs and desires can be perceived as the articulations of a dominant discourse. Rather than express the needs and desires of a universal human (or female) subject, they constitute what, in a particular time and place, counts as a human (or female) subject. Even our most intimate sexual desires can be interrogated for their implications on the level of social relationships, and even as autonomous subjects, we are not simply the sources of our own speech and action, but the contingent outcome of social–symbolic processes of 'subjectification' and 'abjection' (Butler, 1993).

In sum, the feminist rallying cry 'the personal is the political' aptly summarizes the endless ways in which not only the official–political realm – the state – but also the spheres of civil society, the family, and the personal are deeply political and pervaded by power.

CITIZENSHIP

From its very start, modern feminism constitutes a theory and practice which challenges the exclusion or marginalization of women in economic, social, and political life. Feminists have fought for equal rights and opportunities, such as women's right to education, economic independence, or control over their own bodies. These demands for more equality within the existing societal order could not, however, ignore the different roles and identities historically ascribed to and adopted by women. Consequently, struggles for equality and inclusion were often accompanied by demands for particular rights, such as the right to maternity leave or to specific welfare measures for single mothers. Thus, where demands for the equality of women discarded sexual difference, every so often they had to be based on the affirmation of sexual difference. This complicated predicament reminded feminists that the dominant societal order was not a gender-neutral but a masculine order, which structurally favoured male subjects. Nowadays, it is acknowledged that equality and difference are not opposite but rather interdependent strategies, such that political equality rests on the recognition of differences, which in turn implies the recognition of the equal value of these differences (Bock and James, 1992: 10).

Postmodernist thought has led feminist intellectuals to interrogate critically oppositions such as equality versus difference. They are interested in the myriad ways in which such oppositions produce their own 'constitutive outside' in the form of 'hybrid' or 'subaltern' identities and practices. These identities and practices cannot be captured under either pole of a categorical divide, but simultaneously form the matrix that produces these categorizations (Butler and Scott, 1992).

The development in feminist theories of citizenship follows a similar pattern as feminist theory in general. Thus, we can discern tendencies that focus on the equality and *inclusion* of women, arguing that women are to be recognized as full-fledged citizens. A second line of proposals, in drawing attention to the value of female and other differences, aims for the *reversal* of dominant, masculine, or Western conceptions of citizenship. Finally, there are political theorists who wish to deconstruct the dichotomous frameworks altogether, a *displacement* which enables them to develop feminist reconceptualizations of liberal democracy (Squires, 1999).

The strategy of inclusion: women are citizens, too

The American and French Revolutions of the eighteenth century were the first political events in which the subjects of a sovereign power demanded to be acknowledged as equal citizens of their own state. The recognition of the equality of each citizen in the American Declaration of Independence (1776) self-evidently applied to the White, male, Anglo settler – but not to women, Blacks (slaves), or Native Americans (Indians). In a similar manner, in revolutionary France, the Declaration of the Rights of Man and the Citizen (1789), which elevated the status of 'the commons' to that of 'citoyens', excluded women. Their exclusion was defended with the argument that, because women were economically dependent on and legally subordinated to (under coverture of) their fathers or husbands, they were unable to make independent judgements – their social status reflected their naturally dependent status. Consequently, the democratic revolutions reserved citizenship status only for property-owning men who were heads of households. Nevertheless, revolutionary slogans such as 'men are born and remain free and equal in their rights', or 'all men are created equal', were susceptible to the criticism that these ideals were not carried through to their full extent.

The American and the French Revolutions clearly marked the beginning of the *liberal-rights* tradition. Within this tradition, citizenship consists primarily of the status, rights, and entitlements granted by a state to its members. Usually, three kinds of citizenship rights are distinguished: civil rights, which secure the realization of individual freedom, such as freedom of speech and the right to own property; political rights, which allow for active and passive participation in the exercise of government; and social rights, which guarantee each individual a minimum share in economic wealth and social security (Marshall, 1950).

Already in the eighteenth century, revolutionary women like Olympe de Gouge and Mary Wollstonecraft actually took the public stage to argue passionately for the inclusion of women as full-fledged citizens within the political community. They thus presented themselves as active citizens, as individuals who had the competence to speak in public, to write political treatises, to set up a rational argument. In doing so, these women answered to the criteria of good citizenship set by the *civic–republican* tradition, another main theoretical perspective on citizenship. Contrary to the liberal-rights tradition, which conceives of citizenship in terms of status, according to the republican view, citizenship is determined by an individual's active engagement with the public interest. Citizenship here does not so much involve membership in a state, but membership in a community. Rather than start from the assumption of self-interest, the civic–republican tradition expects citizens to cultivate a virtuous self (Connolly, 1991: 74). A good citizen, finally, is expected to exhibit typically manly virtues, such as self-control, impartiality, and civic courage.

To suggest, however, that the approaches of individual liberalism and civic–republicanism are diametrically opposed to one another would be misleading. Within the liberal perspective, the allocation of rights is implicitly made dependent on the fulfilment of certain obligations, such as a citizen's compliance to national laws and regulations. And no modern republican would deny that civic virtues are fostered most in a society which grants its citizens certain rights, such as the civil right of assembly, the political right to vote, and the social right to education. The insight that rights-based and virtue-based approaches to citizenship cannot be separated from each other resonates in contemporary reflections on women's inclusion as equal members of the citizenry. Thus, Ruth Lister (2003) argues for a 'synthetic approach', which conceives of citizenship as both status and practice and acknowledges that civil, political, and social rights are prerequisites for human agency, and that, in turn, agency is needed to acquire individual rights. Susan Moller Okin (1989) pointed out that women will have an equal opportunity to positions of political influence only after the transformation of the family from a patriarchal into a 'gender-free' institution. As long as they remain financially dependent on their husbands, women cannot simply choose to step out of an oppressive relationship, let alone speak up in public. Only when they have a real exit-option will women be able to use their voice and stand up for themselves.

Okin's use of the terms of 'voice' and 'exit', which she adopts from the political theorist Alfred Hirschmann, are particularly insightful with regard to her interventions in recent debates on multiculturalism. Okin took issue with the fact that participants in these debates often parry the question of what to do if claims of special rights by minority cultures clash with the norm of gender equality that liberal states in principle endorse (1998; 1999). With this critique, Okin was the first in a long list of authors who questioned the feminist credentials of multiculturalism (Hirsi Ali, 2006; Wikan, 2002). Each of them chastized adherents to multiculturalism for their attempt to extend the list of liberal rights with a fourth type of rights – cultural rights. Multiculturalists defend the recognition of cultural rights as the logical extension of citizenship rights with the argument that for most individuals, their culture provides them with a meaningful context of choice and a sense of belonging which are essential for their well-being. Hence, it is a fundamental human right for individuals to maintain their own culture (Kymlicka, 1995). Moreover, in an era of ongoing immigration, cultural rights also function as 'rights of integration', allowing non-citizens to become part of civil society on their own terms (Pía Lara, 2002).

To this line of reasoning, liberal feminists object that the crucial difference between civil, political, and social rights and cultural rights is that the first are individual rights whereas the latter are group rights. As group rights, cultural rights are at odds with the liberal value of individual freedom, and their recognition may have devastating consequences, especially for the women members of a group. This conflict, according to Okin, is especially evident when we realize that most cultures are deeply gendered and that our individual sense of self is developed in the private sphere of domestic and family life. Thus we find, first, that most cultures preserve their distinct character and values through regulations of sexuality, reproduction, and family life, which affect the lives of women far more than the lives of men. Second, most cultures are patriarchal cultures, in which women's lives are under the constant control of men, who expect them to serve their every desire and interest. Liberal thinkers who defend multiculturalism on the grounds that one's own culture is an indispensable source for the development of self-esteem and self-respect forget that in most cultures, girls and women are often indoctrinated with the idea that they are of less value than boys, or that their life's sole purpose is to guard the honour of the family. Okin argues that even a defence of group rights only in so far as these rights do not interfere with the freedom of individuals concentrates too much on forms of overt restriction, to the detriment of the far more subtle, but no less influential discriminatory practices in the private sphere of the household and the family. Liberal multiculturalists in particular should be critically aware of such intragroup inequalities. Even in the rare cases that a group has been rightfully granted the right to organize its community life according to its own traditional customs or religious prescriptions, Okin insists that individual members maintain the right to step out of their group whenever they wish to do so. Just as Okin in her earlier reflections endorsed the importance of women having a right to 'exit' from an oppressive marriage, she now emphasizes that liberal societies should do their utmost to lessen the inevitable economic, social, and emotional costs when individuals, especially women, decide to distance themselves from their family, their church, or their cultural–ethnic community – a position with which, for that matter, most liberal multiculturalists wholeheartedly agree.

The strategy of reversal: communitarian and maternal thinking

Liberal feminist critiques of multiculturalism are sometimes countered by precisely the women they claim to stand up for. Ever more Muslim women speak up in public, through interventions in political debates and articles in newspapers and academic books. In Western countries, more Muslim women and girls have taken to wearing the veil, some of them even causing quite a stir when challenging public authorities by attending class or appearing in court dressed in the traditional niqāb. These Muslim women thus manifest themselves as active citizens, initiating and participating in public debates by challenging the liberal–feminist idea that when women are free to choose their own way of life, they will self-evidently choose to live according to the values of secular liberalism. They object to the ethnocentric or 'orientalist' perspective of Western feminists, accusing them of reducing Muslim women to the position of 'inessential Others' (Al-Hibri, 1999: 42). In contrast, Muslim women emphasize their commitment to their own cultural or religious community, which they firmly believe can be changed. They contend that such transformations, however, will not come from the outside, but are possible only from within. For these women, 'Muslim feminism' is not a contradiction in terms, as secular feminists seem to assume. On the contrary, they argue that it offers the only viable strategy really to improve the position of Muslim women. Many Muslim feminists thus take great pains over rereading the Qur'an and the *hadith* (commentary) in order to show that Islam in itself does not offer any legitimation for treating women differently from men. Leila Ahmed emphasizes 'the egalitarian conception of gender inherent in the ethical vision of Islam' (1992: 64), while Azizah Al-Hibri argues that some of the basic Islamic principles imply that women and men are equally entitled to engage in *ijthihad* (the interpretation of the religious texts), that Islam celebrates rather than suppresses diversity, and that Islamic law is meant to be flexible regarding time and place (1999: 43). Muslim feminists also make a point of distinguishing religion from culture, claiming that most woman-unfriendly practices in contemporary Muslim countries and communities can be traced back either to pre-Islamic custom or to their being imposed by conservative exegetes. They also claim that one should understand woman-unfriendly *suras* (Qur'an chapters) in their historical context, rather than holding on to their literal meaning in a world which has undergone dramatic changes (Selim, 2003).

Muslim feminists thus express a different view of feminist citizenship than their liberal and civic–republican counterparts. In many respects, their view can be perceived of as a particular version of *communitarianism*. Modern communitarians have attacked the rights-based approach of liberalism for its assumption of the individual as an 'atomistic' self, to replace it with a conception of the individual as an 'embedded' self. Within the liberal view, an individual can in principle stand back from even her most dearly held convictions. From a communitarian perspective, however, 'our selves are at least partly constituted by ends that we do not choose, but rather discover by virtue of our being embedded in some shared social context' (Kymlicka, 2002: 224). This does not imply that individuals can only obediently follow the traditions in which they are raised. Communitarians subscribe to crucial aspects of modernity, such as the validity of universal human rights. Modernity to them does not so much imply the rejection as the transformation of tradition.

Muslim feminists choose to fulfil their civic duty by voicing their criticism, rather than stepping out of their community altogether. The liberal preference for 'exit' indicates that liberals conceive of communities as voluntary associations, whereas the emphasis on 'voice' is in line with the communitarian view that many of our social ties are not freely chosen, but given. According to this view, most of us have strong emotional bonds with our parents, our family, our neighbourhood; we often find that the language, customs, and habits with which we were raised make us feel more at home in some places than in others. Our attachment to our communal values therefore is not the outcome of some reasonable judgement – it rather is something we discover to be an intimate part of ourselves, to constitute our identity. Communitarians agree with civic–republicans that the responsibility of individuals towards their community comes first. But in their eyes this responsibility does not so much require that citizens actively participate in political decision-making, but that they act decently by fulfilling their basic social obligations.

Muslim feminism can be regarded as the most recent articulation of communitarian approaches to feminist citizenship. An earlier influential strand of communitarian thought in feminism has been elaborated by theorists such as Jean Bethke Elshtain and Sara Ruddick under the denominator of 'maternal thinking'. While these early maternalist thinkers took women's experiences as mothers and feminist philosophies of standpoint as their points of departure, contemporary adherents are especially inspired by the activities of grassroots movements like the women's peace camps at Greenham Common in Britain, the Madres of the Plaza del Mayo in Argentina, the Women in Black (a worldwide peace organization), or indigenous community workers engaged in fighting poverty. Even organizations which initially started out as the purely personal concern of mothers for their children, or which seem to be engaged in 'mere' philanthropic work, often get involved in political activities. As Pnina Werbner phrases it, these women testify to the view that one should 'valorize maternal qualities … as encompassing and anchored in democratic values', and that 'political motherhood' is a viable and much needed alternative conception of active citizenship (1999: 221).

Maternalist thinkers have rightly criticized the false universalism of the traditions of civic republicanism and liberalism. These seemingly neutral conceptions of citizenship are indeed highly gendered. But to simply replace them with a maternalist point of view does not really escape the dichotomous framework of gender. As a consequence, maternalist thinking may easily backfire on women. First, because it tends to essentialize female identity, it runs the risk of imposing the norms of maternalism on all women (Dietz, 1985). Second, it may foster claims to innocent victimhood and moral superiority vis-à-vis men. Third, because it focuses on the 'remoralization' rather than politicization of social life, a maternalist reversal risks playing into the hands of moral conservatism (Squires, 1999: 169).

Comparable risks threaten an all too uncritical espousal of a politics of multiculturalism and group rights by communitarian Muslim feminists. Muslim feminists spend much energy rereading the Qur'an to support their interpretation of its verses as in fact very woman-friendly and emancipatory. However sympathetic, these attempts run parallel to the projects of Islamic fundamentalists in their desire to go back to the original, 'true' meaning of these sacred texts. As such, they run the risk of imposing a new kind of orthodoxy on Muslim women concerning the question of how a 'good Muslima' should live. Indulging in denunciations of orientalist 'othering' and contrasting these dehumanizing gestures with a celebration of the supposedly true humaneness and ethical integrity of Islam may contribute to unproductive feelings of resentment and/or moral superiority towards the Western world in general and towards Western feminism in particular. Despite its emancipatory drive, Muslim feminism, like maternalist thinking, may well relapse into a position of moral conservatism.

For these reasons, many political theorists have opted for a third strategy to give shape to feminist citizenship, the strategy of displacement.

THE STRATEGY OF DISPLACEMENT: FEMINIST CITIZENSHIP AS A PRACTICE OF LIBERAL DEMOCRACY

Politicization to those espousing displacement is the most vital aspect of feminist citizenship. The term comprises the entire gamut of strategies that feminists historically have followed to improve the position of women. As I have indicated earlier, savvy feminist critics may expose any area of public or private life and show how its discursive practices are subtly but deeply contestable. Recently, however, feminists have noted that to label a particular practice as contested, hence political, is in itself a political and therefore contested move. The exposure of private–public boundaries as politically non-innocent constructions does not mean that we should just dispense with them. On the contrary, to mark particular opinions, practices, or domains as matters of private rather than public concern constitutes an important safeguard for our individual liberty.

With such self-reflexive notes, adherents to the strategy of displacement testify to their allegiance to a view of social and political reality as a discursive reality, mediated and sustained by linguistic and narrative conventions. They give a deconstructivist twist to the equal rights and participatory perspectives of inclusion, as well as to the aim of the reversal of dominant masculine or secular Western values by feminist communitarians. Perhaps surprisingly, this radical plea for a more politicized approach to feminist citizenship ends up with what looks like a politically quite moderate position, namely, the revaluation of existing liberal-democratic societies. There seems to be a growing consensus among feminist political theorists that genderized or otherwise differential approaches to citizenship can be displaced only by feminist-informed practices of liberal democracy. This unexpected belief in the emancipatory and empowering potential of liberal democracy is sustained by several insights.

First, feminist liberal democrats subscribe to a constructivist view of identity. Identities, whether sexual, cultural, or religious, are the provisional outcome of dynamic processes of self-identification and ascriptions by others. Boundaries between groups are fluid and permeable and axes of domination are constituted by the intersections and boundary-crossings between different sexual, ethnic, cultural, and religious groups. Consequently, the use of a dichotomous framework of gender provides insufficient insight into the forms of injustice, misrecognition, and exclusion that women from different backgrounds may suffer, nor will it offer viable strategies for political transformation. Instead, feminist citizenship involves the ongoing contestation of identities as given, of the way in which particular issues are framed, and of the tacit norms and values underlying supposedly gender- or value-neutral policy measures. For example, feminist citizenship recognizes that in the context of the welfare state, of which women are the principal subjects, the idiom of 'needs' is not politically innocent but may hide assumptions and controversies concerning who has the authority to decide what people 'really' need, which needs are a matter of legitimate political concern and which a matter of individual responsibility, and to what extent the dominant discourse on needs is in fact a *gendered* discourse. Such practices of contestation can assume all kinds of forms, from strategies of silent withdrawal or articulate resistance by individual clients to formally organized groups combating disciplinary welfare practices (Fraser, 1989).

Second, feminist liberal democrats agree that one of the more effective ways to displace existing hegemonic relationships is through collective identity politics. Such collectivities, however, are preferably not based on primordial links such as motherhood, Muslim or other religious sisterhoods, or ethnicity. The political unity of a collective 'we' is never simply given but the result of the creation and articulation of new political identities (Mouffe, 1992). Donna Haraway evokes the figure of the former slave woman Sojourner Truth, who, with her ironical question 'Ain't I a Woman?', simultaneously claimed and deconstructed the identity of 'woman' (1992: 96). Haraway's earlier 'Manifesto for Cyborgs' can equally be read as an alternative figuration of feminist citizenship, presenting the cyborg as a creature of a post-gender world whose alliances are not based on identity, but on 'affinity' (1991 [1985]). Twentieth-century Black and Latina feminists like

Audre Lorde and Gloria Anzaldúa subscribe to such conscious mobilizations of identity. They suggest a conception of citizenship which allows women of all backgrounds to create commonality by both claiming *and* transfiguring given identities (Bickford, 1997).

According to Seyla Benhabib, from the perspective of an outside observer, cultures appear as if they were unified organic wholes; from the perspective of an insider, however, they rather form 'a horizon that recedes each time one approaches it' (2002: 5). This dual perspective implies that a politics of recognition need not involve the recognition of one particular identity. A politics of recognition might just as well 'initiate critical dialogue and reflection in public life about the very identity of the collectivity itself', allowing for democratic dissent and contestation, possibly leading to the 'reflexive reconstitution of collective identities' (p. 70). This insight opens up space for women's renegotiation of the dominant narratives of identity and difference within their own community. It indicates that women of cultural and religious minority groups are not solely to be seen as 'victims' but also as the potential agents of change, as active citizens able to cross and renegotiate the boundaries between their own cultural or religious community and the wider society.

Third, adherents of the strategy of displacement believe that whether a problematic belongs to the domain of the public or the private, justice or the good life, norms or values, is a matter of contestation – none of these discursive boundaries is sacred, each can be crossed and displaced. This fundamental openness vis-à-vis the subject of debate inevitably affects assumptions concerning the proper *place* for political speech and action, as well as ideas on the required *style* of public speech and action. In a truly open society, there is a plurality of public spheres, ranging from the official sphere of representative institutions to the unofficial spheres of social movements, from voluntary civic associations to grassroots activism, from artistic to religious collectivities. Publics can be distinguished according to lines of ideology, class, or identity, but also regarding their unequal status and their unequal access to discursive resources and positions of power. 'Subaltern counterpublics' may pop up at unexpected places, such as the mosque, the theatre, or the school. They may articulate their views through religious lectures, movies, or clothing. Such alternative styles challenge existing views of legitimate public speech and action by exploring its more affective, rhetorical, and impassioned dimensions, by highlighting the particular rather than the universal, and by appealing to desire rather than reason (Mouffe, 2002; Young, 1997).

Fourth, value pluralism and conflicting interests are considered essential to a vital democracy. A viable theory of democratic citizenship should therefore theorize the ways in which conflicts can be kept alive and tackled at the same time. The relationship between political adversaries should be regulated such that their differences are neither soothed away, nor unnecessarily polarized.

Still, there is significant controversy among adherents of the displacement strategy concerning the ultimate foundations of liberal democracy. Benhabib (1992), for instance, develops the notion of 'interactive universalism' in order to emphasize that the value of liberal democracy lies in its insistence that 'participation precedes universality'. Inspired by Carol Gilligan's ethic of care, Benhabib emphasizes the importance of openness in public deliberations to 'the standpoint of the concrete other'; that is, to the specific needs and interests of people who are different. But this attitude should never become a goal in itself; it should always serve as the critical position from which 'the standpoint of the general other' – the other as an equal bearer of rights and duties – is constantly questioned and revised. The ultimate aim of this responsiveness to particular others is to ensure that our institutions and laws live up to their claims of justice and fairness for all – their claims of universality.

Against this 'deliberative' view, Chantal Mouffe proposes a more 'radical' view of liberal democracy, one which remains distrustful of any appeal to universal values. Democracy, according to Mouffe, is an ancient tradition in which equality and popular sovereignty are the core values. The liberal emphasis on freedom and individual rights, however, is a product of the modern era. Deliberative democrats deny the essential tension between the liberal espousal of individual rights and the democratic emphasis on collective will formation. While democracy is built upon the opposition between 'us' (citizens) and 'them' (non-citizens), liberal principles apply to each individual, no matter her passport or place of residence. According to Mouffe, it is precisely this paradoxical nature of liberal democracy which makes it such a valuable regime. Because any existing configuration of power can be challenged, liberal-democratic regimes have propelled forth important historical political developments. It is therefore of the utmost importance to uphold the 'agonistic' nature of liberal democracy and to distrust any legitimation of the status quo in terms of rational consensus. In the end, it is not public reason, but political passion that motivates citizens to participate actively in the public sphere. However fair the procedures, however reasonable their outcome, democratic struggles will always result in new forms of exclusion, in the hegemony of one particular group interest or form of life to the detriment of others (Mouffe, 2000).

Finally, deliberative and radical democrats alike recognize that, despite the inevitability of value pluralism and conflicting interests, one of the most important public goods in a liberal democracy is 'a viable sense of collective identity' (Benhabib, 1996). A liberal democracy is a *political* community, whose common good cannot be found at the level of substantive beliefs, but must be located at the level of agreed-upon procedures for articulating conflicts and attaining temporary agreement. To this insight, and in line with her agonistic view, Mouffe adds the reminder that a fully inclusive political community can never be realized: each construction of a 'we' implies the constitution of an outside, of a 'them'. She therefore prefers to view the common good of a political community as 'a vanishing point' – something to which we, as citizens, must constantly refer, but that can never be reached (1992: 379).

GLOBALIZATION

Globalization can be seen as the set of economic and cultural processes which simultaneously haunt and evade our contemporary thought on what may count as a political community (see Chapter 10, this volume). Globalization casts doubt on previously self-evident assumptions concerning the power of the nation-state, the boundaries of civil society, and the scope of people to whom we are morally obligated: who do we consider to be part of 'our' community; who should we perceive as our co-citizens? Should we as feminists aim at global justice for all women, or does our civic responsibility require us primarily to care for our co-citizens? Confronted with this choice between the liberal perspective of human rights and the democratic perspective of the rights of sovereign peoples, most feminists do not hesitate. They prefer the 'cosmopolitan' view of citizenship which perceives human beings (men and women alike) as citizens of the global community, over and against the 'internationalist' view according to which individuals primarily belong to, and demand rights and benefits from, a particular political community or nation-state.

However, international women's networks and organizations which attempt to practise global feminist citizenship are acutely aware that their struggles for the greater personal autonomy and equality for all women may not always mesh easily with their demands for a more just global economy (Sen and Onufer Correa, 1999). While the process of economic and cultural globalization has enhanced the empowerment of women world-wide, it has also facilitated the upsurge of religious fundamentalisms which instigated a conservative backlash. Thus, at the Fourth UN World Conference on Women in Beijing in 1995, the Vatican branch of Christian fundamentalism entered into alliances with its Islamic counterparts in demanding that the personal autonomy of women be curbed by strict state regulations concerning dress, sexuality, marriage, and reproduction. Such restrictions are not merely imposed 'from above', they are also supported by many religious women themselves – 'from below'.

This tension between the fight for women's rights and the defence of patriarchal relationships is an apt illustration of the *Janus-face* of globalization as a simultaneous process of modernization and traditionalization. While the outcomes of economic liberalization are embraced almost universally, cultural liberalization is resisted as a form of Western imperialism. Politically conscious women from the East and the South often choose to identify as citizens of their particular religious or ethnic community rather than as citizens of the universal community of humanity. Thus, global civil society seems to be marked by the same tension which troubles liberal multicultural states: the tension between the demands for individual rights for women on the one hand, and demands for collective rights by non-liberal groups and peoples on the other.

Globalization confronts feminist theorists with the problem of the usefulness of the concept of citizenship itself. In the current era of 'deterritorialization', individual rights and responsibilities are less and less tied to the territorial-boundaries of the nation-state. Most Western countries grant specific civil, social, and even some political rights to immigrants who are not (yet) naturalized citizens. On the other hand, social rights of citizens may be violated, for instance when they feel forced to accept jobs in so-called 'free export zones' within their own country. While national governments provide transnational corporations with the infrastructure and energy needed to get their production work done, they at the same time allow them to profit from their 'extraterritorial' status by not paying taxes, evading import and export tariffs, and dodging national regulations concerning minimum payment or maximum working days. As an effect of globalization, contemporary nation-states, especially Western welfare states, are undergoing a significant face-lift: from 'caring' states they are gradually turning into 'competitive' states. Succumbing ever more to the pressures of privatization and liberalization issued by the global market, they lose their power to sustain networks of solidarity amongst compatriots and to safeguard people's basic rights as citizens.

This breakdown of the meaning of national citizenship as a guarantee for individual rights and benefits has been accompanied by the rise of NGOs like Amnesty International and DAWN (Development Alternatives with Women for a New Era), the proliferation of international treaties and conferences (such as UN conferences on the position of women), and the emergence of a worldwide discourse on human and women's rights. We might conclude that the decline of national political communities is somehow made good by the rise of a new political community, that of global civil society. That, however, would be an over-hasty conclusion. For one thing, complaints against violations of human or women's rights only make sense if they can be addressed to institutions with the political and juridical power to condemn and prohibit such practices, and the only institutions endowed with such effective power and jurisdiction are still the institutions of the nation-state. It seems that as yet only as citizens of a particular nation-state can we effectively appeal to our universal rights as human beings. It might be an illusion to think that international institutions, forums, and treaties will, even in the longer run, be able to fill the gap created by the demise of nationhood. Perhaps the ideal of a cosmopolitan 'world republic' is too far-fetched. It might very well be that the promotion of mutual trust and solidarity within particular national communities is the only viable way to achieve more global justice and democracy.

It seems therefore that in the near future, feminist citizenship will have to be practised on two fronts at once. On the one hand, feminists need to strengthen further their international networks and alliances to fight for global justice and democratization for all women. On the other hand, we have to accept that nation-states do remain important transformative agents for achieving a gender-neutral 'community of fate' (Van Gunsteren, 1998). This acknowledgement of the need for a dual strategy makes it even more urgent for feminist theorists to think through the notion of 'global' or 'cosmopolitan' citizenship more thoroughly. For, although it is widely agreed that a feminist practice of citizenship 'cannot stop at the borders of individual nation-states' (Lister, 2003: 199), it is far less clear what such an alternative conception of feminist citizenship should look like in order to be politically effective.

REFERENCES

Ahmed, L. (1992). *Women and Gender in Islam*. New Haven, CT: Yale University Press.
Al-Hibri, A. Y. (1999). Is Western Patriarchal Feminism Good for Third World/Minority Women? In J. Cohen, M. Howard, and M. C. Nussbaum (eds), *Is Multiculturalism Bad for Women?* (pp. 41–46). Princeton, NJ: Princeton University Press.
Benhabib, S. (1992). *Situating the Self: Gender, Community and Postmodernism in Contemporary Ethics*. Cambridge: Polity Press.
Benhabib, S. (ed.) (1996). *Democracy and Difference: Contesting the Boundaries of the Political*. Princeton, NJ: Princeton University Press.
Benhabib, S. (2002). *The Claims of Culture: Equality and Diversity in the Global Era*. Princeton, NJ: Princeton University Press.
Bickford, S. (1997). Anti-Anti-Identity Politics: Feminism, Democracy, and the Complexities of Citizenship. *Hypatia* 12(4): 111–131.
Bock, G., and James, S. (eds) (1992). *Beyond Equality and Difference: Citizenship, feminist politics and female subjectivity*. London: Routledge.
Butler, J. (1993). *Bodies that Matter: About the Discursive Limits of 'Sex'*. New York: Routledge.
Butler, J. and Scott, J. W. (eds) (1992). *Feminists Theorize the Political*. New York: Routledge.
Connolly, W. (1991). *Identity/Difference: Democratic Negotiations of Political Paradox*. Ithaca, NY: Cornell University Press.
Dietz, M. G. (1985). Citizenship with a Feminist Face. The Problem with Maternal Thinking. *Political Theory*, 13(1): 19–37.
Fraser, N. (1989). Struggle over Needs: Outline of a Socialist-Feminist Critical Theory of Late Capitalist Political Culture. In N. Fraser, *Unruly Practices: Power, Discourse and Gender in Contemporary Social Theory* (pp. 161–187). Cambridge: Polity Press.
Fraser, N. (1997). *Justice Interruptus*. New York: Routledge.
Haraway, D. (1991 [1985]). A Manifesto for Cyborgs: Science, Technology, and Socialist Feminism in the 1980s. In D. Haraway, *Simians, Cyborgs, and Women: The Reinvention of Nature* (pp. 149–181). London: Free Association Press.
Haraway, D. (1992). Ecce Homo, Ain't (Ar'n't) I a Woman, and Inappropriate/d Others: The Human in a Post-Humanist Landscape. In J. Butler and J. W. Scott (eds), *Feminists Theorize the Political* (pp. 86–100) New York: Routledge.
Hirsi Ali, A. (2006). *The Caged Virgin: An Emanicipation Proclamation for Women and Islam*. New York: Free Press.
Kymlicka, W. (1995). *Multicultural Citizenship: A Liberal Theory of Minority Rights*. Oxford: Clarendon Press.
Kymlicka, W. (2002, 2nd edition). *Contemporary Political Philosophy: An Introduction*. Oxford: Oxford University Press.
Lister, R. (2003, 2nd edition). *Citizenship: Feminist Perspectives*. Houndmills, Basingstoke: Palgrave Macmillan.
Marshall, T. H. (1950). *Citizenship and Social Class*. Cambridge: Cambridge University Press.
Mouffe, C. (1992). Feminism, Citizenship, and Radical Democratic Politics. In J. Butler and J. W. Scott (eds), *Feminists Theorize the Political* (pp. 369–384). New York: Routledge.
Mouffe, C. (2000). *The Democratic Paradox*. London: Verso.
Mouffe, C. (2002). *Politics and Passion: The Stakes of Democracy*. London: Centre for the Study of Democracy.

Okin, S. Moller (1989). *Justice, Gender, and the Family.* New York: Basic Books.
Okin, S. Moller (1998). Feminism and Multiculturalism: Some Tensions. *Ethics,* 108, 661–684.
Okin, S. Moller (1999). *Is Multiculturalism Bad for Women?* Princeton, NJ: Princeton University Press.
Pía Lara, M. (2002). Democracy and Cultural Rights: Is There a New Stage of Citizenship? *Constellations* 9(2): 207–220.
Selim, N. (2003). *De vrouwen van de profeet: Hoe vrouw(on)vriendelijk is de koran?* Amsterdam: Van Gennep.
Sen, G. and Onufer Correa, S. (1999). Gender Justice and Economic Justice: Reflections on the Five Year Reviews of the UN conferences of the 1990's. Paper, retrieved 7 July, 2004, from http://www.dawn.org.fj/global/health/gender_justice.html
Squires, J. (1999). *Gender in Political Theory.* Cambridge: Polity Press.
Van Gunsteren, H. (1998). *A Theory of Citizenship: Organizing Plurality in Contemporary Democracies.* Boulder, CO: Westview Press.
Werbner, P. (1999). Political Motherhood and the Feminisation of Citizenship: Women's Activisms and the Transformation of the Public Sphere. In N. Yuval-Davis and P. Werbner (eds), *Women, Citizenship and Difference* (pp. 221–245). London: Zed Books.
Wikan, U. (2002). *Generous Betrayal: Politics of Culture in the New Europe.* Chicago: Chicago University Press.
Young, I. M. (1997). Communication and the Other: Beyond Deliberative Democracy. In I. M. Young, *Intersecting Voices: Dilemmas of Gender, Political Philosophy, and Policy* (pp. 60–74). Princeton, NJ: Princeton University Press.

Part V

WORK AND FAMILY

14

Gender and Work

Rosemary Crompton

This chapter examines the parallel changes that have taken place over the last thirty years in gender roles and attitudes, and in paid employment. Women, particularly mothers, have taken up paid employment in ever-increasing numbers, and employment itself has become more flexible and less secure. Although women have gained full rights to equality in the workplace, they remain under-represented in higher-level jobs, and there is a persisting wage gap between men and women. There are a number of explanations for this continued pattern of disadvantage for women. The major explanation lies in the ideology of domesticity, which still allocates the major responsibility for caring work to women. Furthermore, in neo-liberal economies such as Britain and the United States, workplace intensification and increasing career pressures are making 'career' jobs even more problematic for individuals with caring responsibilities, who are usually women.

INTRODUCTION

This chapter examines the parallel changes that have occurred in Western societies over the last sixty years with respect to work, markets, and gender. Since the 1940s, technological change has brought with it the transformation of production systems, as well as developments in areas such as communications and financial intermediation that have contributed to the globalization of markets and cultures. At the same time, the 'feudal' allocation of market work to men and domesticity to women (Beck, 1992) has begun to break down as more married women have entered and remained in paid employment.

Women in the United States, Europe, Scandinavia, and most other advanced industrial countries had secured rights to equal treatment in the world of market work by the 1970s. Nevertheless, despite this formal equality, major inequalities between men and women persist. The structure of employment is still characterized by occupational segregation (men and women are concentrated into different occupations), and there remains a substantial gap between men's and women's pay and lifetime incomes. Women in the United States pay a wage penalty for motherhood that has been estimated at between 5 and 7 per cent per child (Budig and England, 2001; Waldfogel, 1997). In part, the income gap is itself a consequence of occupational segregation, as 'women's' jobs, such as nursing, care, and secretarial work, tend to be not as well paid as 'men's' jobs, such as skilled craft occupations. Women are also more likely to work part-time, and are more likely to take employment breaks. Another contributory factor to women's inequality in the sphere of paid work lies in the fact that even when women enter the same occupations as men, more often than not they fail to rise through organizational and professional hierarchies.

There is no one explanation of the persisting inequalities between women and men in employment. Nevertheless, two major sets of explanations for women's employment inequalities relative to men may be identified. First are those that suggest that women's employment patterns are an outcome of individual and family choices, and second are those that emphasize the persistence of structural barriers (including men's exclusionary practices) to women's progress and job opportunities.

FAMILY AND WOMEN'S EMPLOYMENT CHOICES

Theories relating to the significance of individual choice with regard to women's employment can be categorized within two conflicting traditions. First, there are neo-classical economic theories of the family, which argue that a traditional gendered division of labour is the most rational (and therefore efficient) as far as the family is concerned. Second, there are sociological theories that argue that individual norms or preferences are more significant in determining women's employment patterns.

Drawing on theories of 'human capital', economists have argued that women's 'choice' to specialize in domestic work and men's 'choice' to specialize in market work are economically rational as far as the family unit is concerned (Mincer and Polachek, 1974). As women are likely to suffer employment breaks as a consequence of their caring responsibilities, it is not rational for them to invest their 'human capital' in the paid workplace, and this reasoning will be reflected in their employment experiences. Gary Becker (1991) also assumes that the family unit will, as a rational 'actor', behave so as to maximize its utility. Within the family, however, Becker assumes that motives of altruism prevail, in some contrast to the competitive market context within which it is embedded. Thus, family members (even if they are 'rotten kids') will act so as to maximize the utility function of the senior altruist (or benevolent patriarch). Neo-classical family economics therefore argues that decisions as to the allocation of household and market work between women and men (and thus women's employment patterns) are guided by rational maximization principles that benefit the family as a whole.

Feminist economists have developed an extensive critique of neo-classical family economics. The *de facto* benevolence of the patriarch has been questioned, and much emphasis has been placed on the constraints on choices regarding the type and amount of work performed within the family, which may include 'asymmetric property rights, other institutional rules, social norms, or individual bargaining power' (Braunstein and Folbre, 2001: 29). In short, the feminist critique emphasizes the structural and normative constraints on supposedly rational decision-making.

Many social theorists have argued that contemporary societies are characterized by an increase in levels of individuation and choice (Beck, 1992; Giddens, 1991). Catherine Hakim (2000) has argued that contemporary changes in women's employment reflect this relatively recent capacity of women to exercise their choices. Women's employment patterns, she argues, are different from those of men because of the choices made by different types (or 'preference groupings') of women. She identifies three categories of women: home/family centred, work-centred, and adaptives/drifters. Home-centred women give priority to their families; work-centred women give priority to their employment careers; and adaptive women shift their priorities between family and career over their life cycles.

For Hakim, a major explanation for these male/female differences is biological, namely, variation in testosterone levels (2000: 258ff.). Hakim is emphatic that contemporary women's employment patterns are a consequence of their individual choices rather than any constraints arising from the nature of employment or other structural factors (such as, for example, the availability of non-family care resources): 'self-classification as a primary earner or as a secondary earner is determined by chosen identities rather than imposed by external circumstance or particular jobs' (2000: 275).[1] Hakim further argues that 'preferences' should be the major guide to policy-making: 'policy-making becomes more complex...as policy-makers need to make allowance for at least three distinct household work strategies' (2000: 277). Her arguments have, not surprisingly, found favour in conservative political circles.[2]

An emphasis on the reflexive individual and a focus on individual identities and choice, rather than collective actions and outcomes, have many resonances with economic neo-liberalism, and the promotion of individual rights meshes well with the arguments of those who have criticized the way in which collective provision has disempowered individuals. Thus, as John O'Neill has argued, with the contemporary sociological emphasis on individualization and identity, there has been something of a 'convergence of a postmodern leftism with neo-liberal defences of the market' (1999: 85; also see Frank, 2000). However, as Martha Nussbaum (2000) has argued, preferences are not necessarily the best guide to policy-making, not least because preferences do not exist in thin air, but are shaped by (among other things) habit, low expectations, and unjust background conditions. It is, therefore, vital to explore the context, which will include structural constraints as well as normative assumptions, within which choices are made and preferences developed.

There are some parallels to be drawn between Hakim's approach and that of Simon Duncan and his colleagues, who have emphasized the significance of 'moral rationalities' in shaping mothers' employment decisions (Barlow, Duncan, and James, 2002; Duncan and Edwards, 1999; Duncan, Edwards, Reynolds, and Alldred, 2003). Duncan et al.'s research in Britain identified three broad categories of 'gendered moral rationalities' among the groups they studied: primarily mother, primarily worker, and mother/worker integral. Afro-Caribbean mothers were more likely to be in full-time employment and tended to take a mother/worker integral perspective. That is, they saw their employment as providing a positive role model for their children and saw paid work as being part of 'good' mothering. In contrast, White mothers tended to be ranged along a primarily mother–primarily worker continuum, clustering mainly within the primarily mother category. Duncan and his colleagues argue that because current British government policies are based on the premise of an 'adult worker' model (the assumption that all adults, including mothers, will benefit from paid work), these policies commit a 'rationality mistake'. Here, Duncan and his colleagues are critical of neo-classical assumptions as to the universality of rational, individually maximizing behaviour. Women who define themselves as primarily mothers (whom Hakim might describe as home-and-family centred) will not take up employment even if it is in their economic interest to do so (Barlow et al., 2002).

Ideas about 'the right thing to do', as well as 'preferences' relating to particular combinations of employment and caring, *will* shape individual employment and family decision-making. However, it is difficult to establish conclusively the presence of concrete and stable orientations to work among women, or men, for that matter (Crompton and Harris, 1998a). Qualitative research has demonstrated that women's attitudes (and related behaviour) to employment and family responsibilities vary according to both context and stage in the family life cycle (Crompton and Harris, 1998a; Procter and Padfield, 1998). In practice, as Judith Glover (2002) has argued, most women (and an increasing number of men) seek to achieve some kind of balance between paid work and caring work. How this balance is achieved will depend in part on individual preferences, but in addition, as Glover argues, on a range of other factors, including particular occupational and geographical constraints, the social policy context, as well as broader cultural and normative prescriptions as to 'acceptable' family and employment behaviours (Crompton and Harris, 1998b; Pfau-Effinger, 1999). As Susan McRae argues, both normative *and* structural constraints shape women's decisions (2003: 329). Structural constraints include immediate practicalities such as the availability (and acceptability) of childcare, the demands of a particular job, and so on. However, as McRae has suggested, underlying *class* processes also significantly shape the attitudes and employment behaviour of women. It is an established fact that less well-educated women in the lower levels of the occupational structure are more likely to withdraw from or limit their employment when their children are young, if they can afford to do so (Rake, Davies, Joshi, and Alami, 2000).

The question as to whether attitudes determine behaviour, or vice versa, is one of those chicken-and-egg social science topics that is incapable of unambiguous resolution. Arguments as to the significance of individual choices in determining women's employment patterns, therefore, can emphasize the explanatory value of either rational maximizing behaviour or the overwhelming power of individual norms and values. Both approaches rest on essentialist notions of gender. In the case of neo-classical economics, gender roles are naturalized. Hakim's theory of 'preferences' rests on the 'small but enduring' biological differences between men and women. In contrast, critics of individualistic approaches tend to assert that gender is socially constructed and that the manner of this construction serves to maintain the structural barriers that persist in relation to women's employment opportunities.

GENDER AND EMPLOYMENT

Much of the emphasis in second-wave feminist research and writing focused on the barriers faced by women in the employment spheres dominated by men (Cockburn, 1991; O'Connor, Orloff, and Shaver, 1999: 25; Walby, 1986). Before the advent of legislation against gender discrimination, these barriers were explicit and overt. Women were barred from particular occupations (such as printing) and excluded from access to training and qualifications (such as medicine), as well as subject to direct exclusionary practices in organizations. The women who, increasingly, returned to paid employment in the 1960s and 1970s usually had 'broken' employment careers and only a low level of employment-related credentials and training. Nevertheless, many expressed considerable frustration at the very real and considerable barriers they faced (Crompton and Jones, 1984).

In most Western work organizations, explicitly gendered barriers against women's progress had been formally removed by the 1970s and 1980s, although in some male-dominated occupations, such as engineering, informal barriers are still very much an issue (Bagilhole, Dainty, and Neale, 2000). Throughout the 1980s and 1990s, equal opportunities (EO) policies have been positively encouraged by governments in Britain and the United States (as, indeed, they still are), and widely introduced across the organizational spectrum. As Harriet Bradley has demonstrated for the British case, EO policies have been, to a considerable extent, effective and have had an impact on men and women alike (1999: chs 5, 6).

More women have moved into management and the professions, but women are still under-represented at the topmost levels of the occupational structure. The persisting differences in women's and men's organizational experiences can be explained and understood by a number of overlapping arguments: first, those that focus on the characteristics of women as individuals; second, those that emphasize the characteristics of the organizations themselves and the qualities they require; and third, those relating to the wider context of employment and care.

Up to the 1970s and beyond, traditional bureaucratic careers were overwhelmingly based on men's patterns of work. Women who did have careers (in the sense of upwardly mobile, long-term employment with a single organization) were unlikely to have children. (In career jobs such as banking, women were expected to leave employment during their first pregnancy.) Max Weber's original formulation of the bureaucratic ideal-type characterizes office-holding as a vocation, demanding the 'entire capacity for work for a long period of time' (1958: 198–199). Under the circumstances of the male-breadwinner model, married men would best fulfil these conditions. Wives of managers were widely expected to supply the kinds of domestic supports (entertaining, well-behaved children, clean shirts, etc.) that would help a man in his organizational career. They were, indeed, 'career wives' (Finch, 1983).

One of the more positive aspects of the demise of the bureaucratic career through organizational delayering and the development of the 'portfolio career' might be to reduce women's disadvantage, as modern careers no longer require long-term, unbroken dedication to a single organization. The next section reviews some of the substantial literature that has focused on women's relative failure to progress within organizational contexts.

GENDER AND ORGANIZATIONS

In common with other frameworks that prevailed in social science in the 1960s and into the 1970s, early discussion of women in bureaucratic organizations treated them as if they were gender-neutral. Rosabeth Moss Kanter (1977) argued that bureaucratic organizations were structures of power from which women were excluded. The key, therefore, was to enable women to acquire powerful positions. Male homosociability (the preference of men for working with people like themselves) would have to be overcome, but getting women into positions of power and authority meant equipping them for such jobs via training in assertiveness, getting the right credentials, and ensuring that recruitment to promoted positions was a scrupulously fair process. The focus was on women as individuals, their characteristics, and how the 'right' characteristics might be gained in order that they might progress though the organizational hierarchy. Indeed, the upsurge of qualification levels among women from the 1970s onwards led to suggestions that once women had acquired levels of 'human capital' (qualifications and work experience) equivalent to that of men, they might use the 'qualifications lever' in order to gain higher-level positions (Crompton and Sanderson, 1990).

Others argued that far from being gender-neutral, organizations were gendered, claiming, in particular, that bureaucratic hierarchies are inherently 'masculine', embodying qualities of dominance, hierarchy, and abstract rationality (Ferguson, 1984). Thus 'feminine' qualities were not appropriate or effective in relation to career success in 'masculine' organizational contexts. This essentialist approach counterposed 'feminine' modes of working, based on cooperation and friendship, to 'masculine' bureaucratic hierarchies (Marshall, 1984).

It is not particularly appropriate to regard organizations per se as gender-neutral, masculine, or feminine. Nevertheless, it is important to recognize that organizations are socially situated practices in which gender is constructed and that they have a gendered substructure, defined by Joan Acker as 'the spatial and temporal arrangements of work…the rules prescribing workplace behaviour, and…the relations linking work places to living places. These practices and relations…are supported by assumptions that work is separate from the rest of life and that it has the first claim on the worker' (1990: 142; see also Halford, Savage, and Witz, 1997: 16). Gender is, so to speak, played out in organizations, particularly in respect to overtly sexual aspects of masculinities and femininities:

> Bureaucratic organizations validate and permit forms of male embodiment and invalidate or render impermissible forms of female embodiment…For women, the discursive construct of the reproductive body assumes particular importance in *disqualifying* them from authority positions…The sexualised body represents another discursive construction of female embodiment whereby women have been included, *qualifying* them for certain front-stage and subordinate organizational functions. (Gottfried, 2003: 260–261, emphasis in original)

These cultural assumptions about women have been cited as evidence for the glass ceiling that exists between women and the topmost organizational positions (Davidson and Cooper, 1992). The removal of overt structural barriers against women within organizations, together with improvements in the 'human capital' of individual women, have failed to secure success for women in the highest levels of many areas of employment. The 'cultural turn' in the study of work and organizations was also associated with an increasing focus on the construction of gender within them.[3] For example, Susan Halford et al. (1997: 79) document the shift in retail banking from the old-style, paternalist male manager towards a culture of 'competitive masculinity' in which decisive action and risk-taking predominate.

More generally, many contemporary social theorists have argued that in late capitalist or post-modern societies gender (and sexuality) is in the process of being reconfigured. In 'reflexive modernity', individuals, it is argued, 'make themselves' (Beck, Giddens, and Lash, 1994). As Anthony Giddens has put it: 'We are, not what we are, but what we make of ourselves…what the individual becomes is dependent on the reconstructive endeavours in which he or she engages' (1991: 75). Thus, neither fixed family obligations nor rigid labour market and/or organizational practices serve to determine individual positioning; rather, it is the construction of the self that is of prime importance. For example, Linda McDowell's (1997) study of City (of London) finance workers emphasized how appearance was central to workplace performance for men and women, and how both men and women drew upon particular masculinities and femininities in their work. Increasingly, studies of the workplace now focus on 'a new sovereignty of appearance, image, and style at work, where the performance of stylised presentations of self has emerged as a key resource in certain sectors of the economy, particularly in new service occupations' (Adkins, 2002b: 61).

If the (self-)construction of identity has indeed become of more importance than traditional gender stereotypes in the determination of organizational positioning, then conventional cultural assumptions relating to gender might be becoming less significant as far as women's employment experiences are concerned. However, Heidi Gottfried (2003), for example, has recently demonstrated the overwhelming significance of gendered cultural assumptions in the recruitment and placing of temporary workers in Japan. Patricia Yancey Martin (2003) has argued that 'gendering practices' in the workplace can justify behaviours that systematically discriminate against women, citing, for example, a businessman who had a policy of never dining solo with women colleagues while on business trips. Men who enter occupations where most of the workers are women can find themselves on a 'glass escalator', as organizational superiors hasten to move them into more gender-appropriate supervisory or administrative positions (Williams, 1992).

From a rather different perspective, Lisa Adkins has argued that capacities for 'reflexivity' (or self-construction) are themselves unevenly distributed, and, indeed, that some aspects of identity (for example, women and emotional labour) may be 'naturalized' and thus not capable of being used as employment claims, and that some people – for example, lesbians and gays – may choose to dis-identify in a workplace context (2002b: 125). Therefore, she argues:

> The politics of identity are...not only at the heart of workplace politics but also of the labour process and the organization of production...the significance of issues of identity at work means that a politics of deconstruction (for example, of the hetero/homo binary) is now best suited to the task of addressing workplace struggles. (Adkins, 2002a: 36)

However, it may be argued that workplace injustices in relation to gender are not 'merely sexual' and indeed cannot be addressed at the level of the workplace alone.

My purpose here is not to reject culturalist theorizing. However, its contribution to our understanding of the persisting dominance of men in higher-level positions is somewhat inadequate. Indeed, one criticism of Adkins's arguments is that the assumptions made as to the actual extent of occupational desegregation and the blurring of gender boundaries in the world of work are somewhat sweeping: 'there is increasing evidence of processes of desegregation of occupations in terms of gender, a loosening of the boundaries between "men's work" and "women's work"' (2002b: 60). Notwithstanding the insights that may be gained from the study of gender and sexual identities in organizational cultures and structures, the major explanation for the continuing under-representation of women in higher-level positions may lie in the wider context of employment and care, or the gender division of labour as a whole. Family responsibilities, particularly for childcare, mean that most women do not actively pursue an upwardly mobile occupational career, even when relatively well qualified.

THE IDEOLOGY OF DOMESTICITY

The ideology of domesticity, in particular that of 'moral motherhood' – self-sacrificing, passionless, and devoted to the maintenance of a 'haven in a heartless world' – was crucial to the process of creating a claim for women's moral superiority to men. In turn, the nineteenth century middle-class ideology of separate spheres for men and women built on this moral superiority. As described by Leonore Davidoff and Catherine Hall:

> Their (*the middle classes*') rejection of landed wealth as the source of honour and insistence on the primacy of the inner spirit brought with it a preoccupation with the domestic as a necessary basis for a good Christian life. Evangelical categorizations of the proper spheres of men and women provided the basis for many subsequent formulations and shaped the common sense of the nineteenth century social world. Men were to be active in the world as citizens and entrepreneurs, women were to be dependent, as wives and mothers. (1987: 450)

In the late twentieth century, Joan Williams argues that 'domesticity did not die, it mutated' (2000: 3). Although women (particularly mothers) have increasingly taken up continuous employment, they still retain the primary responsibility for childcare and the organization of domestic life. Employers continue to require 'ideal workers', that is full-time employees who can be presumed to have an immunity from family work (Williams, 2000: 20). Domesticity's capacity for mutation was enhanced by the transformations that were taking place in the world of paid employment at the same time as, with the advent of second-wave feminism, women claimed equality of access to and entry into paid work. The growth of flexible employment has seen an expansion of marginalized jobs that do not necessarily require 'ideal workers'; at the same time, the demands made of 'ideal workers' have increased.

De-industrialization and a shift to service-sector jobs have produced increasing flexibility in employment. In the literature, a distinction is drawn between numerical and pay flexibility, which allows the number of workers or amount of labour time to be varied, and functional flexibility, or multi-tasking. Women's employment has been an integral part of discussions relating to employment flexibility from the 1980s. This is not surprising, given that women have always worked flexibly – in both the numerical and functional senses of the term. Manuel Castells has described new social relationships of production as translating into 'a good fit between the "flexible woman" [forced to flexibility to cope with her multiple roles] and the network enterprise' (2000: 20). The growth of flexible capitalism has been regarded by some as making a contribution to the resolution of the tensions between employment and family work. Thus, the more negative aspects of neo-liberal numerical flexibility are being glossed as a positive contribution to the reconciliation of employment and family life, with employment and families changing in tandem. However, as many authors have noted, flexible employment, which is concentrated among women, is not usually associated with individual success in the labour market, and flexible workers often tend to be in lower-level positions (Perrons, 1999; Purcell, Hogarth, and Simm, 1999).

The growth of service employment supposedly has advantages for women. Stereotypically feminine attributes, such as empathy and the capacity to form and nurture relationships, are key attributes for workers in the service economy. In the flexible, individualized working environments of 'reflexive modernity', it is argued, gender differences will increasingly be eroded. John Macinnes (1998), for example, has claimed that we have reached the 'end of masculinity', and Castells emphasizes the attractiveness of feminine relational skills for employers (1997: 69). Castells goes on to describe a 'crisis of patriarchalism' that 'manifests itself in the increasing diversity of partnership arrangements among people to share life and raise children' (1997: 221).

However, other authors have been more pessimistic about the consequences of increasing employment flexibility and the growth of the 'network society', as described by authors such as Castells. In an influential text, Richard Sennett (1998) argues that the development of global, flexible capitalism has broken social bonds and undermined trust between individuals. Flexible working lives and the end of long-term career predictability have undermined the contribution of employment to the formation of individual identities. In the circumstances of modern organizations, he argues, relationships have been fragmented, as human beings no longer have deep reasons to care about one another. Thus the development of flexible capitalism has resulted in the 'corrosion of character...particularly those qualities of character which bind human beings to one another and furnishes each with a sense of sustainable self' (p. 27).

Sennett's argument, however, ignores gender differences in the impact of these kinds of changes. Most women do not experience career development in the same way, or have the same priorities, as most men, and many express deep conflict over their family responsibilities (Wacjman and Martin, 2002: 995). The playing field between men and women competing as individuals in employment may have been levelled somewhat, but women as mothers and carers face considerable difficulties balancing work and family. As Jane Lewis has argued, 'too often women experience little *genuine* choice to care' (2002: 348). As individuals, women may be seen as equal to men in the sphere of employment, but the normative constructs of domesticity still allocate the major responsibility for care to women: 'our constructs of gendered behaviour emerged from societies in which men had far more cultural and economic power than women. The result can be described as "socially imposed altruism"' (Badgett and Folbre, 1999: 316). Nevertheless, attitudes to women's employment and gender roles *are* changing, and in the next section, I will briefly examine some recent evidence for these changes.

CHANGES IN MOTHER'S EMPLOYMENT AND GENDER ROLE ATTITUDES

In Britain, women's labour force participation rates have been rising since the 1950s and stood at 66 per cent in 1984. The rate then increased markedly during the 1980s, reaching 72 per cent by 2001, and the participation rates of mothers with young children changed rapidly in the last decade of the twentieth century. In 1990, the economic activity rate among mothers with a child under 5 was 48 per cent, but by 2001 had risen to 57 per cent. In contrast, men's labour force participation rates have been falling, from 88 per cent in the 1980s to 84 per cent by 2001 (Dench et al., 2002). The employment of mothers has been rising in all countries in the Organization for Economic Cooperation and Development, although there is still considerable inter-country variation. For example, in 1999, the employment rate of all mothers with a child under 6 was 61.5 per cent in the United States and 55.8 per cent in Britain, but 41.8 per cent in Spain and 45 per cent in Australia. Nevertheless, while the employment rate of mothers remains much lower than that of fathers, the gap has been closing quite rapidly, by around one percentage point per year in the 1990s (OECD, 2001: 133).

Changes in women's employment have been accompanied by changes in once-stereotypical attitudes.[4] There has been a steady decline, among both men and women, in the proportion of respondents who support the once-conventional view that 'a man's job is to earn money, a woman's is to look after the home and family'. Whereas around a third of men took this view in 1989, only a fifth did in 2002. The equivalent change among women has been from a quarter to one in seven. (See Table 14.1.)

Table 14.1 'A man's job is to earn money; a woman's job is to look after the home and family', 1989–2002

Percentage who agree	1989		1994		2002	
Men	32		26		20	
Women	26		21		15	
All	28	(N = 1,307)	24	(N = 984)	17	(N = 1,960)

Source: British Social Attitudes (BSA) surveys

Table 14.2 'Women should stay at home when there is a child under school age', 1989–2002

Percentage who think women should stay at home	1989		1994		2002	
Men	67		60		51	
Women	61		51		46	
All	64	(N = 1,307)	55	(N = 984)	48	(N = 1,960)

Source: British Social Attitudes (BSA) surveys

There has been a corresponding change in attitudes about women's employment, particularly that of mothers. In 1989, over two-thirds of those interviewed thought that a woman should 'stay at home' when she had a child under school age; by 2002, the proportion of people holding this view had declined to under a half. (See Table 14.2.)

Rates of attitudinal change have followed quite closely on actual changes in women's employment behaviour.[5] Women's employment rose most rapidly during the 1980s, and levelled off somewhat during the 1990s, although employment rates among mothers of young children continued to rise. These changes in people's views appear to be permanent. A comparison over the three surveys of people born in the same year suggests that in the older age cohorts, men and women are uniformly becoming more liberal in their attitudes. Changes in behaviour, as well as attitudes, are reflected in the three surveys. In 1989, 62 per cent of the mothers interviewed reported that they had stayed at home with a child under school age, but by 1994, 52 per cent had, and by 2002, the percentage of mothers reporting 'staying at home' had declined even further, to 48 per cent.

Changes in mothers' employment behaviour have been recent and rapid, as the majority of mothers of children born in the 1960s and 1970s simply did not 'go out to work' when their children were young. However, despite this recent and rapid increase in long-term employment among women, and corresponding changes in attitudes about gender roles and mother's employment, the broad contours of occupational segregation still persist, so that women are not the equals of men in the employment sphere. The major factor that explains this persistence seems to be women's continuing responsibility for domestic work and caregiving. Thus, women still predominate as part-time employees; in Britain, 43 per cent of women were employed part-time in 2002 (Duffield, 2002). The mutation of domesticity has brought women into paid employment, but much of this work is marginal in its nature, and other changes in the world of work are serving to make employment even more demanding for 'ideal', full-time workers.

Intensification of work, individualization of careers

It is somewhat paradoxical that as more women and mothers are in long-term employment, the nature of much of this employment would seem to be becoming increasingly less congenial for people who have caring responsibilities outside of the workplace. A wide range of empirical evidence has demonstrated that levels of work intensity have increased (Burchell, Ladipo, and Wilkinson, 2002; Gallie, 2002). In response to the pressures of work intensification, individuals may work part-time, and/or decline to put in the extra hours and effort that is (often implicitly) required by 'high-performance' policies. These individual strategies will have negative consequences for career development, and in the case of a failure to meet targets set by management, possible consequences for pay and job security. In the previous section of this chapter, I was critical of the extent to which the *de facto* priority that many women assign to caring and family responsibilities may be represented as a genuine 'choice'. Current developments in the workplace would seem to be making this 'choice' more difficult if the individual wishes to pursue a career. The erosion of the 'traditional' bureaucratic career may have opened up opportunities for women, but the pressures of individualized career development in contemporary organizations makes career progress for those with caring responsibilities extremely problematic.

As Rosemary Crompton and Nicky Le Feuvre (1996) have argued, women who seek to develop organizational careers are constrained to behave as 'surrogate men', by working full-time and giving priority to their employment over their families, working longer hours when required to do so (see also Crompton, 1999; Crompton and Birkelund, 2000). Many women who are successful in career terms 'choose' to limit their families, or to forgo childbearing altogether. Judy Wacjman's study of senior managers demonstrated that two-thirds of the women managers did not have children living with them, in contrast to the two-thirds of men who did (1998: 139). Halford et al.'s (1997) research found that although women are no longer the focus of direct exclusionary practices within the workplace, in career terms, a new division is opening up within organizations between 'encumbered' and 'unencumbered' workers – that is, those with and without caring responsibilities. As Wacjman argues, 'being a successful manager currently requires an overriding commitment to work. The job consumes most waking hours and dominates life in every respect. While this is true for both women and men, it has very different implications for their personal lives and domestic arrangements' (1998: 156).

WORK–LIFE 'BALANCE'?

The rise in mothers' employment, together with growing pressures within the workplace itself, have led to an increasing focus on the topic of work–life 'balance' by both academic researchers and policy-makers (DTI, 2000; 2003; Hochschild, 1997; Lewis and Lewis, 1996; Moen, 2003).[6] The topic is particularly salient in Britain and the United States because both countries have been characterized by neo-liberal labour market policies that have done much to increase work intensity and thus the difficulties of combining employment and family life. Both Britain and the United States are also characterized by long hours of work. Full-time employees in Britain have the longest working hours in Europe, and the length of the working week in the United States has increased (Schor, 1991).

In Britain, the government is promoting work–life balance through the encouragement of flexible and part-time employment (DTI, 2000: ch. 6). Many women in Britain do work part-time, and Britain has the second highest (after the Netherlands) level of part-time work in Europe. However, as we have seen, the concentration of part-time work among women will contribute to continuing gender inequality, both in respect of incomes as well as in opportunities for upward career mobility.

Organizational culture has also been identified as making a negative contribution to work–life balance (Hojgaard, 1997; Lewis, 1997). Long hours are seen as a measure of organizational commitment, and organizations tend to place the major value on employees who do not allow family commitments to intrude into their working lives. British government policy has encouraged employers to introduce 'family-friendly' policies in order to address work–life balance issues, but has fought shy of any element of compulsion or interference in management's 'right to manage'.[7] Even when 'family-friendly' policies are made available to employees, many do not feel able to use them because of the pressures associated with their work (Crompton, Dennett, and Wigfield, 2003b; Eaton, 2003). An analysis of two large British employment surveys (1992 and 2000) found that appraisal systems, group working practices, and individual incentives (all aspects of 'high-commitment' management practices) increased negative job-to-home spillover (White, Hill, McGovern, Mills, and Smeaton, 2003). They suggest that 'there may...be...practices that employers regard as important for their own success which may exacerbate the work–life balance problem irrespective of the positive contribution of family friendly policies' (2003: 176).

Both the pressures of the market, therefore, as well as at the workplace, make work–life 'balance' problematic. As Phyllis Moen has argued:

> contemporary dual-earner couples are living in a historical time period when they are the norm...over half the workforce is currently married to (or partnered with) another worker...Still, jobs, career paths, community services and family life remain structured in ways that assume that workers have someone else to take care of households, personal affairs, children, and aged or infirm relatives. (2003: 13)

CONCLUSION

The ideology of domesticity has persisted despite extensive changes in gender role attitudes among both men and women, as well as the widespread entry of middle-class mothers of young children into paid employment. The persistence of a modified version of the gendered domestic ideal has in part been facilitated by wider changes in the structure of paid work during the twentieth century that have generated flexible, part-time (and often marginal) jobs that women can combine with their caring responsibilities. At the same time, the demands of 'ideal worker' (full-time) jobs have increased. As a consequence, even well-qualified women in non-marginal employment will often 'choose' to give priority to their caring responsibilities and will not rise as swiftly as men (or not at all) through organizational hierarchies. These difficulties are compounded by the persistence of gendered practices and assumptions about women in contemporary organizations.

Not surprisingly, therefore, the topic of work–life 'balance' has risen to the forefront of the policy agenda, particularly in those countries, such as Britain and the United States, in which neo-liberal policies have resulted in a relative lack of employment and labour market regulation and thus an increasing intensification of work demands. Is it possible to identify any alternatives to this admittedly rather gloomy scenario?

Abstractly, market capitalism undermines the family form through its indifference to the private lives of the labour power it purchases (Seccombe, 1993: 19). As Ulrich Beck has remarked, 'The market subject is ultimately the single individual, "unhindered" by a relationship, marriage, or family' (1992: 116). The 'male-breadwinner' model of the articulation of employment and the family solved the problem of social reproduction within capitalism as well as generating a supply of (male) 'ideal workers' (Folbre, 1994). The cost of this solution was the continuing unequal and subordinate position of women. This situation has changed, from the twentieth century onwards, with the advent and acceptance of women's claims to economic and social equality. These have been powerful (and painful) developments, and their impact has by no means been fully worked through. However, the tensions brought about by these changes are unlikely to be resolved unless (a) men become more like women, and begin to combine both caring and market work over their productive lives (Fraser, 1994), and (b) states and governments confront the necessity of providing greater family supports and regulating 'family-unfriendly' employment. These two strands of change are inextricably inter-related, as men (and women) cannot be expected to participate to any great extent in caring work if they are also expected to work for pay over forty-five hours a week.

The continuing pre-eminence of neo-liberal economic and labour market policies in nations such as Britain and the United States means that such government-sponsored changes are not very likely to happen in these countries. Nevertheless, there are examples of contemporary nation states that have developed policies that have been much more supportive of the consequences of changes in gender relations and women's employment. The most high-profile examples would be the Nordic welfare states, which offer extensive, state-sponsored supports to carers (and those needing care), as well as promoting active policies of gender equality. Women in these countries have achieved a greater level of equality with men, and there is also evidence that employment itself, and the combination of employment with family life, is less stressful (Crompton and Lyonette, 2004; Gallie, 2003). Although it could not be claimed that an optimum 'balance' of gender equality and work–life articulation has been completely achieved in the Scandinavian countries, nevertheless, these examples do serve to demonstrate that policies can, indeed, make a difference (Esping-Andersen, Gallie, Hemerijck, and Myles, 2002).

NOTES

1 Notwithstanding this direct quotation, it should be pointed out that Hakim's arguments tend to be inconsistent and at other points she appears to acknowledge the significance of structural factors.

2 For example, her ideas were enthusiastically adopted in 2002–2003 by the Australian Conservative Government. See the *Sydney Morning Herald*, 7 February and 3 March 2003 (www.smh.com.au).

3 Developments within feminist theorizing also made cultural interpretations increasingly attractive and indeed, in some quarters, more acceptable than 'structural' explanations (see Barrett and Phillips, 1992).

4 Here we draw on evidence for 1989, 1994, and 2002 from the British Social Attitudes surveys (see Crompton, Brockmann, and Wiggins, 2003a).

5 This pattern of attitudinal change – extensive attitudinal change in the 1980s followed by a slowing down in the 1990s – was also found among women interviewed successively in 1980, 1993, and 1999 (see McRae, 2003: 326; see also Crompton et al., 2003a).

6 The EU has also made the topic a policy priority; see 'Employment and social policies: a framework for investing in quality', European Commission paper 2001, p. 313.

7 For example, in 2000, the DTI Work and Parents Task Force raised the possibility of introducing a *right* for both parents to work reduced hours when the mother's maternity leave ends (DTI, 2000: 34). In the original Green Paper, the possibility was also aired that an employee's request might be refused if it caused harm to the business, as well as giving exemptions for small businesses (p. 56). In fact, the legislation finally introduced in the Employment Act of 2001 gave parents a right to 'request' flexible working hours only, and the employers' duty was limited to giving the request 'serious consideration'.

REFERENCES

Acker, J. (1990) 'Hierarchies, jobs, bodies: a theory of gendered organizations', *Gender & Society*, 4(2): 139–158.

Adkins, L. (2002a) 'Sexuality and Economy: Historicisation vs Deconstruction', *Australian Feminist Studies*, 17(37): 31–41.

Adkins, L. (2002b) *Revisions: Gender and Sexuality in Late Modernity*. Open University, Buckingham.

Badgett, M. V. L. and N. Folbre (1999) 'Assigning care: gender norms and economic outcomes', *International Labour Review,* 138(3): 311–326.

Bagilhole, B. M. A., R. J. Dainty, and R. H. Neale (2000) 'Women in the construction industry in the UK: a cultural discord?', *Journal of Women and Minorities in Science and Engineering*, 6(1): 73–86.

Barlow, A., S. Duncan, and G. James (2002) 'New Labour, the rationality mistake and family policy in Britain', in Carling, A., S. Duncan and R. Edwards (eds), *Analysing Families*. Routledge, London.

Barrett, M. and A. Phillips (eds) (1992) 'Introduction', *Destabilising Theory* Polity, Cambridge.

Beck, U. (1992) *Risk Society*. Sage, London.

Beck, U., A. Giddens and S. Lash (1994) *Reflexive Modernisation*. Polity, Cambridge.

Becker, G. (1991) *A Treatise on the Family*. Harvard University Press, Cambridge, MA.

Bradley, H. (1999) *Gender and Power in the Workplace*. Macmillan, Houndmills Basingstoke.

Braunstein, E. and N. Folbre (2001) 'To honor and obey: efficiency, inequality and patriarchal property rights', *Feminist Economics*, 7(1): 25–44.

Budig, M. J. and P. England (2001) 'The wage penalty for motherhood', *American Sociological Review*, 66: 204–225.

Burchell, B., D. Ladipo and F. Wilkinson (eds) (2002) *Job Insecurity and Work Intensification*. Routledge, New York.

Castells, M. (1997) *The Power of Identity*. Blackwell, Oxford.

Castells, M. (2000) 'Materials for an exploratory theory of the network society', *British Journal of Sociology,* 51(1): 4–24.

Cockburn, C. (1991) *In the Way of Women*. Macmillan, Basingstoke.

Crompton, R. (ed.) (1999) *Restructuring Gender Relations and Employment*. Oxford University Press, Oxford.

Crompton, R. and G. Birkelund (2000) 'Employment and caring in British and Norwegian banking: an exploration through individual careers', *Work, Employment and Society*, 14(2): 331–352.

Crompton, R. and F. Harris (1998a) 'Explaining women's employment patterns: "Orientations to work", revisited', *British Journal of Sociology*, 49(1): 118–136.

Crompton, R. and F. Harris (1998b) 'Gender relations and employment: the impact of occupation', *Work, Employment and Society,* 12(2): 297–315.

Crompton, R. and G. Jones (1984) *White-Collar Proletariat*. Macmillan, London.

Crompton, R. and N. Le Feuvre (1996) 'Paid employment and the changing system of gender relations: a cross-national comparison' *Sociology* 30(3): 427–445.

Crompton, R. and C. Lyonette (2004) *Work-Life 'Balance' in Britain and Europe*. City University, London.

Crompton, R. and K. Sanderson (1990) *Gendered Jobs and Social Change*. Unwin Hyman, London.

Crompton, R., M. Brockmann and D. Wiggins (2003a) 'A woman's place...employment and family life for men and women', in Park, A., J. Curtice, K. Thomson, L. Jarvis, and C. Bromley (eds), *British Social Attitudes, the 20th Report*. Sage, London.

Crompton, R., J. Dennett, and A. Wigfield (2003b) *Organizations, Careers and Caring*. Policy Press, Bristol.

Davidoff, L. and C. Hall (1987) *Family Fortunes*. Hutchinson, London.

Davidson, M. J. and C. Cooper (1992) *Shattering the Glass Ceiling*. Chapman, London.

Dench, S. et al. (2002) 'Key indicators of women's position in Britain', Department of Trade and Industry, London.

Department for Trade and Industry (2000) *Work & Parents: Competitiveness and Choice*. Stationery Office, London.

Department for Trade and Industry/HM Treasury (2003) *Balancing Work and Family Life: Enhancing Choice and Support for Parents*. Stationery Office, London.

Duffield, M. (2002) 'Trends in female employment 2002', *Labour Market Trends,* November, 605–616.

Duncan, S. and R. Edwards (1999) *Lone Mothers, Paid Work, and Gendered Moral Rationalities*. Macmillan, Houndmills.

Duncan, S., R. Edwards, T. Reynolds, and P. Alldred (2003) 'Motherhood, paid work and partnering', *Work, Employment and Society*, 17(2): 309–330.

Eaton, S. C. (2003) 'If you can use them: flexibility policies, organizational commitment, and perceived performance', *Industrial Relations*, 42(2): 145–167.

Esping-Andersen, G., D. Gallie, A. Hemerijck, and J. Myles (2002) *Why we Need a New Welfare State.* Oxford University Press, Oxford.

Ferguson, K. E. (1984) *The Feminist Case Against Bureaucracy.* Temple University Press, Philadelphia.

Finch, J. (1983) *Married to the Job.* George Allen and Unwin, London.

Folbre, N. (1994) *Who Pays for the Kids? Gender and the Structures of Constraint.* Routledge, London.

Frank, T. (2000) *One market under God.* New York: Doubleday.

Fraser, N. (1994) 'After the family wage', *Political Theory* 22: 591–618.

Gallie, D. (2002) 'The quality of working life in welfare strategy', in G. Esping-Andersen, D. Gallie, A. Hemerijck, and J. Myles (eds), *Why we Need a New Welfare State.* Oxford University Press, Oxford.

Gallie, D. (2003) 'The quality of working life: is Scandinavia different?', *European Sociological Review*, 19(1): 61–79.

Giddens, A. (1991) *Modernity and Self Identity.* Polity, Cambridge.

Glover, J. (2002) 'The balance model: theorising women's employment behaviour', in Carling A., S. Duncan, and R. Edwards (eds), *Analysing Families.* Routledge, London.

Gottfried, H. (2003) 'Temp(t)ing bodies: shaping gender at work in Japan', *Sociology*, 37(2): 257–276.

Hakim, C. (2000) *Work-Lifestyle Choices in the 21st Century.* Oxford University Press, Oxford.

Halford, S., M. Savage and A. Witz (1997) *Gender, Careers and Organizations.* Macmillan, Basingstoke and London.

Hochschild, A. (1997) *The Time Bind.* Metropolitan Books, New York.

Hojgaard, L. (1997) 'Working fathers; caught in the web of the symbolic order of gender', *Acta Sociological*, 40: 245–261.

Kanter, R. Moss (1977) *Men and Women of the Corporation.* Basic Books, New York.

Lewis, J. (2002) 'Gender and welfare state change', *European Societies*, 4(4): 331–357.

Lewis, S. (1997) 'Family friendly employment policies: a route to changing organizational culture or playing about at the margins?', *Gender, Work and Organization*, 4(1): 1–23.

Lewis, S. and J. Lewis (1996) *The Work-Family Challenge.* Sage, London.

Macinnes, J. (1998) *The End of Masculinity.* Open University Press, Buckingham.

Marshall, J. (1984) *Women Managers.* Wiley, Chichester.

McDowell, L. (1997) *Capital Culture: Gender and Work in the City.* Blackwell, Oxford.

McRae, S. (2003) 'Constraints and choices in mothers' employment careers', *British Journal of Sociology*, 53(3): 317–338.

Mincer, J. and S. Polachek (1974) 'Family investments in human capital: earnings of women', *Journal of Political Economy*, 82: 76–108.

Moen, P. (ed.) (2003) *It's About Time: Couples and Careers.* ILR/Cornell University Press, Ithaca, NY and London.

Nussbaum, M. C. (2000) *Women and Human Development: The Capabilities Approach.* Cambridge University Press, New York.

O'Connor, J. S., A. S. Orloff, and S. Shaver (1999) *States, Markets, Families.* Cambridge University Press, Cambridge.

O'Neill, J. (1999) 'Economy, equality and recognition' in L. Ray and A. Sayer (eds), *Culture and Economy after the Cultural Turn.* Sage, London.

OECD (2001) 'Balancing work and family life: helping parents into paid employment', *Employment Outlook*, ch. 4.

Perrons, D. (1999) 'Flexible working patterns and equal opportunities in the European Union', *European Journal of Women's Studies*, 6: 391–418.

Pfau-Effinger, B. (1999) 'The modernization of family and motherhood in Western Europe', in R. Crompton (ed.), *Restructuring Gender Relations and Employment*. Oxford University Press, Oxford.

Procter, I. and M. Padfield (1998) *Young Adult Women, Work, and Family: Living a Contradiction*. London and Washington, DC, Mansell.

Purcell, K., T. Hogarth, and C. Simm (1999) *Whose Flexibility?* Joseph Rowntree Foundation, York.

Rake, K., H. Davies, H. Joshi, and R. Alami (2000) *Women's Incomes over the Lifetime*. Stationery Office, London.

Schor, J. (1991) *The Overworked American*. Basic Books, New York.

Seccombe, W. (1993) *Weathering the Storm*. Verso, London and New York.

Sennett, R. (1998) *The Corrosion of Character*. W. W. Norton, New York.

Wajcman, J. (1998) *Managing like a Man*. Polity, Cambridge.

Wajcman, J. and B. Martin (2002) 'Narratives of identity in modern management: the corrosion of gender difference?', *Sociology*, 36(4): 985–1002.

Walby, S. (1986) *Patriarchy at Work*. Polity, Cambridge.

Waldfogel, J. (1997) 'The effect of children on women's wages', *American Sociological Review*, 62: 209–217.

Weber, M. (1958) 'Bureaucracy' in Gerth H. and C. W. Mills (eds), *From Max Weber*. Routledge, London.

White, M., S. Hill, P. McGovern, C. Mills, and D. Smeaton (2003) '"High-Performance" management practices, working hours and work-life balance', *British Journal of Industrial Relations*, 41(2): 175–195.

Williams, C. L. (1992) 'The glass escalator: hidden advantages for men in the "female" professions', *Social Problems*, 39: 253–67.

Williams, J. C. (2000) *Unbending Gender: Why Family and Work Conflict and What to do About It*. Oxford University Press, New York.

Yancey Martin, P. (2003) '"Said and Done" versus "Saying and Doing": Gendering practices, practicing gender at work', *Gender & Society* 17: 342–366.

15

Gender, Care, and the Welfare State

Clare Ungerson

This chapter outlines the way in which feminist debates surrounding care have developed, particularly in the latter half of the twentieth century. Much of this debate has been concerned with unpaid 'informal' care which takes place within households, and where it was initially assumed women very much predominated as household carers. The chapter suggests that this assumption was in certain respects oversimplified, and that succeeding debates have taken into account that men care, too, that disabled people feel demeaned by the whole notion of 'care', and that a gendered perspective on care has also to take account of a perspective informed by 'race' and ethnicity. This last perspective has encouraged widening the concept of care to include work carried out within households by non-kin and eventually to a discussion of paid as well as unpaid care. The chapter then goes on to consider various social policies for care as they have recently developed in welfare states and uses a cross-national perspective to discuss the various ways in which different social policies impact on gender and care.

DEVELOPING AN UNDERSTANDING OF CARE IN THE TWENTIETH CENTURY

Western feminism, both first and second waves, has always problematized 'care'. The first wave, around the time of the First World War, was very largely concerned with women's right to vote. But once suffrage had been granted, suffragists, certainly in Britain, turned their attention to the meaning of 'equal citizenship' and, in particular, how mothers both as workers and as carers should be guaranteed equality with men. In debates that continued to the period immediately after the Second World War, they discussed whether or not the care activities encapsulated in the word 'motherhood' should be provided by the state in the form of nurseries for children, or whether mothers should be compensated for the care work they undertook through payment by the state of benefits related to the number of children they cared for. Those who argued for cash support, named by its supporters the 'endowment of motherhood', argued that the receipt of family allowances or child benefits would, at one and the same time, alleviate family poverty, provide mothers with an independent income, and undermine the concept of the 'family wage' which men trade unionists used to boost the wages of men workers (Rathbone, 1917; 1924). Those who argued for state services suggested that cash payments related to care treated women like 'domestic tabby cats' because they relied on the assumption that women were natural carers and homemakers (Nield Chew, 1982). Thus, from the start of the twentieth century onwards, care, particularly the care of children, divided feminists and raised the question as to how care should be provided while at the same time admitting women to full citizenship.

In the second wave of feminism in the late 1960s and 1970s, feminists again took up the question as to how 'care' should be analysed and compensated. At this point, the meaning of the word 'care' expanded to include, quite explicitly, the care of adults with dependencies arising out of what were then called 'handicaps', both mental and physical, and the frailties associated with old age. This expansion reflected two contextual changes which had occurred since the period of suffragist feminism: the ageing of the population and the rapid increase in life expectancy that had occurred across all social classes (but differentially) throughout the twentieth century, and the reversal of long-standing policies (at least two centuries old) that until the 1950s had removed individuals with special needs from their communities and families of origin and sent them to institutions well away from centres of population. The new policies of 'community care' had been fuelled by the discovery of drug therapy for mental illness in the 1950s and by the highly critical analysis, by Erving Goffman and others, of institutional life (Goffman, 1961; Townsend, 1962). Feminist scholarship, by expanding the term 'care' to include, as its objects, *both* adults with special needs *and* children, was simply reflecting a social reality driven by demographic and policy changes. But it was the strength of the analysis brought to bear by feminists on the meaning of 'care' that was to have highly significant impacts on both continuing feminist scholarship into the twenty-first century and, slowly but surely, on the development of policy for people with special needs, and *for their carers*, in the developed welfare states of Western and Northern Europe.

The analysis of 'care' in second-wave feminism, in its early stages and certainly within the British context, emphasized the care of people, both adults and children, with 'special needs' arising out of learning and physical disabilities, mental illness, and the frailty of old age and chronic illness (Finch and Groves, 1980). At the same time, other scholars pursued an analysis of policies for child care and the compatibility of responsibility for child care with participation in paid work (Moss and Fonda, 1980; Sharpe, 1984). This bifurcation of the analysis of care into, on the one hand, the care of people with disabilities and, on the other, the care of 'normal' children was common in the influential British literature. In more recent writing, the influence of feminist analysis, coming particularly from the Nordic countries, has taken the concept of care into the more aggregated phenomenon of care for children as well as care for people with other dependencies (Hobson, Lewis, and Siim, 2002). This chapter will take 'care' to mean, largely, the care of adults with special needs.

The initial impetus for the feminist critique was based on the analysis of the policy-makers' implicit assumption of the availability of women in the home to undertake the care of people with special needs. From the beginning, the analysis was informed by the strands that were then emerging in second-wave feminism. For example, liberal feminists argued from a perspective of equal rights between men and women that even where there were shifting policy recognitions of the role of carers in the provision of welfare, such as the British Invalid Care Allowance,[1] the fact that this social security benefit was not available for married women was a clear infringement of the principle of equal treatment of men and women (Groves and Finch, 1983). It was also a clear demonstration of the gendered construction of family life embedded in social policy. Radical feminists were principally concerned with relations between men and women within the household and the way in which both tasks and resources were allocated between them in the private domain. Care was yet another set of activities where women were organized and driven, within a patriarchal structure, to provide the primary resource for care, to the benefit of men and their kin (Delphy and Leonard, 1992). Socialist feminists, while not rejecting either of these perspectives on care, developed an analysis which emphasized the way in which the paid labour market impacted on the availability of women, rather than men, to care, and how, within specific modes of production and particular welfare states, different forms of care relations emerged, some with more 'woman-friendly' aspects than others (Ungerson, 1990).

Clearly absent from these early forms of second-wave feminist analysis was any strong recognition of difference and diversity, particularly along lines of 'race' and ethnicity, social class, and age. Similarly, there was, as yet, little development of the ideas, prominent now in the North American literature, of an essentialist argument that women learn, from an early age, a distinct moral framework of care (Gilligan, 1982).[2] Without an analysis that incorporated differences among women, once British feminists working at the forefront of this field had identified what they called informal care and the role of women in its provision, they concentrated on identifying why (all) women, rather than (all) men, were the providers of informal care. Much of their analysis was constructed within an argument about culture and what Janet Finch (1989) called 'normative guidelines' prevalent within society that formed the basis for the emergence of carers. Her work, as with many others, tended to take existing literature and small samples as the foundation for their case. Using gender and kin relations as the two main variables, many writers in the early 1980s found evidence of clear 'rules' or 'guidelines' as to who was an appropriate carer. For example, Hazel Qureshi and Alan Walker

(1989) suggested a 'hierarchy of obligation' which identified spouses as first port of call, and then daughters and daughters-in-law.

The strong feature of this early work on motivation was an assumption of a relatively homogeneous contextual culture and very little recognition of how hierarchies of obligation might vary across the many subnational and transnational communities then emerging in multiethnic Western societies with developed welfare states. Moreover, there was a marked absence in the early analysis of men as carers, despite, in the work of Qureshi and Walker, the top 'spot' in their hierarchy of obligation being taken by 'spouses' – of either gender. Scholarship rooted in feminism continued, quite understandably, to put women centre stage. In my small study of carers of elderly people undertaken in the mid 1980s, I had identified men who were carers, in this case, as one might expect, of their wives (Ungerson, 1987). I developed a gendered analysis of motivation to care, suggesting that men did it out of love for and a sense of reciprocity towards their particular wives, while women did it out of a mix of motivations. These were largely founded on a more general sense of duty based on a set of culturally determined norms of what 'women' are expected to do in relation to people with special needs within their kin networks.

The emergence of men as carers became a major issue in the literature, certainly in Britain, in the late 1980s and early 1990s. The shift in focus was largely due to the quantitative data set on informal care that was developed from questions included in 1985 in the government-sponsored national annual survey in Britain known as the General Household Survey. There have since been two repeats of these questions in 1990 and 1995, so that there is now very good longitudinal quantitative data available on informal care activities in Britain. The first report of this data, published in 1988, indicated, to the astonishment of those who had developed the feminist analysis of informal care, that proportionately almost as many men as women were carers – or at least claimed to provide services for someone 'with special needs' in the same household or beyond it (Green, 1988). What was more surprising was that there was even less difference in the proportions of men and women who provided care that consumed a lot of time (over twenty hours a week). Secondary analysis of the GHS data demonstrated that men tended to be concentrated among the carers aged 65 and over who were caring for their wives. Women, on the other hand, while also carers of their husbands, were more likely than men to be caring in their own middle age, and for people with special needs of an older or younger generation. When the particular tasks of care were analysed, it became clear that women were proportionately more than men involved with personal tasks that involved intimate bodily contact.

While these findings accorded with the earlier feminist scholarship that identified women as predominant among carers, it nevertheless became clear, and has been accepted in the literature on gender and informal care, that men care, too (Arber, 1989; Fisher, 1994). The early feminist literature had its origins in the workings of the family and the household. In recognizing the role of men in caregiving, feminist analysts have developed the literature on care such that gender and differences between men and women carers are examined within a framework of work, both paid and unpaid, as well as within a framework of the underpinnings of citizenship for those who care.

The second debate that overtook the early feminist analysis of informal care arose out of a strong critique from disabled feminists writing from a perspective of 'independence' or 'independent living'. They took strong objection to a number of aspects of the early feminist literature (Morris, 1991). First, they objected to the way in which care was construed as necessarily a burden, and complained that the person being cared for was treated as an object of care with no agency, let alone autonomy. The frequent use of the terms 'dependants', 'dependency', 'people with dependencies', 'the cared for', in the early literature was, to disabled people in general and disabled feminists in particular, offensive and inaccurate, describing a passive and dependent state that they were fighting to be free of. Second, they objected to the way in which some feminists, in particular Finch (1984) and Gillian Dalley (1988), had suggested that the solution to the problem of informal care and women's apparent predominance within it lay in the re-establishment of residential care – or, in the case of Dalley, collective and communitarian care – whereby dependent people would be cared for within communal rather than familial settings. Again, such a recommendation was antithetical to the way in which disabled people were developing their analysis of disability. They were campaigning to leave residential care and were promoting 'independent living' whereby they could live independently of *both* formal and informal care through the use of paid personal assistants employed directly by themselves (Morris, 1993). Finally, as some of these disabled feminists pointed out, they were, as mothers, carers themselves (Keith and Morris, 1996). In effect, what their critique pointed out was that just as feminist scholarship had claimed that women had been treated as objects with no autonomy, so feminist scholars who were analysts of care had proceeded to do exactly the same to disabled people.

This argument, along with the recognition that men were carers too, brought into focus the way in which early feminist scholarship had over-generalized the way gender impacted on the emergence and practice of care, and, similarly, had over-emphasized cultural homogeneity in determining motivations and obligations to care. Much of the early literature had failed to recognize difference and diversity across class, racial and ethnic groups, age, and disability. These additional variables have to be taken into account if we are to understand fully the way in which care is constructed, how it emerges within particular configurations of expressed need, and how the practice of informal care is structured within particular welfare states.

Two further strands of scholarship informed the development of a more nuanced analysis. First, the emergence of Black feminism, with its critique of the ethnocentricity of the early second wave, opened up the analysis of care to include care delivered within the private domain by non-kin. (Historically, such care had been the work of Black slaves in ante-bellum North America.) Once home care by non-kin was recognized, it was a small step to include paid care delivered to people who continued to live in their own homes (Graham, 1991).

The second strand of scholarship that fed into the developing analysis of care was the increasing amount of cross-national research and data available, particularly on an EU basis. This data allowed for and encouraged an increasingly sophisticated study of social policy across national boundaries. It steadily became more and more possible to demonstrate that the configuration of care, how it was practised, and who undertook these activities, was at least partially determined by the nature of the particular welfare state in which those activities took place. In this respect, the Scandinavian countries, particularly Sweden and Denmark, rapidly came to be seen as welfare states that were arguably 'woman-friendly' (Hernes, 1987). In these countries, and to a slightly lesser extent in Norway and Finland, the work of care for both elderly and disabled people and for 'normal' children was understood to be an important activity of the state, but where families, and both men and women within them, were recognized as vital deliverers of care. The assumption was that family members worked alongside the state but that the state was on the whole responsible for providing, through paid home and residential care, the practical tasks of care (caring for), thus freeing kin to provide the affective relations of care (caring about) that underpin high-quality care. Moreover, in all the Scandinavian countries, paid employment and a system of care leaves embedded within it was organized in such a way that both men and women could relatively easily combine full-time paid work with the unpaid work of child care and adult care. Using cross-national analysis, scholars were able to develop a more complete understanding of how different welfare states, at a macro level, can profoundly influence, at a micro level, the nature of the informal care relationship, and how and in what way it is gendered (Ungerson, 1990).

THE WELFARE STATE, GENDER, AND CARE

Cross-national research on gender and care has fed into the literature on gendered citizenship. The central difficulty has been that it is very difficult to see how, in welfare states that commonly stress paid work as the preferred route in the acquisition of social rights, care for both 'normal' children and people with special needs can be integrated into a support system where the activity of paid work is treated as morally, symbolically, and practically superior to the activities of unpaid care. Various policy configurations that deal with the conundrum of care and citizenship present themselves, and each has different gendered implications.

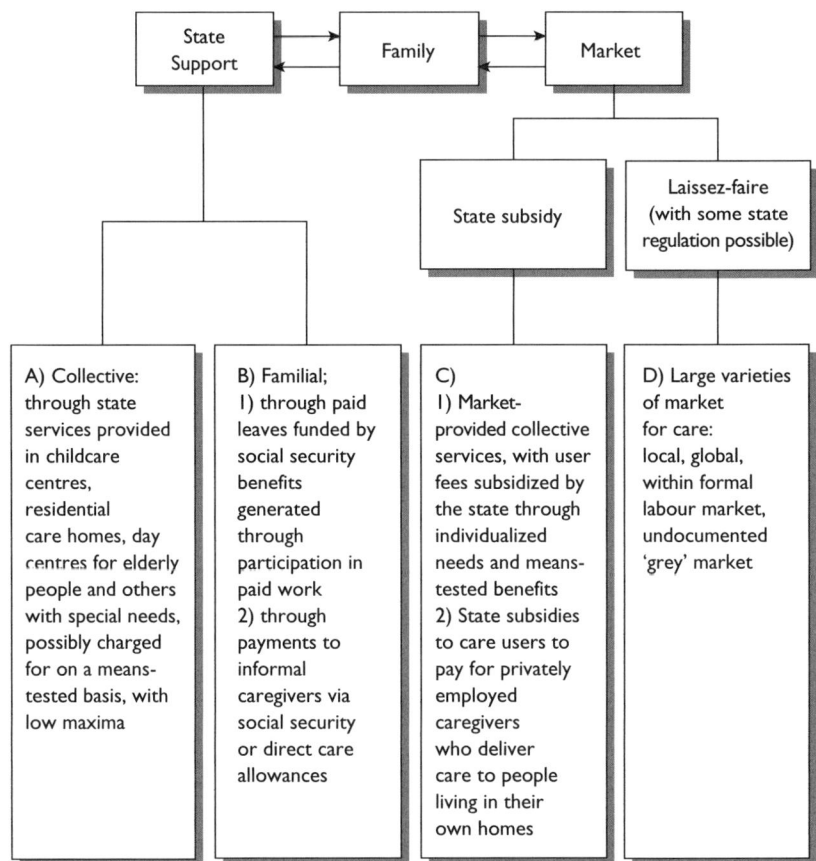

Figure 15.1 Different types of care policy and provision: state and market

In Figure 15.1, a number of the options for state support of care are laid out schematically. The basic distinction is between support from the state for families and households that find themselves faced with the tasks of care, and policy that basically leaves support for people with special needs (and often support for children) to the market and provision to private enterprise. Straddling both state and market in the sense that it has a relation with both is the family or families. First, families pay taxes and individuals within them pay social security contributions. Second, individuals within them are, notionally anyway, the final arbiters of government policy through the democratic process, as well as being consumers of state- and market-provided services. Third, in many welfare state systems, particularly those of Western continental Europe, families are the basis on which needs for services and the charges for them are assessed. Delivery of cash and services to support care is organized in various complex ways in many developed welfare states. Each of these arrangements has profoundly different implications for women, both as paid workers within formally organized care services and as unpaid carers within their families and kin networks. The next section of this chapter outlines some of the gendered impacts and the politics of these different arrangements for care.

The state can and does support care in a wide variety of ways: it can provide care services for both children and people with special needs directly, it can subsidize those who use market-based services, and it can regulate markets. In Figure 15.1, the traditional way in which welfare states support care is outlined in box A. Here, the state directly provides care services which are funded largely through taxation, although there may be some (usually) very low and generally means-tested charges. The front-line care delivery workers within these services are predominantly women state employees. As state employees, they may be privileged compared with care workers employed in for-profit care enterprises, but they are still likely to be low paid. The low pay follows from the assumption that the occupation of care is unskilled and can be competently delivered by any woman, especially if she has gained experience through motherhood. Nevertheless, this type of delivery of care is probably the best situation for paid women care workers to find themselves in. They can organize collectively into trade unions and occupational associations, they may have access to career progression into management, and, increasingly, as welfare states modernize and respond to consumerism, they are likely to have access to training and generally recognized qualifications.

As *consumers* of care in these types of settings, women may well find themselves in difficulties. If the services are of high quality – as they are in the Scandinavian countries – they will almost certainly be heavily rationed, possibly through targeting only to those in very great need, or through long waiting times. Such services may also become stigmatized since, even if they are of high quality, but available only, for example, to children with special needs or at risk of abuse, then mothers and other carers may prefer to find their own solutions. If the services are of low quality – as in the previous command and control economies of the one-time Soviet bloc – then users may prefer, at high personal costs, to stay away from them, and, if they are in need of care, use their kin networks as their support system.

These collective service-based solutions to the problem of care hark back to the old debates, in the early part of the twentieth century, as to whether care is best supported through services or through cash and which form of support underwrites women's citizenship the best. The collective-based service solution tends to be associated with the politics of the left; it is not surprising, therefore, in a period where collectivism is in decline relative to individualism to find that individualistic arrangements via both state and market are now in the ascendancy in most developed welfare states.

The first of these kinds of individualized arrangements is suggested in box B. These are systems which are funded by the state and which provide income maintenance for those who care for their own children or adults with special needs within their kin networks in their own homes. The system under B1 is based on generous rights to paid leave to care for a sick or very young child or someone elderly or terminally ill, rights generated by participation in paid work. Individual citizens in these welfare states are treated as *both* workers *and* carers: the expectation is that all citizens will engage in paid work, and it is through that primary activity that they accumulate generous social rights. Again, the Scandinavian countries are at the forefront of developing paid leave as the means whereby care of many different kinds can be best supported. The amount of payment is highly earnings related, and individuals have rights to return to their previous occupations at the end of the leave.

Some systems, notably in Norway and Sweden, have developed incentives within the leave system itself so that the gendered division of labour, whereby mothers rather than fathers take time off to care for newborns, begins to break down (see Leira, 1998, for an analysis of the Norwegian 'Daddy leave'). These individualized solutions to the problem of care have embedded within them an idea that the best and most preferred form of care is that provided by kin in a domestic and intimate setting. In the case of care of elderly people, the provision of care leaves for workers means that, in effect, support is being given for intragenerational care, rather than intergenerational care.

It is a small step from this form of state-supported care to systems which, rather than using social rights to income maintenance during periods of care leave, instead actually pay carers to stay at home to care for their children or adults with special needs. An example is the system of Finnish Home Care Allowances, which pay parents and other caregivers who stay at home to care for their children and adults with special needs at rates similar to those generated in the paid labour market for care work. These kinds of payment could be construed as constituting what early second-wave feminists called 'wages for housework'. While they clearly constitute a form of compensation and recognition of formerly unpaid care work, it is more difficult to build in gender-bending incentives, since the levels of the allowances tend to be relatively low and therefore unattractive to high earners.

The home care allowances may compensate and recognize care, but they tend to embed a highly gendered division of labour. In 2004, the British Conservative Party discussed the Finnish Home Care Allowance as a possible basis for the development of an allowance (£150 a week) which they considered would be enough to encourage British mothers of pre-school children to stay at home to care for their children. They have since abandoned these ideas in favour of benefits which encourage mothers to enter paid work as well as care but would allow them to pay their children's grandparents (for 'grandparent' read 'grandmother') with childcare benefits. Such cash-based solutions to the problem of care are therefore, potentially, a policy of the right. If allowances are paid only to mothers, they embed a gendered division of labour and reintroduce a traditional model of family life, based on the breadwinner husband/carer wife model.

Increasingly, welfare states are pursuing a mix of individualized solutions to the problem of care, including support for the development of private markets for its provision. Some of this support comes in the form of means-tested supplemental benefits for care users who enter private for-profit residential and nursing care (if they are frail and elderly, for example) or employ carers to work in their homes. These kinds of market solutions to the problem of care are outlined in box C in Figure 15.1.

The gender implications of each of these types of state-subsidized market activities are complex. In the first place, any means testing for consumers of care who are themselves elderly is highly likely to mean that the chief beneficiaries of lower or subsidized fees for service will be women, since, given their biographies of low pay and unpaid work, women are much more likely to be poor in old age than men are. So, if a means-testing system works properly, at least those on very low levels of income should benefit. But they will be buying a service provided for them by other women who are *currently* low paid and working for profit-making care enterprises determined to extract maximum labour for the least cost. Many of these women paid caregivers will be part of the global care market sucked into the vortex of highly developed welfare states which seek care labour wherever they can find it (Anderson, 2000; Ehrenreich and Hochschild, 2002). Much of that care labour will consist of documented women migrants from the poorer nations of transitional Europe and the very poor nations of the Second and Third Worlds.[3] Not all the paid care workers will be migrants; there will also be local labour, again predominantly women, providing care in people's homes and in residential care facilities. Most of them will be low paid and lacking in qualifications.[4] In sum, it is a feature of the private sector care market that it draws on both local and global labour, of whom the huge majority are women.

Other types of state support for the private market come in the form of subsidizing care users' effective demand so that they are able to employ their own labour to deliver care for them in their own homes. The names for these types of payment in different countries – 'direct payments in Britain,' 'consumer-directed care' in the United States, 'personal budgets' in the Netherlands, 'companion payments' in Italy – indicate that care users are free to spend the money as they wish. The assumption in most of these schemes is that they will use it to employ their own caring labour directly. There are large variations among these systems, but the two most important are whether or not the cash can be used to employ and pay relatives, and whether or not there are any regulations to ensure that those who are employed are covered for social security and other employment rights (Ungerson, 2004).

The gendered implications of these schemes, which are rapidly growing in importance, are considerable. In those schemes which allow care users to pay their relatives, we have a very clear example of the commodification of intimate caring relationships – wages are being paid for informal care which was, until the scheme was introduced, wageless. Once again, this has echoes of the old 'wages for housework' debate and whether the payment of wages for work in the domestic domain carried out by family members is a form of recognition of the importance of domestic labour or whether, in practice, it is demeaning for women (and men who care for their wives) and likely to trap them into the demanding and isolating tasks of care delivered at home.

The question of regulation also raises issues of gender, since, in the systems where regulation is strict, it can ensure that care workers are properly covered for social security and related rights and thus escape the common fate of unpaid carers who usually lose full social security and pension entitlements. In the Dutch 'personal budget' scheme, for example, relatives including spouses can be paid and are elaborately contracted to do so, and at the same time they are included in formal labour market regulation, fully integrated into social security and taxation systems, and entitled to holiday rights and other work-related benefits. Not surprisingly, paid caregivers (and the great majority of them are women) in this kind of system report high levels of satisfaction and a sense of full citizenship (Ungerson, 2003). There are also gendered implications for the schemes that are not regulated, for it is here that care labour can be most easily recruited from undocumented migrants and from local labour seeking, illegally, to supplement low social security benefits. Given the highly feminized nature of care work, it is most likely that these entirely unprotected workers will be women, but given the invisibility of this type of 'grey' labour located within the domestic domain, it is impossible to quantify gender breakdowns. Such labour is easily exploited, especially if the workers are co-resident with the people they care for. Many such workers, with no rights of residence, seek out live-in work to resolve their own housing needs. Of course, that means they lose their own living space and control over their own time (Ungerson and Yeandle, 2005).

Box D in Figure 15.1 depicts the situation where the state takes little interest in the way people satisfy their care needs and largely ignores the care market, on both the demand and supply sides. There may be some attempt to regulate the market through incentives encouraging the registration of workers for tax and social security,[5] but on the whole, this market and the workers in it are left to their own devices. Typically, such markets exist alongside residual state services which are heavily targeted towards those in highest need and/or to those on lowest incomes. Such free markets cater to those who are not eligible for the more regulated state services or for subsidies for collectively provided private sector services. The workers will again almost certainly be women, many of them migrants without documents, and so in the most vulnerable position in terms of their social and employment protection.

Thus, the debates about the future of care, in particular long-term care of elderly people, and the way in which it is gendered are closely tied to the way in which welfare states are developing. In particular, the trends towards individualism, consumerism, and privatization are moving the site of care, except for the very frail elderly, into the home and into the control, through cash injection, of care users. This market-based care is a highly gendered world – of elderly women in need of care and of younger low-paid women, some of them deeply vulnerable to exploitation, who provide it for them through paid labour markets. Where care users cannot afford to employ their own carers or cannot afford, despite some subsidy, to access private sector residential care, they must seek out unwaged, informal care in their kin networks, where, paradoxically, the gender division of care is not so pronounced since, informally, men care, too. The alternative to this type of policy solution, which is a feature of liberal and corporatist welfare states, is that pursued in the social democratic welfare states of Scandinavia, where workers are entitled to care leaves. Within a system of care leaves, some incentives can be built in to break down the gendered division of care, but so far such incentives have been developed only in relation to the care of very young children.

INTO THE FUTURE

The traditional choice between family, state, and market as far as care is concerned is no longer straightforward, and the way in which these three institutions interact within particular policy and welfare state contexts is complex. When gender is taken into account, the possible policy choices and debates become even more difficult to untangle.

The long-standing discussion among feminists about whether motherhood in particular, or care in general, should be supported by collective services or by cash supplements, and whether care is best carried out by kin whose work is recognized and compensated for, is still unresolved. Moreover, it is impossible to ignore the impact of care policy on both the care user and the caregiver, both of whom, particularly when it comes to the care of the elderly, are likely to be women (except where elderly men are caring for their wives). The care issue is additionally complicated by the development of a globalized care labour market where those in the developed world import women workers, some undocumented.

At the core of the care issue is the question of how high-quality care can best be delivered, and whether this can be done informally by kin who are compensated and recognized as caregivers, or by paid workers who are fully protected. Welfare states are increasingly concerned with the quality of care, and in many countries, training for care and care qualifications are proliferating which, it is argued, provide the basis for high-quality care. The early assumptions made by policy-makers that 'community care' could be based on the untrained, unwaged labour of women caregivers are now giving way to an argument that high-quality care should not be based on experience but rather on expertise. In other words, high-quality care is now regarded as a *skill*. As a result, credentialism and its concomitant, occupational hierarchy, are beginning to proliferate in the field of hands-on care delivery. Slowly but surely, the kinds of occupational and organizational structures put into place in nursing in the nineteenth and early twentieth centuries are developing in the formal care delivery sector. The outcome for women care workers working within the better organized care delivery sector, whether public or private, is likely to be considerable improvement in their working conditions and the development of a clear career structure.

But there are two profound paradoxes embedded here. First, the development of a care profession will entail higher wages and therefore higher care costs. Such labour will be too expensive for many welfare states to provide extensively or for many care users to afford to purchase. Hence, the growth of a care profession will also drive an added dependence on the caring labour of close kin – many of whom will be women caregivers who are unwaged and without social protection – and a dependence on the much cheaper grey labour of undocumented and illegal women care workers in the global/local care market. The second paradox is that even as welfare states try to improve the quality of care by introducing compulsory qualifications for formally employed care workers, so they are also seeking to maintain the informal care sector, sometimes through direct cash support to caregivers, but also by providing them with support services such as respite from care duties. Clearly, there is an ambivalence here – either high-quality care is based on training and qualification or it is not. And yet we have the spectacle of welfare states currently trying to ride two horses, arguing that care delivered by women who are not the kin of the people they care for has to be carried out by skilled professionals, whereas kin care, especially if delivered by untrained women caregivers, is 'good enough' care.

Future feminist scholarship in the area of gender and care will inevitably be concerned with these issues, many of which are very long-standing. How can care users and caregivers and workers best be protected, and what is the best configuration of family, state, or market in relation to care delivery and its gendered implications? Is 'care' a skill, and, if so, what are the implications of the professionalization of care? And how can caring labour be found that will provide for the ageing populations of the First World that does not pull out of the Third World their mothers and nurturers? There are no easy solutions to these issues, but their careful analysis will continue to demand feminist attention, since the rights and biographies of women across the globe lie at their core.

NOTES

1 This social security benefit, introduced in 1977, compensated carers of working age who were not working in paid labour but were providing care in the home for someone with dependencies for at least thirty-five hours a week. All men between 16 and 65 years old were eligible; all women, except married women, between 16 and 60 were eligible. The law was only changed to include married women after a test case on grounds of gender discrimination was taken to the European Court of Justice in 1987.

2 Carol Gilligan's moral framework was later developed by Joan Tronto (1993) and Selma Sevenhuijsen (1998) into their feminist conceptualization of an 'ethic of care'.

3 Typically, these workers are Mexicans for California, Latin Americans for Italy, North Africans for France, Filipinas, Malaysians, West and East Africans, and Afro-Caribbeans for Britain, Turks and Central and Southern Europeans for Germany and Austria.

4 In Britain, there are now considerable efforts, under the *Care Standards Act, 2000* to ensure that at least 50 per cent of such care workers have a minimum care qualification by 2008.

5 In France, for example, there are voucher schemes for care users which are contingent on the employment of documented workers.

REFERENCES

Anderson, Bridget (2000) *Doing the dirty work? The global politics of domestic labour*, London: Zed Books.

Arber, Sara (1989) 'Men, the forgotten carers', *Sociology*, vol. 23, no. 1, pp. 111–118.

Dalley, Gillian (1988) *Ideologies of caring: rethinking community and collectivism*, Basingstoke: Macmillan Education.

Delphy, Christine and Diana Leonard (1992) *Familiar exploitation: a new analysis of marriage in contemporary Western societies*, Cambridge: Polity Press.

Ehrenreich, Barbara and Arlie Russell Hochschild (eds) (2002) *Global woman: nannies, maids and sex workers in the new economy*, London: Granta Books.

Finch, Janet (1984) 'Community care: developing non-sexist alternatives', *Critical Social Policy*, Issue 9, Spring.

Finch, Janet (1989) *Family obligations and social change,* Cambridge: Polity Press.

Finch, Janet and Dulcie Groves (1980) 'Community care and the family: a case for equal opportunities?', *Journal of Social Policy*, vol. 9, no. 4, pp. 487–511.

Fisher, Mike (1994) 'Man-made Care: Community Care and Older Male Carers', *British Journal of Social Work*, vol. 24, pp. 59–80.

Gilligan, Carol (1982) *In a different voice: psychological theory and women's development*, Cambridge, MA and London: Harvard University Press.

Goffman, Erving (1961) *Asylums: essays on the social situation of mental patients and other inmates*, Garden City, NY: Anchor Books.

Graham, Hilary (1991) 'The Concept of Caring in Feminist Research: the case of domestic service', *Sociology*, vol. 25, no. 1, pp. 61–79.

Green, Hazel (1988) *Informal carers: a study carried out on behalf of the Department of Health and Social Security as part of the 1985 General Household Survey*, London: HMSO.

Groves, Dulcie and Janet Finch (1983) 'Natural selection: perspectives on entitlement to the Invalid Care Allowance', in Janet Finch and Dulcie Groves (eds), *A labour of love: women, work and caring*, London: Routledge and Kegan Paul.

Hernes, Helga Maria (1987) *Welfare state and woman power: essays in state feminism*, Oslo: Norwegian University Press.

Hobson, Barbara, Jane Lewis, and Birte Siim (eds) (2002) *Contested concepts in gender and social politics*, Cheltenham: Edward Elgar.

Keith, Lois and Jenny Morris (1996) 'Easy Targets: a disability rights perspective on the "children as carers" debate', in Jenny Morris (ed.), *Encounters with Strangers: feminism and disability*, London: Women's Press.

Leira, Arnlaug (1998) 'Caring as Social Right: Cash for Child Care and Daddy Leave', *Social Politics*, Fall.

Morris, Jenny (1991) *Pride against prejudice: a personal politics of disability*, London: Women's Press.

Morris, Jenny (1993) *Independent lives? Community care and disabled people*, Houndmills: Macmillan.

Moss, Peter and Nickie Fonda (eds) (1980) *Work and the family*, London: Temple Smith.

Nield Chew, Doris (1982) *Ada Nield Chew: the life and writings of a working woman*, London: Virago Press.
Qureshi, Hazel and Alan Walker (1989) *The caring relationship: elderly people and their families*, Basingstoke: Macmillan.
Rathbone, Eleanor (1917) 'The remuneration of women's service', *Economic journal*, vol. 27, pp. 55–68.
Rathbone, Eleanor (1924) *The disinherited family: a plea for the endowment of the family*, London: Arnold.
Sevenhuijsen, Selma (1998) *Citizenship and the ethics of care: feminist considerations on justice, morality and politics*, London: Routledge.
Sharpe, Sue (1984) *Double identity: the lives of working mothers*, Harmondsworth: Penguin.
Townsend, Peter (1962) *The last refuge: a survey of residential institutions and homes for the aged in England and Wales*, London: Routledge & Kegan Paul.
Tronto, Joan (1993) *Moral boundaries: a political argument for an ethic of care*, New York and London: Routledge.
Ungerson, Clare (1987) *Policy is personal: sex, gender and informal care*, London: Tavistock.
Ungerson, Clare (ed.) (1990) *Gender and caring: work and welfare in Britain and Scandinavia*, New York and London: Harvester Wheatsheaf.
Ungerson, Clare (2003) 'Commodified Care Work in European Labour Markets', *European Societies*, vol. 5, no. 4, pp. 377–396.
Ungerson, Clare (2004) 'Whose empowerment and independence? A cross-national perspective on "cash for care" schemes', *Ageing & Society*, vol. 24, no. 2, pp. 189–212.
Ungerson, Clare and Sue Yeandle (2005) 'Care Workers and Work-Life Balance: the Example of Domiciliary Workers', in Diane Houston (ed.), *Work-Life Balance in the 21st Century*, London: Palgrave.

16

Blending into Equality

Family Diversity and Gender Convergence

Molly Monahan Lang and Barbara J. Risman

Two major trends occurred in gender and families in the last half of the twentieth century in Western post-industrial societies: an increasing diversity of family structures and a trend toward what we call gender convergence between women's and men's life patterns, both inside families and outside of them. Economic and cultural revolutions, including deindustrialization and feminist social movements, have led to an increasing assortment and acceptability of family forms, as well as a weakening of previously rigid gender expectations. The trend toward gender convergence can be seen in families headed by two parents or one, gay or straight. It has also been encouraged – and discouraged – by governmental family policies. While these trends are not occurring without controversy, they are expected to continue well into the twenty-first century.

INTRODUCTION

As families change, so does gender. As gender changes, so do families. Two major trends occurred in gender and families in the last half of the twentieth century in Western post-industrial societies. First, there was clearly a trend toward a diversity of family structures. Families now come in a variety of shapes and forms and include married couples with and without children, cohabiting couples with children, single mothers, childless lesbian and gay couples and many with children, grandparents raising their grandchildren, remarried parents with their biological and stepchildren, and many other configurations. Second, there is a trend toward what we call *gender convergence* between women and men in terms of their life patterns, both inside families and outside of them. Men's and women's lives are becoming more like one another as they are less likely to be forced into social roles because of rigid gender expectations.

These trends toward family diversity and gender convergence began in the twentieth century, but we argue that they are progressing and will become even more pronounced in the twenty-first. In the past, people in Western societies were expected to live under parental guidance until marriage, when men were expected to earn a living for their families. Women were expected to focus their primary attention on childbearing, childcare, and running their homes, even if they had to work for pay. Men proved their worth as men by earning a living, while women proved their worth as women by being good wives and mothers (Berk, 1985). They 'did gender' by fulfilling their expected family roles. We argue here that the social forces that have led to increased diversity in family structures have also led to more similar expectations for women and men and how they 'do gender' – in other words, to gender convergence. We also suggest that as women and men do gender differently than before, they further change the kinds of families that come to be accepted in their society and thus further diversify what we think of as family.

We begin this chapter with a theoretical discussion of how the processes of family diversity and gender convergence have developed. We then provide some evidence for gender convergence among heterosexual married couples, single mothers and their kinship groups, and gays and lesbians. In each type of family, we note how the trends are different by class and racial ethnic groupings, if that information is available. We end with a discussion of current social policy toward gender in families in the United States and Western Europe.

THE CHANGING FAMILY

There is no one type of family that has existed throughout history. Families always reflect the technological, economic, and cultural forces in their societies. In a society where women are legally barred from owning property, their ability to survive is based on their acceptance of the patriarchal dictates of fathers and then husbands. As women come to be financially self-sufficient, they are freer to reject patriarchal marriages and either remain single or negotiate more egalitarian partnerships. What we have come to see as a natural division of labor in families is socially constructed and historically specific.

A quick descriptive overview shows evidence of remarkable family diversity in today's world. At present, one-third of American children are born to women who are not married, and that rate is more than doubled for African American children (Ventura, Martin, Curtin, Mathews, and Park, 2000). Two-thirds of American married mothers work in the labor force. In Sweden, most children are born to cohabiting, not married, couples (Badgett, 2004). In some countries, such as Spain and Germany, children are becoming such a scarce commodity that a pressing social issue is whether or not the society will shrink so quickly that jobs will go unfilled. A new stage of life has emerged, young adulthood, where a majority of women and men in their twenties linger between their parental family and one that they may make. In this new individualist and autonomous moment of life, friends often serve as surrogate family (Furstenberg, Kennedy, McLoyd, Runbaut and Settersten, 2004). Gay and lesbian couples are demanding the right to marry, and an increasing number of children are being raised by gay and lesbian parents.

While there is no one simple explanation for social change, we can look to the economic and technological revolutions that change society and therefore shape the landscape for families. In Western societies, industrialization and urbanization radically changed the lives of families who previously lived primarily on family farms or worked together in family shops (Mintz and Kellogg, 1988). The expectation of father as breadwinner began when work migrated from farms to factories. No longer could fathers work at home alongside their families; now, their main task as providers was to bring home wages. This financial imperative effectively constituted their roles as fathers and husbands.

The notion of separate spheres for women and men that ensued included a cult of domesticity that required women to make the home a welcome and relaxing alternative to the dark, noisy, and dangerous factory. This ideal of femininity was defined by middle- and upper-class wives who could specialize in running their homes, usually with the help of poorer women servants to do the hard labor. While the reality of separate spheres was only possible for the wealthy, the ideal that married women should be shielded from paid labor became widespread. Many poor families could never meet the separate spheres' ideal; wives of poor men worked at cottage industries in the home or in shops and factories. Yet the desire for domestic wives trickled down from the top (Coontz, 1992). The goal of domesticity for wives became a strong part of the union movement where men fought for a 'family wage' to allow working-class women to leave their jobs and become full-time homemakers. The organization of work during the early industrial era created what became known as the traditional family, where men specialize in employment and women in domesticity (Skolnick, 1991).

Economic transitions were not the only social changes affecting families and gender. The industrial era also brought an ideology of meritocracy, a belief that one could change one's position in life through hard work. Individuals came to see themselves as autonomous actors, beyond the total control of families, free to follow job opportunities. Such ideas spread to women. By the early part of the twentieth century, the first wave of feminism had given women the right to vote. Some women came to envisage a life beyond their roles as wives and mothers. The flapper era of the 1920s began the divorce between sexual pleasure and the marriage bed, at least for the avant garde (Skolnick, 1991). Marrying for love and desire – rather than assuming love and desire would follow marriage – became more acceptable. In addition, divorce rates began the steady climb that would continue for most of the twentieth century. Clearly, the rigid gender expectations of an earlier age were giving way to a greater array of socially acceptable ways to be men and women.

In the United States, the momentous events of the Great Depression and World War II halted – if briefly – the changes that were already occurring in family life. Rather than continuing the trends toward sexual freedom and women's equality, families reverted to the patterns of bygone eras. Immediately after World War II, the US government accommodated returning veterans (mostly men) with easy access to education and jobs that paid 'family wages' (Coontz, 1992). The cult of domesticity had a strong resurgence in the United States, with high rates of marriage and unusually high fertility and low divorce rates. Men felt the pressures of breadwinning as strongly as at any point in American history; indeed, the percentage of all men in the labor force with wives working exclusively in their homes reached its peak in the United States during the 1950s.

Similar patterns were in evidence in Europe as well. After World War II, people began marrying earlier, divorce rates spiked but then lowered, and birth rates began to rise, although without the same kind of baby boom as in the United States. Families headed by men who were the exclusive breadwinners became more numerous. The European families' return to traditional patterns that had been disappearing in the twentieth century started slighter later than in the United States and ended later as well (Coontz, 2005). After the chaos of World War II, social pressure that dictated one path of gendered expectations returned, if temporarily.

But then came the 1960s, with a faster pace of cultural changes, an era marked by the youth and civil rights social movements. While the US civil rights movement fought economic and racial discrimination that still plagued African Americans, women organized to fight against the barriers that had always been in place but had hardened during the postwar period. Educated middle-class White women in particular fought to enter the labor force because of the problem that as yet had no name – dissatisfaction with lives devoted entirely to small families and lack of access to roles that allowed them to use their educational attainment (Skolnick, 1991). This trend set in motion the modification of appropriate femininity to include employment outside the home for life. The percentage of all women in the labor force in the United States and in Europe has been climbing steadily ever since (Fullerton, 1999).

While feminism was making waves in Western industrial countries, and middle-class women were adopting cultural and ideological views that challenged traditional family life, economic changes were continuing to affect families as well (England and Farkas, 1986). By the 1970s, American men's wages had stagnated, and deindustrialization processes began as developed countries moved toward the Information Age and service economies. Those blue-collar jobs that had once paid family wages were now being exported to cheaper labor markets. Even when men kept their jobs, inflation rates, particularly for homes, rose faster than wages. Working-class married women, the last to have the opportunity to leave the labor force to pursue the goal of domestic wife, were forced back into the labor force in order to help pay their rents or mortgages (England and Farkas, 1986; Stacey, 1990).

These economic and cultural forces worked together to change families, particularly to increase divorce rates. There is ongoing scholarly debate about why divorce rates began to climb precipitously in the 1970s in the United States and Western Europe. We think both economic and cultural changes played a part. Families struggling economically are more likely to dissolve. At the same time, women who can support themselves are less likely to remain in marriages that are emotionally unsatisfying or abusive. Once women are seen as independent actors in the workplace, and not primarily as wives and mothers, men are no longer judged amoral if they delay marriage far into adulthood, choose not to marry at all, or leave their wives when they are dissatisfied with the marriage (Ehrenreich, 1983). Thus, marriage comes to be seen as a voluntary instead of an obligatory relationship, further increasing rates of divorce. In sum, as Roderick Phillips (1988) argues in an expansive history of divorce in the Western world, women's employment and the increasing acceptance of divorce together are the primary explanations for divorce-prone modern Western societies.

At the present time, divorce rates in Europe and the United States have been stable for two decades, but so high that marriage has come to be seen as serial, rather than for life (Coltrane and Collins, 2001). Serial marriages may benefit economically independent adults, but many children whose mothers are not economically self-sufficient may suffer. More and more poor women who have few prospects of marrying men who will contribute financially to their homes have children without husbands. Just as sexual pleasure was separated from the marriage bed in the twentieth century, it appears as if childbearing and marriage may be split in the twenty-first. This trend has led, unfortunately, to the feminization of poverty in countries where the state does not help support children or ensure that men who can do so contribute to their children's welfare, as many women still do not earn wages high enough to allow their children to enjoy a decent standard of living on their wages alone. With a high divorce rate, remarriage, and cohabitation, adult wages may have to stretch across several families.

Increasing acceptance of openly gay and lesbian households also adds to the changing face of modern families. Extended kinship networks surrounding a heterosexual couple and their children have been replaced by complex kin and pseudo-kin networks of support for heterosexual and homosexual parents (Gerson, 2002; Stacey, 1990; Weston, 1991). Thus, complex forces, including changing cultural norms, rising divorce and remarriage rates, and shifts in the economy all lead to changes in families, which further change gender expectations.

So is there still an ideal family? Do people choose to live in diverse families because they want to, or are they forced into them by circumstances beyond their control? We would argue that marriage remains an ideal in American society, though this is less clear in Europe. Opinion polls suggest that most Americans want to marry, and the current fierce battle for the right to do so by gay men and lesbians suggests that this desire is not limited to heterosexuals. Similarly, although the majority of poor African American children are born to single mothers, those women and their partners tell researchers that they hope to marry in the next few years, although few of them do so (England, 2004). When American couples do not marry despite the desire to do so, they cite the lack of jobs and financial insecurity as reasons that deter them from making matrimonial commitments. While many Europeans live together without marriage, most eventually marry after the birth of their first child. High divorce rates do not necessarily indicate a desire to live alone, but rather may indicate the importance women and men give to good relationships and the push they feel to finding one, even if it means changing partners.

Family diversity is now the norm (Coontz, 1992). Children live with one or two parents, who may be gay or straight. And most children live through some transitions during childhood, from one to two parents and back again, from living with mother alone to living with mother and grandparents, from being an only child to having step-siblings. Today's families are best described as post-modern, with new sets of complicated relationships that must be negotiated: step-grandparents, ex-brothers-in-law, mothers-in-law who remain kin even after divorce (Stacey, 1990).

What we see as the continuing and emerging changes are that women, and increasingly men, will not remain boxed into traditional gender norms, either doing all the housework because they are expected to, or shouldering the entire burden of supporting the family. This is the social landscape we see creating the historical trend toward gender convergence. In the following section, we provide evidence, and when appropriate, counter-evidence, for the trends toward gender convergence in attitudes and behavior in family life. We begin with a discussion of heterosexual couples. Here, the trends differ tremendously by social class. It is unclear to us whether trends differ by ethnicity within social classes, although some have argued that they do. We then discuss whether convergence applies at all to single mothers who are raising children alone or with the help of kin. And finally, to conclude this section, we discuss how gender convergence is applicable to gay and lesbian couples.

GENDER CONVERGENCE AMONG HETEROSEXUAL COUPLES

The trend toward women entering the labor force is far advanced in the United States and most European countries. There is a convergence in labor force participation rates between husbands and wives and an increase in women who are co-breadwinners of families (Gershuny, 2000). There are important national variations, however, as mothers in some countries, such as Sweden, are likely to work part-time, while in other countries, such as in Finland and the United States, mothers working full-time have become the norm. Married women in the Netherlands work only half as many hours as their husbands, while Finnish wives work nearly the same hours (93 per cent). US couples fall somewhere in the middle, with wives working 80 per cent, on average, of the hours husbands work (Jacobs and Gerson with Gornick, 2004).

While men's roles in families have not changed in any way commensurate with this massive entry of wives into paid labor, there is no doubt that the roles of father and husband have grown to include more involvement in childcare and housework than in eras past (Coltrane, 1989). Studies of the division of household labor in the United States and elsewhere show a trend toward equality. In a study of men's roles in family life, Scott Coltrane (1996) suggests that as women move into jobs that require uninterrupted career commitment, and their families come to rely on their income, more participation of men in domestic work and childcare is likely. Recent cross-national research shows that as women's education and income increase, so does their husbands' participation in household labor (Davis and Greenstein, 2004). The goal may not be gender convergence, but that may be the eventual outcome.

These trends do not mean that men and women are now free from traditional gender expectations. Though we are experiencing a trend *toward* gender convergence, it is not at all a full reality, nor may it even be desired by two-job families. Women are still expected to do the bulk of caring work in society, and nurturance is not yet a fully acceptable activity for men (Cancian and Oliker, 2000; Davis and Greenstein, 2004). Dominant definitions of masculinity are still tied to breadwinning and are uneasily stretched to include housework and childcare. These connections – between femininity and nurturance, between masculinity and work outside the home – are centuries in the making and will not be dissolved entirely any time soon. Change is slow and sometimes painful. Couples who believe in equality but have yet to put it into practice may feel conflicted and at odds about sharing the second shift of domestic labor (Hochschild, 1989). Indeed, changes in gender expectations may lead to the dissatisfaction that causes marriages to dissolve. But today's families do not feel as bound to these traditional definitions as in the past; there has clearly been a shift in attitudes and behavior.

One study suggests that among middle-class families, Black men contribute more to family work in the home than do White men (Landry, 2000). Black middle-class couples may have developed a gender-converged family structure because the pattern of wives working for pay is more established in African American culture. Shirley Hill (2005) argues that men's participation in household work is greater primarily among African American couples who themselves grew up in middle-class homes and thus are comfortable with their middle-class status. Hill's research suggests that first-generation middle-class African Americans often hold to very traditional gender norms in order to lay claim to their newly acquired class status.

There have been several small qualitative studies of families where husbands and wives intentionally share parenting and organize their family life without concern for traditional gender expectations (Coltrane and Collins, 2001; Dienhart, 1998; Risman, 1998). Most of the couples in these studies are privileged heterosexual professionals who have the labor force power and financial means to choose flexible work schedules. It appears that for full gender convergence to succeed, the institutional barriers of inflexible full-time work schedules must be overcome, and both partners must share an ideological commitment to equality. Although we have focused thus far on gender convergence in families with couples including one man and one woman, this pattern is also apparent, though in a slightly different fashion, in both single-parent and gay-identified families.

GENDER CONVERGENCE AMONG UNMARRIED PARENTS?

More and more families are headed by single parents, at least for a time. While more single fathers exist now than in the past, the substantial majority of single-parent families consist of women and children. Single parents, as a group, are less well-to-do than couples (Coltrane and Collins, 2001). Single parents have often been both mother and father to their children, and in that way are perhaps the first and most appropriate model for gender convergence. Some single parents do very well economically, but many more struggle.

In the United States, single-mother households are particularly common among poor families, and so we need to focus particular attention on their families. Single African American women and their children are most likely to be living near or below the poverty line (Aulette, 2002). Indeed, African American femininity has never protected women from labor (whether in the fields, the factory, or elsewhere) the way that traditional notions of femininity have protected middle-class White women. Single mothers, including a disproportionate number of African American women, have always had to take on the task that has traditionally defined men's family roles – breadwinning. In the past, single mothers often had strong kinship groups who helped to share their childrearing responsibilities (Stack, 1974), but current research suggests that such extended family support is rare today (Hill, 2005). Not only have single mothers been living this gender convergence longer than other women, but today, they often do so alone, without strong kinship groups or much help from men who do not live with them.

Where do the men in these poor single mothers' lives fit into this scheme? Economic and cultural factors have combined to discourage gender convergence among this group. The shift away from a manufacturing-based economy and the movement of jobs out of the inner cities in recent decades have packed a dual punch for these men (Wilson, 1996). We believe that gender convergence is much more likely to happen from positions of strength. When women or men can take for granted success at traditional roles, they are freer to envision moving toward non-traditional behavior. Without stable and legitimate employment (the signature of the traditional breadwinner role in families), men cannot envision sharing more feminine tasks, such as childcare and housework. Indeed, urban, poor men often adopt cultural expectations that highlight tough hyper-masculinity, perhaps to offset the inability to find jobs that could provide economically for their children. They fail at the traditional male family role and so prove their maleness in other ways, such as an increase in display of physical aggression or toughness. For them, the movement toward gender convergence is unlikely (Froyum, 2004).

Not all single parents are poor or struggling. Single mothers who can be the prime parent and also support their children by themselves are proof of the possibility of successful convergence of traditionally male and female responsibilities in one woman's roles. For the small but growing number of men who share the physical custody of their children after divorce, gender convergence is evident in their lives as well. Some fathers who are not married to their children's mother are primary parents. While still a minority pattern, a growing percentage of men are either the primary parent or share physical custody. Research suggests that when they have to, men can be effective nurturing parents – good 'mothers' (Risman, 1987; 1998). In fact, being a single parent seems to increase a man's self-image as a caring, warm, and nurturing person. When men take care of their children after divorce, they behave more like women – gender convergence in its purest form.

GENDER CONVERGENCE AMONG SAME-SEX COUPLES?

The increasing visibility and acceptance of gay and lesbian families also shows that modern societies are becoming less rigid in gender expectations. There is growing acceptance of the idea that two men or two women can effectively perform all the family tasks (Stacey and Biblarz, 2001). However, they do not necessarily interchange duties, but rather often split them along domestic–breadwinner lines. Christopher Carrington's (1999) research on gay and lesbian households suggests that economic factors explain who is responsible for homemaking in the absence of gender difference. People with higher wages avoid cleaning toilets whether they are in a gay or heterosexual couple. Although these couples exhibited gender convergence in their behavior – a man was doing the family work in gay couples, a woman was doing the breadwinning in lesbian couples – the family structure was tacitly heterogendered. Ironically, the couples were likely to insist that the family work was evenly divided because that is the expectation in gay and, especially, in lesbian households.

If heterogendered couples adopted a financially pragmatic division of labor, women in high-paying, high-powered jobs would be the breadwinners, and men with lower pay would be stay-at-home or part-time parents. Currently, women still do not 'marry down'; career-committed women are often married to career-committed men. When they come under pressure from competing commitments, they are likely to give in to the moral imperative that women are mothers and cut back on their work lives (Blair-Loy, 2003).

SOCIAL POLICY AND FAMILIES

Family structures and the potential for gender convergence are significantly influenced by government policies. In welfare state economies, families are the direct beneficiaries of child allowances, subsidized childcare, and paid parental leave. Many countries with extensive government-provided services employ women professionals and administrators, and so their policies on work–family balance can become a model for private work organizations. In free-market economies, taxation policies are important instruments, fostering or discouraging marriage and having children. However, families often change without government support, even in the face of government hostility, as in the case of gay and lesbian households.

Family leave

The trend toward gender convergence in the United States cannot be said to be the result of government policy. Indeed, it appears that this trend has been occurring despite the US government, as there is not yet any national systematic policy to help solve the dilemmas that accompany the reality that more than half of mothers of infants and toddlers work in the paid labor force, and yet there are no public accommodations for their children (Williams, 2000). The sole US federal policy that addresses the struggle of combining work and family is the Family Medical Leave Act of 1993, which does not include wage replacement. Its qualifying conditions – limited to those in firms with fifty or more employees who have worked 1,250 hours in the previous year – result in almost half of US workers lacking coverage. Even among those who are covered, usage has been sporadic at best (Waldfogel, 2001).

Rather than seeing work–family balance as something that should be addressed at the national level, the US government has left it to individual employers in the private sector. Some employed Americans work for a few major companies that have generous work–family policies, but most families struggle to patch together their own strategies. The trend toward combining full-time work with childrearing continues to gain speed among women and men, suggesting that the changes in families will continue to require changes in other institutions. To the extent that gender convergence continues, and both women and men struggle to combine family and caretaking work, the demand for government policies that help organize family-friendly workplaces will grow stronger.

European countries, on the other hand, have a longstanding tradition of offering paid leave and financially supporting care giving as part of health and social service programs (Waldfogel, 2001). They vary in the types of benefits offered, however: universal or means-tested; parental leave, childcare, or both; and level of generosity. The package of policies offered by each country indicates their cultural encouragement of, or opposition to, the trend toward married mothers' employment outside the home (Henneck, 2003).

In some European countries, for example Switzerland and Portugal, policies indicate a discomfort with full-time employment of married mothers. Their policies encourage women to focus on care giving in the home and men to concentrate on employment. Germany is an example of a country that offers particularly generous parental (read maternal) leave with fourteen weeks at 100 per cent of earnings and the possibility of three years at an income-tested rate, but little public support for childcare. This type of policy maximizes the amount of time a mother can spend with her children, as it gives women an incentive not to return to paid employment (Henneck, 2003). The inadequate provision of childcare creates significant conflict between short school days and long work hours. These policies decrease gender equity because if women do return to paid employment after several years, they have lost a great deal of experience and seniority. The stated intent of such policies has been to increase the numbers of children born, but the opposite has often occurred. While women who remain unemployed have large families, growing numbers of employed women decide not to have any children at all or to have only one. In addition to the unintended consequence of low national fertility, such policies discourage couples from pursuing gender convergence.

At the other end of the spectrum are Nordic countries such as Sweden and Norway, whose policies indicate a clear desire to encourage mothers to stay in the labor force (Jacobs and Gerson with Gornick, 2004). By default, they also encourage an increasing convergence in the family behavior of men and women. The social welfare system in these countries provides a comprehensive array of universal benefits and services to families, from birth payments and monthly child allowances, to childcare centers and extensive parental leave (Henneck, 2003). Benefits in these countries were originally gender-neutral, so that either men or women could take advantage of parental leave and subsidized childcare, but research showed clearly that the leaves were used more by mothers.

Structural shifts in women's labor force participation and ideological shifts toward the belief that both men and women should contribute to childrearing equally have not yet led to full gender convergence, even in countries like Norway. In 1999, only 3 per cent of Norwegian couples had ideal work schedules for shared parenting. The most common pattern was for women to work fewer hours for pay than their husbands. Still, the average Norwegian wife works almost as many hours a week as her husband (Jacobs and Gerson with Gornick, 2004). Recently, however, Norway has implemented a 'daddy leave' opportunity to close even that small gap in working time. A 'daddy leave' reserves some parental caretaking time for fathers only (Cancian and Oliker, 2000). It is a purposeful attempt to redistribute the caring burden between men and women in families. Sweden, too, has recently implemented leave policies focused on men because the earlier gender-neutral policies had not led to remaking families as much as the feminist policy-makers had hoped. The new 'daddy month' off was pushed by men, instead of by women. This new daddy month can, however, be spread over several years and is often used to expand holiday weekends and vacation times rather than to intensively bond with a child.

Clearly, changing the gendered expectations for parenting is harder than simply dictating new government policy. The structure of jobs, the definition of a good worker, and cultural beliefs about parenting must all change in addition to government policy. Gender convergence is far from complete, even in countries where it is a social goal. In a recent comparative analysis of social policy, Janet Gornick suggests that there is an apparent contradiction between family policy designed to reduce the stress on dual-earner families by subsidizing women's time off from market work and policies that support gender equity and convergence (Jacobs and Gerson with Gornick, 2004). Following Arlie Hochschild's (2003) suggestion of a 'warm modern' approach, we advocate a shorter work week that is as flexible as possible in terms of how and where those hours are completed, coupled with both parental leave and a commodification of further services from which to choose. Such policies would promote both gender equity and gender convergence.

Single-parent poverty

There have been, and will continue to be, divergent views on how to respond to the poverty that accompanies much single parenthood in the United States, which is one of the few post-industrial Western nations that does not provide government support for childcare or a generous safety net for those unable to work full-time. Many social scientists suggest that economic changes such as job creation and living wages for low-tier employment would enable more women and men to be gainfully employed. They argue that there will be greater commitment to families and that the families will be more gender-equal if both women and men have jobs that pay a living wage. Conservatives and functionalist social scientists, on the other hand, counter that cultural changes are essential for encouraging men to stay with families out of a sense of financial and moral obligation, thereby contributing to the stable (and more traditional) functioning of families.

Preliminary results from the first national study of unmarried parents and their children in the United States – the Fragile Families and Child Wellbeing

Study – confirm that such couples are more likely than married parents with children to live near or below the official poverty line (see England, 2004; Parke, 2004). Contrary to stereotypes, the great majority of unmarried parents in the study were romantically involved at the time of their child's birth. Although most value marriage, they are not likely to marry unless numerous financial and relational obstacles are first overcome. Rather than seeing the presence of a child as the primary reason for marriage, these couples tend to want long-term financial security and assurances that the quality of their relationship is high enough to be maintained. They see both maternal and paternal employment – an important part of gender convergence – as important prerequisites for a marital commitment.

Right to marry

Gay men and lesbians are increasingly demanding full citizenship rights, including marriage. In Europe, a kaleidoscope of laws permits legal same-gender unions. Scandinavian nations have what are called 'registered partnerships' for homosexual couples, where they receive virtually the same rights as married couples. The Netherlands and Belgium opened marriage to same-gender couples in 2001, and Spain did so in 2004, generating discussion of the effects on heterosexual marriages (Badgett, 2004).

In the United States, the issue is being battled out in the states and in the federal government. The Supreme Court in Massachusetts declared it unconstitutional to deny marriage rights to same-gender couples in 2003; previously, the state of Vermont granted homosexual couples the right to state-recognized civil unions. Civil unions are now widely considered a conservative compromise in the United States, allowing each state to legally recognize (or deny) homosexual relationships without legalizing same-gender marriage. The issue is highly contentious, as the US 2004 election showed, when every state that voted on the issue banned marriage between two people of the same gender, and some have banned even civil unions. They may, however, have to recognize domestic partners with legal unions from other jurisdictions. Few gay men and lesbians in any Western society appear to be willing to settle for the second-class citizenship offered by 'unions,' as the fight for the right to marry indicates.

FAMILY DIVERSITY, GENDER CONVERGENCE, AND FEMINIST THEORY AND POLITICS

We have suggested that economic and cultural forces have created a diversity of family forms and a trend toward gender convergence in men's and women's family responsibilities. We see no reason to expect these social forces will shift direction or lose strength. Social forces, however, do not mysteriously change people's lives but create conditions for change. Women have mobilized in feminist movements all around the world to demand more equal rights, both inside their homes and outside of them. Women and men are choosing possibilities created by economic and cultural changes. Women's labor force employment appears to be moving more towards men's patterns, with fewer interruptions for childcare. Men, at least in survey data, appear to desire fewer hours in the labor force and more time for their family duties (Williams, 2000). While women do more household labor and childcare, the long-term trends are clear: they do less every generation and every decade (Sullivan, 2004). As women have more economic clout and more education, men tend to do a higher proportion of family work (Davis and Greenstein, 2004). We expect these signs of gender convergence in heterosexual couples to become more apparent as we move further into the twenty-first century.

From a feminist point of view, these trends point to greater gender equality. As feminist scholars, we argue that both men and women should be expected to contribute to the family income, engage in housework, and provide care. Not only would this lead to more fulfilling partnerships, where deep friendship is truly possible (Schwartz, 1994), it would undo the harmful and unnecessary value distinction between paid and unpaid contributions to society (Cancian and Oliker, 2000). As feminist proponents of gender convergence, we suggest that what matters is how families operate, the process and interaction between members, and not whether the parents are traditionally gendered, or even whether the parents are the same or opposite gender. In this view, kinship is about mutual care and commitment through illness and death, and families of all kinds can provide this emotional support for one another. In this model, family process counts far more than family structure, and feminist policy recommendations focus on changing economic and political structures so that families of any form can function better (Cherlin, 2002). At the very least, government policy should insure that women and men have the right to equal status in the labor force and the right to devote time outside of paid work time to childcare and other family responsibilities.

The trends for gender convergence evidenced by single-parent families are more complicated and less symmetrical for women and men. Single mothers have long shown they are capable of childcare, domestic work, and earning a living. By breadwinning and nurturing, they have long since shown the logical possibility of gender convergence, especially where governments supply support for childcare and schooling. Single fathers taking primary care or sharing the custody of their children also show gender convergence in action. Most single men, however, are totally removed from any of the caretaking work that children involve and are less likely even to take good care of themselves (Waite and Gallagher, 2000). Unemployed single men, in particular, appear to adopt hyper-masculine identities that are opposed to moving toward incorporating activities traditionally identified as feminine. We have suggested that gender convergence depends on success at traditional roles and then expansion to those of the other gender. We therefore suggest that unemployed poor single men are not likely to move toward gender convergence unless they move into good jobs and feel successful in traditional masculine territory. The best policy for supporting gender convergence among heterosexuals who live in poverty is to provide a living wage to both women and men, so that each will be better off single or partnered.

Homosexual couples appear to break down many stereotypes about the gender appropriateness of social roles. As they become more visible in our societies and more accepted, their very existence contradicts the logic of gender dichotomies, at least as they relate to differences between women and men. Two mommies or two daddies cannot rely on gender differences to organize their family life (Sullivan, 1996). They may not be equal sharers of domestic and paid work, and their family structure may look like mother/wife, father/husband in a gendered world, but it is a model for gender convergence. They have led the way in providing evidence that gender does not necessarily predict social roles. Future research should pay more attention to gender performance of such couples as they provide much information to heterosexual couples moving toward gender convergence.

CONCLUSION

We have argued that the movement of women into paid labor and the cultural shift toward individual rights for women as well as men have led to more diverse families and a trend toward gender convergence within families. These social forces provide the opportunity for such changes, but social movements such as feminism and gay rights are the catalysts for the speed of such transformations and for their acceptance as lasting changes. The acceptance of diverse families in Western post-industrial societies and the movement toward gender convergence depend not only on structural social forces, but also on the actions of social movement activists and their supporters.

As feminist sociologists, we see our role in the feminist movement toward equality as providing analytic tools in order to help shape a more just world. In our view, the only path to a more just world for women and men is gender convergence. At the present time, we are in a moment of change. While some countries are more in flux than others, the direction of change toward convergence and equality seems clear. But we have far to go. In a just world, women would not feel guilt over childrearing if they did it less intensely than as a full-time occupation. And men would feel much more moral responsibility for the daily caretaking of their own offspring. We will know we have arrived at a just world when hearing that your baby 'is a girl' does not give you any different image for her future, than if the new human being is a boy. As Judith Lorber (2005) and Barbara Risman (1998) have argued, a world beyond gender is a world where women and men can be equal.

REFERENCES

Aulette, Judy R. (2002) *Changing American Families*. Boston, MA: Allyn and Bacon.

Badgett, M. V. Lee (2004) 'Will providing marriage rights to same-sex couples undermine heterosexual marriage? Evidence from Scandinavia and the Netherlands,' Discussion paper, Council on Contemporary Families. http://www.contemporaryfamilies.org

Berk, Sarah Fenstermaker (1985) *The Gender Factory: The Apportionment of Work in American Households*. New York: Plenum Press.

Blair-Loy, Mary (2003) *Competing Devotions: Career and Family Among Women Executives*. Cambridge, MA: Harvard University Press.

Blankenhorn, David (1995) *Fatherless America: Confronting Our Most Urgent Social Problem*. New York: Harper Collins.

Cancian, Francesca M. and Oliker, Stacey (2000) *Caring and Gender*. Thousand Oaks, CA: Pine Forge Press.

Carrington, Christopher (1999) *No Place Like Home: Relationships and Family Life Among Lesbians and Gay Men*. Chicago: University of Chicago Press.

Cherlin, Andrew J. (2002) *Public and Private Families* (3rd edition). New York: McGraw-Hill.

Coltrane, Scott (1989) 'Household labor and the routine production of gender,' *Social Problems*, 36(5): 473–490.

Coltrane, Scott (1996) *Family Man: Fatherhood, Housework, and Gender Equity*. Oxford: Oxford University Press.

Coltrane, Scott, and Collins, Randall (2001) *Sociology of Marriage and the Family* (5th edition). Belmont, CA: Wadsworth.

Coontz, Stephanie (1992) *The Way We Never Were: American Families and the Nostalgia Trap*. New York: Basic Books.

Coontz, Stephanie (2005) *Marriage, A History: From Obedience to Intimacy, or How Love Conquered Marriage*. New York: Viking–Penguin.

Davis, Shannon N. and Greenstein, Theodore N. (2004) 'Cross national variations in the division of household labor,' *Journal of Marriage and the Family*, 66(5).

Dienhart, Anke (1998) *Reshaping Fatherhood: The Social Construction of Shared Parenting*. Thousand Oaks, CA: Sage.

Ehrenreich, Barbara (1983) *The Hearts of Men: American Dreams and the Flight from Commitment*. New York: Anchor Books/Doubleday.

England, Paula (2004) 'Fragile family study,' Paper presented at the Council on Contemporary Families Conference, Houston, Texas.

England, Paula and Farkas, George (1986) *Households, Employment, and Gender: A Social, Economic, and Demographic View*. New York: Aldine.

Froyum, Carissa M. (2004) '"Doing what I do": African-American teenagers, gender, and sexuality in an inner city,' Master's thesis, North Carolina State University, Raleigh, NC.

Fullerton, Howard (1999) 'Labor force participation: 75 years of change, 1950–98 and 1998–2025,' *Monthly Labor Review*, December: 3–12.

Furstenberg, Frank F. Jr., Kennedy, Sheela, McLoyd, Vonnie C., Runbaut, Rubén G., and Settersten, Richard A. Jr. (2004) 'Growing up is harder to do,' *Contexts*, 3(3): 33–41.

Gershuny, Jonathan (2000) *Changing Times: Work and Leisure in Postindustrial Society*. Oxford: Oxford University Press.

Gerson, Kathleen (2002) 'Moral dilemmas, moral strategies, and the transformation of gender: Lessons from two generations of work and family change,' *Gender & Society*, 16(1): 8–28.

Henneck, Rachel (2003) 'Family policy in the U.S., Japan, Germany, Italy, and France: Parental leave, child benefits/family allowances, childcare, marriage/cohabitation, and divorce,' *Working Paper series*, Council on Contemporary Families. http://www.contemporary families.org

Hill, Shirley A. (2005) *Black Intimacies: A Gender Perspective on Families and Relationships*. Walnut Springs, CA: AltaMira Press.

Hochschild, Arlie R. (1989) *The Second Shift: Working Parents and the Revolution at Home*. New York: Viking Press.

Hochschild, Arlie R. (2003) *The Commercialization of Intimate Life: Notes From Home and Work*. Berkeley, CA: University of California Press.

Jacobs, Jerry A. and Gerson, Kathleen with Gornick, Janet C. (2004) *The Time Divide: Work, Family and Gender Inequality*. Cambridge, MA: Harvard University Press.

Landry, Bart (2000) *Black Working Wives: Pioneers of the American Family Revolution*. Berkeley, CA: University of California Press.

Lorber, Judith (2005) *Breaking the Bowls: Degendering and Feminist Change*. New York: W.W. Norton.

Mintz, Steven and Kellogg, Susan (1988) *Domestic Revolutions: A Social History of American Family Life*. New York: Free Press.

Parke, Mary (2004) 'Who are "fragile families" and what do we know about them?', Center for Law and Social Policy: Couples and Marriage Series, Policy Brief No. 4: January.

Phillips, Roderick (1988) *Putting Asunder: A History of divorce in Western Society*. Cambridge: Cambridge University Press.

Risman, Barbara J. (1987) 'Intimate relationships from a microstructural perspective: Mothering men,' *Gender & Society*, 1(1): 6–32.

Risman, Barbara J. (1998) *Gender Vertigo: American Families in Transition*. New Haven, CT: Yale University Press.

Schwartz, Pepper (1994) *Peer Marriages: How Love Between Equals Really Works*. New York: Free Press.

Skolnick, Arlene (1991) *Embattled Paradise: American Families in an Age of Uncertainty*. New York: Basic Books.

Stacey, Judith (1990) *Brave New Families: Stories of Domestic Upheaval in Late Twentieth-Century America*. New York: Basic Books.

Stacey, Judith and Biblarz, Timothy J. (2001) '(How) Does the sexual orientation of parents matter?', *American Sociological Review*, 66(2): 184–203.

Stack, Carol (1974) *All Our Kin: Strategies for Survival in a Black Community*. New York: Basic Books.

Sullivan, Maureen (1996) 'Rozzie and Harriet? Gender and family patterns of lesbian coparents', *Gender & Society*, 10(6): 747–767.

Sullivan, Oriel (2004) 'Changing gender practices within the household: A theoretical perspective,' *Gender & Society*, 18(2): 207–222.

Ventura, Stephanie J., Martin, Joyce A., Curtin, Sally C., Mathews, T. J., and Park, Melissa M. (2000) Births: Final data for 1998. National Vital Statistical Reports, 48(3), March 28, Centers for Disease Control and Prevention.

Waite, Linda and Gallagher, Maggie (2000) *The Case for Marriage: Why Married People Are Happier, Healthier, and Better Off Financially*. New York: Random House/Doubleday.

Waldfogel, Jane (2001) 'International policies toward parental leave and child care,' *Future of Children*, 11(1): 99–111.

Weston, Kath (1991) *Families We Choose: Lesbians, Gays, Kinship*. New York: Columbia University Press.

Williams, Joan (2000) *Unbending Gender: Why Family and Work Conflict and What to Do About It*. New York: Oxford University Press.

Wilson, William J. (1996) *When Work Disappears: The World of the New Urban Poor*. New York: Knopf.

Part VI

INTIMATE RELATIONSHIPS AND SEXUALITIES

17

Thinking Straight, Acting Bent

Heteronormativity and Homosexuality

Chrys Ingraham

Thinking straight – heteronormativity, the belief system underlying institutionalized heterosexuality – constitutes the dominant paradigm in Western society. It secures a division of labor and distribution of wealth and power that requires gender, racial categories, class, and sexual hierarchies as well as ideological struggles for meaning and value. In this chapter, I argue that the preoccupation with gender in feminist scholarship obscures the significance of heterosexuality as a primary institution complete with organizing rituals and disciplining practices that regulate acting bent. While gender is a central feature of heteronormativity, it is institutionalized heterosexuality that is served by dominant or conventional constructions of gender, not the other way around. Shifting the focus from gender to heteronormativity, theorizing what it means to think bent, holds enormous potential for feminist theory and research.

INTRODUCTION

Media coverage in the days following the attacks on the World Trade Center towers in New York City on September 11, 2001, was full of stories about heroes and families. Human interest journalists filled our imaginations with tales of young fathers leaving behind widows and children, young wives and daughters pleading with the public for any news about their loved ones, newlyweds whose dreams would no longer be realized, brave firemen who died being heroic, and mothers grieving for their lost children. In all these stories of lives changed forever, it was what the media left out that captured my attention. Where were the tales of women heroes, women in occupations historically held by men – firefighters, police officers, construction workers? Who did all those cars belong to that were abandoned in the commuter lots of regional train stations? What happened to the stories of those who did not have husbands, wives, children, mothers, but lost someone they loved, nevertheless? Where were the reports on grieving partners of homosexual couples who had also lost their families, their futures? Finally, the lack of coverage about people of color and immigrants – many of those killed were from other countries – was shocking. In the days following this (inter)national crisis, we had all we could do to think straight – except when it came to telling the stories. Thinking straight – foregrounding heteronormativity and the dominance of men – was the role of the news media. From this standpoint, the lives of people who do not fit the dominant paradigm – those who act bent – are marginalized, made invisible, or rendered irrelevant.

For gender and women's studies scholars, reading the gaps, silences, and invisibilities in the popular narratives about the events and effects of September 11, 2001, provides a wealth of information about the state of gender and racial relations and the interests at stake in those relations. Judith Lorber's presidential address to the Eastern Sociological Society in 2002, for example, provided a gender analysis of the ways *The New York Times* and *The New Yorker*, as sophisticated mainstream media outlets, relied on conventional gender depictions of heroes and of masculinity while simultaneously focusing on the complexity of women's status in Islamic societies (Lorber, 2002). Lorber's powerful 'degendering' of this historical conjuncture offers dramatic insight into the media's use of 'superficial social constructions of masculinity and femininity' as well as of the gender politics of the event now commonly referred to as 9/11. Arguing that a degendering analytic undermines consequential ideologies and actions, Lorber explains how prevailing depictions of the male hero, the female widow, the traditional (White middle-class) family, as well as depictions of the oppressive lives of Islamic women, set the conditions for war, violence, and continued acts of terrorism.

Feminist philosopher Judith Butler's *Precarious Life: the Powers of Mourning and Violence* offers another valuable, if not unusual, feminist appraisal of 9/11. Theorizing the relationship between vulnerability and aggression, Butler critiques the use of violence as a response to loss and censorship as a necessity for war or patriotism. Disturbed by politicians' appropriation of feminism's demand for the liberation of women in Afghanistan as a justification for war, Butler cautions feminists to be more reflexive. Feminism, she argues, is 'unequivocally identified with the imposition of values on cultural contexts' and as such should be ever alert to its complicity with First World presumptions that can 'use the resources of feminist theory, and activism, to rethink the meaning of the tie, the bond, the alliance, the relation, as they are imagined and lived in the horizon of a counterimperialist egalitarianism' (2004: 42).

To achieve this objective, Butler argues, feminists need to embrace the value of feminist critique and use conjunctural moments such as 9/11 to 'provide all kinds of responses.' Like many feminists today, Butler and Lorber understand the historical necessity of feminist analyses for advancing the interests of democracy. Lorber's analysis makes visible the potentiality conventional gender tales create for the social legitimation of violence and revenge as well as for advancing men's dominance, while Butler cautions us to pursue a feminism that does not participate in its own demise or in the destruction of all forms of alterity. Implicit in their critiques are questions concerning the stakes in how events are depicted and in the responses they evoke. For example, who benefits from cultural dependencies on conventional gender, racial, and familial narratives and what ends do these depictions serve? To answer questions such as these requires a continuous and lively debate over the starting points for feminist theory and research.

Gender analysis of 9/11 gives us insight into the meanings and values attached to masculinity and femininity, hegemonic men's dominance, and the hierarchical weighting embedded in those gendered constructions. When the meanings we attach to masculinity as a form of dominance incorporate a valuing of violence, militarism, and retribution as necessary for our survival in the face of terrorism, the most popular voices and images are those that mirror these values. A gender analytic gives us this insight and helps us to identify the points of intervention necessary to create social change. It leaves incomplete the explanation of the media's attachment to stories of thwarted betrothals and ruined wedding plans. How do we analyze the heteronormative gaps, silences, and invisibilities present in media narratives of the events and effects of 9/11? Do we give primacy to a gender analytic? Is it applicable to such questions or does it limit our understanding and, worse, participate in the very conditions we seek to interrupt?

In the days following 9/11, the media made clear whose sadness was most valued, whose lives and work were most important, and whose relationships earned our attention. To provide a critique of this historical conjuncture requires an analytic capable of revealing the significance of heterosexuality, family, and Whiteness for relations of ruling in Western society. By shifting our locus of analysis from gender to the ends gender serves, our perspective alters and, along with that, the explanations and interventions we seek.

In this chapter I will argue that thinking straight – heteronormativity, the belief system underlying institutionalized heterosexuality – constitutes the dominant paradigm in Western society. It is the basis for the division of labor and hierarchies of wealth and power stratified by gender, racial categories, class, and sexualities. It also underlies ideological struggles for meaning and value. Gender is a central feature of heteronormativity, but it is institutionalized heterosexuality that is served by dominant or conventional constructions of gender, not the other way around. To critique the operation of gender as imbricated in racial, class, and sexual relations to the exclusion of institutionalized heterosexuality is to bracket off the ends served by prevailing and dominant gender constructions and practices. We need to revisit this question: Would gender exist were it not for its organizing relationship to institutionalized heterosexuality?

CURRENT ASSUMPTIONS ABOUT GENDER

In current gender theory, there are several foundational assumptions that remain unexamined. First and foremost, most feminist and gender scholars provide definitions of gender as a relational concept, built on the presumption of relations between biological males and biological females. These sources typically refer to gender as based on 'the sexes' or one's 'sex' or one's 'maleness or femaleness' as the basis for gender.[1] The taken-for-granted notion that gender is about males and females living in relation to one another implies that the most salient feature of male and female behavior has to do with relating across groups (male to female) not within groups (female-to-female; male-to-male). The presence of this assumption throughout gender theory and research suggests that gender's purpose is primarily to organize relations between males and females – the process necessary for institutionalizing heterosexuality or, to minimize the role of sexuality here, institutionalizing hetero*relationality*.

The second but related assumption operating in these definitions is the notion that there are only two sexes, male and female, and that they are fixed and stable categories – beyond construction – operating naturally and without need for debate or discussion. Notions such as these have been challenged and debunked in recent years by researchers from across the disciplines.[2] While it is true that the institution of science and its authority in relation to the production of biological knowledge has significant legitimating power, it is also true that biology – or any science – is also subject to cultural influences and bias.

The third assumption in definitions of gender is that of 'oppositeness': males vs. females, men vs. women, heterosexuals vs. homosexuals. It is not clear what constitutes an opposite and why we are so attached to binary categories rather than the idea that human physiology and anatomy, desire, and social behavior are all variable. Even with the high degree of sensitivity to these topics in gender theory and research, references to the 'opposite' sex (not the 'other' sex or sexes) permeate gender theory and research. We have come to rely on the category rather than the variability of human behavior as object of study. In other words, if we begin social inquiry from the standpoint of categories, it is the categories or what they reveal that we end up studying. If we start from the assumption of human behavior as variable, then it is the variability or reality in human behavior that we study. We may find it useful to conclude with categories, but they serve an explanatory purpose rather than a legitimizing function. Shifting our starting point and questioning the assumptions upon which we base our categories and concepts, we reduce the risk of reproducing the very conditions we seek to change. As Butler warns in *Precarious Life*, we must be ever alert to our complicity in presumptions that may unintentionally result in securing oppressive interests. The remedy, she argues, is to keep the debate open and continue to question our own assumptions.

GENDER AND HETEROSEXUALITY

As it stands currently, most contemporary theory and research on gendered behavior participates in 'thinking straight' or what I have defined in earlier writings as the *heterosexual imaginary*:

> [It is] that way of thinking that conceals the operation of heterosexuality in structuring gender and closes off any critical analysis of heterosexuality as an organizing institution. The effect of this depiction of reality is that heterosexuality circulates as taken for granted, naturally occurring, and unquestioned, while gender is understood as socially constructed and central to the organization of everyday life. (Ingraham, 1994: 203–4)

By treating heterosexuality as normative (heteronormative) or taken for granted, we participate in establishing heterosexuality – not sexual orientation or sexual behavior, but the way it is organized, secured, and ritualized – as the standard for legitimate and prescriptive socio-sexual behavior, as though it were fixed in time and space and universally occurring. Even given the recent emergence of critical heterosexual studies, gender and sexuality scholars from across the disciplines continue to pursue the study of heterosexuality as either a natural form of sexual or relationship behavior or as the default category for institutions such as marriage and family. In other words, they examine heterosexuality from the standpoint of heteronormativity. These approaches frequently obscure the ways in which ascribed or prescribed behaviors for women and men – gender – actually organize and serve the interests of *institutionalized* heterosexuality. The consequence is missed opportunities for understanding the material realities of institutionalized existence, for providing insights into the inconsistencies and incoherences of those lived realities, and for de-naturalizing oppressive social practices.

Even within queer theory and contemporary feminist debates on sexuality throughout the 1990s, there was little agreement on how to understand the relationship of gender to heterosexuality. For example, feminist sociologist Stevi Jackson, most notable for her book *Heterosexuality in Question* (1999), has made an enormous contribution to critical heterosexual studies but consistently argues that while gender is indeed linked to heterosexuality, it exists prior to the institution of heterosexuality. She says:

> While gender and heterosexuality are so closely entwined that it is not easy to unravel their intersections, we should retain the capacity to tease out the tangled web of connections between them. Hence it seems necessary to maintain an analytical distinction between gender, as the hierarchical relation between women and men, and heterosexuality, as a specific institutionalized form of that relation…[W]hile I remain convinced that gender is logically prior to sexuality (erotically significant desires, practices, relationships and identities) I am far more uncertain about how much weight it should be given in relation to institutionalized heterosexuality. (2005: 27)

Jackson's thoughtful theoretical approach to critical heterosexual studies leaves room for gender as a starting point while holding open the possibility that gender is primarily a product of institutionalized heterosexuality.

Sociologists Diane Richardson (1996) and Steven Seidman (1995), as well as historian Jonathan Katz (1996), have also addressed the issue of heterosexuality as an organizing concept. For example, Richardson's work focuses on the social construction of citizenship as grounded in heteronormative assumptions. Drawing on both feminist and gay/queer studies, Richardson argues:

> The notion of the normative category citizen as heterosexual is not, however, limited to lesbian/feminist analysis. Some queer/gay male writers have also acknowledged the relationship between citizenship and the institutionalization of heterosexuality.[3] This is, perhaps, hardly surprising given that the concept of 'heteronormativity' has been central to queer theory, which in common with feminist approaches has problematized the heterosexual/homosexual binary (Warner, 1993). Having said this, the importance of earlier feminist work on developing critical analyses of heterosexuality, laying the foundations for later work, is not always acknowledged by queer theorists. (2005: 64)

To date, we have not adequately determined if what we consider gender or gendered behavior would even exist if not for its relationship to the institution of heterosexuality. Furthermore, we have not engaged a pubic debate on the merits (or lack thereof) of the ways we have organized heterosexuality, except for the indirect ways the current gay marriage question brings these issues into consideration.

DROPPING THE CATEGORIES

Our attachment to categories, with their implied discrete and rigidified boundaries, has limited our explanations of gender and sexuality as fluid and complex forms of human behavior.[4] Categories such as lesbian, gay, bisexual, heterosexual, transsexual, transgendered, and transvestite provide us with the illusion of belonging (comfortably or uncomfortably) to a particular identity or of describing various social practices, but they actually restrict our understanding of either gender or sexuality as variable behaviors. For example, how do we categorize the woman who has lived to mid-life as a married heterosexual with an active (and enjoyable) extra-marital sex life with men who falls in love with a woman and commits herself to a *same*-sex relationship, but still finds men attractive? Or, the married transvestite (cross-dresser) who has five children and a very feminine partner – is he really a lesbian? There are numerous variations in the lived realities of people's experiences with gender and sexuality.

As we move more fully into the twenty-first century, the historically variable regulative forces controlling gender and sexuality continue to shift and change. Behaviors that were previously underground – acting bent – have become more visible – e.g., transsexual, transgender – while those that have been taken for granted are continually challenged – e.g., heterosexuality, lesbian, gay. Thinking straight positions us to see all things as grounded in heterosexuality and prevents us from seeing the widely variant social/sexual world. By shifting away from the heterosexual imaginary and not thinking straight, we are able to see that gender and sexuality are historically variable and constantly changing over the lifespan. The variation and flexibility permitted in gender and sexuality are in direct proportion to applied or challenged regulative forces.

Heteronormativity

Before we can understand the implications of thinking straight for gender and women's studies, it is important to trace the evolution of the concept of heteronormativity. In the 1970s, second-wave feminists began to theorize and examine heterosexuality as normative and as a primary source of women's oppression. One of the earliest examples is an essay authored by a Dutch group, Purple September, entitled 'The Normative Status of Heterosexuality' (1975). Breaking from traditional notions of heterosexuality as biological, they argued that heterosexuality is a normalized power arrangement that limits options, privileges men over women, and reinforces and naturalizes men's dominance. Ti-Grace Atkinson (1974), The Furies Collective, Redstockings (1975), Rita Mae Brown (1976), and Charlotte Bunch (1975) all contributed to these debates, arguing that heterosexuality is a highly organized social institution rife with multiple forms of domination and ideological control. In a representative statement of this idea, Bunch said:

> Heterosexuality – as an ideology and an institution – upholds all those aspects of female oppression…For example, heterosexuality is basic to our oppression in the workplace. When we look at how women are defined and exploited as secondary, marginal workers, we recognize that this definition assumes that all women are tied to men…It is obvious that heterosexuality upholds the home, housework, the family as both a personal and economic unit. (1975: 34)

Considered by many to be the most pivotal contribution to early debates regarding normative heterosexuality is Adrienne Rich's essay on compulsory heterosexuality and lesbian existence (1980). Rich confronts the institution of heterosexuality head on, asserting that heterosexuality is neither natural nor inevitable but is instead a compulsory, contrived, constructed, and taken-for-granted institution that serves the interests of men's dominance. She said:

> Historians need to ask at every point how heterosexuality as institution has been organized and maintained through the female wage scale, the enforcement of middle-class women's leisure, the glamorization of so-called sexual liberation, the withholding of education from women, the imagery of high art and popular culture, the mystification of personal sphere, and much else. We need an economics which comprehends the institution of heterosexuality, with its doubled workload for women and its sexual divisions of labor, as the most idealized of economic relations. (1980: 27)

Understanding heterosexuality as compulsory and as a standardized institution with processes and effects is what makes Rich's contribution ground-breaking.

Monique Wittig's 'The Category of Sex,' originally published in 1976, takes the argument to a different level, declaring heterosexuality a political regime. The category of sex, she claims, is the political category that founds society as heterosexual:

> As such it does not concern being but relationship…The category of sex is the one that rules as natural the relation that is at the base of (heterosexual) society and through which half of the population, women, are heterosexualized…and submitted to a heterosexual economy…The category of sex is the product of a heterosexual society in which men appropriate for themselves the reproduction and production of women, and also their physical persons by means of a contract called the marriage contract. (1992: 7)

According to Wittig, the heterosexual regime depends upon the belief that women are sexual beings, unable to escape or live outside of men's rule. Wittig's theory claims that the categories of sex and gender would not exist were it not for the regime of heterosexuality. Arguing that the very notion of 'woman' is a product of heterosexual society, Wittig links the regime of heterosexuality to the social production of both sex and gender. In so doing, she opens up the possibility that the meaning given to such categories as woman and man is not self-evident but the product of patriarchal heterosexual dominance. The theoretical opening Wittig provides for feminist theory foregrounds the dependency of sex and gender on the regime of heterosexuality. Wittig's 'The Straight Mind,' published in 1980, challenged feminist theories of gender to examine the interests served by the social constructions of sex/gender and prepared the field for the further development of critical heterosexual studies.

As if to answer this need, another generation of feminist theorists emerged. These new works produced an epistemological break with earlier notions of biologically based heterosexuality.[5] They challenged the centrality of a naturalized body-based heterosexuality in favor of an institutionalized and normative model, opening the way for a systematic analysis of heterosexuality – critical heterosexual studies. In their view, the relevance of naturally occurring or biologically based sexual orientation became less urgent than understanding how heterosexuality is organized, how we give it meaning, and what interests are served by these processes. Joining in these efforts, the simultaneous and sometimes overlapping emergence of queer theory in the 1990s pressured and invigorated this new wave of critical analyses of heterosexuality.[6] Jonathan Katz's book *The Invention of Heterosexuality* (1996) provided a substantial catalyst for continuing development of this field. His historical genealogy of the term and his revealing finding that as a concept *heterosexual* is only about a hundred years old make a powerful case against sexuality as some form of immutable nature. His history of the development of the terms *heterosexual* and *homosexual* outlines the path by which heterosexuality attained the status of norm.

In 1923 *Webster's* defined 'heterosexuality' as a 'Med.' term meaning 'morbid sexual passion for one of the opposite sex.' Not until 1934 does the definition of 'heterosexuality' first appear in *Webster's Second Edition Unabridged* as a 'manifestation of sexual passion for one of the opposite sex; normal sexuality' (Katz, 1996: 92). According to Katz, there was substantial historical evidence to support the argument that what we think of as natural heterosexuality had, in fact, been invented, socially produced. Katz's history gave further weight to the argument that normative heterosexuality must be studied as a phenomenon that is socially produced not naturally occurring.

Concurrent with the emergence of these works arose a host of new concepts. Among the first were ideas that could be used to identify the structured inequality and discrimination embedded within the institution of heterosexuality, concepts such as heteronormativity, heterosexism, heterogender, or the heterosexual imaginary. Of these, 'heteronormativity' became the most useful as shorthand for countering notions of a naturalized sexuality. Credited with creating the term, Michael Warner, in his anthology *Fear of a Queer Planet*, argues:

> So much privilege lies in heterosexual culture's exclusive ability to interpret itself as society. The culture thinks of itself as the elemental form of human association, as the very model of inter-gender relations, as the indivisible basis of all community, and as the means of reproduction without which society wouldn't exist…Western political thought has taken the heterosexual couple to represent the principle of social union itself. (1993: xxi)

In this passage Warner rearticulates Wittig's notion of heterosexuality as a social contract: 'To live in society is to live in heterosexuality…Heterosexuality is always there within all mental categories' (1992: 40). Like Whiteness in a White supremacist society, Warner argued, heterosexuality is socially produced as dominant, systemic, taken for granted, and universalized. This is so much the lived reality that society itself becomes viewed as inseparable from heterosexuality.

In sum, heteronormativity can be defined as the view that institutionalized heterosexuality constitutes the standard for legitimate and expected social and sexual relations. Heteronormativity insures that the organization of heterosexuality in everything from gender to weddings to marital status is held up both as a model and as 'normal.' Thinking straight means employing ways of thinking that assume the centrality and universality of heteronormativity. In other words, to think straight is to apply the prevailing meanings and ideological messages that organize heterosexuality. It is to view the world according to the social, economic, cultural, and political codes of institutionalized heterosexuality as normative.

Consider the following examples:

- Thinking straight means understanding heterosexuality as naturally occurring, not as an extensively organized social arrangement or means for distributing power and wealth.
- Thinking straight is confusing *institutionalized* heterosexuality with something that is naturally occurring.

- Thinking straight means believing that the world is only and has always been heterosexual – the way we think about this category – not historically or regionally variant or as a cultural invention (Katz, 1996).
- Thinking straight means believing that institutionalized heterosexuality is universal, practiced the same way in all societies as well as in the animal world, when there is substantial evidence to the contrary (Lorber, 1994; Roughgarden, 2004).
- Thinking straight is embracing a sense of entitlement, social and economic, just by virtue of participating in the dominant form of heterosexual life – marriage – regardless of the ways that entitlement denies non-participants access to equal opportunity and citizenship.
- Thinking straight is living in romance or the illusion of well-being that the ideology of institutionalized heterosexuality promises, not in its varied realities.
- Thinking straight means believing that sexuality can be categorized, e.g., that a man and a woman in a relationship are heterosexual or that two women in a same-gender relationship are lesbian.
- Thinking straight means relying on authorized prescriptive notions of relational behaviors.

Thinking straight can include everything from boy/girl seating at a party or asking for marital status on institutional forms to global economic assumptions about the division of labor. Using the earlier example of media coverage of 9/11, covering only those stories that mirror institutionalized and normative heterosexuality is a prime example of thinking straight.

But what if we shift our standpoint away from one that embraces heteronormativity? Would that have changed the media coverage of 9/11, for example? What happens to the scholarship on gender and women's studies?

RESEARCHING HETERONORMATIVITY

Shifting the starting point of feminist inquiry from gender (as independent of heterosexuality) to gender as an organizing concept for institutionalized heterosexuality (heteronormativity) could potentially provide us with significantly enhanced insights into the organization of male and female behavior and the gendered categories of men and women. Some recent examples include research on proms (Best, 2000), weddings (Ingraham, 1999; 2005), citizenship (Richardson, 2005), and poverty (Walsh, 2005). In each of these studies, the focus is on the operation and consequences of institutionalized heterosexuality, shifting the paradigm beyond the boundaries of traditional gender analysis.

Since the publication of *White Weddings: Romancing Heterosexuality in Popular Culture* (Ingraham, 1999), several new works have emerged exploring this highly utilized and commodified ritual. Most notable among them are *Cinderella Dreams: The Lavish Wedding* by Cele Otnes and Elizabeth Pleck (2003), and *The Wedding Complex: Forms of Belonging in Modern American Culture* by Elizabeth Freeman (2002). While these works are very different from each other, combined with Amy Best's sociological study, *Prom Night* (2000), they represent a developing body of research into established heterosexual practices.

Prior to the mid-1990s, very little investigation had been conducted into the taken-for-granted ritual of the wedding, a pervasive tradition long considered women's domain. Starting with *White Weddings* (1999), studies of weddings and wedding culture have proliferated. This growing body of research offers a revealing and valuable contribution to our understanding of the heterosexual imaginary and its organizing effect on gender. Viewing this tradition for how it is integral to institutionalized heterosexuality brings to light the myriad ways the wedding–industrial complex and the vast wedding market rely *not* on notions of gender so much as on constructions of gender in relation to heterosexuality – heterogender. Both *White Weddings* and *Cinderella Dreams* make visible the pervasive effect wedding marketers have on what counts as wedding traditions. For example, white wedding gowns and diamond rings have a relatively short history as so-called wedding traditions but are perceived by many to be long-standing heterosexual (and sacred) traditions. In reality, they are *not* traditions but the outcome of very effective marketing campaigns (Ingraham, 1999; Otnes and Pleck, 2003).

Among the most powerful insights offered by wedding research is the way in which the wedding industry both produces and relies upon the fantasy of the fairy tale romance. From toys targeted at young girls to the marketing of everything from prom dresses to wedding gowns, this research shows the overdetermined consequence of what Otnes and Pleck call 'Cinderella dreams.' From childhood to adulthood, the potential bride is socialized to prepare for the day when her handsome prince will sweep her away into a happily-ever-after life, free from class and sex oppression and away from the abuses of the workplace. They offer many examples of the way this story is woven throughout the history of the lavish wedding and offer insights into how it gives meaning to everything from the wedding gown to the Barbie doll. The consequence of this pervasive and far-reaching socialization and marketing process is the solidification of what is valued and acceptable as women's work. This modern-day Cinderella story is played over and over again in movies and popular culture, securing the illusion that the lavish wedding is necessary for guaranteeing the happy ending and the heterosexual imaginary.

Amy Best's ground-breaking study *Prom Night* explores the meaning-making processes embedded in representations of proms in popular films and in the real-life enactment of the high school prom. In a passage illustrative of her examination of heteronormativity, Best explains:

> Normative heterosexuality is actively reinscribed through the film's prom scene in two distinct, though interrelated ways. While erasing the fact of queerness from the historical landscape, this scene also works to naturalize heterosexuality. Heterosexuality is presumed to be enduring and timeless. In this way, this film, like so many other popular cultural images targeting teen audiences, reproduces heterosexuality as a normative feature of American cultural life of both past and present, and at the same time embeds heterosexual ideology within American mainstream youth culture. (2005: 193–4)

Again, what Best explores is another significant instance of socialization that constructs gender to meet the needs of institutionalized heterosexuality.

Diane Richardson's work is a particularly powerful example of this paradigm shift because she mines the core of one of the most essential features of social existence – what it means to be a citizen and how citizenship functions as a form of heterosexual regulation. In her essay 'Claiming Citizenship,' Richardson demonstrates how our notions of citizenship are based upon assumptions about sexuality, specifically 'hegemonic heterosexuality.' She asserts:

> The main focus of such work is to demonstrate how citizens are normatively constructed as (hetero)sexual subjects and, related to this, offer a way of analyzing the resultant inequalities faced by 'excluded' citizens in terms of the institutionalization of heterosexuality…what we have conventionally understood as 'citizenship' is itself a hegemonic form of sexual citizenship. (2005: 65)

In each of these areas of inquiry, the shift in standpoint from gender studies to critical heterosexual studies opens up dynamic and expansive insights into the ways in which institutionalized heterosexuality and its ideological framework, heteronormativity, organize most of our social, political, and economic lives. At the very least, these new works raise profound new questions for continued debate and investigation.

THINKING BENT: THE FUTURE OF FEMINIST SCHOLARSHIP

Feminist scholarship has a long tradition of pushing the boundaries of accepted and traditional fields of inquiry, challenging their foundational assumptions and opening up new knowledge about the lives and practices of people previously overlooked. Thinking bent, theorizing and studying the lives and practices of non-dominant groups and pressuring the ways of thinking that keep them invisible, is the foundation of feminist thinking and scholarship. In other words, thinking bent is another way to queer all knowledge, reducing the risk of merely reproducing the status quo and embracing a standpoint that enables further investigation by attending to the lives and practices of the Other.

As we move into the twenty-first century, we find more and more evidence that a body-based model of gender is slippery. We understand more fully how gender and sexuality operate flexibly and variably over the lifespan. We are living in an historical moment where this reality is increasingly more visible. Culturally, we are giving more permission and acceptance to peoples and behaviors that appear 'bent' – operate outside the dominant gender and sexuality paradigms. As this variability becomes more apparent, so does our awareness that very little is actually about the body. We can study the prevalence of eating disorders or sexual or domestic violence only to discover that they are not about the body but about how we give meaning to the body. In these instances, the body functions as metaphor, as symbolic of such things as gender and sexuality, not as the thing itself. The materiality of the body is instead about power, the division of labor, and the distribution of economic resources – not the body itself.

The future of feminist scholarship resides in keeping the debates open, in exploring those areas of social life that are typically considered 'bent,' and in finding new ways to expand our thinking and our methods. More important, the promise of feminism resides in questioning our own foundational assumptions and maintaining our critical edge. By doing so we keep open the greatest possibility for the continued relevance of feminism in all its aspects.

ACKNOWLEDGEMENTS

Thank you to Ilene Kalish for 'thinking straight,' to Anita Roddick for her gentle guidance in titling this work, and to Eileen Brownell for her royal museness and support. Many thanks to Judith Lorber for this opportunity and for her gentle guidance.

NOTES

1 *Blackwell Dictionary* (Johnson, 2000) (see also Kramer, 2001; Renzetti and Curran, 2003; Rubin, 1975).

2 As in various references (e.g., Fausto-Sterling, 1985; 2000; Kessler, 1990; Lorber, 2005; Roughgarden, 2004).

3 See, for example, M. B. Kaplan (1997).

4 Patricia Hill Collins (2000) and Dorothy Smith (1989) have each argued that research on the lives of women and people of color is limited by our attachment to rigidified categories. Each offers an alternative starting point to address the specificity and standpoint of sociological inquiry.

5 As can be found in various references (e.g., Butler, 1990; de Lauretis, 1987; Fuss, 1991; Hennessy, R., 1995; 2000; Ingraham, 1994; Jackson, 1996; Ramazanoglu, 1995; Richardson, 1996).

6 Discussed by several authors (e.g., Katz, 1996; Sedgwick, 1990; Seidman, 1991; 1992; 1995; Warner, 1993).

REFERENCES

Atkinson, Ti-Grace (1974). *Amazon odyssey*. New York: Links Books.
Best, Amy (2000). *Prom night: Youth, schools and popular culture*. New York: Routledge.
_____ (2005). The production of heterosexuality at the high school prom, in C. Ingraham (ed.), *Thinking straight*. New York: Routledge.
Brown, Rita Mae (1976). *Plain brown rapper*. Baltimore, MD: Diana Press.
Bunch, Charlotte (1975). Not for lesbians only. *Quest: A Feminist Quarterly* Fall.
Butler, Judith (1990). *Gender trouble*. New York: Routledge.
_____ (2004). *Precarious life: The powers of mourning and violence*. London: Verso.
Collins, Patricia Hill (2000). *Black feminist thought: Knowledge, consciousness, and the politics of empowerment*. New York: Routledge.
de Lauretis, Teresa (1987). *Technologies of gender: Essays on theory, film, and fiction*. Indianapolis: Indiana University Press.
Fausto-Sterling, Anne (1985). *Myths of gender: Biological theories about men and women*. New York: Basic Books.
_____ (2000). *Sexing the body: Gender politics and the construction of sexuality*. New York: Basic Books.
Freeman, Elizabeth (2002). *The wedding complex: forms of belonging in modern American culture*. Durham, NC: Duke University Press.
Fuss, Diana (1991). *Inside/Out: Lesbian theories, gay theories*. New York: Routledge.
Hennessy, Rosemary (1995a). Queer theory, left politics. *Rethinking Marxism* 7(Spring): 85–111.
_____ (1995b). Queer visibility in commodity culture. *Cultural Critique* 29(Winter): 31–76.
_____ (2000). *Profit and pleasure: Sexual identities in late capitalism*. New York: Routledge.
Ingraham, Chrys (1994) The heterosexual imaginary: Feminist sociology and theories of gender. *Sociological Theory* July.
_____ (1999). *White weddings: Romancing heterosexuality in popular culture*. New York: Routledge.
_____ (2005). *Thinking straight: The power, the promise, and the paradox of heterosexuality*. New York: Routledge.
Jackson, Stevi (1996). Heterosexuality and feminist theory, in D. Richardson (ed.), *Theorising heterosexuality*. Buckingham: Open University Press.
_____ (1999). *Heterosexuality in Question*. London: Sage.
_____ (2005). Sexuality, heterosexuality, and gender hierarchy: Getting our priorities straight, in C. Ingraham (ed.), *Thinking straight*. New York: Routledge.
Johnson, Allan (2000). *Blackwell dictionary of sociology*. London: Blackwell.
Kaplan, M. B. (1997). *Sexual justice: Democratic citizenship and the politics of desire*. New York: Routledge.
Katz, Jonathan (1996). *The invention of heterosexuality*. New York: Penguin.
Kessler, Susanne (1990). The medical construction of gender: Case management of intersexed infants, *Signs* 16(1): 3–26.
Kramer, Laura (2001). *Sociology of gender*. New York: Roxbury.
Lorber, Judith (1994). *Paradoxes of gender*. New Haven, CT: Yale University Press.
_____ (2002). Heroes, warriors, and burqas: a feminist sociologist's reflections on September 11. *Sociological Forum* 17: 377–96.
_____ (2005). *Breaking the Bowls: Degendering and Feminist Change*. New York: W. W. Norton.
Otnes, Cele and Elizabeth Pleck (2003). *Cinderella dreams: the allure of the lavish wedding*. Berkley, CA: University of California Press.
Purple September Staff (1975). The normative status of heterosexuality, in *Lesbianism and the Women's Movement*. Baltimore, MD: Diana Press.
Ramazanoglu, Caroline (1995). Back to basics: Heterosexuality, biology, and why men stay on top, in M. Maynard and J. Purvis (eds), *(Hetero)sexual politics*. London: Taylor and Francis.

Redstockings Collective (1975). *Feminist revolution*. New York: Random House.
Renzetti, Claire and Daniel Curran. (2003). *Women, men, and society*. Boston, MA: Allyn and Bacon.
Rich, Adrienne (1980). Compulsory heterosexuality and lesbian existence. *Signs*, 5 (Summer): 631–60.
Richardson, Diane (1996). Heterosexuality and social theory, in D. Richardson (ed.), *Theorizing heterosexuality: Telling it straight*. Buckingham: Open University Press.
_____ (2005). Claiming citizenship? Sexuality, citizenship and lesbian feminist theory, in C. Ingraham (ed.), *Thinking straight*. New York: Routledge.
Roughgarden, Joan (2004). *Evolution's rainbow: Diversity, sexuality, and gender in nature and people*. Berkeley, CA: University of California Press.
Rubin, Gayle (1975). The traffic of women: Notes on the political economy of sex, in R. Reiter (ed.), *Toward an Anthropology of Women*, New York: Monthly Review Press, pp. 157–210.
Sedgwick, Eve (1990). *Epistemology of the closet*. Berkeley, CA: University of California Press.
Seidman, Steven (1991). *Romantic longings: Love in America, 1830–1980*. New York: Routledge.
_____ (1992). *Embattled Eros: Sexual politics and ethics in contemporary America*. New York: Routledge.
_____ (1995). *Queer Theory/Sociology*. London: Blackwell.
Smith, Dorothy (1989). *The everyday world as problematic*. Boston, MA: Northeastern University Press.
Walsh, Margaret (2005). Out of wedlock: why some poor women reject marriage, in C. Ingraham (ed.), *Thinking straight*. New York: Routledge.
Warner, Michael (1993). *Fear of a queer planet: Queer politics and social theory*. Minneapolis: University of Minnesota Press.
Wittig, Monique (1992). *The straight mind and other essays*. Hemel Hempstead: Harvester Wheatsheaf.

18

Foregrounding Friendship

Feminist Pasts, Feminist Futures

Sasha Roseneil

Friendship is an understudied yet vitally important topic for gender and women's studies. Looking back over the history of feminist writings on women's same-sex friendships, the first section of the chapter explores the importance placed on friendship by earlier generations of feminists across the twentieth century. Focusing on polemical, theoretical and empirical considerations of friendship, I suggest that friendship has been fundamental to feminist politics, identities and communities. The second part of the chapter then sets out an argument for the centrality of friendship – same-sex, male and female, and cross-sex – to feminist research agendas, now and in the future. The lens of friendship facilitates a radical challenge to the heteronormativity of the social sciences, and draws our attention to the ways in which intimate life is being reconfigured at the start of the twenty-first century.

INTRODUCTION

Personal and political, private and public, a source of pleasure and sometimes pain, friendship is indubitably a feminist issue. Without powerful, chosen bonds of affection and care between women, feminism would be unthinkable, women's movements impossible, everyday life in inhospitable environments lonely. Yet, in relation to its importance in feminist lives and politics, friendship has received little attention within the field of gender and women's studies. Unlike most of the topics addressed in this volume, it rarely has whole courses dedicated to its study, and there are few feminist scholars for whom friendship is a primary field of research. It is not just gender and women's studies which have neglected friendship; right across the disciplines – philosophy, history, sociology, anthropology, psychology – as a non-institutionalized, particularistic, affective relationship, friendship has been marginal to dominant themes and perspectives. This is starting to change. With the widespread cultural revaluing of the sphere of the personal in the wake of the women's liberation movement, there is emerging a corpus of research and writing about friendship.[1]

Friendship offers feminism a focus on the agentic, non-institutional, emotional, and pleasurable aspects of social life. It suggests a different theoretical worldview from one which attends primarily to the structures of gender oppression, to the institutional arenas through which domination and subordination are reproduced. While friendship is never outside the relations of power which shape the social world, neither is it is ever fundamentally contained or defined by the core social institutions of family, work, and nation.[2] Friendship may arise in families and in workplaces, and discourses of friendship and enmity between men, of men's homorelational affiliation and preference, have historically grounded nation-states, but friendship is characteristically and distinctively interstitial, unregulated, voluntary and driven by the pursuit of pleasure. It contrasts, therefore, with formal, legally regulated, and institutionalized personal relations between husband and wife, parent and child, citizen and state, which are more usually the subject of academic study.

Part retrospective review, part manifesto for future feminist agendas, this chapter stakes a claim for the centrality of friendship to gender and women's studies, arguing that foregrounding friendship is a radical move for feminism, in multiple meanings of the word 'radical'. The first section – the retrospective review – focuses on key twentieth-century feminist writings on women's same-sex friendships, encompassing polemical, theoretical, and empirical engagements with the topic. It takes feminism back to its roots historically, back to the importance placed on friendship by earlier generations of feminists, to friendship as the root or base of feminism, as an inherent, fundamental part of feminism. The second section argues for the importance of friendship more broadly – same-sex, men and women, and cross-sex – in feminist research. I suggest that the lens of friendship is an important one for feminist futures because it enables a challenge to the heteronormativity of the social sciences and facilitates attention to some of the radical transformations in the organization of intimate life which characterize the early twenty-first century.

FEMINISM ON WOMEN'S FRIENDSHIPS

At the heart of twentieth-century Western feminist writing about women's same-sex friendships is a shared belief in the necessity of ties of affection between women as part of the project of transforming gender relations. Woven through this body of work, more or less explicitly, are two understandings of friendship, which explain why feminism values women's friendship: friendship is seen as political solidarity, as constitutive of feminist movements and the basis of collective identity, and it is seen as a mode of personal support, intimacy and care, and, as such, productive of self-identity. I will approach the literature in terms of four distinct, but interrelated, moves which are made within it: identifying the importance of women's friendships; writing histories of women's friendships; debating the meanings of women's friendships; and revaluing women's friendships. The discussion is necessarily highly selective, but offers an overview of key writers, issues, and moments in the development of feminist engagements with friendship.

Identifying the importance of women's friendships

One of the first disquisitions on the importance of women's friendships was Virginia Woolf's essay, *A Room of One's Own* (1993). Originally delivered as a lecture at Girton, a women's college of Cambridge University, in 1928, the year equal suffrage was finally extended to women in Britain, it is one of a number of polemical pieces of non-fiction in which Woolf explores the disadvantages suffered by women as a result of their exclusion from men's homosocial worlds of public school and Oxbridge. In the course of an extended consideration of the material and social conditions which constrain women's creativity, particularly in relation to writing, she discusses the disruptive, thought-provoking impact a novel by Mary Carmichael had on her:

> Then I may tell you that the very next words I read were these –'Chloe liked Olivia…': Do not start. Do not blush. Let us admit in the privacy of our own society that these things sometimes happen. Sometimes women like women.
> 'Chloe liked Olivia', I read. And then it struck me how immense a change was there. Chloe liked Olivia perhaps for the first time in literature. Cleopatra did not like Octavia. And how completely *Antony and Cleopatra* would have been altered has she done so! As it is, I thought, letting my mind wander a little from *Life's Adventure*, the whole thing is simplified, conventionalized, if one dared say it, absurdly. Cleopatra's only feeling about Octavia is one of jealousy. Is she taller than I am? How does she do her hair? The play, perhaps, required no more. But how interesting it would have been if the relationship between the two women had been more complicated. All these relationships between women, I thought, rapidly recalling the splendid gallery of fictitious women, are too simple. So much has been left out, unattempted. And I tried to remember any case in the course of my reading where two women are represented as friends. (1993: 74–75)

In the literary classics, Woolf notes, 'almost without exception' women 'are shown in their relation to men', with the effect that only a very limited part of women's lives are represented. She goes on to ponder how it would be if 'men were only represented in literature as the lovers of women, and were never friends of men, soldiers, thinkers, dreamers; how few parts in the plays of Shakespeare could be allotted to them; how literature would suffer!' It is important, she suggests, in Carmichael's novel, that Chloe and Olivia 'shared a laboratory', that their friendship existed outside the confines of the domestic sphere 'which will of itself make their friendship more varied and lasting because it will be less personal'. Here she is identifying the importance of women's friendships as relationships not just of the private sphere, but as part of their presence in the public world, from which they had for so long been excluded. Once women's relationships with each other become representable, 'something of great importance has happened':

> For if Chloe likes Olivia and Mary Carmichael knows how to express it she will light a torch in that vast chamber where nobody has yet been. It is all half lights and profound shadows like those serpentine caves where one goes with a candle peering up and down, not knowing where one is stepping. (1993: 76)

Women's experience, in all its complexity and diversity, becomes explorable, because women are no longer seen just in relation to men. And from the moment when Chloe's affection for Olivia is written, it also becomes possible, Woolf suggests, to write more truthfully – more critically – about men.

As Michèle Barrett (1993) points out, Woolf had a great capacity to anticipate concerns which would preoccupy feminists in the future. While very much of its time, and reflecting Woolf's class position and her preoccupations as 'the daughter of an educated man', *A Room of One's Own* is suggestive of important issues in later feminist work on women's friendships. First and foremost, it identifies the cultural neglect of women's friendships and links this neglect to the limited roles and representations of women that have been culturally available. Presaging much later feminist analyses of 'heteroreality' (Raymond, 1986), and queer usage of the concept of heteronormativity, it identifies, without naming it as such, the heterorelational worldview which can only see women in relation to men, and which thereby obscures women in relation to other women. It also points to the impact of this heterorelationality on the representation of women as individuals – to the way in which this restricts vastly the conceptualization of what women can do, be, and feel.

The possibility of friendship between women, particularly outside the private sphere, opens up vistas of creativity and experience that are otherwise unimaginable when women are only seen in relation to men. In addition, a debate can be seen to begin, which comes to characterize feminist writing on women's friendship, about the meaning of Woolf's 'woman-oriented' position in this essay. '"*Chloe liked Olivia…*": *Do not start. Do not blush. Let us admit in the privacy of our own society that these things sometimes happen. Sometimes women like women*' can certainly be read as suggestive of lesbianism as much as of feminism. Barrett (1993: xxiii) points to Woolf's own prediction, with reference to the publication of *A Room of One's Own*, that 'I shall be attacked for a feminist and hinted at for a Sapphist', and to the fact that she wrote it during the period of her intense relationship with Vita Sackville-West, and around the time of the publication of *Orlando*, her tribute to their relationship.

Writing histories of women's friendships

In the context of the women's liberation movement, with its emphasis on the importance of women working and creating communities together, and as part of the political project of revaluing women's friendships, a body of research emerged from the mid-1970s onwards which sought to document the history of women's friendships, networks, and communities. Largely relying on personal letters and diaries, feminist historians engaged with the challenge of writing the history of intimate relationships which by their very nature lack public documentation. Much of this work focused on the eighteenth and nineteenth centuries, when industrialization and the separation of work and home which accompanied it had established in the Western middle and upper classes a structure and ideology of separate spheres for men and women.

Caroll Smith Rosenberg's groundbreaking essay (1975) explores the 'female world of love and ritual' which existed in the intense homosocial networks of women between the mid-eighteenth and mid-nineteenth centuries. She was concerned with the passionate emotional and often erotic ties between married women within which they offered each other psychological support, and which were entirely culturally acceptable. This women's culture is further explored by Nancy Cott (1977), whose study of New England between 1780 and 1835 researched the development of a shared gender identity among women through common experiences of life and work. Cott emphasizes that models of women's friendship were consciously developed, and argues that the feminist political movement of the nineteenth century emerged out of women's shared experiences under the doctrine of separate spheres. A few years later Lillian Faderman (1985) published what was to become a much debated book on 'romantic friendship and love between women' from the Renaissance onwards. Her research suggests that 'it was virtually impossible to study the correspondence of any nineteenth century woman, not only of America but also of England, France, and Germany, and not uncover a passionate commitment to another woman at some time in her life' (p. 16). 'Romantic friendships' between women were considered noble and virtuous in the eighteenth century, and in the nineteenth century several terms to describe love relationships between women were in common usage–'sentimental friends', 'Boston marriages', and 'the love of kindred spirits'.

Taken together, this body of work suggests that close, primary friendships between women were widespread in this period, and that these existed within a culture which was broadly supportive of such relationships. These friendships were characterized by high degrees of self-revelation and intimacy and extensive participation in shared activities, such as charitable, religious, moral, and educational associations. They offered emotional support and companionship, and there are many examples of how, for particular women, they underpinned and facilitated movement into the world of feminist public work and/or political activism. Carol Lasser's (1988) discussion of Antoinette Brown and Lucy Stone's forty-seven-year-long intimate friendship, for instance, emphasizes how the mutual supportiveness of their 'elective sisterhood' sustained them in their respective work, Brown in the women's suffrage movement and Stone in developing a feminist engagement with Protestant theology. Phillipa Levine's (1990) study of friendship among nineteenth-century English feminists identifies passionate friendships between many women and holds that these relationships were the basis for feminist political activism. She describes the role that women's clubs, which were established in most major cities, played in the formation of such friendships, and then the way in which friendships served to support women in their political work. Heloise Brown and Krista Cowman (1999), in their essay on friendships within the British suffrage movement, argue that friendship became an important part of suffrage discourse, and that it differed from the notion of comradeship which served as a mobilizing discourse in the male-dominated socialist movement. They cite Ethel Smyth's suffrage anthem, 'The March of the Women', which was regularly sung at gatherings of activists, as highlighting the political nature of friendship within the movement:

> Firm in reliance, laugh a defiance
> (Laugh in hope for sure is the end)
> March, march, many as one
> Shoulder to shoulder and friend to friend
>
> (Smyth and Hamilton, 1911, in Brown and Cowman, 1999: 122)

Faderman (1985) seeks to explain why the positive cultural value attributed to the intense relationships between women in the eighteenth and nineteenth century changed in the early years of the twentieth century. She argues that such friendships came to be pathologized, particularly by psychoanalysis and sexology, which labelled formerly unclassified behaviour as erotic, so that passionate love for a friend of the same sex came to signal a deviant sexual identity.[3] She links this 'morbidification', the shift in attitudes to women's same-sex relationships, to the increased possibility of their economic independence from men, and identifies a patriarchal impetus to rein women into heterosexual bonds. With the decline in the separateness of the worlds of men and women, as women entered education and paid work, companionable and intimate heterosexual bonds emerged as the desired arena of intimacy. By the mid-twentieth century, there had developed a new culture emphasizing mutual disclosure between husband and wife, and valuing the importance to the marriage of socializing as a couple and participating in joint leisure activities. While intimate friendships persisted between women, they had far less cultural recognition and validation than a century earlier.

Debating the meaning of women's friendships

As we have seen, already in the 1920s Virginia Woolf was well aware of the possibility that her discussion of Chloe and Olivia's mutual affection could be read as 'Sapphic'. It is not surprising, then, that in the context of the emergence of lesbian feminism as a powerful intellectual current and political force within the women's liberation movement, a vigorous debate developed about the extent to which women's friendships of earlier times should be understood as sexual. Smith Rosenberg's (1975) article draws attention to the homoerotic dimensions of the relationships she was studying, and Blanche Wiesen Cook's (1977) study of the female support networks of women activists of the late nineteenth and early twentieth century (Lillian Wald, Chrystal Eastman, Emma Goldman) explored the possibility of sexual relationships among her subjects. Wiesen Cook argues women's networks of this era included relationships which ranged from acquaintanceship to long-term sexual relationships. Both Smith Rosenberg and Wiesen Cook suggest that there was a continuum of women's same-sex relationships, and grant a place to the sexual in their analyses. However, Faderman differs in her construal of nineteenth-century romantic friendships from Smith Rosenberg and Wiesen Cook. Regarding them as 'love relationships in every sense except perhaps the genital', she argues that prior to the twentieth century women 'internalized the view of females as having little sexual passion'. So, 'they might kiss, fondle each other, sleep together, utter expressions of overwhelming love and promises of eternal faithfulness, and yet see their passions as nothing more than effusions of the spirit' (1985: 16). While not denying the possibility of *any* sexual contact between romantic friends, she downplays the importance of the sexual, explaining it in terms of dominant cultural constructions of femininity. Nonetheless, she is prepared to call these intense, sex-free passions between women 'lesbian' (p. 19).

Faderman has been widely criticized, by, for instance, Martha Vicinus (1992), Liz Stanley (1992), and Judith Halberstam (1998), for assuming the asexual nature of women's same-sex relations in the past, and for at the same time being prepared to call them 'lesbian'.[4] Indeed, the publication of the extensive and highly explicit diaries of a nineteenth-century English landowner, Anne Lister, in which she describes her sexual relationships with, and conquests of, other women, underlines the problems with Faderman's analysis (Whitbread, 1988; 1992). But this does not necessarily mean that it is useful to use the term 'lesbian' to describe relationships between women which might have been sexual. As Halberstam points out, from a Foucauldian history of sexuality perspective, 'lesbian' refers to same-sex desire between women in the mid- to late twentieth century, in the context of the rise of feminism and a politics of homosexual 'reverse discourse'; it does not work as a transhistorical term for all same-sex activity between women (Halberstam, 1998: 51). There are problems, therefore, *both* with labelling such connections 'lesbian' *and* with denying the possibility of sexual dimensions. Ultimately, the sexual nature of particular close relationships between women in the past is a matter for empirical investigation and creative speculation, and often, given the nature of the sources available, the question will remain open. The lens of friendship, if combined with a willingness to acknowledge same-sex desire and sexuality, should, as Stanley (1992) argues, enable the full range of relations between women to be investigated, and their meanings for the women themselves, and for present day readers, to be explored.

Revaluing women's friendship

Central to the theory and practice of second-wave feminism was a belief that solidarity between women was vital. Writing in the late 1940s, in her groundbreaking treatise *The Second Sex*, Simone de Beauvoir clearly articulated the cultural problems feminism faced in this regard, demonstrating the necessity of a consciously pro-woman politics:

> Young girls quickly tire of one another. They do not band together…for their mutual benefit; and this is one of the reasons why the company of boys is necessary to them. (1968: 335)

> Women's fellow feeling rarely rises to genuine friendship, however. Women feel their solidarity more spontaneously than men; but within this solidarity the transcendence of each does not go out towards the others… each is against the others. (1968: 544)

> In fact, the theme of woman betrayed by her best friend is not a mere literary convention; the more friendly two women are, the more dangerous their duality becomes. (1968: 545)

Whether de Beauvoir was empirically correct or not in her observations, it is clear that she was articulating a widely held view about the impossibility of true friendship between women, a notion which survives in popular ideas that women together are inclined to 'bitchiness' or 'cattiness'.

In second-wave feminism, it was radical feminists – Mary Daly (1978), Adrienne Rich (1980), and Janice Raymond (1986), in particular – who initially took up the challenge of shifting such attitudes, developing an explicit agenda that sought to revalue women's friendships. In Mary Daly's *Gyn/ecology*, 'woman-loving Spinsters/Lesbians' are held to be the true carriers of feminist politics, for whom friendship is at the core of politics and life, and all love relationships are based on friendship. She emphasizes that feminist friendship must be between whole, independent selves, as opposed to 'bonding out of weakness' (1978: 342). Poet and essayist Rich sets out both to challenge the historical denial of lesbian existence and to valorize all forms of female relationality in her polemical essay 'Compulsory Heterosexuality and Lesbian Existence'. There, she coined the controversial concept of the 'lesbian continuum', which she explains thus:

I mean the term to include a range – through each woman's life and throughout history – of woman-identified experience, not simply the fact that a woman has had or consciously desired genital sexual experience with another woman. If we expand it to embrace many more forms of primary intensity between and among women ... we begin to grasp the breadths of female history and psychology which have lain out of reach as a consequence of limited almost clinical definitions of *lesbianism*. (Rich, 1980: 51–52)

It is beyond the scope of this chapter to discuss the extensive debate which ensued about Rich's essay, because it takes us away from our central concern with friendship. Suffice it to say that there are clear parallels between the controversy about whether Rich's expansive definition of lesbian existence served to erase sexuality as the core of lesbian identity, and to deny the specificity of the lesbian lives and history, including the costs and dangers of lesbian identity,[5] and the controversy about whether some of the friendships of women in the past should be understood as lesbian.

Raymond's *A Passion for Friends* carries forward Daly's project of centring friendship in feminism and is one of the few book-length feminist engagements with friendship. She traces genealogies of women's friendship ('gyn/affection') across the centuries and explores how it has been both the source of great pleasure and strength for women and the subject of philosophical and literary neglect, social and cultural disapprobation, and sanctions. Raymond argues that 'heteroreality', the worldview that woman exists always in relation to man ('heterorelations'), can be challenged by women's friendships with each other, which (in Aristotelian tradition) in turn depend on women's affinity with their own 'vital Self'. She offers a philosophical engagement with the question of the cultural value attached to women's friendships, the values, ethics, and political implications of friendship, and the micro and macro gender politics within which women's friendships are lived. Her work also highlights the ontological question of relationship between 'the self' and 'the friend'.

It was in the day-to-day practice of second-wave feminism that the project of revaluing women's friendships really took hold and began to effect social change. Activists in the women's liberation movement in the 1970s initially adopted a discourse of sisterhood to express solidarity between women – 'sisterhood is powerful' – but it was elective bonds of friendship between women which proved to be vital in sustaining feminist communities, collectives, households, projects, and political groups. For instance, my research (Roseneil, 1995; 2000a) on the Greenham Common Women's Peace Camp and the wider women's peace movement in Britain in the 1980s suggests that through involvement in women's movement activism, women came to revalue friendship with other women. Women involved in the movement formed intense and close relationships with each other, which were very different from friendships they had experienced with women before. They realized that they had learnt not to value other women's company and that their social orientations had been constructed as heterorelational:

I found out what it was like to be really close to women and to be really friends with women, and how good women are together. All that was new to me. (Barbara Rawson)

I'd never really had friendships with women on their own. When you're married, you have friendships with another couple…When we first formed the group in Derby it just opened my eyes. I'd never seen anything like it. It was amazing…It was the way that women could be together and be friends and talk about things and do things together. It was something I hadn't encountered. I'd been brought up to think that anything that you did with women was really secondary, your marriage was the thing and your husband, and the things you did with your husband. If you went and had coffee with another woman that was just a bit of frivolity. It wasn't your real life. (Leah Thalmann)

And, reminiscent of de Beauvoir's position:

So many women said to me, 'it's so nice living with women. I never thought it would be'. And it was clear that they had these concepts that obviously patriarchy fosters, that women together are just a disaster, that they squabble and fight, and they can't get anything done. (Katrina Allen)

(Roseneil, 2000a: 281)

As a community and a social movement Greenham cohered as much, if not more, through the emotional ties of friendship, love, and sexual intimacy between the women who were part of it, as through shared politics and philosophies. Indeed, a valuing of all forms of same-sex affection, love, and care was fundamental to the politics and philosophy of Greenham. This was seen both as part of the feminist political project of transforming the dominant social relations of gender and sexuality, and as an everyday, life-sustaining pleasure.

FRIENDSHIP AND FUTURE FEMINIST AGENDAS

Thus far I have shown how women's same-sex friendships were important to twentieth-century feminism. In this section I go on to propose that the study of friendship should be central to twenty-first-century feminist agendas. The question of how people organize their personal lives, loving and caring for each other in contexts of social, cultural, and economic changes which increasingly demand the pursuit of individual life strategies, is a key concern for social scientists and policy-makers, and a major issue for feminist researchers internationally. It is my argument that if we are to understand the current state, and likely future, of intimacy and care, we need to foreground friendship as a social relationship, and de-centre the 'family' and the heterosexual couple in our intellectual imaginaries. While the idea of 'family' retains an almost unparalleled ability to move people, both emotionally and politically, much that matters to people in terms of intimacy and care increasingly takes place beyond 'family', in and among networks of friends. Indeed, as feminist historical work on friendship discussed above suggests, it is probably the case that far more of people's affective lives has always taken place outside 'family' than has been recognized by social scientists.

As the global distribution and mainstream success of a plethora of television shows such as *Friends*, *Seinfeld*, *Ellen*, and *Will and Grace* attests, popular culture is proving rather better at proffering stories which explore the burgeoning diversity of contemporary practices of intimacy and care than are academic researchers. If we were to seek our understanding of cultures of intimacy and care from the social scientific literature, we would be given to believe that they are still almost solely practiced under the auspices of 'family'. This is not to deny that the gender and women's studies scholars have sought to meet both the empirical challenge of social changes in family and gender relations and the theoretical challenge of anti-essentialist, postmodern, Black and minority ethnic feminist, and lesbian and gay emphases on difference and diversity. They have responded by pluralizing the notion of 'family', so that they now always speak of 'families', and they emphasize the diversity of family forms and experiences, how the membership of families changes over time, as they break down and re-form, and they welcome lesbian and gay 'families of choice' into the 'family tent' (Stacey, 2002). This shift has been an important one, particularly as a counter to the anti-feminist and anti-gay public political discourse of 'family values', which developed in the United States and Britain during the 1980s and 1990s. However, these moves to pluralize notions of 'family', even when they embrace the study of lesbian and gay families, are insufficient to the task of understanding both the contemporary and the future experience of intimacy and care for two reasons. First, they leave unchanged the heteronormativity of the social scientific imaginary, and second, they are not grounded in an adequate analysis of contemporary social change because they do not recognize the increasing importance of friendship. Let us look at each of these issues in turn.

Challenging heteronormativity: friendship matters

Gender and women's studies, as well as sociology, continue to marginalize the study of love, intimacy, care, and sociality which takes place beyond what they define as 'family'; even though the definition of 'family' – or at least 'families of choice' – may have been expanded in scope. Heteronormative assumptions continue to produce analyses which are overwhelmingly focused on monogamous, dyadic, co-residential (and primarily hetero) sexual relationships, particularly those which have produced children, and on changes within these relationships. Jo Van Every's (1999) systematic survey of British research and writing on families and households published in one year, 1993, found that there was 'an overwhelming focus on the "modern nuclear family"': that is, on married couples who lived together in households only with their children. She argues convincingly that 'despite all the sociological talk about the difficulty of defining families and the plurality and diversity of family forms in contemporary (postmodern?) societies, sociologists were helping to construct a "normal" family which looked remarkably similar to that which an earlier generation of sociologists felt confident to define' (1999: 167).

The 'non-standard intimacies' (Berlant and Warner, 2000) created by those living non-normative sexualities pose a particular challenge to a field which has studied intimacy and care primarily through the study of families. Although some lesbians and gay men refer to their emotional networks quite consciously — often with a knowing irony — as 'family', the adoption of the term 'families of choice' by writers such as Kath Weston (1991), Jeffrey Weeks, Brian Heaphy, and Catherine Donovan (2001),[6] and Judith Stacey (2004) to refer to lesbian and gay relationships and friendship networks actually serves to direct attention away from the extra-familial, counter-heteronormative nature of many of these relationships.

There is considerable evidence to suggest that friendship, as both a practice and an ethic, is of foundational and particular importance in the lives of lesbians and gay men.[7] Networks of friends, which often include ex-lovers, form the context within which lesbians and gay men tend to lead their personal lives, offering emotional continuity, companionship, pleasure, and practical assistance. Building and maintaining lives outside the framework of the heterosexual nuclear family, and sometimes rejected or marginalized by their families of origin, lesbians and gay men ground their emotional security and daily lives in their friendship groups. Weeks et al. (2001), Sasha Roseneil (2000, a; c), and Jacqueline Weinstock and Esther Rothblum (2004) draw attention to the blurring of the boundaries of, and the movement between, friendship and sexual relationships which often characterizes contemporary lesbian and gay intimacies: friends become lovers, and lovers become friends — and many have multiple sexual partners of varying degrees of commitment (and none). Moreover, an individual's 'significant other' may not be someone with whom she or he has a sexual relationship (Preston with Lowenthal, 1996: 1). These practices de-centre the primary significance that is commonly granted to sexual partnerships and challenge the privileging of conjugal relationships in research on intimacy. Non-normative intimacies — those between friends, non-monogamous lovers, ex-lovers, partners who do not live together, partners who do not have sex together, those which do not easily fit the 'friend'/'lover' binary classification system — and the networks of relationships within which these intimacies are sustained (or not) largely fail to be registered in a literature which retains an imaginary which, without ever explicitly acknowledging it, sees the heterosexual couple as the heart of the social formation, as that which pumps the life-blood of social reproduction. It is time for this heterosexual imaginary to change and for research which focuses both on friendship and on 'non-conventional' forms of sexual/love relationships — and the interconnections between the two — a move that was heralded in some of the feminist work on the history of women's same-sex friendships discussed earlier.[8]

Analysing social change: friendship is becoming more important

As we have seen from these feminist histories, friendship is a socially constructed relationship whose meanings and practices change over time. The second element of my argument that feminism should take friendship seriously suggests that we do so because friendship is a relationship of increasing social significance in the contemporary world.

The version of friendship which emerged in the mid-twentieth century, which promoted the companionate intimate heterosexual couple as the primary arena of intimacy and emphasized a new culture of mutual disclosure between husband and wife and the importance of joint leisure activities, has recently started to be unsettled. Shifts in gender and family relations, processes of individualization, and the postmodernization of relations of sexuality are socially and culturally de-centring heterorelations and destabilizing – or *queering* – the distinctions between heterosexual and homosexual ways of life.[9] As geographical mobility increases, as marriage rates drop and marriage takes place later in life, as divorce rates have soared over the past thirty years, as births outside marriage, and indeed outside any lasting heterosexual relationship, increase steeply, as the proportion of people living in single-person households rises, and the proportion of women not having children climbs, patterns of sociability – as well as the more widely discussed patterns of intimacy – are undergoing transformation (Beck and Beck Gernsheim, 1995; Giddens, 1992). A smaller proportion of the population is living in the heterosexual nuclear family of idealized mid-twentieth-century form, and fewer people are choosing or able to construct their intimate relations according to the symmetrical family, intimate-couple model. In 2003, only 22 per cent of households in Britain comprised a heterosexual couple with dependent children (National Statistics, 2004). This increasingly means that ways of life that might previously have been regarded as distinctively 'homosexual' are becoming more widespread. As Weeks, et al. have suggested, 'one of the most remarkable features of domestic change over recent years is…the emergence of common patterns in homosexual and heterosexual ways of life as a result of these long-term shifts in relationship patterns' (2001: 85).

The significance of these processes of individualization calls for attention to the relationship and caring practices of those living at the leading edge of social change. Evidence from the British Household Panel Study shows that men and women who are divorced are more likely to see a close friend during the week than those who are married. Moreover, the British Social Attitudes report suggests that people are more likely to have seen their 'best friend' than any relative who does not live with them in the previous week. While there has been a decline in the proportion of respondents seeing relatives or friends at least once a week between 1986 and 1995, the decline in contact with friends was considerably smaller (Pahl, 1998). Peter Willmott's (1987) research also suggests that friends were, by the mid-1980s, more important than relatives or neighbours in terms of providing practical help with everyday tasks. It seems highly unlikely that this trend will suddenly change and that there will be a reversion to the forms of familial and neighbourly assistance which were reported in the working-class localities researched in the British community studies of the 1950s (such as Hodges and Smith, 1954; Young and Willmott, 1957).

There is a new cultural emphasis on *post-heterorelational* friendship and a popular celebration of it. It is no coincidence that *Friends* is consistently the most popular television comedy across the Western world. The show speaks to the experience, desires, and hopes of a generation which is constructing its lives outside mid-twentieth-century notions of heterosexual intimate relationships, and which seeks comfort, stability, and companionship in networks of friends rather than in a dyadic relationship. As the theme song declares, friends are there for you, every day, when life is going well and when it's going badly. Many other television programmes which have captured the popular imagination share this focus on lives built around friends in which sexual relationships come and go but friends remain: *This Life, Men Behaving Badly, Seinfeld*, for instance. Magazines for women and girls seem to be placing a stronger emphasis on the importance of same-sex friendship, with the focus on 'getting and keeping' a man losing its centrality. In the 1990s, the pop group Spice Girls' valorizing of girls' and women's same-sex friendships with each other extended a pro(to)feminist emphasis on same-sex friendships into a younger age group. Perhaps even more significantly, men are now constantly enjoined by agony uncles, opinion writers, and advertisers to spend time and emotional effort developing their friendships with other men, to go out to dinner with a close male friend, to telephone their male friends for a chat, and to talk about their feelings with any friend, man or woman, who will listen.

Case-study example

Research I have carried out with Shelley Budgeon (Roseneil and Budgeon, 2004) adds weight to the idea that friendship is an increasingly socially significant relationship. This research has investigated how the most 'individualized' in our society – people who do not live with a partner – construct their networks of intimacy, friendship, care, and support. We wanted to find out who matters to people who are living outside conventional families, what they value about their personal relationships, how they care for those who matter to them, and how they care for themselves. We carried out in-depth interviews with fifty-three people aged 25 to 60 years old in three locations – a former mining town that is relatively conventional in terms of gender and family relations; a small town in which alternative, middle-class, 'down-shifted' lifestyles and sexual non-conformity are common; and a multi-ethnic, inner-city area characterized by a range of gender and family practices, a higher-than-average proportion of women in the labour force, and a large number of single-person and non-couple households. We talked to men and women with and without children, of a diversity of ages, ethnic origins, occupations, and sexual orientations, with varying relationship status and living arrangements. This gave us detailed insight into the texture of people's emotional lives.

We found that across a range of lifestyles and sexualities, friendship occupies a central place in the personal lives of our interviewees. Whether they were in a heterosexual couple relationship or not, the people we interviewed were turning to friends for emotional support. Jools, a heterosexual woman of 28 from a former mining town, spoke for many people when she said: 'I think a friendship is for life, but I don't think a partner is…I'd marry my friends. They'd last longer.' There was a high degree of reliance on friends, as opposed to biological kin and sexual partners, particularly for the provision of care and support in everyday life, and friendship operated as a key value and site of ethical practice for many. Far from being isolated, solitary individuals who flit from one unfulfilling relationship to another, most of the people we interviewed were enmeshed in complex networks of intimacy and care, and had strong commitments and connections to others. In contrast to the mythology of the singleton in desperate search for a marriage partner – exemplified by Bridget Jones – very few showed any yearning to be part of a conventional couple or family. A great many, both those with partners and those without, were consciously placing less emphasis on the importance of the couple relationship. Instead, they were centring their lives on their friends. Of those with partners, almost all had *chosen* not to live together. Very few saw cohabitation as the inevitable and desirable next stage of their relationship.

Many of the interviewees had experienced the ending of a marriage or a long-term cohabiting relationship, and the pain and disruption the break-up had caused had made them question the wisdom of putting all of their emotional eggs in one basket. The people who mattered were either friends or a combination of friends, partner, children, and family. This was not a temporary phase, and people did not return to conventional couple relationships as soon as an opportunity arose. Re-interviewing people eighteen months later, we found a remarkably consistent prioritization of friendship.

Friends were an important part of everyday life in good times and bad. Most of the people we spoke to put considerable effort into building and maintaining friendships in the place where they lived. A good number had moved house, or had persuaded friends to move house, with the aim of creating local friendship networks that could offer reciprocal childcare and help in times of illness, as well as pleasurable sociability. It was friends far more than biological kin who offered support to those who suffered from emotional distress or mental health problems and who were there to pick up the pieces when love relationships ended. Many of the people we interviewed were opening up their homes to people who were not part of their conventionally defined family. It was not just the twenty-somethings who spent much of their leisure time hanging out with friends at each other's homes or having people in to dinner, parties, and barbecues. Friends were invited to stay during periods of homelessness, when out of work, or when they were depressed or lonely.

What this research suggests is that researchers have often failed to recognize the extent to which, as a matter of preference, people are substituting the ties of friendship for those of blood, particularly with regard to everyday care and emotional support. If gender and women's studies are interested in thinking about the social world of the twenty-first century, a shift in gaze beyond the study of 'the family' as the privileged locus of practices of intimacy and care is necessary, and a refocusing on friendship is vital. In the context of processes of individualization and the destabilization of the homosexual/heterosexual binary, there is a need for an approach which is able to grasp the ways in which what matters to people in terms of intimacy increasingly exceeds the category of 'family'.

CONCLUSION

This chapter has explored the significance of friendship for feminism and gender and women's studies in the past, and for current and future research agendas. One of the most exciting aspects of the topic of friendship is the way in which it is able to build a bridge between the practices and theoretical concerns of feminists of previous eras and the social transformations of the contemporary world. Indeed, the increasing importance of friendship as a social relationship, which I argued in the second section of the chapter, can be seen, in part, as related to the radical social changes set in train by the feminist politics and theory of earlier times. It is no longer the case that women can only be represented in relation to men. Women's friendship is culturally valued and recognized in ways unimaginable to Virginia Woolf, and women (and men) are building lives outside heterorelations in ever greater numbers, grounding themselves psychically and socially in friendship, as feminists of the second wave were keen to promote. While the organizations, collectives, and communities of the feminist movements of the nineteenth and twentieth centuries have largely faded away, the value they placed on bonds of affection and care outside the familial has permeated contemporary Western societies.

Taking friendship seriously can offer feminism important discursive resources. First, it provides an important counterpoint to the work of public intellectuals such as Zygmunt Bauman (2001; 2003), Robert Putnam (2000), and Richard Sennett (1998), whose ideas have been taken up in a widespread discourse about a supposed crisis in personal relationships and community. These patriarchal pessimists bemoan the demoralizing, anomic impact of individualization and the social transformations of the past three decades on intimacy, community, and personal character, expressing a conservative hankering after a lost golden age of stable families and seemingly more secure structures of care. A recognition of the value that people place on friendship and the care and support that it offers also challenges the familialism that still characterizes the policies of many Western governments. From this recognition we can start to map a political agenda which moves beyond the rhetoric of 'supporting families' (Home Office, 1998), to consider how we can support and recognize the importance of friendship.[10] For instance, work–life balance policies can be framed in terms of the range of important personal relationships and commitments within which people live their lives, rather than narrowly with reference to family responsibilities. Employment benefits should be redefined to extend bereavement leave to apply to all the people about whom an employee cares or with whom he or she shares a special relationship. More radically, it is time to press for the extension of civil partnerships for lesbian and gay couples, now legal in many Western states, to recognize any significant relationship – sexual or otherwise – and to open up fiscal benefits, inheritance, and other rights to those whose intimate lives are not covered by a policy framework which focuses on conjugal couples and families.[11] A progressive feminist policy agenda needs to enable all of those who care for others, whoever they are, to do so with maximum social support and recognition.

That said, friendship is not a universal panacea. It cannot promise to solve all of the problems which face feminism. As a personal relationship which tends to bind together people who are socially similar, it cannot resolve all the political and ethical issues feminism faces, not least the problem of its constitutive outside – the enemy and the stranger. If we are to develop a politics that is not just concerned with those within the charmed circle of love, affection, and care, we have to consider our collective obligations to the lonely, the unloved, and the uncared for. We have to recognize what we all know from personal experience: that friendship is not always easy, that it can struggle with difference, and that it sometimes flounders when friends misrecognize each other. Friendship can cause us pain, as well as offering us care and support. But, nonetheless, foregrounding friendship casts light on feminism's radical past and allows us to understand better how people are living and loving today.

NOTES

1 On gender differences in friendship see Martínez Alemán (1997) and Knickmeyer, Sexton, and Nishimura (2002). For a review of the wider literature on women's friendships see Connor (1992).
2 See Adams and Allan (1998) on the structuring of friendship.

3 However, Stanley (1992) disagrees with Faderman on the role of sexology in this process.
4 See also Traub (2002) for a theoretically engaged history of lesbianism, focusing on early modern England, which takes issue with Faderman.
5 For critiques of the 'lesbian continuum' see Bowles (1984) and Zimmerman (1985).
6 Weeks et al. (2001) discuss the differences between their interviewees in relation to the adoption of the term 'family' to describe their intimate relationships, and acknowledge that many reject the term.
7 See for example, Altman, 1982; Nardi, 1992; 1999; Preston with Lowenthal, 1996; Weeks, 1995; Weeks et al., 2001; Weston, 1991.
8 On the narrowness of the heterosexual imaginary, see Chrys Ingraham in this volume.
9 For a detailed exposition of my 'queering of the social' thesis see Roseneil (2000b; 2002).
10 A Law Commission of Canada (2002) report sets out an agenda for the support of close personal relationships beyond conjugality.
11 The opening up of relationship recognition to friends has occurred in France, with the introduction of the PACS (Pacte Civil de solidarité/Civil solidarity pact), and in 2003, in Tasmania.

REFERENCES

Adams, R. G. and G. Allan (eds) (1998) *Placing Friendship in Context* Cambridge: Cambridge University Press.
Alemán, M. (1997) 'Understanding and Investigating Female Friendship's Educative Value', *Journal of Higher Education*, 68(2): 119–159.
Altman, D. (1982) *The Homosexualization of America* New York: St. Martin's Press.
Barrett, M. (1993) 'Introduction', in V. Woolf *A Room of One's Own, and Three Guineas* Harmondsworth: Penguin. First published 1929.
Bauman, Z. (2001) *The Individualized Society* Cambridge: Polity.
Bauman, Z. (2003) *Liquid Love* Cambridge: Polity.
Beck, U. and E. Beck Gernsheim (1995) *The Normal Chaos of Love* Cambridge: Polity.
Berlant, L. and M. Warner (2000) 'Sex in Public', in L. Berlant (ed.), *Intimacy* Chicago: Chicago University Press.
Bowles, G. (1984) 'Adrienne Rich as Feminist Theorist', in J. R. Cooper (ed.), *Reading Adrienne Rich: Reviews and Re-visions, 1951–1981* Ann Arbor: University of Michigan Press.
Brown, H. and K. Cowman (1999) 'Exploring Suffrage Friendships', in R. Symes, A. Kaloski, and H. Brown (eds), *Celebrating Women's Friendship: Past, Present and Future* York: Raw Nerve Books.
Connor, P. (1992) *Friendships between Women: A Critical Review* Hemel Hempstead: Harvester Wheatsheaf.
Cott, N. (1977) *The Bonds of Womanhood: 'Woman's Sphere' in New England, 1780–1835* New Haven, CT: Yale University Press.
Daly, M. (1978) *Gyn/ecology: The Metaethics of Radical Feminism* Boston, MA: Beacon Press.
de Beauvoir, S. (1968) *The Second Sex* (translated and edited by H. M. Parshley). London: Jonathan Cape.
Faderman, L. (1985) *Surpassing the Love of Men* London: Women's Press.
Giddens, A. (1992) *The Transformation of Intimacy: Sexuality, Love and Eroticism in Modern Societies* Cambridge: Polity.
Halberstam, J. (1998) *Female Masculinity* Durham, NC: Duke University Press.
Hodges, M. W. and C. Smith (1954) 'The Sheffield Estate', in T. Simey (ed.), *Neighbourhood and Community* Liverpool: Liverpool University Press.
Home Office (1998) *Supporting Families: A Consultation Document* London: HMSO.

Knickmeyer, N., K. Sexton, and N. Nishimura (2002) 'The Impact of Same-Sex Friendships on the Well-Being of Women: A Review of the Literature', *Women and Therapy*, 25(1): 37–59.

Lasser, C. (1988) '"Let Us Be Sisters Forever": The Sororal Model of Nineteenth-Century Female Friendship', *Signs: Journal of Women in Culture and Society*, 14(1): 158–181.

Law Commission of Canada (2002) *Beyond Conjugality*. http://www.cga.state.ct.us/2002/olrdata/jud/rpt/2002-R-0172.htm

Levine, P. (1990) 'Love, Friendship and Feminism in Later Nineteenth Century England', *Women's Studies International Forum*, 13: 63–78.

Nardi, P. (1992) 'That's What Friends Are For: Friends as Family in the Gay and Lesbian Community', in K. Plummer (ed.), *Modern Homosexualities: Fragments of Lesbian and Gay Experience* London: Routledge.

Nardi, P. (1999) *Gay Men's Friendships: Invincible Communities* Chicago: Chicago University Press.

National Statistics (2004) *Social Trends No. 34* London: Office for National Statistics.

Pahl, R. (1998) 'Friendship: The Social Glue of Contemporary Society?', in J. Franklin (ed.), *The Politics of Risk Society* Cambridge: Polity.

Preston, J. with M. Lowenthal (eds) (1996) *Friends and Lovers: Gay Men Write about the Families They Create* New York: Plume.

Putnam, R. D. (2000) *Bowling Alone: The Collapse and Revival of American Community* New York: Simon and Schuster.

Raymond, J. (1986) *A Passion for Friends: Toward a Philosophy of Female Affection* London: Women's Press.

Rich, A. (1980) 'Compulsory Heterosexuality and Lesbian Existence', *Signs: Journal of Women in Culture and Society*, 5(4): 631–660.

Roseneil, S. (1995) *Disarming Patriarchy: Feminism and Political Action at Greenham* Milton Keynes: Open University Press.

Roseneil, S. (2000a) *Common Women, Uncommon Practices: The Queer Feminisms of Greenham* London: Cassell.

Roseneil, S. (2000b) 'Queer Frameworks and Queer Tendencies: Towards an Understanding of Postmodern Transformations of Sexuality', *Sociological Research Online*, 5(3): 1–19. http://www.socresonline.org.uk/5/3/roseneil.html

Roseneil, S. (2000c) 'Why we Should Care about Friends: Some Thoughts about the Ethics and Practice of Friendship', ESRC Research Group for the Study of Care, Values and the Future of Welfare Working Paper, 2000, pp. 19. http://www.leeds.ac.uk/cava

Roseneil, S. (2002) 'The Heterosexual/Homosexual Binary: Past, Present and Future', in D. Richardson and S. Seidman (eds), *The Lesbian and Gay Studies Handbook* London: Sage, pp. 27–44.

Roseneil, S. and S. Budgeon (2004) 'Cultures of Intimacy and Care Beyond the Family: Personal Life and Social Change in the Early Twenty-First Century', *Current Sociology*, 52(2): 135–159.

Sennett, R. (1998) *The Corrosion of Character: The Personal Consequences of Work in the New Capitalism* New York: Norton.

Smith Rosenberg, C. (1975) 'The Female World of Love and Ritual: relations between women in nineteenth century America', *Signs: Journal of Women in Culture and Society*, 1(1): 1–29.

Stacey, J. (2002) 'Fellow Families? Genres of Gay Male Intimacy and Kinship in a Global Metropolis', CAVA International Seminar Paper.

Stacey, J. (2004) 'Cruising to Familyland: Gay Hypergamy and Rainbow Kinship', *Current Sociology*, 52(2): 181–198.

Stanley, L. (1992) 'Feminism and Friendship', in *The Auto/biographical I* Manchester: Manchester University Press.

Traub, V. (2002) *The Renaissance of Lesbianism in Early Modern England* Cambridge: Cambridge University Press.

Van Every, J. (1999) 'From Modern Nuclear Family Households to Postmodern Diversity? The Sociological Construction of "Families"', in G. Jagger and C. Wright (eds), *Changing Family Values* London: Routledge.

Vicinus, M. (1992) '"They Wonder to Which Sex I Belong": The Historical Roots of the Modern Lesbian Identity', *Feminist Studies*, 18(3): 467–498.

Weeks, J. (1995) *Invented Moralities: Sexual Values in an Age of Uncertainty* Cambridge: Polity.

Weeks, J., B. Heaphy, and C. Donovan (2001) *Same Sex Intimacies: Families of Choice and Other Life Experiments* London: Routledge.

Weinstock, J. and E. D. Rothblum (eds) (2004) *Lesbian Ex-lovers: the Really Long-Term Relationships* New York: Harrington Park Press.

Weston, K. (1991) *Families We Choose: Lesbians, Gay Men and Kinship* New York: Columbia University Press.

Whitbread, H. (ed.) (1988) *I Know My Own Heart: The Diaries of Anne Lister, 1791–1840* New York and London: New York University Press.

Whitbread, H. (ed.) (1992) *No Priest but Love: Excerpts from the Diaries of Anne Lister, 1824–1826* Otley, West Yorkshire: Smith Settle.

Wiesen Cook, B. (1977) 'Female Support Networks and Political Activism: Lillian Wald, Chrystal Eastman, Emma Goldman', *Chrysalis*, No. 3.

Willmott, P. (1987) *Friendship Networks and Social Support* London: Policy Studies Institute.

Woolf, V. (1993) *A Room of One's Own, and Three Guineas* Harmondsworth: Penguin. First published 1929.

Young, M. and P. Willmott (1957) *Family and Kinship in East London* London: Routledge and Kegan Paul.

Zimmerman, B. (1985) 'What Has Never Been: An Overview of Lesbian Feminist Criticism', in E. Showalter (ed.), *The New Feminist Criticism: Essays on Women, Literature, and Theory* New York: Pantheon.

19

Transgendering
Blurring the Boundaries of Gender

Wendy McKenna and Suzanne Kessler

'Transgender' is a complicated and contested term, whose meaning has considerable historical and situational specificity. This chapter considers the various meanings of transgender over the last thirty years and relates these meanings to some theoretical questions that have emerged from various academic and non-academic discussions, especially as they suggest directions for feminist inquiry. Transgendering radically deconstructs the meaning of gender categories and presents feminist scholars with possibilities for linking theory and practice.

> Students recently voted to change the words 'she' and 'he' to 'the students' in the constitution of the student government association of Smith College. The move was instituted by students to make the document more welcoming to those who, although biologically female, do not identify themselves as women, said a representative of the women's college in Northampton, Mass. (*The Journal News*, May 26, 2003)

INTRODUCTION

For many years we have been writing about the social construction of gender and how transsexuality and intersexuality – categories that would seem to challenge the gender dichotomy – are paradoxically used to support it by being filtered through the *natural attitude* toward gender (Kessler, 1998; Kessler and McKenna, 1978). The *natural attitude* is a phenomenological construct proposed by the philosopher Edmund Husserl (1931) and later adopted by sociologist Alfred Schutz (1962). It refers to members' unquestionable axioms about a world that appears to exist independently of particular perceptions or constructions of it. Within the *natural attitude*, gender exists as a quality independent of any particular example of maleness or femaleness. Harold Garfinkel (1967), in developing ethnomethodology, an offshoot of phenomenology, described how the *natural attitude* forms the foundation of everyday, as well as scientific, thinking about gender and showed how that thinking both creates and reflexively supports the categories of female and male.

Ethnomethodology was the theoretical perspective through which we began our examination of gender. In developing Garfinkel's ideas we detailed eight beliefs that constitute the *natural attitude* about gender (Kessler and Mckenna, 1978: 113–114):

1 There are two and only two genders.
2 One's gender is invariant.
3 Genitals are the essential sign of gender.
4 Any exceptions to two genders are not to be taken seriously.
5 There are no transfers from one gender to another except for the ceremonial.
6 Everyone must be classified as a member of one gender or another.
7 The male/female dichotomy is a *natural* one.
8 Membership in one gender or another is *natural*.

By treating transsexuals and intersexuals as 'mistakes' that need to be rectified through various medical treatments and legal remedies, these eight beliefs about gender are 'proved.' The assertion that 'male,' 'man,' 'female,' 'woman,' are social constructions, inextricably tied to the natural attitude, rather than independently existing categories in nature, has come to be known as the social construction orientation. Social construction, as articulated by Peter Berger and Thomas Luckman (1972), rests on assumptions that absolute claims should not be made about the world and that social categories like gender have no meaning until they are put in a human context and interpreted through human eyes (Gergen, 1994; Hacking, 1999; Handel, 1982). Social construction *does not* imply that these categories are irrelevant, arbitrary, or easily eradicated. Rather, it is a critique of essentialism, the assertion that there are objective facts that exist independently of history and culture, and that the way to uncover the facts of this world is through research using the scientific method.

When the term 'transgender' was first proposed by Virginia Prince in 1979, she argued that it should replace the term 'transsexual' because people could never change their essential biological sex, no matter what they did to their bodies. She believes that genital surgery would not change a person's sex, and therefore the status of 'transsexual' is an impossibility. Prince's usage of 'transgender' reinforces the biological dichotomy of male versus female sex, even if gender (man versus woman) is seen as not so immutable. In 2004, the meaning of 'transgender' bears little resemblance to its earliest proposed usage. It is clear that the contemporary usage of 'transgender' is increasingly becoming a challenge to, rather than a reinforcement of, the natural attitude.

Our goal in this chapter is to consider what transgender has meant and what it means today, and to give some examples of the theoretical questions that have emerged from various academic and non-academic discussions, especially as they suggest directions for feminist inquiry. Although this chapter contains citations to a number of important writings, we acknowledge that other significant works may not be referenced here, especially since books, articles, and websites on transgender seem to be appearing at an increasing rate. In addition, while our focus is theoretical and academic, we, as authors, and you, as readers, must always be aware that transgender is not just a subject for analysis, any more than race or gender is. Those whose experience we draw on in any discussion of transgender live real lives in real worlds, where their actions and decisions are not merely theoretical.[1] We will return to this point at the end of the chapter. In addition, we must always remember that the origins of feminist, women's, queer, and gender studies lie in political movements whose goals have not yet been reached, and, therefore, it is our responsibility to always reflect on the ways in which our theory might inform and support action.

THE EMERGENCE OF TRANSGENDER

In the late 1970s, our assertion that the essentialist dichotomy of biological 'sex' was not independent of people's methods for creating the dichotomy was basically ignored by those engaged in studying gender and sexuality.[2] Now, social construction is a taken-for-granted assumption of gender studies. It is important to understand some of the parameters of this transformation. In order to document the emergence of transgender and differences in the term's usage over time and across disciplines, we searched six academic electronic databases and one general newspaper database. What the searches showed was that something began to happen around 1995 that led to an explosion by the year 2000 in theorizing, scientific and legal research, and personal narratives involving transgender. (See Table 19.1.) In addition, these searches provide a general overview of how various fields organize and understand gender and transgender.

MEDLINE archives articles in the field of medicine, including psychiatry. Although there were fifty-eight citations for 'transsexual' between 1991 and 1994, there was only one citation for 'transgender.' That was in a public health journal and dealt with phalloplasty for a born female. In the last decade, typical topics in articles using the term 'transgender' include AIDS care in transgender communities and factors that differentiate kinds of transsexuals and transvestites. For the most part, material indexed by *MEDLINE* uses transgender as a synonym for transsexual.

The *PsycINFO* database archives articles in the field of psychology. In the four articles that used the term 'transgender' from 1990 to 1994, transgender

Table 19.1 *Number of citations for 'transgender' in seven indexes since 1990*

	MEDLINE	Psyc INFO	Social Science	Women Studies	Gender Watch	Humanities	News Source Index
1990–1994	1	4	1	9	18	0	0
1995–1999	19	50	12	81	257	29	9
2000–2004	33	118	37	103	304	30	1,998,382

is a synonym for 'transsexual.' In the five years following, the number of citations increased more than twelve-fold and then doubled again from 2000 to 2004. In the more recent articles, largely from clinical psychology and education disciplines, applied issues like treatment and public policy are the main topics. These writings typically add transgendered people to gays, lesbians, and bisexuals as another discrete population that needs to be served or taught about. Transgender is not differentiated from transsexual. It is taken for granted that the reader will understand, at least in general, what is meant by transgender. A smaller subset of articles from the *PsycINFO* database deals with more theoretical issues like defining transgender and deconstructing identity, and these overlap with citations from humanities and social science databases.

Social Science Index and the *Women Studies International* database mirror this same pattern of few citations before 1995 and a huge increase after that. *Gender Watch Index*, a database that archives gay/lesbian academic journals as well as popular/alternative gay-related media, recorded 18 citations between 1990 and 1994, 257 from 1995 to 1999, and 304 from 2000 to 2003.

Humanities Abstracts, which includes philosophical and literary analyses (from which the discipline of queer studies emerged), had no citations for transgender before 1995, twenty-nine citations between 1995 and 1999, and thirty between 2000 and 2003. (The relatively low numbers are due to the fact that this database searches key words only and not the text or title.) Because the articles indexed are almost always theoretical, the use of the term 'transgender' reflects the expanding interest in transgender as a challenge to essentialism, rather than just signaling a shift in terminology from transsexual to transgender as in the other databases.

Transgender is also a term that has entered popular culture since 1995. An unobtrusive measure of the degree to which this has happened is that a *Google* search for transgender had no 'hits' for 1994, 3,300 'hits' in 1999, and 816,000 'hits' in March, 2004.[3] This surge is also reflected in the number of citations in the *Newspaper Source Index* (of 194 major news sources, including *The New York Times* and *The Los Angeles Times*). There were no citations for transgender before 1995, 9 between 1995 and 1999, and 1,998,382 between 2000 and 2003! In the last five years of the twentieth century, with gay and lesbian issues already having a familiar place in public discourse, with 'gender' having replaced 'sex' in discussions of being male and female (Haig, 2004), and with the Internet transforming communication networks and information access, what had been thought of and treated as a 'disorder' was becoming an identity category that both reflects and shapes changes in theoretical and practical understandings of gender.[4]

In trying to understand the diverse and seemingly contradictory connotations of transgender, we have found it useful to consider the various meanings of the prefix 'trans' (McKenna and Kessler, 2000). The first meaning of 'trans' is *change*, as in the word 'transform.' In this sense, transgendered people change their bodies from those they were born with to those matching the genders they feel they are. They change from male to female or vice versa. Transgender in this sense is synonymous with 'transsexual,' and it would be appropriate to refer to someone as 'a transgender' just as it is common to refer to someone as 'a transsexual.' As the term transgender entered academic and popular discourse, this was the most common meaning of the term. For example, in 1997, the first year that the *International Journal of Transgender* was published, seventeen of the articles had transgender in the title and twenty-two had transsexual in the title. Despite this distinction, both terms seemed to refer to the transsexual usage, which is still the meaning implied in much of the medical and psychological literature. Although much of the professional literature on transsexualism has important practical and clinical implications, for the rest of this chapter our focus is on two other meanings of trans – *crossing* (gender) and *moving beyond* (gender). As we will argue below, both of those meanings reflect a social construction perspective on gender, unlike the essentialist perspective implied by *changing* (gender).

TRANS AS *CROSSING*: GENDER THEORY AND ACADEMIC DISCOURSE

Even social construction usages of transgender do not share a uniform meaning. Many writers who use the term transgender are careful to explain what they mean (and do not mean) by it, usually in the first endnote. Some provide a general definition, using words like 'crossing,' 'blending,' 'non conformity,' or 'discordance.' For example, Anne Bolin considers transgender '[T]hat group of people whose genitals, status, appearance and behaviors are not in congruence with the Western schema that mandates an essential relationship between sex and gender' (1994: 590). Other writers list categories of people who can be considered transgendered. Here are some typical examples:

> Transgenderism…includes people whose gender expression is non-conformant with gender role expectations of males and females in a given territory or society. Cross-dressers, transvestites, and transsexual are all often covered under the transgender category. Moreover, people of any sexual orientation whose gender expression remains outside of a rigid or gender conformist system often identify as transgenders…I use transgender and transsexual [making no distinction] to refer to individuals who chose to identify with a gender different from that assigned at birth

and who have made strides to accommodate to that gender construct…Individual [s who] dress as another gender for erotic purposes, as well as people who are blending gender, or being playful about their gender presentation are excluded from this term's use. (Vidal-Ortiz, 2002: 224–225)

Those who might fall under the umbrella term of transgender…includ[e] transvestites, transsexual, crossdressers, transgenderists, gender blenders, gender benders, drag queens, bi-genders, feminine men, androgynes, drag kings, intersexuals, masculine women, passing men, gender dysphorics and others who might consider themselves a 'gender outlaw.' (Broad, 2002: 263)

As these definitions point out, there are many categories, identities, and behaviors associated with transgender that force a confrontation with the natural attitude toward gender. Specifically, transgender challenges three major beliefs of the natural attitude: (1) that there are two, and only two, genders; (2) that a person's gender never changes; and (3) that genitals are the essential sign of gender. Transsexualism, on the other hand, has never created such a challenge because it has been conceptualized as surgically changing a person's *genitals,* not changing their ('real') *gender.* The assumption that one could be born into the wrong body supports the belief that there are right bodies and wrong bodies for each of the two essential genders. Thus, transsexualism, although on the surface a rather radical concept, is reconcilable with the belief that gender is invariant and there are no transfers (Kessler and McKenna, 1978). This deep conservatism probably accounts for transsexualism's relative acceptance.

In the second meaning of 'trans,' *across* (as in the word 'transcontinental'), the transgendered person moves across genders, or maybe just certain aspects of the person crosses from one gender to another. Gender is no longer packaged as a unity. Because this meaning does not imply surgical intervention or even surgical intent, it has a more fluid connotation than the first meaning of transgender, which equated it with transsexual.[5] Without genital surgery, there is more of a sense that the crossing does not have to be permanent, although it might be. At the time of this writing, the connotation of crossing is the most common meaning of transgender. It names some deviation from dichotomous gender expectations, in dress, behavior, bodily changes (other than genital), and choice of sex partner, but avoids the language of diagnosis and etiology that suffuses discussions of transsexuality and transvestism. This meaning of 'trans' has added the phrase *non-op* or *'can't afford' op* to what had been the limited choices of *pre-op* or *post-op.*

In spite of this more social construction perspective, the transgendered person who crosses genders does not leave the realm of two genders. For example, some transgender people assert that, although they are the other gender, they do not need to change their genitals. Such a person might say, 'I want people to attribute the gender "female" to me, but I'm not going to get my genitals changed. I don't mind having my penis. Penises do not only belong to men.' Although the language is still bigendered, there is a radical potential to this stance of not treating the penis as a sign of maleness or the lack of a penis as a sign of femaleness.

The disentangling of genitals from gender has motivated some writers to include intersexuals under the transgender umbrella. Intersexuality (previously known as *hermaphroditism*) refers to any one of many conditions characterized by a lack of concordance among genitals, gonads, and/or chromosomes or an atypical form of any of those. In cases where the genitals of an infant are atypical, the standard medical treatment has been to 'correct' them so that they look normal to the parents and support whatever gender is assigned to the child.

Since 1995, a politicized and organized movement (led by members of the Intersex Society of North America) has argued for a moratorium on infant genital surgeries, except for the rare case when the condition is life-threatening (Kessler, 1998). The basis for that argument is not only that the surgeries create more physical damage than has been acknowledged by medical professionals, but that people do not need to have perfect-looking genitals. They can be male or female with genitals that are atypical. Even if they are not damaging, the surgeries restrict the intersexed person's options because early surgery would make it difficult to cross from one gender to another as an adult. Many intersexuals see their diagnostic category as socially constructed and identify as transgendered, but not all people with an intersexed condition experience themselves that way.

People who cross from one gender category to another, without necessarily having or wanting the genitals that traditionally signal the crossing, are doing something new. Having a public gender identity that does not depend on the matching genital is new. Having serial genders is new. What is *not* new is that there is still only male or female, even if one's lived experience combines both in some way.

TRANS AS *BEYOND*: QUEERING GENDER

Originally a homophobic slur, the term 'queer' was appropriated by young gay and lesbian activists in the 1990s and became part of intellectual discourse within the cultural analysis known as queer theory. To 'queer' is to render 'normal' sexuality as strange and unsettled (Goldberg, n.d.; Warner, 1993). This challenge to dichotomous sexuality assumes that heterosexuals can be queer and homosexuals are not necessarily queer and that to not feel homosexual does not mean one must feel hetero- or bisexual. Consistent with this fluid view of sexuality, discussions of gender non-conformity began to reflect the concept of queering gender. Those who queer gender raise the issue of not just what kind of sex 'real' men or women have, but whether there are 'real' men or women in the first place.

By the end of the 1990s, many individuals who had aligned themselves with queer politics began to identify as members of 'the transgender community.' These were mainly young people, mainly 'born women,' who did not identify as either women or men. Many of them made this transition while in college, within a community of similar and supportive others, referring to themselves as tranny boys, transmen, FtMs,[6] or 'bois' (cf. Kaldera, n.d.). Their analyses of gender, which usually come out of their own experiences, have been compelling and reflect a third meaning of 'trans': *beyond* or *through*, as in the word 'transcutaneous.' Many of those who identify as transgender in this third meaning commonly display, on a deep level, the understanding that gender is socially constructed, that it is an action, not a noun or an adjective, and that to not feel like a female does not mean to feel like a male. Everything is open to analysis, revision, and rejection. Rather than call them 'transgenders,' or 'transgendered persons,' the phrase 'transgendering persons' best captures this meaning.[7] This is a challenge to the natural attitude because within the natural attitude, not only is moving through (trans) gender impossible, but transgendering is nonsensical, because gender is not an activity that is implied by the '*ing*.' From the standpoint of the natural attitude, 'gendering' is as nonsensical as 'heighting.'

In this third sense, a transgendering person is one who has gotten through gender – is beyond it, although probably never really 'over it.' That no clear gender attribution can be made is not seen as problematic. Gender is refused. It ceases to exist as a cross-situational essential attribute for the person and for those with whom they interact. This meaning of transgender is the least common but the one of greatest importance to gender theorists who are interested in the possibility, both theoretical and real, of eliminating gender oppression.

TRANSGENDERING, FEMINIST THEORY, AND WOMEN'S STUDIES

Feminism, grounded in the axiom that the basis for women's oppression is the reality created by (White) men, can be troubled by transgender. From almost the beginning of the women's movement, some feminists responded very negatively to the challenge of transsexualism. Their reactions included direct hostility and exclusion (MacDonald, 1998). Most vehement was Janice Raymond's attack on male-to-female transsexuals (1980).[8] More recently, some feminists have regarded female-to-male transgendered people with suspicion. The 'womanist' perspective is that M-to-F people, raised with male privilege, cannot ever be women, and F-to-M people, seduced by the power of patriarchy, have been duped and have defected to the enemy. This perspective has treated transgender as at best irrelevant to feminist causes and at worst a way of deflecting energy from the struggle for gender equality. The resultant feminist separatist activism has been responsible for empowering many women and for redefining how to meet our diverse needs. These needs must be addressed, but the theory that underlies 'womanism' is an essentialist one, and, in excluding the possibility of transgender in any of its meanings, this type of feminism misses the opportunity to undermine a gender system whose constitution both creates and sustains the oppression of women.

In the last few decades many postmodern-influenced feminist and queer theorists have embraced transgender as a way of revealing gender as an activity. Gender transgression is characterized as liberating. Many of these theorists are themselves transgendered and have been, with few exceptions, 'born women.'[9] Even those theorists who are not transgendered tend to be 'born women.' Although a detailed analysis of why awaits future work, we suggest that those who developed their consciousness on the margins are much better positioned to uncover and analyze what is taken for granted in defining the borders of a social reality. 'If we really want to be free, women must realize that at the end of the struggle, we will not be women anymore. Or at least we will not be women in the way that we understand the term today' (Califia-Rice, 1997: 90; see also Wittig, 1980).

A common misunderstanding of those who reject transgender's relevance to feminism is that eradicating gender as a meaningful social category is not the same as asserting that physical bodies do not exist or that bodies do not affect experience and identity. It is the intractable status hierarchy given to gender categories by tying them to dichotomous physical attributes like genitals that is being questioned by feminists like ourselves.

For many years, and in different ways, a case has been made that it is important for feminist activism that gender be destabilized.[10] One might argue that the discipline of women's studies is predicated on there being women, but surely feminist studies is not. What, then, could those involved in feminist studies do to encourage gender destabilization? We suggest analyzing when and where gender is invoked and then challenging the criteria for determining what 'female' and 'male' mean in each particular case. In other words, feminists should be uncovering what is revealed by refusing to gloss gender. The following are two examples.

Some people argue that only a man and a woman can marry because the basic purpose of marriage is reproductive. From that argument it would follow, then, that one member of the pair must produce viable sperm and the other must have viable eggs. The absurdity of this requirement is highlighted by the fact that no one has to pass such a test in order to get married, and no one's marriage license is revoked when they fail to reproduce. In this case (as in all cases where gender is examined rather than glossed), the putative theoretical criteria fail when confronted with gender-as-lived.

Another example comes from the practical management of transgender in society. Colleges are grappling with providing housing for transgender students (Klein, n.d.). The existence of transgender students creates a problem for room assignments and forces an examination of assignment rules. Typically, college students are assigned a 'same-sex' roommate. For as long as students have been assigned roommates, this criterion has gone unexamined. Rarely is it asked, 'What do we mean by "same-sex" and why do we think roommates should be the "same-sex"?' If the underlying purpose of assigning same-sex roommates is to avoid sexual tension in close quarters, clearly this is based on the false assumption that all college students are heterosexual. If the assumption is that people with more similar bodies are more likely to get along well together, then why not also use criteria of height, weight, and skin, eye, and hair color?

TRANSGENDERING: THEORY AND PRACTICE

The insistence that gender is a natural dichotomy is historically grounded in religion and now also in science; thus, it has been at the core of Western European intellectual inquiry. As gender theorists confront more fluid constructs of gender within our contemporary culture, we should remember and acknowledge that we are not the inventors of gender fluidity. 'Transgender is a complicated and contested term whose meaning has considerable cultural, historical, and situational specificity, not just over many years and lives but also within a single day and life. In fact, when people use the label transgender to refer to themselves, there is no way of knowing which meaning is being referenced. There is no assumption that the user even intends a particular (limited) meaning. On the one hand, this presents a practical problem. Is this a person who intends to become the other gender – surgically and/or legally – or is this someone who is refusing to be a particular gender and is challenging the gender system? On the other hand, the looseness of the meaning forces us to conceptualize transgender (and by extension, *gender*) as a fundamentally fluctuating phenomenon.

What does transgendering mean for feminist theorists, researchers, and clinicians, many of whom are not transgendered? First of all, it provides further warrant for questioning an essentialist view of gender. There is a body of provocative writing by transgendering people for non-transgendering people to learn from.[11] Treating this work seriously will help advance gender theory, improve clinical practice, and suggest social action. The last should not be overlooked, since our theoretical discussion is taking place at a time when hate crimes against transgendering people are at an all-time high (Moser, 2003). People whose gender is unconventional have real-life concerns, including better trans medicine, clearer legal strategies, and more supportive psychological interventions. They need help in order to negotiate meaningful and safe lives in a society that is not ready for them. Whether they are *changing, crossing*, or *moving beyond* gender categories, they are objects of 'transoppression' (Feinberg, 1998).

The issues raised by transgendering are not limited to gender alone. Eleanor MacDonald argues that transgendering raises questions about the issue of identity itself: '[T]he experience of being transgender problematizes the relationship of the self to the body, and the self to others…[I]t problematizes issues of identity boundaries, stability and coherence' (1998: 5). Additional questions about physical bodies, social meanings, and individual experience of self are raised in Bernice Hausman's (2001) analysis of various aspects of transgender in her review of books on that topic.[12]

The social reality of transgendering and the refusal to gloss gender provides many subversive possibilities for those of us engaged in feminist scholarship. The fact that transgendering threatens something basic is a good indication that radical social change can result from it. The 'warning' in our closing quote, a quote endorsed by the Traditional Values Coalition, is, from our perspective, a statement of promising possibility.

> The promotion of 'sex changes' and the normalization of severe gender identity disorders by radical feminists, pro-same-sex-attraction disorder activists, and sexual revolutionaries is part of their larger agenda – namely, the destabilization of the categories of sex and gender. (O'Leary, 2002)

ACKNOWLEDGEMENTS

We would like to thank Judith Shapiro and Judith Lorber for their helpful comments on an earlier version of this chapter.

NOTES

1 Jacob Hale (n.d.) has written important guidelines for non-transgender people who write about trans issues, including such directives as not treating transgender as exotic, giving credence to non-academic voices, and asking what transgender can teach about everyone's gender. We have tried to hold to these standards and hope we have succeeded.

2 See Judith Gerson (2005) for a review essay bringing this work to contemporary attention.

3 On May 28, 2005, there were 2,710,000 hits on Google for transgender, with a link to a definition page http://www.answers.com/transgender&r=67 (JL).

4 In this cultural climate, Judith Butler's *Gender Trouble* (1990) was the right book at the right time, providing a theoretical framework for a politicized transgender movement as well as stimulating the development of gender studies.

5 Bolin (1994) argued that one important factor in this development was the closing of university-affiliated gender clinics in the 1980s. The fact that transsexuals were finding it more difficult to obtain surgery pushed many of them to consider the possibility/ advantage of crossing genders without genital change. Another related factor was the general politicization of the transgender movement. Grassroots organizations adopted a political agenda, wanting a voice in their treatment and a desire to define their 'condition' for themselves. They, like gay people before them, wanted to take their name and their conceptualization out of the hands of the medical professionals.

6 The usage of 'FtM' is not merely shorthand for 'female-to-male.' It is, we believe, an explicit way of signaling that neither male nor female is 'there' any more and that the 't' is a permanent part of the identity, not a transition.

7 Richard Ekins' (1997) coinage of the term 'male femaling' might seem to foreshadow transgendering, but his discussion of the various ways that 'genetic males' (his usage) appropriate female/feminine properties maintains the sex/gender distinction.

8 Richard Ekins and Dave King, writing in the first issue of the *International Journal of Transgenderism*, claimed that 'the influence of writers such as Janice Raymond effectively silenced transgenderists for many years' (1997: 9).

9 These few exceptions e.g., Kate Bornstein (1995), Dallas Denny (1992), and Riki Wilchins (1997) – have, of course, contributed a great deal to gender theory.

10 See Kessler and McKenna (1978), Judith Shapiro (1982), and Judith Lorber (2000; 2005).

11 Much of this writing is not conventionally published but only available on the Internet, and feminist scholars/practitioners must access information from this source in order to stay knowledgeable.

12 Most of these books have already been referenced in this chapter. Three important works that have not are *FTM: Female to male transsexuals in society* (Devor, 1997); *Second Skin: The body narratives of transsexuality* (Prosser, 1998); and *Female Masculinity* (Halberstam, 1998).

REFERENCES

Berger, P. L. and Luckman, T. (1972) *The Social Construction of Reality: A treatise in the sociology of knowledge*. New York: Doubleday.

Bolin, Anne (1994) 'Transcending and Transgendering: Male-to-Female Transsexuals, Dichotomy and Diversity,' in Gilbert Herdt (ed.), *Third Sex, Third Gender*. New York: Zone Books, 447–485.

Bornstein, Kate (1995) *Gender Outlaw*. New York: Vintage Books.

Broad, K. L. (2002) 'Fracturing transgender: Intersectional constructions and identization,' in Patricia Gagne and Richard Tewksbury (eds), *Gendered Sexualities*. Amsterdam: Elsevier, 235–266.

Butler, Judith (1990) *Gender Trouble*. New York: Routledge.

Califia-Rice, Patrick (1997) *Sex Changes: The politics of transgenderism*. San Francisco: Cleis Press.

Denny, Dallas (1992) 'The politics of diagnosis and a diagnosis of politics,' *Chrysalis Quarterly* 1(3): 9–20.

Devor, H. (1997) *FTM: Female to Male Transsexuals in Society*. Bloomington: Indiana University Press.

Ekins, Richard (1997) *Male Femaling: A grounded theory approach to cross-dressing and sex changing*. New York: Routledge.

Ekins, Richard and King, Dave (1997) 'Blending Genders: Contributions to the emerging field of transgender studies,' *The International Journal of Transgenderism* 1(1). http://www.symposion.com/ijt/ijtc0101.htm

Feinberg, Leslie (1998) *Trans Liberation: Beyond Pink or Blue*. Boston, MA: Beacon.

Garfinkel, Harold (1967) *Studies in Ethnomethodology*. Englewood Cliffs, NJ: Prentice Hall.

Gergen, Kenneth J. (1994) *Realities and Relationships: Surroundings in social construction*. Cambridge, MA: Harvard University Press.

Gerson, Judith (2005) 'There is no sex without gender,' *Sociological Forum* 20: 179–181.

Goldberg, Michael (n.d.) http://www.bothell.washington.edu/faculty/mgoldberg/queer.htm

Hacking, I. (1999) 'Are you a social constructionist?' *Lingua Franca* May–June: 65–72.

Haig, David (2004) 'The inexorable rise of gender and the decline of sex: Social change in academic titles, 1945–2001,' *Archives of Sexual Behavior* 33(2): 87–96.

Halberstam, Judith (1998) *Female Masculinities*. Durham, NC: Duke University Press.

Hale, Jacob (n.d.) *Suggested rules for non-transsexual writing about transsexuals, transsexuality, transsexualism, or trans____*. http://sandystone.com/hale.rules.html

Handel, Warren (1982) *Ethnomethodology: How people make sense*. Englewood Cliffs, NJ: Prentice Hall.

Hausman, Bernice L. (2001) 'Recent transgender theory,' *Feminist Studies* 27(2): 465–490.

Husserl, Edmund (1931) *Ideas*. New York: Humanities Press.

Kaldera, Raven (n.d.) http://astroqueer.tripod.com/charts/raven.html
Kessler, Suzanne and Mckenna, Wendy (1978) *Gender: An ethnomethodological approach*. Chicago: University of Chicago Press.
Kessler, Suzanne (1998) *Lessons from the Intersexed*. New Brunswick, NJ: Rutgers University Press.
Klein, Alana (n.d.) 'A Question of Gender'. http://www.universitybusiness.com/page.cfm?p=551
Lorber, Judith (2000) 'Using gender to undo gender: A feminist degendering movement,' *Feminist Theory* 1(1): 79–95.
Lorber, Judith (2005) *Breaking the Bowls: degendering and feminist change*. New York: W. W. Norton.
MacDonald, Eleanor (1998) 'Critical identities: Rethinking feminism through transgender politics,' *Atlantis* 23(1): 3–11.
McKenna, Wendy and Kessler, Suzanne (2000) 'Who put the "trans" in transgender?' *International Journal of Transgenderism* 4(3). http://www.symposion.com/ijt/gilbert/kessler.htm
Moser, Bob (2003) 'Disposable people', *The Southern Poverty Law Center's Intelligence Report* 112: 10–20.
O'Leary, Dale (2002) 'Sex and Gender: The case of the transgendered student (National Association for Research and Therapy on Homosexuality'. www.narth.com/docs/transgendered.html
Prince, Virginia (1979) 'Charles to Virginia: Sex research as a personal experience,' in Vern Bullough (ed.), *The Frontiers of Sex Research*. Buffalo, NY: Prometheus Books, 167–175.
Prosser, Jay (1998) *Second Skin: The body narratives of transsexuality*. New York: Columbia University Press.
Raymond, Janice (1980) *The Transsexual Empire: The making of the she-male*. London: Women's Press. Teachers College Press: Reissue edition (March 1, 1994).
Shapiro, Judith (1982) 'Women's Studies: A note on the perils of markedness,' *Signs* 7(3): 717–721.
Schutz, Alfred (1962) *Collected Papers I: The problem of social reality* (ed.), M. Natanson. The Hague: Nijhoff.
Vidal-Ortiz, Salvador (2002) 'Queering sexuality and doing gender: Transgender men's identification with gender and sexuality,' in Patricia Gagne and Richard Tewksbury (eds), *Gendered Sexualities*. Amsterdam: Elsevier, 181–233.
Warner, Michael (1993) 'Introduction,' in Michael Warner (ed.), *Fear of a Queer Planet: Queer Politics and Social Theory*. Ann Arbor: University of Michigan Press, xxvi–xxvii.
Wilchins, Riki (1997) *Read My Lips: Sexual subversion and the end of gender*. Ann Arbor, MI: Firebrand Books.
Wittig, Monique (1980) 'The Straight Mind,' *Feminist Issues* Summer: 103–111.

Part VII

EMBODIMENT IN A TECHNOLOGICAL WORLD

20

Gendered Bodies
Between Conformity and Autonomy

Sharyn Roach Anleu

A major challenge for feminist scholars is to articulate the continual tension between individual women's choices to present, maintain, alter, or use their bodies in certain ways and the social requirement to conform to gender norms, which often reinforce women's inequality and powerlessness and limit the capacity for individual autonomy. Feminist research indicates that social norms and cultural values governing women's bodies, behaviour, and appearance generally are far more restrictive and repressive than those regulating men's bodies. The chapter illustrates these theoretical issues first, with a discussion of the medicalization of women's bodies. It then discusses the relationship between the ways women manage and alter their bodies and the dominant ideals limit feminine beauty and the normal woman and whether and when these limit women's autonomy. The chapter investigates the ways or circumstances in which conformity to gender norms can compromise, reduce, or even enhance women's autonomy and power. It does not posit powerlessness or empowerment as a zero-sum equation: conformity to one set of gender norms may reduce women's autonomy in some respects but expand opportunities for mobility and empowerment in other respects.

INTRODUCTION

In all societies – past and present – bodies are subject to considerable normative evaluation and regulation (Shilling, 1993; Turner, 1992). Many of these norms are deeply gendered and construct inequalities between men and women (Weitz, 2003). Evaluation and regulation of bodies can entail medical attention, when bodies are diagnosed as diseased or sick and subject to medical treatment and intervention. Mostly, a myriad of everyday norms and their associated sanctions – both formal and informal – regulate bodies and their functions (Nettleton and Watson, 1998). Such norms specify appropriate body shapes, sizes, appearance, gestures, movements, types of adornment, and clothing. Feminist scholarship identifies the social construction of women's and men's bodies and the cultural and historical underpinnings of femininity and masculinity. In contemporary Western societies, femininity tends to be defined as the absence of masculinity, and gender norms specify separate roles and expectations for men and women. The socially constructed differences between men and women and ideas about men's and women's bodies are usually constituted as bases for inequality with women less powerful than men and femininity inferior to masculinity.[1]

This chapter examines the gendered assumptions about the nature and place of the female body in contemporary Western societies. It first discusses critical feminist analyses of bodies and gender that address some of the ways gendered norms regulate the (re)presentation of bodies. There is a major tension between the impact, on the one hand, of dominant social norms regarding body management and the imperative of feminine ideals that constrain women's options for success and well-being and, on the other, individual women's experience and exercise of choice regarding their bodies. Conformity to dominant gender norms can provide individual women with resources and power. Indeed, women are often aware that they are complying with social norms that emphasize women's difference and inferiority to men, but nonetheless rationally decide to conform.

The chapter focuses on two topics that illustrate the tension between women's agency and conformity to gendered norms that result in social control: reproduction and body maintenance and alteration. A major feminist issue is whether women who conform are passive dupes of patriarchal power or are rationally considering their options and exercising choice and control over their bodies. I suggest that this is not an either/or proposition, but that compliance with gendered norms (which can be conscious or not) might limit autonomy in some respects but empower in other respects. For example, conformity with feminine appearance norms in the workplace might provide individual women with more legitimacy and credibility and expand opportunities within the organization at the same time that these norms reinforce conventional feminine ideals and differences from men. The chapter concludes by returning to the theoretical issues in feminist analyses of gendered bodies.

THEORIZING THE BODY

Critical feminist analyses examine the myriad ways in which female bodies are constructed and constrained and the ways in which gender is constituted and performed (Butler, 1993). There is considerable focus on issues involving women's bodies, including abortion, contraception, maternity, reproduction, childbirth, sexuality, pornography, prostitution, and rape (Grosz, 1995: 31). A challenge is not to adopt essentialist modes of thought or biological determinism to explain gendered bodies. Essentialism attributes characteristics assumed to be related to women's biology, such as nurturance, empathy, and emotional support, which are supposedly exhibited by all women at all times (Grosz, 1995: 47). The contrasting view is that the body not a natural entity, but is culturally coded and socially constructed (see Price and Shildrick, 1999). Viewing the body as constructed and infinitely malleable can ignore the materiality and limits of human bodies (Negrin, 2002). Nonetheless, 'patriarchal oppression justifies itself, at least in part, by connecting women much more closely than men to the body and, through this identification, restricting women's social and economic roles to (pseudo) biological terms' (Grosz, 1994: 20).

The social norms and cultural values governing women's bodies, behaviour, and appearance are far more restrictive and repressive than those regulating men's bodies. They tend to reinforce women's lower social status and emphasize women's association with the body and appearance rather than the mind and rational thought. Feminine gender norms valorize passivity, weakness, pathology, and irrationality in contrast to strength, normality, and rationality, which are more associated with masculine gender norms. Racial identity, ethnicity, and class also affect these social norms so that expectations for 'normal' women's and men's bodies differ in different social groups (De Casanova, 2004; Leeds Craig, 2002; Lovejoy, 2001).

Feminist analyses recognize the power of gender norms that regulate self-presentation and bodily practices and yet acknowledge that women have some agency in making choices about their bodies. Sandra Lee Bartky (1988), following Michel Foucault (1979), offers a fairly deterministic account of the disciplinary practices that produce a body in which size, gesture, and appearance are recognizably feminine. In this view, the body is docile and self-imposes patriarchal disciplinary practices. The woman concerned about her feminine appearance has become 'just as surely as the inmate of the Panopticon, a self-policing subject, a self committed to a relentless self-surveillance' (Bartky, 1988: 81). However, individual women might experience their self-surveillance and concern with bodily presentation as a source of empowerment and choice (Bordo, 1993a; 1993b). A cultural determinist position claims that the sense of control is false consciousness, women's 'duping' by dominant cultural ideals.

A major challenge for feminist scholars is to articulate the continual tension between individual women's choices, or at least their experience of choice, to present, maintain, alter, or use their bodies in certain ways and the social requirement to conform to gender norms that often reinforce women's inequality and powerlessness and limit the capacity for individual choice (Davis, 1991; 1995). In her nuanced enquiry into cosmetic surgery, Kathy Davis confronts the tension head on:

> My analysis is situated on the razor's edge between a feminist critique of the cosmetic surgery craze (along with the ideologies of feminine inferiority which sustain it) and an equally feminist desire to treat women as agents who negotiate their bodies [as do men] and their lives within the cultural and structural constraints of a gendered social order. (1995: 5)

Many feminists do identify the range of discourses, human diversity, flexibility, and ability to change among women (Hubbard, 1990: 134). They also note that 'women are no more subject to this system of corporeal production than men' (Grosz, 1994: 144). Men and masculinity are not more or less cultural constructs than are women and femininity, but for women, the construction of femininity is the construction of powerlessness, whereas for men, masculinity confers power. Many discussions of women's interaction with the (predominantly male) medical system emphasize their powerlessness and vulnerability.

MEDICALIZATION OF WOMEN'S BODIES

The medicalization of women's bodies, especially in regard to their reproductive capacities, is a well-documented source of social control and disempowerment for women. Women's bodies are subject to medical intervention and designation as sick or diseased in the contexts of fertility and reproductive issues, including abortion, pre-menstrual tension, and menopause (Roach Anleu, 2006). They are sites in which women, both individually and collectively, struggle for autonomy and power vis-à-vis medical dominance.

Fertility and childbirth

The medical intervention and diagnostic testing during pregnancy, the movement from home to hospital births, and men physicians' progressive exclusion of women midwives from the birthing process are all aspects of women's loss of control over pregnancy and childbirth (Rothman, 1982; 1986). However, many women make a conscious choice to participate in a medicalized childbirth because they expect little support from a male partner after the birth and want to be sure they will have the strength to care for a newborn (Fox and Worts, 1999; Zadoroznyj, 2001).

Infertility is also designated a condition requiring medical treatment and intervention, rather than a social problem stemming from the stigma of childlessness (Strickler, 1992: 113–15). Women who are unable to conceive (because either they or their partner are physically infertile) experience considerable shame that can have profound effects on their social identity and behaviour (Miall, 1986). A study of forty-three couples undergoing a medical evaluation for infertility found that the treatment heightened their sense of deviance from cultural norms and abnormality in terms of body function and image (Becker and Nachtigall, 1992: 463–5). While many women experience infertility as a devastating role failure spoiling their ability to live normal lives, men perceive infertility as disappointing but not devastating, so long as it is assumed that the cause of the problem is the female partner

(Greil, Leitko, and Porter, 1988: 181). Fertile women partnered with men with documented infertility tend to adopt a 'courtesy stigma' allowing others to believe that the origin of the problem was their own biological defect, not that of their male partner (Miall, 1986: 271–8). Now that *in vitro* fertilization can be used in many instances of male infertility, fertile women who could become pregnant via heterosexual intercourse undergo debilitating assisted reproduction techniques so that their partner can have a biological child (Lorber, 1989; Lorber and Bandlamudi, 1993).

Another aspect of how reproductive technology undermines women's autonomy is the way ultrasound and electronic fetal monitoring facilitate a conception of the fetus as distinct from the pregnant woman's body (Petchesky, 1987: 271). According to fetal rights advocates, the interests of the woman and the fetus are not necessarily compatible; an adversarial relationship may exist in which the woman becomes liable for any birth defects or neonatal problems (Johnsen, 1986: 613). Fetal rights discourse has justified court-ordered medical intervention such as caesarean sections and blood transfusions to benefit the fetus. It is the woman's body that is the site of the medical intervention, and this signals her loss of control and decision-making capacity.

The meaning of reproductive autonomy is a point of debate among liberal and radical feminists. Liberal feminists see the new reproductive technologies as extending individual control over conception and pregnancy. Radical feminists suggest that, rather than extending women's choices and autonomy, medically assisted reproductive techniques narrow them, subjecting women to social control and pathologizing their bodies. For many radical feminists, a woman who participates in assisted reproduction succumbs to the power of medical science and the medical profession, and accepts a passive, compliant role in the process. They claim that the availability of such programmes reinforces pro-natalist ideals and places additional pressures on women unable to conceive; the technology also reinforces motherhood as a necessary status for 'normal' women. Participants in IVF programmes may have little scope for making choices to refuse or vary treatments. Thus, the only sphere where women have some distinctive power and control – motherhood – is being eroded steadily by increasing medical intervention (Rothman, 1989: 152–8).

On the other side, liberal feminists reject the victim image of women who participate in assisted reproduction programmes. They argue that women who use this technology are not succumbing to male domination or passively complying with the desires of a husband to 'father' children and the demands of the mostly male medical doctors (Wikler, 1986: 1053). They maintain that such imagery trivializes women who have decided to participate in an IVF programme and denies that the desires of women who are unable to conceive are real and concrete, not merely ephemeral or socially constructed (Sandelowski, 1990: 41).

Pre-menstrual syndrome and menopause

Further examples of the medicalization and social control of women's bodies are the supposed pathological syndromes of pre-menstrual tension (PMT) or pre-menstrual syndrome (PMS) and menopause. Medical and popular literatures describe the negative and debilitating effects of PMS. Popular discourses that identify the causes as physiological focus on women's hormones as the source of such problems as dizziness, backache, concentration lapses, mood swings, and irritability (Markens, 1996: 46–8; Parlee, 1994; Rittenhouse, 1991). However, such symptoms may stem from other pressures in women's lives, and the possibility of a legitimate sick role, i.e. suffering from PMS, may be a coping mechanism that helps individual women manage diverse obligations and responsibilities (Parlee, 1982).

Similar assumptions about the nature of women and hormones inform the medical definition of menopause as a 'deficiency' disease. Biomedical explanations of menopause and the associated descriptions of the effects on women's bodies dominate socio-cultural accounts. Nonetheless, medical definitions legitimate and explain the symptoms that many women experience so they are not dismissed as figments of women's imagination or attributed to hypochondria (Bell, 1987: 540). Menopause differs from PMS as the condition itself, not just its effects, is constituted as a medical problem (Lorber and Moore, 2002: 82).

Until recently, medical discourse persuasively maintained that hormone replacement therapy (HRT) was the best single way to manage the 'debilitating' effects of menopause. Extensive clinical trials sponsored by the US Women's Health Initiative showed that HRT use beyond the immediate post-menopausal period could cause heart attacks and strokes. Nonetheless, a small research study in Australia suggests medical practitioners reconstruct menopause as a series of health risks: the risks of menopause and the risks of using HRT. Practitioners present information on the comparative health risks of menopause and HRT as a series of choices that only the woman as patient can make. In this model, as rational consumers of medical science, women must weigh the risks and then decide whether or not to commence a programme of HRT (Murtagh and Hepworth, 2003).

The medicalization of menopause and PMS does confer some advantages on women, as various symptoms – physiological and psychological – are given credibility by a medical label. However, medicalization too easily generalizes the observed symptoms as expected for all women at particular stages of life and automatically attributes various conditions to hormones rather than to other causes or social events in women's lives. Moreover, presenting various options to women and then asking them to decide on their treatment does not necessarily expand autonomy, given the power of medical discourse and the social risks in not following medical advice.

Abortion

Abortion is one issue where legal, medical, and moral evaluation and regulation of women's bodies and reproductive capacities intersect. Questions of autonomy and choice are pre-eminent in feminist arguments about abortion and women's capacity to control their bodies. In most Western industrial societies, abortion became a crime in the early nineteenth century, although certain terminations (if deemed therapeutic) were legal if carried out by a medical practitioner (Petersen, 1993). By the 1960s access to abortion had become a central platform of the women's movement. Feminist proponents of legalization maintain that abortion is neither a medical nor a legal issue but a woman's right to control her own body and realize reproductive autonomy.

Different political and legal structures and ideologies shape the abortion debates and the strategies for change adopted by activists in various countries (Farr, 1993: 169; Gibson, 1990: 181–5; Ferree, 2003: 314–18). Legalization does not provide women with an absolute right to abortion but allows medical practitioners to perform abortions under certain circumstances. Thus, the 'right to choose' is usually ringed with restrictions. After legalization in the United States, battles have centred on such restrictions as time limits, parental consent, and type of procedure. In the United Kingdom and some Australian jurisdictions, an abortion is legal only if performed by a registered medical practitioner after two practitioners find that the duration of the pregnancy is within a specified time period, and that the termination is necessary to avoid injury to the pregnant woman's physical or mental health (which often includes social factors). Other countries have shifted between more and less restrictive policies on abortion.

Medicalization and social control

In sum, the medicalization of women's bodies around reproduction shifts control and intervention from women as a group to the medical profession and other experts. Traditionally, in Western societies (and currently in many non-Western societies) fertility, childbirth, and life-cycle issues generally were managed by women family members and neighbours. The medicalization of reproduction and women's life-cycles means that women are subject to medical diagnoses and intervention, including medication, diagnostic testing, and surgery, with variable scope for non-medical interpretation or intervention. Nonetheless, medicalization offers women a raft of options and choices. Women do make rational choices to seek medical attention and intervention and are able to evaluate, to some extent, the medical service and choose whether to continue to comply.

However, the concept of free choice in the context of medicalization is constrained by the power and persuasiveness of medical advice, and the perceived risks of non-compliance. The risks of not following medical advice may implicate individual women as accountable for any outcome perceived to be socially undesirable. The choice to comply does give individual women some sense of agency while not disrupting dominant cultural expectations.

BODY MAINTENANCE/BODY-ALTERING WORK

Women's maintenance and alteration of their bodies to conform to gender norms is another area where they seem to have lost control over their bodies but in a different view may be exerting agency. Much has been written about the beauty/fashion industries whose mostly women customers spend large amounts of money in their quest to attain the dominant ideals of heterosexual feminine attractiveness and sexuality (Faludi, 1992; Wolf, 1990). The imagery of beauty and elegance conveyed by these industries is very narrow and unattainable by most women, but it can have a powerful influence on their sense of self.

Women's body maintenance activities vary in their level of routine, normality, or naturalness. There are daily grooming activities, including use of cosmetics, less frequent routines such has hair removal and hair styling, which might include visits to the beauty parlour, and finally medical intervention in the form of cosmetic surgery. The vast majority of women in Western societies, regardless of their feminist orientation, remove hair from their legs or underarms in the quest for greater femininity and attractiveness. While such hair removal is habitual, that is routine and normal for most women, it endorses the assumption that the female body is abnormal or unacceptable as is (Tiggemann and Kenyon, 1998: 879–84). To be hairy and a woman contravene conventional notions of appropriate femininity and risk the negative labels of being lazy, dirty, unattractive (to heterosexual men), and masculine (Toerien and Wilkinson, 2003: 341). Hairlessness also conveys youthfulness, a pre-pubescent stage in contrast with the hairy, virile man. Merran Toerien and Sue Wilkinson suggest that 'constructed as masculine, hair has no rightful place on the feminine body' (2003: 341).

Feminist scholars have pointed out the contradictions between individual women's choices to present, maintain, alter, or use their own bodies and gender norms that often reinforce women's inequality and powerlessness (Davis, 1991; 1995; Dellinger and Williams, 1997; Weitz, 2001). An overly individualistic model emphasizes choice and self-determination with little attention to powerful social institutions, including the fashion/beauty industry, the sex industry, and the medical profession. A deterministic model sees women as having little autonomy and simply being duped by cultural images and heterosexual social expectations. Neither model captures women's experiences of body maintenance. For example, an investigation of beauty therapy shows that the procedures can be relaxing and pleasurable, and they are paid for by women with their own disposable income. Yet overarching feminine or beauty ideals are continually reinforced by the advertisements of cosmetic companies gracing the walls and shelves of beauty salons (Black and Sharma, 2001: 109; Gimlin, 1996).

Conventional attractiveness can be a realistic route to power for women in both intimate relationships and careers; doing femininity well can be empowering (Jackson, 1992). From this vantage point, women are rational actors making choices in the light of their personal resources and their knowledge of cultural and social expectations. Rose Weitz studies hair to explore the ordinary ways in which women struggle daily with cultural ideas about the female body. She argues that 'women are neither "docile bodies," nor free agents; rather, they combine accommodation and resistance as they actively grapple with cultural expectations and social structures' (2001: 669). But 'because these strategies do not challenge the cultural ideologies supporting subordination, at best they can improve the position of an individual woman, but not of women as a group' (Weitz, 2001: 675). The gains such strategies provide are usually tenuous and short-term but may reap the particular benefits women seek at the time.

Cosmetic surgery is an area of the regulation of the body where the body is viewed as incomplete, as a potentiality and as physically changeable (with the assistance of medical intervention), usually to attain greater conformity with culturally specific appearance norms.

Cosmetic surgery

Cosmetic surgery in particular presents a confronting paradox between self-determination and disempowerment and the lack of real options for diversity and difference. Some women (and men) might perceive benefits from cosmetic surgery in the context of socially conferred rewards for conformity to certain appearance norms. Critics contend that the use of cosmetic surgery attests to the over-bearing influence of gendered social norms and narrow conceptions of beauty: 'More often than not, what appear at first glance to be instances of choice turn out to be instances of conformity to norms of beauty and heterosexuality' (Morgan, 1991: 36). Many feminists feel discomfort in viewing the recipients of medical intervention as misguided, deluded by the power of medicine and advertising, rendering them victims of larger social forces to which they passively comply (Davis, 1995; 1997). Empirical research reveals that those who have cosmetic surgery are not 'simply the duped victims of the beauty system. Cosmetic surgery is, first and foremost, about identity; about wanting to be ordinary rather than beautiful' (Davis, 1995: 12). Though, as one commentator observes: 'the limitation of cosmetic surgery is that it offers a technological solution to a social problem', namely, dominant definitions of acceptable female appearance (Negrin, 2002: 25).

One way of resolving this dilemma is to conclude that 'conformity to social and cultural norms may on the one hand represent collusion by women in dominant constructions of femininity; nevertheless at the individual level it may also be rational and empowering' (Gillespie, 1996: 82). Women may accurately assess that their employment prospects will improve if they undergo plastic surgery, especially as body presentation is an increasingly important part of the contemporary workplace. Interviews with surgeons who perform cosmetic surgery and with individuals who had such surgery find that many described it as 'normal' and 'natural', comparable to buying makeup and going to the hair salon (Dull and West, 1991; Gimlin, 2000). Some clients exhibit a desire to return to their own more youthful state and perceive an opportunity to conform to particular norms of beauty or youthful appearance. Others identify problems with racial and ethnic features. Those who are not White, Anglo-Saxon, and Protestant, for example some Jewish and Italian women, have rhinoplasties; Asian women have their eyes reshaped (Kaw, 2003). Surgeons and former clients tend to describe the surgery as a reconstructive project that focuses on various body parts that need correction or repair. While presented as an 'objective' assessment, the repair was always in accord with gendered, ethnically specific ideals of beauty (Dull and West, 1991: 66–7). Many of the women who undergo plastic surgery express enormous satisfaction with the procedures that fix a particular 'flaw' and enable them to acquire a set of racial features considered more prestigious (Gimlin, 2000: 80; Kaw, 2003: 190–1). Far more ambivalence exists about men's choice to undergo cosmetic surgery; men who do are often viewed as less masculine (Davis, 2002: 58–60).

Bodies, food, and diet

The relationship between the body and food for women can be a complex mix that varies along class and racial ethnic dimensions (Lupton, 1996). On the one side, the purchase or production, preparation, and serving of food are typically women's work both in the paid workforce and in their own domestic realm. It is low-paid work, but a way of conveying emotional care for family members (DeVault, 1991). On the other side, strong cultural imperatives induce many women to attempt to control their eating habits and the quantity of food they consume. Weight is a much greater concern for women than for men in Western societies; they tend to feel overweight, diet more, express more body consciousness, and indicate that weight interferes with their social activities (Tiggemann, 1994: 327–8; Tiggemann and Pennington, 1990: 306). Anglo-Saxon young women seem to be overwhelmingly dissatisfied with their current body shape, and they rate their current figures as larger than their ideal and actual figures. Psychological research shows that 'fat talk' among female undergraduates in the United States involves daily self-disparaging body talk, for example 'I feel fat.' Such talk reinforces the shared dislike of fat and affirms the value of thinness. It also invites continuous surveillance of body size (Gapinski, Brownell, and LaFrance 2003). Non-White racial ethnic groups, however, may have entirely different conceptions of sexy, attractive female bodies, favouring large breasts and buttocks and overall plumpness, despite a problematic history of racial stereotyping (Hobson, 2003; Magubane 2001; Wallace-Sanders, 2002).

A qualitative study of pre-menopausal, healthy women in the Sydney area who had a history of dieting to lose weight shows that they distinguish between good and bad food, with the latter being associated with pleasure and temptation. They placed themselves under a form of self-surveillance by aspiring to the 'ideal' female body and reinforcing the thin ideal on other women via comments and gestures. Many of the participants were aware that by dieting regularly, they were making a trade-off with their health; dieting and health were seen to some extent as mutually exclusive (Germov and Williams, 1996).

Weight watching, dieting, and body maintenance or body work in general can be implicit (or even explicit) requirements of many occupations. The work of the flight attendant, for example, involves such body work, and management strategies of recruitment, training, and supervision as well as uniform and grooming regulations enforce the importance of body maintenance and self-surveillance (Tyler and Abbott, 1998: 439–45). Men and women flight attendants must engage in body work, though for men routine grooming might be sufficient.

In upper- and middle-class Western societies, where the ideal female body is defined as small, slender, and taking up little space, women who are defined as large or fat are subject to negative sanctions and stigmatization. In these social groups, women designated 'fat' are considered to have 'let themselves go', indicating deviance from the norms of restraint and control (Hartley, 2001: 63). Even after childbirth, women are advised by popular magazines on 'getting one's body back' by engaging in a regime of exercise (Dworkin and Wachs, 2004: 616). Fat people are often discriminated against as unhealthy, taking up too much space, physically lazy, sexually unattractive, and abnormal. They are subject to stares, comments, and difficulties in public spaces, including seats on buses, planes, and trains and in many auditoriums. As a result, there have been attempts in the United States to use discrimination laws to protect overweight people's right to access public places and job opportunities (Roehling, 2002). The New Jersey Supreme Court recently ruled that obesity is a disability where the condition was a result of a genetic metabolic disorder (Gallagher, 2002). This case suggests that moral distinctions will be made between fat people who can demonstrate that their weight is a result of a medical condition and those perceived as overweight because of overeating.

The development of fitness classes and body building provides new normative opportunities for control of fat levels to produce a new body shape. While men as well as women are criticized for fatness and strive for a more desirable body, women are under greater social pressure in societies with thinness norms to resist food temptations and closely monitor themselves. These pressures can tip self-control into eating disorders.

Eating disorders

In contemporary societies, self-starving women who aspire to bodily health, slimness, and self-control share similarities with medieval women who denied themselves food to achieve spiritual salvation. In both instances, their over-conformity can be a source of social approval, but then the negative consequences lead to disapproval (Garrett, 1998).

According to the current biomedical/psychiatric definition, a person suffering from anorexia nervosa refuses to maintain a minimally normal body weight, is intensely afraid of gaining weight, and demonstrates a significant disturbance in the perception of their body shape or size. The fear of becoming fat is not reduced by weight losses. Anorexia nervosa and bulimia nervosa (typically binge eating followed by self-induced vomiting or other purging activities) are most common in industrialized Western societies and appear to be increasing, especially among White, middle-class teenage girls (American Psychiatric Association, 1994: 539–50). Lovejoy (2001) argues that Afro-American women adopt a positive evaluation of their appearance and an alternative beauty aesthetic to Whites. Their different concept of beauty means that they are less prone to anorexia than their Euro-American counterparts.

Susan Bordo suggests that the anorexic embodies the intersection between the pursuit of slenderness through the denial of appetite and the attractiveness of 'masculine' values of self-control, determination, emotional discipline, and mastery[2] (1993b: 139–64; also Brumberg, 1998). By discovering what it is like to transcend and resist her craving for food, the young woman achieves a sense of power over others via superior will and control. At the same time, food denial can be a protest (perhaps non-articulated or unconscious) against cultural ideals about women and slenderness and the emphasis on dieting and suppression of appetite (Bordo, 1989: 18–23). The medicalization and stigmatization of anorexia nervosa create two moral/medical categories – a healthy thinness and an unhealthy thinness – thereby not undermining the dominant ideals surrounding the 'normally' slender female body (McKinley, 1999: 98–9).

This discussion shows that the range of 'normal' body types for women in Western societies is fairly narrow and deviation from these norms can result in medical intervention and social control. Being 'too fat' or 'too thin' can be met with opprobrium and attempts to alter women's eating behaviour. This is especially true in interactive service work where women's bodies and their emotions become part of the service or product purchased by clients or customers. Tensions between women's autonomy and identities and the power of gender norms also emerge in the context of women's bodies, exercise, and sports.

Exercise and 'fitness'

'Dieting is one discipline imposed upon a body subject to the "tyranny of slenderness,"; exercise is another' (Bartky, 1988: 65). Bartky asserts that even though men and women exercise, their motivations to do so are different: men exercise for health and fitness, while women exercise for appearance and body shaping as well as health and fitness. Many women experience exercise and fitness as sites of power and agency where they reject narrow or conventional constructions of femininity and where they can embrace physical power and independence.

Some forms of exercise and fitness, for example aerobics, are seen as appropriate for women. Moya Lloyd argues that the discourses around aerobics and dieting are components of the general requirements of femininity that gauge the 'the female body as inferior, unruly and in need of discipline, and which converges with other practices to produce a decorated and resculpted body as the symbol of female selfhood' (1996: 87). The proliferation of various exercise programmes has not resulted in 'a diversification of images of femininity, but rather to the reification of dominant cultural standards of beauty' (Lloyd, 1996: 90). Nonetheless, men and women do have some choice and autonomy in the exercise programmes they pursue, though these choices are constrained by resources and gender norms.

A study of the clients of fitness centres identified a range of factors affecting women's choice of activities. To a great extent, they reflected 'negotiating commonsense ideas about muscle and women's biology, bodily knowledge and experiences, and ideologies about what women's bodies should do' (Dworkin, 2003: 244). Many of the women participants articulated an upper limit in the quest for muscular strength and bulk and expressed both fear and repulsion for female bodybuilders' bodies. Women often structured fitness practices that emphasized health and femininity, thus complying with normative expectations of women's bodies. Even successful women bodybuilders with large musculature (which may be the result of steroids) are rewarded in competitions for maintaining such traditional markers of the feminine as makeup and hairstyling (Mansfield and McGinn, 1993).

For women, body maintenance and body-altering work can be experienced as personally empowering and central to their identities while simultaneously reinforcing powerful gender norms which devalue women's diversity and social status. While many women engage in pursuits often considered quintessentially masculine, for example weightlifting and other sports, a socially constrained desire to remain feminine limits women's engagement in these activities. Yet a desire to fit in and have access to a range of other resources, including employment and promotion, shapes some women's decisions to engage in this body-altering activity.

Sports

Historically, and to a lesser extent in contemporary societies, there is a tension between athletic excellence and heterosexual femininity (Messner, 2002). Strong women athletes may be viewed as masculine, assumed to be lesbian, and unattractive to heterosexual men (Cahn, 2003). They are therefore mixed role models for young girls and women spectators. In contrast, sporting prowess and physical competence are usually seen as confirming men's gender identity and heterosexuality, making it harder for men athletes to declare their homosexuality (Anderson, 2005). Men athletes' sexuality, masculinity, and physical power can thus be experienced vicariously by hegemonic men sport spectators and emulated as role models by boys (Connell, 1995; Messner, 1992; Miller, 1990).

Sports are a path to upward mobility for poor and working-class boys, even though few become successful professional athletes. Those who break into professional teams have only a few years to make it, and they play with injuries and use pain-dulling and muscle-building drugs (Messner, 1992; Messner and Sabo, 1994; Sokolove, 2004). The payoff for successful athletes in men's sports is very high income and fame. Successful women athletes do not receive the same amount of income, media coverage, or prestige (Messner, 2002). Media images of men athletes glorify their strength and power, even their violence. Media images of women athletes tend to focus on their feminine beauty and grace, downplaying their muscular strength. The model female athlete often seems to be a young gymnast with a thin, small, wiry, androgynous body.

CONCLUSION

Notions like the healthy body, the beautiful body, and the fit body conveyed via popular culture – magazines, television, billboard advertising, and the Internet – tend to be highly normative, gender-specific, and biased by White Anglo-Saxon middle-class standards of beauty and body shape. The images portray the types of bodies (a small range) that will link to occupational and emotional success. Normalization occurs as the images function as models against which the self continually measures, judges, disciplines, and corrects (Bordo, 1993b). Some feminists, following Foucault, underscore the role of self-regulation as the woman concerned about her appearance engages in continual self-surveillance, thereby affirming gendered cultural norms that reinforce inequalities between men and women (Bartky, 1988: 81). This fairly deterministic view does not allow sufficient scope for the experiences and circumstances of individual women and the choices that conscious, rational women can make in their self-interest. Dominant social norms can simultaneously constrain women's actions and provide space for individual women to make choices that may empower them in their everyday lives. This paradox, as well as women's resistance to dominant gender norms, needs to be explained, and that is not possible within a determinist theoretical framework.

A study of beauty therapists highlights some of the ambivalence regarding the trappings of femininity. The therapists refused to agree that their work is about the reproduction of disempowering feminine ideals; in their eyes, it is about enabling clients to make the best of their attributes and providing treatments to enable ordinary women to look and feel better (Black and Sharma, 2001). Others argue that disciplines of diet, exercise, and beauty that reproduce dominant normative feminine practices train women in docility and obedience to cultural requirements. The effect is sustained because the controls are personally experienced as empowering (Bartky, 1988: 64–8; Bordo, 1993b).

It is important not to posit powerlessness or empowerment as a zero-sum equation: conformity to one set of gender norms may reduce women's autonomy in some respects but expand opportunities for mobility and empowerment in other respects.

ACKNOWLEDGEMENTS

I would like to extend appreciation to Steven Talbot for research assistance and to the Flinders University Faculty of Social Sciences for a Research Support Programme grant that enabled completion of this chapter. I also appreciate suggestions from Jason Pudsey.

NOTES

1 See Rosi Braidotti (1994), Elizabeth Grosz (1987; 1994; 1995), Ruth Hubbard (1990), Edwin Schur (1984), and Rose Weitz (2003).

2 Male athletes are also prone to eating disorders due to pressures of competition and consequent need to control weight and weight gains.

REFERENCES

American Psychiatric Association (1994) *Diagnostic and Statistical Manual of Mental Disorders*, 4th edition. Washington, DC: APA.

Anderson, Eric (2005) *In the Game: Gay Athletes and the Cult of Masculinity*. Albany, NY: State University of New York Press.

Bartky, Sandra Lee (1988) 'Foucault, femininity, and the modernization of patriarchal power', in Irene Diamond and Lee Quinby (eds), *Femininity and Foucault: Reflections of Resistance*. Boston, MA: Northeastern University Press.

Becker, Gay and Nachtigall, Robert D. (1992) 'Eager for medicalisation: The social production of infertility as a disease', *Sociology of Health & Illness*, 14: 456–71.

Bell, Susan E. (1987) 'Changing ideas: The medicalization of menopause', *Social Science and Medicine*, 6: 535–42.

Black, Paula and Sharma, Ursula (2001) 'Men are real, women are "made up": Beauty therapy and the construction of femininity', *Sociological Review*, 49: 100–16.

Bordo, Susan R. (1989) 'The body and the reproduction of femininity: A feminist appropriation of Foucault', in Alison Jagger and Susan Bordo (eds), *Gender/Body/Knowledge: Feminist Reconstructions of Being and Knowing*. New Brunswick, NJ: Rutgers University Press.

Bordo, Susan (1993a) 'Feminism, Foucault and the politics of the body', in Caroline Ramazanoglu (ed.), *Explorations of Some Tensions Between Foucault and Feminism*. London: Routledge.

Bordo, Susan (1993b) *Unbearable Weight: Feminism, Western Culture, and the Body*. Berkeley, CA: University of California Press.

Braidotti, Rosi (1994) *Nomadic Subjects: Embodiment and Sexual Difference in Contemporary Feminist Theory*. New York: Columbia University Press.

Brumberg, Joan (1998) *The Body Project: An Intimate History of American Girls*. New York: Vintage Books.

Butler, Judith (1993) *Bodies that Matter: On the Discursive Limits of 'Sex'*. New York: Routledge.

Cahn, Susan K. (2003) 'From the "muscle moll" to the "butch ballplayer": Mannishness, lesbianism, and homophobia in U.S. sports', in Rose Weitz (ed.), *The Politics of Women's Bodies: Sexuality, Appearance & Behavior*. New York: Oxford University Press.

Connell, R.W. (1995) *Masculinities*. Berkeley, CA: University of California Press.

Davis, Kathy (1991) 'Re-making the she-devil: A critical look at feminist approaches to beauty', *Hypatia*, 6: 21–43.

Davis, Kathy (1995) *Reshaping the Female Body: The Dilemma of Cosmetic Surgery*. New York: Routledge.

Davis, Kathy (1997) '"My body is my art": Cosmetic surgery as feminist utopia?', *European Journal of Women's Studies*, 4: 23–37.

Davis, Kathy (2002) '"A dubious equality": Men, women and cosmetic surgery', *Body & Society*, 8: 49–65.

De Casanova, Erynn Masi (2004) '"No ugly women": Concepts of race and beauty among adolescent women in Ecuador', *Gender & Society*, 18: 287–308.

Dellinger, Kirsten and Williams, Christine L. (1997) 'Makeup at work: Negotiating appearance rules in the workplace', *Gender & Society*, 11: 151–77.

DeVault, Marjorie L. (1991) *Feeding the Family: The Social Organization of Caring as Gendered Work*. Chicago: University of Chicago Press.

Dull, D. and West, C. (1991) 'Accounting for cosmetic surgery: The accomplishment of gender', *Social Problems*, 38: 54–70.

Dworkin, Shari L. (2003) '"Holding back": Negotiating a glass ceiling on women's muscular strength', in Rose Weitz (ed.), *The Politics of Women's Bodies: Sexuality, Appearance & Behavior*. New York: Oxford University Press.

Dworkin, Shari L. and Wachs, Faye Linda (2004) '"Getting your body back": Postindustrial fit motherhood in *Shape Fit Pregnancy* magazine', *Gender & Society*, 18: 610–24.

Faludi, Susan (1995) *Backlash: The Undeclared War Against Women*. London: Chatto and Windus.

Farr, Kathryn Ann (1993) 'Shaping policy through litigation: Abortion law in the United States', *Crime & Delinquency*, 39: 167–83.

Ferree, Myra Marx (2003) 'Resonance and radicalism: Feminist framing in the abortion debates of the United States and Germany', *American Journal of Sociology*, 109: 304–44.

Foucault, Michel (1979) *Discipline and Punish: The Birth of the Prison*, trans. Alan Sheridan. New York: Vintage.

Fox, Bonnie and Worts, Diana (1999) 'Revisiting the critique of medicalized childbirth: A contribution to the sociology of birth', *Gender & Society*, 13: 326–46.

Gallagher, Mary P. (2002) 'Obesity ruled a protected status under state LAD', *New Jersey Law Journal*, 169: 1, 14.

Gapinski, Kathrine D., Brownell, Kelly D., and LaFrance, Marianne (2003) 'Body objectification and "fat talk": Effects on emotion, motivation, and cognitive performance', *Sex Roles*, 48: 377–88.

Garrett, Catherine (1998) *Beyond Anorexia: Normative Spirituality and Recovery*. Cambridge: Cambridge University Press.

Germov, John and Williams, Lauren (1996) 'The sexual division of dieting: women's voices', *Sociological Review*, 44: 630–47.

Gibson, Suzanne (1990) 'Continental drift: The question of context in feminist jurisprudence', *Law and Critique*, 1: 173–200.

Gillespie, Rosemary (1996) 'Women, the body and brand extension in medicine: Cosmetic surgery and the paradox of choice', *Women and Health*, 24: 69–85.

Gimlin, Debra (1996) 'Pamela's place: Power and negotiation in the hair salon', *Gender & Society*, 10: 505–26.

Gimlin, Debra (2000) 'Cosmetic surgery: Beauty as commodity', *Qualitative Sociology*, 23: 77–98.

Greil, Arthur L., Leitko, Thomas A., and Porter, Karen L. (1988) 'Infertility: His and hers', *Gender & Society*, 2: 172–99.

Grosz, Elizabeth (1987) 'Notes towards a corporeal feminism', *Australian Feminist Studies*, 5: 1–16.

Grosz, Elizabeth (1994) *Volatile Bodies: Towards a Corporeal Feminism*. Bloomington: Indiana University Press.

Grosz, Elizabeth (1995) *Space, Time and Perversion: The Politics of Bodies*, St Leonards: Allen and Unwin.

Hartley, Cecilia (2001) 'Letting ourselves go: Making room for the fat body in feminist scholarship', in J. E. Braziel and K. Le Besco (eds), *Bodies Out of Bounds: Fatness and Transgression*. Berkeley, CA: University of California Press. pp. 60–73.

Hobson, Janell (2003) 'The 'batty' politic: Toward an aesthetic of the black female body.' *Hypatia* 18: 87–105.

Hubbard, Ruth (1990) *The Politics of Women's Biology*. New Brunswick, NJ: Rutgers University Press.

Jackson, Linda (1992) *Physical Appearance and Gender: Sociobiological and Sociocultural Perspectives*. Albany, NJ: State University of New York Press.

Johnsen, Dawn E. (1986) 'The creation of fetal rights: Conflicts with women's constitutional rights to liberty, privacy, and equal protection', *Yale Law Journal*, 95: 599–625.

Kaw, Eugenia (2003) 'Medicalization of racial features: Asian-American women and cosmetic surgery', in Rose Weitz (ed.), *The Politics of Women's Bodies: Sexuality, Appearance & Behavior*. New York: Oxford University Press.

Leeds Craig, Maxine (2002) *Ain't I a Beauty Queen: Black Women, Beauty and the Politics of Race*. New York: Oxford University Press.

Lloyd, Moya (1996) 'Feminism, aerobics and the politics of the body', *Body & Society*, 2: 79–98.

Lorber, Judith (1989) 'Choice, gift, or patriarchal bargain? Women's consent to *in vitro* fertilization in male infertility', *Hypatia*, 4: 23–36.

Lorber, Judith and Bandlamudi, Lakshmi (1993) 'Dynamics of marital bargaining in male infertility', *Gender & Society*, 7: 32–49.

Lorber, Judith and Moore, Lisa Jean (2002) *Gender and the Social Construction of Illness*, 2nd edition. Walnut Creek, CA: AltaMira.

Lovejoy, Meg (2001) 'Disturbances in the social body: Differences in body image and eating problems among African American and white women', *Gender & Society*, 15: 239–61.

Lupton, Deborah (1996) *Food, the Body and the Self*. London: Sage.

Magubane, Zine (2001) 'Which bodies matter? Feminism, poststructuralism, race, and the curious theoretical odyssey of the "Hottentot Venus"', *Gender & Society*, 15: 816–34.

Mansfield, Alan and McGinn, Barbara (1993) 'Pumping irony: The muscular and the feminine', in David Morgan (ed.), *Body Matters*. London: Farmer Press.

Markens, Susan (1996) 'The problematic of "experience": A political and cultural critique of PMS', *Gender & Society*, 10: 42–58.

McKinley, Nita Mary (1999) 'Ideal weight/ideal women: Society constructs the female', in Jeffery Sobal and Donna Maurer (eds), *Weighty Issues: Fatness and Thinness as Social Problems*. New York: Aldine De Gruyter. pp. 97–115.

Messner, Michael A. (1992) *Power at Play: Sports and the Problem of Masculinity*. Boston, MA: Beacon Press.

Messner, Michael A. (2002) *Taking the Field: Women, Men, and Sports*. Minneapolis: University of Minnesota Press.

Messner, Michael A. and Sabo, Don F. (1994) *Sex, Violence, and Power in Sports: Rethinking Masculinity*. Freedom, CA: Crossing Press.

Miall, Charlene E. (1986) 'The stigma of involuntary childlessness', *Social Problems*, 33: 268–82.

Miller, Toby (1990) 'Sport, media and masculinity', in David Rowe and Geoff Lawrence (eds), *Sport and Leisure: Trends in Australian Popular Culture*. Sydney: Harcourt Brace Jovanovich. pp. 74–95.

Morgan, Kathryn Pauly (1991) 'Women and the knife: Cosmetic surgery and the colonization of women's bodies', *Hypatia*, 6: 25–53.

Murtagh, Madeleine J. and Hepworth, Julie (2003) 'Menopause as a long-term risk to health: Implications of general practitioner accounts of prevention for women's choice and decision-making', *Sociology of Health & Illness*, 25: 185–207.

Negrin, Llewellyn (2002) 'Cosmetic surgery and the eclipse of identity', *Body & Society*, 8: 21–42.

Nettleton, Sarah and Watson, Jonathan (eds) (1998) *The Body in Everyday Life*. London: Routledge.

Parlee, Mary Brown (1982) 'Changes in moods and activation levels during the menstrual cycle in experimentally naïve subjects', *Psychology of Women Quarterly*, 7: 119–31.

Parlee, Mary Brown (1994) 'The social construction of premenstrual syndrome: A case study of scientific discourse as cultural contestation', in M. G. Winkler and L. B. Cole (eds), *The Good Body: Asceticism in Contemporary Culture*. New Haven, CT: Yale University Press.

Petchesky, Rosalind Pollack (1987) 'Fetal images: The power of visual culture in the politics of reproduction', *Feminist Studies*, 13: 263–92.

Petersen, Kerry A. (1993) *Abortion Regimes*. Aldershot: Dartmouth.

Price, Janet and Shildrick, Margrit (eds) (1999) *Feminist Theory and the Body*. New York and London: Routledge.

Rittenhouse, C. Amanda (1991) 'The emergence of premenstrual syndrome as a social problem', *Social Problems*, 38: 412–25.

Roach Anleu, Sharyn L. (2006) *Deviance Conformity and Control*, 4th edition Sydney: Pearson Education.

Roehling, Mark V. (2002) 'Weight discrimination in the American workplace: Ethical issues and analysis', *Journal of Business Ethics*, 40: 177–89.

Rothman, Barbara Katz (1982) *In Labor: Women and Power in the Birthplace*. New York: W.W. Norton.

Rothman, Barbara Katz (1986) *The Tentative Pregnancy: Prenatal Diagnosis and the Future of Motherhood*. New York: Viking.

Rothman, Barbara Katz (1989) *Recreating Motherhood: Ideology and Technology in a Patriarchal Society*. New York: W.W. Norton.

Sandelowski, Margarete J. (1990) 'Fault lines: Infertility and imperiled sisterhood', *Feminist Studies*, 16: 33–51.

Schur, Edwin M. (1984) *Labeling Women Deviant: Gender, Stigma and Social Control*. New York: Random House.

Shilling, Chris (1993) *The Body and Social Theory*. London: Sage.

Sokolove, Michael (2004) 'The lab animal: In pursuit of doped excellence', *New York Times Magazine*, January 18: 28–33, 48, 54, 58.

Strickler, Jennifer (1992) 'The new reproductive technology: Problem or solution?', *Sociology of Health & Illness*, 14: 111–32.

Tiggemann, Marika (1994) 'Gender differences in the interrelationships between weight dissatisfaction, restraint, and self-esteem', *Sex Roles*, 30: 319–30.

Tiggemann, Marika and Kenyon, Sarah J. (1998) 'The hairlessness norm: The removal of body hair in women', *Sex Roles*, 39: 873–85.

Tiggemann, Marika and Pennington, Barbara (1990) 'The development of gender differences in body-size dissatisfaction', *Australian Psychologist*, 25: 306–13.

Toerien, Merran and Wilkinson, Sue (2003) 'Gender and body hair: Constructing the feminine woman', *Women's Studies International Forum*, 26: 333–44.

Turner, Bryan S. (1992) *Regulating Bodies: Essays in Medical Sociology*. London: Routledge.

Tyler, Melissa and Abbott, Pamela (1998) 'Chocs away: Weight watching in the contemporary airline industry', *Sociology*, 32: 433–50.

Wallace-Sanders, Kimberly (ed.) (2002) *Skin Deep, Spirit Strong: Critical Essays on the Black Female Body in American Culture*. Ann Arbor: University of Michigan Press.

Weitz, Rose (2001) 'Women and their hair: Seeking power through resistance and accommodation', *Gender & Society*, 15: 667–86.

Weitz, Rose (ed.) (2003) *The Politics of Women's Bodies: Sexuality, Appearance & Behavior*. New York: Oxford University Press.

Wikler, Norma Juliet (1986) 'Society's response to the new reproductive technologies: The feminist responses', *Southern California Law Review*, 59: 1043–57.

Wolf, Naomi (1990) *The Beauty Myth*. London: Vintage.

Zadoroznyj, Maria (2001) 'Birth and the "reflexive consumer": Trust, risk and medical dominance in obstetric encounters', *Journal of Sociology*, 37: 117–39.

21

The Natural World and the Nature of Gender

Irmgard Schultz

This chapter presents a survey on how the field of gender studies approaches research on the environment and environmental problems. The survey is divided into three main sections. The first elucidates the principal theoretical debates on women and nature, presenting the main epistemological approaches on (post-)gender and the environment. The second identifies the main gender issues and gives some examples of research in this field. The third is a brief outlook on upcoming challenges to this research field in gender studies. The whole chapter focuses on questions of integrating gender into interdisciplinary and transdisciplinary social–ecological research.

INTRODUCTION

'Environment' is a scientific and political category that includes the question, Whose environment? In contrast, 'nature' is primarily a philosophical category and one common to everyday life. Contemplating 'nature' raises the question, What is not nature? Is culture 'not' nature? Is society? Rationality? Men? Technology? God? And to what extent does the distinction between nature and 'not nature' explain the problems and relations that humans associate with these categories? Against the background of these considerations, this chapter presents a survey on how the field of gender studies approaches research on the environment and environmental problems. I start with the principal theoretical debates on and approaches to women and nature, (post-)gender, and the environment. Second, I identify the main gender issues and offer some examples of research in this field. I conclude with a brief outlook on upcoming challenges to this research field in gender studies.

THEORETICAL DEBATES

In environmental studies, feminist theoretical debates have focused on the relationship between women and nature. These debates go back to the nineteenth century. Current debates use twentieth-century critical theory and look forward to an integrative post-modern approach.

Assumptions about the relationship between women and nature

Assumptions about the relationship between women and nature strike at the core of feminist debates because they have to deal with societal idealizations and normative regulations about how images of 'the woman' and 'the feminine' are constructed. In modern European thinking at the end of the nineteenth century, the 'inner nature' of woman was related in a special way to 'outer nature', combining it with the question of woman's morality and identity (Schultz, 2001a). The first European women's movement at the beginning of the twentieth century sparked a controversial debate about the nature of women. This debate defined women in a moral way as closely connected with nature, in contrast to men, who were seen as connected with culture. Against the background of Darwin's nascent evolutionary theory, Mendelian laws, and genetics, there was a strong scientific and public discussion about the sexual instincts of women and their part in heredity. The predominant discourse in physiology and early psychology combined the question about the nature of women with the issue of women's sexuality and morality. Richard von Krafft-Ebing, head of the first psychiatric university hospital in Vienna, exemplified this view in his 1886 study, *Psychopathia sexualis*.[1] In the predominant moral discourse of that time prostitutes, who were portrayed as having a strong sexual desire, were contrasted with the ideal woman, who was a moral housewife with almost no sexuality. Prostitutes were given as examples to demonstrate what kind of woman is 'not natural'.

At the *fin-de-siècle* there was a vast, popular body of gender literature that gave educational advertisements and instructions to mothers and daughters warning them against becoming a 'brain woman'. This literature defined the nature of women as moral reproduction. Because of its misogyny, Paul J. Möbius' 1906 pamphlet 'Über den Schwachsinnn des Weibes' ('On the Imbecility of the Wife') was a famous example of this new sort of literature. In his pamphlet, Möbius argued that the reproductive function of a woman's uterus suffers when a woman uses her brain too much. Feminists rejected the misogyny of this argument, but they were in conflict about the question of women and their relation to nature (*Feministische Studien*, 1984). In her well-known 'Kritik der Weiblichkeit' ('Critique of Feminity', 1922), the feminist Rosa

Mayreder refuted the dominant idea that women have a special bond with nature. Instead, she argued that women are able to do cultural work in the same way that men do. Her argument criticized, in particular, the position of the feminist psychoanalyst Lou Andreas Salome, who had accredited a certain closeness of women to nature, seeing women as more self-centered and more bound with the cosmos than men.[2]

Despite the fact that this discussion took place almost a hundred years ago, one experiences a certain 'déjà vu effect' when examining more recent debates on the question of whether women are closer to nature than men. First-wave feminists argued for or against a special bond between women and nature, but they did not depart from the frame of the hierarchical dichotomous worldview that posited women and men as separate and related to nature and culture, respectively. After World War II, however, second-wave feminists began to examine this hierarchical constellation critically.

The anthropologist Sherry Ortner asked in 1974, 'Is Female to Male as Nature is to Culture?' An emphatic answer to Ortner's question was given by the French feminist Françoise d'Eaubonne (1974). In her radical feminist manifesto *Le Feminisme ou la mort* (*Feminism or Death*), d'Eaubonne linked the question of the relationship between women and nature to the 'ecological question', which examined whether human activities were destroying Earth's ecosystems. D'Eaubonne argued that the success of women's struggle is the only way to guarantee the survival of the entire human species. The term 'eco-feminism', as defined by d'Eaubonne, is an important approach in gender research on the environment. The subject matter is not the philosophical idea of nature but the natural environment of human beings, women and men, and their society.

Radical feminist thinkers of the 1970s and 1980s argued philosophically that the exploitation and commodification of women is similar to the way humans treat nature. In a more poetic manner, Susan Griffin, in her 1978 *Woman and Nature*, argued that patriarchal thinking is grounded on the principle of separating and dividing from wholeness and thus converts the living wholeness of nature into dead material. Similarly, in her popular book *Death of Nature* (1980), Carolyn Merchant presented historical evidence of the violent character of the simultaneous oppression of nature and women in the emergence and implementation of a new mechanistic worldview in Europe in the sixteenth and seventeenth centuries.

Since the 1980s, the eco-feminist approach has been closely connected with Vandana Shiva in India and Maria Mies in Germany. Shiva sees the linkage between nature and women as the result of a gendered cultural development that led to a deeper spiritual connection between women and nature than men have. She shows this connection by the example of *pankriti*, which is a principle in Indian mythology. In modern society, *pankriti* has been replaced by Eurocentrism, which has succeeded with a mechanistic concept of sciences, colonialism, and the Western model of development (Mies and Shiva, 1993; Shiva, 1988; see also Von Werlhof, Bennholdt-Thomsen, and Faraclas, 2002).

Materialistic eco-feminists, such as Maria Mies and Mary Mellor in England, see the privileged bond of women with nature as the product of an historical development that devalued the ability to give birth and excluded life-giving experiences from the historical record (Mellor, 2001).

As these examples show, there are strong theoretical differences among eco-feminist approaches (see also Biehl, 1991; Plant, 1989; Plumwood, 1986). Some eco-feminists are closely connected to spiritual thinking while others are linked with psychological or materialistic arguments. Despite the different theoretical positions, all forms of eco-feminism stress in some way women's privileged bond with nature. In emphasizing this relationship, eco-feminists are reversing the predominant evaluation and giving nature (Mother Earth) more worth. Because of their argument of a special bond between women and nature, eco-feminist approaches have provoked responses from other feminists, who disagree with eco-feminism's undifferentiated generalizations and view of women as a 'naturalized' category.

New feminist approaches to the question of gender and nature

Epistemologically grounded theoretical positions, which are diametrically opposed to eco-feminism, are presented by post-structural feminists, on one hand, and by feminists in the tradition of critical theory, a feminist approach in Germany, on the other. Both theoretical positions stress, in different ways, a logic of identity as a prerequisite in the epistemology of eco-feminism. They do not agree with the assumption that all women have a 'female identity' that can become the basis of feminist policies and political action.

In Germany, a feminist critique of a logic of identity refers to the critical theory of the philosophers Theodor W. Adorno, Max Horkheimer, and Walter Benjamin (Becker-Schmidt, 1999; Kulke and Scheich, 1992; O'Neill, 1999; Scheich, 1996). Following Adorno, this approach looks for 'mediations' between abstract oppositions. Critical theory distinguishes the 'outer nature' from the 'inner nature' of human beings in a special way. In their book *Dialectics of Enlightenment* (1944/1972), Adorno and Horkheimer argue that 'enlightenment' entails the intellectual surmounting of natural myths and the generation of an objective, rational understanding of nature. But this rationality, which was successful in developing technology, capsized and became a myth itself. Rationality, which levels all qualitative aspects of societal living and de-emphasizes emphatic emotions that human beings could have with each other and with other natural beings, became the character of a 'second nature'.

Critical theory is an important approach for gender research in the environmental field because it constitutes a critical understanding of gender relations within the frame of a gender order that distinguishes among questions relating to the symbolic order, the economic and political order, and the social organization of sexuality (Becker-Schmidt, 1999). Yet, it is not the prominent 'instrumental reason' argument that makes the dialectic between inner and outer nature attractive to feminists.[3] Instead, it is critical theory's philosophical reference to *mimesis*, which visualizes in art a capacity for integrated feeling and reflecting by acting with each other and nature. If the idea of *mimesis* were viewed not only with respect to cultural productions, but also with regard to developments within natural sciences, it would open access to new venues of reflection. Searching for an example of a quality like *mimesis* within the natural sciences, feminists embraced the biologist Barbara McClintock, who won the Noble Prize in 1954 for her work on genetic transposition in cell genetics. Her biographer, Evelyn Fox Keller (1983), underlined the surprising way in which McClintock's investigative procedures differed from the 'male-objective standards' in biological research. McClintock developed a deep connection with the corn plants she observed every day, which could be described as a quality of *mimesis* (Schultz, 1992).

With new forms of techno-scientific mediation, which recombines 'the enfleshed and the technological' (Braidotti, 1997) in genetic cell transplantation technology as well as in many new technology fields, there is a need for a new approach in gender studies in the area of the environment. Such an approach should provide a distinct and critical perspective on natural sciences and technical design in their multiple interconnections with the social and economic sciences and societal developments.

With respect to natural and technical sciences, the post-structuralist perspective of natural scientist Donna Haraway is predominant in environmental gender studies.[4] Haraway criticizes the postulate of scientific objectivity by focusing on the principle of generalization. She shows that the goal of transferability of scientific assertions extracted from specific (gender) situations is as constitutive for an epistemological position of a universal perspective 'from Nowhere' (that means a perspective that is not self-reflective, not located and not embodied). In contrast to this kind of objectivity of the 'techno-sciences', Haraway demands a 'situated knowledge' (Haraway, 1988).

In the international discourse on science, Haraway became famous because of her practice of deconstructing the dichotomies of nature and culture, living and dead material, and humans and non-humans, which are deeply grounded in modern dualistic thinking and language (Haraway, 1989). In feminist environmental research, it is not her method of discourse, but rather her epistemological point of 'situating' and 'recontextualizing knowledge' that is utilized as the feminist perspective on technology and consumer products. The first attempts to use this approach to innovate socio-technical constructions demonstrated that the idea must be further developed before it can make additional contributions in the field (Weller, Hayn, and Schultz, 2002). What is needed is a series of new methods and categories to combine the deconstructive perspective of 'situating' and 'recontextualizing knowledge' with reconstructive perspectives. The feminist historian of science Londa

Schiebinger (1997: 203) names this change in the perspective of feminist critiques on natural sciences to reconstruction, 'sustainable science'.[5]

Societal relations to nature and the double-sided perspective on gender relations

The Institute for Social–Ecological Research (ISOE) in Frankfurt am Main uses a modified version of critical theory's idea of theory-guided empirical research. Its interdisciplinary approach on societal relations to nature takes the philosophical critique on the abstract general – that it can be approximated only by reflections. This idea, promulgated by Adorno and Horkheimer, has serious consequences for research, as it posits that theory must be developed further within its subject matter – the society – by empirical studies (not only 'proved' by empirical studies). But, the approach of societal relations to nature goes beyond the epistemological reflections of critical theory on society by separately examining the prerequisites and impacts of natural sciences as well as those of social sciences. This approach also values the interconnections between social scientific and natural scientific explanations (Becker and Jahn, 2004; Schultz, 2001a). It refers to Albert Einstein's theory of relativity and especially to Niels Bohr's concepts of complementarity and correspondence in early quantum physics, which are examples of scientific self-reflectivity and are, in a certain sense, postmodern perspectives within natural sciences.[6] Thus, the approach of societal relations to nature opens a space for a double-sided critique that scrutinizes the predominant epistemological prerequisites, concepts, and methods of social sciences as well as those of natural and technical sciences.

Within the framework of a dualistic worldview, the relationship between nature and society can be theoretically conceptualized in two mutually exclusive ways: as a *naturalizing of society* or as a *culturalization of nature*. These alternatives divide theoretical discourse on the relationship between nature and society into two camps: naturalist and culturalist. Taking this argument as a new form of dualism opens a double-sided critique and a new position for socio-ecological thinking: against naturalization of societal relations to nature (naturalism), on one hand, and against culturalization of societal relations to nature (culturalism), on the other (Becker and Jahn, 2004: 12). This double-sided critique opens new starting points for scientific reflection and problem-oriented research. It takes the Nature–Culture opposition not as substantial dualism (worldview), but as scientific distinction within environmental problems.

With respect to an understanding of gender, the concept of societal relations to nature starts with the strong theoretical assumption that the interconnections of the natural sciences with the social sciences are grounded in symbolic, abstract, and fragmented inventories of knowledge about gender relations. This assumption can be proved by considering the history of sciences. Since the formation of the disciplines of sociology and economy in the eighteenth and nineteenth centuries and the different disciplines of evolutionary biology, physiology, medicine, and psychology in the nineteenth and twentieth centuries, there has been an ongoing knowledge transfer about gender issues between the two scientific cultures, with normative implications (Schultz, 2001a). This 'gender knowledge' was basic for the construction of gendered relations in different societal and scientific fields.[7] As a result of this dynamic knowledge transfer, gender can be reconstructed only through interdisciplinary research and cooperation between the two scientific cultures.

The double-sided critique against the naturalization of gender relations, on one hand, and against the culturalization of gender relations, on the other, can be connected by situating and recontextualizing knowledge through problem-oriented research. These practices of critique according to the approach of societal relations to nature result in a *new understanding of the difference between sex and gender*: 'sex' is seen in a constructive way, but nevertheless remains different from 'gender'. 'Sex' implies the descriptions of gender relations by medical, technical, and natural sciences, while 'gender' means the descriptions of the same gender relations from cultural, social, and economic perspectives. In this perception of gender relations both sides are understood from a (de)constructive and reconstructive perspective (Schultz, 2001a).

MAIN GENDER ISSUES AND RESEARCH IN FEMINIST ENVIRONMENTAL STUDIES

Thus far, the theoretical feminist debate on the environment has been strongly influenced by the discourse on development policy strategies within the international women's movement and the UN's incorporation of women's issues.

Political issues and feminist studies on the environment from a global perspective

At the World Conference on Women in Nairobi in 1985, the 'women and environment' issue was brought into public consciousness through the example of the Chipko movement in the Himalayan region. By embracing the trees, which they owned commonly, the Chipko women tried to protect them against commercialization and destruction. The woodland was their reservoir for food, materials for house building, and small non-timber products. Governmental and industrial interests denied the Chipko people their traditional right to the commons and tried to expropriate them.

Since that time, there have been strong 'women for the environment' movements in the countries of the South. They struggle for women's right to own land and for the preservation of subsistence economies, in which women generally have a more powerful position. They fight against the pollution of rural and urban environments, the depletion of resources, and hazardous large-scale technical projects, such as large dams in India.[8]

In the 1980s and early 1990s, these types of debates and studies were subsumed under the women, environment, and development (WED) debate. The WED debate is anchored in a critical view of development policies and focuses on the link between modernization and technology, on the one hand, and environmental deterioration, on the other. One very important aspect of this debate thus far has been the empowerment approach of Development Alternatives with Women for a New Era (DAWN, see www.dawn.org.fj), a network of women scholars and activists from the economic South that, since 1984, has engaged in feminist research and analysis of the global environment. DAWN conducts research with the goal of developing a global theory of the interdependencies between the macroeconomic level and the everyday life of women. Central to DAWN's analysis is the perspective of women's empowerment. This perspective argues that formal equity for women is not enough; what is needed is an improvement in the actual power relations with a specific focus on the transformation of global societal relations, including nature (DAWN, 1985).

The UN Conference on Environment and Development (UNCED) in Rio de Janeiro in 1992 provided further important input into feminist environmental studies by establishing the political perspective of sustainable development as a major frame of reference for international and UN policies. After UNCED, many issues from the WED debate were grouped under the concept of sustainable development. Many international women's NGOs, above all the Brazilian section of WEDO (Women's Environment and Development Organization, see www.wedo.org), an international advocacy network that seeks to increase the power of women worldwide, were very active in preparing for UNCED. WEDO and other women's organizations and activists brought women's issues into the agreements of the conference. The commitment to overcome gender inequality and the objective of necessary, full, and equal participation of women form the essential components of Agenda 21, one of the most important agreements to come out of UNCED. Since then, the debate surrounding sustainable development has constituted a frame of reference for environmental and feminist studies in this field, mainly in Europe and Canada. Nevertheless, the understanding of what sustainable development is differs considerably, most of all between the countries of the South and the countries of the North. In the countries of the South, sustainability is seen more with respect to development and more in terms of its promise of better economic and social conditions. In contrast, in the countries of the North, the normative aspect of preserving the environment for the next generation is emphasized more (Becker and Jahn, 1999).

In the last decade, the debate on women, environment, and development has become more and more connected with the questions of basic rights to livelihood, control over reproduction, and environmental justice and equity. At venues such as the most recent World Conference on Women in Beijing in 1995, new issues have been raised. These include (a) the interdependency between women's poverty and environmental degradations in their living conditions; (b) the important role of women in preserving healthy food and nutrition; (c) the preservation of women's and Indigenous traditional knowledge against commercialization by biotechnological firms; (d) the effects of organic pollutants on women's and men's reproductive health; and (e) the debate on population policies, which were discussed in Beijing in the context of human rights, reproductive and sexual rights, and self-determination for women. Poverty elimination, information provision, and capacity building for women are seen as the most important objectives (Ogunleye and Hemmati, 2000: 8ff.)

In feminist ecological studies which refer to the international debate, there is another approach that can be characterized as more pragmatic. Indian feminist ecologist Bina Agarwal provides a good example. Agarwal (1992) argues, in opposition to eco-feminist approaches, for a 'feminist environmentalism' that reflects the predominant power structures of policy and economics. In this perspective, the environment is not seen as a vital subject, 'Nature', but as an ecological system that is described by natural sciences and (trans)formed by human cultural work. Agarwal raises issues about the policies of gender relations in connection with environmental management strategies in concrete contexts and stresses the role of customs, laws, and social structures in determining women's relationship to their environment. In this perspective, the different forms of relationship to the environment are seen as caused by different forms of interaction between human beings and their material interests. The feminist environmentalist approach opens scientific space for empirical feminist studies by going beyond normative reflections.

It is very important for these gender studies, which are framed by political and normative strategies and concepts, such as gender equity, environmental justice, and sustainability, to reflect in an analytical way on the normative dimension of research. Maggie O'Neill emphasizes this point for gender studies in general in her introduction to the edition *Adorno, Culture and Feminism*: 'We have to face the moral as well as the analytical issues' (1999: 5).

European gender mainstreaming and environmental studies

Within its strategy of gender mainstreaming, the European Commission launched, in 2001, gender impact assessment (GIA) studies in order to introduce a critical dimension in the way gender issues are treated throughout the Fifth European Framework Program for Research, Technology Development and Demonstration (RTD). The GIAs are part of an ongoing monitoring process by the European Commission that aims to take the gender dimension more fully into account within research policy. To this end, seven studies were carried out, one of which was entitled 'Environment and Sustainable Development' (ESD).[9]

The ESD subprogram contained seven thematic research fields, which reflected the dominance of natural and technical sciences in environmental studies. These fields included: (1) urban sustainability; (2) global change, climate, and biodiversity; (3) sustainable marine ecosystems; (4) sustainable management and quality of water; (5) natural and technological hazards; (6) earth observation technologies; and (7) socio-economic aspects of environmental change in the perspective of sustainable development. A state-of-the-art report described the results of gender research on the environment and sustainable development in general and in the seven research fields in particular (ISOE, 2003; Schultz, Hummel, Hayn, and Empacher, 2001). The report identified three main gender dimensions in environmental research:

1 Work: the gendered division of labor and women's work
2 Body: the organization of intimacy
3 Science: the shaping power of women and men in science, technology and environmental policies

These three components are characterized as gender dimensions in environmental studies, and they incorporate a list of highly gendered issues within environmental and sustainability research. Gender dimensions in gender impact assessments (Verloo and Roggeband, 1996) are a heuristic concept to identify and, according to the approach of mainstreaming, to integrate gender issues into research and politics. To identify gender issues in this field is, in contrary to some research fields of social sciences, still very avant garde. One important finding of the gender impact assessment of the ESD subprogram was that the program did not mention gender issues explicitly and concretely with respect to the different sub-research areas. As a result, from a total of 2,125 research proposals, only one mentioned gender in the abstract. Thus, the identification of gender issues in environmental research is important to bring those issues into research programs.

Assuming that gendered power relations are at the core of all gender dimensions, the three gender dimensions correspond with three main theoretical and political debates on women and gender studies: a feminist understanding of work, a feminist understanding of the body, and the feminist debate about science:

1 *A feminist understanding of work*: This gender dimension focuses on the connections between paid and unpaid labor, between work inside and outside the home, and between gendered tasks and professions such as market-mediated labor and domestic work, subsistence work, care work, 'informal' and 'illegal' work.[10] Within environmental studies this gender dimension is strongly connected with a daily life perspective.[11]
2 *A feminist understanding of the body*: The feminist debate about the body[12] is connected with questions of gendered identities and a critical

perspective on heterosexuality. This is not the case in environmental studies so far. In environmental research, the issue of health and risk perception is predominant. The example of the different impacts of radiation on women, men, children, seniors, and others illustrates that a perspective on different vulnerable bodies, such as pregnant women and ill men, is needed, one that does not ignore knowledge from physics and (feminist) medicine and is able to differentiate between the symbolic gender order, sexual politics, and physical gender differences.[13]

3 *The feminist debate about science*: Feminist reflections on science are numerous, especially with respect to epistemological prerequisites such as rationality and objectivity.[14] However, the empowerment approach in the women's movement and in gender studies of the 1980s and 1990s focused on an exclusively social and economic perspective. Even within the debate surrounding sustainable development, the assumption that science functions as a 'motor' of unsustainable development was very seldom examined. In connection with its environmental research, the women's movement needed to expand its approach to include a perspective on empowerment with relation to the sciences.

Against this background, the approach of gender and environment within social–ecological research focused on empowerment of feminist perspectives within the sciences and combined it with the sustainable development framework (Schultz, 2001b; Schultz and Weller, 1995). One key challenge for the empowerment perspective in the sciences is to develop inter- and transdisciplinary research. In order to achieve such gender studies, environmental research has to be changed at the level of standards, methods, instruments, and tools as well as at the content level. The blending of the gender approach with the natural sciences and technological research cannot be achieved by simply adding the gender perspective to existing approaches. What is needed is the development of new concepts and methods to integrate the different perspectives, including those of different scientific disciplines and those of different laypersons and civil society groups. The difficulty in overcoming this challenge is exacerbated by the fact that, even in feminist and gender research, 'interdisciplinary' is often understood as between the social, cultural, and historical sciences only. Research examples that integrate perspectives from natural sciences and feminist critique on natural sciences are rare.

The next section provides examples of environmental studies in each gender dimension: work, body, and science. In the interest of brevity, I describe only one example for each gender dimension.

Work: sustainable production and consumption patterns

Pollution was the leading issue when the new research field of environmental studies was being developed in the 1970s and 1980s in Europe. The pollution problem was elaborated with respect to air, water, soil, and forests. A significant amount of 'end-of-the-pipe technology' was developed to avoid pollution, such as filters in the chimneys of industrial plants. Women's studies could hardly be found in this research. Today, the issue of pollution is no longer focused on end-of-the-pipe technologies, and new methods of evaluating environmental costs are available. The life-cycle analysis (LCA) of products calculates environmental loads with respect to different life phases of a product. In addition to the production phase of a product and its waste disposal, the LCA includes the use of the product as a possible source of environmental pollution. Thus, the issue of consumption became an environmental issue. After UNCED in Rio and its call for sustainable consumption patterns, especially in the countries of the North, a broader field in environmental research was established: sustainable production and consumption. This field includes different economic, ecological, and social scientific approaches, such as demonstrating the effects of energy use in households and examining consumer behavior in different areas with respect to material flows. In this type of research, socio-economic environmental approaches dominate, and gender studies play a significant role.[15]

The gender perspective in this research stresses the importance of everyday life for environmental strategies, which is a feminist conceptualization of the issue. The feminist perspective is based in debates and theories about the gendered division of labor and women's work. To conceptualize waste work in a household or the special tasks of consumption work from a gender perspective, for example, one needs a critical gender analysis of new forms of housework and everyday life. To this end, a number of different social scientific approaches have been elaborated, including the concept of daily life organization (Jurczyk and Rerrich, 1993) and the concept of everyday life ecology within socio-ecological research (see www.isoe.de). A prominent economic feminist approach in this field is that of 'provident economy', which aims for the satisfaction of needs rather than abstract values (Busch-Lüty, Jochimsen, Knobloch, and Seidl, 1994). Similar to provident economy, but from a more global perspective is the subsistence perspective (Bennholdt-Thomsen and Mies, 1997). There are some empirical studies on consumption patterns in general or with respect to specific fields of consumption, such as the use of energy, water, and traffic and mobility.[16] Most recently, food consumption has arisen as a prominent issue. Within this framework, two analytical trends are becoming more important for gender studies in environmental research. The first trend is research on gendered time patterns (Adam, 1994), and the second is a greater focus on gendered patterns of using public and private space (Paravicini, 1999). In general, reflections on new concepts of time and space in environmental gender studies can be frequently found.

Despite new developments in the content of research, the methods and instruments of measuring environmental degradation and environmental loads (material flows) have not been thoroughly questioned from a gender perspective. Only a few studies have begun to consider these methods and their standards as being gendered as well (Weller et al., 2002). Furthermore, only a few feminists from the natural and technological sciences have begun to work on conceptual questions of material development and product design with a (re)constructive approach (Weller, 2004).

Body: the issue of vulnerability

There are a growing number of feminist environmental studies about risk perception and disaster research that focus on the important issue of vulnerability. To take a prominent example, in Europe, environmental issues were seldom discussed at the beginning of the women's movement. This changed considerably after the nuclear accident in Chernobyl in 1986. Women in many European countries organized demonstrations against nuclear technology. In Finland, women called for a 'birth strike' against nuclear technologies, and in Germany, even a year after the accident occurred, there were still more than 1,000 groups of Mothers Against Nuclear Technology. The first studies from a feminist perspective appeared soon after the accident and led to a lively discussion on the risks of nuclear technologies. This discussion incorporated a wide spectrum of arguments that shape research on technological risks from a gender perspective.

Research on attitudes towards environmental issues showed, and continues to show, that risk perception is highly gendered. In the German feminist debate on the effects of the nuclear accident, the concept of gendered vulnerability was discussed for the first time. Mothers Against Nuclear Technology criticized those strategies that were aimed at minimizing radioactivity to so-called limit-values. They criticized not the method to set limit-values, but instead the fact that the limit-values were modeled for an average, healthy man, instead of taking into account the special vulnerability (with respect to radioactivity) of pregnant women, the ill, and children. The issue of environmental impacts on the health of diverse vulnerable groups has since been a core topic of gender research in this field. Feminist studies in medicine and gynecology are the epicenters of such research.

Fifteen years after the Chernobyl accident, the German Federal Ministry for the Environment, Nature Conservation, and Nuclear Safety (BMU) undertook the project 'Gender Impact Assessment in the Field of Radiation Protection and the Environment', which evaluated the renewed Radiation Protection Ordinance (RPO). The GIA focused on new provisions that regulated the overlapping area between radiation protection, protection of reproductive health, and protection of the unborn child. The new RPO repealed the general ban on pregnant women's access to workplace areas that are exposed to radiation and replaced it with a concept of differentiated protection. These new regulations targeted those persons exposed to radiation working as medical, research, and other staff at nuclear facilities or in airline crews. The GIA focused, in particular, on the question of why different gender-specific regulations are applied to women and men with respect to reproductive health. Since the RPO contains additional limits for women, the researchers investigated whether men could be disadvantaged in the sense of protection and women in the sense of access to working places and career. However, the latest status of medical research justifies gender-specific provisions, citing differing degrees of incorporation of radioactivity in the ovaries and uterus, on the one hand, and in sperm, on the other (Hayn and Schultz, 2002).

This example shows that environmental research, when referring to questions of bodily needs and physical vulnerability, sometimes has to take into account physical differences between the two sexes (and within them), even if the differences appear to be socially constructed. From a perspective of the empowerment of women, the stereotypical idea of associating reproductive health only with women must be critically examined. Men's vulnerability is an equally important issue in environmental gender studies.

Science: genetically transformed organisms

One current field of environmental research deals with genetically transformed organisms in agriculture, and is conducted with the aim of sustaining biodiversity. This research shows that new scientific methods are required to expand the influence of women in science, technology, and environmental policies. The areas of biotechnology and genetic–technological research, which deal with the risks of development and analysis of agriculture, nutrition, and the protection of nature in the wider sense, are also incorporated into this field.[17]

Today, there are many women researchers in the field of genetically transformed organisms. They are very active in NGOs working on this theme, in ethics commissions, and in the women's organization Diverse Women for Diversity. Similar to feminist approaches in the field of economic development (Busch-Lüthy et al., 1994), many feminists stress the ethical point of techno-economical developments in genetic transformation. They view ecological developments with respect to an 'ethic of precaution'. A specific gender approach that includes natural scientific perspectives has yet to be fully elaborated in this research field. A preliminary attempt at gender-sensitive research on genetically transformed organisms was made by the German state of Bremen in its monitoring of the environmental impacts of genetically modified plants (Weller, 2003). The monitoring, which was carried out in a GIA of environmental research projects, focused on conceptual and methodological questions of situating and contextually reconceptualizing knowledge.

With respect to empowerment that reflects gendered daily life conditions in technological development, several groups of research questions should be combined. These include questions of the health of vulnerable groups of women and men, agricultural sustainable development and everyday nutrition, giving special attention to the use of 'novel' food, which contains genetically modified substances. Methods of risk assessment fall into three different fields: (1) agriculture/ecology, (2) health/medicine, and (3) daily life and society. Initially, each of these fields needs to be elaborated independently. Then, they have to be combined with new methods of research integration. These results must be viewed within the context of the gendered daily lives of different social groups. Thus far, these three research fields are separated. With respect to methodological questions, the clarification of the perspective of evaluation is indispensable for the elaboration of new methods of integrating social, ecological, and medical impact analyses. In this case, that means clarifying the normative dimension by defining the 'precautionary principle'. Here, the ethical debates within feminist and scientific discourses are crucial.

OUTLOOK FOR THE FUTURE

In her book *Silent Spring* (1962, see Hynes, 1989), the US biologist Rachel Carson first described the catastrophic consequences that the use of agricultural pesticides has on human beings and nature. Many environmentalists claim that the environmental movement began with this book and with Carson's involvement. Carson accurately depicted how pesticides move from plants sprayed with DDT to other plants that were not sprayed. From the trees, the pollution reaches birds, which eventually die from the toxins; therefore, the silent spring is the spring when the birds no longer sing. Before Carson's book, there was little scientific knowledge about these ecological interdependencies, and such connections would not have been accepted if Carson had not demonstrated them by using the language of natural sciences and the methods and measurements of biology and biochemistry. Carson's call for an end to environmental pollution formed the nucleus of the nascent environmental movement. Later, the movement led to a ban on the use of DDT and to the implementation of the Environmental Protection Act in the United States. A new governmental institution, the Environmental Protection Agency, was founded, and new scientific methods within natural sciences and technology were developed, namely, environmental impact assessments and technological risk assessments.

In the forty years since the publication of *Silent Spring*, the environmental movements in the United States, Australia, and Western Europe have seen their ups and their downs. They received a push by the movement for 'globalization from below'. In Eastern Europe and in some Asian, Latin American, and African countries, the movements are very active in dealing with local and regional conflicts and needs. Women and feminists, like the Kenyan Nobel Prize winner Wangari Maathai, play an important role within these movements all over the world. There are strong women's networks with respect to different environmental issues, such as Women in Europe for a

Common Future (WECF), the international network on Gender and Sustainable Energy (ENERGIA), the German Focal Point Gender Justice and Sustainability (GENANET), and the Gender and Water Alliance. GIA methods were developed to mainstream gender issues similar to the mainstreaming of environmental impact assessments.

Despite these advances, the women's movement still requires a greater contribution in environmental studies by feminists like Rachel Carson, simultaneously scientifically oriented, innovative, and engaged. The field of environmental science has never been exclusively defined by natural sciences, as is the case with quantum physics, for example. To examine an environmental problem such as biodiversity means to observe and measure the loss of biological species while at the same time evaluating why this loss happens. By its very nature, this research demands an understanding of social, economic, technical, and natural interconnections and dynamics. In other words, it requires an understanding of the constant transformation in societal relations to nature. Gender studies within environmental science have advanced significantly in the analysis of social and economic interactions and planning demands.

In this respect, the example of urban research and city planning is significant. Gender approaches in academic urban research, research networks, and professional associations have been established successfully in many different countries. New planning instruments and concepts in gendered urban planning are being elaborated. However, the core of knowledge on material construction in physics, chemistry, and some disciplines of engineering remains without a feminist perspective.

To bring gender issues into the hard sciences would mean to open their disciplinary boundaries to so-called social issues. A gender perspective functions in this sense as an eye opener for social questions. Thus, it requires interdisciplinary and transdisciplinary approaches. In the European landscape of gender studies, first experiences with a new type of transdisciplinary, gender-sensitive research occurred through special research programs in Germany, Austria, and Switzerland.[18] To identify gender issues and integrate them into a project involving different disciplines, professionals, and laypersons is a new and difficult task. Predominant themes of gender-sensitive, social–ecological research projects deal with the highly complex set of interactive natural and social systems: *life-support systems* for water, energy, and food. They are embedded in fragile natural environments which require intelligent regulation in order to satisfy the needs of a growing population now and in the future.

Projects of this new type of transdisciplinary, gender-sensitive research analyze the privatization of communal water services and the European and national shaping of the new emissions trading systems. One research project developed with explicitly feminist perspective is 'Supplying the population – interactions among demographic trends, needs and supply systems' (Hummel, Hertler, Niemann, Lux, and Schulze, 2003). These examples show that one tendency within environmental gender studies is to go 'mainstream'.

Mainstreaming gender requires elaborate concepts of scientific critique with respect to social as well as to natural and technical sciences and their reconstructive integratation. In the words of the feminist historian of sciences Londa Schiebinger:

> It is not enough to understand how sciences had been made; we need to develop more practical, constructive ways to employ tools of gender analysis creating what I will call 'sustainable science.' Only when gender analysis becomes an integral part of science research programs will the problem of women in science be solved. (1997: 203)

NOTES

1 Nike Wagner (1987) gives a detailed overview of this discourse.

2 For an overview of Salome's work, see Biddy Martin (1991).

3 In fact, the authors of *Dialectics of Enlightenment* refer to an understanding of natural sciences that does not consider the new epistemological frames of Einstein's theory of relativity and quantum physics. Thus, their generalizing critique on natural sciences fails its subject.

4 To a certain extent, Haraway's perspective on 'situated knowledges' (1988) corresponds with the feminist critique of 'female identity' and Adorno's critique of the 'abstract general'. Adorno's critique focuses on the dialectics of the general and the concrete of concepts and terms. By reflecting the power of concepts and terms, and thus the power of language, this philosophical approach opens more space for 'the unspeakable' and thus for a certain 'agency' of nature.

5 Haraway's work has influenced another post-structuralist position associated with a post-colonialist approach to the question of identity within the frame of global development. Post-colonialism departs from dualistic thinking and the dichotomy of nature and culture. One proponent is Rosi Braidotti, who assumes 'border-crossing and dislocated subjectivity' instead of fixed (female or male) identities (Braidotti, 2002).

6 The Danish physicist Niels Bohr introduced the idea of complementarity in 1927. Complementarity refers to micro objects that are, under different experimental conditions, describable by means of two different statements, each of which seems to logically exclude the other, yet each of which must be held to be empirically true. 'It was already clear to Bohr that the physical principle of complementarity and its related principle of correspondence were simply special cases of an idea with significance far beyond physics. This is the idea that observers are part of what they observe and that they can only observe something by changing it' (Becker and Jahn, 2004: 14).

7 See Dorothea Mey (1987) for the knowledge transfer about normative gender relations between moral physiology and medicine in the middle of the nineteenth century in France, on the one hand, and avant-garde sociology (in the work of the 'parents of sociology', Proudhon, Comte, and Michelet), on the other.

8 A number of feminist environmental studies refer to these struggles all over the world (Braidotti, Charkeiwitz, Häusler, and Wieringa, 1994; Harcourt, 1994; Rocheleau, Thomas-Slayter, and Wangari, 1996; Rodda, 1991; Roy, 1998; Shiva, 1988).

9 The seven studies include: (1) Quality of Life and Management of Living Resources, (2) User-friendly Information Society, (3) Energy, (4) Environment and Sustainable Development, (5) Confirming the International Role of Community Research, (6) Promotion of Innovation and Encouragement of Participation of Small and Medium-sized Enterprises, and (7) Improving the Human Research Potential and the Socio-economic Knowledge Base. For the results of all seven studies, see Linda Maxwell, Karen Slavin, and Kerry Young (2002).

10 See the documentation of the Women's University in Hannover, 2000, on this theme in Regina Becker-Schmidt (2002).

11 See the feminist debate on work and the environment in Beate Littig (2001: 57–84).

12 See the documentation of the Women's University in Hannover, 2000, on this theme in Barbara Duden and Dorothee Noers (2002).

13 With respect to the feminist sex–gender debate in life sciences, see Ineke Klinge and Mineke Bosch (2001).

14 For a critique of specific forms of rationality and objectivity, see Sandra Harding (1986).

15 For an overview of these studies, see ISOE (2003: 113–135); see also Lucia Reisch and Inge Røpke (2004).

16 For more on the field of energy use, see the main findings of the GIA study on the energy program in Maxwell et al. (2002). For water use see the findings on 'sustainable water management' in ISOE (2003: 85–96). For traffic use and mobility see the findings in ISOE (2003: 41–47).

17 See the findings on biodiversity research in ISOE (2003: 62–70). See also the findings in the GIA study on the European Program Quality of Life and Management of Living Resources in Klinge and Bosch (2001).

18 In Germany, this occurred in the *Program on Social–Ecological Research*, which is financed by the Federal Ministry of Education and Research. Very advanced in interdisciplinary feminist research are the projects of the *Lower Saxony Research Association for Women's and Gender Studies in the Natural Sciences, Technology and Medicine* (see Paravicini and Zemple-Gino, 2003). Similarly in Austria, the *Program Kulturlandschaftsforschung* and actually the *Pro-Vision* program of the Austrian Ministry of Sciences, and in Switzerland, the *Program Mensch – Gesellschaft – Umwelt*, which was supported by a private foundation.

REFERENCES

Adam, Barbara (1994) 'Time for Feminist Approaches to Technology, Nature and Work', in T. Eberhart and C. Wächter (eds), *Feminist Perspectives on Technology, Work and Ecology*, 2nd European Feminist Research Conference, Graz. pp. 5–9.

Adorno, Theodor W. and Horkheimer, Max (1944/1972) *Dialektik der Aufklärung*. Frankfurt/Main: Fischer Verlag.

Agarwal, Bina (1992) 'The Gender and Environment Debate: Lessons from India', *Feminist Studies*, 18(8).

Becker, Egon and Jahn, Thomas (eds) (1999) *Sustainability and the Social Sciences: A Cross-disciplinary Approach to Integrating Environmental Considerations into Theoretical Reorientation*. London, New York: Zed Books.

Becker, Egon and Jahn, Thomas (2004) 'Societal Relations to Nature: Outline of a Critical Theory'. Institut für sozial-ökologische Forschung (ISOE), Frankfurt/Main.

Becker-Schmidt, Regina (1999) 'Critical Theory as a Critique of Society: Theodor W. Adorno's Significance for a Feminist Sociology', in M. O'Neill (ed.), *Adorno: Culture and Feminism*. London, Thousand Oaks, CA, New Delhi: Sage. pp. 104–118.

Becker-Schmidt, Regina (ed.) (2002) *Gender and Work in Transition: Globalization in Western, Middle and Eastern Europe*. Opladen: International Women's University, Verlag Leske und Budrich.

Bennholdt-Thomsen, Veronika and Mies, Maria (1997) *Eine Kuh für Hillary. Die Subsistenzperspektive*. München: Frauenoffensive.

Biehl, Janet (1991) *Rethinking Ecofeminist Politics*. Boston, MA: South End Press.

Braidotti, Rosi (1997) 'Meta(l)morphoses', *Theory, Culture and Society*, 14(2): 67–80.

Braidotti, Rosi (2002) 'Identity, Subjectivity and Difference: A Critical Genealogy', in Gabriele Griffin and Rosi Braidotti (eds), *Thinking Differently: A Reader in Women's Studies*. London: Zed Books. pp. 158–180.

Braidotti, Rosi, Charkeiwitz, E., Häusler, S., and Wieringa, S. (eds) (1994) *Women, the Enviroment and Sustainable Development.* London: Zed Books.

Bundesministerium für Umwelt, Naturschutz und Reaktorsicherheit (BMU) (2002) *Environment – Sustainability – Gender Justice: German Activities from Rio to Johannesburg.* Berlin.

Busch-Lüthy, Christiane, Jochimsen, Maren, Knobloch, Ulrike, and Seidl, Irmi (eds) (1994) 'Vorsorgendes Wirtschaften: Frauen auf dem Weg zu einer Ökonomie der Nachhaltigkeit', *Politische Ökologie*, 6(special issue).

DAWN (Development Alternatives with Women for a New Era) (1985) *Development, Crisis and Alternative Visions: Third World Women's Perspectives.* Stavanger.

D'Eaubonne, Françoise (1974) *Le Feminisme ou la mort.* Paris: C. Pierre Horay.

Duden, Barbara and Noers, Dorothee (eds) (2002) *Auf den Spuren des Körpers in einer technogenen Welt.* Opladen: Internationale Frauenuniversität, Verlag Leske und Budrich.

Feministische Studien (1984) 'Die Radikalen der alten Frauenbewegung', 3(1).

Griffin, Susan (1978) *Woman and Nature: The Roaring Inside Her.* San Francisco: Sierra Club Books.

Haraway, Donna J. (1988) 'Situated Knowledges: The Science Question in Feminism as a Site of Discourse on the Privilege of Partial Perspective', *Feminist Studies*, 14: 575–600.

Haraway, Donna (1989) *Primate Visions: Gender, Race and Nature in the World of Modern Science.* New York: Routledge.

Harcourt, Wendy (ed.) (1994) *Feminist Perspectives on Sustainable Development.* London: Zed Books.

Harding, Sandra (1986) *The Science Question in Feminism.* Ithaca, NY: Cornell University Press.

Hayn, Doris and Schultz, Irmgard (2002) 'Gender Impact Assessment in the Field of Radiation Protection and the Environment'. Concluding Report (English version) on behalf of the (BMU), Frankfurt/Main.

Hummel, Diana, Hertler Christine, Niemann, Steffen, Lux Alexandra, and Schulze, Kay Oliver (2003) *Die Versorgung der Bevölkerung – Wirkungszusammenhänge von demographischen Entwicklungen, Bedürfnissen und Versorgungssystemen.* Frankfurt/Main: Interdisziplinäre Nachwuchsforschungsgruppe im BMBF-Förderschwerpunkt Sozial-ökologische Forschung.

Hynes, Patricia (1989) *The Recurring Silent Spring.* New York: Pergamon Press.

ISOE (2003) 'Research on gender, the environment and sustainable development: Studies on gender impact assessment of the Fifth Framework Program for RTD "Environment and Sustainable Development"', Brussels: European Commission (EUR 20313).

Jurczyk, Karin and Rerrich, Maria (1993) *Die Arbeit des Alltags. Beiträge zu einer Soziologie der alltäglichen Lebensführung.* Freiburg im Breisgau: Lambertus.

Keller, Evelyn Fox (1983) *A Feeling for the Organism.* New York: Freeman.

Klinge, Ineke and Bosch, Mineke (2001) 'Gender and Research: Gender Impact Assessment of the specific programs of the Fifth Framework Program "Quality of Life and Management of Living Resources"', Brussels: European Commission.

Kulke, Christine and Scheich, Elvira (eds) (1992) *Zwielicht der Vernunft: Die Dialektik der Aufklärung aus der Sicht von Frauen.* Pfaffenweiler: Centaurus.

Littig, Beate (2001) *Feminist Perspectives on Environment and Society.* Harlow: Pearson Education.

Martin, Biddy (1991) *Woman and Modernity: The Lifestyles of Lou Andreas-Salome.* Ithaca, NY: Cornell University Press.

Maxwell, Linda, Slavin, Karen, and Young, Kerry (eds) (2002) 'Gender and Research: Conference Proceedings, Brussels 8–9 November 2001, Brussels: European Commission 2001/EUR 20022.

Mayreder, Rosa (1922) *Zur Kritik der Weiblichkeit.* Jena: Eugen Diedrichs.

Mellor, Mary (2001) 'Nature, Gender and the Body', in A. Nebelung, A. Poferl, and I. Schultz (eds), *Geschlechterverhältnisse – Naturverhältnisse.* Opladen: Leske und Budrich. pp. 121–140.

Merchant, Carolyn (1980) *The Death of Nature: Women, Ecology and the Scientific Revolution*. San Francisco: Harper Collins.
Mey, Dorothea (1987) *Die Liebe und das Geld. Zum Mythos und zur Lebenswirklichkeit von Hausfrauen und Kurtisanen in der Mitte des 19. Jahrhunderts in Frankreich*. Weinheim, Basel: Beltz Verlag.
Mies, Maria and Shiva, Vandana (1993) *Ecofeminism*. London: Zed Books.
Ogunleye, B. and Hemmati, Minu (eds) (2000) 'Women and Sustainable Development 2000–2002, Recommendations in Agenda 21 and Related Documents and Suggestions for a Review of Implementations', Paper presented at the CSD NGO Women's Caucus, New York.
O'Neill, Maggie (ed.) (1999) *Adorno, Culture and Feminism*. London, Thousand Oaks, CA, New Delhi: Sage.
Ortner, Sherry (1974) 'Is Female to Male as Nature is to Culture?', in M. Z. Rosaldo and L. Lamphere (eds), *Woman, Culture and Society*. Stanford, CA: Stanford University Press. pp. 67–88.
Paravicini, Ursula (1999) 'Social Role and Social Use of Public Spaces: A Gender Perspective', Paper presented at El Renacimiento de la Cultura Urbana 29, Rosartio, Argentina.
Paravicini, Ursula and Zempel-Gino, Maren (eds) (2003) Dokumentation Wissenschaftliche Kolloquien 1999–2002, Wissenschatliche Reihe NFFG (Niedersächsischer Forschungsverbund für Frauen-/Geschlechterforschung in Naturwissenschaften, Technik und Medizin), Band 2, Hannover.
Plant, Judith (ed.) (1989) *Healing the Wounds. The Promise of Ecofeminism*. Philadelphia: New Society.
Plumwood, Val (1986) 'Critical Review: Ecofeminism: An Overview and Discussion of Positions and Arguments', *Australian Journal of Philosophy*, 64: 120–138.
Reisch, Lucia and Røpke, Inge (eds) (2004) *The Ecological Economics of Consumption*. Cheltenham: Edward Elgar.
Rocheleau, D., Thomas-Slayter, B., and Wangari, E. (eds) (1996) *Feminist Political Ecology*. London: Routledge.
Rodda, Annabel (ed.) (1991) *Women and the Environment*. London: Zed Books.
Roy, Arundhati (1998) *The Cost of Living*. London: Harper Collins.
Scheich, Elvira (ed.) (1996) *Vermittelte Weiblichkeit: Feministische Wissenschafts- und Gesellschaftstheorie*. Hamburg: Hamburger Edition HIS.
Schiebinger, Londa (1997) 'Creating Sustainable Science', *Osiris: A Research Journal Devoted to the History of Science and its Cultural Influence*, 12: 201–216.
Schultz, Irmgard (1992) 'Julie & Juliette und die Nachtseite der Geschichte Europas: Naturwissen, Aufklärung und pathische Projektion in der 'Dialektik der Aufklärung', in Christine Kulke and Elvira Scheich (eds), *Zwielicht der Vernunft*. Pfaffenweiler: Centaurus. pp. 25–40.
Schultz, Irmgard (2001a) 'Umwelt- und Geschlechterforschung: eine notwendige Übersetzungsarbeit', in A. Nebelung, A. Poferl, and I. Schultz (eds), *Geschlechterverhältnisse – Naturverhältnisse*. Opladen: Leske und Budrich Verlag.
Schultz, Irmgard (2001b) 'Der blinde Fleck zwischen Politik und Technikwissenschaften: Strategien eines scientific-technological empowerment als Perspektive feministischer Wissenschaft und Politik', *femina politica*, 10(2).
Schultz, Irmgard and Weller, Ines (eds) (1995) *Gender & Environment. Ökologie und die Gestaltungsmacht der Frauen*. Frankfurt/Main: IKO-Verlag.
Schultz, Irmgard, Hummel, Diana, Hayn, Doris, and Empacher, Claudia (2001) 'Gender in Research: Gender Impact Assessment of the specific programs of the Fifth Framework Program "Environment and Sustainable Development"', Brussels: Eurpean Commission (EUR 20019).
Shiva, Vandana (1988) *Staying Alive: Women, Ecology and Development*. London: Zed Books.
Verloo, Mieke and Roggeband, C. (1996) 'Gender Impact Assessment: The Development of a New Instrument in the Netherlands', *Impact Assessment*, 14(1): 3–21.

Wagner, Nike (1987) *Geist und Geschlecht: Karl Kraus und die Erotik der Wiener Moderne.* Frankfurt/Main: Suhrkamp.

Von Werlhof, Claudia, Bennholdt-Thomsen, Veronika, and Faraclas, Nicholas (eds) (2002) *There is an Alternative: Subsistence and Worldwide Resistance to Corporate Globalization.* London: Zed Books.

Weller, Ines (2003) 'Gender-Vision zur Forschungsthematik "Stoffliche Verwertung von Faserverbundwerkstoffen"', in I. Weller, K. Fischer, D. Hayn, and I. Schultz (eds), *Gender Impact Assessment der Angewandten Umweltforschung Bremen.* Abschussbericht Bremen.

Weller, Ines (2004) *Nachaltigkeit und Gender*, Neue Perspektiven für die Gestaltung und Nutzung von Produkten. München: ökom Verlag.

Weller, Ines, Hayn, Doris, and Schultz, Irmgard (2002) 'Geschlechterverhältnisse, nachhaltige Konsummuster und Umweltbelastungen', in Ingrid Balzer and Monika Wächter (eds), *Sozial-ökologische Forschung. Ergebnisse der Sondierungsprojekte aus dem BMBF-Förderschwerpunkt.* München: ökom Verlag.

22

From Science and Technology to Feminist Technoscience

Jutta Weber

In this chapter I introduce and discuss feminist approaches in science and technology studies not only with regard to their epistemological and ontological framework, but in the light of contemporary sociopolitical developments, prevailing technological practices, artifacts, and material cultures. My aim is to develop a stance which goes beyond euphoric affirmation or pessimistic refusal of technoscience as the 'Other'. Rather, I articulate a perspective from which the refiguring of central concepts like nature, body, and identity, and the omnipresence of technoscientific discourses and practices in our daily lives becomes visible and thereby available for feminist analysis. I interpret recent cultural studies of science and technology as reactions to the new epistemological and ontological challenges induced by technoscientific developments and the reorganization of knowledge culture in our messy global world.

INTRODUCTION

> taking responsibility for the social relations of science and technology means refusing an anti-science metaphysics, a demonology of technology, and so means embracing the skillful task of reconstructing the boundaries of daily life … It is not just that science and technology are possible means of great human satisfaction, as well as a matrix of complex dominations…It means both building and destroying machines, identities, categories, relationships…(Haraway, 1985: 181)

In most of contemporary Western theory, science and technology are regarded as a central part of culture with discourses and practices tightly interwoven with our daily lives. In the mid 1980s, when feminist science studies scholar Donna Haraway wrote the lines cited above, this understanding of science and technology was not self-evident. Science was often thought of in terms of classical sciences, such as physics, mathematics, biology, or chemistry, disciplines many of us 'well-educated girls' were not very fond of at school. In the Cold War period, most science studies scholars directed their attention towards so-called 'Big Science' (Price, 1963). Researchers equated science and technology with hierarchically organized scientific and technological projects planned and undertaken by governments and the military. Huge technological systems like nuclear power plants, weapon systems, and undertakings like the Manhattan Project or ARPANET[1] were the prototypes of the technology of that time. No wonder that feminist or critical theory stressed science and technology as 'masculine culture' (Wajcman, 1991), partly driven by masculinist dreams of omnipotence or ruled by fantasies of death (Keller, 1985). Equating science and technology with government projects and the military often led to a 'demonology' of technology in feminist and other critical theory.

A good example is the critique of reproduction technologies in the 1970s and 1980s. These technologies were regarded as not driven by fantasies of death, but by the longing to unveil the secrets of life. Since the birth in the1970s of Louise Brown, the first *in vitro* fertilization child, reproduction technologies evoked fears of masculinist appropriation of women's reproductive abilities, leading to a repressive population policy. There were many women activists fighting against these new technologies, like the well-known group FINRRAGE, founded by Gena Corea, Maria Mies, and others. To them, reproductive technologies turn the female body into a laboratory for the industrialized production of living beings (Corea et al., 1985; Wajcman, 1991). These technologies were regarded as another means to prolong the subordination of women. Shulamith Firestone (1970) was one of the few feminists who celebrated the new reproductive technologies as a possible means to liberate women.

TECHNOLOGY, SCIENCE, AND MASCULINITY

Technology is often described as a genuine 'masculine culture' grounded in patriarchal structures, gender relations, and identity politics. While some feminists interpreted the desire for technologies as grounded in a 'natural' tendency of men towards aggression and an obsession with control, others insisted on distinguishing 'between different forms of masculinity in relation to different areas of technology. To say that control over technology is a core element of masculinity is not to imply that there is one masculinity or one technology' (Wajcman, 1991: 143). Not only does this view stereotype masculinity, but other feminists reminded us that the emphasis on male-dominated technologies like the cyber and life sciences 'reproduces the sterotype of women as technologically ignorant and incapable' (Wajcman, 1991: 136). Against this view, Ruth Schartz Cowan and Judith Wajcman, among others, stress the importance of the 'technological revolution in the home' (Cowan, 1976: 33).

The feminist lack of interest in science and technology studies until the late 1980s was mostly grounded in the understanding of science and technology as military-biased 'Big Science' and 'masculine culture', while household technologies, new media, as well as new technosciences were, for the most part, disregarded. The increased use of television, video, cable, personal computers, and other developments in communication and information technology as well as the proliferation of biotechnology in agriculture, medicine, and procreation challenged the identification of science and technology with centralized, top-down research projects and huge technological systems. Since the late 1980s, it has become more and more obvious that science and technology are deeply interwoven into our everyday lives.

Donna Haraway (1985), Elvira Scheich (1989), and others have shown how central humanist concepts like nature, body, and identity get refigured through technoscientific discourses and practices. The relations of nature and technology and concomitantly those of gender are profoundly reshaped in the process of appropriating nature in Western societies, facilitating the idea of the co-construction of science, technology, society, and gender. To give an example, when reprogenetics or sex change becomes a common commercial practice for many people or care robots are developed to take over the former 'feminine' task of caring for children or sick people, old borders between sex and gender, between private and public, between a so-called masculinist technology and a feminine *Lebenswelt*, implode. The constructionist move in feminist and other science studies challenges the borders of the social and the technoscientific.

Feminist theorists also articulated a new bonding of technoscience with transnational capitalism, arguing that new technologies contribute to 'increasing capital concentration and the monopolization of the means of life, reproduction and labor' and to 'global deepening of inequality' (Haraway, 1997: 60). The effects are twofold. On the one hand, relations of domination are becoming more complex and opaque. On the other hand, the reshaping of central categories through technoscientific practices opens up new options for refiguring gender, nature, and sociotechnical systems. As structures of domination are getting more and more complex and the reshaping of old hierarchical categories seems possible, the demonology of technology appears more and more inadequate as a critical attitude towards our technoscientific culture.

CONTINUING THE STORY

Today's feminist critique often uses the former demonology of technology as a point of departure to tell a story of progress from liberal to postmodern feminism.[2] According to this narrative, liberal and Marxist feminist critiques failed to critically analyze science and technology because they considered the latter as neutral or did not pay attention to the symbolic dimension of technoscience. However, the Marxist feminist critique is acknowledged at least for analyzing gender in terms of social structure, while it is conceded that radical and ecofeminist approaches successfully elaborated the symbolic dimensions of science, technology, and masculinity. However, these perspectives are blamed for locating 'women's essence…in their biology' (Gill and Grint, 1995: 5). Unlike the liberal and Marxist feminist approaches, early social construction feminism understood that 'women's alienation from technology is a product of the historical and cultural construction of technology as masculine'. Social construction, however, did not succeed in fully explicating 'the relations between the key terms, "men" or "males", "masculinity" and "patriarchy"' (Gill and Grint, 1995: 12).

I have deliberately exaggerated this somewhat Hegelian story of progress to clarify my argument that as knowledge is situated, it always takes a perspective. The problem is how to write a *non-linear and complex* historiography of theories and practical engagements, as well as the artifacts of science and technology. It might help to avoid linear stories of feminist theory by reflecting not only on the epistemological and ontological framework of earlier approaches, but also by rethinking these frameworks in the light of contemporary sociopolitical developments as well as prevailing technological practices, artifacts, and material cultures.[3]

Recent studies question essentialist understandings of science and technology partially because of their cumulative fusion. When science, technology, society, and industry amalgamate into dense networks, and the sociocultural and the technological are tightly interwoven, the idea that a masculinist technology determines a feminine *Lebenswelt* appears ridiculous. Technology as an intimate part of our lives is no more the 'Other', as it was often understood in the age of 'Big Science', but rather part of our human condition. The demonization of technology becomes counterproductive as it hinders understanding of our life conditions in the age of technoscience and the refiguring of ontological realms of science, technology, society, and gender.

I will, therefore, tell my story of feminist science and technology studies in this chapter using a situated sociocultural and historically grounded approach. I concentrate on the close ties between changing theoretical approaches of science and technology studies and the material, symbolic, and sociopolitical dimensions of science and technology. My aim is to develop a stance which goes beyond euphoric affirmation or pessimistic refusal of technoscience, and, rather, articulates a perspective from which the omnipresence of technoscientific discourses and practices in every realm of our daily lives becomes visible and thereby available for analysis.

GENDERED AND OTHER CRITIQUES OF SCIENCE

In the first decades of women's studies in the 1960s and 1970s, it was mostly women scientists confronted with discrimination via institutional and gender identity politics who engaged in critical science and technology studies.[4] They reconstructed the achievements of other women scientists, rendering them visible for a broader audience and analyzing the mechanisms of their exclusions.[5] By discovering the large number of women scientists who had to live on the margins of intellectual and academic life, they contributed to a growing mistrust of the self-ascribed values of neutrality and objectivity in science.

In addition to the analysis of the professional politics of gender, inquiries into scientific constructions of sex differences resulted in a misogynist portrait of science (Bleier, 1984; Fausto-Sterling, 1985; Hubbard, Henifin, and Fried, 1979). Feminist analysis showed that the construction of sex differences in biology revolves around 'errors of the following sort: (a) the world of human bodies is divided into two kinds, male and female (i.e., by sex); (b) additional (extraphysical) properties are culturally attributed to those bodies (e.g., active/passive, independent/dependent, primary/secondary: read *gender*)' (Keller, 1995a: 87). For example, the process of conception was until recently described as a 'passive egg' waiting for the heroic, active sperm (Martin, 1991). According to Ruth Hubbard, we find manifold versions of the 'sociobiologist's claim that some of the sex differences in social behavior that exist in our society (for example, aggressiveness, competitiveness, and dominance among men; coyness, nurturance, and submissiveness among women) are human universals that have existed in all times and cultures' (1988: 8).

The so-called 'objective' knowledge of male experts was also radically challenged by critical practices in the women's movement. For example, the famous workshop on 'women and their bodies', held in Boston in 1969, promoted alternative forms of health care. The workshop group continued to meet and compile information about women's bodies and health care. Their discussion papers were assembled and published in 1970 as the first version of *Our Bodies, Ourselves*; in the last thirty years, OBOS has been translated and adapted to many different cultures all around the world (Davis, 2002). Challenging men's expertise 'was an extension of this recognition of the power of scientific ideas to define women's sense of bodily awareness, sense of self and sense of reality that propelled the feminist analysis of science to investigate the historical emergence of particular constructions of women and the natural within scientific discourse' (McNeil and Franklin, 1991: 134).

In addition to the women's movement, other social movements, such as the Radical Science Movement in Britain, the anti-war movement, and the ecology movement, contributed to questioning the privileged status of scientific knowledge. The battles against reproductive technologies, biotechnological products, bio-piracy, the Human Genome Diversity Project, and the patenting of living beings have helped to question technoscientific practices. At the same time, they demonstrated their growing impact on everyday life. In view of ecological disasters caused by industrialization, ecofeminism and radical feminism criticized the Anglo-American understanding of nature as the 'Other', as feminine, inferior, and uncanny, that has to be controlled by an autonomous subject (a White man). They fostered the insight that nature should not be reduced to a resource and passive material for men's ends, but regarded as an active agent endowed with its own logic. As many critics pointed out, the hybridization of science, technology, the military, industry, and politics in the last decades also helped to undermine the understanding of science as the only legitimate producer of knowledge. These movements questioned so-called truths 'discovered' by science about the nature of nature, of woman, and of sex.

The growing interest in science and technology studies is partly attributable to the deconstruction of the grand narratives of progress, scientific truth, and objectivity. It also made technoscience a promising field for women's and gender studies. But the challenge to positivism and the rise of the social construction perspective are not due only to the radical critique of the practices and discourses of technoscience by feminists and 'other Others'. They are also related to changes in the theoretical premises in science and technology which formed the basis for the emergence of new technosciences. Wave/particle duality in quantum physics is probably the most famous example for challenging objectivity through scientific theories and practices. Haraway (1985; 1991), Katherine Hayles (1999), and others have analyzed the departure from the classical Cartesian heritage, with its dualism of observer and observed, subject and object, body and mind, towards constructivist epistemologies and 'posthuman' concepts of cybernetics, artificial intelligence, immunology, and brain research.

In view of the decline of classical scientific values, feminism strengthened the insight that trying to speak for nature – to interpret its own logic – always involves a politics of representation implying epistemological, ontological, and thereby political claims. Challenging the scientific and technological discourses of truth, feminism argued that nature, sex, and biology are not given nor are they beyond representation, rather they are agents in a high-stakes game, a dynamic relationship as well as a product, constructed and taking part in, or even constructing discourses and practices. The so-called 'natural laws' and empirical data of technoscience were reinterpreted as the outcome of cultural practices with many different human as well as non-human actors. At present, feminist and other critical science studies ask how and for whom knowledge, technologies, agents, and hybrids have been employed so far and continue to be employed:[6]

> with the hope that the technologies for establishing what may count as the case about the world may be rebuilt *to bring the technical and the political back into realignment so that questions about possible livable worlds lie visibly at the heart of our best science.* (Haraway, 1997: 39; my emphasis)

Feminist approaches reflect on the need for political reflexivity in theory, which is often neglected in mainstream science and technology studies. At the heart of feminist studies lies the search for better, or at least more visible, ways to design and use categories, knowledge, and technologies, to shape objects, artifacts, and worlds in order to make exclusions visible and to overcome the hardships of gender-asymmetries, reductionism, and injustice.[7]

In sum, the critique of positivism and naturalist rhetorics became possible through many different factors: the liberal feminist critique of an unfair and misogynist science, the ecofeminist critique of Western hyperproduction, social movements challenging the privileged status of science, and the postmodern critique of ventriloquial politics of representation. Posthumanist reconfigurations of so-called natural entities like nature, sex, and body also made visible the changed epistemological and ontological groundings of science, which were induced by critical as well as technoscientific discourses and practices. The merging of science and technology, as well as that of technoscience, industry, and politics, all raise questions about the idea of technological determinism.

In the following sections, I will map out movements of denaturalization, dematerialization, and renaturalization in constructionist technoscience and contemporary feminist science and technology studies. The merging of boundaries between nature/culture (*Denaturalizing nature*), sex/gender (*Constructing sex and gender*), and science/technology/society (*Technoscience*) are at the heart of the current epistemological and ontological reconfigurations of our age. Cultural studies of science and technology (*Technoscience as cultural practice and practical culture*) can be seen as an answer to the new epistemological and ontological challenges induced by technoscientific developments. I conclude with conditions of knowledge production (*The reorganization of knowledge cultures in a messy global world*) and make suggestions for future directions.

DENATURALIZING NATURE: CONSTRUCTIONISM IN CONTEMPORARY TECHNOSCIENCE(S)

Major concepts, such as nature, matter, and body, are profoundly refigured in contemporary technosciences. With the rise of system theory, cyberscience, and new life sciences, there is a move towards the molecularization of matter, breaking up organisms or cells into micro-parts down to the subatomic level (Kay, 1996). This miniaturization enabled 'the translation of the world into a problem of coding, a search for a common language ... and all heterogeneity can be submitted to disassembly, reassembly, investment, and exchange'. Information becomes 'just that kind of quantifiable element...which allows universal translation' (Haraway, 1985: 164).

Technosciences nowadays do not see themselves as primarily engaged in subjugating nature and its processes through creating artificial natures via technological artifacts and systems, but through designing and engineering nature in the sense of reshaping and improving it. 'The claim of technoscience not to create but to continue the work of nature by rebuilding, converting and perfecting it, gives the border between nature and culture its chimerical character' (Weber, 1999: 470). Nature becomes a toolkit and the world a realm of endless possibilities of recombination – with evolution tinkering around to find new ways of development and investment (see, among others, Jacob, 1977). Similar to this logic, organisms are not regarded as something static and given, but as evolving, parallel, and distributed networks, that is a 'fast, responsive, flexible and self-organizing system capable of constantly reinventing itself, sometimes in new and surprising ways' (Hayles, 1999: 158). Attention is given to the creation of spontaneous entities and the logic of emergent behavior. In other words, a constructionist understanding of nature, organisms, and even sex can be found not only in critical feminist theory but also in contemporary technosciences.

Engineering nature makes technoscientific practices even more efficient (Haraway, 1997). This approach relies on a constructionist stance – which implies radical changes in the understanding of science and nature in general. While modern scientific theories linked women and nature, under the assumption that they were both immutable, the refigured posthuman body departs from these essentialist and naturalizing premises. The body is no longer considered as 'natural' and 'given' in the sense of static, unchangeable, and governed by teleological and harmonious principles. With this move, the radical feminist and other critiques of the naturalist or essentialist grounding of the natural sciences became partly obsolete.

This new denaturalization notwithstanding, there has been a strong movement of renaturalization emerging in the rhetorics of popular science, technosciences, and popular culture at the same time. Spontaneity, change, and dynamics are often reinterpreted as natural, evident, and given by 'Mother Nature'. The French molecular biologist François Jacob describes organisms as 'historical structures: literally creations of history. They present not a perfect product of engineering, but a patchwork of odd sets pieced together when and wherever opportunities arose. For *the opportunism of natural selection ... reflects the very nature of a historical process full of contingency*' (Jacob, 1977: 1166, my emphasis). After all, it seems to be 'Mother Nature' which rendered organisms as patchwork creations via natural selection. The change of ontological and epistemological groundings in the technosciences is made invisible by declaring the turbulent, evolving body not as an effect of the change of paradigm in (techno)science but as natural.

CONSTRUCTING SEX AND GENDER IN THE AGE OF REPROGENETICS AND SEX-CHANGE SURGERY

Given the centrality of gender for feminist scholarship in general, science and technology studies are concerned with how 'gendered artifacts may constitute the glue that sometimes keeps gender relations stable, sometimes on the move' (Berg and Lie, 1995: 346). These studies ask how gender, understood as a product of diverse material, symbolic, and sociopolitical processes 'was at stake in key reconfigurations of knowledge and practice that constituted modern science' (Haraway, 1997: 27). Feminist scholars are 'particularly interested in the question how scientists have constructed "woman" as a natural category' (Oudshoorn, 1996: 123).

What is the meaning of categories like 'woman', 'sex', or 'gender'? Thinking about the category of gender highlights the performative character of feminist theory and science studies, which are themselves a cultural practice and as such are entangled in language games, sociopolitical experiences, and values. One can understand sex/gender as a 'boundary object' (Bowker and Star, 1999), as a classification system which holds together a globalized but predominantly Anglo-American feminist discourse. The differentiation of sex and gender which pervades many feminist discourses in different languages shapes theoretical frames, perspectives, and questions. It is a historical and situated classification which produces a segmentation of the world which fosters strict differentiations between the social and the biological.[8]

The suspicion that every possible differentiation between biology and society, nature, and culture in feminist theories, too, only prolongs dubious definitions of the natural and reifies old normative descriptions of 'woman' might be only the flip side of difficulties in mediating the social and the biological.[9] Sometimes these fears result in a hyperproductive stance, whereby a dogmatic denaturalization of gender and the body turns into their dematerialization. In this conceptual frame of idealism, matter or bodies are conceptualized as the exclusive product of history, society, or discourse. Trying to overcome the dual sex/gender system and the separation of the biological and social often leads to an ignorance or even negation of material, bodily aspects.

While contemporary postmodern approaches favored denaturalization and even dematerialization of the gendered body, they often ignored the strong development towards construction and denaturalization in technoscience itself. Many sociotechnical developments already undermine the dual sex/gender system and the natural in a more profound way than many postmodern theorists had ever dreamed of: new reproduction technologies, cosmetic surgery, and sex-change procedures are radically denaturalizing (and sometimes renaturalizing) the category of sex (Stone, 1993; Stryker, 2000). For example, with the possibility of sex change in the second half of the twentieth century sex becomes – at least in principle – an open, free-floating category.[10] Technoscientific practices and artifacts such as reconstructive surgery and hormones render radical physical sex change possible. Thus the dual sex/gender system is destabilized by making it (at least theoretically) a matter of technological investigation and individual choice in Western societies.

The denaturalization of bodies is the ontological ground which makes it possible to think of bodies as a toolkit, breaking them down into small parts and reorganizing them in technoscientific practices. Bodies are fragmented into different functions, organs, cells, molecules, genes. A case in point is collaborative reproduction, in which body parts from different, sometimes anonymous donors are made to fit together in the laboratory. The laboratory product – an artificially fertilized egg – is subsequently implanted in a woman, who is not necessarily the child's genetic mother. Collaborative reproduction becomes possible by the separation of sex, sexuality, reproduction, and kinship through which new complex relations of social and biological kinship emerge. These denaturalizing technoscientific practices also produce new social and economic relations in the process of reproduction. But these new practices of reproduction are made invisible at the same time by renaturalizing rhetorics of 'blood ties' and the right to a 'child of one's own'.[11]

TECHNOSCIENCE: A NEW UNDERSTANDING OF SCIENCE AND TECHNOLOGY

With the growing interest in technoscience, we find more feminist science studies which try to mediate de/constructionist with materialist and realist positions. They share central epistemological and ontological premises, like commitment to self-reflexivity, contextuality of knowledge, and interest in empowerment. They reflect on 'standardization and local experience, (on) that which is between the categories, yet in relationship to them' (Star, 1991: 39). They are projects of political intervention and critique highlighted processes of domination and resistance. The goal is to enable empowerment, particularly of those who do not fit the standard or who are on the margins of the production of knowledge and culture.

While earlier approaches in the 1970s and 1980s[12] mainly investigated the social and political conditions of science (often using a 'classical' concept of society), the separation of science and society is now being challenged, along with other separations such as 'science and politics ... or science and culture. At the very least, one such category cannot be used to explain the other, and neither can be reduced to the status of context for the other' (Haraway, 1997: 62). These challenges are due to fundamental dissolutions of borders between the ontological realms of science, technology, industry, and society and the refiguring of central epistemological concepts. At present, we are experiencing a changed understanding of technology not only in theory, but in the emerging technosciences themselves, which materializes in concrete sociotechnical changes.

In pre-modern societies, technology was understood mostly in the sense of human knowledge, while in modernity, technology's most important connotation was that of the artifact. Today, the contemporary dimension of technology as system and process becomes more and more important. Technological systems are regarded as networks with tightening connections and an organization of material and non-material components which rely on scientific knowledge, engineers, and juridical, economic, and other agents (Hughes, 1986). This new perspective makes visible the 'seamless web' of science, technology, society, industry. Strict distinctions between the socio-cultural and the technical are no longer plausible. In addition, the differences between nature and culture are undermined by technosciences which conduct their research mainly in the laboratory as they construct the nature they are investigating.

The term 'technoscience' marks the merging of science, technology, industry, and the military, as well as the intensified amalgamation of science and technology, of society fusing with the technological, and of a new efficiency in industrial technologies which refigures the organic in a new and most efficient way. These developments are accompanied by radical changes in the ontological premises of (techno)sciences as well as some of their rhetorical strategies and politics of representation (Weber, 1999; 2003). With these multifaceted changes, new epistemologies and methodologies arise which stress the constructionist character of categories such as science, technology, and society.

TECHNOSCIENCE AS CULTURAL PRACTICE AND PRACTICAL CULTURE

With the hybridization of science, technology, industry, and society, it becomes much easier to acknowledge that science and technology, deeply intermeshed in culture, are central sites for the production of ideology. It also becomes easier to grant oneself the right to intervene: 'we have a right, and in fact a duty, to debate, contest, modify and perhaps even to transform' (Balsamo, 1998: 294). Even if we are not trained and socialized in technosciences and even if we are not part of that community of knowledge producers, we are, nevertheless, required to reflect on technoscientific developments which are shaping our world in profound ways.

Today, hybrids, artifacts, and cyborgs populate feminist theories and narratives. There has been a shift within and outside many disciplines (sociology, cultural studies, art, philosophy, literature, anthropology) towards analyzing discourses and practices of technoscience and its growing impact on everyday life. While early approaches in feminist science and technology studies mainly focused on classical sciences, it is now the so-called technosciences – artificial intelligence, biotechnology, neurosciences – which are at the center of feminist scholars' attention. Now that science and technology have been identified as deeply interwoven with many other ontological realms, they are understood as 'cultural practice and practical culture' (Haraway, 1997: 66). Culture is understood as a social practice, as an always situated, heterogeneous, and complex process in which many different agents like concepts, machines, humans, and animals produce meanings and thereby maintain or refigure cultural boundaries.

With this perspective, it becomes much easier to develop approaches which go beyond either the euphoric affirmation of science and technology or their abstract negation. Feminist science studies scholars now want to challenge boundaries and to refigure concepts and frames of thought by inventing powerful stories and different socio-material practices. To strive for more livable worlds beyond the hegemonic tales of progress, of technoscience as biological, and technological determination means also to reinterpret what counts as nature, as sex, or as gender. The central premises of recent feminist science and technology studies are that science and culture are deeply interwoven, that facts are theory-laden, and that theories are not neutral but can better be seen as stories. There are close linkages between metaphors and factuality, between semiotic and material processes. The relationships between science, technology, knowledge, and society are increasingly viewed as open and dynamic. Intervention into semiotic–material configurations of humans, non-humans, and machines is now seen as not only a possible but a necessary political practice.[13]

THE REORGANIZATION OF KNOWLEDGE CULTURES IN A MESSY GLOBALIZED WORLD

Contemporary science and technology studies use theories and methods from very divergent disciplines and prefer no unified methodology. Inter- or transdisciplinarity is grounded in a radical challenge of the popular idea of two separate cultures of 'hard' and 'soft' science, which was introduced by Charles Percy Snow (1959) and was revived in the science wars in the 1990s:

> The current 'two cultures' discourse assumes a division of labor: humanities researchers are critics who write commentaries on art and ideas, while scientists, engineers, and physicians find out facts about the real world and fix real problems. More succinctly, the humanities are for reflection and the sciences are for investigation…[C]ultural studies of science, technology, and medicine violate this division of labor and violate our conventions of expertise. (Reid and Traweek, 2000: 7)

With the breakdown of borders between science and society, between nature and culture, and with the understanding of science as a cultural practice, it becomes more and more obvious that all sciences are determined by cultural values, language games, and politics of representation. Moreover, these values and ideas cannot be categorized in terms of different cultures of knowledge. They travel between different disciplines, realms, and discourses. Take, for example, the notable metamorphosis of system theory in the twentieth century. Starting with biology, it went on to become a central part of cybernetics and molecular biology, and later an important approach in the social sciences, especially sociology. Other frequent transdisciplinary travelers are the concepts of network, emergence, and cyborg, which lose and gain new connotations, change shape, and transport frames of meanings.

The (re)naissance of inter-/transdisciplinarity today seems due not only to developments in critical theory, but also to the floating of concepts and frames of meanings between the disciplines. While transdisciplinary exchange between cultures of knowledge has not been unknown to modern science, I would claim that this exchange rapidly increased with the emergence of technosciences in the post-World War II period. It might be an irony of history that exactly at the time when Snow complained about the advancing gap between scientists, intellectuals, and the public because of the specialization of science and technology, an advancing exchange emerged between scientists and intellectuals in new (techno)scientific fields. Many technoscientists had the feeling that the classical approaches could not provide answers to new demands and questions. Therefore they started to work transdisciplinarily out of a need for new methods and conceptional frames. For example, the transdisciplinary field of cybernetics or, as Evelyn Fox Keller calls it, cyberscience 'was developed to deal with the messy complexity of the postmodern world' (1995b: 85). This might be true as well for other research fields like molecular biology, immunology, and others.

Science studies scholars Egon Becker and Thomas Wehling stress that the transfer of concepts became a 'central element of the dynamic of science and of theories' since the 1950s (1993: 42; my translation). But the effects of these transfers had not been analyzed within the disciplines themselves. Since the 1990s several feminist science studies scholars have reconstructed the transfer of metaphors and concepts throughout divergent disciplines. For example, Lily Kay (1999) analyzed the use of linguistic metaphors and concepts in the life sciences; Elvira Scheich (1993) has shown the major impact of system theory on the social sciences. Crossing the borders between different disciplines, between the so-called hard and soft sciences, seems to be much more common than scientists and intellectuals in either 'culture' realized.

It is my contention that the intensified permeability of the borders of disciplines is linked to recent transformations in science, technology, and society. By this, I mean the reorganization of the cultures of knowledges in our globalized world. I will not draw here on the new organization of knowledge through education policy, restructuring of academic fields, and redistribution of resources (infrastructure, funding, and so on) in the context of multifaceted processes of globalization. What I want to stress here is that knowledge is restructured not along disciplines but primarily along certain theoretical fault lines. Mainstream research areas are currently operating at a level of metalanguage, that is formal systems and models. They succeed in making divergent objects compatible through a contemporary logic of translation and coding which abstracts from material aspects of these objects (Knapp, 1998: 49).

System theory is a good example of this move as is the already-mentioned dominant concept of information in cyberscience, which has been conceptualized as a quantifiable element beyond materiality and meaning thereby allowing universal translation. The decontextualization of knowledge allows the development of powerful theorems that can be applied to nearly every field and context, regardless of their contextual meaning and material grounding. The logic of universal translation is especially attractive in a global world where compatibility becomes a central value. These formal approaches also support the invisibility of political hierarchies and economic injustices – not the least between North and South, West and East.

Today successful fields of research (in terms of funding) are those that follow these new cognitive and epistemological premises. Others that are unable or unwilling to do so often lack funding and, therefore, many so-called old-fashioned academic institutes have closed down. This development might give some clues as to why such divergent disciplines as microbiology, bioethics, and robotics are advancing fields, while disciplines like zoology, philosophy of history, or botany are on the decline.

The reorganization of cultures of knowledge is not only shaped by processes of transnational capitalism and reorganized along theoretical fault lines, but also the outcome of new questions and objects of study emerging in a globalized word. As feminist science studies recognize the reorganization of knowledge cultures, I think it becomes a necessity to focus not only on the production of artifacts and practices but also on hegemonies of cognitive and epistemological frames of thought. Up to now we have no or only a few studies on the contemporary epistemology in terms of hegemonic styles and frames of thought (Foucault, 1970).

FUTURE DIRECTIONS

After all, in the present world 'after modernity,' there is much to learn and much to do. To be sure, in a climate of polemics, thoughtful interdisciplinary reflection is hard to come by. (Reid and Traweek, 2000: 15)

Keeping in mind recent epistemological and ontological shifts in the age of technoscience, the emergence of posthuman bodies, nature(s), gender(s) as well as the reorganization of knowledge cultures, I want to make some suggestions concerning future directions for feminist studies.

Feminist science studies scholars analyzing transdisciplinary cultures of knowledge should not only be aware of the multifaceted transfer of concepts, methods, frames, and theories, but also adapt these insights to their own analysis. Reflecting on one's own conceptual frame requires at the very least a kind of second-order reflection that keeps in mind that theory itself is imprinted by the traveling concepts, epistemological approaches, and visual and rhetoric practices of the technosciences being analyzed. Thus, the critique of the discourses and practices of technosciences should question its own ontological and epistemological groundings and its entanglement with our technoculture. It is my hope that this kind of second-order reflection will enable alternative research which moves beyond euphoric celebrations of the most recent concepts and ideas from the technosciences as well as pessimistic and abstract negation of the so-called 'other' culture of technoscience – a stance that predominated gender studies for such a long time. Perhaps such a second-order reflection could also foster a critical usage of semiotic–material fields linked to the technosciences, which were so long imagined as the 'Other', as alien and rejected in the abstract. If feminist science and other critical studies succeed in showing the intensified blurring of the science and culture, it could help to overcome old dichotomies of euphoric affirmation of technology or its pessimistic refusal.

In my view, it is quite important that feminist studies continue to elaborate that *the technical is the political* for all the divergent fields of science and technology, showing and analyzing the ongoing co-construction of gender, science, and technology. In order to take part in the shaping of contemporary sociotechnical practices and discourses, we need to engage with today's scientific, cultural, and social turbulences, to engage in contests about what counts as nature, intelligible bodies, or efficient machines. To question techno-pragmatic and hegemonic forms of rationality and the dominant logic of efficiency, usability, and common sense, we need to intervene and challenge hierarchical sociotechnical relations by developing new theories of our age of technoscience.

ACKNOWLEDGEMENTS

I am very grateful to Kathy Davis who read and commented on several drafts of the original chapter. Many thanks also to Judith Lorber and Mary Evans.

NOTES

1 ARPANET was the forerunner of the Internet and developed to promote computer networks for military use.

2 See, for example, Rosalind Gill and Keith Grint (1995) and Sandra Harding (1986).

3 In my usage, 'ontology' signifies the assumptions every theory has to make with regard to the existence (of constellations) of things, entities, etc. The core assumptions are contained in the meta-theoretical principles. These general principles encompass not only syntactical structures and criteria of critique but ontological options. The last are responsible for what counts as a fact, as being.

4 For the study of gender in science through history, see Londa Schiebinger (2000). Beside women scientists, there were also feminist sociologists (Berg, Cockburn, Wacjman), philosophers (Code, Harding, Longino, Merchant), anthropologists (Lie, Star, Suchman, Traweek), and a few historians (Duden, Schiebinger) who were engaged in the field of critical science and technology studies in the early days of the second women's movement.

5 For an overview, see Schiebinger (1989) and Renate Tobies (2001).

6 See Haraway (1985; 1997), Harding (1986) Susan Leigh Star (1991), and Lucy Suchman (1987).

7 See, for example, Lorraine Code (1987), Haraway (1988), Nancy Hartsock (1983), Helen Longino (1990), and Hilary Rose (1983).

8 On paradoxes of gender, see also Judith Lorber (1994).

9 See Wendy Cealey Harrison, in this volume.

10 This choice remains in the dual-sex system and is only given in few countries under strict juridical, medical, and financial restrictions.

11 See, for example, Heidi Hofmann (2003).

12 For example, the Sociology of Scientific Knowledge (SSK) and, respectively, the 'Strong Programme' of the Edinburgh School, ecofeminism, or radical/cultural feminism.

13 See, for example, Haraway (1997) and Reid and Traweek (2000).

REFERENCES

Balsamo, Ann (1998) An Introduction, *Cultural Studies*, Special Issue: Cultural Studies of Science and Technology, 12, 3, 285–299.

Becker, Egon and Wehling, Thomas (1993) Wissenschaft und Modernisierung, in Becker, Egon and Wehling, Thomas, *Risiko Wissenschaft. Ökologische Perspektiven in Wissenschaft und Hochschule*. Frankfurt a.M./New York: Campus, pp. 35–59.

Berg, Anne-Jorunn and Lie, Merete (1995) Feminism and Constructivism: Do Artifacts Have Gender?, *Science, Technology & Human Values*, 20, 3, 332–351.

Bleier, Ruth (1984) *Science and Gender. A Critique of Biology and Its Theories on Women*. New York: Pergamon.

Bowker, Geoffrey C. and Star, Susan Leigh (1999) *Sorting Things Out. Classification and Its Consequences*. Cambridge, MA/London: MIT Press.

Code, Lorraine (1987) *Epistemic Responsibility*. Hanover, NH: University of New England Press.

Corea, Gene, et al. (1985) *Man-Made Women: How New Reproductive Technologies Affect Women*. London: Hutchinson.

Cowan, Ruth Schartz (1976) The 'Industrial Revolution' in the Home: Household Technology, in Patrick D. Hopkins (ed.) (1998) *Sex/Machine. Readings in Culture, Gender and Technology*. Bloomington: Indiana University Press, pp. 33–49 (originally published in *Technology and Culture*, 17, 1, 1976).

Davis, Kathy (2002) Feminist Body/Politics as World Traveller: Translating Our Bodies, Ourselves, *European Journal of Women's Studies* 9, 3, 223–247.

Duden, Barbara (1987/1991) *Geschichte unter der Haut. Ein Eisenacher Arzt und seine Patientinnen um 1730*. Stuttgart: Cotta.

Fausto-Sterling, Anne (1985) *Myths of Gender. Biological Theories about Women and Men*. New York: Basic Books.

Firestone, Shulamith (1970) *Dialectic of Sex*. New York: Morrow.

Foucault, Michel (1970) *The Order of Things: An Archeology of the Human Sciences*. New York: Vintage Books.

Gill, Rosalind and Grint, Keith (1995) The Gender-Technology Relation: Contemporary Theory and Research, in Grint, Keith and Gill, Rosalind (eds), *The Gender-Technology Relation. Contemporary Theory and Research*. London/Bristol, PA: Taylor & Francis.

Haraway, Donna J. (1985) Manifesto for Cyborgs: Science, Technology, and Socialist Feminism in the Late Twentieth Century, in Haraway, Donna (1991) *Simians, Cyborgs, and Women: the Reinvention of Nature*. London: Routledge (originally published in *Socialist Review*, 80, 1985).

Haraway, Donna J. (1988) Situated Knowledges: The Science Question in Feminism as a Site of Discourse on the Privilege of Partial Perspective, in Haraway, Donna (1991) *Simians, Cyborgs, and Women: the Reinvention of Nature*. London: Routledge (originally published in *Feminist Studies*, 14, 3, 575–599).

Haraway, Donna J. (1991) *Simians, Cyborgs, and Women: the Reinvention of Nature*. London: Routledge.

Haraway, Donna J. (1997) *Modest_Witness@Second_Millenium.FemaleMan©_Meets_Onco- Mouse™. Feminism and Technoscience*. New York/London: Routledge.

Harding, Sandra (1986) *The Science Question in Feminism*. Ithaca, NY: Cornell University Press.

Hartsock, Nancy (1983) The Feminist Standpoint: Developing the Ground for a Specifically Feminist Historical Materialism, in Harding, Sandra and Hintikka, Merill B. (eds), *Discovering Reality. Feminist Perspectives on Epistemology, Metaphysics, Methodology and Philosophy of Science*. Dordrecht: Reidel, pp. 283–310.

Hayles, N. Katherine (1999) *How We Became Posthuman: Virtual Bodies in Cybernetics, Literature, and Informatics*. Chicago/London: Chicago University Press.

Hofmann, Heidi (2003) Reproduktionstechnologien bedeuten soziokulturelle Veränderungen, in Weber, Jutta and Bath, Corinna (eds), *Turbulente Körper, soziale*

Maschinen. Feministische Studien zur Technowissenschaftskultur. Opladen: Leske & Budrich, pp. 235–250.

Hubbard, Ruth (1988) Some Thoughts about the Masculinity of the Natural Sciences, in Mary McCanney Gergen (ed.), *Feminist Thought and the Structure of Knowledge.* New York: New York University Press, pp. 1–15.

Hubbard, Ruth, Henifin, Mary Sue, and Fried, Barbara (eds) (1979) *Women Look at Biology Looking at Women: A Collection of Feminist Critiques.* Cambridge, MA: Schenkman.

Hughes, Thomas P. (1986) The Seamless Web: Technology, Science, Etcetera, Etcetera, *Social Studies of Science*, 16, 281–292.

Jacob, François (1977) Evolution and Tinkering, *Science*, 196, 4295, 1161–1166.

Kay, Lily E. (1996) Life as Technology: Representing, Intervening, and Molecularizing, in Sahotra Sarkar (ed.), *The Philosophy and History of Molecular Biology: New Perspectives.* Dordrecht/Boston/London: Kluwer, pp. 87–100.

Kay, Lily E. (1999) In the Beginning Was the Word? The Genetic Code and the Book of Life, in Biagioli, Mario (ed.), *The Science Studies Reader.* New York/London: Routledge.

Keller, Evelyn Fox (1985) *Reflections on Gender and Science.* New Haven, CT/London: Yale University Press.

Keller, Evelyn Fox (1995a) The Origin, History, and Politics of the Subject called 'Gender and Science', in Jasanoff, Sheila, Markle, Gerald E., Petersen, James C. and Pinch, Trevor (eds), *Handbook of Science and Technology Studies.* Thousand Oaks, CA/London/New Delhi: Sage, pp. 80–94.

Keller, Evelyn Fox (1995b) *Refiguring Life. Metaphors of Twentieth-Century Biology.* New York: Columbia University Press.

Knapp, Gudrun-Axeli (1998) Beziehungssinn und Unterscheidungsvermögen, *Potsdamer Studien zur Frauen- und Geschlechterforschung*, 2, 45–56.

Longino, Helen (1990) *Science as Social Knowledge.* Princeton, NJ: Princeton University Press.

Lorber, Judith (1994) *Paradoxes of Gender.* New Haven, CT/London: Yale University Press.

Martin, Emily (1991) 'The Egg and the Sperm: How Science Has Constructed a Romance Based on Stereotypical Male–Female Roles, *Signs*, 16, 485–501.

McNeil, Maureen and Franklin, Sarah (1991) Science and Technology: Questions for Cultural Studies and Feminism, in Franklin, S., Lury, C. and Stacey, J. (eds), *Off-Centre. Feminism and Cultural Studies.* London/New York: HarperCollins, pp. 129–146.

Oudshoorn, Nelly (1996) A Natural Order of Things? Reproductive Sciences and the Politics of Othering, in Robertson, George et al. (eds), *FutureNatural. Nature/Science/Culture.* London/New York: Routledge, pp. 122–132.

Price, Derek J. de Solla (1963) *Little Science, Big Science.* New York: Columbia University Press.

Reid, Roddey and Traweek, Sharon (2000) Introduction: Researching Researchers, in Reid, Roddey and Traweek, Sharon (eds), *Doing Science and Culture. How Cultural and Interdisciplinary Studies Are Changing the Way We Look at Science and Medicine.* New York/London: Routledge.

Rose, Hilary (1983) *Hand, Brain, and Heart: A Feminist Epistemology for the Natural Sciences, Signs*, 9, 1, 73–90.

Scheich, Elvira (1989) Frauen-Sicht. Zur politischen Theorie der Technik, in Beer, Ursula (Hg.) *Klasse Geschlecht. Feministische Gesellschaftsanalyse und Wissenschaftskritik.* Bielefeld, pp. 132–161.

Scheich, Elvira (1993) *Naturbeherrschung und Weiblichkeit. Denkformen und Phantasmen der modernen Naturwissenschaften.* Pfaffenweiler: Centaurus.

Schiebinger, Londa (1989) *The mind has no sex? Women in the Origins of Modern Science.* Cambridge, MA: Harvard University Press.

Schiebinger, Londa (2000) Gender, in Hessenbruch, Arne (ed.), *Reader's Guide to the History of Science.* London/Chicago: Fitzroy Dearborn, pp. 283–285.

Snow, Charles Percy (1959) *The Two Cultures and the Scientific Revolution.* Cambridge: Cambridge University Press.

Star, Susan Leigh (1991) Power, Technology and the Phenomenology of Conventions: on Being Allergic to Onions, in Law, John (ed.), *A Sociology of Monsters. Essays on Power, Technology and Domination.* London/New York: Routledge, pp. 26–56.

Stone, Sandy (1993) The 'Empire' Strikes Back: A Posttranssexual Manifesto, in http://www.actlab.utexas.edu/%7Esandy/empire-strikes-back, pp. 1–30 (last accessed July 2000).

Stryker, Susan (2000) Transsexuality: The Postmodern Body and/as Technology, in Bell, David and Kennedy, Barbara M. (eds), *The Cybercultures reader.* London: Routledge, pp. 588–597.

Suchman, Lucy (1987) *Plans and Situated Actions: The Problem of Human–Machine Communication.* Cambridge, MA: Cambridge University Press.

Tobies, Renate (2001) Women and Mathematics, in *NTM*, 9, 191–198.

Wajcman, Judith (1991) *Feminism Confronts Technology.* University Park, PA: Pennsylvania State University Press.

Weber, Jutta (1999) Contested Meanings: Nature in the Age of Technoscience, in Mittelstraß, Jürgen (ed.), *Die Zukunft des Wissens. XVIII. Deutscher Kongreß für Philosophie.* Konstanz: UVK, pp. 466–473. http://www.univie.ac.at/soziale_maschinen/PDF/WeberNatureTechnoscience.pdf

Weber, Jutta (2003) *Umkämpfte Bedeutungen: Naturkonzepte im Zeitalter der Technoscience.* Frankfurt a.M./New York: Campus.

Part VIII
MAKING CHANGE

23

Moral Perspectives
Gender, Ethics, and Political Theory

Joan C. Tronto

Beginning from the historical exclusion of women from most ethical and political concerns, feminist scholars in these fields try to understand how to think ethically and act politically to end women's oppression. The challenges of this task are not only to determine the nature of oppression, but to challenge faulty claims that men's experiences, concerns, and ways of knowing are the only possible ones. Feminist scholars must confront such basic questions as: How is the subject of human action, 'what can she know?' How can one persuade others about the necessity for moral and political reform or revolution? This essay explores these questions by focusing on feminist advances in thinking about human diversity: Who are women? What is knowledge about morality and politics? How do people develop their moral views? Standpoint epistemology and its resolution in a thick moral contextualism, the multifaceted subject, a feminist ethic of care, and a concern with the nature of evil are among the most distinctive advances in gender, ethics, and political theory.

INTRODUCTION

Ethics considers the fundamental questions: How ought we to live our lives? What should be our goals? How should we act towards others? Ethics is intertwined with the study of political theory, which asks: How should we best structure institutions and practices so that we may live our lives to allow people to achieve their goals? Although women have always been a part of humanity, and although throughout history women have made contributions to answer these questions, their contributions have usually been ignored and their lives and experiences left out in thinking about these questions (Minnich, 1990). Recent feminist thinkers offer critiques of the old answers and provide new ways to think about these questions.

As one of the older disciplines, and one that considers itself at the center of the Western intellectual tradition, contemporary philosophy has been quite wary about including feminist insights into its disciplinary perspectives.[1] Within professional philosophy, ethics has until recently been considered a less central aspect of the discipline as well. As a twice-forgotten subfield, feminist ethics has developed on its own and also has been related to the broader currents in women's studies. Feminist political theory has also had a somewhat marginal status in political science.[2] Most fields in feminist scholarship have a similar pattern to their history: scholars began by noticing the neglect of women in the canonical account of their field; they began slowly to 'add women and stir,' (Bunch, 1987) and later, they began to change substantially the concepts of the field. In both ethics and political theory, there are clear trends to include women and feminist perspectives, but a total paradigm shift has not yet occurred. This chapter describes the ways in which the fields of feminist ethics and political theory have emerged, the main debates in the fields today, and some prospects for future change.

BROADENING ETHICS AND POLITICAL THEORY: CHANGING THE STARTING ASSUMPTIONS

As feminists began to wonder about women's lives from the standpoint of these two disciplines, they noticed similarities in the ways that ethics and political theory approach the world. Andrea Nye described ethics in this way:

> Like religious ethics, the form of secular modernist morality is deductive. Philosophers lay down first principles – natural freedom, universal value of pleasure, universalizability – and from them make inferences to lesser principles and applications. The model is law, a body of prohibitions, mutually coherent and authoritative, that justify action. The problems of moral philosophy are defined accordingly. Is there a clear application of principle? How can the actions prohibited or enjoined be defined? What happens when principles conflict? (1995: 140–141)

While not all political theory is equally rigid in following what Margaret Walker (1998) eventually called a 'theoretical–juridical' conception, political theory shares with ethics a search for a universal perspective. Looking at this philosophical tradition, feminist scholars found that two critical aspects of women's lives were ignored. Neither ethics nor political theory provided a way to explain women's oppression, and neither provided a way to take as central the importance of women's moral experiences (Jaggar and Rothenberg, 1993).

Several major directions of feminist thinking have begun to transform the nature of political theory and ethics. Many of these trends are part of a broader movement in political thought and philosophy questioning the boundaries around these subdisciplines and reflecting interdisciplinary and less Eurocentric concerns throughout the world.

Within political theory, scholars have focused on its historical and conceptual dimensions. Political theory remains one of the most canonical of fields, teaching students about political thought through its history. Feminist scholars included new theorists and texts to the canon (Mary Wollstonecraft and J. S. Mill's *On the Subjection of Women*, for example), and made feminist interpretations a vital part of ongoing readings of classic texts. Both Jean Bethke Elshtain (1981) and Susan Moller Okin (1979) offered early readings of women's place in the history of political theory that presaged scores of outstanding articles and books. Carole Pateman's *The Sexual Contract* (1988) offers a rereading of the historical social-contract tradition.

Other political theorists focused on conceptual change. In a collection published in the mid-1990s, Mary Lyndon Shanley and Uma Narayan (1997) collected some of the work that reflects fundamental transformations in such concepts as freedom, power, and autonomy. Among the most important conceptual innovations is the focus on the changing border between 'public' and 'private' life. The relationship of public and private life has a long history in political theory, as it appears in Aristotle's *Politics* in Book I and is a central part of the analysis of J. S. Mill's account of liberty. Nevertheless, as feminist scholars began to think about the ways in which the containment of women in the private sphere furthered women's oppression, the insight that the public and private are intertwined, not separate, was critical.

A number of perspectives on the relationship of public and private life are possible, and in a way, this issue frames some of the most important continuing debates within contemporary liberal political theory. For Aristotle, the relationship of public and private life was simple: private life was a prerequisite for the more important realm of public engagement. For traditional liberals, individuals exercise their vital rights to comprise the meaning of their life in the private sphere, but the public sphere exists to regulate the private. How might feminists best understand the relationship of public and private life?

One of the key questions that feminists put onto this agenda is the question of how public and private life are framed and constituted. Aristotle saw economic life as a part of the private sphere. For Marxists, economic activity is centrally a public concern. Insofar as broad-scale change occurs in the public arena, feminists began to puzzle through why and how women and their concerns had been so completely excluded from the public arena. Pateman (1988) argued that the shape of the private sphere, what counts as 'private,' is constituted in the public sphere, and only those who are permitted access to engagement in the public sphere have the power to set the boundaries between them. Women's relegation to the private sphere and their exclusion from political life was determined by men in the public sphere, and women had no way of contesting this decision, since they had no public life. The social contract was imposed on women by men through their arbitrary exclusion from the public sphere.

The place of ethics in feminist philosophy

In ethics, the critical conceptual issue has not been the relationship of public and private life, since ethical questions arise in both spheres. Relatively little attention has been paid to the ways in which ethical issues might be different in the two realms (Hampshire, 1978). Instead, the feminist discussion in ethics has been parallel to a larger discussion about the centrality of ethics in philosophy and the connection between ethics and other branches of philosophy, such as epistemology and metaphysics.

Throughout much of the twentieth century, the presumption was that ethics was at best a lesser field of philosophy, given its closer association with the messy realities of human life and its less clear focus and status as an abstract realm of thought (cf. Lloyd, 1993). In recent years, spurred largely by the question of where women are in philosophy, the field of ethics has re-emerged as a vital philosophical field. A large part of feminist argumentation, however, has been devoted to challenging the terms for the philosophical hierarchy of concerns within the discipline and the treatment of different parts of philosophy as if they are entirely discrete. A number of important discoveries in feminist ethics have not really been in ethics at all, but in related fields of philosophy.

Standpoint epistemology and feminist ethics

Feminist transformations in epistemology – the philosophy of knowledge – provide an important starting point for feminist ethics. Feminist epistemologists have insisted that knowledge is contextual, that is, knowledge is generated in a particular historical and geographical location. It is also embedded in bodily experience (Lloyd, 1993). Lorraine Code (1991) has suggested that the unequal distributions of power and privilege in society are reflected in the authority that different people have in making knowledge claims. Thus, the ideal that knowledge can be independent of its human knowers, who are themselves always embodied in social settings, appears to be an illusion. Once knowledge is so situated, how does that affect ethics? One possibility is that it makes ethics, understood as the process by which universal laws are derived, a suspect enterprise. Many feminists, though not all, have thus been highly suspicious of universal ethical claims. It also means, most importantly, that all ethical thought needs to be contextualized.

Nancy Hartsock first raised the question of what has come to be called standpoint epistemology (1978; 1998). Following Georg Lukács' reading of Marx, Hartsock argued that the objective and structural location of some people made them better situated to understand their own circumstances and those of others around them. Thus, Lukács posited that the working class were better equipped to understand the nature of capitalism than capitalists, since they understood their own positions as well as those of their bosses. This approach was different from the previous Marxist view, which had given equal or greater weight to the more powerful to understand the nature of the world around them. Hartsock similarly argued for the radical idea that women's subordinate position provides them with a way to understand the world more completely, since they must understand the world both from their own perspective and from the perspective of dominant men. In both cases, Lukács and Hartsock make the claim that those who are less well off are actually in a better place to understand the world than the more powerful.

This feminist standpoint, however, is not the same thing as the subjective sensibilities of women. In the first place, it is possible not to be genuinely observant of one's circumstance. More seriously, though, being in a situation where one might be able to see the world more clearly is no guarantee that one will see the world with clarity. It is possible to be misled or deceived. People might be unwilling to recognize the reality around them. Marxists frequently call such forms of deception or partiality 'false consciousness.' False consciousness seems to be a difficult epistemological tool for feminists, though. Feminist thinkers have found it difficult to be in a position to say that mainstream philosophy has ignored women's experience only to turn around and say that some women are deluded by a kind of 'false consciousness' and do not understand their own experience (Grant, 1993).

There is also the question of whether there is only one possible feminist perspective. Feminist scholars who focus on the experiences of women of color quickly observed that just as women might have access to a different kind of knowledge because they are women and suffer from sexist oppression, so, too, women of color experience and know how systems of racist oppression affect them and the racially privileged. Lesbians made a similar point about heterosexist forms of privilege. Soon, the neatness of the feminist standpoint seemed to dissolve into the complexity of multiple standpoints.

In answering these charges, feminist scholars (including Hartsock herself in 1998) have agreed that multiple standpoints are possible. Nevertheless, it is still possible to describe how a standpoint provides knowledge that is different, and more comprehensive, than knowledge understood as simply facts about the world around us. Knowledge from a standpoint always involves an analysis and a realization of the power differentials operating among different individuals. It requires recognition of multiple ways of seeing, and of understanding why the centrally powerful way of seeing operates to exclude other points of view. Although feminists no longer believe that there is a single 'feminist standpoint,' standpoint epistemology, and the knowledge that comes from taking multiple perspectives, continue to be powerful tools for understanding feminist ethics and politics.

Feminist ethics and politics from multiple standpoints

Given multiple standpoints, how might feminists interested in ethics proceed? Throughout the twentieth century, ethics proceeded as a field of study from the recognition of a reliable way to produce knowledge. With multiple points from which to gain knowledge, is all of feminist ethics open to the charge of relativism? If there is no certain and universal moral knowledge, is ethics possible at all? The question of how the study of ethics should proceed, metaethics, is the subject of Margaret Urban Walker's *Moral Understandings* (1998). Urban Walker draws a contrast between two ways of moral theorizing. Traditionally, ethics has used a 'theoretical-juridical' conception of morality, which aims to produce impersonal, action-guiding rules that are timeless, context-less, and pure. In contrast, Urban Walker urges feminists to think of ethics in terms of an 'expressive-collaborative' model, in which social practices, and the ways in which ethics actually operates in people's lives, are primary. As Urban Walker writes:

> Morality is always something people are actually doing together in their communities, societies, and ongoing relationships. It s not up to academic philosophers to discover it or make it up... Without already knowing a good deal about (what we call) moral reasoning, moral rules, moral responsibility, and so on, we wouldn't know where to begin or what we are talking about. We're all in the same boat, epistemically, in this way. Feminist, race, gay and lesbian, and post-colonial philosophy has taken this farther: what we know about the social relations that embody our moral ones, and so what we are inclined to identify as the subject matter of ethics, is likely to be directly related to which places in our particular ways of life we occupy, and what the particulars of those ways of life are. (Walker, 2002: 175)

These 'particulars' that Walker (1998) describes are similar to the thick descriptions of the multiple standpoints that Hartsock invokes, as well as to the question of context in all non-universal forms of ethics. Particularities raise another important issue to feminist ethics – the definition of a moral person.

Ontology and feminist ethics

Another key question within philosophy that has a bearing on feminist ethics is the question of ontology, or being itself. What does it really mean to be a person? What is the notion of the self? This issue is central for feminist thinkers, many of whom have argued, in a variety of ways, that the category 'human,' and the very notion of what it means to be human, have been mainly inflected by the lives of men. Since Kant, most philosophers have presumed that what it means to be a human individual is to be autonomous, that is, literally, capable of making one's rules for oneself. Feminist scholars have noted how often the experience of oppression distorts this capacity for making one's own choices. In recent years, feminist philosophers have begun to describe humans as possessed of 'relational autonomy,' that is, an autonomy that is not absolute but also needs to be contextualized (Mackenzie and Stoljar, 2000).

Finally, feminists have insisted that philosophers cannot ignore the intersection of their disciplinary concern with 'ethics,' how we ought to live, and moral psychology, what actual human beings are capable of doing, in terms of moral reasoning and action. A recent collection considers how feelings, our capacities for memory, and so on, affect our ethical possibilities (DesAutels and Walker, 2004).

All of these findings in philosophy have consequences for the shape of contemporary feminist debates in ethics. The main effect of all of these discoveries is similar: it is no longer possible to describe ethics as the kind of field where scholars fix the rules and think about their consequences without reference to the actual people who will be responsible for applying them. Thus, feminists have revitalized ethics by reintroducing questions that were, until recently, considered somewhat passé. Among them are the nature of virtues, the nature of moral action, and large questions such as the nature of evil. Once this basic point is admitted, though, a number of challenges remain for feminist ethics.

CURRENT DEBATES

The great progress made in adding the question of context to feminist ethics and political theory is an accomplishment of note. Nevertheless, difficult questions lie ahead. How should we think about the aspects of human contexts that are relevant to ethical discussions? In this section, I will consider the issues that currently concern feminist scholars in ethics and political theory. These include the nature of the self, the definition of 'women,' the care–justice debate, and the problems of evil and responsibility for wrongs.

Who is the subject/self?

In both ethics and political theory, the question of who constitutes the subject of the inquiry remains a thorny and unavoidable issue. After all, in order for 'someone' to act, there has to be a someone to do it. Or does there? One of the most ferocious debates throughout feminism in the last twenty years has concerned the status of postmodern or poststructuralist thought, and whether these currents are useful and important to feminists. Postmodernism and poststructuralism are not the same, and there are many varieties of these systems of thought. In general, though, postmodernism refers to the social condition of being in a new historical era. In this new moment, humans are made by a variety of competing and dizzying forces. Material and symbolic forces are all accorded importance and then produce much flux in the relationship of fixed 'realities' and apparent constructions of gender, race, nationality, senses of self, and so forth. Poststructuralism refers to the conceptual location that is beyond the assumption that there are enduring and deep structures, especially in human language, that provide a foundation for knowledge and action. Both postmodernism and poststructuralism pose the same challenge to the idea in ethics and political theory that there is a fixed self who can make decisions about the best course of action or the best way to structure institutions.

Part of the virulence over this discussion is the fact that in their most severe academic forms, neither side is very appealing. On the one hand, postmodernists accuse their critics of 'essentializing,' that is, fixing and exaggerating the realities that they see around them. On the other hand, non-postmodernists accuse poststructuralists and postmodern feminists of ignoring the realities of women's lives and offering a description of social reality that leaves little space for real action. In truth, feminist theorists all remain committed to fundamental social change, but this struggle over the best strategies for doing so cuts to the core of the relationship between feminist activity as thinkers and feminist political action.

In political theory, the discussion of the self quickly branches into the topic of poststructuralist concerns. If there is no self, then how can one make a coherent argument for political activity that will culminate in a political movement (Moi, 1999)? Some feminist thinkers have argued that the need for a coherent and whole self is not necessary in order to make political theory meaningful (for example, Brown, 1995).

Judith Butler's pathbreaking account of how gender is *constructed* and *performed*, rather than biological or set, is an important example of how poststructuralist thought operates (1990). Butler argues that gender is not so much a fixed category as a set of contested pieces that are constantly in negotiation. In saying this, Butler does not mean that anyone can invent her own idea of gender, but that the categories that seem to be fixed are in fact malleable. Butler's work has inspired an entire generation of scholars, especially those in cultural studies and queer studies, to deconstruct seemingly fixed moments and practices.

Martha Nussbaum is one critic of postmodern and poststructuralist thought. In a strong attack on Butler in particular, she argued that postmodern thought is too far removed from the lives of actual women (1999a). To Nussbaum, Butler's poststructuralist writings can quickly become an arcane exploration of social forms. In her view, too great an appreciation of multiplicity and fluidity results in a kind of relativism that lacks power to make clear arguments about what is wrong with such forms. For Nussbaum, categories such as justice are too vital for assessing harm to allow them to be deconstructed. Nussbaum (2000) continues to find a more universal account of human needs, the necessary conditions for human flourishing, as a way to evaluate women's lives.

The question of whether the search for a self is a meaningful one is complicated when we recognize how this question intersects with categories such as race, ethnicity, religion, sexual orientation, and so forth. On the one hand, racial identity is a good example of a socially constructed category that is 'essentialized' by social practices and forces. To deny this construction its power would be a liberating step, indeed. On the other hand, as thinkers such as Patricia Williams have argued, women of color have been denied their identity, their rights, and their dignity in many ways; at this moment when they are about to gain recognition, what is the point of a discourse that argues that no such thing exists (1991; 1995)? Clearly, for Williams, some appreciation of poststructuralist insights is necessary, while at the same time, it is not appropriate to abandon entirely the frameworks of rights.

There are other and more complicated questions that arise from the nature of the self. Are all selves the same? Some feminist thinkers have been able to write highly nuanced and thoughtful accounts of human lives from deep reflection of what 'selves' do (Bartky, 1990; Meyers, 1994). Just as feminist scholars have gone beyond the notion that only epistemology and ontology are central concerns in ethics, moral psychology has become an increasingly important part of the study of feminist ethics. How does a 'self' come to be the person that she is? Is there is a fixed 'self' of some kind? To what extent does one's social status affect and determine what kind of person one will be?

One way that this idea of the self has been expressed in political and ethical terms is around the question of 'identity.' What does it mean for a person to have a particular identity? How central is identity to one's self-conception? To what extent does identity also function as a kind of privilege, since some women can use their accounts of their identity without running afoul of entrenched social privileges and prejudices, while others cannot? To what extent does the brute fact that women occupy female bodies affect how women negotiate the moral and political world?

One such identity that has been extremely important in the formulation of feminist ethics is a lesbian identity. Numerous scholars have noted how important sexuality is for one's sense of self.[3] Some writers, such as Monique Wittig (1992), have emphasized that to be a lesbian is to have a different sensibility about the entire world. Other scholars have taken an approach that makes no claims about lesbians' ultimate differences from other women, but have stressed the ethical difficulties forced upon lesbians by their status as outcasts from society.

What, in the end, does the question of identity mean for feminist ethics and political theory? Some feminists have been highly critical of the practices of 'identity politics' because it seems to narrow and constrain women's possibilities and to rely upon, and thus to reinforce, categories that have been used rigidly for purposes of oppressing women (Brown, 1995). One political theorist who has proposed a solution to this problem is Nancy Fraser (1997), who has argued that the key issues facing women in their struggles to end oppression are both redistribution (gaining equality and access to resources) and recognition (having others treat one as fully human). To think of recognition as a solution, though, requires an ability to solve a difficult and fundamental philosophical question: How does one conceive of the self in relationship to others? Is the creation of 'others' a necessary part of our self-definition, as some philosophers seem to have argued? Or is it possible for us to see our self in relation to others, as Walker (1998) would suggest that we must, and to be certain that the moral conclusions that we draw do not simply rest on our embedded assumptions about social life?

Who are 'women?'

A second ongoing debate in feminist political theory and ethics is the question of multiculturalism. Feminist scholars have been leading advocates for the position that, given the centrality of context in ethical and political theory, one needs constantly to be sensitive to the differences among women and among their varying experiences. Racial category, sexual orientation, ethnicity, religion, linguistic capacities, disability – all of these conditions affect how a given woman is able to live her life and engage in political and moral activity. Women of color raised these criticisms early and continuously as an attempt to make feminists aware of the limitations of their theories.[4] Third World women also raised these concerns and pointed to the limitations of viewing the world only through Western eyes.[5]

But a serious question arises about whether, at some point, one has been too accommodating to cultural differences, obscuring the main point of feminist critique. Susan Moller Okin raised such a criticism in the important article 'Is Multiculturalism Bad for Women?' (Okin et al., 1999). Okin et al. argued that, on balance, cultural deference was likely to give power to religious leaders, damaging the possibility of creating coherent support for women's lives throughout the globe. Many critics accused Okin et al. of being insensitive to cultural differences in general, and to making arguments that would not, strategically, yield strong arguments that women could use to improve their life circumstances.

Nussbaum (1999b; 2000) is another thinker who has criticized feminists for their too ready acceptance of multiculturalism. Following the work of the economist Amatyra Sen, Nussbaum posits that it is possible to identify some categories for human flourishing. This approach, called the human capabilities model, identifies a number of essential capabilities that all humans have, and argues that any decent society will try to make certain that all of its people are able to develop these capabilities to the fullest. Thus, in societies where girls are forced to leave school while their brothers continue their education, because boys are more likely to get good-paying jobs, the girls are deprived of the equal development of their capabilities. Because these capabilities will be defined by local practices, Nussbaum believes that she is sensitive to context. Nevertheless, she argues that feminists can retain a standard for making universal judgments.

Another standard by which some scholars advocate making universal judgments is that of international human rights. Although the language of rights is an old and foundational part of the liberal intellectual tradition, the language of 'human rights,' as embodied in the Universal Declaration of Human Rights (1945), makes a clear set of claims that lay out the basic rights every human is entitled to have honored. The Declaration has been adopted by virtually every government in the world, and human rights have become a rallying call and a point for expanding political participation and discussion throughout the globe. Over half a million human rights organizations exist now in the world; they do not all share the starting premises of Lockean individualism, but they do all subscribe to the same Declaration.

Women's groups have been especially successful in changing some aspects of the focus of the discussion of international human rights. While the first rights described in the Declaration consider political and civil rights that are most likely to be violated by the state itself, women have argued that often the greatest threats to them do not come from the state but from the failure of the state to protect them against violators of their human rights and dignity, who may operate in their own society. Violence against women, the threat of rape, and the threat of domestic violence all reduce women's capacities to enjoy their human rights. Increasingly, human rights advocates have also begun to assert the importance of human security, arguing that the state's duties to secure itself are not over when it has protected its borders from physical attack, but only when it also protects its citizens from others and from each other. Children and women are especially vulnerable to such internal attacks, and the logic of human security, extended from the desire to enjoy human rights, is an attempt to persuade all states to take such concerns seriously.

These discussions raise critical questions for feminist thinkers. To what extent should people be able to make judgments about the lives of others? To allow no such judgments would require that everything collapses into relativism. On the other hand, is it not equally insulting for some women to presume that their understandings of the world make sense, not only for themselves, but for everyone? One issue, for example, that has been much discussed by Western feminists is the question of female genital cutting in parts of Africa and the Middle East. Feminists have written about their outrage at this practice, at the same time expressing their appreciation for the rights of women in different cultures to make decisions for themselves.[6] Yet it is somewhat disturbing that this practice has received so much attention while other issues of women's health, such as the remarkable and widening gap of global inequalities in access to health care, and other issues, such as vulnerability to HIV infection and AIDS, remain less fully explored.

Within political theory as well, feminist scholars have begun to recognize the need to think beyond the experiences of women in Europe and the Americas, and this broader perspective now informs feminist theorizing.[7] As to the problem of relativism in ethics and political action, Walker provided this solution:

> I don't mind being some kind of relativist, as long as I am not the kind that renders individuals' or societies' moral self-criticism incoherent, or that declares intergroup or intercultural moral evaluation and criticism impossible or forbidden. (1998: 6)

Care ethics and the justice/care debate

Another current key debate in feminist ethics and political theory is the discussion of care and justice. Feminists have made important contributions in understanding justice; Iris Young provides a rich rethinking of justice (Young, 1990), as does Nancy Fraser (1997). But the care–justice debate arose out of feminist discourse, not out of the philosophical mainstream. This debate originated in the writing of Carol Gilligan, whose pathbreaking text, *In a Different*

Voice (1982), posited that the progress of moral development charted by her mentor, Lawrence Kohlberg, had been too narrow because it left out women. Kohlberg's original research on stages of moral development had been conducted only with men as subjects. When women subjects were added, they seemed to be less moral because they scored less high on Kohlberg's single hierarchical scale. This discrepancy led Gilligan to posit that there were, in fact, two ways to describe moral development, a difference characterized 'by theme, not gender.' Nonetheless, Gilligan has been read as arguing that women have a different course of moral development. She identified this alternative account as 'an ethic of care' as opposed to 'an ethic of rights.' What distinguishes the ethics of care, Gilligan argued, are three aspects. First, the ethic of care is about different moral concepts; it is about responsibility and relationships rather than rights and rules. Second, it is about concrete circumstances rather than abstract and formal rules. Third, it expresses morality best not as a set of principles but as an activity.

Based on a liberal understanding of moral psychology, Gilligan's correction of Kohlberg was treated by mainstream philosophers as a contribution to an understanding of private morality. Around the same time, though, Nel Noddings (1984) had begun to explore the meaning of care, starting from an Heideggerian perspective. She argued that care was not simply an added approach to morality, but a way to think about morality that started from one's existing situation and was somewhat constrained by the necessarily close and dyadic nature of care. Thus, Noddings argued that care is essentially unprincipled; it is guided by the needs of those to whom we are closest.

Feminist scholars reacted in two ways. Many were very wary of the similarity between such an ethic of care and the tradition of responsibility for others that had oppressed women's lives. Others enthusiastically embraced the idea that women's lives were to be the starting point for a serious rethinking of the values that had driven men to structure social and political institutions as they had (Held, 1993). I suggested one approach to breaking this impasse when I argued that care was best understood not as a *gendered* account of ethics, but as an alternative way to think about ethics. Although it had been eschewed by the mainstream intellectual tradition and thus appeared more closely associated with the moral positions advocated by women, US minorities, and others outside the intellectual mainstream, there was no reason to reject an ethic of care as not an adequate and worthy approach to ethics (Tronto, 1987).

As time has gone on, virtually all feminist scholars agree that care and justice are related approaches to ethics; neither is complete without including some of the insights of the other perspective.[8] Nevertheless, the question of how to reconcile the two perspectives remains a serious and ongoing concern. Is there such a thing as care, or can what feminists describe as care be described in other terms? Is care a different kind of moral theory, more closely related to approaches that emphasize virtues, than to principled approaches to justice? Can care be well accommodated in traditional liberal frameworks? Eva Kittay (1998), who uses a Rawlsian framework, demonstrates how necessarily unequal burdens of care in private life need to be accommodated in public accounts of justice. Kittay notes that some humans, such as children and those with a severe disability, are inevitably and completely dependent on others, and their caregivers have a burden that affects their equal opportunity to participate fully in the rest of life. Not to notice this inequality, Kittay argues, is unjust.

For some theorists of care, the most profound challenge returns to some of the questions about the nature of ethics raised earlier. From the standpoint of care, if morality is measured as an activity, it cannot be presumed that the moral actor is always an autonomous self, acting on the basis of set ethical principles and possessed of all of the requisite knowledge to act morally. After all, humans are all always (though at some times more than at other times) care receivers as well as care givers. The care perspective requires that we think about the moral dimension of receiving care as well as that of giving care. It requires that we reflect upon the place of dependency, illness, insecurity, and death in human life. These have not been the central concerns of moral philosophy and political theory. Furthermore, exploring the personal provision of care makes clear how limited our individual capacities are and how much we depend upon others for guidance and direction. Even the seemingly most 'natural' of caring acts, mothering, is a complex set of human practices that are well served by constant moral reflection (Ruddick, 1989).

Whatever the final outcome of this discussion on care and justice, it nevertheless demonstrates the basic insight of feminist explorations in ethics: the ongoing and deep importance of context. In response to the claim that care is only about private life with details of moral relations that remain to be worked out after the larger questions of 'justice' have been settled, feminist political theorists and ethicists have insisted that, in fact, justice is also context-dependent (Tronto, 2000; Sevenhuijsen, 1998; White, 2000). They have begun to pay attention to the larger contexts within which both care and justice must be situated. Julie White (2000), for example, has insisted that care practices that are divorced from concerns for democratic practices are not good care practices. Selma Sevenhuijsen (1998) has argued that care requires trust.[9] It is the ongoing concern with context, with recognizing that morality is embedded in social institutions and our capacity to make broader moral judgments, that continues to make the outcome of the care–justice debate crucial.

Evil, responsibility, and complicity

Another set of questions that feminist thinkers have begun to explore is the nature of evil. In a way, all feminist ethics starts from a presumption of at least one evil: gender oppression. But partly in response to the ever-growing sophistication about the relationship of women to questions of victimhood and agency (Brown, 1995), the question of what constitutes 'evil' and what to do about complicity becomes more real. Claudia Card (1999) finds it useful to refer to moral locales, following Primo Levi, as gray zones. Card's insistence on the gray middle is important in observing that virtually all people are complicit in some way in systems that deny people their moral agency.

Another dimension of this concern with wrong-doing is what Walker calls moral repair. How should individuals make up for wrongs done in the past? How should they come to understand these wrongs, and how should they act to correct them? Walker's argument extends her claim that feminist ethics needs to be an 'ethics of responsibility,' that is, 'a normative moral view [that] would try to put people and responsibilities in the right places with respect to each other' (1998: 78).

As important as it is to understand the questions of evil and of responsibility, what does it mean when a group of feminist moral theorists have decided that they are central questions? Partly it arises out of a sense that they wish to avoid making mistakes that are similar to the ones that they criticize from the past. But it is also probably a sign of the historical maturity of the women's movement. No longer motivated by a hope that a fundamental and transformative revolution is around the corner, the discussions in feminist theory lack some of the urgency and assertiveness that characterized the debates of twenty years ago. Then, it seemed as if all that feminists needed to do was to determine the proper framework for change within which to devote their energies. Feminist scholars now are much more aware of their own location in a position of relative privilege in a world that does not much engage in theoretical activities, and in which discussions of broad-based change seem not to be at the center of possibilities. In such a setting, the ongoing and haunting questions of whether to apply universal standards or to recognize local context, who may make judgments for whom, and who are the subjects and objects of feminist change, remain knotty.

FUTURE DIRECTIONS

The increasing concern of feminist thinkers with evil and moral repair also points towards another change that has occurred in feminist writing. It is no longer possible to portray women simply as the victims of a patriarchal order that oppresses them. While this shift of view makes the prospects for simple arguments and answers less bright, it also makes possible a more genuine contribution to ethics and politics. The lack of consensus in feminist political theory and ethics reflects the complicated realities of the world. Feminism began with a hope to liberate women from patriarchal oppression, but the variety and depth of oppressive mechanisms and the complicity of all or some women in their operation has made liberation much more difficult than early feminist thinkers hoped. In confronting the study of political thought and ethics, feminists have come to insist on the importance of placing all knowledge into its social setting, and, as a result, recognizing the positions from which philosophers and theorists begin their work.

Feminists have insisted that ethics and political theory as fields of study must start from the real world of power and oppression. As a result, ethics and political theory now more accurately reflect the complexities of self, society, political institutions, and the nature of change. Whatever the future brings, feminist scholars will continue to insist that our hopes start from a global, complex, and morally inclusive vision.

NOTES

1 'Of all the intellectual disciplines, none appeared more blatantly and unremittingly sexist than philosophy. From the homo-eroticism of ancient Greece, through the manly virtuousness of Rome, to the Latinate priestliness of medieval and renaissance universities and the professionalized careerism of the twentieth-century academy, the entire philosophical tradition seemed to function like a male club expressly designed to keep women out' (Rée, 2002: 641). There are some accounts of the place of feminist ethics within philosophy (see, especially, Brennan, 1999; Walker, 1998; 2003a; 2003b) and other important collections and works in feminist ethics (Bar On and Ferguson, 1998; Card, 1991; Code, 2000; Daly, 1978; DesAutels and Walker, 2004; DesAutels and Waugh, 2001; Fiore and Nelson, 2003; Fricker and Hornsby, 2000; Frye, 1983; Jaggar, 1983; Jaggar and Rothenberg, 1993; Jagger and Young, 1998; Kittay and Meyers, 1987; Kourany et al., 1992; MacKinnon, 1989; McLaughlin, 2003; Zaleha et al., 1995).

2 For an outstanding recent survey of the state of the discipline, see Mary Dietz (2003). See also Shanley and Narayan (1997).

3 Sandra Bartky (1990) has insisted on the importance of heterosexuality for one's identity; much more has been written about lesbian ethics (see, for example, Frye, 1983; Hoagland, 1988; Mohin, 1996).

4 As discussed by various authors (see, among others, Collins, 1990; hooks, 1984; Lorde, 1982; 1984;1996; Moraga and Anzaldúa, 1981).

5 As described by various authors, for example Mohanty, 2003; Mohanty et al., 1991; Narayan, 1997; Spivack, 1987.

6 Discussed by various authors (see, among others, Abusharaf, 2001; Gruenbaum, 2000; Hernlund and Shell-Duncan, 2000; James, 1994; 1998; Obermeyer, 1999; Robertson, 1996).

7 As presented by various authors (see, for example, Ackerly, 2000; Petchesky, 2003; Petchesky and Judd, 1998; Petchesky and United Nations Research Institute for Social Development, 2000; Smith, 2000).

8 There are two excellent collections of essays on the care–justice debate (namely, Held, 1995; Larrabee, 1993), among many other works on care (Bowden, 1997; Bubeck, 1995; Cannon, 1988; Collins, 1990; Groenhout, 2004; Kittay, 1998; Noddings, 2002; Robinson, 1999; Sevenhuijsen, 1998; Tronto, 1993). There is also a large literature in nursing ethics on care.

9 Other important feminist scholars in ethics who have emphasized the nature of trust are Annette Baier (1994) and Marilyn Friedman (1993).

REFERENCES

Abusharaf, Rogata Mustafa. (2001). 'Virtuous Cuts: Female Genital Mutilation in an African Ontology.' *Differences: A Journal of Feminist Cultural Studies* 12: 112–140.

Ackerly, B. A. (2000). *Political Theory and Feminist Social Criticism*. Cambridge; New York: Cambridge University Press.

Baier, A. (1994). *Moral Prejudices: Essays on Ethics.* Cambridge, MA: Harvard University Press.

Bar On, B.-A. and A. Ferguson (eds) (1998). *Daring to Be Good: Essays in Feminist Ethico-Politics.* New York: Routledge.

Bartky, S. L. (1990). *Femininity and Domination: Studies in the Phenomenology of Oppression.* New York: Routledge.

Bowden, P. (1997). *Caring: Gender-Sensitive Ethics.* London; New York: Routledge.

Brennan, S. (1999). 'Recent Work in Feminist Ethics.' *Ethics* 109(4): 858–893.

Brown, W. (1995). *States of Injury: Power and Freedom in Late Modernity.* Princeton, NJ: Princeton University Press.

Bubeck, D. (1995). *Care, Justice and Gender.* Oxford: Oxford University Press.

Bunch, C. (1987). *Passionate Politics: Feminist Theory in Action: Essays, 1968–1986.* New York: St. Martin's Press.

Butler, J. (1990) *Gender Trouble: Feminism and the Subversion of Identity.* New York: Routledge.

Cannon, K. G. (1988). *Black Womanist Ethics.* Atlanta, GA: Scholars Press.

Card, C. (ed.) (1991). *Feminist Ethics.* Lawrence, KS: University Press of Kansas.

Card, C. (1999). 'Groping Through Gray Zones.' *On Feminist Ethics and Politics.* C. Card. Lawrence, KS: University Press of Kansas.

Code, L. (ed.) (2000). *Encyclopedia of Feminist Theories.* London; New York: Routledge.

Code, Lorraine (1991). *What Can She Know? Feminist Theory and the Construction of Knowledge.* Ithaca, NY: Cornell University Press.

Collins, P. H. (1990). *Black Feminist Thought: Knowledge, Consciousness, and the Politics of Empowerment.* Boston, MA: Unwin Hyman.

Daly, M. (1978). *Gyn/ecology: the Metaethics of Radical Feminism.* Boston, MA: Beacon Press.

DesAutels, P. and M. U. Walker (eds) (2004). *Moral Psychology: Feminist Ethics and Social Theory.* Lanham, MD: Rowman and Littlefield.

DesAutels, P. and J. Waugh (2001). *Feminists Doing Ethics.* Lanham, MD: Rowman & Littlefield.

Dietz, M. G. (2003). 'Current Controversies in Feminist Theory.' *Annual Review of Political Science* 6: 399–431.

Elshtain, J. B. (1981). *Public Man, Private Woman: Women in Social and Political Thought.* Princeton, NJ: Princeton University Press.

Fiore, R. N. and H. L. Nelson, (eds) (2003). *Recognition, Responsibility and Rights: Feminist Ethics and Social Theory.* Lanham, MD: Rowman and Littlefield.

Fraser, N. (1997). *Justice Interruptus: Critical Reflections on the 'Postsocialist' Condition.* New York; London: Routledge.

Fricker, M. and J. Hornsby (eds) (2000). *The Cambridge Companion to Feminism in Philosophy.* Cambridge: Cambridge University Press.

Friedman, M. (1993). *What are Friends for? Feminist Perspectives on Personal Relationships and Moral Theory.* Ithaca, NY: Cornell University Press.

Frye, M. (1983). *The Politics of Reality: Essays in Feminist Theory.* Trumansburg, NY: Crossing Press.

Gilligan, C. (1982). *In a Different Voice.* Cambridge, MA: Harvard University Press.

Grant, J. (1993). *Fundamental Feminism: Contesting the Core Concepts of Feminist Theory.* New York: Routledge.

Groenhout, R. E. (2004). *Connected Lives: Human Nature and an Ethics of Care.* Lanham, MD: Rowman & Littlefield.

Gruenbaum, Ellen (2000). *The Female Circumcision Controversy: An Anthropological Perspective.* Philadelphia: University of Pennsylvania Press.

Hampshire, S. (ed.) (1978). *Public and Private Morality.* New York: Cambridge University Press.

Hartsock, N. C. (1998). *Feminist Standpoint Revisited: And Other Essays.* Boulder, CO: Westview Press.

Hartsock, N. C. M. (1978). *Money, Sex and Power: Toward a Feminist Historical Materialism.* Boston, MA: Northeastern University Press.

Held, V. (1993). *Feminist Morality: Transforming Culture, Society and Politics.* Chicago: University of Chicago Press.

Held, V. (1995). *Justice and Care: Essential Readings in Feminist Ethics.* Boulder, CO: Westview Press.
Hernlund, Ylva and Bettina Shell-Duncan (eds) (2000). 'Female Circumcision.' *Africa: Culture, Controversy, and Change.* Boulder, CO: Lynn Rienner.
Hoagland, S. L. (1988). *Lesbian Ethics: Toward New Value.* Palo Alto, CA: Institute of Lesbian Studies.
hooks, b. (1984). *Feminist Theory From Margin to Center.* Boston, MA: South End Press.
Jaggar, A. M. (1983). *Feminist Politics and Human Nature.* Totowa, NJ: Rowman & Littlefield.
Jaggar, A. M. and P. S. Rothenberg (eds) (1993). *Feminist Frameworks: Alternative Accounts of the Relations Between Women and Men.* New York, McGraw-Hill.
Jaggar, A. M. and I. M. Young (1998). *A Companion to Feminist philosophy.* Malden, MA: Blackwell.
James, Stephen A. (1994). 'Reconciling Human Rights and Cultural Relativism: The Case of Female Circumcision.' Bioethics 8(Nov. 1): 1–26.
James, Stephen A. (1998). 'Shades of Othering: Reflections on Female Circumcision/Genital Mutilation.' *Signs* 23: 1031–1048.
Kittay, E. F. (1998). *Love's Labor: Essays on Women, Equality and Dependency.* New York: Routledge.
Kittay, E. F. and D. T. Meyers (1987). *Women and Moral Theory.* Totowa, NJ: Rowman & Littlefield.
Kourany, J. A. et al. (eds) (1992). *Feminist Philosophies: Problems, Theories, and Applications.* Englewood Cliffs, NJ: Prentice Hall.
Larrabee, M. J. (1993). *An Ethic of care: Feminist and Interdisciplinary Perspectives.* New York: Routledge.
Lloyd, G. (1993). *The Man of Reason: 'Male' and 'Female' in Western Philosophy.* New York: Routledge.
Lorde, A. (1982). *Zami, a New Spelling of my Name.* Trumansburg, NY: Crossing Press.
Lorde, A. (1984). *Sister Outsider: Essays and Speeches.* Trumansburg, NY: Crossing Press.
Lorde, A. (1996). *The Audre Lorde Compendium: Essays, Speeches, and Journals.* London: Pandora.
Mackenzie, C. and N. Stoljar (eds) (2000). *Relational Autonomy: Feminist Perspectives on Autonomy, Agency, and the Social Self.* New York: Oxford University Press.
MacKinnon, C. A. (1989). *Toward a Feminist Theory of the State.* Cambridge, MA: Harvard University Press.
McLaughlin, J. (2003). *Feminist Social and Political Theory: Contemporary Debates and Dialogues.* Basingstoke, Hampshire; New York: Palgrave Macmillan.
Meyers, D. T. (1994). *Subjection and Subjectivity: Psychoanalytic Feminism and Moral Philosophy.* New York: Routledge.
Minnich, E. K. (1990). *Transforming Knowledge.* Philadelphia: Temple University Press.
Mohanty, C. T. (2003). *Feminism Without Borders: Decolonizing Theory, Practicing Solidarity.* Durham, NC; London: Duke University Press.
Mohanty, C. T. et al. (1991). *Third World Women and the Politics of Feminism.* Bloomington: Indiana University Press.
Mohin, L. (1996). *An Intimacy of Equals: Lesbian Feminist Ethics.* New York: Harrington Park Press.
Moi, T. (1999). *What is a Woman? And other Essays.* Oxford; New York: Oxford University Press.
Moraga, C. and G. Anzaldúa (1981). *This Bridge Called my Back: Writings by Radical Women of Color.* Watertown, MA: Persephone Press.
Narayan, U. (1997). *Dis-Locating Cultures.* New York: Routledge.
Noddings, N. (1984). *Caring: A Feminine Approach to Ethics and Moral Education.* Berkeley, CA: University of California Press.
Noddings, N. (2002). *Starting at Home: Caring and Social Policy.* Berkeley, CA: University of California Press.
Nussbaum, M. C. (1999a). 'The Professor of Parody.' *The New Republic* 220(8): 37–45.

Nussbaum, M. C. (1999b). *Sex and Social Justice*. New York: Oxford University Press.
Nussbaum, M. C. (2000). *Women and Human Development: The Capabilities Approach*. Cambridge; New York: Cambridge University Press.
Nye, A. (1995). *Philosophy and Feminism: At the Border*. New York: Twayne.
Obermeyer, Carla Mahklouf. (1999). 'Female Genital Surgeries: The Known, the Unknown, and the Unknowable.' *Medical Anthropology Quarterly* 13: 79–106.
Okin, S. M. (1979). *Women in Western Political Thought*. Princeton, NJ: Princeton University Press.
Okin, S. M. et al. (1999). *Is Multiculturalism Bad for Women?* Princeton, NJ: Princeton University Press.
Pateman, C. (1988). *The Sexual Contract*. Stanford, CA: Stanford University Press.
Petchesky, R. P. (2003). *Global Prescriptions: Gendering Health and Human Rights*. London; New York: Zed Books.
Petchesky, R. P. and K. Judd (1998). *Negotiating Reproductive Rights: Women's Perspectives Across Countries and Cultures*. London; New York: Zed Books.
Petchesky, R. P. and United Nations Research Institute for Social Development (2000). *Reproductive and Sexual Rights: Charting the Course of Transnational Women's NGOs*. Geneva: United Nations Research Institute for Social Development.
Rée, J. (2002). 'Women Philosophers and the Canon.' *British Journal for the History of Philosophy* 10(4): 641.
Robertson, C. (1996). 'Grassroots in Kenya: Women, Genital Mutilation, and Collective Action, 1920–1990.' *Signs* 21: 615–641.
Robinson, F. (1999). *Globalizing Care: Ethics, Feminist Theory, and International Relations*. Boulder, CO: Westview Press.
Ruddick, S. (1989). *Maternal Thinking: Toward a Politics of Peace*. Boston: Beacon Press.
Sevenhuijsen, S. (1998). *Citizenship and the Ethics of Care: Feminist Considerations on Justice, Morality, and Politics*. London; New York: Routledge.
Shanley, M. L. and U. Narayan (eds) (1997). *Reconstructing Political Theory: Feminist Perspectives*. University Park, PA: Pennsylvania State University Press.
Smith, B. G., (ed.) (2000). *Global Feminisms Since 1945*. London; New York: Routledge.
Spivack, Gayatri (1987). *In Other Worlds: Essays in Cultural Politics*. London: Methuen.
Tronto, J. (1987). 'Beyond Gender Difference to a Theory of Care.' *Signs* 12(4): 644–663.
Tronto, J. C. (1993). *Moral Boundaries: A Political Argument for an Ethic of Care*. New York: Routledge.
Tronto, Joan C. (2000). 'Demokratie als fürsorge Praxis' (Democracy as a Caring Practice) trans. Regina Othmer. *Feministische Studien* extra 2000: 25–42.
Walker, M. U. (1998). *Moral Understandings: A Feminist Study in Ethics*. New York: Routledge.
Walker, M. U. (2002). 'Morality in Practice: A Response to Claudia Card and Lorraine Code.' *Hypatia* 17(1): 174–182.
Walker, M. U. (2003a). *Moral Contexts*. Lanham, MD: Rowman & Littlefield.
Walker, M. U. (2003b). 'The State of Feminist Philosophy.' Annual Meeting of the Eastern Division of the American Philosophical Association. Washington, DC.
White, J. A. (2000). *Democracy, Justice and the Welfare State: Reconstructing Public Care*. University Park, PA: Pennsylvania State University Press.
Williams, P. J. (1991). *The Alchemy of Race and Rights*. Cambridge, MA: Harvard University Press.
Williams, P. J. (1995). *The Rooster's Egg*. Cambridge, MA: Harvard University Press.
Wittig, M. (1992). *The Straight Mind and Other Essays*. Boston, MA: Beacon Press.
Young, I. M. (1990). *Justice and the Politics of Difference*. Princeton NJ: Princeton University Press.
Zaleha, K. et al. (1995). *Women's Issues: Women's Perspectives*. Petaling Jaya, Selangor, Malaysia: Women's Affairs Secretariat IIUM.

24

Having It All
Feminist Fractured Foundationalism

Sue Wise and Liz Stanley

While the theory and practice of feminist research is central to the development of feminist scholarship, once vibrant debates about feminist methodology have presently reached an impasse. After overviewing the main themes in recent discussions of grounded feminist research, we discuss the work of some interesting 'border crossers'. There is, however, a fissure or fault-line in this work, an impasse introduced by failing fully to confront the differences between normative/realist epistemology and anti-foundationalist epistemology. The way out, and a means of 'having it all', resists the notion of warring binary epistemologies and involves the development of a 'feminist fractured foundationalism'. Its main characteristics are delineated and discussed, and it is presented as a 'toolkit' for practical use rather than an abstract system to be repetitiously re/stated.

INTRODUCTION

Feminist research is fundamental to feminist scholarship of all kinds. *Research*, investigating something in depth, is closely related to *method*, a systematic procedure for collecting relevant information, and to *methodology*, a mode of investigation in which method, operational procedures, and theory are dovetailed. They have a more indirect relationship with *epistemology*, a theory of knowledge in which knowledge, knowers, the nature of facts, and ways of adjudicating between competing knowledge-claims are specified. The theory and practice of feminist research, method/ology, and epistemology are crucial to the feminist project of remaking knowledge, and debates about it were at the cutting edge of feminist scholarship from the late 1970s for around two decades.

Having once been keenly involved participants in these debates (Stanley and Wise, 1979; 1983a; 1983b; 1990; 1992; 1993), we think the liveliness and innovation of early discussions have been replaced by weariness and analytical impasse (Stanley and Wise, 2000; Wise and Stanley, 2003), with much writing about feminist research over the last decade rehashing old debates, and even the best making only minor adjustments to existing arguments. In the next section of the chapter, we overview broad areas of work regarding feminist research and discuss why this impasse has come about. Although many people situate themselves within one of these areas, others – for us, the most interesting – engage in 'border crossings' and think outside narrow frameworks, and in the section following we look at work by Lorraine Code, Patricia Hill Collins, Sandra Harding, Shulamit Reinharz, and Sylvia Walby, as well as the germinal writings of Dorothy Smith, as examples of border crossing. In spite of the strengths of this work, we detect a problem: an oscillation between what we see as fundamentally differing epistemological positions without fully dealing with the differences. In the final section, therefore, we sketch out some ideas about how to 'have it all'.

GROUNDED RESEARCH AREAS AND EPISTEMOLOGY POSITIONS

During the 1970s, a broad-based feminist critique of mainstream/malestream academic research was produced which rejected 'positivist' or 'scientistic' approaches that over-dichotomized the social world and assumed that only a single unseamed social reality existed – that seen from the perspective of (some) men. A number of recurrent themes emerged from this critique, which still provide a basis for much feminist work.[1] The underlying theme is that knowledge is constructed from where the researcher/theoretician is situated, and so feminist knowledge should proceed from the location of the feminist academic and work outwards. Consequently, feminist knowledge-claims should acknowledge their partial remit and avoid the false universalizing claims of the mainstream/malestream.

Moreover, the social world, including in its gendered aspects, is complex and multi-dimensional; consequently, multi-dimensional means of investigating, knowing, and representing it are needed in configuring feminist research. Relatedly, feminist knowledge production should be done in an accountable way, rather than bracketing or dismissing the process involved as unimportant, as most mainstream/malestream writing does. In addition, importance lies in the broad methodological procedures that underlie social investigation, rather than the particular method or technique of data-gathering utilized ('It isn't what you do, it's how you do it, and what you claim for it.'). And also, feminist research praxis entails refusing to interpret and theorize the social world through conventional binaries such as researcher/subject, theory/research, research/life, investigation/action, and requires a different epistemological frame.

Certainly there were – and are – feminists who have rejected various aspects of these ideas, misrepresenting this work as rejecting 'hard' or quantified and favouring 'soft' or qualitative methods and promoting a distinct method that only feminists could use.[2] But in fact almost no feminist methodologist promoted the idea of a distinct feminist method; the large majority of work was instead concerned with methodology (broad procedural ideas about social investigation) in relation to grounded research practices (how these shape up in specific projects) and to epistemology, and feminist research actually utilized the entire range of methods. In addition, the ideas that knowledge is structured by gender and 'race', and that interpretation plays a strong role in understanding the complexities of social reality, were seen as 'off the wall' by critics of (post-)Marxist realist persuasion, even though these ideas are located within a long Western intellectual heritage (in social science from Dilthey and Weber on, in philosophy from Kant on). However, wider changes in Western intellectual life have meant that these ideas subsequently became almost mainstream because of the impact of poststructuralist and deconstructionist thinking.

While the intellectual changes associated with poststructuralism and deconstructionism have been largely liberating and enabling, some dimensions are more troubling. One concern is their imperialist and colonizing aspect, in which the diverse intellectual origins of these ideas have 'vanished', which seems to be the fate of the feminist contribution to this pantheon of new thinking. Another concern is the seminal (we use the word advisedly) role of a particular style of philosophy, together with its feminist variant, in determinedly occupying a canonical position in relation to 'Theory'. There is of course nothing 'wrong' with feminist philosophy and its particular 'take' on research matters, nor its approach to social theory more widely. However, there *is* something problematic for feminist scholarship overall when feminist research and methodology morphs into abstract Theory, not least because the very different concerns of (for the sake of shorthand) 'research practitioners' and 'abstract social theorists' are lost sight of as a consequence. One result has been characterized as the 'feminist methodology wars' (Stanley, 1997), a damaging period of debate in which, on the one hand, developing ideas about feminist methodology were dismissed as relativist nonsense by some feminists, and on the other, these critics were depicted as peddling unreconstructed malestream ideas. With hindsight, we conclude there is quite a simple explanation for why these passionate disagreements occurred, connected with the warring existence of two very different epistemological positions within feminism, something we discuss later.

Growing out of the 'methodology wars', the vast majority of feminist research was highly practical in its concerns and approaches, exploring a wide range of empirical substantive areas of social life and changing the nature of academic inter/disciplines in the process.[3] Not surprisingly, much of this new work threw up practical issues and problems concerning feminist research. Discussions of these have mainly failed to explore the wider epistemological reverberations.[4] More recent work of this particular kind has clustered around five main themes.

1. *Power and hierarchy in research situations.* Work here ranges from emphasizing that even well-intentioned feminist research is potentially exploitative, especially regarding the developing world and 'Other' women. More nuanced accounts describe the often complex to-ings and fro-ings of power dynamics between researchers and researched, and also the closeness between the practitioners and participants that occurs in long-term projects.[5]
2. *Ethical issues.* Discussions here mainly concern the emotional responses and the analytical concerns of feminist researchers when researching difficult and sometimes dangerous topics, including matters relating to physical safety and anxieties about this.[6]
3. *Issues in feminist ethnography.* Issues here concern power and the relationship of feminist ethnographers to 'Other' women, ethnographic research processes, and writing and representation, considered around empowerment and reciprocity. There is also a strong interest in new approaches to representational matters which are concerned with writing, texts, and discourse, with some of it having an ebullient 'let's get on with it' character.[7]
4. *Whether Western feminist research and theory 'travels'.* Work here concerns the specificity of US and other Western feminist ideas, which are seen as not 'travelling' to and being inapplicable in other parts of the world; however, some 'Other' feminists have protested that theory especially does travel and makes a difference.[8]
5. *Writing and representation.* Concerns here centre on writing as part of the analysis of research materials and also as a crucial representational medium that needs to be theorized and reworked as a key feminist method/ology. It ranges from seeing 'different writing' as an end in itself, to using 'messy texts' to put across complex ideas, to a communicative concern with reaching a wider popular audience.[9]

A separate body of work from that sketched out above has shifted discussions of feminist methodology into those of epistemology. The emphasis here has been on debating the pros and cons of two very different epistemological projects, with the proponents of the 'other' position often denied intellectual validity, in a way replicating the 'war' character of the earlier debate.

Normative epistemology is an epistemological project concerned with distinguishing the features of knowledge- and truth-claims in (aspiring) universalist terms. It proceeds from abstractions, rather than exploring how knowledge-making works in grounded real-world practice. Consequently, normative epistemology either denies the epistemological significance of, or else backgrounds, differently situated knowledge practices. It shares many of the same assumptions and concerns as critical realism in social theory. Its feminist variant privileges some knowledge over others, wants to specify criteria for grounding truth and knowledge, at basis perceives one social reality, and positions the feminist scholar around (sometimes modified) notions of epistemological privilege, while sometimes also attempting to recognize local knowledges. Grounded research practices, apart from those characterizing theorizing, are outside the domain of its interests apart from general or abstract terms.[10]

Everyday knowledge practice or anti-foundationalist epistemology emphasizes empirical explorations of situated knowledges (Schmidt, 2001). It suspends or brackets evaluating these against external a priori notions of truth, instead investigating how fact and reality judgements are articulated in grounded social situations. It rejects foundationalism, the view that one single social reality exists which can be fully apprehended by properly scientific practitioners of various kinds. People in general, not just researchers, are seen here as competent knowers reflexively engaged in making sense of the social world, including through routinely adjudicating between competing truth- and knowledge-claims. Feminist researchers and their analyses are located *within* such practices, rather than external to them; and while for some proponents grounds for a priori epistemological privilege for feminist research are claimed, for others research is seen as having different rather than superior qualities from everyday practices because it involves more formal procedures and outcomes. For some proponents, there is also a commitment to egalitarian research practices, transparency in the analyses provided, and conclusions drawn (not just the research activities engaged in). Also grounded research practices are bracketed away in some work of this kind and explicated in others.[11]

BORDER CROSSINGS

Some work evades confinement in one of the above areas of activity and is instead characterized by its border crossing concerns. It may, for example, raise policy issues regarding epistemological stances in feminist scholarship, or challenge the realist epistemological project while still making strong knowledge-claims, or recognize that the complicated, often messy, character of grounded research does not necessarily prevent analytical precision or theoretical break-through. The work of Sylvia Walby, Sandra Harding, Lorraine Code, Shulamit Reinharz, Patricia Hill Collins, and Dorothy Smith provides examples of different kinds of border crossings, with that of Smith constituting the most considerable attempt to 'think outside the boxes'. In addition, we see our own work (we hope not too immodestly) in these terms, for it was conceived throughout as a border crossing enterprise that resists pigeonholing as either realist/normative or anti-foundationalist.

In a number of recent publications, Sylvia Walby (2000; 2001a; 2001b) has usefully attempted to think through what she, like us, perceives as an impasse, a 'no through road', in feminist methodology and epistemology because of the dominance of debates therein by feminist philosophy. Hers is a bold, indeed at times swingeing, argument that overrides complexities to make some strongly held points and is to be welcomed for setting out a platform for a feminist realist position in an untrammelled way. Walby builds on Susan Hekman's (1997a; 1997b; 1999) critique of standpoint theory, which both perceive as emanating from women's experiences and therefore producing separate knowledges.[12] Consequently, Walby insists that feminist epistemologists 'hinder feminist research by their strictures on method' (2001b: 537) because social structural changes benefiting women require strong feminist knowledge-claims, which need to be general, pertaining to the whole of social life. Indeed, she finds feminist standpoint, and feminist epistemology generally, unhelpful for the 'hegemonic feminist knowledge project' she desires (2001a: 486). This is because she views them as promoting relativism, which she associates with a retreat into situated knowledges, which in turn gives rise to the 'epistemological chasms' she assigns to relativism.

Walby recognizes that Harding, and also Vandana Shiva (1989), Patricia Hill Collins (1997), Nancy Hartsock (1997), and Donna Haraway (1988), all accept the necessity of criteria for privileging some knowledge over others, but still she criticizes them for seeing the grounds for this as 'women's experience'. Consequently, while it is clear that she dislikes women's experience as a grounding, even in her terms they *do* want to ground knowledge and so her charge of relativism does not hold, in relation to these theorists at least. In addition, Walby seems unaware that variant relativisms exist, for she reduces all interpretational complexities to 'radical relativism' and characterizes this (we think wrongly) as necessarily denying any vantage-point from which to advance knowledge-claims (2001a: 495). Her worries about 'epistemological chasms' are related, because all thinking about the social in terms of fractures and complexities cuts across her realist convictions and hegemonic aspirations. Thus, she wants a 'rigorous methodology for feminist questions and an argument that feminist analysis can and should claim that it generates the best knowledge while rejecting the two poles of absolutism…and relativism' (2001a: 503), proposing that there is a 'world out there' which provides a reality check for theory development and knowledge-claims.

Walby's not only is a strong normative/realist approach which claims hegemony, but also seemingly perceives no problems in invoking a 'world out there' that is supposedly interpretation-free. Her argument has few internal tensions, largely because her views about social reality, research, truth, and knowledge are over-simplified and viewpoints different from her own are collapsed into radical relativism, which she (mis-)characterizes as a priori preventing feminist knowledge from changing the world. We certainly welcome Walby's attempt to think outside the frame of positions about feminist research minutely added to – indeed, we have found it refreshing to read someone who actually wants to argue something definite. But we also conclude she falls considerably short of her goals, because she misunderstands relativism and proceeds from an unreconstructed critical realist position that seems unable to contemplate, let alone theorize, social complexities.

Sandra Harding's work[13] has helped construct standpoint theory through her succession of overviews and amendments, and her influence has been all the greater because few of the key people she associates with standpoint theory actually describe their work as such.[14] Recently, Harding has restated standpoint theory as an epistemological position concerned with knowledge from the standpoint of women, identified its main themes, and explored controversies regarding the natural sciences (2004: 29–39). She distinguishes standpoint theory from mere 'perspectivalism', because it studies 'up' to explore the impact of structures and organizations on women and goes beyond 'what women…in fact say or believe to identify these distinctive standpoint insights' (2004: 31), claiming knowledge and privilege for the feminist analyses thus produced. Harding also presents standpoint theory as eschewing 'excessive constructionism', which she characterizes as a 'damaging relativism' going against 'the realities of nature's order' (2004: 38), a strong realist claim about a 'natural' order purportedly existing beyond the social. Instead, she favours 'reasonable constructionism', quoting Haraway's argument in favour of both partial perspectives *and* a 'commitment to faithful accounts of a "real" world' (Haraway, 1991: 187).

In fact, disentangling what has been argued by the 'names' described as standpoint theorists from Harding's formulations of standpoint theory as a generalized 'position' can be difficult.[15] Moreover, there is a major tension between the social construction that on one level Harding acknowledges exists, and her desire for feminist science that can advance strong knowledge-claims, largely because her realist ideas about relativism are confined to dismissing the 'radical' version. 'What she knows' is that there are everyday knowledge practices, situated knowledges, and partial perspectives, but she is unable to reconcile them with the realist perception of an objective reality and the privileged knowledge-claims of the feminist social scientist.

For Lorraine Code (1991; 1993; 1995), the gender of the knower significantly impacts on knowledge-production: what can be known and how it can be known depends on where knowers are situated (Code, 1991: 1–26). Code is fully aware there are issues with the normative/realist epistemological project, while there is also a normative base to her own approach. She insists, for instance, that feminist politics requires strong truth- and reality-claims, (over)stating that if there is no objective reality then there can be no feminist project (1991: 319–20). She combines this with accepting the situated nature of knowledge because she recognizes (unlike Walby and Harding) that there are different kinds of relativism: 'Participants in standard objectivist/realist debates work with a false dichotomy…epistemological relativism does not entail antirealism' (1991: 319). Consequently, she opts for 'mitigated relativism', which accepts that a reality exists 'out there' which 'constrain[s] possibilities of knowledge and analysis' (1991: 320), but also recognizes the perspectival locatedness of knowledge. Wanting to avoid the 'homogenizing effect' of the traditional normative project, Code chooses mitigated relativism as a 'middle ground' position and as 'a political act that refuses confinement within the narrow, cramped space that the adversarial paradigm allows' (1991: 322).

Code's emphasis on notions of truth and her desire to make strong feminist knowledge-claims suggests that 'mitigated objectivism' actually better characterizes her position. Thus, for her, the feminist project can still claim that 'feminists can know better what is going on, what needs to be put right' (1995: 110), because stronger versions of relativism have to be rejected. Certainly treating realism and relativism in less absolutist terms is useful; but Code's 'feminists can know better' claim provides little help for feminist social researchers grappling with a social reality most often composed by shades of grey and complexities of understanding, while her 'mitigation' leaves the binary positions intact.

Shulamit Reinharz's (1979; 1983) ideas about 'experiential analysis' have been developed as a feminist social researcher wanting to make sense of such complexities in operationalizing feminist research. Experiential analysis involves strategies for practising feminist research, including analysing social life in natural settings, rejecting separating research processes from research products, conducting collaborative forms of research, and providing self-reflexive analyses of research materials. Experiential analysis includes mixing the subjective and objective, being accurate but innovative, focusing on meaning-making in social life, recognizing the unique features of particular social settings, and emphasizing that social research always involves partial analyses of ongoing events and that generalizing concepts should always specify their limitations. These strategies for research practice are also interestingly related to Reinharz's later work (1992; 1993), which focuses on how methods are used in practice by feminist social researchers. Therein Reinharz recognizes that the 'same' method can be used very differently. Method is never 'just method': what it 'is' depends on the context of use, including the theoretical concerns and epistemological assumptions of the researcher, and how reality and truth are seen and adjudicated by people in the social contexts being investigated.

Experiential analysis brings together method, methodology, and epistemology around the everyday knowledge practices of both feminist researchers and those researched in a way that eschews claims to epistemological privilege. It is also (ideally) fully collaborative and involves the participation of 'the researched' at all stages, including analysis and publication. But as well as considerable strengths, a major limitation arises from this, because it requires feminist research to focus specifically on 'good women'. Our own research has included projects concerning 'evil men' (including serial killers) and 'bad women' (including child abusers), which could not have involved collaborative research and which necessitated making feminist knowledge-claims over, and sometimes against, those of the people concerned. Consequently, our reservations stem from what we see as an overly narrowed focus for feminist research – all the world must be our province, not just a sub-component of the category 'women'.

Something of a similar tack to Reinharz's has been taken by Collins (1990; 1997; 2000a; 2000b) in seeing the Black feminist researcher as a member of Black women's communities carrying out dialogue-based research around notions of empowerment. She rejects mainstream precepts such as distancing the researcher from the researched, objectifying subjects, and banishing emotion. For Collins, this Black feminist epistemology brings its own tensions but also creates useful possibilities, including seeing concrete experience as a criterion of meaning, using dialogue and interconnections to assess knowledge-claims, recognizing the importance of an ethics of care, and emphasizing personal accountability. The result 'opens up the question of whether what has taken to be true can stand the test of alternative ways of assessing truth' (Collins, 1990: 219), but at the same time, there is no one-dimensional privileging of '(Black) women's experience' here. Although *collective* experience is at the centre (Collins, 1997), Collins sees this as one 'angle of vision', a partial perspective (1990: 234). She also resists a 'positivist' or normative approach, that the researcher necessarily has a clearer view of the truth, *and* she rejects relativism of a kind that sees all perspectives as equally valid, seeing both as ignoring inequalities between different social locations.

Collins avoids claiming epistemological privilege by locating the researcher firmly within Black women's communities and standpoint and by recognizing the partialities of both 'angles of vision'. She also does this by focusing on how Black women's communities construct a shared standpoint in the context of oppressive circumstances, rather than adjudicating notions of truth and fact between elements of this and dominant forms of knowledge. That is, Collins' narrowed focus enables considerable consistency between the different components of her approach. This is highly commendable but we conclude it would still have difficulty in encompassing, for example, 'bad' Black women or, more simply, themes and topics in which 'race' plays little part, including those occurring within Black women's communities.

Dorothy Smith[16] has produced the most considerable body of work on feminist methodology, and on feminist sociology more widely, in thinking outside the confines of the malestream academy. Her work emphasizes everyday knowledge practices, positions the feminist researcher as participant within the social world she studies, recognizes the complexity of social reality and the partiality of knowledge-claims, and still provides the feminist social researcher with grounds from which to make distinctive knowledge-claims.

Smith's 'sociology for women' starts from the disjunctures between women's experiences, and how experience is represented (including by women researchers) within the academic mode, in which the social world is conceptually pre-structured and so 'pre-known'. For her, sociology and other disciplines are part and parcel of the 'relations of ruling', a subtle concept concerned with the intersection of institutional and organizational processes for organizing and regulating society and people's everyday life-worlds, operating in multiple sites of power/knowledge and crucially involving constructions of the social world made in and by texts of different kinds.

Smith's work does not just critique present methods: it proceeds in a different way, around 'how to make ourselves as women the subject of the sociological act of knowing' (1987: 69) without then transforming these subjects into objects. Simply focusing on good and bad methods is insufficient to ground a feminist sociology, nor is merely changing the relationship between researcher and researched enough. For Smith, the problem for feminism is not an ethical one concerning non-exploitative behaviour, nor of technique, but the more fundamental matter of disciplines being organized around translating lives into pre-given conceptual categories.

Smith sees women subjects as actors and competent knowers, as active experiencing subjects, and her approach 'makes space' for the presently absent 'woman subject' (1987: 107). At the same time, she perceives women as outside of the 'extralocal', located in a local life-world organized by social relations 'not observable within it' (1987: 89). She relatedly perceives women's lives as outside 'textually mediated discourse' – thus, commenting on women as wives and secretaries, she sees them as 'confined' to the local and particular. However, none of our friends and colleagues who are 'wives' and/or secretaries are limited in this way, for many women are involved in the 'extralocal', not just feminist academics. For Smith, however, while people can tell social researchers what happens, they cannot be relied on to understand the wider social relations that shape the everyday, and so she concludes that what is required is 'a specialized enterprise, a work, the work of a social scientist' (1987: 110).

We certainly agree with Smith that feminist social science must go beyond the 'authentic speaking of women', having little truck with this romanticized view of women and of feminist research. However, while we think her comments about women, people, and the local demonstrate a fault-line in Smith's thinking, clearly it is one she herself is happy with in wanting to 'speak truth with confidence' concerning the grounded investigations she has conducted. Her position here is actually surprisingly similar to Walby's, for in grounding such claims Smith turns to the 'ontological basis' of social life and to checking such claims against 'the very character of the social itself' (1987: 122), with the feminist sociologist providing a route to a 'faithful telling' (1987: 143). We do not accept this line of argument, for two reasons. First, we perceive the ontological base as fractured and complicated, so that only rarely can any incontrovertible 'character of the social' provide a basis for unproblematically checking research results against. Thus, what Smith perceives as an 'end to interpretation problems' seems to us as actually a key site for their occurrence. Second, Smith's stance on this indicates a surprisingly referential basis to her 'sociology for women', while we cannot accept referentiality claims as an adequate means of grounding the knowledge-claims of feminist or indeed any other research.

It is important to consider why so perspicacious a commentator as Smith remains attached to the epistemological privilege of the feminist researcher over the supposedly 'local' lives of women. One reason is that, notwithstanding her border crossings, Smith remains very much a committed sociologist and buys into a considerable amount of its underpinnings, in spite of her wide-ranging criticisms of its conceptual apparatus. Another is that of course *all* feminist academics have to consider what we are 'for' and what value our research endeavours add, and Smith has clearly thought this through in terms that make good sense for her. Nevertheless, we think there are important feminist reasons for eschewing epistemological privilege, as discussed later.

Most of the border crossers we have discussed, apart from Walby and in a different way Collins, want to have the epistemological privilege that comes from advocating strong, certain, and, at basis, realist knowledge-claims, while also recognizing (to different degrees) that there are 'situated knowledges and partial perspectives'. Some are located in one 'camp' and some in the other, but for all of them there are fault-lines or fissures in their arguments because they are attempting to reconcile irreconcilables. Even Code's work leaves these binary positions intact while tacking together bits of both, while Walby's argument is the most consistent and represents what we earlier called an 'untrammelled' approach. Our stance is different again: we refuse the idea that there are two, and only two, battling binary epistemological positions for feminism, those of normative/realist epistemology *versus* anti-foundationalist epistemology. As far as we are concerned, 'in life' it isn't a matter of 'either/or', but rather *both*. So how to have both, without doing what we said these other border crossers do, struggling to reconcile things which cannot be reconciled? We move on to this discussion.

HAVING IT ALL: FEMINIST FRACTURED FOUNDATIONALISM AND ITS ANALYTICAL TOOLKIT

The idea of 'feminist fractured foundationalism' and the 'analytical toolkit' that comprises it provides our framework for 'having it all', an approach that is both 'untrammelled' and also refuses the binary game. Feminist researchers who eschew making normative or realist kinds of truth-claims still need to provide a reasoned account of 'what they are for' and what kinds of claims they want to make. Along with this, if feminism rejects conventional notions of foundationalism, there still has to be some notion of a grounding for the alternative kind of knowledge being claimed. Our response has been the determination both to recognize that there is a materially real social world that is real in its consequences, *and* to insist that differently situated groups develop often different views of the precise realities involved. Material reality has to be recognized, but the complexities of interpretation also have to be grappled with in ways that do not position feminist researchers as overriding the understandings of the women and men who are the researched with a priori statements of epistemic privilege. We think feminist fractured foundationalism enables this.

Fractured foundationalism is concerned with 'out there', with understanding social life as the fundamental 'it' that feminist researchers grapple with, doing so like other society members but also more formally as researchers. But feminist fractured foundationalism (FFF) is about 'in here' as well, for it proceeds from making transparent the practices and understandings of feminist research, which is located within the academy and is at least in part implicated in its relations of ruling. What brings 'out there' and 'in here' together for FFF is *methodology*, not in Harding's simple 'perspective' sense, but rather as operational strategies which enable thinking and conceptualizing, grounded research practice, writing about research data, and theorizing from these, to be thought of as a coherent whole. Consequently, we see the relationship between FFF (that is, an epistemological position) and feminist methodology (that is, a research praxis) as inextricably intertwined. That is what we mean by an 'analytical toolkit'; and the particular analytical toolkit for FFF is composed of the components outlined below.

The fractured ontological base

FFF is predicated on the ontological position that social life is intersubjectively constructed around ideas and practices concerning structures understood as 'social facts' that are external to and constraining upon society members. Social life is at one and the same time experienced as independent of social construction, but is also constituted by it, and knowledge is always already grounded because it necessarily has an ontological basis. That is, there is always a knower situated in time and place with other people, going about the business of knowing the social world. Ontology is the basis, grounding knowledge and knowers as well as social life itself (Stanley and Wise, 1979; 1992). Because different collectivities of people understand realities and facts from where (geographically, socially, politically) they are situated, everyday kinds of fractures of understanding and meaning – reality disjunctures – frequently arise; however, these are negotiated (sometimes successfully, sometimes with remaining disagreements) around the shared premise that there is real meaning, facts, and truth – a social reality – to be arrived at (Stanley, 1994).

Succinctly, for us, ontological relativism marches hand in hand with strong everyday foundationalist claims and practices (Stanley and Wise, 1992), and ontological problematics always have epistemological consequentiality (Stanley, 1997). Thus, our epistemological position rejects the 'false dichotomy' of the warring normative/realist versus anti-foundationalist binaries and advances the alternative of a fractured foundationalist epistemology.

A modest 'internalist' approach to feminist knowledge production

Some key sites for feminist research production include the researcher/researched relationship, emotion in research, intellectual auto/biography, managing competing versions of reality, and power in research and writing about this (Stanley and Wise, 1990). FFF does not take sides on basic reality matters: it sees social facts and social reality as both constructed *and* experienced as external and constraining. Its concern is instead with how fractures and disjunctures are managed, and order and regularity or change produced. There may indeed be one 'really real social reality'; however, we are not so much agnostic about this as concerned with something else – the 'reality, for all practical purposes' that is multiply produced in social life and how feminist research might go about understanding it. While many feminist approaches see the grounding for feminist knowledge-claims as solely lying in possession of 'the facts', indeed better or best facts, for FFF the grounding lies in 'moral knowledge', accountable knowledge produced by the 'knowing subject'.

Feminist realists are concerned with 'out there' and with how to change oppressive circumstances by means of producing better or hegemonic feminist facts, seen as the most effective way to produce social and policy change of a kind that will benefit women. But replacing masculinist science with this unreconstructed feminist version will only replicate the relations of ruling with women still as object, but this time to hegemonic feminist science – and, anyway, just and egalitarian goals cannot be reached by unjust and inegalitarian means (as argued powerfully by Rose, 1994). Also, the realist contention begs serious questions about how social change takes place: while some academics like to think that it occurs by means of 'serious research', the evidence strongly suggests otherwise. However, while the realist approach is a grand 'externalist' one, in contrast, that of FFF is a modest 'internalist' one, concerned with the 'in here' of academic feminism as it goes about the business of crafting knowledge in a feminist form.

The feminist research labour process

FFF is built on and proceeds from the fractured ontological nature of social life. Feminism as a politics centres a radical social ethics, and, for FFF, necessitates producing feminist knowledge in an open, accountable, and defensible way. There are a number of elements to this, starting with the research labour process of the academic mode of production and its relations and forces of production (Stanley, 1990b). In particular, FFF is concerned with analytical processes concerning how knowledge is produced and the claims made for it.

For FFF, method in the narrow sense is neither here nor there: methods are merely techniques for getting certain kinds of things done, and what matters is why and how they are used and for what purpose. We have certainly used a wide range of methods, from textual analysis to interviewing, institutional and other ethnography, historical research, large-scale surveys, secondary data analysis, abstract theorizing, all within the framework of FFF. FFF is more concerned with analytical reflexivity of a kind which uses retrievable data, so as to provide key elements of evidence, argument, and interpretation in texts that readers can 'argue back to', because provided with the detail to reach their own conclusions. We do not claim referentiality for such texts – they are not directly reflective of the settings that gave rise to them, but they *will* contain good, bad, or indifferent analyses and arguments of their kind. Consequently, readers should be able to evaluate their adequacy and 'validity', and a key concern for FFF is to enable readers to make such evaluations. Much purportedly radical social science writing actually disempowers readers quite as thoroughly as conventional kinds; we want to reconfigure the reader-position so as to enable readers to 'bite back'.

The knowing subject

At an epistemological level, FFF involves a double-take on what 'knowledge' consists of. It is what is constituted as such within everyday knowledge practices, and it is also what the feminist (or other) researcher makes of and does with it (and these may conflict, of course). All society members are engaged in such activities, because all of social life revolves around practical knowledge matters. However, while researchers engaged in social enquiry will certainly produce knowledge in a more structured and formal way, FFF does not see these activities as different in kind from everyday practices (Stanley, 1994). FFF also sees feminist researchers as investigating 'necessary' topics (Stanley, 1996). Here, the feminist researcher is an active knowing agent in producing analyses and conclusions, someone who interprets and so constructs, not just reflects, research situations and data. The research writings that result are never directly referential of the social contexts and events they are about, always analytically artful selections and interpretations around an interpretive frame deriving from the intellectual (and political, and…) concerns of feminism in the academy (Stanley and Wise, 1993).

Moreover, FFF strenuously resists seeing women or men as immersed in the local and unable to discern the wider relations and structures of ruling. Nor is the feminist researcher able to see further or better, nor is she magically able to check her analyses against the 'really real' ontological reality of the extralocal. There is no god's eye view for feminist research, although the enquiries that the feminist researcher engages in are likely to be different in degree, and the resultant analyses of social life will usually be directed to different purposes.

Moral epistemology

Epistemology always has a 'moral' or ethical dimension: claims to know are made against or over others, not everyone is deemed a competent knower, and so on. 'Moral knowledge' is knowledge that is transparent, produced through non-exploitative means, makes defensible knowledge-claims, produces open accounts of 'findings' and conclusions, and is fundamental to FFF (Stanley, 2004; Stanley and Wise, 1993). Also FFF involves a *feminist*, rather than *women's*, standpoint, organized around ensuring transparent and accountable good practice for feminist social research concerning the activities involved and the knowledge-claims and written or other knowledge products that result. We emphasize again the modest compass and practical basis for FFF: it is predicated on a social ontology and has an epistemological basis and concerns, but its *raison d'être* is neither epistemological nor ontological, but instead political, ethical, and methodological. Its practitioners should certainly reject passing as the disembodied 'experts' who have objectified women in countless research projects and claimed authority as authoritative knowers of the lives of mere 'subjects'. Working within a mainstream methodological framework, as some feminist research does, leaves these relations of ruling and knowing intact, and thus we attempt to move beyond it (Stanley, 1997).

Analytical reflexivity

The knowledge practices and products of FFF reflect a specifically feminist politics and ethics, requiring that ontology and epistemology are brought under the sign of feminist methodology. And for us, analytical reflexivity is key to ensuring transparency and accountability. The descriptive variety of reflexivity is concerned with providing contextualizing descriptions only; however, analytical reflexivity focuses on the acts of knowing and what goes into this, looking in detail at the analytical processes involved and the supporting evidences (Stanley, 2004). Analytical reflexivity entails writing an open research text that adduces evidence in retrievable form that is appropriate and sufficient for the argument being made, outlines all stages of the argument properly evidenced, in which each successive level is properly supported by those prior. It accounts for interpretations and conclusions by closely linking these to evidence and argument and provides sufficient detail regarding all of the above for readers to be able to make their own interpretations and so evaluate conclusions and claims.

Knowers and competing knowledge-claims

The response of FFF to the question of who can be a 'knower' (in the 'having authority' sense) is that it all depends on where people are situated within the relations of ruling and the operations of power/knowledge in particular contexts or situations. 'Women's experience' has been both fiercely disputed and incredibly productive for feminist enquiry (Stanley, 1995). Certainly, subjugated knowledges can be given greater or even privileged status (on a variety of grounds) by some persons and in some contexts, and this is precisely the re-evaluation given by feminism to the category 'women'. However, while FFF involves re-evaluating the perspectives and knowledges of subjugated and dominant *groups*, those of *particular* women or particular men are not necessarily viewed as preferential or devalued: that will depend on persons and circumstances. Concerning how competing knowledge-claims are to be evaluated and adjudicated, for FFF again this depends on context or situation, the people involved, how 'the facts' are seen, and whose facts and evidence are deemed convincing or flawed. In addition to the actions and responses of others, the analytical frame for FFF includes what the feminist researcher makes of it all, the interpretational acts she engages in, and the conclusions she draws.

Grounding feminist knowledge

Like other (canonical and contrary) feminist approaches, FFF may advance preferential knowledge-claims on grounds of 'the facts', but the grounds can also include ethical or political values and preferences. However, we are unhappy with epistemological privilege being accorded to feminist research and feminist knowledge in any a priori hegemonic way. While we view some knowledge as better than others, *all* knowledge-claims need to be evaluated and responded to *on their specific merits*. It is also important to recognize that claims that 'feminists know better' really do assume a 'god trick' and are intellectually and politically highly dubious. Whether feminism in general, or any particular feminist researcher, 'knows' in an authoritative sense will all depend on the appropriateness and sufficiency of the evidence for the conclusions drawn, on the plausibility of interpretations and conclusions, and also and crucially on their reception by target audiences and in 'public life' more widely. These comments are not intended to duck 'how can she know?' questions, but to emphasize that FFF's recognition of the fractured ontological base of social reality means there are no easy answers. Any knowledge-claims made by FFF will concern *specific* examples and contexts and be grounded in *particular* evidence and interpretations.

Unalienated knowledge

Bracketing or cancelling out the act of knowing is highly consequential in feminist terms: it renders invisible the indexical properties of knowledge within a false 'universalism', and by denying the labour involved, it alienates knowledge work as a devalued commodity (Stanley, 1990b). Important dimensions of an unalienated feminist knowledge include grounding the feminist researcher and her research as an actual person at work in a concrete setting, recognizing that understanding and theorizing are material activities which can be accounted for, and linking the 'act of knowing' (research process) with claims about what is known (research product). There is nothing about unalienated labour in social research terms that ties it specifically to a feminist approach (Stanley and Wise, 1990). However, while other researchers can work in this way, most elect not to, because of conviction, or because critics may reject such work on *ad personam* (against the person) grounds. What is distinctive about unalienated knowledge is that feminists working in an 'unalienated' way will focus on knowledge production as an ontology, a way of being, rooted in inscribing the investigative and interpretive acts of feminist researchers.

A BRIEF CONCLUSION

A conclusion in the usual sense is not an appropriate end for this chapter, because it has been concerned with pinpointing what we perceive as problems in a body of feminist work and detailing what we see, in the shape of FFF, as a way out. FFF is intended as a *practical* way of 'having it all'; hence our description of it as an analytical *toolkit*. It is, then, intended for use, by us and by others: it is not for redescribing in endless repetitious restatements of positions minutely adjusted, but instead for operationalizing, evaluating, and reconfiguring in the light of grounded research enquiries.

For us, feminist scholarship is a political and ethical choice put into research practice. The ontological grounding of FFF has nothing to do with women as a 'natural' category, and everything to do with analysing 'from the inside' and working outwards. It resists binaries and conjoins emotion and analysis, method and theory, idealism and materialism, subjectivity and objectivity; its goal is to help ensure 'at long last, that knowledge has a human face and a feeling heart' (Stanley and Wise, 1993: 232).

NOTES

1 See Linda Alcoff (1987), Linda Alcoff and Elizabeth Potter (1993), Gloria Bowles and Renate Klein (1983), Mary Fonow and Judith Cook (1991), Harding (1987a), Kathleen Lennon and Margaret Whitford (1994), Liz Stanley (1990a), Sue Wilkinson (1986). Various aspects of this work are discussed in Stanley (1990b) and Stanley and Wise (1990; 1993); see also Carolyn Ramazanoglu with Janet Holland (2002) and Gayle Letherby (2003). For an inward-looking philosophy take, see Alessandra Tanesini (1999).

2 See Stanley and Wise (1993: 1–15, 186–233) and Ramazanoglu with Holland (2002) and Letherby (2003). In fact, feminist and gender social research ranges across all possible methods (DeVault, 1996; 1999; Letherby, 2003) and most was, and indeed still is, quantitative.

3 For overviews, see Cheris Kramarae and Dale Spender (1992) and Spender (1981).

4 For work which does, see Mary Maynard (1994), Mary Maynard and June Purvis (1994), and Jane Ribbens and Rosalind Edwards (1998).

5 See, for example, Julia Droeber (2003), Bev Gatenby and Maria Humphries (2000), Sarah Goode (2000), Carolina Ladino (2002), Donna Luff (1999), Regina Scheyvens and Helen Leslie (2000), and Ning Tang (2002).

6 See, for example, Sevaste Chatzifotiou (2000), Stephanie Linkogle and Geraldine Lee-Trewick (2000), Jo Reger (2001), Sara Scott (1998), and Sue Wise (1999).

7 See, for example, Elizabeth St Pierre and Wanda Pillow (2000), Kamala Visweswaran (1994), Diane Wolf (1996), and Marjorie Wolf (1996).

8 See, for example, Jane Gaskell and Margrit Eichler (2001), Diana Mulinari and Kerstin Sandell (1999), Anne Seller (1994), Tang (2002); but see also Andrea Pető (2001).

9 See, for example, Arthur Bochner and Carolyn Ellis (2001), Carolyn Ellis (2004), Patti Lather (2000; 2001), Patti Lather and Chris Smithies (1997), Wendy Morgan (2000), and Laurel Richardson (1994; 1997).

10 But see the later discussion of Harding's and Walby's work, and the more ambiguous work of Code. See also Janet Chafetz (1997; 2004), Haraway (1988; 1991), Lynn Hankinson Nelson (1990; 1993), and Ann Oakley (1998a; 1998b; 2000).

11 See the later discussion of Collins' and Reinharz's work, also Smith's, in some ways straddling this and normative epistemology. See also Kum-Kum Bhavnani (1993).

12 Although not standpoint theorists ourselves, we still consider this a large oversimplification.

13 (1986; 1987a; 1987b; 1991; 1993; 1997; 1998; 1999; 2003; 2004).

14 Thus Harding has noted Smith and Hartsock (1983; 1997; 1998) as key standpoint theorists concerned with women's perspective, but Smith (1997) has denied membership of such a collectivity, while Hartsock (1998) has emphasized she has no interest in *women's* standpoint and is instead theorizing a specifically *feminist* one.

15 As Smith (1997) has pointed out (contra Hekman, 1997a), seeing it as a 'position' requires bundling together, as though 'the same', theorists whose work was conceived at different times and in different places and deals with different things. While Harding (2004: 40) says she agrees with Smith's objection, actually she disregards it.

16 (1974a; 1974b; 1978; 1987; 1990a; 1990b; 1997; 1999; 2001; 2003).

REFERENCES

Alcoff, Linda (1987) 'Justifying feminist social science', *Hypatia*, 2: 107–27.
Alcoff, Linda, and Potter, Elizabeth (eds) (1993) *Feminist Epistemologies*. New York: Routledge.
Bhavnani, Kum-Kum (1993) 'Tracing the contours: feminist research and feminist objectivity', *Women's Studies International Forum*, 16: 95–104.
Bochner, Arthur and Ellis, Carolyn (eds) (2001) *Ethnographically Speaking: Autoethnography, Literature, and Aesthetics*. Lanham, MD: AltaMira Press.
Bowles, Gloria and Klein, Renate (eds) (1983) *Theories of Women's Studies*. London: Routledge.
Chafetz, Janet (1997) 'Feminist theory and sociology: underutilized contributions for mainstream theory', *Annual Review of Sociology*, 23: 97–120.
Chafetz, Janet (2004) 'Some thoughts by an unrepentant "positivist" who considers herself a feminist nonetheless', in Sharlene Hesse-Biber and Michelle Yaiser (eds), *Feminist Perspectives on Social Research*. New York: Oxford University Press. pp. 320–9.
Chatzifotiou, Sevaste (2000) 'Conducting qualitative research on wife abuse: dealing with the issue of anxiety', *Sociological Research Online*, 5: http://www.socresonline.org.uk/5/2/chatzifotiou/html
Code, Lorraine (1991) *What Can She Know? Feminist Theory and the Construction of Knowledge*. Ithaca, NY: Cornell University Press.
Code, Lorraine (1993) 'Taking subjectivity into account', in Linda Alcoff and Elizabeth Potter (eds), *Feminist Epistemologies*. New York: Routledge. pp. 15–48.
Code, Lorraine (1995) *Rhetorical Spaces: Essays on Gendered Locations*. New York: Routledge.
Collins, Patricia Hill (1990) *Black Feminist Thought: Knowledge, Consciousness, and the Politics of Empowerment*. Boston, MA: Unwin Hyman.
Collins, Patricia Hill (1997) 'Comment on Hekman', *Signs*, 22: 375–81.
Collins, Patricia Hill (2000a, 2nd edition) *Black Feminist Thought: Knowledge, Consciousness, and the Politics of Empowerment*. New York: Routledge.
Collins, Patricia Hill (2000b) 'What's going on? Black feminist thought and the politics of postmodernism', in Elizabeth St Pierre and Wanda Pillow (eds), *Working the Ruins: Feminist Poststructural Theory and Methods in Education*. New York: Routledge. pp. 41–73.

DeVault, Marjorie (1996) 'Talking back to Sociology: distinctive contributions of feminist methodology', *Annual Review of Sociology*, 22: 29–50.

DeVault, Marjorie (1999) *Liberating Method: Feminism and Social Research*. Philadelphia: Temple University Press.

Droeber, Julia (2003) 'Woman to woman – the significance of religiosity for young women in Jordan', *Women's Studies International Forum*, 26: 409–24.

Ellis, Carolyn (2004) *The Ethnographic I: A Methodological Novel About Autoethnography*. Lanham, MD: AltaMira Press.

Fonow, Mary and Cook, Judith (eds) (1991) *Beyond Methodology: Feminist Scholarship As Lived Research*. Buckingham: Open University Press.

Gaskell, Jane and Eichler, Margrit (2001) 'White women as burden: on playing the role of feminist "experts" in China', *Women's Studies International Forum*, 24: 637–51.

Gatenby, Bev and Humphries, Maria (2000) 'Feminist participatory action research: methodological and ethical issues', *Women's Studies International Forum*, 23: 89–105.

Goode, Sarah (2000) 'Researching a hard-to-access and vulnerable population: some considerations on researching drug and alcohol-using mothers', *Sociological Research Online*, 5: http://www.socresonline.org.uk/5/1/goode.html

Haraway, Donna (1988) 'Situated knowledges: the science question in feminism and the privilege of partial perspective', *Feminist Studies*, 14: 575–99.

Haraway, Donna (1991) *Simians, Cyborgs and Women: The Reinvention of Nature*. London: Free Association Press.

Harding, Sandra (1986) *The Science Question in Feminism*. Buckingham: Open University Press.

Harding, Sandra (ed.) (1987a) *Feminism and Methodology*. Buckingham: Open University Press.

Harding, Sandra (1987b) 'The method question', *Hypatia*, 2: 19–35.

Harding, Sandra (1991) *Whose Science? Whose Knowledge? Thinking From Women's Lives*. Buckingham: Open University Press.

Harding, Sandra (1993) 'Rethinking standpoint epistemology. "What is strong objectivity"?', in Linda Alcoff and Elizabeth Potter (eds), *Feminist Epistemologies*. New York: Routledge. pp. 49–82.

Harding, Sandra (1997) 'Comment', *Signs*, 22: 382–91.

Harding, Sandra (1998) *Is Science Multi-Cultural? Postcolonialism, Feminisms and Epistemologies*. Bloomington: Indiana University Press.

Harding, Sandra (1999) 'The case for strategic realism: a response to Lawson', *Feminist Economics*, 5: 127–33.

Harding, Sandra (2003) 'Representing reality: the critical realism project', *Feminist Economics*, 9: 151–9.

Harding, Sandra (2004) 'A socially relevant philosophy of science? Resources from standpoint theory's controversiality', *Hypatia*, 19: 25–47.

Hartsock, Nancy (1983) 'The Feminist Standpoint: Developing the Grounds for a Specifically Feminist Historical Materialism', in Sandra Harding and Merrill Hintikka (eds), *Discovering Reality: Feminist Perspectives on Epistemology, Metaphysics, Methodology and Philosophy of Science*. Dordrecht: Reidel. pp. 283–311 (also republished as ch. 6 of Hartsock 1998).

Hartsock, Nancy (1997) 'Comment on Heckman', *Signs*, 22: 367–74.

Hartsock, Nancy (1998) *The Feminist Standpoint Revisited and Other Essays*. Boulder, CO: Westview Press.

Hekman, Susan (1997a) 'Truth and method: feminist standpoint theory revisited', *Signs*, 22: 399–402.

Hekman, Susan (1997b) 'Reply to Hartsock, Collins, Harding and Smith', *Signs*, 22: 341–65.

Hekman, Susan (1999) *The Future of Differences: Truth and Method in Feminist Theory*. Cambridge: Polity Press.

Kramarae, Cheris and Spender, Dale (eds) (1992) *The Knowledge Explosion: Generations of Feminist Scholarship*. New York: Teachers College Press.

Ladino, Carolina (2002) '"You make yourself sound so important." Fieldwork experiences, identity construction, and non-Western researchers abroad', *Sociological Research Online*, 7: http://www.socresonline.org.uk/7/4/ladino/html

Lather, Patti (2000) 'Drawing the line at angels: working the ruins of feminist ethnography', in Elizabeth St Pierre and Wanda Pillow (eds), *Working the Ruins: Feminist Poststructural Theory and Methods in Education*. New York: Routledge. pp. 284–311.

Lather, Patti (2001) 'Postbook: working the ruins of feminist ethnography', *Signs*, 27: 199–27.

Lather, Patti and Smithies, Chris (1997) *Troubling the Angels: Women Living With HIV/AIDS*. Boulder, CO: Westview/HarperCollins.

Lennon, Kathleen and Whitford, Margaret (eds) (1994) *Knowing the Difference: Feminist Perspectives in Epistemology*. London: Routledge.

Letherby, Gayle (2003) *Feminist Research in Theory and Practice*. Buckingham: Open University Press.

Linkogle, Stephanie and Lee-Trewick, Geraldine (2000) *Danger in the Field: Risk and Ethics in Social Research*. London: Routledge.

Luff, Donna (1999) 'Dialogue across the divides: "moments of rapport" and power in feminist research with anti-feminist women', *Sociology*, 33: 687–703.

Maynard, Mary (1994) 'Methods, practice and epistemology: the debate about feminism and research', in Mary Maynard and June Purvis (eds), *Researching Women's Lives From a Feminist Perspective*. London: Taylor & Francis. pp. 10–26.

Maynard, Mary and Purvis, June (eds) (1994) *Researching Women's Lives From a Feminist Perspective*. London: Taylor & Francis.

Morgan, Wendy (2000) 'Electronic tools for dismantling the master's house: poststructuralist feminist research and hypertext poetics', in Elizabeth St Pierre and Wanda Pillow (eds), *Working the Ruins: Feminist Poststructural Theory and Methods in Education*. New York: Routledge. pp. 130–49.

Mulinari, Diana and Sandell, Kerstin (1999) 'Exploring the notion of experience in feminist thought', *Acta Sociologica*, 42: 287–98.

Nelson, Lynn Hankinson (1990) *Who Knows: From Quine to a Feminist Empiricism*. Philadelphia: Temple University Press.

Nelson, Lynn Hankinson (1993) 'Epistemological communities', in Linda Alcoff and Elizabeth Potter (eds), *Feminist Epistemologies*. New York: Routledge. pp. 121–59.

Oakley, Ann (1998a) 'Science, gender, and women's liberation: an argument against postmodernism', *Women's Studies International Forum*, 21: 133–46.

Oakley, Ann (1998b) 'Gender, methodology and people's ways of knowing: some problems with feminism and the paradigm debate in social science', *Sociology*, 32: 707–31.

Oakley, Ann (2000) *Experiments in Knowing: Gender and Method in the Social Sciences*. Cambridge: Polity Press.

Petö, Andrea (2001) 'An empress in a new-old dress', *Feminist Theory*, 2: 89–93.

Ramazanoglu, Carolyn with Holland, Janet (2002) *Feminist Methodology: Challenges and Choices*. London: Sage.

Reger, Jo (2001) 'Emotions, objectivity and voice: an analysis of a "failed" participant observation', *Women's Studies International Forum*, 24: 605–16.

Reinharz, Shulamit (1979) *On Becoming A Social Scientist*. San Francisco: Jossey-Bass.

Reinharz, Shulamit (1983) 'Experiential analysis', in Gloria Bowles and Renate Klein (eds), *Theories of Women's Studies*. London: Routledge. pp. 162–91.

Reinharz, Shulamit (1992) *Feminist Methods in Social Research*. Oxford: Oxford University Press.

Reinharz, Shulamit (1993) 'Neglected voices and excessive demands in feminist research', *Qualitative Sociology*, 16: 69–76.

Ribbens, Jane and Edwards, Rosalind (eds) (1998) *Feminist Dilemmas in Qualitative Research: Public Knowledge and Private Lives*. London: Sage.

Richardson, Laurel (1994) 'Writing: a method of inquiry', in Norman Denzin and Yvonna Lincoln (eds), *The Handbook of Qualitative Research*. London: Sage. pp. 516–29.

Richardson, Laurel (1997) *Fields of Play: Writing an Academic Life*. New Brunswick, NJ: Rutgers University Press.

Rose, Hilary (1994) *Love, Power and Knowledge: Towards a Feminist Transformation of the Sciences*. Cambridge: Polity Press.

St Pierre, Elizabeth and Pillow, Wanda (eds) (2000) *Working the Ruins: Feminist Poststructural Theory and Methods in Education*. New York: Routledge.

Scheyvens, Regina and Leslie, Helen (2000) 'Gender, ethics and empowerment: dilemmas of developmental fieldwork', *Women's Studies International Forum*, 23: 119–30.

Schmidt, Volker (2001) 'Oversocialised epistemology: a critical appraisal of constructivism', *Sociology*, 35: 135–57.

Scott, Sara (1998) 'Here be dragons: researching the unbelievable, learning the unthinkable. A feminist sociologist in uncharted territory', *Sociological Research Online*, 3: http://www.socresonline.org.uk/3/3/scott/html

Seller, Anne (1994) 'Should the feminist philosopher stay at home?', in Kathleen Lennon and Margaret Whitford (eds), *Knowing the Difference: Feminist Perspectives in Epistemology*. London: Routledge. pp. 230–48.

Shiva, Vandana (1989) *Staying Alive: Women, Ecology and Development*. London: Zed.

Smith, Dorothy (1974a) 'Theorising as ideology', in Roy Turner (ed.), *Ethnomethodology*. Harmondsworth: Penguin. pp. 41–4.

Smith, Dorothy (1974b) 'Women's perspective as a radical critique of Sociology', *Sociological Quarterly*, 44: 7–13.

Smith, Dorothy (1978) 'A peculiar eclipsing: women's exclusion from men's culture', *Women's Studies International Quarterly*, 1: 281–96.

Smith, Dorothy (1987) *The Everyday World As Problematic: A Feminist Sociology*. Buckingham: Open University Press.

Smith, Dorothy (1990a) *The Conceptual Practices of Power: A Feminist Sociology of Knowledge*. Boston, MA: Northeastern University Press.

Smith, Dorothy (1990b) *Texts, Facts and Femininity: Exploring the Relations of Ruling*. London: Routledge.

Smith, Dorothy (1997) 'Comment on Hekman', *Signs*, 22: 392–8.

Smith, Dorothy (1999) *Writing the Social: Critique, Theory, and Investigations*. Toronto: University of Toronto Press.

Smith, Dorothy (2001) 'Texts and the ontology of organizations and institutions', *Studies in Cultures, Organizations and Societies*, 7: 159–98.

Smith, Dorothy (2003) 'Rigoberta Menchu and David Stoll: contending stories', *Qualitative Studies In Education*, 16: 287–305.

Spender, Dale (ed.) (1981) *Men's Studies Modified: The Impact of Feminism on the Academic Disciplines*. Oxford: Pergamon Press.

Stanley, Liz (ed.) (1990a) *Feminist Praxis: Research, Theory and Epistemology in Feminist Sociology*. London: Routledge.

Stanley, Liz (1990b) 'Feminist praxis and the academic mode of production', in Liz Stanley (ed.), *Feminist Praxis: Research, Theory and Epistemology in Feminist Sociology*. London: Routledge. pp. 3–19.

Stanley, Liz (1994) 'The knowing because experiencing subject: narratives, lives and autobiography', in Kathleen Lennon and Margaret Whitford (eds), *Knowing the Difference: Feminist Perspectives in Epistemology*. London: Routledge. pp. 132–48.

Stanley, Liz (1995) 'Speaking "as a....", speaking "for the...": on the mis/uses of the category "experience" in recent feminist thought', *Women's Studies Review*, 3: 19–29.

Stanley, Liz (1996) 'The mother of invention: necessity, writing and representation', *Feminism and Psychology*, 6: 45–52.

Stanley, Liz (1997) 'Methodology matters!', in Victoria Robinson and Diane Richardson (eds), *Introducing Women's Studies*. London: Macmillan. pp. 198–219.

Stanley, Liz (2004) 'A methodological toolkit for feminist research: analytical reflexivity, accountable knowledge, moral epistemology and being "a child of our time"', in Heather Piper and Ian Stronach (eds), *Educational Research: Difference and Diversity*. Aldershot: Ashgate. pp. 3–9.

Stanley, Liz and Wise, Sue (1979) 'Feminist research, feminist consciousness and experiences of sexism', *Women's Studies International Quarterly*, 2: 259–4.

Stanley, Liz and Wise, Sue (1983a) *Breaking Out: Feminist Consciousness and Feminist Research*. London: Routledge.

Stanley, Liz and Wise, Sue (1983b) 'Back into the person, our attempt to construct feminist research', in Gloria Bowles and Renate Duelli Klein (eds), *Theories of Women's Studies*. London: Routledge, pp. 192–209.

Stanley, Liz and Wise, Sue (1990) 'Method, methodology and epistemology in feminist research processes', in Liz Stanley (ed.), *Feminist Praxis: Research, Theory and Epistemology in Feminist Sociology*. London: Routledge.

Stanley, Liz and Wise, Sue (1992) 'Feminist epistemology and ontology', *Indian Journal of Social Work*, 53: 343–65.

Stanley, Liz and Wise, Sue (1993) *Breaking Out Again: Feminist Ontology and Epistemology*. London: Routledge.

Stanley, Liz and Wise, Sue (2000) 'But the Empress has no clothes! Some awkward questions about the "missing revolution" in feminist theory', *Feminist Theory*, 1: 261–88.

Tanesini, Alessandra (1999) *An Introduction to Feminist Epistemologies*. Oxford: Blackwell.

Tang, Ning (2002) 'Interviewer and interviewee relationships between women', *Sociology*, 36: 703–21.

Visweswaran, Kamala (1994) *Fictions of Feminist Ethnography*. Minneapolis: University of Minnesota Press.

Walby, Sylvia (2000) 'Beyond the politics of location: the power of argument in a global era', *Feminist Theory*, 1: 189–206.

Walby, Sylvia (2001a) 'Against epistemological chasms: the science question in feminism revisited', *Signs*, 26: 485–510.

Walby, Sylvia (2001b) 'Reply to Harding and Sprague', *Signs*, 26: 537–40.

Wilkinson, Sue (ed.) (1986) *Feminist Social Psychology: Developing Theory and Practice*. Buckingham: Open University Press.

Wise, Sue (1999) 'Reading Sara Scott's "Here Be Dragons"', *Sociological Research Online*, 4: http://www.socresonline.org.uk/4/1/wise.html

Wise, Sue and Stanley, Liz (2003) 'Looking back and looking forward: some recent feminist sociology reviewed', *Sociological Research Online*, 8: http://www.socresonline.org.uk/8/3/wise.html

Wolf, Diane (ed.) (1996) *Feminist Dilemmas in Fieldwork*. Boulder, CO: Westview Press.

Wolf, Marjorie (1996) 'Afterword: musings from an old grey wolf', in Diane Wolf (ed.), *Feminist Dilemmas in Fieldwork*. Boulder, CO: Westview Press. pp. 215–21.

25

From Autonomy to Solidarities
Transnational Feminist Political Strategies

Manisha Desai

In this chapter I use a transnational perspective to examine feminist political strategies used by women around the world in the past fifty years. I do so by focusing on three arenas: (1) the redefinition of politics: what constitutes politics and political issues, the nature of political activism, and the changing political discourses from feminism to human rights; (2) the nature of feminist politics: its autonomy vis-à-vis the state, political parties, and other social movements; and (3) the sites of political activism from the personal to the familial, local, national, and transnational. In each arena, I highlight the historical and diverse nature of the debates, the transnational flows of feminist politics, and the successes and limitations of feminist political strategies.

INTRODUCTION

This chapter presents a transnational overview of feminist political strategies of women's movements, primarily in India and the United States,[1] that spans the second half of the twentieth century. I highlight the key debates about what constitutes feminist activism and effective strategies. My location in an academic institution in the United States and work on the women's movements in India and around sites such as the UN and the World Social Forum mean that I draw primarily from academic and activist sources published in English in the United States and English, Hindi, and Marathi sources from India. I do not endeavor to present an exhaustive discussion of all political strategies used by feminists in the two countries, but rather have chosen to focus on three that are key. They are (1) broadening the definition of 'politics' to include issues relegated to the 'private realm' and developing autonomous women's organizations, (2) working in and against the state, and (3) gendering political discourse and building coalitions and networks with women's and other movements locally and transnationally.

The above mix has led to rethinking the nature of strategies in the social movement literature.[2] As a variant of an 'old social movement' interested in transforming society (not necessarily taking over the state) and a 'new social movement' involved in identity formation and practising its values and visions. Feminist movements have used multiple strategies from both old (in and against the state) and new movements (redefining and gendering politics). Hence, the literature on women's social movements has moved away from elaborating effective strategies to recognizing the need for multiple strategies based on context and purpose and addressing the varied consequences of different strategies.

The main feminist political strategies can be grouped as (1) making women's personal issues political in autonomous women's organizations, (2) developing policies and taking action both in and against the state, and (3) building coalitions and transnational networks. As I will show, the consequences of the three kinds of strategies have been mixed. They have made the issue of women's inequalities central to public debate, created new organizations and organizational practices, led to legal reform, and changed public and private understanding of the gendered divisions within social relations and institutions. Despite significant and wide-ranging changes, women still lack power in most economic, social, and political institutions as well as access to and control of material resources. To further women's structural empowerment in the current context of neo-liberalism, religious fundamentalism, and increasing militarism, we need a neo-radical politics that can combine more effectively the 'old' and 'new' politics.

THE PERSONAL IS POLITICAL: DEVELOPING AUTONOMOUS ORGANIZATIONS

Beginning in the late 1960s and 1970s, there was a resurgence in feminist women's movements around the world.[3] A major contribution of the feminist second wave was to redefine the term 'politics' to include issues that were relegated to the private realm.[4] This is best captured in the slogan of the times, 'the personal is political.' Issues like violence against women, women's control over their bodies, and sexuality were articulated as issues of public concern and politics.[5] The opening up of the 'private' realm to activism led to the development of numerous kinds of autonomous women's organizations, including consciousness-raising (CR) groups, self-help centers and service organizations, cooperatives and businesses, and women's studies centers.

CR groups emerged in the United States in response to women's experiences in the new left and the civil rights movements, where White women were marginalized by being relegated to kitchen and secretarial duties. In India and

Latin America, the CR groups came out of women's participation in peasant and workers' movements, where women's issues were subordinated or considered secondary to the primary issues of class. The experience of subordination led women activists to join with other women to develop feminist principles and processes of organizing on their own behalf. Autonomy was articulated at different levels: analytic autonomy from patriarchy as a concept not subsumed by class, political autonomy from parties and other movements, and organizational autonomy, forming women-only groups. In both the United States and India, the members of these autonomous group were primarily educated women from the dominant social groups: White, middle-class in the United States, and upper-caste, Hindu women in India.

In these groups, women practiced and debated feminist organizational structures and principles of participatory decision-making that eschewed hierarchy and leadership. Later analysts have critiqued this much celebrated 'structure-lessness,' and over the years many feminist organizations have also developed hierarchical structures, but most still practice a variation of participatory decision-making, even at the transnational level. Developing autonomous feminist organizations and practices has been one of the enduring contributions of the second-wave feminist movement (Ferree and Martin, 1995; Gandhi and Shah, 1991).

Self-help centers were another kind of organization that feminists formed in countries around the world. While issues of health and sexuality dominated the discussions in women's self-help groups in the United States, in India the earliest groups dealt with violence against women, primarily rape in police custody, dowry deaths and then wife-battering. In both countries, in response to women's needs, activists set up women's centers where battered women could receive emotional, legal, and medical counseling. In the United States (and also in Europe), the self-help centers became more institutionalized as hot lines and shelters and more professionalized both in the state welfare system and outside it. The result was the contradiction of trying to practice non-hierarchical feminist values and principles, but also having to meet state mandates in order to obtain financing. In India (and in Africa, Asia, and Latin America), given the lack of social services in general, many centers became NGOs with financial support from foreign donors to supplement what they got from their governments.

There was a boom in women's NGOs during the UN International Women's Decade, 1975–1985, and after the 1995 UN Beijing Conference, when women's unequal status in all societies gained international attention, and member-states of the UN made a commitment to address those inequalities.[6] Most of these NGOs over the decades have become service providers or gender experts to the state and other donors interested in funding research and programs for women's empowerment. This trend has led to a depoliticization of women's movements, as many NGOs are neither committed to feminist practice nor work with women's movements, but serve merely as service providers (Alvarez, 2000). In addition to these more or less political activities, Europe and the United States saw a proliferation of women-owned cooperatives, such as book stores, cafés, and music stores. Given the lack of capital and consumer power, these cooperatives were not a major trend in other parts of the world. The last decade, however, has seen an increase in transnational fair-trade cooperatives as an alternative to corporate globalization.

An important expansion of feminist activity was the establishment of women's studies programs in colleges and universities, and outside the academy, research and documentation centers that focused on women's issues. Both the United States and India as well as many countries in Africa, Asia, and Latin America have such academic and non-academic research centers that have begun to network, as I will discuss in the last section. The UN decade and its accompanying four conferences on women and NGO forums facilitated the establishment of such research spaces by providing visibility as well as resources for institutionalizing women's issues in the state and the academy.[7] The UN decade, however, was not unproblematic or uncontentious, as I will highlight later. What it did do is bring together activists and academics from the women's movement with their counterparts in the development movement. They enabled feminists from around the world to confront each other's assumptions, issues, and differences and facilitated the formation of transnational solidarities and practices which, I will argue, has become the dominant strategy of women's movements today (Desai, 1999; Moghadam, 2005).

In India and the United States, the early autonomous women's politics and analysis were seen to reflect the views and issues of middle-class, educated, White or high-caste women. Beginning in the 1970s and continuing in the 1980s, women of color in the United States and Dalit and Muslim women in India began to critique that feminist analysis and broaden it to include issues of race, caste, and religion.[8] Similar questions of inclusion are now being discussed vis-à-vis Indigenous and African women in Latin America. In India, issues of class had always been part of the feminist analysis, as most feminists came out of poor people's movements, but it was issues of caste and religion that became thorny.

The critique of feminist discourse took place in the academy as well as in movement organizations. Post-colonial feminists, located in US academies but with origins in India and other post-colonial societies, also began to offer a more nuanced analysis of women's varied social locations and what they might mean for feminist solidarities across those locations.[9] Sisterhood, therefore, could not be assumed but had to be forged in concrete struggles. The critique of early feminism also led to the development of a new generation of autonomous feminist organizations devoted to issues of women of color, Dalit and Muslim women, lesbian women, and transgendered people. This has led to a proliferation of women's organizations working on multiple issues. Feminists as well as social movement analysts see this as a contradictory development. On one hand, it has meant that more issues are being addressed, but it has also led to the fragmentation of the women's movement. Despite the emergence of complex intersectional analysis and transversal politics in feminist discourses around the world, the reality of transnational feminist politics has yet to include women from varied social, geographic, and economic locations.

In sum, the strategy of redefining politics and developing autonomous organizations has been extremely effective in pushing women's issues to the center of public debate and in providing women with safe organizational space to develop political positions and analyses, gain skills and employment, and provide much needed help. But it also tended to isolate women's issues and politics from other political discourses and organizations. However, feminists were not just involved in developing new identities and organizations, they were simultaneously working through the state machineries as well.

IN AND AGAINST THE STATE

Feminists in India and the United States conceptualized the state simultaneously as the target against which feminists struggle and a site for the expansion of gender equity and women's empowerment. Feminists worked with the state at various levels, seeking legal reform, promoting policy changes, and gendering state machineries. In both countries, feminists have succeeded in gaining some legal changes for women, like reproductive rights, protection for battered women, pay equity, and anti-sexual harassment and sex discrimination laws. In India, women have also succeeded in passing legislation to criminalize dowry murders and prevent sex-selective abortions.[10]

Following the UN decade and the 1995 UN World Conference in Beijing, many women's movements used international agreements to initiate reform at national level, a practice that has been called the boomerang effect (Tarrow, 2003). While most countries still do not have a gender-equitable legal system, many have more legal protection for women than before. Of course, laws on the book are not sufficient, as most women do not have access to the legal system, and most laws are not always implemented. But they represent a normative commitment that is an important first step. The United States, however, has still to ratify the Convention on All Form of Discrimination Against Women and tried, unsuccessfully, to introduce anti-abortion language onto the Beijing Platform at the joint meeting of the UN General Assembly and the 49th session of the Commission on Status of Women, which convened in New York City in 2005 to evaluate the progress of the world's governments in their commitments to women's rights. The US government and the women's movement's role vis-à-vis the UN has been problematic. The United States sees the UN as a space to help the 'developing world,' not a space where it is accountable for its own policies and actions. Therefore, the US women's movement also does not use the space of the UN to work on domestic gender issues. Most US women's organizations that do work at the UN focus on women's issues outside the United States.

In addition to lack of implementation of laws, feminists in the United States and India have realized that they do not have the political support for truly radical legislation. In the United States, despite intense mobilization, the ERA (Equal Right Amendment) failed to be ratified (Ryan, 1992). In India, despite similar mobilization, the government of Rajiv Gandhi passed the Muslim Women's Bill which would limit Muslim women's access to the civil courts for matters of marriage, divorce, inheritance, and child custody among other matters. But as recent research has shown, this bill had unintended, positive consequences for Muslim women. Flavia Agnes (1999) shows how lawyers and judges have interpreted the bill in accordance with local customs and awarded women larger alimonies and child support than warranted in the bill. The rise of religious fundamentalism in both countries has also demonstrated that feminists cannot make claims on behalf of all women in their countries. Women have been active in the fundamentalist movement in both countries, showing the lack of support for feminist issues not just from the established polity but also from women themselves (Klatch, 1987; Sarkar and Butalia, 1995). That has made it necessary in both countries for feminists to reach out to supporters, both men and women, in other progressive movements.

Reforming legislation, however, has not been the only strategy of the women's movements in relation to the state. Feminists have also worked to establish women's commissions at the state and national level in both countries and, through these, have had some success in effecting policy changes (Stetson and Mazur, 1995). In India, the National Commission on Women, along with other committees and activists from the movement, has been instrumental in gendering a lot of public policy discussions. During debates on the 2005 budget, the finance minister made a commitment to undertake a gender budget analysis. Writing about feminists employed by the Australian welfare state, Hester Eisenstein (1995) demonstrates that feminists can make a progressive difference in policy design and implementation when located in strategic positions within the state bureaucracy. She argues that feminist bureaucrats or 'femocrats' helped place feminist issues on the political agenda and established 'a range of feminist institutions funded by governments' in Australia during the early 1970s and later 1980s. However, feminists located within state institutions are also constrained in their ability to counter the disciplining function of social policy and the depoliticization of their advocacy roles (Naples, 1998b). Other research has shown that when there is a mobilized women's movement that can pressure the state, feminists within the state can be more effective (Stetson and Mazur, 1995). The success also depends on the extent to which women within the state feel responsible to a women's movement.

As the above discussion suggests, feminists have been successful in reforming legislation that directly relates to women's issues, such as violence against women and health and reproductive issues, although these are constantly being threatened in the United States under conservative administrations. Feminists have been less successful when politicians view issues as 'general,' such as welfare reform in the United States, which was not considered a women's issue but an economic measure to put people to work. Similarly, in India the Muslim Women's Bill was seen as an issue of religious freedom, even though it would discriminate against Muslim women.

Women need greater political power to act effectively in the arena of formal politics as well as new political arenas. Although feminists have struggled with the idea of quotas for women in government, many countries have begun to use political quotas for women. India passed legislation reserving 33 per cent of seats in local elections for women, but the bill for the national level is stalled in parliament. In the United States, there have been many groups and caucuses that have supported increasing the number of women in power, but they have not taken up the issue of quotas. A recent comprehensive analysis of the issue of quotas for women around the world found that how the quotas were implemented, the discourse surrounding it, and the relationship of elected women to women's movements shaped how effectively women in power could bring about gender equity within the government (Dahlerup and Freidenvall, 2005; IDEA, www.idea.int). Clearly, this is an issue that has to be addressed by feminists all over the world if they are to gain the political support they need to eliminate gender inequality.

GENDERING POLITICS, BUILDING COALITIONS

Another strategy that women have followed to further gain political support is through gendering political discourse and forming alliances with other movements. Even as feminists were forming autonomous organizations, they were also developing analyses to gender the discourses of other movements. In the United States, women of color and lesbians forced White feminists to first broaden their own gender-based discourse to include issues of race, class, and sexuality (Moraga and Anzaldúa, 1981). Early socialist and Marxist feminists had tried to integrate gender and class analytically, but there were few feminist organizations that were consciously diverse on class. There were, however, many community-based movements of poor women, White women, and women of color, who were organizing around housing, welfare, and other issues (Naples, 1998a). These groups enabled feminists to gender other political discourses (*Gender & Society*, 1999). They argued not only that feminism was about 'women's issues' but that all issues like capitalism, militarization, colonialism, poverty, environmental degradation, among other oppressions, must be understood through a gendered lens (Enloe, 1990; Omvedt, 1993; Sen, 1990). They simultaneously argued that issues associated with women, such as child care, reproductive rights, and adequate food, have profound effects on all members of households and communities regardless of gender.

While feminists have successfully gendered political discourse, at least at an academic level and among social movements if not at the level of political parties, their efforts at coalition building have not been as successful. Early coalition building began with other women's groups nationally and then, during the course of the UN decade for women, transnationally (Desai, 2002). Networks became the organizational expression of this coalition-building activity. As Valentine Moghadam (2005) shows, there are many transnational feminist networks across issues and regions that have emerged since the 1980s. Most of these networks are composed of educated, middle-class women from the North and the South. Much of the actual networking involves sharing information, research, advocacy, and support or 'communicative power.' Unfortunately, these networks often reproduce inequalities among women within countries and between countries, especially when the networks are funded by private donors or the aid agencies of Northern countries, as many are. Analysts such as Amrita Basu (2004) argue that transnational feminism is a new version of 1970s' 'sisterhood is global' feminism; it, too, was composed of a particular group of women but purported to make claims on behalf of all women.

But in addition to such elite networks, there are also networks of grass-roots movements, such as GROOTs (Grass Roots Organizations Operating Together) and Women in Informal Economy Globalizing and Organizing (Batliwala, 2002). These networks bring together poor women and men who have been impacted by globalization to develop strategies to confront its forces. Most of these networks work in partnerships with NGOs and academics to gain funding for their work. Grass-roots networks have succeeded in bringing poor people's claims to the political table and establishing their members as knowledge experts with solutions to their issues, not just as victims of globalization. However, within institutions of global governance, such as the UN and the World Bank, their radical language is depoliticized into programs such as gender mainstreaming or participatory governance while the policies that lead to marginalizing the poor continue. In India, the major networks of the women's movement are the National Network of Autonomous Women's Groups, which was organized in 1985, and the National Alliance of Women, which emerged after the 1995 Beijing Conference. These networks have enabled women's organizations in different parts of the country to communicate and work together. Like the UN conferences, their meetings have been contentious, with women from different parts of the political spectrum disagreeing over strategies. In the United States, while there are many coalitions of women's movements, there is no overarching network.

In addition to networking with other women's organizations nationally and transnationally, feminists have also formed coalitions and alliances with other movements (Keck and Sikkink, 1998; Naples and Desai, 2002). In India, among the major coalitions are the National Alliance of People's Movements, which works primarily on the local impact of globalization, and Slum and Shack Dwellers International, which works on housing rights for the urban poor. In the United States, such coalitions were formed during the struggle against the North American Free Trade Agreement.

Most coalitions of feminists and other activists tend to be issue-based rather than ongoing. They have not incorporated gender issues into the visions of other movements, nor have they worked jointly on strategies of structural change. While early coalition activity was around supporting mass mobilizations and common issues, in the age of the Internet a lot of network activity is exchange of information. Transnational economic issues are symbolically framed as matters of global justice and human rights, which have become the dominant discourses in most movements, with problematic consequences. Human rights discourse has tended to leave the state unproblematized. It focuses on individual as opposed to collective rights, and, most importantly, reinforces a regulative rather than redistributive discourse. Mass mobilizations are an exception and, despite their success in bringing out huge numbers of people, have not altered the course of economic globalization or prevented the invasion of Iraq.

As I have argued elsewhere (Desai, 2005) much transnational feminist activism post-Beijing has taken place in such sites as the UN and the World Social Forum. These spaces privilege popular intellectuals who act as knowledge experts in shaping discourse. There is dialogue among members of diverse organizations, but no substantive changes in national policies or actual redistribution of economic, political, or social power. Coalition building has not translated into political power for the feminist movement at home or in global governance.

NEO-RADICAL FEMINIST POLITICS

Feminist strategies of the last thirty years have been very effective in making women's issues central to political discourse, but they have not been as successful in altering women's inequalities. As UN Secretary-General Kofi Annan's report on the implementation of the Beijing Platform noted, the progress towards women's equality has been uneven.[11] The major achievement the report highlights is the increase in global awareness of women's inequalities and how new forces like globalization, HIV/AIDS, and armed conflicts contribute to such inequalities, as well as the commitment of national governments and international agencies to address these inequalities. The specific achievements noted were an increase in girls' education, women's economic empowerment, women's expanded political participation, and legal changes. But it also noted the challenges in the areas of continuing violence against women, including in armed conflict, the spread of HIV/AIDs among women and girls, discrimination in employment, decline in sexual and reproductive health, and limited access to land and property. Thus, as Shirin Rai (2004) notes, we have women's empowerment without real transfer of resources. In the context of neo-liberal globalization, rising religious fundamentalisms, and militarism, many gains that women have made are threatened or have been undermined.

While feminists have recognized the need to 'reinvigorate feminism as a political project' (Feminist Dialogues, 2005) and build links with other movements, the strategies they continue to use are a mix of the three outlined above. There is a need for a neo-radical agenda to combat the neo-liberal agenda, which will have to include strategies that deal not only with the question of power at the micro-discursive level but also with the structural power of the state, transnational corporations, and multilateral institutions of global governance. While keeping in mind the lessons we have learnt of our differences and multiple identities, and continuing to use feminist principles of participatory politics, we need to develop coalition politics that directly confronts structures of power so we can have redistributive and not just regulative justice for women.

ACKNOWLEDGEMENTS

I would like to thank Nancy Naples for her comments and suggestions on an earlier draft.

NOTES

1 The strategies we discuss for India and the United States are similar to strategies used by feminists in other parts of the world and I refer to these as appropriate. However, due to lack of space, I focus on the two countries with which I am most familiar.

2 See, for example, M. Bahati Kumba (2001), Arturo Escobar and Sonia Alvarez (1992), Jeff Goodwin and James Jasper (2004), and Jackie Smith, Charles Chatfield, and Ron Pagnucco (1997).

3 See, for example, Basu (1995), Catherine Eschle (2001), and Raka Ray and A. C. Korteweg (1999).

4 While I find the concept of waves of feminist movements problematic as an analytical category, as it overlooks the continuities between waves and ignores the latent activism between waves, I use it here as a temporal descriptor.

5 See, for example, Alice Echols (1989), Myra Marx Ferree and Beth Hess (2000), Nandita Gandhi and Nandita Shah (1991), and Radha Kumar (1993). Unless otherwise specified, my analysis of the women's movements in the United States is based on Echols (1989) and Ferree and Hess (2000) and my analysis of the women's movements in India is based on Gabriele Dietrich (1992), Gandhi and Shah (1991), Kumar (1993), Gail Omvedt (1993), and Ilina Sen (1990).

6 The UN declared 1975 as the International Women's Year and then 1975–1985 as the International Women's Decade with world conferences to mark the decade in 1975 (Mexico City), 1980 (Copenhagen), 1985 (Nairobi), and then another one in 1995 in Beijing (United Nations, 1995).

7 There have also been nine Women's World International Interdisciplinary Conferences meeting every three years in universities around the world. They started in Haifa, Israel, in 1981 (Safir, 2002).

8 See, for example, Agnes (1999), Combahee River Collective (1982), Dietrich (1992), Cherrie Moraga and Gloria Anzaldúa (1981), and Anupama Rao (2003).

9 See, for example, Jacqui Alexander and Chandra Talpade Mohanty (1997), Inderpal Grewal and Caren Kaplan (1994), and Chandra Mohanty (2003).

10 But this has often resulted in criminalizing the victims as shown by cases discussed in Agnes (1999).

11 The report is based on questionnaires that member-states filled out. It was published on the occasion of the 49th session of the Commission on the Status of Women's Beijing Plus Ten Review session. Available on the CSW website http://www.un.org/womenwatch/csw.

REFERENCES

Agnes, Flavia (1999). *Law and Gender Inequality: The Politics of Women's Rights in India*. New Delhi: Oxford University Press.

Alexander, M. Jacqui, and Chandra Talpade Mohanty (1997). *Feminist Genealogies, Colonial Legacies, and Democratic Futures*. New York: Routledge.

Alvarez, Sonia (2000). 'Translating the Global: Effects of Transnational Organizing on Local Feminist Discourses and Practices in Latin America.' *Meridiens* 1(1): 29–67.

Bahati, Kumba, M. (2001). *Gender and Social Movements*. Walnut Creek, CA: AltaMira Press.

Basu, Amrita (2004). 'Women's Movements and the Challenge of Transnationalism.' *Curricular Crossings: Women's Studies and Area Studies*.

_____ (ed.) (1995). *The Challenge of Local Feminisms: Women's Movements in Global Perspectives*. Boulder, CO: Westview Press.

Batliwala, Srilatha (2002). 'Grassroots Movements as Transnational Actors: Implications for Global Civil Society.' *Voluntas* 45(8): 732–755.

Combahee River Collective (1982). 'A Black Feminist Statement.' Pp. 13–22 in *All the Women are White, All the Blacks are Men But Some of Us are Brave*. Old Westbury, NY: Feminist Press.

Dahlerup, Drude and Lenita Freidenvall (2005). 'Quota as a "Fast Track" to Equal Representation for Women.' *International Journal of Feminist Politics* 7(1): 26–48.

Desai, Manisha (2005). 'Transnationalism: The Face of Feminist Politics Post Beijing.' *International Social Science Journal*. 185: 493–504.

_____ (2002). 'Transnational Solidarity: Women's Agency, Structural Adjustment, and Globalization.' Pp. 15–33 in Nancy Naples and Manisha Desai (eds), *Globalization and Women's Activism: Linking Local Struggles to Transnational Politics*. New York: Routledge.

_____ (1999). 'From Vienna to Beijing: Women's Human Rights Activism and the Human Rights Community.' Pp. 184–196 in Peter Van Ness (ed.), *Debating Human Rights: Critical Essays From U.S. and Asia*. New York: Routledge.

Dietrich, Gabriele (1992). *Reflections on the Women's Movement in India: Religion, Ecology, and Development*. New Delhi: Horizon India Books.

Echols, Alice (1989). *Daring to Be Bad: Radical Feminism in America, 1967–1995*. Minneapolis: University of Minnesota Press.

Eisenstein, Hester (1995). 'The Australian Femocratic Experiment: A Feminist Case for Bureaucracy.' Pp. 69–83 in Myra Marx Ferree and Patricia Yancey Martin (eds), *Feminist Organizations*. Philadelphia: Temple University Press.

Enloe, Cynthia (1990). *Bananas, Beaches, and Bases: Making Feminist Sense of International Politics*. Berkeley, CA: University of California Press.

Eschle, Catherine (2001). *Global Democracy, Social Movements, and Feminism*. Boulder, CO: Westview Press.

Escobar, Arturo and Sonia E. Alvarez (eds) (1992). *Making of Social Movements in Latin America: Identity, Strategy, and Democracy*. Boulder, CO: Westview Press.

Feminist Dialogues (2005). 'Concept Note for the Feminist Dialogues.'

Ferree, Myra Marx and Beth B. Hess (2000). *Controversy and Coalition: The New Feminist Movement across Three Decades of Change*. New York: Routledge.

Ferree, Myra Marx and Patricia Yancey Martin (1995). *Feminist Organizations: Harvest of the New Women's Movement*. Philadelphia, PA: Temple University Press.

Gandhi, Nandita and Nandita Shah (1991). *Issues at Stake: The Theory and Practice in the Contemporary Women's Movement in India*. New Delhi: Kali for Women.

Gender & Society. (1999). Special Issue on Gender and Social Movements 13(1).

Goodwin, Jeff and Jasper, James, M. (eds) (2004). *Rethinking Social Movements: Structure, Meaning, and Emotion*. Lanham, MD: Rowman and Littlefield.

Grewal, Inderpal and Caren Kaplan (eds) (1994). *Scattered Hegemonies: Postmodernity and Transnational Feminist Practices*. Minneapolis: University of Minneapolis Press.

Keck, Margaret and Kathryn Sikkink (1998). *Activists Beyond Borders: Advocay Networks in International Politics*. Ithaca, NY: Cornell University Press.

Klatch, Rebecca (1987). *Women of the New Right*. Philadelphia, PA: Temple University Press.

Kumar, Radha (1993). *The History of Doing: An Illustrated Account of Women's Rights and Feminism in India 1800–1990*. New Delhi: Kali for Women.

Moghadam, Valentine (2005). *Globalizing Women: Transnational Feminist Networks*. Baltimore, MD: Johns Hopkins University Press.

Mohanty, Chandra (2003). *Feminism without Borders: Decolonizing Theory, Practicing Solidarity*. Durham, NC: Duke University Press.

Moraga, Cherríe and Gloria Anzaldúa (1981). 'Introduction.' Pp. xxiii–xxvi in *This Bridge Called My Back: Writings by Radical Women of Color*. Berkeley, CA: Third Woman Press.

_____ (eds) (2002) (3rd edition). *This Bridge Called My Back: Writings by Radical Women of Color*. Berkeley, CA: Third Woman Press.

Nancy, Naples (ed.) (1998a). *Community Activism and Feminist Politics: Organizing Across Race, Class, and Gender*. New York: Routledge.

_____ (1998b). *Grassroots Warriors: Activist Mothering, Community Work, and the War on Poverty*. New York: Routledge.

Naples, N. and M. Desai (2002). *Globalization and Women's Activism: Linking Local Struggles to Transnational Politics*. New York: Routledge.

Omvedt, Gail (1993). *Reinventing Revolution: New Social Movements and the Socilaist Tradition in India*. New York: M.E. Sharpe.

Rai, Shirin (2004). 'Gendering Global Governance.' *International Journal of Feminist Politics* 6(3): 579–601.

Rao, Anupama, (ed.) (2003). *Gender & Caste: Issues in Contemporary Indian Feminism*. New Delhi: Kali for Women.

Ray, Raka and A. C. Korteweg (1999). 'Women's Movements in the Third World: Identity, Mobilization, and Autonomy.' *Annual Review of Sociology* 25: 47–71.

Ryan, Barbara (1992). *Feminism and the Women's Movement: Dynamics of Change in Social Movement Ideology and Activism*. New York: Routledge.

Safir, Marilyn P (2002). 'How it all began: The Founding of Women's Worlds Congress and International Network.' Sociologists for Women in Society *Network News* Winter: 6–8.

Sarkar, Tanika and Urvashi Butalia (eds) (1995). *Women and the Hindu Right*. London: Zed Books; New Delhi: Kali for Women.

Sen, Ilina (1990). *A Space Within the Struggle: Women's Participation in People's Movements*. New Delhi: Kali for Women.

Smith, Jackie, Charles Chatfield, and Ron Pagnucco (1997). *Transnational Social Movements and Global Politics: Solidarity Beyond the State*. Syracuse, NY: Syracuse University Press.

Stetson, Dorothy and Amy Mazur (eds) (1995). *Comparative State Feminism*. Thousand Oaks, CA: Sage.

Tarrow, Sidney (2003). 'Global Movements, Complex Internationalism, and North–South Inequality.' Paper presented at Workshop on Contentious Politics, Columbia University, Oct. 27, and Seminar on Inequality and Social Policy, Harvard University, Nov. 17.

United Nations (1995). *Women and the UN: 1945–1995*. New York: UN Press.

26

Utopian Visions

In this final chapter, the editors offer their views on what social changes they would most like to see, and how these can be accomplished. They are unanimous in their enthusiasm for the challenge that the study of gender makes to conventional thinking, but offer different suggestions about the part that feminist politics can play in producing a more equal and peaceful social world.

A WORLD WITHOUT GENDER?[1]

Judith Lorber

Feminists have long tried to attain gender equality by changing the dynamics of interaction between women and men, redressing gender imbalances in politics and control of valued resources, altering gender-discriminatory social practices, and challenging the invisibility and 'naturalness' of what is taken for granted about women and men. But after an initial revolutionary foray, they have not pushed these agendas to the point of calling for the abolition of gender boundaries and categories, with the goal of doing away with them altogether. I argue here that it is the bureaucratic and legal binary structure of gender that initiates gender inequality and therefore needs to be dismantled. I raise the question of whether it is possible to have a world without gender.

THE PERSISTENCE OF GENDER

The social construction perspective on gender recognizes the equal importance of agency (what people do) and structure (what results from what they do). Gender operates at one and the same time to give individuals status and identities and to shape their everyday behavior, and also as a significant factor in face-to-face relationships and organizational practices. Each level supports and maintains the others, but – and this is the crucial aspect of gender – the effects of gender work top down.

Because it works from social categorization to the individual, the gendered social order is very resistant to individual challenge. Its power is such that people act in gendered ways based on their position within the gender structure without reflection or question. We 'do gender' and participate in its construction once we have learned to take our place as a member of a gendered social order. Our gendered practices construct and maintain the gendered social order. But our practices also change it. As it changes, and as we participate in different social institutions and organizations throughout our lives, our gendered behavior changes.

I am arguing here that we have to go further than changing gendered practices and modifying the content of the gendered social order to achieve gender equality. To have a gender revolution, we have to challenge the whole institution based on the binary divisions of gender that are deeply rooted in every aspect of social life and social organization in most societies. In the sense of an underlying principle of how people are categorized and valued, gender is differently constructed throughout the world and throughout history. But the basic principle – a social order built on two sets of different types of people – remains.

At the present time in the Western post-industrial world, the gendered social order persists without much rationale. Women and men have legal equality, supported by a public rhetoric of equal rights and equal responsibilities for family support, household maintenance, and child care, as well as for individual economic independence – none of which are translated into laws. There are still occasional claims for men's 'natural' domination over women and women's 'natural' subordination, ostensibly backed by research on brain organization, hormonal input, or personality structure, but these claims are increasingly delegitimated by the presence of women prime ministers, university presidents, and Nobel prize winners.

Unfortunately, the rhetoric and legality of gender equality mask the underlying structure of gender inequality. Modern machinery and computers even out physical capabilities, and women are often better educated than men, but the post-industrial gendered social order still reproduces gender inequality in the job market and in wage scales. Men can run vacuum cleaners and change diapers, but women are still the main household workers and managers and the primary parents and so lose out in the job market. Men still think they have a right to women's bodies, to exploit them sexually and to dictate whether or not they should have children. Women's presence in the political arena varies widely. Wars and violent national conflicts especially perpetuate gender divisions.

As pervasive as gender is, because it is constructed and maintained through daily interaction, it can be resisted and reshaped through degendering practices. We need gender trouble-makers to challenge the way gender is still built into the Western world's overall social system, interpenetrating the organization of the production of goods and services, kinship and family, sexuality, emotional relationships, and the minutiae of daily life.

Gendered practices have been questioned, but the overall legitimacy of the gendered social order is deeply ingrained and currently bolstered by scientific studies on supposed inborn differences between females and males. The ultimate touchstone is pregnancy and childbirth. Yet procreative and other biological differences are part of the gendered social order, which is so pervasive that the behavior and attitudes it produces are perceived as natural, including women's greater predisposition to nurturance and bonding. This belief in natural – and thus, necessary – differences legitimates many gender inequalities and exploitations of women.

Feminist movements have focused on the inequalities and exploitations, especially in the gendered work world and domestic division of labor, but have found that as one set of gendered practices is eliminated, others rise to take their place. To keep women down, differences from men must be maintained and used as a rationale for women's inferior status. Feminists have either minimized these differences, to little effect, or maximized and valorized them, also to little effect. The problem is that the focus has been on differences between women and men as individuals or as social actors. These differences are a means to an end – legitimation and justification of gendered social orders. It is the foundation of gendered social orders, gender itself, gender as a social institution, that must be delegitimized.

But aren't biological sex differences the ultimate barrier to degendering? And what about sexuality? Won't degendering flounder on sexual desire for a member of the opposite or same gender? My argument is two-fold: biological sex and sexuality themselves are not clear binary opposites, and both are deeply intertwined with the social aspects of gender. The complexities of the gender system – it is a hierarchy of race and ethnicity and social class as well – complicate the categories of biological sex, sexual identities, and sexual desire. None of these are binary, and none produce gender. Genes, hormones, physiology, and bodies (what is summarized as 'sex differences') are socially constructed as gendered in Western society; they are not the source of gender as a social status. Like bodies, sexuality is socially gendered but has multiple manifestations that create more than one 'opposite sex.' Sexuality follows gender scripts; it does not create them. If sexual behavior were the source of gender categories, there would be many more than heterosexual man, heterosexual woman, gay man, lesbian woman.

Gender is so deeply embedded in our lives because it is a *social institution*. It creates structure and stability, seeps into the practices of many social roles, has a long history, and is virtually unquestioned. Institutionalized patterns of acting and thinking are learned so early and reinforced that they seem impervious to change. Nonetheless, institutions evolve as societies evolve. The institution of gender has certainly evolved in Western societies – women and men now have *formal* equality in all the major social spheres. In many countries, no laws prevent women from achieving what they can, and many laws help them do it by preventing discrimination and sexual harassment. More and more countries are ratifying laws to protect women's procreative and sexual rights, and to designate rape, battering, and genital mutilation as human rights crimes.

But women are still responsible for child care and men for economic support of children, skewing women's wages in the job market and chances for career advancement. The continued gendered division of labor in the job market and in the home is the bedrock of gender inequality. At the very least, the gendered division of family work and the gendered practices of work organizations and their interconnections need to be degendered if we are to create true and permanent gender equality.

DEGENDERING IN PRACTICE

Degendering as a viable form of resistance has to be deliberate, structural, and independent of sexed bodies if existing gendered social orders are to be transformed. Degendering needs to be focused on how people are sorted and allocated tasks in work organizations, schools, small groups, families, and other familiar social groupings. Degendering means not assigning tasks in the home and workplace by gender. Degendering means not grouping children by gender in schools. Degendering means confronting gender expectations in face-to-face interaction and underplaying gender categories in language (not saying 'ladies and gentlemen' but 'colleagues and friends').

Many people already use the degendered and legally neutral terms 'partner,' 'constant companion,' 'significant other,' or 'beloved' for the person in their long-term emotional relationships. Degendered kinship designations, such as 'child,' 'parent,' and 'sibling' could liberate us further from stereotypical gendered expectations. Especially important is to stop comparing children by gender and not ever saying 'boys will be boys' or 'just like a girl.'

Where language itself is built on gender categories, developing gender-neutral ways of addressing and referring to people will be a major and revolutionary enterprise, but its accomplishment would go a long way towards structural degendering. Similarly, in theocracies where the state religion separates women and men and treats them markedly unequally through religious law, degendering cannot take place unless personal status laws are secularized and made gender-neutral. Non-state religions should be free to continue to separate women and men.

Even with degendering, people who wish to can continue to identify themselves as men, women, girls, boys, and to display femininity or masculinity, as they define it, in names, clothing, and behavior. Displays of dominance or aggression, however, would not be a prerogative of men, nor would displays of subordination or submission be confined to women; with degendering, such currently gendered behavior could be expected of anyone. People can be consistent in their gender presentation and display in all phases of their lives, or varied by situation.

What is most important about degendering is that formal bureaucratic categories and the formal structures of organizations not be built on gender divisions, nor should workplaces, households, and child care.

As degendering agents in our everyday lives, we can confront the ubiquitous bureaucratic and public gender binaries just as transgenders do – by thinking about whether we want to conform or challenge. We could stop ticking off the M/F boxes at the top of every form we fill out or ask about the need for them. Shannon Faulkner, a girl, got into the Citadel, an all-boys military school, because the admission form did not have an M/F check-off box; it was assumed that only boys would apply. All her credentials and biographical information qualified her for admission, but when the Citadel administration found out she was a girl, she was immediately disqualified. The person didn't change; her qualifications remained the same. The *legal status* – and all the stereotypical baggage about capabilities that comes with it – changed. It was on that basis that she successfully claimed gender discrimination and challenged the all-male status of the Citadel. That is precisely what degendering would do.

In societies where women are severely disadvantaged, degendering may not be the best strategy to achieve women's rights. Gender sensitivity may be necessary to bring attention to how seemingly neutral policies are insidious for women. It may also be necessary to compare women and men in the economic sphere, but here the effects of education, income, and social class standing often mean that women and men cannot be treated as homogeneous global categories.

If we are going to conduct a campaign of degendering, it can be everywhere and ongoing, because gender so imbues our lives. If this sounds like the 'good old days' of pervasive personal politics, it is – but rather than just fighting sexism or the oppression of women by male-dominated institutions, it includes men and attends as well to other subordinating social statuses. Most of all, degendering directly targets the processes and practices of gendering and their outcome – gendered people, practices, and power. Deliberate degendering is not ignoring gender, which allows gendered processes and practices to proceed unhindered. To *deliberately degender*, you have to attend to those processes and practices in order to not do them.

Degendering will not do away with wars and hunger and economic disparities. But I do think that degendering will undercut the patriarchal and oppressive structure of Western societies and social institutions and give all of us the space to use our energies to demilitarize, work for peaceable solutions to conflicts, grow and distribute food, level the gaps between social classes.

The feminist task of gaining citizenship rights and economic equality for most of the world's women is undeniably of first priority, but I will suggest a second task that can be done where women are not so terribly unequal – challenging the binary structures just a little bit more by asking why they are necessary at all. I think that it is only by undercutting the gender system of legal statuses, bureaucratic categories, and official and private allocation of tasks and roles that gender equality can be permanently achieved.

NOTE

1 Adapted from Judith Lorber (2005), *Breaking the Bowls: Degendering and Feminist Change*. New York: W. W. Norton.

GETTING REAL: CONTEXTUALIZING GENDER

Mary Evans

In this handbook we, as editors, are deeply indebted to those authors who have vividly brought together the range and vitality of current writing about the issue of gender. It is impossible to read this handbook without a sense of pride in the academic achievements of those individuals who have contributed to the gendering of the human subject in the university (and indeed outside it) and, through this, to the recognition that human knowledge might in the past have been inadequate or blind in its discussion of the human condition. People, it is now recognized, come in two sexes and even if we differ about where to take this fact of existence, its very presence has played a crucial part in opening up new debates and indeed new possibilities in social life.

It is, however, around the question of the nature of social life that I would like to offer my hopes for the future. More precisely, I should like to propose that those working in gender/women's studies begin to forge alliances around the nature of the real world. I very deliberately do not put apostrophes around the word real here, because I want to suggest that there is a real world in which individuals of both genders have markedly different experiences of the world according to their class and their ethnicity. Indeed, I would like to go further and propose that it is only necessary to read Barbara Ehrenreich (2002) or Beverley Skeggs (2004) or Linda McDowell (2003) and see that the 'cultural turn' in the social sciences may have liberated and enlarged intellectual horizons, but it has made little impact on the economic and material divisions in which people live.

Beverley Skeggs in particular has written about the impact of television programmes such as *Sex and the City* and *Friends*, which take huge assumptive leaps towards the normalization of White middle-class experience and leave untouched (and indeed marginalized) the worlds of the poor and the socially excluded. The world of Western Bridget Joneses needs, I would argue, more critical attention than it sometimes receives. It is not difficult to recognize the infantilization of women which Bridget Jones represents, but perhaps more pernicious is the taking for granted of an ethic of trivial entitlement which Bridget Jones – and similar characters – represent. In *Love's Work*, her final work before her death, Gillian Rose (1995) wrote of the way in which, in her view, we have become more sentimental towards ourselves and more ruthless towards others in the late twentieth (and early twenty-first) centuries. Indeed, the sense of entitlement which seems to be endemic in some Northern cultures has arguably become the major threat to the planet.

The above is of course a view of the world which is contentious; raising it is a prelude to posing the question of where feminism, and the question of gender, should stand, and does stand, in the social world. The majority of Western societies have achieved legal and civic equality between women and men, even though gender still impacts upon all aspects of social life. But 200 years after the end of the Enlightenment we are still living in a world in which male authority remains greater than that of women: step out of the West and men can dictate how women dress. A dramatic example – and of course an example in which women are often complicit with that male authority – but nevertheless an example of the way in which the world as a whole has a very considerable way to go before it becomes 'de-gendered'. If we decide that we should become gender blind in determining institutional access then we leave unchanged the nature of those institutions; yes, women have entered the military and certain religious institutions but in doing so they have to accept – and 'buy into' – the values explicit in those contexts. Back in the early days of second-wave feminism many authors spoke of the 'second shift' which women in paid employment worked, the housework and the work in paid work. To extend the range of that comment, I would argue that feminism and gender/women's studies have to continue to work something of an intellectual double shift – that is, we can never solely write about gender, we must always contextualize it. So to adapt the plea of Tony Blair and British 'New Labour' for 'education, education, education' I would argue for 'context, context, context'.

The strength of this position, it seems to me, is that it allows women's studies – and feminism – to step beyond that criticism made of it that it is a movement of and about middle-class White women. It is not that feminism has not achieved great things (notably around issues of sexuality and personal autonomy) but that it often founders on the very sharp rocks of employment and motherhood. Employment throughout the world is hierarchical, and there is little escape from the equally universal truth that some paid work is badly paid and terrible to perform. The problem for all societies is that much of this work is essential. Speaking for those who do this work (and abandoning the fantasy world of work in *Sex and the City*) is a campaign which would enormously benefit millions of women and men. Equally, motherhood is universal, if not universally desired. But one of the most chilling aspects of public policy in the United States and Britain in recent years has been the redefinition of motherhood, in the case of poor mothers (the 'welfare' mothers of the United States) as a social problem. Here we see the sharpest possible impact of class and gender: poor mothers must enter paid work, regardless of the personal costs and the statutory blindness to individual needs. Indeed, one of the great paradoxes of the individualism of the West is that it can often make us blind to the individuality of others.

The history for the world in the past 200 years suggests that state attempts to abolish gender differences are a feature of totalitarian societies, whilst the emphasis on gender difference is a mark of the most theocratic. At the beginning of the twenty-first century there are some grounds for supposing that the world's most powerful society, the United States, is moving towards a form of secular theocracy: Christian fundamentalism becoming the dominant form of social morality, whilst a huge secular culture of pornography and the manipulation of sexual difference contribute to the maintenance of sexual inequality. It is within this new politics that we need to situate our discussion of gender, to see the limitations of liberal feminism but also to defend liberal values at a time when they are demonstrably under attack. It is, of course, another 'second shift' but a second shift which has the very real value of making gender politics relevant, of taking gender out of the dream factory and into the politics which determines, often in the most brutal ways, individual lives.

Real is not a matter for apostrophes, it is a matter (to follow Barbara Ehrenreich's title) of nickels and dimes. We should be able to acknowledge the reality of the capitalist social world (and also acknowledge that even if grand narratives have disappeared the narrative of capitalism has not) but we also question the acceptance of its values.

REFERENCES

Ehrenreich, Barbara (2002) *Nickel and Dimed*. London: Granta.
McDowell, Linda (2003) *Redundant Masculinities*. Oxford: Blackwell.
Rose, Gillian (1995) *Love's Work*. London: Chatto and Windus.
Skeggs, Beverley (2004) *Class, Self, Culture*. London: Routledge.

FEMINIST POLITICS OF LOCATION

Kathy Davis

The present volume represents the 'state of the art' of women's and gender studies. The authors have done a remarkable job of mapping the achievements of Western feminism. The handbook shows how contemporary feminist scholarship has developed new ways of thinking about differences between the sexes – from the old distinction of sex and gender to abolishing the distinction and focusing on the performance of gender (à la Judith Butler) to Judith Lorber's radical plea for a total 'degendering' of the social world. The contributions explore the variegated experiences of women of different class backgrounds, ethnicities, 'race,' and sexual orientations, paying special attention to their individual and collective histories of struggle. Taken together, they critically interrogate the dualistic and gendered binaries of our Enlightenment heritage (mind–body, culture–nature, White–Black, the 'West and the rest'), which provide the justifications for everything from masculinist science to unbridled technological expansion at the expense of environment and health, to nationalism, genocide, and war. The contributions maintain a strong and heart-felt commitment to an egalitarian and just society, for both women and men.

It is not coincidental that the contributions have come from feminist scholars from what is – somewhat problematically – referred to as 'the West,' i.e., the United States, the United Kingdom, Australia, and (Western) Europe. There were many practical reasons for this selection, given the origin of the discipline of women's studies and its stronghold within academic settings throughout these parts of the world, not to mention the expediency of gathering contributions by authors fluent in English as lingua franca. Nor is it my intention to deny the substantial efforts on the part of many of the authors in this volume to reflect critically on the hegemony of Western feminist scholarship, in particular, and the 'West' in general. Nevertheless, we clearly have a volume which not only is somewhat parochial, but also raises some rather serious political concerns about the representation of feminism in this age of globalization. Thus, with an eye toward a more truly 'global' handbook on women's and gender studies at some as yet to be determined date in the future, I would like to engage in some utopian reflection on what a global feminist 'politics of location' might entail.

POLITICS OF LOCATION

The term 'politics of location' was coined by Adrienne Rich (1986) and was initially intended to counter the ethnocentrism of mainstream US feminism. It was a response to the longstanding critique from women, who had been marginalized within mainstream feminism by virtue of their color, class, ethnicity, sexual orientation, or nationality. 'Politics of location' meant acknowledging difference, retrieving previously marginalized perspectives, and compelling, in particular, White US or Western women to become accountable about their own locations. It was about naming the ground we are standing on and critically examining conditions we have always taken for granted. It stood for a desire for plurality within feminism and an increased willingness to reflexively and critically situate one's own perspective.

Since Rich wrote this essay, the meaning of 'politics of location' has shifted. The centrality given to 'difference' and the reluctance of – notably – White Western feminists to address their complicity in hierarchies of power among women have been broadened to include a more expansive theoretical and political agenda for women's studies. The 'politics of location' as envisioned by feminist scholars like Chandra Talpade Mohanty (2003), Avtar Brah (1996), Inderpal Grewal and Caren Kaplan (1994), and many, many others refers to relationships of exchange across *all* borders, especially those of nation and culture. While still concerned with differences among women, this 'politics of location' situates differences among women (and men) within global hierarchies of power and explores how these hierarchies shape all encounters, both locally and globally. It is less concerned with the reflexivity of US or Western feminists *within* the academy than with decentralizing the priority given to Western scholarship and providing ways to understand how feminism travels, both in theory and in practice.

This new and revised 'politics of location' in a global context opens up a whole new set of questions about how feminism 'travels,' how feminist knowledge and knowledge practices are 'translated' in different cultural locations, and what this might mean for feminist encounters transnationally. Applied to the field of women's and gender studies, this suggests (at least) three new directions: how we write feminist history, how we produce feminist theory, and, last but not least, how we practice feminist politics.

FEMINIST HISTORY

The history of academic feminism has often been situated in the 'West,' where it becomes a standard against which feminisms in other parts of the globe are measured. Even ostensibly international or comparative studies of feminism tend to give precedence to the history – the events and struggles – of feminism in the West. This somewhat myopic focus has led to a series of problems, ranging from overlooking feminist struggles in other parts of the world to overestimating the importance of what is essentially a specific local version of Western feminism. Susan Stanford Friedman (1998) has argued for replacing what she calls an overdeveloped concern for 'our' history within US/Anglo/European feminism with a more well-developed 'geographical imagination.' Let's think 'geographically' instead of just 'historically.' This is not just a call for a more comparative approach – that is, taking the time to learn about women's struggles in different parts of the world. At a time when the accelerating pace of economic globalization and transnational cultural traffic have made national borders increasingly permeable, it perhaps makes more sense to explore feminism (in theory and in practice) as a *glocal* phenomenon. In my utopian vision, future histories within women's studies would no longer focus on national or regional histories of feminism, but would track its migratory and transcultural formations, making it viewable as both more ubiquitous (global) than we (in the West) had imagined and more specifically located within temporal and spatial frameworks than we (in the West) have liked to admit.

FEMINIST THEORY

Many feminist scholars have been concerned with how global power relations are played out in the production and reception of theory, noting that feminist theory, writ large, tends to be located in the West, while the writings of non-Western women are treated as un-theoretical. Gayatri Chakravorty Spivak (1988) has provided a particularly forceful critique, mercilessly attacking the powerful division of labor in feminist theory which represent feminists in the West as the subjects who make theory, while non-Western women are treated as the objects of feminist theory. As effective as this critique has been in deconstructing problematic notions about Western superiority, it remains focused on feminist theory *in* the West. In the interests of a true 'de-centering' of Western feminist theory, it would behoove us to treat feminist theory as – to borrow Edward Said's (1983) famous metaphor – 'traveling theory.' This would mean exploring how feminist theory moves from place to place. What kinds of theories get taken up in different parts of the world? Does the fact that a particular theory 'travels' from the affluent West to other parts of the globe make it reprehensible – a kind of feminist cultural imperialism? Or, to put a bit differently, what makes a specific feminist theory oppositional – in the sense of opening up – often unforeseen – possibilities for new forms of critical engagement? In my wishful thinking about the future, Western feminist theory would become less concerned with its own conditions of production and more concerned with the circulation and transformation of feminist knowledge in a global framework.

FEMINIST POLITICAL PRACTICE

Western feminism has always had an ideological commitment to internationalism. Virginia Woolf's well-known statement, 'As a woman, I have no country. As a woman I want no country. As a woman my country is the whole world' (1938: 109) is a case in point. This vision, while shared by many feminist scholars, has also been heavily criticized. Caren Kaplan (1996) has argued that, however well-intentioned, it remains insensitive to the fact that feminist alliances are infused with global inequalities of power. However much we, like Virginia Woolf, might like to disassociate ourselves from our national histories of slavery, imperialism, genocide, or colonialism, we remain, often to our own dismay, imbricated in them and, therefore, responsible for understanding how our positions of relative privilege shape encounters across lines of difference, both within and outside our national contexts.

Many contemporary feminist scholars in the West have taken differences between women (in experiences, histories, struggles) as a starting point for feminist political practice. It seems to me that the task of a truly transnational feminist political practice would be to find ways to create dialogues where differently situated women (and men) could begin to engage with issues which are of concern to us all. In my utopian vision of the future, it would be this 'working across borders,' which could generate a sequel to the present volume – a truly transnational handbook of women's and gender studies.

REFERENCES

Brah, Avtar (1996) *Cartographies of Diaspora.* London: Routledge.
Friedman, Susan Stanford (1998) *Mappings: Feminism and the Cultural Geographies of Encounter.* Princeton, NJ: Princeton University Press.
Grewal, Inderpal, and Caren Kaplan (1994) *Scattered Hegemonies.* Minneapolis: Minnesota University Press.
Kaplan, Caren (1996) *Questions of Travel.* Durham, NC: Duke University Press.
Mohanty, Chandra Talpade (2003) *Feminism Without Borders.* Durham, NC: Duke University Press.
Rich, Adrienne (1986) *Blood, Bread, and Poetry.* New York: W.W. Norton.
Said, Edward (1983) *The World, the Text, the Critic.* Cambridge, MA: Harvard University Press.
Spivak, Gayatri Chakravorty (1988) *In Other Worlds.* New York: Routledge.
Woolf, Virginia (1938) *Three Guineas.* London: Harcourt Brace Jovanovich.

Index

9/11 attacks 307–9

Aboriginal women 98
abortion 363
Abu Ghraib Prison 204, 223
academia, gendered
  epistemology in 59
academic feminism
  anxieties and vitalities
    13–15, 27–8
  autonomy/integration
    debate 15, 16–21
  depoliticisation 22
  development of 17, 478
  future of 28–9
  integration of 'forgotten'
    women's culture 75, 76
  international context 20–1,
    25–6
  link with activism 17–18
  location and biography 15,
    21, 22, 24–5, 27–9
  'naming' debate 15, 22–6, 27
  Western bias 214–15, 216–17,
    218, 477, 478, 479
academic markets 19–20, 21
Acker, J. 259
activism
  feminist *see* feminist
    political practice
  fundamentalist 103
Adkins, L. 260–1
Adorno, T.W. 379
Africa 62, 94, 220
African National Congress 216
Agarwal, B. 384
agency
  and body maintenance/
    modification 364–70
  and gender 469
  and medicalization 359,
    363–4
  and regulation of bodies
    359, 370–1
  of women in conflict 216,
    219, 224, 225, 227
agential realism 160
Agnes, F. 462

agriculture 389, 390
Ahmed, L. 241
Al-Hibri, A. 241
Alcoff, L. 161–2
alcohol consumption 113, 116
Allen, S. 198
American Revolution 238
Amnesty International 248
analytical reflexivity 448, 449
analytical toolkit for fractured
  foundationalism 445–51
Andermahr, S. 127, 128, 130
androcentricity, of
  epistemology 147, 148
Annan, K. 465
anorexia nervosa 368
Anthias, F. 198
anthropology 55
anti-foundationalist
  epistemology 439
anti-psychiatry movement 78–9
anti-social behaviour 114
anti-war politics 224
Anzaldúa, G. 245
Appiah, K. 128
archeological–genealogical
  project 75
Aristotle 419
art 74–5, 78, 86–7
Asia 61, 62, 221, 225–7
Asian Institute of Technology 87
atheism 100
Australia 26, 61, 98
autobiography 82
autonomous women's groups
  458–61
autonomy
  of academic feminism
    15, 16–21
  relational autonomy 422
  see also agency

Bacchetta, P. 226
ballet dancers 47
Banerjee, S. 205
Barad, K. 160
Barrett, F. 120
Barrett, M. 325

Bartky, S.L. 359, 369
Basu, A. 141–2, 464
beauty therapy 364–5, 371
Beauvoir, S. de 38, 81, 329
Beck, E.T. 95
Beck, U. 267
Becker, E. 409
Becker, G. 254
Belarus 205
Belgium 299
Benhabib, S. 133, 245–6
Benwell, B. 117–18
Berger, P. 343
Best, A. 317–18
Bhabha, H. 188
Bhasin, K. 221
Big Science 398, 399
binary categories 74, 83, 310,
  436, 471
  see also dichotomies
binary divisions 74
binge drinking 113, 116
biography 15, 22, 27–9
biological sciences
  and body/mind interface
    47–8
  challenges to 83
  construction of sex
    differences 401
  gendered assumptions in
    41–2
biological sex differences 36–7,
  39, 401, 471
  and women's cultural
    production 77, 78
  and women's
    employment 255
biotechnology 86, 389
Black feminism 276–7, 443
Black Studies 222
Black women's cultural
  production 81–2
Bly, R. 59
bodies
  agency and conformity 359,
    361, 363–71
  in concept of gender 318–19
  denaturalization of 405–6

bodies *(cont.)*
  evaluation and regulation of 357–8, 359, 370–1
  in feminist environmental studies 385–6, 388–9
  feminist study of 358–60
  food, diet and 366–9
  and knowledge 61
  maintenance and modification of 47, 86–7, 364–70
  medicalization of 360–4
  pre-enlightenment understanding of 39
  sexual categorization 37–8, 39–40, 43–4
  shaped by cultural context 46–8
  in technoscience constructionism 404
  and women's cultural production 77, 78, 79–80, 86–7
  women's workshops on 401
  see also embodiment
body building 367, 369
Bohr, N. 381
Bologna Declaration 21
boomerang effect 461
Bordo, S. 151, 368
Bosnia 218, 219, 222
Boxer, M.J. 13
boxers 47
boys' education 113, 114, 118, 175–7
Bradley, H. 116, 257
Brah, A. 192
Braidotti, R. 17, 24, 25
Britain
  concepts of nation 201, 205–6
  Islamic veiling debates 97
  work–life balance 266
Brown, A. 327
Brown, E.B. 134
Brown, H. 327
Brown, W. 22, 24, 141
Brownmiller, S. 219
Buddhism 99
Budgeon, S. 335–7
bulimia nervosa 368
Bunch, C. 313
bureaucratic careers 258
bureaucratic hierarchies 259
Butalia, U. 220, 226
Butler, J. 37, 42, 133, 134, 140, 308, 309, 310, 424
Bynum, C.W. 39

Cahoone, L. 127, 130
Cannon, W.B. 48
capability approach 179

capitalism
  and education 173–4
  and technoscience 399
  and women's employment 267
Card, C. 429–30
care
  and citizenship 277, 282
  concept of 273
  concepts of disability 276
  cross national research 277
  and ethnicity 276–7
  feminist analyses of 272–7, 283
  informal care by men 275
  interaction of provision 283
  motivations for informal 275
  payment for informal 280, 281–2
  state support of informal 277, 278, 279–83, 284
  types of policy and provision 278–83
  see also childcare
care workers 279, 281, 282, 283–4
care–justice debate 427–9
careers 258, 265
carers 275, 280, 283
Carmichael, M. 324–5
Carson, R. 390
Castells, M. 111, 121, 262
Catholicism 204
CEDAW (Convention on the Elimination of all forms of Discrimination Against Women) 193, 461
Chernobyl nuclear accident 388
Chicago, J. 78
Chicana identity 162–3
childbirth 360–1
childcare
  gender convergence 294–5, 300
  parental leave 296–8
  single-parent families 294–5, 298–9
Chipko movement 382
Chow, E.N-l. 189–90, 191
Christ, C. 101
Christianity 95, 100, 102
Churchill, C. 78
citizenship
  and care 277, 282
  feminist study of 235
  displacement strategy 243–6
  equality and difference 238
  and globalization 247–9
  inclusion strategy 238–40
  reversal strategy 241–3

citizenship *(cont.)*
  feminist use of term 234–5
  global or national 235
  and heteronormativity 312, 318
  multiculturalism and feminism 235
  and nationalism 206–7
  and same-sex marriage 299
civic-republican tradition 239
civil rights 238, 239, 248
civil society, as public/private 236
Cixous, H. 79
Clark, J. 78
class
  and body perceptions 367
  differences between women 81
  and education 169, 174, 176
  and employment choices 257
  and gender convergence 293, 294
  and gender norms 359
  and masculinity 58, 61, 118
  and nation 205
  and other social categories 58, 134, 191
  and women's movements 459, 460, 463, 464
coalitions 463–5
Cock, V. 216
Cockburn, C. 204, 207–8
Code, L. 160–1, 420, 441–2
coeducation 168–9, 172
cohabitation 288, 292
coherentist epistemology 161–2
collaborative reproduction 405–6
collective identities
  and citizenship 244–5, 246
  see also communitarianism
  and sexual violence 221–2
Collins, P.H. 443
colonialism 94, 222
Coltrane, S. 293
combat, women in 216, 223–7
combination approach to women's studies 16–17
communitarianism 241–2
community care 273
complicity 429–30
Connell, R.W. 36, 46–7, 59, 111
consciousness-raising 156
consciousness-raising (CR) groups 458–9
constructionism
  in contemporary technoscience 404
  see also social construction
consumerism 85

consumption 387
context
　body shaped by 46–8
　feminism in global 478–80
　gender in 474–6
contextual empiricism 154
Convention on the Elimination of all forms of Discrimination Against Women (CEDAW) 193, 461
cooperatives 460
Copelon, R. 218
cosmetic surgery 86–7, 359, 365–6
Cott, N. 326
counterpoint 141
couple relationships 336
　see also marriage
Cowman, K. 327
crisis in masculinity 115, 121–2
　concept of 109–10, 117–18
　and cultural production 84
　historical analysis 119–20
　limitations of model 115–21
　men's understandings of 120–1
　models 110–12
　previous crises 119
　symptoms 110, 112–15
crisis in patriarchy 111, 117–18, 121–2
critical heterosexual studies 314, 318
Critical Research on Men in Europe (CROME) 62
critical theory 379–80, 381
Croatia 207, 218
Crompton, R. 265
cross national research on care 277
cultural context, of bodies 46–8
cultural difference, and defining women 426
cultural genitals 38
cultural production by women 73–4
　differences between women 80–2
　focus on body 77, 78, 79–80, 86–7
　histories of 75
　popular culture 83–4
　rediscovery of 75–7, 78–9
　sites of 75–6
　specificity of 77–80
cultural rights 240
cultural turn 86, 87–8, 474
culturalism 381
culturalization of science 86

culture
　men's relationship with 377, 378
　and technoscience 407–8
　use of term 74
curriculum subjects 169, 171, 172
cybernetics 409
cyborg 87

'daddy leave' 298
Dalley, G. 276
Daly, M. 95, 329
dancers 47
Davidoff, L. 261
Davis, K. 359
DAWN (Development Alternatives with Women for a New Era) 248, 383
d'Eaubonne, F. 378
Declaration of Independence (1776) 238
Declaration of the Rights of Man and the Citizen (1789) 238
deconstructionism 437
degendering 470–1, 472–4
Delphy, C. 36, 37, 38
dematerialization of gendered body 405
denaturalization
　of gendered body 405–6
　of nature 403–4
Denmark 277
depoliticization of feminism 22
developing countries
　education in 178–80
　masculinities in 62, 63
　see also Third World
Development Alternatives with Women for a New Era (DAWN) 248, 383
Dewey, J. 162
diasporic minority identities 187–8
dichotomies 151, 347
　see also binary categories
diet 366–8
difference
　and citizenship 238
　and feminist postmodern epistemologies 157
　and politics of location 477–8
　versus equality 215, 237–8
　see also biological sex differences
diplomacy 198
disability 81, 134, 273, 276
disciplinary autonomy/integration 15, 16–21

discursive-political sphere 236
displacement strategy of citizenship 243–6
disruption, in feminist method 137, 138, 139
division of labour 254–5, 263–4, 289, 293, 295–6, 300, 470, 472
　and ideology of domesticity 261–3, 267, 289, 290
divorce 289–90, 291, 292
domesticity
　ideology of 261–3, 267, 289, 290
　see also household labour
Duncan, S. 256
Dwyer, L. 198

eating disorders 368–9
ecofeminism 378–9, 399–400, 401
ecological thinking 161
economic analysis of masculinity 64
economic change
　and crisis in masculinity 111
　impact on families 289, 290–1
economic neo-liberalism 255
economy, global 185–6
écriture féminine 79–80
education
　1970s coeducation debates 172
　1980s approaches and debates 173–4
　1990s changing approach 174–8
　and crisis in masculinity 113, 114, 118
　current trends 178–80
　degendering 473
　in developing countries 178–80
　feminist debates and activism 170–2
　history of 167–9, 180–1
　and religion 95
　see also teaching
education policy 171–2
educational achievement 114, 175–7
Eisenstein, H. 462
El-Bushra, J. 224
elderly, care of 273
Elgin, S.H. 76
Elshtain, J.B. 242, 419
emancipation of women by war 215, 219, 224, 225, 226–7

embodiment
  in feminist epistemologies 157, 160
  and gender in organizations 259
  of knowledge 61
  of nation in woman 200
Emmanuel, S. 216, 221
empiricism 59–60
  feminist 152, 153–5
employment
  barriers to women's 257–8
  and body maintenance 367
  care workers 279, 281, 282, 283–4
  changing attitudes to women's 263–5
  changing nature of 253, 262, 293
  family leave 296–8
  gender convergence 292–3, 300
  and ideology of domesticity 261–3, 289
  individualization of careers 265
  intensification of work 265
  and masculinity 111, 112, 116–17
  occupational segregation 254–5, 261, 264–5
  in organizations 258–61
  paid leave for carers 280, 283
  parental leave 296–8
  in real world context 475
  work–life balance 266, 267, 268, 296, 338
  see also labour force; work
employment choices 254–7
employment flexibility 262, 266, 294
employment inequalities 253–4
empowerment
  by body maintenance/modification 359, 368, 369
  by education 179
  and environmental studies 386
  by femininity 365, 366
  and regulation of bodies 359
  by religion 103
  by war 215, 219, 224, 225, 226–7
Enloe, C. 198, 199, 224–5
environment, concept of 376
Environment and Sustainable Development (ESD) study 385
environmental movements 390–1

environmental studies
  future of 391–2
  gender and nature 379–81
  mainstreaming gender 384–6, 392
  societal relations to nature 381–2
  women and nature 377–9
  see also feminist environmental studies
epistemology 138, 139, 435
  anti-foundationalist 439
  definition 136
  feminist critiques of 151–3
  feminist disruption of 147–50
  and gender 146–7
  normative 438–9
  and societal relations to nature 381–2
  standpoints and feminist ethics 420–2
  in study of masculinities 59–61
  in study of women and nature 379–81
  and technoscience 406
  see also feminist epistemology
epistemology of ignorance 163
equal opportunities (EO) policies 257
equal pay 170
Equal Right Amendment (ERA) (USA) 462
equal rights to benefits 274
equality see gender equality
equality-versus-difference debate 215, 237–8
ESRC 116
essentialism 140, 358–9
ethic of care 428
ethics 417
  feminism in 418
  in feminist philosophy 419–20
  in feminist research 438
  perspective of 418
  see also feminist ethics
ethnic identity
  and globalization 187, 188
  intersection with gender 58, 190–1
Ethnic studies 23
ethnicity
  and care 276–7
  and education 174, 176
  and employment 256
  and gender convergence 293, 294
  and gender norms 359

ethnicity (cont.)
  and masculinity 61, 118
  and nation 205
  and women's cultural production 81–2
  see also race
ethnocentrism 477
  see also Western feminism
ethnography 438
ethnomethodology 343
ethology 49
Eurocentrism 216–17, 218, 378
Europe
  family structure 290
  women's organizations 460
European Commission 384–5
European gender mainstreaming 384–6
European Union 62
European Women's Studies Thematic Network 21
everyday knowledge practice 439
evidence-based practice 175
evil 429–30
exercise 367, 369–70
exit 240, 242
experiences, and feminist epistemology 158
experiential analysis 442
explanation, in feminist method 136, 137, 138
expressive-collaborative model 422

Faderman, L. 326, 328
false consciousness 421
Faludi, S. 112
familialism, in social policy 338
families of choice 333
family
  concepts of 332–3
  friendship outside 331–2, 333
  informal care in 278
  and masculinity 111–12
  as public/private 236–7
  single parents 291, 294–5, 298–9, 300–1
  and social policy 296–9
  and transnational migration 190
  and women's employment 254–7
family friendly employment policies 266
family leave 296–8
family structures
  changing patterns of 289–91, 334, 338
  diversity of 287, 288–9, 291–2, 299–301

Fausto-Sterling, A. 41, 44, 133
Featherstone, M. 188
Feinberg, L. 351
female figures, revalorizing 101
female genital cutting 427
feminine gender norms 358, 359, 364–6, 367, 368, 369–70
femininity
  in coverage of 9/11 308, 309
  and domesticity 289
  and nation 198, 199
  and nurturance 293
  in organizations 259–60
  sexual violence, victimization and 219–20
  and war 216
feminism
  approach to method 129, 136–9
  approaches to gender 132–5, 316
  backlash against 84–5
  and crisis in masculinity 111, 114
  critiques of epistemology by 151–3
  disruption of epistemology by 147–50
  equality-versus-difference debate 215, 237–8
  gender, epistemology and 146–7
  modern and postmodern thought in 127–35, 139–42
  and multiculturalism 235
  and political theory 236–7, 418–19
  second wave 3, 290, 458–61
  thinking bent 318–19
  and transgender 349–51
  see also academic feminism
feminist academics 15–16, 26
feminist consciousness-raising 156, 458–9
feminist empiricism 152, 153–5
feminist environmental studies
  European gender mainstreaming 384–6
  global perspective 382–4
  research on body 385–6, 388–9
  research on science 386, 389–90
  research on work 386–8
feminist environmentalism 384
feminist epistemology 152, 436–9
  agential realism 160
  border crossing research on 439–45

feminist epistemology *(cont.)*
  coherentist epistemology 161–2
  ecological thinking 161
  empiricism 152, 153–5
  fractured foundationalism 445–51
  new directions 162–4
  postmodern theories 157–9
  situated knowledges 159–60, 380, 436, 439
  society and nature 381–2
  standpoint theories 60–1, 133, 155–7, 420–2, 440, 441
  women and nature 379–81
feminist ethics
  care/justice debate 427–9
  defining women 425–7
  evil, responsibility and complicity 429–30
  future of 430–1
  nature of self 423–5
  and ontology 422–3
  and standpoint epistemology 420–2
feminist ethnography 438
feminist fractured foundationalism (FFF) 445–51
feminist history 478–9
feminist knowledge
  range of 18
  specificity of 478
feminist methodology wars 437
feminist philosophy
  ethics in 419–20
  and feminist research 437
feminist political practice 479–80
  and academic feminism 17–18
  difference and inclusion 460–1
  friendship as basis of 327, 329, 330
  and maternal thinking 242
  see also women's movements
feminist political strategies 457–8
  in and against the state 461–3
  building coalitions 463–5
  developing movements 458–61
  gendering politics 463–5
  neo-radical 465–6
feminist political theory
  care/justice debate 427–9
  defining women 425–7
  evil, responsibility and complicity 429–30

feminist political theory *(cont.)*
  future of 430–1
  nature of self 423–5
feminist politics of location 477–8
feminist postmodern epistemologies 157–9
feminist research 435–6
  border crossings 439–45
  feminist fractured foundationalism (FFF) 445–51
  labour process 447–8
  research areas and epistemologies 436–9
feminist sci-fi 76
feminist spirituality movement 95, 101
feminist standpoint theories 60–1, 133, 155–7, 420–2, 440, 441
feminist study of bodies 358–60
feminist study of care 283
  Black feminists' work 276–7
  disabled feminists' work 276
  first wave feminist debates 272–3
  second wave feminist analysis 273–5
feminist study of citizenship 235
  displacement strategy 243–6
  equality and difference 238
  globalization 247–9
  inclusion strategy 238–40
  reversal strategy 241–3
feminist study of friendship 337–8
  future agendas 331–7
  histories of women's 326–7
  importance of women's 322, 323–5
  meaning of women's 328–9
  revaluing women's 329–31
feminist study of men 53–4
feminist study of nationalism 24, 198–9
feminist study of religion 94–8, 103–4
  interpretation and authenticity 98–9
  lesbianism 102–3
  secularism and atheism 100
  spirituality 100–2
feminist study of science and technology
  construction of sex and gender 404–6
  critiques of orthodox 400–3
  future directions 410–11
  knowledge production 408–10

feminist study of science and
    technology *(cont.)*
  lacking 398–9
  perspectives 399–400
  reproduction
    technologies 398
  technoscience 406–8
feminist study of war 214–18,
    227–8
  sexual violence in war
    218–23, 227
  women's participation 216,
    223–7
feminist study of women and
    nature
  critical theory 379–80
  eco-feminism 378–9
  first wave 377–8
  post-structuralism 380–1
feminist theory 479
  applicability of 438, 478
  appropriation of 310
Feminist and Women's Studies
    Association 20
feminization of labour
    market 116
feminization of poverty 291
femocrats 173, 462
fertility 360–1
fetal rights discourse 361
Fifth European Framework
    Program for Research,
    Technology Development
    and Demonstration
    (RTD) 384
film 85–6
Finch, J. 274
Finland 19, 25, 277, 280, 293
FINRRAGE 398
Firestone, S. 398
First World
  study of masculinities in 63
  see also West
fitness 367, 369–70
Flax, J. 133
flexible capitalism 262
flexible employment 262,
    266, 294
flight attendants 367
food 366–9
Foucault, M. 43–4, 127, 130,
    141, 158
foundationalism
  feminist 445–51
  rejection of 439
fractured foundationalism 446
  feminist 445–51
Fragile Families and Child
    Wellbeing Study 298–9
France 17, 96–7
Franklin, S. 191

Fraser, N. 425
French feminism 79–80
French Revolution 238
Freud, S. 79
Fricker, M. 163
Frieden, B. 81
Friedman, S.S. 478
Friends 335
friendship 337–8
  future agendas 331–7
  and heteronormativity 332–3
  histories of women's 326–7
  importance of women's
    322, 323–5
  increasing importance of
    334–7
  meaning of women's 328–9
  neglect of 322–3
  revaluing women's 329–31
Frosh, S. 110
Frye, M. 81, 163
Fukuyama, F. 186
funding 19, 20
Fuss, D. 133

g-r-r-r-l culture 83–4
Gadamer, H.-G. 161
Gapova, E. 205
Garfinkel, H. 343
gay families 289, 291
  gender convergence
    295–6, 301
gay marriage 299
gay men
  and friendship 333
  and gender norms in
    sport 370
  and nationalist
    discourse 202
gay pupils and parents 174
gay studies 23
gender
  absent from globalization
    theory 189–91
  assumptions 310
  central to nation 197, 198,
    199–200, 206
  concept of body in 318–19
  conceptualizing 2, 35–6,
    37–8, 85, 310, 312, 382
  and coverage of 9/11
    307–8, 309
  critical theory on nature
    and 379–80
  in cultural production 73–4
  degendering 470–1, 472–4
  destabilizing 350
  in education research 171
  and epistemology *see*
    epistemology
  and globalization 193–4

gender *(cont.)*
  and heterosexuality 309,
    311–12
  intersection with other social
    categories 57–9, 134,
    177, 190–1, 204–5, 217
  modern and postmodern
    approaches to 128–9,
    132–5
  natural attitude toward
    342–3, 347, 349
  and organizations 258–61
  post-structuralism on
    nature and 380–1
  in real world context 474–6
  in scientific study 391
  social construction
    perspective 469–70
  and societal relations to
    nature 381–2
  technoscientific construction
    of 404–6
  see also transgender
gender attribution 46
gender-bending 82–3, 85
gender convergence 287–8
  and feminism 299–301
  heterosexual couples 292–4
  same-sex couples 295–6
  and social policy 296–8
  unmarried parents 294–5
gender and development
    (GAD) 178
gender difference 2, 471, 476
  see also biological sex
    differences
gender displays 49
gender equality 470, 472
  in education 169, 171
  as political goal of
    feminism 236
  see also gender inequality
gender equality policy,
    masculinities and policy
    on 61, 62, 63
gender hierarchies, war as
    means of retaining 224
gender impact assessment
    (GIA) studies 384–5,
    388–9
gender inequality
  in employment 253–4, 258
  limited progress against
    465, 470
gender mainstreaming, in
    environmental studies
    384–6, 392
gender norms 358, 359, 364–6,
    367, 368, 369–70
gender relations, and violent
    conflict 224

gender revolution 470
gender roles
  attitudes to employment and 263–5
  impact of violent conflict on 224
  see also sex roles
gender studies
  autonomy and integration 18–21
  concept of 2, 3–4
  naming 22–6, 27
gendered social order
  degendering 470–1, 472–4
  pervasiveness of 470–2, 475
gendering
  of epistemology 59
  of politics 463–5
gene modification technology 86
General Household Survey 275
generational model of masculinity crisis 112
genetic research 44, 86
genetically transformed organisms 389–90
genital difference 37–8, 39–40, 43–4
genital surgery 348
genitals
  female genital cutting 427
  in women's cultural production 78, 80
genus studies 24
Germany 288–9, 297
Geurrilla Girls 83–4
Giddens, A. 189, 259
Gilligan, C. 133, 246, 427
Gillis, S. 22
girls' education 94, 167–9, 179
Global Campaign for Women's Human Rights 192
global context of feminism 478–80
global crisis of masculinity 119
global economy 185–6
global perspective in feminism 382–4
global production networks 190
global theory, local use of 141–2
globalization
  and citizenship 247–9
  concepts of 185–7
  and diasporic minority identities 187–8
  and gender 58, 193–4
  gender absent from theories of 189–91
  and masculinity 64, 111
  and transnational feminist movements 191–3, 464

Glover, J. 256
'god-trick' 149, 160
Goffman, E. 48–9
Golden, D. 201
Gornick, J. 298
Gottfried, H. 260
Gouge, O. De 238–9
government
  support of women's and gender studies 19, 24
  women in 463
Grass Roots Organizations Operating Together (GROOTs) 464
Greenham Common Women's Peace Camp 330–1
Grewal, I. 201
Griffin, G. 24, 25
Griffin, S. 219, 378
Gross, R. 95, 99
grounded feminist knowledge 450
grounded research areas 436–9
grounded research practices 437
Gutmann, M. 58

Hakim, C. 255
Halberstam, J. 328
Halford, S. 259, 265
Hall, C. 261
Hanmer, J. 54
Haraway, D. 87, 140, 141, 149, 156, 159–60, 244, 380, 397, 403
Harding, S. 136, 152, 441
Hartsock, N. 133, 420
Harvey, D. 130
Hausman, B. 352
Hayden, R. 221
Hayles, K. 402
health
  environmental impact on 388–9
  and medicalization 360–4
  men's 113, 118
Hekman, S. 440
hermaphroditism see intersexuality
hermeneutics 138
heteronormativity 309, 311, 312, 313–16
  and friendship 325, 332–3
  media coverage of 9/11 307–8, 309
  researching 316–18
heterorelationality 310, 325, 330–1
heterosexual couples, gender convergence 292–4

heterosexuality
  and gender norms in sports 370
  institutional 309, 311–12, 313–14, 315, 316–18
  link with nation 202
  as political regime 314
  relationship with gender 309, 311–12
  social construction of 314–15
  and women's friendships 327
hierarchy
  bureaucratic 259
  of gender in war 224
  and religion 93
  in research situations 438
hierarchy of obligation 275
higher education 168, 169, 170, 172, 175–6
hijab debates 96–8, 99
Hill, S. 293
Hinds, H. 16–17
Hinduism 102
Hindutva movement 205, 226–7
Hirschmann, A. 239
Hirst, P. 186
historical research on masculinities 57, 119–20
histories of women's friendships 326–7
history of education 167–9, 180–1
history of feminism 478–9
Hobsbawm, E. 197, 200
Home Care Allowances 280
homosexuality
  and coverage of 9/11 308
  and education 174
  and epistemology 163
  and gender norms in sports 370
  in nationalist discourse 202
  and religion 102
  see also gay men; lesbianism
Horkheimer, M. 379
hormone replacement therapy (HRT) 362
household labour
  division of 293, 470, 472
  gender convergence 295–6, 300
  see also domesticity
household technologies 399
households
  changing patterns 334
  see also family
Hubbard, R. 401
human capabilities model 426
human capital 254, 259

human rights 96, 192, 207, 248, 426–7, 465
Husserl, E. 342
hybridized identities 186–7, 188

iconography 204
identity
  and citizenship 244
  collective 221–2, 244–5, 246
  erosion of masculine 111, 112
  gender, nature and 379
  hybridized 186–7, 188
  impact of globalization on 187–8
  political and ethical concept of 425
  racial/ethnic 58, 187, 188, 190–1, 424
  self-construction of 259–60
  and transgendering 351–2
  see also social categories
ignorance, epistemologies of 163
imperialism 201
inclusion strategy of citizenship 238–40
income 254, 279
independent living 276
India
  academic feminism 19
  coalitions 464–5
  feminism and state 461, 462, 463
  nation 205
  violence 220, 221, 222
  women's organizations 458–9, 460
  women's participation in conflict 225, 226–7
indigenous religions 98, 101–2
  Western interest in non-Western 101–2
individual choice, of employment 255–6
industrialization 289
inequality see gender inequality
infertility 360–1
Ingraham, C. 317
Institute for Social–Ecological Research (ISOE) 381
institutional heterosexuality 309, 311–12, 313–14, 315, 316–18
institutionalization of feminism see academic feminism
integration, of academic feminism 15, 16–21
internalist approach to knowledge 447

international affairs, women's role 198
international agreements 461
international concern with masculinities 62–3
International Criminal Tribunal for former Yugoslavia 219–20
international cultural turn 87–8
international flow of staff and students 21, 25–6
international women's movement 192
  see also transnational feminism
interpretive understanding 138
intersectionality of social categories 57–9, 118, 134, 177, 190–1, 204–6, 217
intersexuality 39, 43–4, 343, 348
Invalid Care Allowance 274
Iraq war 204, 223
Ireland 204
Irigaray, L. 80, 140
irony 140–1
Islam
  feminist rereading of 241, 243
  hijab debates 96–8, 99
  and religious interpretation 99
  study of masculinities and 62
Islamic Salvation Front (FIS) 103
Israel 203
Italy 17, 26, 80

Jackson, D. 57, 118
Jackson, S. 311
Jacob, F. 404
Japan 61
Jayawardena, K. 198
Jegerstedt, K. 24
jilbah 97
Judaism 95, 102
justice 220, 427–9

Kabeer, N. 179
Kahlo, F. 78
Kandiyoti, D. 206
Kane, S. 84
Kant, I. 60
Kanter, R.M. 258
Kaplan, C. 479
Kašić, B. 221
Katz, J. 314–15
Kay, L. 409
Keller, E.F. 151–2, 380

Kenya 222
Kesic, V. 207
Kessler, S. 37–8, 39, 46, 133
Kim, J. 190–1
Kimmel, M. 119
Kittay, E. 428–9
Klein, R. 22
knowledge
  challenging scientific 401–2
  feminist challenges to 148–50
  modern and postmodern approaches to 135
  and power 449
  situated knowledges 159–60, 380, 436, 439
  women absent from 147
  see also epistemology; feminist knowledge
knowledge production, in science and technology 408–10
Kohlberg, L. 428
Koontz, C. 216
Krafft-Ebing, R. von 377
Kristeva, J. 79
Krog, A. 220
Kruks, S. 158

labour force
  and education 176
  and transnational migration 190, 191
  see also employment
laddism 114
ladette culture 83, 84
Langton, R. 147, 163
language
  degendering 472
  and nation 205
  and women's cultural production 77, 79
Laqueur, T. 38–9, 40–2, 43, 133
Lasser, C. 327
Latin America 61, 62, 459
Le Feuvre, N. 265
legal remedies for war crimes 219–20
legal system, and feminism 461, 462, 463
legislation 171, 461, 462–3, 470, 472
leisure, and masculinity 112
Lennon, K. 157
lesbian athletes 370
lesbian continuum 329–30
lesbian cultural production 82
lesbian families 289, 291
  gender convergence 295–6, 301
lesbian friendship networks 333

lesbian identity 425
lesbian marriage 299
lesbian pupils and parents 174
lesbian sex wars of 1980s 82
lesbian studies 23
lesbianism
  and religion 95, 102–3
  and standpoint
    epistemology 421
  and women's friendships
    325, 328–30
Levine, P. 327
Lewis, J. 263
liberal democracy 243–6
liberal feminism 215, 274,
  361, 399
liberal thought 236
liberal-rights tradition 238,
  239, 240, 241–2
life-cycle analysis (LCA) 387
Lindio-McGovern, L. 190
Lister, A. 328
Lister, R. 239
literature
  Black women's 81–2
  Third World women's 82
  women's absence and
    rediscovery 75–7, 78–9
  women's publishers 75–6
liver failure 113
Lloyd, G. 151
Lloyd, M. 369
local use of global theory
  141–2
location, of feminist study 21,
  22, 24–5, 28
Longino, H. 154
Lorber, J. 132, 308, 309
Lorde, A. 245
Lovejoy, M. 368
Luckman, T. 343
Lukacs, G. 420
Lyotard, J-F. 130

McClintock, B. 152, 380
MacDonald, E. 351–2
McDowell, L. 111, 116, 119,
  120, 260
Macinnes, J. 262
McKenna, W. 37–8, 46
McRae, S. 256–7
Magarey, S. 26
magazines 335
male breadwinner model
  114–15, 289, 290, 293, 295
male culture
  and crisis in masculinity 115
  laddism 114
male gender norms and
  sport 370
male sex role 56, 64

marriage
  changing ideology of
    289–90, 291, 292
  and concept of gender 350
  same-sex 299
  weddings 316–17
Martin, E. 41
Martin, P.Y. 260
martyrdom 220
Marxism 420, 421
Marxist feminism 399
Marxist sociology of
  education 173
masculine, challenging 2–3
masculine gender norms
  358, 359
masculine identities, erosion of
  111, 112
masculinities
  concept of 55, 117, 118
  in coverage of 9/11 308, 309
  and education 177
  and gender convergence
    293, 295, 300–1
  growing research on 56–7
  link with science and
    technology 398–9
  and nation 198, 199, 202
  in organizations 259–60
  studying see men and
    masculinities research
  and war 216
masculinity in crisis 115, 121–2
  concept of 109–10, 117–18
  and cultural production 84
  historical analysis 119–20
  limitations of model 115–21
  men's own understandings
    of 120–1
  models 110–12
  previous crises 119
  symptoms 110, 112–15
masculinity studies 54, 222
materiality of sex 37
maternal thinking 242–3
Mayer, T. 197–8
Mayreder, R. 377–8
media coverage of 9/11 307–8,
  309
medicalization 360–4
men
  as carers 275
  paternity leave 298
  relationship with culture
    377, 378
  role in household labour 293
  as single parents 295
  in teaching 169–70
  as victims of sexual violence
    222–3
  as warriors 200

men and masculinities
  research 2
  epistemological issues 59–61
  framing studies 53–4
  future study 63–4
  general approach 57
  intersectionality of
    categories 58–9
  methodologies 57
  naming 54–5
  political and policy issues
    61–3
  social construction 55–7
  see also masculinities
Menon, R. 221
menopause 362
men's health 113, 118
men's studies 54–5
Merchant, C. 378
meritocracy 289
Mertus, J. 219–20
Messerschmidt, J. 222
methodology 138, 435, 436, 437
  and border crossing
    research 439–45
  definition 136
  and fractured
    foundationalism
    445–51
  for studying men and
    masculinities 57
methods 136, 138, 435, 437,
  442, 447–8
  feminist approach to 129,
    136–9
Mibenge, C. 220, 222
Mies, M. 378
Milan Women's Bookstore
  Collective 80
Milić, A. 17
militarism 202, 203, 216, 225
military, women's role 198,
  224–5
Mills, C. 163
mimesis 380
miniaturization in
  technoscience 403
mitigated relativism 441–2
Möbius, P.J. 377
modernism
  approach to gender 128,
    132–5
  concept of 127, 128, 129–30
  in feminist debates 127,
    129–30
  and method 137
  tension between
    postmodernism and
    139–42
modernization, masculinities
  and 62

Moen, P. 266
Moghadam, V. 464
Mohanty, C.T. 191, 206
moral conservatism 243
moral development 428
moral epistemology 448–9
moral knowledge, and fractured foundationalism 447
moral motherhood 261
moral panics 117, 119
moral psychology 425
moral rationalities 256
moral repair 430
morality, women, nature and 377
Mosse, G. 200
motherhood 272–3, 475–6
    and employment 256, 261, 263–5, 297–8
Mothers Against Nuclear Technology 388
Mouffe, C. 246
Moya, P. 162–3
multiculturalism 235, 239–40, 425–7
Munford, R. 22
Muslim feminists 241–2, 243
Muslim Women's Bill 462, 463

Narayan, U. 419
nation
    and class 205
    concept of 197–8
    and ethnicity 205
    gender as central to 197, 198, 199–200, 206
    insiders and outsiders 197–8, 201
    and racism 205–6
    and religion 204–5
    and sexuality 201–4, 207
nation states, in global world 186, 206–7, 247, 248
nation-building 196, 198
National Alliance of People's Movements (India) 464
National Alliance of Women (India) 464
National Commission on Women (India) 462
National Network of Autonomous Women's Groups (India) 464
national reproduction 202–4
nationalism
    and citizenship 206–7
    feminist work on 24, 198–9
    and militarism 203
natural attitude 342–3, 347, 349
natural sciences 381–2

naturalism 381
naturalization of behaviour 48–9
naturalized empiricism 155
naturalized epistemology 155, 159, 161
nature
    challenging scientific concepts of 401–2
    concept of 376
    critical theory on gender and 379–80
    denaturalization of 403–4
    post-structuralism on gender and 380–1
    relations with technoscience 399
    societal relations to 381–2
    women and 377–9
    see also environmental studies
Nazi movement 216
needs 244
Nelson, L.H. 155
neo-classical economic theory 254
neo-Marxist sociology of education 173
neo-radical feminist politics 465–6
Netherlands 282, 293, 299
new laddism 114
NGOs (non-governmental organizations) 18, 24, 459
Niarchos, C. 219
Nicholson, L. 128
Noddings, N. 428
normative epistemology 438–9
normative guidelines on care 274–5
Norway 277, 280, 297–8
nuclear technologies 388–9
Nussbaum, M. 179, 255–6, 424, 426
Nye, A. 418

Oakley, A. 36
obesity 367
objectification 147
objectivity 149–50, 151, 154, 401, 402
occupational segregation 254–5, 261, 264–5
O'Donnell, M. 113, 118
official-political sphere 236
Ohmae, K. 185
O'Keefe, G. 78
Okin, S.M. 239–40, 419, 426
Olsen, T. 75
one-sex model 39, 40
O'Neill, J. 255

O'Neill, M. 384
ontology
    and feminist ethics 422–3
    and fractured foundationalism 446
    and technoscience 406
oppression, women's shared 74
organizations 258–61, 266
Orlan 86–7
Ortner, S. 3, 378
othering 197–8, 201, 206, 401
Otnes, C. 317
Oudshoorn, N. 45–6

Page, D. 44
Pakistan 193, 220, 221
pankriti 378
Papic, Z. 18
parental leave 296–8
parenting
    and gender convergence 294
    see also motherhood
Parker, R. 74, 78
participatory decision-making 459
Pateman, C. 419
paternity leave 298
patriarchal dividend 111, 122
patriarchy 2, 173–4, 430
    crisis in 111, 117–18, 121–2
Pattman, R. 110
peace-politics 224
Pease, B. 57
Pederson, S. 222
peer pressure 114
performativity of gender 133
pesticides 390
Peterson, S. 206
Philippines 190
Phillips, R. 291
philosophy
    of science 152, 159
    see also ethics; feminist philosophy; political theory
Phoenix, A. 16–17, 110
plastic surgery 86–7, 359, 365–6
Pleck, E. 317
pluralism 160, 163
Poland 204
policy
    and masculinities 61–3
    and women's commissions 462
    see also social policy
political action
    place and style of 245
    see also feminist political practice
political issues in study of men and masculinities 61–3

political power, and religion 93
political regime, heterosexuality as 314
political right wing, women in 215, 226
political rights 238, 239, 248
political theory
  and feminism 236–7, 418–19
  see also feminist political theory
politicization 236, 237, 243–4
politics
  feminist redefinition of 458
  gendering 463–5
  modern and postmodern approaches 134–5
politics of location 477–8
politics of representation 402
Pollock, G. 74
pollution 386–7, 390
polysemic language 79
popular culture 76–7, 85–6, 332, 335
portfolio careers 258
Portugal 297
post-feminist cultural production 84
post-heterorelational friendship 335
post-positivist empiricism 153
post-positivist realism 162–3
post-positivist theories of knowledge 149
postcolonial theory 60, 64, 95, 222
postmodern epistemologies 157–9
postmodernism
  approach to gender 128–9, 132–5
  and biology 83
  concept of 128, 130–1
  on equality versus difference 237–8
  in feminist debates 127, 131–2
  and method 136, 137, 138, 139
  and nature of self 423–4
  tension between modernism and 139–42
poststructuralism
  and academic feminism 22, 27–8, 437
  and education 177
  on gender and nature 380–1
  and masculinities 64
  and nature of self 423–4
poverty 291, 294, 298–9

power
  and feminist epistemologies 158
  and knowledge 449
  and masculinities 56
  and medicalization 361, 363–4
  modern and postmodern approaches 134–5, 158
  and nation 197, 199, 200
  and religion 93–4
  in research situations 438
  and women's popular culture 83–4
Power, M. 226
pragmatism, in feminist epistemology 162–3
pragmatist–feminist standpoint theory 162
pre-menstrual syndrome (PMS) 362
Prince, V. 343
private sector care 278, 281
private sphere
  politics of 458
  public/private distinction 236–7, 419
production 387
provident economy approach 387
psychoanalysis 55, 78–9, 177
public/private distinction 236–7, 419
publishers 75–6
Purple September 313

queer studies 23
queer theory 83, 314, 348
Quine, W.V.O. 155
quotas, for women in government 463
Qureshi, H. 274–5

race
  and body perceptions 367, 368
  and coverage of 9/11 308
  and education 171, 176
  and gender norms 359
  and masculinities 58, 62
  and other social categories 58, 134
  and standpoint epistemology 421
  and women's cultural production 81–2
  see also ethnicity
racial identity 424
racism, and nation 205–6
Radiation Protection Ordinance (RPO) 388–9

radical feminism
  on care 274
  on nature 378, 401
  on reproductive technology 361
  on technoscience 399–400
  on war 215
  on women's friendships 329
Radicalesbians 74
Rai, S. 465
Rajasingham-Senanayake, D. 226
rape 203–4, 218–23
rational knowledge 151
rationalist epistemology 59, 60
rationality 111, 121, 379
rationing of care services 279
Raymond, J. 330, 349
real world, gender in 474–6
reason, feminist critiques of 151
reflexive modernity 259
reflexivity 448, 449
Reid, R. 408
Reinharz, S. 442
relational autonomy 422
relationships see couple relationships; friendship; marriage
relativism 427, 440, 441
religion
  cultural adaptation of 93–4
  and degendering 472
  feminist critiques of 94–8
  feminist study of 103–4
  hijab debates 96–8, 99
  interpretation and authenticity 98–9
  lesbianism 102–3
  and nation 204–5
  and power 93–4
  secularism and atheism 100
  spirituality 100–2
religious conservatism 96
religious fundamentalism 97, 103, 243, 247, 462
religious texts 98–9
renaturalization 404
representation 135, 402, 438
reproduction, and nature of women 377
reproductive technologies 86, 361, 398, 405–6
Research Assessment Exercise (RAE) 20
residential care 276, 281
resistance, religion as vehicle of 93, 95
responsibility 430
reversal strategy of citizenship 241–3
Rich, A. 76, 313, 329–30, 477

Richardson, D. 23, 312, 318
right wing politics 215, 226
rights
    and citizenship 238, 239,
        240, 248
    see also human rights
Riley, D. 133
risk perception 388
Robinson, V. 23
romantic friendships 326, 328
Rome (ancient) 98
Rooney, E. 140
Rose, G. 475
Roseneil, S. 330, 335–7
Roy, A. 223, 226
Rubin, G. 132
Ruddick, S. 242
Rutherford, J. 120
Rwanda 218, 220, 222

SADF (South African Defence
    Force) 216
Salome, L.A. 378
same-sex couples see gay
    families
same-sex roommates 350–1
Sarkar, T. 226
Sassen, S. 193
Scandinavia 61, 299
Scandinavian model of care
    277, 280, 283
Scheich, E. 409
Schiebinger, L. 381, 392
schools, Muslim dress in 97
Schutz, A. 342
Schwalbe, M. 57
science and engineering
    171–2
science fiction 76
science and technology
    concepts of 397–8
    constructing sex and gender
        41–2, 404–6
    critiques of 380–1, 400–3
    culturalization of 86
    denaturalizing nature
        403–4
    and feminist environmental
        studies 386, 389–90
    feminist perspectives 87,
        399–400
    gender issues in 391
    knowledge production
        408–10
    link with masculinity 111,
        398–9
    natural sciences 381–2
    technoscience 406–8
science and technology studies
    400–1
Scott, J 13
second-order reflection 410

second-wave feminism 3, 290,
    458–61
secularism 100
Sedgwick, E.K. 163
self 259–60, 423–5
self-harm 177
self-help centres 459
semiotic language 79
Sen, A. 179
Sennett, R. 262
serial marriages 291
service sector 111, 262
Sevenhuijsen, S. 429
sex
    conceptualizing 36–8, 39–42,
        43–6, 83, 310, 382
    scientific construction of
        404–6
sex change procedures 405
sex differences see biological
    sex differences
sex hormones 45–6
sex roles 55–6, 64
    see also gender roles
sex/gender distinction
    35–8, 42–3, 46–8, 83,
    132, 405
sexual behaviour 62
sexual health 62, 63
sexual identity 83–4
sexual violence in war 203–4,
    218–23, 227
sexuality
    categorizing 312
    and education 174
    and epistemology 163
    and gendered social
        order 471
    intersection with other
        social categories 58,
        134, 207
    and nation 201–4, 207
    and national reproduction
        202–3
    women, nature and 377
    see also heterosexuality;
        homosexuality;
        transsexualism
Shanley, M.L. 419
Sharpe, J. 222
Sharpe, S. 113, 118
Sheriden, S. 26
Shiva, V. 378
Singapore 97, 203
single-gender schools
    169, 172
single-parent families 291,
    294–5, 298–9, 300–1
situated knowledges 159–60,
    380, 436, 439
situatedness 141
Skeggs, B. 13, 474

Slum and Shack Dwellers
    International (India)
    464–5
Smith, D. 443–5
Smith Rosenberg, C. 326, 328
Smith, V. 222
Snow, C.P. 408–9
social categories
    intersectionality of 57–9,
        118, 134, 177, 190–1,
        204–6, 217
    problems of 312
social change
    and crisis in masculinity
        110–12, 115
    and friendship 334–7
social construction 343
    of bodies 359
    of masculinities 55–7
    of sex hormones 45–6
social construction feminism,
    on technoscience 400
social construction
    perspective on gender
    469–70
social contract 419
social control
    and medicalization 363–4
    and women's bodies 363–4,
        365–6, 368, 370–1
social institution, gender as
    471–2
social movements 458
    alliances 463–5
    see also women's movements
social order see gendered
    social order
social policy
    and academic feminism 18
    and care 278–83
    and families 296–9
    and friendship 338
social rights 238, 239, 248
social sciences 55–6, 381–2
socialist feminism 80, 274
society, relation to nature
    381–2
South Africa 220
South African Defence Force
    (SADF) 216
South Asia 221, 225–7
space 387
Spain 19, 288–9, 299
spirituality 95, 100–2
Spivak, G.C. 82, 139,
    140, 479
sport
    and body modification 47
    commercialization 112
    and gender norms 370
Sri Lanka 221, 225
Stacey, J. 16–17

standpoint theory 60–1, 133, 155–7, 420–2, 441
  critique of 440
state
  feminist debates over care and 272–3
  feminist politics in and against 461–3
  women, religious conservatism and 96
state benefits 273, 274
state care services 272–3
state subsidies, for private care 281
state support of informal care 277, 278, 279–83, 284
Stone, L. 327
strategic essentialism 140
Stromquist, N. 178
strong objectivity 154
structural barriers to women's employment 256–7, 259
structure 469–70, 471
subaltern counterpublics 245
subaltern studies 82
subject, nature of 423–5
subjectivity 133, 157, 158
subjugated knowledges 158
subordination 155–6
subsistence perspective 387
suffrage movement 327
suicide 113–14, 116, 177
Sullivan, S. 162
sustainable development 383, 385, 386
sustainable production and consumption 387
sustainable science 381, 392
Sweden 277, 280, 288, 293, 297, 298
Switzerland 297
symbolic language 79
symbolism 40–1
symbols of nation 200

Tamil Tiger militants 221
Taylor, D. 221
teaching 169–70, 174, 175
technology *see* science and technology
technoscience 406–8
television 76, 83, 332, 335
terrorist attacks 307–9
theoretical-juridical model 422
thinking bent 318–19
thinking straight 315–16
Third World
  women's cultural production 82
  women's role in combat 216
  see also developing countries; Rwanda

Third World feminists, study of war 217
Third World resources 88
Thompson, G. 186
time 387
transactional knowing 162
transdisciplinarity 391, 408–9
transgender
  concepts of 346–9, 351
  emergence of term 343, 344–6
  and feminism 349–51
  living 351
transgender studies 23
transgendering 349, 350–1
transnational corporations 190–1, 193, 248
transnational feminism 141–2, 191–3, 207, 464, 465, 480
transnational migration 190, 191
transsexualism 343, 346, 347, 349–50
transversal politics 207–8
Traweek, S. 408
Tronto, J.C. 428
truth 161
Turkey 97

Ugresic, D. 203
UN (United Nations) 62–3, 224, 461–2, 465
UN Conference on Environment and Development (UNCED) (1992) 383
UN International Women's Decade (1975–1985) 459, 460
UN World Conference on Women (1985) 382
UN World Conference on Women (1995) 247, 384, 459
unalienated knowledge 450–1
understanding, in feminist method 137, 138
Ungerson, C. 275
UNICEF 179
Universal Declaration of Human Rights (1945) 426
universality 140, 246, 418, 420
unmarried parents 294–5
urban research 391
urbanization 289
USA
  Black women's cultural production 81–2
  coalitions in 465
  concern with men 61
  family leave 296–7
  family structure 288, 290, 292

USA (cont.)
  feminism and state 461–2, 463
  feminist critiques of religion 94–5
  gender convergence 293, 294
  national reproduction 203
  same-sex marriage 299
  sexual violence 222
  single-parent poverty 298–9
  women's employment patterns 293
  women's organizations 458, 459, 460
  women's studies 24, 25–6
  work-life balance 266, 296

value neutrality 149–50, 157
Van Every, J. 332
veiling 96–8, 99
vestal virgins 98
victimization of women in war 218–20, 227
victims of sexual violence 220–3
violence
  international concern with 192
  self-help centres 459
  study of men's 62
  in women's cultural production 84
  see also sexual violence in war
voice, and citizenship 239, 242
vulnerability 388–9

Wacjman, J. 265
Wacquant, L. 47, 58
wages for housework 280, 281–2
Walby, S. 439–40
Walker, A. 274
Walker, M.U. 422, 427, 430
Walkerdine, V. 49–50
war
  feminist study of 227–8
  classical studies 214–18
  sexual violence 218–23, 227
  women's participation 216, 223–7
  and masculinity 112
Warner, M. 315
Weber, M. 258
weddings 317
Weeks, J. 334
Weeks, K. 139
Wehling, T. 409
Weisen Cook, B. 328
Weiss, A. 193
Weitz, R. 365
welfare benefits 280
welfare state 244, 277, 278, 279–80

Werbner, P. 242
West
    cultural influence of 186
    interest in non-Western
        religions by 101–2
    religious influence in 100
Western approach to difference
    426, 427
Western feminism
    applicability of 438, 478
    bias of 214–15, 216–17, 218,
        477, 478, 479
    critiques of religion 94–5
White, J. 429
White, M. 266
Whitehead, S. 120
Whitford, M. 157
Williams, J. 261
Williams, P. 159, 424
Willmott, P. 334–5
Wittig, M. 81, 314, 425
Wolf, N. 85
Wolkomir, M. 57
Wollstonecraft, M. 238–9
woman
    in concepts of nation 200,
        201–4, 206, 207
    concepts of 25, 74, 81, 85,
        191–2, 425–7
women
    absent from knowledge 147
    changing status of 112
    and culture see cultural
        production by women
    differences between 80–2,
        274, 276, 425–7, 460–1,
        477–8
    as focus of feminist study
        22–3
    fundamentalist 462
    and nature 377–9
    as participants in conflict
        216, 223–7
    revalorizing 101
    role in nation–building 198
    in teaching 169–70
    as victims of violence 220–3

Women in Black 202
women care workers 279, 281
women and development
    (WID) 178
women, environment and
    development (WED)
    debate 383–4
Women in Informal Economy
    Globalizing and
    Organizing 464
women religious leaders 104
women scientists 400–1
women's bodies
    agency and conformity 359,
        363–71
    maintenance and
        modification 47, 86–7,
        364–70
    medicalization of 360–4
    and women's cultural
        production 77, 78,
        79–80, 86–7
    women's workshops on 401
women's commissions 462
women's culture see cultural
    production by women
women's employment 267, 291
    barriers to 257–8
    changing attitudes 263–5
    employment choices 254–7
    gender convergence
        292–3, 300
    and ideology of domesticity
        261–3, 289
    in organizations 258–61
    work–life balance 266, 267,
        268, 296, 338
Women's Environment and
    Development Organization
    (WEDO) 383
women's environmental
    movements 390–1
women's friendships
    future agendas for study
        331–7
    histories of 326–7
    importance of 322, 323–5

women's friendships (cont.)
    meaning of 328–9
    revaluing 329–31
women's movements 458
    and academic feminism 17
    and class 459, 460,
        463, 464
    demands of 170
    environmental 383
    fragmentation of 460–1
    and scientific
        knowledge 401
    second wave emergence
        458–61
    shared oppression 74
    transnational 141–2, 191–3,
        207, 464, 465, 480
women's peace movement
    330–1
women's spirituality
    movement 95, 101
women's studies
    autonomy and integration
        16–17, 18–21
    concept of 1–2, 3
    emergence and growth of
        172, 173, 174, 460
    naming 22–6, 27
    and transgender 350
    views of 13–14
Woolf, V. 75, 77, 324–5, 479
work
    feminist environmental
        study of 385, 386–8
    see also employment;
        labour force
work-life balance 266, 267,
    268, 296, 338
writing 438

young adulthood 289
Yugoslavia (former)
    concepts of nation 202, 203,
        205, 207
    feminism 17, 18
    war rapes 218, 219–20, 221
Yuval-Davis, N. 198, 207

HQ 1180 .H355 2006

Handbook of gender and women's studies

FEB 1 2 2008